Dialect and Language Variation

Academic Press Rapid Manuscript Reproduction

Dialect and Language Variation

Edited by

Harold B. Allen

Departments of English and Linguistics
University of Minnesota, Minneapolis
Minneapolis, Minnesota

Michael D. Linn

Department of English
University of Minnesota, Duluth
Duluth, Minnesota

1986

ACADEMIC PRESS, INC.
Harcourt Brace Jovanovich, Publishers
Orlando   San Diego   New York   Austin
London   Montreal   Sydney   Tokyo   Toronto

ACADEMIC PRESS, INC.
Orlando, Florida 32887

United Kingdom Edition published by
ACADEMIC PRESS INC. (LONDON) LTD.
24–28 Oval Road, London NW1 7DX

LIBRARY OF CONGRESS CATALOG CARD NUMBER: 85-48209

ISBN: 0-12-051130-4

PRINTED IN THE UNITED STATES OF AMERICA

86 87 88 89   9 8 7 6 5 4 3 2 1

Contents

Social Dialects and Language Variation   **237**

Preface

Although we editors had directed a side glance at the subject matter of this book in preparing a previous publication, *Readings in Applied English Linguistics,* ed. 3 (Alfred A. Knopf, 1982), numerous colleagues reported their continuing need for an anthology concerned exclusively with language variation.

Consideration of that demand did indeed indicate that none of the current textbooks treating dialects would quite satisfy the instructor of a class in language variation, whether the course emphasized regional or social differences or sought a balance of emphasis. At the same time, it was clear that so much activity had recently occurred in both of these fields that it would not suffice simply to revise the out-of-date anthology that the senior editor, with Gary Underwood, had prepared some 15 years earlier *Readings in American Dialectology* (Appleton-Century-Crofts, 1971).

The present collection actually includes only 4 of the essays of the 1971 anthology. The remaining 35, all published since 1971, deal variously with the theoretical, general, and specific aspects of regional dialects and social dialects. The collection, unhappily, could not be as comprehensive as was first planned. The imperative requirement that the cost of the ultimate book be kept within the textbook range imposed a space limitation that compelled us to reject about 250 pages of material that would have expanded several of the present sections besides adding one on British regional speech and another on dialects and literature.

Even so, we believe that this anthology offers a more than adequate representation of the current scene, certainly enough to provide in one term both a broad and an intensive view of the extent of present-day research in language variation.

We believe, further, that somewhere in the liberal arts curriculum this representation is invaluable in counteracting both the popular and the theoretical view of language, even so-called standard English, as monolithic. True, primarily we think of these essays as desirable for students in classes variously designated as American English, The English Language, American Dialectology, Social Dialects, Sociolinguistics, Sociology of Language, and Language Variation. But although such courses are likely to be offered in departments of English, American studies, linguistics, sociology, and anthropology, we would also submit that since the content of the book is so nontechnical that, except perhaps for the minimal use of phonetic transcription, it demands no prerequisites except a degree of maturity, this introduction to the field of language variation is valuable collateral reading for all upper division and graduate students.

When the predecessor of this collection appeared in 1971, theoretical linguistics, focusing largely upon generative theory, dominated the professional scene. Linguistic or dialect geography was emerging from a holding operation, and concern with the social dimension of language variation was just beginning to move in from the wings to center stage. Today, while linguistic theory about innate universals retains a prominent place in language study, it no longer overshadows concern with a number of other historical and contemporary interests, including that of language variation. Renewed activity in regional dialect projects and lexicography has been matched by research in social dialectology stimulated by the sociopolitical problems raised by attitudes toward Black vernacular English. But such research has reached out also into the productive relationships being explored by William Labov and his students.

Indeed, it is probably appropriate to repeat here a declaration that appeared in the preface to the 1971 precursor of this textbook:

> Whatever universals, innate or not, contemporary theoretical linguists may eventually settle upon as essential in human language—those underlying links that bind the facts of linguistics with those of psychology and philosphy—the correlations of overt language manifestations with place and social class will always prove, at the other end of the scale, equally interesting and far from trivial. This collection focuses upon these correlations and their significant interpretation.

And so does this collection!

Dialect and Language Variation

DIALECT THEORY

Although the three articles in Part I need not be studied first, they should not be omitted. It is a truism, unhappily often ignored, that no understanding of the present is complete without understanding the past. Implicit in the skill of the medical doctor is an underlying awareness of the distant contributions of Hippocrates, Aristotle, Galen, and Vesalius, as well as of the more recent work of Harvey. Luckily for the student, the history of linguistic geography is much shorter.

That a language exhibits variation within its geographical limits is not, of course, a modern discovery. The Greeks knew it; the Romans knew it; Chaucer recognized it; and Shakespeare used it. A collection of dialect terms actually was printed in England in 1674.

But it was in Germany that the theories stemming from the beginning of historical and comparative linguistics led to the first dialect research based upon a carefully planned program of collecting regional variations. The concept that dialect differences deserve scholarly study instead of being considered bizarre deviations from a standard norm led Georg Wenker in 1878 to undertake what was to become a decades-long project, Der deutsche Sprachatlas, the linguistic atlas of Germany. Wenker used a postal questionnaire to elicit from more than 44,000 schoolteachers their written dialect translations of 44 sentences in Standard High German. Though not trained investigators, these schoolmasters did provide a vast mine of information about vocabulary as well as some about gross differences in pronunciation.

A quite different way to obtain dialect data requires a trained fieldworker to interview informants in their home communities and record their responses in a phonetic transcription that as closely as possible represents the individual features of pronunciation. This procedure Jules Gilliéron initiated in France when he sent Edmond Edmont into the field to cover the entire country with his interviews of peasants and other rural dwellers. The result was the monumental *Atlas Linguistique de la France*, published between 1904 and 1910.

Because the practical and theoretical implications of the French atlas are relevant to later dialect studies in North America, we chose to open this collection with the article by the late Professor Bottiglioni, an Italian dialectologist. He draws upon Gilliéron's data to establish various historical and current linguistic relationships and makes clear the theory underlying Gilliéron's approach to dialect data.   Although the article refers to American work only in passing, the kind of inference it draws and other uses of the data are like those that can be derived from the materials of American dialect geography.   Indeed, it may be desirable to give this article only a quick once-over reading at this time and then return to it for close study after the completion of Parts II and III.

But none of the studies proliferating from the French and German atlases were in the mold of the developing structuralism of linguistic theory.   Dialectologists had been dealing with item comparison on a geographical basis only; they did not treat items as features within an over-all system, within a structure of structures.   Whether such a comprehensive comparison could indeed be made was the tenor of much criticism of dialect geography, particularly in the article by the late Uriel Weinreich.   Although Weinreich's examples are from Yiddish, his seminal approach opened the door to subsequent American research, notably by his one-time student, William Labov, whose own recent studies are represented in this book.

American structuralism, however, was rather abruptly checked when Noam Chomsky's *Linguistic Structures* appeared in 1957. It was not long before some linguiists sought to apply Chomsky's generative grammatical theory to the study of dialect.   This development K. M. Petyt follows in some detail in the third article. He describes the effort to fit dialect variation into a system, perhaps a "diasystem," but with a new theoretical underlying structure as the base from which rule-governed variations or transformations develop surface structure.

Petyt continues with a discussion of developments caused by greater attention to variation than to structural uniformity, that is, to a dynamic approach recognizing change rather than to the quantitative or static approach of the generativists.   David De-Camp, Charles-James Bailey, and Derek Bickerton are among the innovating scholars whose work in this frontal area of research demands discussion.

Students desirous of a more comprehensive treatment of the background and progress of dialect theory may profitably read Chapter 7 of W. N. Francis's *Dialectology: An Introduction*, New York and London, Longman, 1983.   Also valuable is Wolfgang Viereck's article, "The growth of dialectology," *Journal of English Linguistics* 7 (1973):69-86.

LINGUISTIC GEOGRAPHY: ACHIEVEMENTS,

METHODS, AND ORIENTATIONS

Gino Bottiglioni

The development of science includes both the discovery of new facts and the successive equalization of the methods of interpretation. As the methods increase in accuracy, it becomes possible to study other truths which, when they were first noted, seemed to darken that part of the horizon that had appeared clear to still earlier researchers. We have an unceasing contrast of shades and lights that, however, softens and composes itself harmonically to the eyes of those who observe the succession with serene minds while even the latest acquisitions of science get old in the course of time. The same may be said about linguistic geography, which is already half a century old. Now, with the fervor of the first neophytes calmed down and their comprehensible, but often too easy, enthusiasm moderated, linguistic geography can rightly fill the place it deserves among the methods of linguistic studies.

Linguistic geography owes its origin to the comparative method started by Bopp and his close successors who deduced the kinship of Indo-European languages from the observation of the corresponding linguistic phenomena, building their theory on the basis of those phonetic series that were improperly called laws and, in the wrong estimation of Schleicher and even more of the neogrammarians, were interpreted and applied as laws of the physical world.

But since H. Schuchardt[1] opposed naturalism and strict neogrammarian uniformity with his spiritualistic interpretation of language, considered in the essence of its historical reality, new methodological needs appeared on the horizon of linguistics. And when Paul Meyer,[2] in conformity with the "Wellentheorie" of Schmidt[3] and in a polemic against Ascoli,[4] demonstrated that the location of different isoglottic lines did not coincide in one linguistic area, it became necessary to represent and study each linguistic fact separately, abstracting oneself from those dialectical limits to which Meyer had denied any real objective existence. Among those who agreed with Meyer were also Antoine Thomas and Gaston

From *Word*, Vol. 10 (1954) pages 357-387. Reprinted by permission of Johnson Reprint Corporation.

Paris.   The latter, in *Les parlers de France*,[5] showed the way
later followed by his pupil Jules Gilliéron, the master of the
linguistic geography, a way which became an organic part of
linguistics, improving and renewing the comparative method with
a broader and more realistic view of developmental factors.   As a
matter of fact, after the first discoveries of Gilliéron, the grave
deficiencies of traditional etymology became evident, particularly
in the field of the Romance languages.   It became clear that
traditional etymology, confining itself to the relation between the
starting-point of an evolution and its conclusion, ignored all intermediate phases, sometimes distorting the history of the word.
With perhaps an excess of assurance and absolutism, Gilliéron
proclaimed "the failure of phonetic etymology."

The new views of that multiform prism which is human language, illustrated by Gilliéron and his school, evoked a general
echo of consent.   When in 1919 his lecture on *La faillite*[6] appeared, the *Atlas linguistique de la France* (*ALF*)[7] had already been
published, a "monumentum aere perennius"[8] which, as the first
geographic representation of linguistic facts seen in a moment of
their development, offered to historical-reconstructive research
an effective means for the investigation of the complex reasons
of their divergence.   The principle and the procedure were obvious: just as the geologist moves from the morphological aspect
of the ground to discover the sedimentary processes that have
determined it, so the linguist needs a faithful representation of
the linguistic area to reconstruct its history.   Dictionaries were
not and are not enough for this purpose.   Though no atlas
contains as much material as a dictionary, it can, with a limited
number of grammatical and lexicological examples, offer a representation, even if synthetic and only sketchy, of a linguistic
zone characterized in time and space.   In addition, a careful
observation and an ingenious comparison of the maps of the *ALF*
revealed a series of developmental facts unnoticed by former linguists, and the processes through which innovation takes place
appeared in all their complexity.

When Gilliéron undertook his task he may not have realized
the consequences that would come from the study of the materials
that Edmont, his wise and tireless cooperator, submitted to him,
and that he was sketching in on outline maps of France.   However,
these consequences became evident soon afterwards, upon the
completion of the great work, in the studies of Gilliéron himself
and of his most faithful disciples, Jean Mongines and Mario
Roques.[9]   These studies devoted particular attention to phenomena
of a psychological nature which had not been considered significant
before and stressed expressive peculiarities peculiar to the different social classes, the sexes, and the age groups of the speakers
which had been submerged in the levelled neogrammarian studies.

Ethnic reactions and substratum phenomena brought out in
Ascoli's learned work were subjected to stricter discipline through
areal comparison.   Thus for instance the occurrence of cacuminal
sounds (such as -ḍ(ḍ)- < LL-) in the amphizone of the Mediterranean

and farther up to the Indian peninsula actually helps delimit the area of the peoples that were overpowered by Indo-European waves.[10]

The genesis and expansion of innovating currents crossing, interweaving, being superposed on one another, became evident. In an area of mixed languages like Corsica, areal comparison leads us to recognize the most ancient ethnic linguistic aspects (common to Sardinia and Sicily, too) which are partly obscured by the Tuscan stratum;[11] and we can follow the succeeding and more recent French penetration from the principal centers (Bastia, Aiaccio).[12] And if the Corsican sonorization of the voiceless intervocalis occlusives, originally intact, is to be attributed to Tuscan influence, as I think I have demonstrated, the *vexata quaestio* about the priority of Tuscan series like *ago* < ACU over the series *fuoco* < FOCU[13] is explained and settled.

The processes of Latin linguistic expansion could be traced in a new light through the successive strata of Romanized territory. In Sardinia we find derivations of Lat. JANUA, FORNU, ĪLEX, and also of Lat. JENUA, FŬRNU, and ĒLEX; the presence of the former in the central zone, the most conservative in the island, and of the latter in the peripheral zones, reveals two chronologically different moments of Sardinian Latinization.[14]

The phonetic decay that may bring about the destruction of the form of a word or create homonymies that are intolerable for the linguistic feeling of the speakers, now was ranked among the most important developmental factors in lexical history. A language strengthens weakened words, abandons and replaces embarrassing homophones.[15] The reason why the Romance languages retain CAMBA and not CRUS is to be sought in the weak resistance of the Latin word. In the Gallo-Roman territory especially, where evolution is quicker and more destructive, many Latin monosyllables, dissyllables, and trisyllables show a tendency to disappear if they are not strengthened by a suffix, so that SOLICULU > *soleil*, ACUCULA > *aiguille*, CORBICULA > *corbeille*, AETATICU > *âge* replace the doomed words SOLE, ACU, CORBE, AETATE. Against the few, marginal, and weak survivals of APIS > *ef*, *es*, we have the flourishing of substitute designations which Gilliéron studied in their genetic relations with so much - perhaps too much - ingenuity.[16] Prov. *clavel* < CLAVELLUS replaces *claus* < CLAVUS which clashed with *claus* < CLAVIS;[17] *traire* < TRAHERE replaces *moudre* < MULGĒRE, which merged in the struggle with *moudre* < MOLĒRE;[18] in the Gascon area, the cock becomes a vicar (*bégey* < VICARIUM) or a pheasant (*hazan* < PHASIANUM) as GALLUS and GATTUS in the long run converge into the single ambiguous form *gat*;[19] the success of *viande* < VIVENDA is due to the Parisian pronunciation in which *char* < CARNE, pronounced *cher*, gets confused with *chère* < CARA.[20] The innovating effect of these phonetic and semantic conflicts may take place at any time and place, for instance - leaving the French sphere - we notice that in a part of the Italian territory bounded by Sillaro, Santerno, and Senio (Emilia-Romagna) the "hedge" is referred to by derivations of Lat. SAEPE (> *sęva*, *sęve*, *siv*, *sęv*); in another part, these are replaced by derivatives of a deverbative of CLAUDERE (> *cǫ́da*, *kiǫda*). The reason for this substitution becomes evident if we observe that in the same territory, the derivations of Lat. SALVIA become *sęv* in the zone of *cǫ́da* (*kiǫda*), so that superposing the two areas of *cǫ́da* and *sęv* < SALVIA, we get perfect congruence.[21]

Besides the comparison of linguistic areas, we derive from linguistic geography the criteria for understanding not only the lexical evolution due to homonymy, but also to different aspects of monosemy and polysemy. If instead of starting from the *idea* reflected in its various denominations (onomasiology) we start from the *word*, we can construct semantic maps where different meanings of the same word characterize mutually exclusive areas (e.g. in Friuli *linda* < *LIMITA "eaves" and *linda* "lodge"), others where the two semantic values are superimposed on one another (e.g. in the north of Italy, *balcone* "window" and *balcone* "shutter"), and still others where the process of superposition is not completed but where it can be seen in action, or where semantic areas recede and lose contact with each other. The various reasons and conditions of polysemy may be seen in the comparison of semantic areas: thus the meanings have less stability and are weaker in the periphery of a zone, while in the middle they struggle more vigorously until they reach a definite order; the literary language avoids polsemy as much as possible; polysemy is frequent in dialectal speech especially when two ideas are included in the same sphere of human activity; and so forth.[22]

Areal comparison yields results not only in the field of lexicology, but is useful also in the fields of phonetics, morphology,[23] and syntax. Everywhere there is a ferment of studies aiming toward a biology of language, probing deeply into the analysis of thought and of its expression considered as the creative act of the individual in a socially determined environment.

Linguistic geography draws its origin from Gilliéron's *Atlas*; none of the earlier works of a similar nature [24] had a sufficient rigor or breadth of view to launch it. Considering the value of the first results of the new methods, one can easily understand the enthusiasm of the master and his disciples and their belief that they had overthrown the whole edifice built up in a century of work by the pioneers of linguistic science and by the neogrammarians. Gilliéron, an eminently critical and caustic mind, thought that the comparison of geographical areas could in itself resolve the most vexed linguistic problems, and thus worked almost exclusively with the materials of the *Atlas*. Notwithstanding the deficiencies pointed out by many people, he thought the *Atlas* to be essentially reliable and used it to destroy the myth of a phonetic law working, like a force of nature, blindly, rigorously, and inescapably. The Gilliéron critique nearly coincides with that of the linguists following Benedetto Croce's idealisms;[25] they, too, in stressing correctly the spiritual value of the creative act of language, opposed the neogrammarian naturalism. But at bottom,

Gillieronians and Crocians followed fundamentally different principles and moved from different points of view.   The former
started from the system, considered in its arrangement, and from
perturbations coming from expressive necessities incident to its
equilibrium; the latter began with the word in the immediacy of
its poetic creation.[26]   In addition, both, though working together
to throw down the last bulwarks of neogrammarian resistance and
to clear the way of science toward new goals, had a one-sided
view of the truth, which still escapes us.   As we progress in
our studies, we continue to discover the faults of our predecessors.

Gilliéron thought that he could discard the services of the
historical-comparative method.   But as the errors in some of his
most daring constructions came to light,[27] the scope of geographical comparison was reducing itself to its proper limits.[28]   For, if
geographical comparison can point, for example, to homophony as
the cause of a creative impulse, it can say nothing or very little
about the reasons why the innovation becomes established in the
mind of the speaker in one way rather than in another.[29]

"Quelle est," asks Millardet,[30] "la valeur primitive de l'image
contenue dans *bégey* < VICARIUM 'coq'?   Est-ce l'echo d'une
satire anticléricale, nous reportant à l'inspiration des fabliaux?
Ou bien le 'coq' est-il le vice-roi du poulailler, ou bien autre
chose encore?   Dans quel milieu social a pu se developper tout
d'abord le sens nouveau?   Le mot est-il savant ou héréditaire?"
We cannot answer all these questions by means of linguistic
geography alone.   But we must also observe that the conception
of the death of words due to phonetic decay was based on that
very historical phonetics towards which Gilliéron and his first
aides showed so much disdain; we can say that the phonetic law
or, better, the phonetic series, which had been driven out through
the door came in again through the window.   The followers of
Gilliéron have been speaking of superseding the traditional method,
but the work of those who discovered and studied the phonetic
"laws" could not have been in vain if many of these "laws" have
withstood the sharpest criticism and some of them have been
allowed the reconstruction of forms which were subsequently confirmed by historical documents.   The pronominal form EO (< EGO),
resulting from Romance comparison (Sard, *eo*, Prov. Port. *eu*,
It. *io*, Span. *yo*, etc.) found its confirmation in the manuscripts
of the sixth century from which we may presume[31] the existence
of that form in a former epoch.   From the historical sources we
derive the certainty which is missing in the results both of mere
phonetic comparison and of areal comparison.   Fetishists have
made great claims for each of the latter methods, but it would be
difficult to say which of them is farther from the truth when
each of them sticks to positions which are not sustained by the
facts.   The numerous aspects of the phenomenon of language
need different methods of study which must all contribute their
best to its reasonable explanation.   The facts which are beyond
the scope of both phonetic comparison and geographic comparison
are numerous.   The latter cannot produce the reason for the

semantic evolution of *pagus* "pale limiting a property" into *pagus* "village", of *paganus* "inhabitant of the pagus" into *paganus* "worshipper of the gods", of *vicus* "block of houses" into *vicus* "a street", of *aedes*, -*is* "fireplace, temple" into *aedes*, -*ium* "house of many stories". The innovations *casa* and *mansio*, preserved in the Romance languages instead of *domus* and *aedes*, are due to political and social causes and depend on factors of civilization[32] which explain also the vitality of *germanus* and the luck of *fratellus* against *frater*; and the reasons for the gradual abandonment of *patruus* and *matertera* and of the prevalence of the pair *avunculus* --*amita*, of the victory of the Graecism *zio*, -*a* < THIUS < *thetos* are of affective character.[33]   The foreign elements, which often penetrate a language and become an integral part of it, are also discovered and arranged chronologically through phonetic and grammatical comparison[34] and through history, rather than through areal comparison.   Moreover, we must not forget that homonyms and homophones are not always intolerable to the linguistic feeling of the speakers, and they can coexist conserving their different meaning, e.g. *riso* from "ridere" and *riso* "graminaceae", *rombo* from "rombare" and *rombo* "a sea fish", *canto* of the voice and *canto* "corner", *ratto* "rape" and *ratto* "rat", *mondo* "the earth, the universe" and *mondo* from "mondare", *fondo* from "fondare" and *fondo* from "fondere", *porto* from "portare" and *porto* "harbor"; *louer* < LAUDARE and *louer* < LOCARE; similarly, though they are spelled differently, *verre* "a glass", *vair* "various", *vert* "green", *vers* "towards"; *cou* "neck" and *coup* "stroke", etc., etc.   It follows that homonymy and homophony considered as developmental factors should be used with great caution and not with the almost absolute faith in them which Gilliéron showed in his resourceful constructions.

On the other hand, the certainty of Gilliéron's reasonings and presumed conclusions is opposed at least by the poverty of the materials offered by each linguistic atlas, the richest of which can capture and represent in outline only the most general character of the linguistic territory, displaying it in broad strokes, while the most significant meanings escape it.[35]   To this fundamental defect of all the works we are dealing with we should add the unavoidable mistakes made by the explorer of a zone, mistakes that are due, among others, to the way in which the plan of a linguistic atlas is organized and carried out.   In so far as the *ALF* itself is concerned, the checks made in the course of time have subsequently revealed its grave deficiencies;[36] and since the atlas is the base on which the promoters of linguistic geography must build, we understand why in the works inspired afterwards by their masters, they have tried to re-examine the methodological standards in the light of the facts produced.

The importance of Gilliéron's teaching and the success of the *ALF* appear also from the considerable number of linguistic atlases that were published in Europe and elsewhere from 1910 to 1950 or are still in the process of study or completion.[37]   They are

all interesting, and some are indicative of new orientations and
recent advances in the geographic sector of linguistic study.

It would be useful to deal here in particular with the later
atlases, keeping an eye on the methodological criteria followed by
Gillieron, and comparing them with those which have been adopted
since.   Such criteria concern chiefly: (1) the choice of the
points of inquiry; (2) the compilation of the work sheets; (3)
the character of the fieldworker; (4) the character of informants;
(5) the method of questioning.

1.   As is known, Gilliéron chose the points of inquiry of the
ALF quite mechanically, in a geometrical pattern, as it were.
Consequently, Edmont was compelled to modify the plan as he
went along.[38]   This is obviously prejudicial to the objectivity
which is required of a fieldworker, for it involves him in the
analysis of the materials he is collecting and a comparison of the
different zones - jobs which are the duty rather of the future
user of the atlas.   That is why I have long maintained[38] that
the network of points must be made in advance, chiefly on ethno-
linguistic principles derived from previous reliable knowledge of
the area under study.   This is now done in practice by most
people, even by those who do not acknowledge it formally.

2.   The drawing up of work sheets, or questionnaires, has
also proceeded quite differently since Gilliéron.   He had said
that "le questionnaire . . . pour être sensiblement meilleur,
aurait dû être fait après l'enquête";[40] hence the best work sheets
are those which fit the specific character of the area under
study and which result from previous studies of that very area.
This is what most people have been doing since the *ALF*.

3.   Another of Gilliéron's standards that we may now consider
quite surpassed concerns the fieldworker.   According to the
Master, he should not be a linguist in order that a maximum of
objectivity may prevail and lest he criticize while he collects.[41]
Now it is a fact that the field workers of all linguistic atlases
since the *ALF* have almost all been linguists: Oscar Bloch, Griera,
Gauchat, Tappolet, Scheuermeier, Rohlfs, Wagner, Pop, Kurath
and his assistants, etc. etc.   This is because we now realize
that the autosuggestion and the prejudice feared by Gilliéron
cannot influence the man who, linguist or not, is devoted with
all his mind to the difficult task of selecting an informant,
establishing rapport, and transcribing so smoothly and so quickly
as not to interrupt the contact which has been forming and binds
the questioner to the questioned.   The field worker, even if he
is a specialist in linguistics, is so absorbed with this exhausting
work that he could not, though he would, think of rules, phonetic
laws, linguistic schemes.

The advantages that a native fieldworker may have over a
foreigner in the area under study have also been discussed; but
since it is now agreed that the area should be well known by
those who work in it, it is plain that a native collector, with
training and other necessary qualifications, will always produce
better results.   Hence a large territory which is linguistically

diverse, like Italy or France, should be explored by a staff of fieldworkers, each of them able to get deeply into the specifics of the area in his charge. Gilliéron was not of this opinion, and his skepticism is shared by those who think it is impossible to get among the various fieldworkers that uniformity of procedure which is necessary to get methodologically uniform materials. I will not try to resume here my discussion of this problem of over twenty years ago.[42] I think that my arguments have since been proved correct by my colleagues, Hans Kurath and his nine able assistants who together compiled the New England Atlas,[43] and by Tomàs Navarro Tomàs who entrusted to eight explorers the collection of the materials for the Atlas of the Iberian Peninsula (*ALPI*), which is to be published soon.[44]

4. Concerning the criteria of a good informant (sex, age, familiarity with surroundings, amount of education, etc.), we can see both extremes. On the one hand, the authors of the Italian-Swiss Atlas (*AIS*),[45] which marked a considerable advance in methodology, think that "the fieldworker's rule must be not to stick to any rule." [46] Scheuermeier, one of the able fieldworkers, confirms this; "il n'y a pas de règle infaillible pour le choix d'un bon sujet." [47] On the other hand, Pop requires a rigorous method[48] and enumerates as many as sixteen criteria[49] followed by him in the choice of his subjects for the Rumanian Atlas (*ALR*).[50] No one else, as far as I know, before or after Pop, has felt it necessary to stick to these or similar rules. We may conclude, I think, that except for certain irreducible requirements (certain knowledge of local speech, good pronunciation, intelligence, etc.), the choice of a good informant is entrusted to the intuition and experience of the fieldworker.

What remains to be ascertained is whether a single informant is superior to a group of two or more. Most linguistic atlases record the answer of one informant; but even Edmont sometimes had to question two or three persons, and the same happened to Griera for his Catalan Atlas (*ALC*),[51] to Scheuermeier and to other fieldworkers for the Italian-Swiss Atlas,[52] and to Pellis for the Italian Linguistic Atlas (*ALI*).[53] Pop distinguishes an inquiry made in a whole country, for which he allows the necessity of several informants, from that made in a given territory, where a single informant is preferable, though the possibility of parallel inquiries remains even here[54]; Bloch, for his Vosges Atlas[55] questioned, besides the principal informant, from two to six secondary ones.[56] For my Atlas of Corsica (*ALEIC*)[57] I used a single informant who was, as it were, responsible, but I admitted the help or corrections of other informants. Thus, even those who accepted the rule of the single informant (authors of the *ALF*, *ALC*, *AIS*, etc.) were often forced to resort to different informants, so that even this principle of the Gilliéron procedure may now be considered superseded once and for all.

5. Let us deal at somewhat greater length with the use of the work sheets, that is, of the questioning method, for on this point there has been an inclination to carry to the limit a procedure

hinted at by Gilliéron, but which is to be attributed particularly to the directors of the *AIS*, followed by Pop and a few others.

I have discussed this subject on several occasions[58] and will briefly recapitulate here. It is a fact that Gilliéron's scheme has no strict rules,[59] so that Edmont, in using, for instance, his herbarium, added certain supplementary explanations which he did not report.[60] We may conclude that neither Gilliéron nor Edmont cared about the strict uniformity of questioning. The same goes for O. Bloch,[61] Le Roux [62] (when he thought he was not well understood, he made an additional interview[63]), and Gardette,[64] whose work sheets were changed several times during the inquiry.[65] On the contrary, the uniformity of questioning is an essential rule of the linguistic collection in the Italian-Swiss Atlas, and it was strictly observed by Pop and Pellis, the late lamented collector of the Italian Linguistic Atlas. This group thought that the answers of different informants are not comparable if they are not elicited in the same way; they lost sight of the true aim of this research, namely, to discover and record for each place the most exact expression of the idea proposed in the work sheets, an expression which will really be useful for the comparative purposes.

Is it possible that informants of different character, habits, and culture when questioned in a uniform way, should reveal that objective truth which we are looking for? A hunter, well versed in the form and life of birds, will react properly when faced with a good picture or drawing, but a worker chosen at random will need detailed, circumstantial oral explanations; moreover, the opportunities which keep arising during the interview for pointing out to the informant an object for whose name we are looking are numberless, and to disregard them seems naive, to say the least.

The conviction that the best answer is the first, given by the informant as a reaction to the first stimulus of the question itself, goes hand in hand with the belief that the uniformity of the question is essential to the comparative goal. And those who adhere to this method strictly know and admit that the materials they collect do not represent the maximum degree of objective truth, but only the effects that a uniform stimulus produces on different subjects. But this is a subjective truth which does not interest a future user of the atlas; he would like to be able to consider the material offered as a true image of the linguistic conditions in a given territory. For my own part, I have got rid of what I consider as prejudices and, as I have written several times, it is my opinion that the work sheet represents not the *means*, but the *aim* of the inquiry. By a series of words, it sets forth the impressions we want to produce in the informants; the expressions we may want of him may be stimulated and directed by any suitable means and at any occasion that arises during the interview. It follows that those who study an atlas compiled by the so-called impressionistic method (uniformity of question, answer at one stroke) may be comparing mistakes, too, while those who use an atlas made without the handicap of any such rules will be comparing the materials that synthesize the real average speech, checked by the one responsible informant. And it will be granted that everybody aims at this, even the adherents of the impressionistic method, so that for instance Sever Pop, who is among the latter, takes care to avoid the danger of "présenter des cartes linguistiques qui ne reflètent pas le parler de la majorité des individus employant encore le pathois dans leur entourage."[66]

All agree, then, on the aim: both those whom we should call *rigorists*, that is adherents of a rigorous and mechanical method, like Pop, and the *free collectors*, like the writer himself, who follow a method corresponding to reality and free from the handicap of strict and tyrannic rules. We could continue this discussion, but the remarkable progress of linguistic geography, from the year when the *ALF* appeared to the atlases that now are being planned or completed, can be easily inferred from the preceding discussion. These atlases show that the method of the free collectors is being improved and the number of its followers is growing as the checking of the already published atlases proceeds and experience increases. In fact, the analysis of the deficiencies of the *ALF* has prompted the work of the regional atlases of France, inspired and directed by Albert Dauzat[67] in conjunction, and in full agreement on purpose and method, with the well known Mgr. Gardette, who after the Lyons Atlas is now working on that of the Massif Central. Similarly, work is proceeding on regional atlases in the framework of the impressive Linguistic Atlas of the United States and Canada, as reported by Harold B. Allen in *Orbis* 1.89-94 (1952); the inquiries of R. Hotzenköcherle[68] for the *Linguistic and Ethnographic Atlas of German Switzerland*[69] are also in progress. Spain, too, is working hard: the materials of the *ALPI* should be published soon, while Luis Cortés Vasquez of Salamanca University is at work on the *Atlas lingüistico de Sanabria* - an interesting region in which four linguistic currents join and influence one another. In Italy the publication of the materials collected by the late Ugo Pellis for the *ALI* is now eagerly awaited; while the standards of the field work are not those demanded today, the collection itself is valuable.

There is, then, everywhere intense research and study[70] which shows that linguistic geography has become an essential part of linguistic science. We may say that there is no longer any scholar of historical-reconstructive linguistics who does not feel the need of recourse to areal comparison; such comparison may not be decisive as often as Gilliéron and his first pupils thought, but is always informative on problems not only of modern languages but even of the most ancient ones.[71] It is enough to recall, for the latter, how the theory of the marginal areas started and promoted, after the discovery of Tokharian,[72] a new conception of the original Indo-European guttural in the contrast of the *kentum* and *satem* languages, and illustrated the Basque-Caucasian connections in the frame of Mediterranean languages. Finally, it is likely that further achievements of linguistic geography may contribute enormously to reconcile the Saussurian dualism[73] in the modern orientation of structural linguistics that studies hetero-genesis and endogenesis in the perpetual development of different systems. Linguistic geography may yet open to science those new fields outlined more than twenty years ago by N. S. Troubetzkoy when he called for the geographical-phonological description of the languages of the world.[74]

FOOTNOTES

[1] *Über die Lautgesetze. Gegen die Junggrammatiker*, Berlin, 1855.

[2] In *Romania*, 4.294-296.

[3] J. Schmidt, *Die Verwandschaftsverhältnisse der indogermanischen Sprachen*, Weimar, 1872.

[4] See *Archivio Glottologico Italiano*, 2.385ff. (1876).

[5] Reprinted in *Mélanges linguistiques*, publiés par Mario Roques, Paris, 1909, 432ff.

[6] Jules Gilliéron, *Étude sur la défectivité des verbes. La faillité de l'étymologie phonétique*; résumé de conférences faites à l'École pratique des Hautes Études; Neuveville, Beerstecher, 1919.

[7] Paris, Champion, 1902-12; *ALF Corse*, 1914.

[8] This was defined by Meyer-Lübke himself (in *Litteraturblatt für germanische und romanische Philologie*, June, 1902), who in his sincere enthusiasm did not foresee the uncompromising struggle Gilliéron would wage against the neogrammarian school.

[9] Among the many studies of linguistic analysis and reconstruction, we should mention here Gilliéron's *Généalogie des mots qui désignent l'abeille d'après l'Atlas linguistique de la France*, Paris, Champion, 1918.

[10] Bottiglioni, Indice fonetico per l'area di espansione ligure (Abstract from *Atti del 1° Congresso Internazionale di Studi Liguri*, 1950); L. Heilmann, Il problema delle cerebrali indiane, in *Seritti in onore di Alfredo Trombetti*, 287-304.

[11] Bottiglioni, La penetrazione toscana e le regioni di Pomonte nei parlari di Corsica, *L'Italia Dialettale* 2.156-210 and 3.1-69.

[12] Bottiglioni, Elementi costitutivi delle parlate còrse secondo l'Atlante Linguistico Etnografico Italiano della Corsica, *Memorie Accad. Bologna, Classe Sc. morali*, S. IV, V. ii (1934/41).

[13] Bottiglioni, Il còrso pretoscano nella classificazione delle lingue romanze, *Archivum romanicum* 21.524 (1937).

[14] See M. L. Wagner, La stratificazione del lessico sardo, *Revue de linguistique romane* 4 (1928), num. 13-14.

[15] See J. Gilliéron, *Pathologie et thérapeutique verbales*, Paris, Champion, 1918.

[16] *Généalogie, cit.*, passim.

[17] Gilliéron, *L'aire "clavellus" d'après l' "Atlas linguistique de la France*," Neuveville, 1912.

[18] Gilliéron-Mongin, Études de géographie linguistique III. Traire, mulgere et molere, *Revue de philologie francaise* 20.90-98 (1906).

[19] Gilliéron-Roques, Etudes de géographie linguistique XII. Mots en collision. A. Le coq et le chat, *Rev. phil. franç.* 24.278-288 (1910).

[20] Gilliéron, *Pathologie, cit.*, I, 2ff.

[21] See Antonio Quarneti, Un caso di omofonia nei dialetti delle alte valli del Síllaro, Santèrno e Sénio, *Memorie Accad. Bologna*, S. IV, V. iii (1939-41).

[22] For this study of semantic areas, see K. Jaberg, *Aspects géographiques de langage.* Deuxième conférence (aires sémantiques), Paris, 1936, 43-77.

[23] See Jaberg, *Aspects géographiques, cit.* Troisiéme conférence (aires morphologiques), 79-106.

[24] Like the *Petit atlas phonétique du Valais roman* (sud du Rhône), Paris, Champion, 1880, also by Gilliéron; the *Sprachatlas von Nord- und Mitteldeutschland*, Strassburg, 1881 and the 28 maps added to the *Geographie der Schwäbischen Mundart*, Tübingen, 1895.

[25] B. Croce, *Estetica come scienza dell'espressione e linguistica generale*, Barl, 1922; La filosofia del linguaggio e le sue condizioni presenti in Italia, *La Critica* 39 (1941).

[26] See Karl Vossler, *Positivismus und Idealismus in der Sprachwissenschaft*, Heidelberg, 1904; *Sprache als Schöpfung und Entwickelung*, Heidelberg, 1905.

[27] E. g. in the *Abeille* (*cit.*) where, however, Gilliéron shows all the acuteness of his mind and his exquisite linguistic sensibility. For the criticism on this, see Dauzat, *La géographie linguistique*, Paris, Flammarion, 1922, 46ff.; Georges Millardet, *Linguistique et dialectologie romanes* , Paris, Champion, 1933, 42ff., 379ff., and passim.

[28] Karl Jaberg, *Aspects géographiques du langage*, Paris, Droz. 1936, 42: "La géographie linguistique n'a pas la prétention de créer un corps de doctrines particulières. Elle n'est pas, non plus, comme le feraient croire certaines travaux de nôtre maitre Gilliéron, fier de la nouvelle voie qu'il avait ouverte, une sorte de "trobar clus". Elle peut cependant revendiquer quelques mérites. . . ." See also M. Grammont, *Rev. Lang. Rom.*, 63:319 (1926): "si le comparatisme historique a trop longtemps régné seul, il serait funeste que le comparatisme géographique régnât seul après l'avoir détrôné. On ne saurait faire oeuvre utile et solide qu'en combinant ensemble toutes les informations fournies par l'un et l'autre, et en outre toutes les autres ressources dont on peut disposer."

[29]See Walther v. Wartburg, *Problèmes et méthodes de la linguistique*, translated from German by Pierre Maillard, Paris, 1946, 124ff.

[30]Millardet, *Linguistique et dialectologie*, *cit.*, 66.

[31]Schuchardt, *Vokalismus des Vulgärlateins*, Leipzig, I, 129.

[32]See Alfred Ernout, *Philologica*, Paris, Klincksieck, 1946, 103-118.

[33]See Paul Aebischer, *Annali della R. Scoula Normale Superiore di Pisa* 5.1-52 (1936); Vittorio Bertoldi, *Linguistica storica* (*Questioni di metodo*), second edition, Roma, Soc. Dante Alighieri, s.a., 67-71.

[34]I cite, from among many, the now classic work of Alfred Ernout, *Les éléments dialectaux du vocabularie latin*, Paris, 1909.

[35]Wartburg, *Problemes*, *cit.*, 1933: "L'image qu'il donne du trésor linguistique ressemble à un paysage de collines dans une mer de nuages: seuls les sommets émergent; quant aux dépressions sur lesquelles s'élèvent ces hauteurs et forment le lien organique entre elles, elles restent dissimulées sous le voile opaque des nuages."

[36]See e.g. Dauzat, *cit.*, 11ff., 127ff.; Louis Remacle, Présentation de l'Atlas linguistique de la Wallonie (the first volume of which was published 1953) in *Essais de philologie moderne* (1951); Bibliothèque de la Faculte de Philosophie et Lettres de l'Université de Liège, fasc. CXXIX, Paris, 1953, p. 245. For the maps of Corisa, P. E. Guarnerio, *Rendiconti Istituto Lombardo* 48.517ff; C. Salvioni, *ibid.*, 49.705ff; V. Bertoldi, Vocabolari e atlanti dialettali, *Riv. della Soc. Filol. friul. G. I. Ascoli*, Anno V. fasc. II; Bottiglioni, La penetrazione toscana e le regioni di Pomonte, *cit.*, passim.

[37]They are listed, with satisfactory descriptions of their structure, but with judgments of methodological order which are not always reliable, in the weighty and highly meritorious work of Sever Pop (*La Dialectologie. Aperçu historique et méthodes d'enquêtes linguistiques*. Parties I (*Dialectologie romane*), II (*Dialectologie non romane*), i-xxi, 1-1334, Louvain, 1950), as supplemented by Albert Dauzat's remarks and additions, *Le francais moderne*, 19º année, num. 3, 1951, 225ff. See also my own remarks in *Rendiconti dell'Istituto di Glottologia dell'Universita di Bologna* (IV, 1952), Bologna, S.T.E.B., 1953, pp. 3-4, and in Questioni di metodo nella preparazione degli atlanti linguistici, *Cultura Neolatina* 12.144ff. (1952). For other interesting reports of the latest plans of linguistic Atlases see *Orbis. Bulletin intern. de documentation ling.* 1.87ff. (1952); 2.49ff. (1953).

[38]"De fait il n'est guère de département où nous ayons maintenu le nombre de points d'enquête qui avait fait été fixé primitivement" (*Atlas linguistique de la France, Notice*, Paris, 1902, p. 4).

[39]In Le inchieste dialettali e gli Atlanti Linguistici, *Atti della XX riunione (settembre, 1931) della Societa per il progresso delle Scienze (SIPS)*, Milano, 1932, Vol. I, 413-492.

[40]*Études de géographie linguistique. I. Pathologie et thérapeutique verbales*, Neuveville, 1915, p. 45.

[41] *Abeille, cit.*, p. 3.

[42] In *Atti della XX riunione della SIPS, cit.*, (footnote 39).

[43] *Linguistic Atlas of New England,* Providence, Rhode Island, Brown University, 1939-43.

[44] *Atlas lingüistico de la Penìnsula Ibérica*; See M. Sanchiz Guarner, *La cartografia lingüistica en la actualidad y el Atlas de la Penìnsula Ibérica*, Instituto Miguel de Cervantes, Palma de Mallorca, 1953.

[45] K. Jaberg und J. Jud, *Sprach- und Sachatlas Italiens und der Südschweiz*, Bande I-VIII, Zofingen, 1928-40. Among the great merits of this atlas is the addition of the study and comparison of ethnographic data to those of linguistic facts.

[46] Jaberg-Jud, *Der Sprachatlas als Forschungsinstrument*, Halle (Saale), 1928, p. 191.

[47] P. Scheuermeier, Observations et expériences personnelles faites au cours de mon enquête poul l'Atlas linguistique et ethnographique de l'Italie et de la Suisse méridionale, *Bulletin de la Société de linguistique de Paris*, 23.104 (1932).

[48] Pop, *La Dialectologie, cit.*, p. 1156.

[49] *Ibid.*, pp. 723ff.

[50] *Atlasul linguistic român*, sub conducerea lui Sextil Puscariu, part I (by Sever Pop), II (by Emil Petrovici), Cluj, 1938-40.

[51] A. Griera, *Atlas lingüistic de Catalunya*, Montserrat, 1923-39. Interrupted at the 5th volume. See Pop, *La Dialectologie, cit.*, p. 372.

[52] See Pop, *La Dialectologie, cit.*, p. 579.

[53] Promoted by the Società Filologica Friulana G. I. Ascoli, directed by the late Professor Matteo Bartoli; Ugo Pellis, also deceased, collected almost all the materials now at the University of Turin. See Pop, *La Dialectologie, cit.*, 598ff.

[54] *La Dialectologie, cit.*, p. 726.

[55] *Atlas linguistique des Vosges méridionales*, Paris, Champion, 1917.

[56] See Pop, *La Dialectologie, cit.*, p. 96.

[57] G. Bottiglioni, *Atlante Linguistico Etnografico della Corsica*, Pisa, 1933-41-42.

[58] Inchieste dialettali, *cit.*; Questioni di metodo, *cit.*; Il valore unitario e quello obiettivo degli Atlanti Linguistici, *Annali della R. Scuola Normale Superiore di Pisa*, S. II, Vol. (1932), 167ff.; Come si preparano e comme si studiano gli Atlanti linguistici, *ibid.*, S. II, Vol. ii (1933), 126ff.

[59] *Notice, cit.*, p. 4.

[60] Pop, *La Dialectologie, cit.*, p. 118.

[61] *Ibid.*, p. 94.

[62] In the *Atlas linguistique de la Basse-Bretagne*, Paris, 1924-43.

[63] See Pop, *La Dialectologie, cit.*, p. 949.

[64] In the *Atlas linguistique et ethnographique du Lyonnais* (ALL), Institute de Linguistique Romane, Facultés Catholiques de Lyon.

[65] See *Bulletin de l'Institut de Linguistique Romane de Lyon* I, 1953; Pop, *La Dialectologie, cit.*, p. 224.

[66] Pop, *La Dialectologie*, *cit*, p. 1156.

[67] *Nouvel atlas linguistique de la France par régions* (*NALF*). To round out the information in *Le français moderne*, April, 1939, pp. 97-101 and January 1941, pp. 1ff. (see also Pop, *La Dialectologie, cit.*, 136ff.), I can add here the latest reports according to a personal communication from Dauzat. The first volume of 220 maps of the Gascon Atlas entrusted to Jean Séguy, Professor of the University of Toulouse, is going to be published, the Atlas Poitu-Charente is almost finished, Miss Massignon having completed the fourth part of the definitive inquiries; M. Loriot has done the field work for the Atlas of the North and Picardy in the whole South of the zone; Dauzat himself is doing with youthful vigor (in spite of his 76 years) the fieldwork for the Arvernian and Limousin Atlas; intensive work is also going on for the Atlas of Provence, entrusted to Ch. Rostaing, who will do the field work at Bouches du Rhônes, his native town; M. Camproux, Luis Michel and Alibert are working on the Atlas of Languedoc; R. Sincou is busy with Quercy, the center of an Atlas Guyenne-Albigeois; the Atlas of the West will be directed by Abbe Guillaume; the Atlas of Normandy has been entrusted to F. Lechanteur who has almost completed his fieldwork on Cotentin and Bocage; Loriot will explore the Seine Inférieure. Further reports will appear in *Le français moderne*. The enthusiasm of my colleague Dauzat is obviously spreading among his able aides and the grand task to which they are devoting themselves will be completed.

[68] See *Bulletin de Lyon, cit.*

[69] See the report on it in *Essais de philologie moderne, cit.*, pp. 115ff.

[70] For the various Atlases which are being issued and drawn or planned, see Pop, *La Dialectologie, cit.*, cont. vol. II, pp. 1197-1198.

[71] The set of rules of spatial linguistics Matteo Bartoli dictated in 1925 (*Introduzione alla neolinguistica*, Biblioteca dell' *Archivum Romanicum*, S. II, Vol. xii, Genève) and applied during all his active life devoted to study (see *Saggi di linguistica spaziale*, Torino, 1945) is still very useful in this connection.

[72] See G. Campus, *Due note sulla questione delle velari arioeuropee*, Torino, 1916.

[73] See F. de Saussure, *Cours de linguistique générale*, Paris, 1931.

[74] CF. *Travaux du Cercle Linguistique de Prague*, 6.228ff. (1931).

IS STRUCTURAL DIALECTOLOGY POSSIBLE?

Uriel Weinreich

1. In linguistics today the abyss between structural and dialectological studies appears greater than it ever was. The state of disunity is not repaired if "phoneme" and "isogloss" occasionally do turn up in the same piece of research. Students continue to be trained in one domain at the expense of the other. Fieldwork is inspired by one, and only rarely by both, interests. The stauncher adherents of each discipline claim priority for their own method and charge the others with "impressionism" and "metaphysics," as the case may be; the more pliant are prepared to concede that they are simply studying different aspects of the same reality.

This might seem like a welcome truce in an old controversy, but is it an honorable truce? A compromise induced by fatigue cannot in the long run be satisfactory to either party. The controversy could be resolved only if the structuralists as well as the dialectologists found a reasoned place for the other discipline in their theory of language. But for the disciplines to legitimate each other is tantamount to establishing a unified theory of language on which both of them could operate. This has not yet been done.

While the obstacles are formidable, the writer of this paper believes that they are far from insurmountable. The present article is designed to suggest a few of the difficulties which should be ironed out if the theories of two very much disunited varieties of linguistics, structural and dialectological, are to be brought closer together. A certain amount of oversimplification is inevitable, for the "sides" in the controversy are populous and themselves far from unified. The author would not presume to function as an arbitrator. He simply hopes, without a needless multiplication of terms, to stimulate discussion with others who have also experienced the conflict of interests--within themselves.

If phonological problems dominate in this paper, this is the result of the fact that in the domain of sounds structural and non-structural approaches differ most;[1] semantic study has (so far, at least) not equalled sound study in precision, while in the

From *Word*, Vol. 10 (1954) pages 388-400. Reprinted by permission of Johnson Reprint Corporation.

domain of grammar, specifically structural points of view have had far less to contribute.

2. Regardless of all its heterogeneity, structural linguistics defines a language as an organized system. It was one of the liberating effects of structural linguistics that it made possible the treatment of a language as a unique and closed system whose members are defined by opposition to each other and by their functions with respect to each other, not by anything outside of the system. But since organization must have a finite scope, one of the major problems in a structural linguistic description is the delimitation of its object, the particular system described. Only in ideal cases can the linguist claim to be describing a whole "language" in the non-technical sense of the word. In practice he must delimit his object to something less. One of the steps he takes is to classify certain items in his data as intercalations from other systems, i.e. as "Synchronically foreign" elements (e.g. *bon mot* in an otherwise English sentence). Another step is to make certain that only one variety of the aggregate of systems which the layman calls a "language" is described. These steps are taken in order to insure that the material described is uniform. This seems to be a fundamental requirement of structural description.

To designate the object of the description which is in fact a subdivision of the aggregate of systems which laymen call a single language, the term "dialect" is often used. But if "dialect" is defined as the speech of a community, a region, a social class, etc. the concept does not seem to fit into narrowly structural linguistics because it is endowed with spatial or temporal attributes which do not properly belong to a linguistic system as such. "Dialects" can be adjacent or distant, contemporary or non-contemporary, prestigious or lowly; linguistic systems in a strictly structural view can only be identical or different. It is proposed that the term "dialect" be held in reserve for the time being and that, for purposes of structural analysis as set forth here, it be replaced by "variety."

In deference to the non-structural sense of "dialect" as a type of speech which may itself be heterogeneous, some linguists have broken down the object of description even further to the "idiolect" level. This term has been used in the United States to denote "the total set of speech habits of a single individual at a given time." The term has been seriously criticized on two grounds: (1) constancy of speech patterns may be more easily stated for two persons in a dialogic situation (a kind of *dialecte à deux*) than for a single individual; (2) there are differences even within an "idiolect" which require that it be broken down further (e.g. into "styles").

"Idiolect" is the homogeneous object of description reduced to its logical extreme, and, in a sense, to absurdity. If we agree with de Saussure that the task of general linguistics is to describe all the linguistic systems of the world,[2] and if description could proceed only one idiolect at a time, then the task of structur-

al linguistics would not only be inexhaustible (which might be
sad but true), but its results would be trivial and hardly worth
the effort.

The restriction of descriptive work to homogeneous material
has led to a paradox not quite unlike that proposed by Zeno
about motion. A moving arrow is located at some point at every
moment of time; at intermediate moments, it is at intermediate
positions. Therefore it never moves. Rigidly applied, the typical
elements of structural description--"opposition" and "function of
units with respect to other units of the same system"--have come
close to incapacitating structural analysis for the consideration of
several partly similar varieties at a time. Fortunately, the progress
of research no longer requires absolute uniformity as a working
hypothesis.[3]

Structural linguistic theory now needs procedures for constructing systems of a higher level out of the discrete and homogeneous systems that are derived from description and that represent each a unique formal organization of the substance of expression and content. Let us dub these constructions "diasystems,"
with the proviso that people allergic to such coinages might safely
speak of supersystems or simply of systems of a higher level. A
"diasystem" can be constructed by the linguistic analyst out of
any two systems which have partial similarities (it is these similarities which make it something different from the mere sum of two
systems). But this does not mean that it is always a scientist's
construction only: a "diasystem" is experienced in a very real
way by bilingual (including "bidialectal") speakers and corresponds
to what students of language contact have called "merged system."[4]
Thus, we might construct a "diasystem" out of several types of
Yiddish in which a variety possessing the opposition /i~I/ is
itself opposed to another variety with a single /i/ phoneme. Be
it noted that a Yiddish speaker in a situation of dialect contact
might find information in the confusion of /i/ and /I/ of his
interlocutor, which is opposed, on the diasystem level, to his
own corresponding distinction. It might tell him (in a "symptomatic" rather than a "symbolic" way) where, approximately, his
interlocutor is from.

It may be feasible, without defining "dialect" for the time
being, to set up "dialectological" as the adjective corresponding
to "diasystem," and to speak of dialectological research as the
study of diasystems. Dialectology would be the investigation of
problems arising when different systems are treated together
because of their partial similarity. A specifically structural dialectology would look for the structural consequences of partial differences within a framework of partial similarity.

It is safe to say that a good deal of dialectology is actually
of this type and contains no necessary references to geography,
ethnography, political and cultural history, or other extra-structural factors. In Gillieron's classic studies, the typical (if not
exclusive) interest is structural rather than "external." In the
diasystem "French," we may very well contrast the fate of *gallus*

in one variety where $-ll->$-d- with its fate in another variety where this phonological change did not take place, without knowing anything about the absolute or even relative geography or chronology of these varieties. Non-geographic, structural dialectology does exist; it is legitimate and even promising. Its special concern is the study of partial similarities and differences between systems and of the structural consequences thereof. The preceding is not to say, of course, that "external" dialectology has been surpassed; this subject will be referred to below (section 7).

Dialectological studies in the structural sense are, of course, nothing new.   Binomial formulas like "Yiddish *fus*/*fis* 'foot'," which are often condensed to f''_is , etc. have always been the mainstay of historical phonology.   But it should be noted that structural dialectology need not be restricted to historical problems to the extent to which it has been in the past.   Consequences of partial differences between varieties can be synchronic as well as diachronic.   The following is an example of a "synchronic consequence." In one variety of Yiddish (we stick to Yiddish examples for the sake of consistency), the singular and plural of "foot" are distinguished as (*der*) *fus* vs. (*di*) *fis*, while in another variety, both numbers are *fis*. Now, in the number-distinguishing variety, the singular, *fus*, occurs also as a feminine (with *di*); even so, the distinction between singular and plural can still be made in terms of the vowel: *di fus* "sg."--*di fis* "pl." In the other dialect, *fis* is invariably masculine, perhaps as a consequence of, or at least in relation to, the fact that there only a masculine could distinguish between sg. *der fis* and pl. *di fis*.[5]

If structuralism were carried to its logical extreme, it would not allow for the type of comparisons suggested here: it could only study relations within systems; and since in a perfect system all parts are interrelated ("tout se tient"), it is hard to see how systems could even be conceived of as partially similar or different; one would think that they could only be wholly identical or different.   Considerations of this nature prevented orthodox Saussureanism of the Geneva school from undertaking the study of gradually changing systems, since it was felt that languages could only be compared, if at all, at discrete "stages."[6]   But a more flexible structuralism has overcome this hurdle by abandoning the illusion of a perfect system, and is producing notable results in the diachronic field.[7] We should now take the further step of asserting the possibility of a synchronic or diachronic dialectology based on a combined study of several partially similar systems.

This step in structural linguistic theory would, it seems, do much to bring it closer to dialectology as it is actually carried on.

3.   We come next to dialectology's share in the proposed rapproachement.   The main objection raised by structuralists against dialectology as usually practised might be formulated thus: in constructing "diasystems" it ignores the structures of the constituent varieties.   In other words, existing dialectology usually

compares elements belonging to different systems without sufficiently stressing their intimate membership in those systems.

In the domain of sounds, this amounts to a non-phonemic approach. A traditional dialectologist will have no scruples about listening to several dialect informants pronounce their equivalents of a certain word and proclaiming that these forms are "the same" or "different." Let us assume four speakers of a language who, when asked for the word "man," utter (1) [man], (2) [man], (3) [mȧn], (4) [mȧn], respectively. On an impressionistic basis, we would adjudge (1) and (2) as "the same," (3) and (4) as "the same," but (1) and (2) as "different" from (3) and (4). Yet suppose that informant (1) speaks a variety in which vowel length is significant; phonemically his form is 1/mãn/. Informant (2) does not distinguish vowel length, and has given us 2/man/. We can further visualize a variety represented by informant (3) where a vowel with maximum degree of opening has the positional variant [ȧ] between /m/ and /n/; phonemically, then, we have 3/man/. In the fourth variety, no such positional variation exists; that form is perhaps 4/mon/. The structural analysis is thus different from the non-structural one: (2) and (3) now turn out to be possibly "the same" (but only, of course, if the systems are otherwise also identical), while (1) and (4) appear to be different. Structural linguistics requires that the forms of the constituent systems be understood first and foremost in terms of those systems, since the formal units of two non-identical systems are, strictly speaking, incommensurable.[8]

A similar requirement could be made about the units of content, or "semantemes." It would not do to say, for instance, that the word *taykh* in one variety of Yiddish is "the same" as *taykh* in another if, in the one, it is opposed to *ózere* "lake," and hence means only "river," while in the other it is not so opposed and stands for any sizable "body of water." Similar structural cautions would be required with respect to "synonyms" in the diasystem. In the diasystem "Yiddish," *baytn*, *shtékheven*, and *toyshn* all signify approximately "to exchange," but they cannot be synonyms on the variety level if they do not all exist in any one variety.

A grammatical example might also be cited. In terms of function within the system, it would not be justified to identify the feminine *vaysl* "Vistula River" of two Yiddish varieties if in the one it is opposed to a neuter *vaysl* "eggwhite," while in the other it is completely homonymous with the (also feminine) word for "eggwhite." It is even doubtful whether any two feminines in these two varieties could be legitimately identified in view of the fact that one of the varieties does not possess a neuter gender altogether.

The dialectologist is used to comparing directly the "substance" of different varieties. The demand of the structural linguist that he consider the train of associations, oppositions, and functions that define linguistic forms seems to the dialectologist complicating, unreasonable, and unnecessary ("metaphysical"). To show up the disagreement most clearly, let us represent the phonic

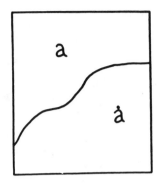

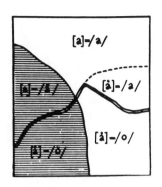

Map 26.1: Traditional   Map 26.2: Structural

THE VOWEL IN "MAN" IN LANGUAGE X

*On Map 26.2, a continuous single line divides areas with differ-
ent phonemic inventories (shaded area distinguishing vowel
length, unshaded area not distinguishing it). The double line
separates areas using different phonemes in this word (difference
of distribution). The dotted line separates allophonic differences.*

problem just discussed on a map and compare the traditional and
the proposed structural treatments of it. Obviously the structural
approach involves complications, but the dialectologist will become
convinced of their necessity when he realizes that phonemics,
like structural linguistics generally, represents not a special
technique for studying certain problems, but a basic discovery
about the way language functions to which structural linguists
are completely committed.

Since, in the structural view, allophonic differences between
sounds are in a sense less important than phonemic differences,
the "substantial" isogloss (Map 26.2) which separates [å] from
[a] in the overall /å/ area is structurally somehow less important
than the purely formal isogloss which separates pronunciations of
[man] = /mån/ from those of [mån] = /mon/; the latter isogloss
may not reflect any difference in "substance" at all; it would not
show up on the non-structural map (Map 26.1). The traditional
dialectologist naturally wonders what he stands to gain by the
drawing of such "metaphysical" lines. But if dialectological maps
are considered diachronically as snapshots of change, and if it
can be shown that the difference between phonemes and allophones
can be material in determining sound change, it may be possible

to convince the dialectologist that the structural map is after all more true to the reality of functioning language. Similar arguments, perhaps, could also be persuasive insofar as they are pertinent to grammatical and lexical matters.

If dialectologists would consider the functions of the elements which they use in their comparisons, their conception of a "diasystem" would come close to that proposed here for structural linguistics and might lead to the unified theory which is so badly needed.

4. The partial differences which are proposed as the specific subject matter of dialectologic study may be of two kinds: differences of inventory and differences of distribution. While the latter are the standard material of comparative study, the former have not received their due stress.

As an example of a difference in inventory, let us take a simple phonemic case first. In the following discussion, single slashes enclose sets of phonemes and single tildes designate phonemic oppositions in a variety identified by a preceding subscript number; oppositions in the constructed diasystem are characterized by double tildes, and the formulas for the diasystems are surrounded by double slashes. Given two varieties with identical five-vowel systems, we might construct the following diasystem: $_{1,2}//i \approx e \approx a \approx o \approx u//$. Now let us assume that in one of the varieties, the front vowel of the intermediate degree of openness is more open than in the other; choosing a phonemic transcription which would reflect this fact, we might indicate the difference in the diasysteem thus:

$$_{1,2}\left|\left| i \approx \frac{1^e}{2} \approx a \approx o \approx u \right|\right|.$$

Given two varieties, one of which (1) distinguishes three front vowels, the other (2) distinguishing four, we might formulate the corresponding part of the vowel diasystem thus:

$$_{1,2}\left|\left| \frac{1/i \sim e \sim \ae /}{2/i \sim e \sim \varepsilon \sim \ae /} \approx a \approx o \ldots \right|\right|.$$

Here is the actual vowel inventory of Yiddish considered as a diasystem of three dialects, 1. Central ("Polish"), 2. Southwestern ("Ukrainian"), and 3. Northwestern ("Lithuanian"):

$$_{1,2,3}\left|\left| \frac{\frac{1/i:\sim i/}{2/i \sim I/}}{3i} \approx e \approx \frac{1/a:\sim a/}{2,3a} \approx o \approx u \right|\right|.$$

Similarly differences in inventory of grammatical categories might be stated, e.g. between varieties having two against three genders, three as against four conjugational types, and the like. All examples here are tentative and schematic; the possibilities of a more analytical statement of the diasystem, based e.g. on relevant features, remain to be investigated.

One thing is certain: In the study of language contact and interference (see section 5), a clear picture of differences in inventory is a prerequisite.[9]

Differences in distribution cannot be directly inferred from a comparison of the differences in inventory, although the two ordinarily stand in a definite historical relationship. For example, in the diasystem "Yiddish" described above, the phoneme 3 /i/ in variety 3 usually corresponds to either 2 /i/ or 2 /I/ in cognates of variety 2, and to either 1 /i:/ or 1 /i/ in cognates of variety 1 (3/sine/: 2/sIne/: 1/sĩne/ "enmity"). This is, as it were, a correspondence between the nearest equivalents. But many 3 /o/'s correspond to /u/'s in variety 1 and 2, even though all three varieties today possess both /o/ and /u/ phonemes. Thus, /futer/ means "father" in varieties 1 and 2, but "fur" in variety 3; /meluxe/ means 1,2"craft" and 3"state"; /hun/ means 1,2"rooster" and 3"hen." For the tens of thousands of speakers for whom the contact of these varieties is an everyday experience, these "Yiddish" sound sequences are not fully identified until the particular variety of Yiddish to which they belong is itself determined. Now no one would deny that a form like Yiddish [fĩ˘l] (1,2"full," "many") is identified fully only in conjunction with its meaning in one of the varieties, i.e. when account is taken of the differences in distribution of sounds in cognates occurring in the several varieties. The less obvious point made here is that the form is not fully identified, either, if relevant differences in *inventory* are not accounted for, i.e. if it is not rendered in terms of the phonemes of one of the concrete varieties: [fil] = 1/fĩl/, 2/fIl/, 3/fil/.

Recent descriptive work on American English phonemics has come close to treating the language as a "diasystem" without, however, satisfying the requirements set forth here. The widely adopted analysis of Trager and Smith[10] provides a set of symbols by which forms of all varieties of American English can be described. It makes it possible, for example, to transcribe Southeastern /pæys/ *pass* in terms of some of the same symbols used in /pæt/ *pat* of the same dialect or in /pæs/, /bəyd/ *bird*, etc. of other varieties. This violates the principle advocated here that the phonemic systems of the varieties should be fully established before the diasystem is constructed. We are not told whether in the phoneme inventory of Southeastern American English, the /æy/ of *pass* does or does not correspond as an inventory item to the /æ/ of other varieties. We cannot tell if the [o] of *home* of Coastal New England is the same phoneme, or a different phoneme, from the [ow] in *go* in the same variety. For reasons of this type, the system has been criticized as providing not a phonemic description or a set of descriptions, but a "transcriptional arsenal."[11] Yet the remaining step toward the establishment of a phonemic diasystem is not difficult to visualize.

5. We might now restate and specify the suggested position of structural dialectology in linguistics as a whole. SYNCHRONIC DIALECTOLOGY compares systems that are partially different and analyzes the "synchronic consequences" of these differences within the similarities. DIACHRONIC DIALECTOLOGY deals (a) with DIVERGENCE, i.e. it studies the growth of partial differences at the expense of similarities and possibly reconstructs earlier stages of greater similarity (traditionally, comparative linguistics); (b) with CONVERGENCE, i.e. it studies partial similarities increasing at the expense of differences (traditionally, substratum and adstratum studies, "bilingual dialectology,"[12] and the like).

The opposite of dialectology, which hardly needs a special name, is the study of languages as discrete systems, one at a time. It involves straight description of uniform systems, typological comparisons of such systems, and diachronically, the study of change in systems considered one at a time.

6. It was stated previously that diasystems can be constructed *ad hoc* out of any number of varieties for a given analytic purpose. Constructing a diasystem means placing discrete varieties in a kind of continuum determined by their partial similarities. However, in passing from a traditional to a structural dialectology, the more pressing and more troublesome problem is the opposite one, viz. how to break down a continuum into discrete varieties. What criteria should be used for divisions of various kinds? Can non-technical divisions of a "language" into "dialects," "patois," and the like be utilized for technical purposes?[13]

Before these questions can be answered, it is necessary to distinguish between standardized and non-standardized language. This set of terms is proposed to avoid the use of the ambiguous word, "standard," which among others has to serve for "socially acceptable," "average," "typical," and so on. On the contrary, STANDARDIZATION could easily be used to denote a process of more or less conscious, planned, and centralized regulation of language.[14] Many European languages have had standardized varieties for centuries; a number of formerly "colonial" tongues are undergoing the process only now. Not all leveling is equivalent to standardization. In the standardization process, there is a division of functions between regulators and followers, a constitution of more or less clearcut authorities (academies, ministries of education, *Sprachvereine*, etc) and of channels of control (schools, special publications, etc.). For example, some dialectal leveling and a good deal of Anglicization has taken place in the immigrant languages of the United States, and we might say that a word like *plenty* has become a part of the American Norwegian koinê.[15] But in a sense proposed here, there is no "standardized" American Norwegian which is different from Old-World Norwegian, and from the point of view of the standardized language, *plenty* is nothing but a regional slang term.

Now it is part of the process of standardization itself to affirm the identity of a language, to set it off discretely from other languages and to strive continually for a reduction of differences within it. Informants of standardized languages react in a peculiar way; moreover, it is much easier to deal with samples of a standardized language, to make generalizations about it and to know the limites of their applicability. On the level of non-standardized or FOLK LANGUAGE,[16] a discrete difference between one variety and others is NOT a part of the experience of its speakers, and is much more difficult to supply. For example, it is easy to formulate where standardized Dutch ends and standardized German begins, but it is a completely different matter to utilize for technical purposes the transition between folk Dutch and folk German.

On the whole dialectologists have avoided dealing with standardized languages and have restricted themselves to folk language.[17] Consequently, in practice as well as in theory the problem of dividing and ordering the continuum of language is especially serious with respect to the folk level and not the standardized level. Time was when the continuum of folk language used to be divided on the basis of (usually diachronic) structural features, e.g. the geographic limits of a certain phonological development. Either one isogloss which the linguist considered important was selected (e.g. k/x as the line between Low and High German), or a bundle of isoglosses of sufficient thickness was used as a dividing line. In either case, the resulting divisions were not, of course, all of the same degree; they were major, minor, and intermediate, depending on the thickness of the bundle or the relative importance of the key isogloss. It is evident that no unambiguous concept of dialect could emerge even from this optimistic methodology any more than a society can be exhaustively and uniquely divided into "groups."

Classificatory procedures of this type are today virtually passé. Dialectologists have generally switched to extra-structural criteria for dividing the folk-language continuum. The concept of language area (*Sprachlandschaft*) has practically replaced that of "dialect" (*Mundart*) as the central interest in most geographic work,[18] and ever more impressive results are being obtained in correlating the borders, centers, and overall dynamics of language areas with "cultural areas" in a broader sense. Instead of speak-ing, for instance, of the *helpe/helfe* and *Lucht/Luft* isoglosses as the border between the Ripuarian and Mosell-Franconian "dialects" of the German Rhineland, linguistic geographers now speak of the Eifel Barrier between the Cologne and Trier areas. This Eifel mountain range happens to be the locus not only of those two random isoglosses, but, among others, also the dividing line between *kend* and *keŋk* "child," *haus* and *hus* "house," *grumper* and *erpel* "potato," *heis* and *gramm* "hoarse"; between short-bladed and long-bladed scythes, grey bread in oval loaves and black bread in rectangular loaves, New Year's twists and New Year's pretzels, St. Quirin as the patron saint of cattle and the same as the patron of horses, two different types of ditty addressed to the ladybug, etc.[19] The line is meaningful as a reflex of a medieval boundary which can in turn be accounted for by more permanent climatic, orological, hydrographic, and other geographic factors. [20]

The search for ways to divide the folk-language continuum has also led to statistical correlation methods. [21]   Rather than plotting the border lines of single selected structural features, which may be impossible in areas of amorphous transition, the following procedure is used.   Inquiries are made at various points concerning the presence or absence of a whole list of test features; then the correlation between the results at some reference point and at all other points is computed, and may be represented catographically, points with similar correlation coefficients being surrounded by lines which have variously been called "isopleths" or "isogrades."   Theoretically related to this procedure are the tests of mutual intelligibility between dialects. [22]   All these procedures must depend on an arbitrary critical constant (or constants) for the drawing of a dividing line (or lines, of various degrees of importance), but they do yield an insight into the makeup of a continuously varying language area which supplements, if it does not supersede, the results derived by other methods.

In the domain of dialect sociology, where transitions are perhaps even more continuous and fluid than in dialect geography, the use of extra-linguistic correlations and statistical sampling techniques offers promising possibilities of research in an almost untrodden field. [23]

The use of the social-science tools of "external dialectology" can do much to supplement the procedures outlined for a structural

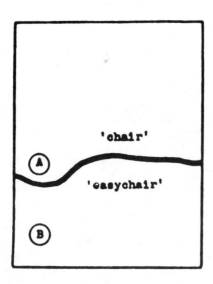

Map 26.3: Meaning of shtul *in East European Yiddish (Schematized).*

dialectology.   One problem for combined structural and "external" linguistic investigation is to determine what structural and non-structural features of language have in fact helped to break up the folk-language continuum into the non-technical units of "dialects," "patois," etc.   This combined research might get to the heart of the question of diasystems as empirical realities rather than as mere constructs.   One of its by-products might be the formulation of a technical concept of "dialect" as a variety or diasystem with certain explicit defining features.

7.   Finally a word might be said about the interrelationship of structural and "external" points of view applied to a specific dialectological problem.   Given a map showing an isogloss, the "external" dialectologist's curiosity is likely to concentrate on the locus of that isogloss.   Why is it where it is?   What determines the details of its course?   What other isoglosses bundle with it? What communication obstacle does it reflect?

The structural dialectologist has another set of questions, stemming from his interest in partial differences within a framework of partial similarity.   To take up the semasiological example of Map 26.3 (which is schematized but based on real data), if *shtul* means "chair" in zone A, but "easychair" in zone B, then what is the designation of "easychair" in A and of "chair" in B? Every semasiological map, due to the two-faceted nature of linguistic signs, gives rise to as many onomasiological questions as the number of zones it contains, and vice versa.   If we were to

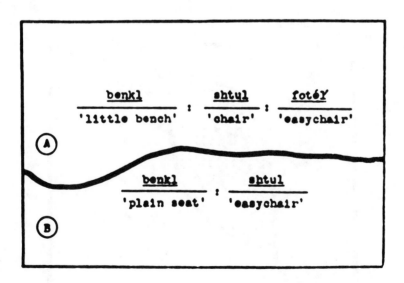

Map 26.4:   Designations of Seats in East European Yiddish (Schematized).

supply the information that in zone A, "easychair" is *fotél'*,
while in zone B "chair" is *benkl* , a new set of questions would
arise: what, then, does *fotél'* mean in B and *benkl* in A?[24]
This implicational chain of questions could be continued further.
The resulting answers, when entered on a map, would produce a
picture of an isogloss dividing two lexical systems, rather than
isolated items (see Map 26.4).   This would be the "structural
corrective" to a traditional dialect map.

It is easy to think of dialectological field problems for the
solution of which "external" and structural considerations must
be combined in the most intimate manner.   Such problems would
arise particularly if the cartographic plotting of systems should
produce a set of narrowly diverging isoglosses.   Assume that an
isogloss is drawn between a variety of a language which distinguishes short /u/ from long /u:/ and another variety which
makes no such quantitative distinction.   The structuralist's
curiosity is immediately aroused about length distinctions in other
vowels.   Suppose now that the variety that distinguishes the
length of /u/ does so also for /i/; but that the isoglosses,
plotted independently, are not exactly congruent (Map 26.5).
Some intriguing questions now arise concerning the dynamics of
the vowel pattern of the discrepant zone.   Nothing but an on-the-
spot field study closely combining structural analysis and an
examination of the "external" communication conditions in the area
could deal adequately with a problem of this kind.

8.   In answer to the question posed in the title of this
paper, it is submitted that a structural dialectology is possible.
Its results promise to be most fruitful if it is combined with
"external" dialectology without its own conceptual framework being
abandoned.

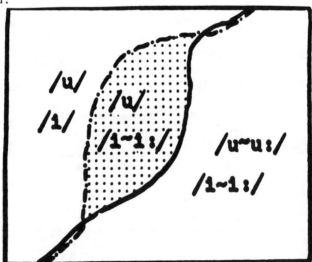

Map 26.5:   Non-Congruent Vowel-Length Isoglosses in Language Y.

FOOTNOTES

[1] Some of the phonological points made here were inspired by N. S. Troubetzkoy's article on linguistic geography, "Phonologie et géographie linguistique," *TCLP* 4.228-34 (1931); reprinted in his *Principes de phonologie*, Paris, 1949, pp. 343-50.

[2] Ferdinand de Saussure, *Cours de linguistique générale*, Paris, 1949, p. 20.

[3] André Martinet, in preface to Uriel Weinreich, *Languages in Contact*, Linguistic Circle of New York, Publication no. 1, 1953, xii + 148 pages, p. vii.

[4] *Languages in Contact*, pp. 8f.

[5] For an example of synchronic consequences in phonemics, see Anton Pfalz, "Zur Phonologie der bairisch-österreichischen Mundart," *Lebendiges Erbe; Festschrift . . . Ernst Reclam*, Leipzig, 1936, pp. 1-19, which is at the same time one of the rare instances of German phonemics and of structural dialectology.

[6] Albert Sechehaye, "Les trois linguistiques saussuriennes," *Vox romanica* 5.1-48 (1940), pp. 30f.; H[enri] Frei, "Lois de passage," *Zeitschrift für romanische Philologie* 64.557-68 (1944).

[7] Cf. the bibliography of diachronic phonemics by Alphonse G. Juilland in *Word* 9.198-208 (1953).

[8] *Languages in Contact*, pp. 7f.

[9] *Ibid.*, pp. 1f.

[10] George L. Trager and Henry Lee Smith, Jr., *An Outline of English Structure* (=*Studies in Linguistics, Occasional Papers 3*), Norman (Okla.), 1951, esp. pp. 27-29.

[11] Einar Haugen, "Problems of Bilingual Description," *Report of the Fifth Annual Round Table Meeting on Linguistics and Language Teaching* (=[Georgetown University] *Monograph Series on Languages and Linguistics* no. 7), in press.

[12] For an essay in bilingual dialectology, see Uriel Weinreich, "*Sábesdiker losn* in Yiddish: a Problem of Linguistic Affinity," *Word* 8.360-77 (1952).

[13] The possibility of introducing some scientific rigor into existing loose terminology has been explored by André Martinet, "Dialect," *Romance Philology* (1953/54), in press. The article by Václav Polák, "Contributions á l'étude de la notion de langue et de dialecte," *Orbis* 3.89-98 (1954), which arrived too late to be utilized here as fully as it deserves, suggests that we call "language" a diasystem whose partial similarities are grammatical while its partial differences are phonological and lexical.

[14] Cf. *Languages in Contact*, pp. 99-103. An interesting book about standardization is Heinz Kloss, *Die Entwicklung neuer germanischer Kultursprachen von 1800 bis 1950*, Munich, 1952.

[15] Einar Haugen, *The Norwegian Language in America*, Philadelphia, 1953, p. 588.

[16] Interesting parallels could be developed between the sociolinguistic opposition "standardized"--"folk" and the social anthropologist's opposition between the clusters of complex (industrialized) and folk societies or strata of society; cf. e.g. George M. Foster, "What Is Folk Culture?" *American Anthropologist* 55.159-73 (1953).

[17] Some people are not averse to calling modern standardized languages "Indo-European dialects," or speaking of "literary dialects." Dialectology in the sense proposed in this paper need not restrict itself to the folk level, but such usage is one more reason why the term "dialect" ought to be held in abeyance.

[18] This is particularly evident in the methodologically most advanced German Swiss work; cf. the publications series *Beiträge zur schweizerdeutschen Mundartforschung* edited by Rudolf Hotzenkocherle.

[19] Linguistic data from Adolf Bach, *Deutsche Mundartforschung*, Heidelberg, 1950, pp. 123ff; ethnographic data from Adolf Bach, *Deutsche Volkskunde*, Leipzig, 1937, p. 228.

[20] In the United States, Hans Kurath (*A Word Geography of the Eastern United States*, Ann Arbor, 1949), has successfully combined strictly linguistic with "external" criteria in breaking down the relatively undifferentiated American folk-language area.

[21] See David W. Reed and John L. Spicer, "Correlation Methods of Comparing Idiolects in a Transition Area," *Language* 28.348-60 (1952).

[22] Cf. for example C. F. Voegelin and Zellig S. Harris, "Methods of Determining Intelligibility Among Dialects of Natural Languages," *Proceedings of the American Philosophical Society* 95.322-29 (1951).

[23] See the interesting paper by Stanley M. Sapon, "A Methodology for the Study of Socio-Economic Differentials in Linguistic Phenomena," *Studies in Linguistics* 11.57-68 (1953). A scheme for the classification of varieties of a language according to their function (ecclesiastic, poetic, scientific, etc.) to replace the unsatisfactory terminology of "styles" has been proposed by Yury Serech, "Toward a Historical Dialeectology," *Orbis* 3.43-56 (1954), esp. pp. 47ff.

[24] The actual answer is that *fotél'* is not current in zone B, while *benkl* means "little bench" in zone A.

OTHER RECENT APPROACHES

K. M. Petyt

I. GENERATIVE DIALECTOLOGY

In 1957 a young American linguist, Noam Chomsky, published a slim volume entitled *Syntactic Structures*, which was to initiate a major revolution in linguistics: in it he argued for a *generative* approach to linguistic description. For the previous thirty years or so structural linguists had largely been concerned with analysing the data they had collected in field work, and then producing a description of this material in terms of phonetics, phonology, morphology, and syntax. Chomsky argued that a description of a corpus of observed data in any language is not sufficient; a language is more than a corpus of material - many sentences which have never been uttered before and so are not in a corpus will be grammatical. In fact a speaker is constantly producing, hearing, and understanding sentences that have never occurred in precisely that form before; this 'creativity' is perhaps the most essential property of human language, so a complete grammar must account for all the infinite number of possible sentences in a language: it must *generate* all the grammatical sentences and no ungrammatical ones.

A *generative grammar* consists of a set of rules, which are essentially statements of the regularities of the language; applying these rules will produce grammatical sentences, which may or may not have actually occurred in this precise form. A grammar will have several sections or *components*: in a fuller work published in 1965, Chomsky expanded and in some respects reformulated his view of a generative grammar, saying that it would have syntactic, semantic, and phonological components. Work on the phonological component, *generative phonology*, had been pioneered by Morris Halle,[1] and later he and Chomsky collaborated in this.[2] Since the greatest number of dialect differences concern phonology, and since most works on generative dialectology have concentrated on this area, the discussion here will be similarly restricted.

From *The Study of Dialect*, The Western Press, 1980, pp 171-197. Reprinted with permission from Basil Blackwell Ltd.

35

But the same general principles would apply in the case of grammatical differences between dialects. [3]

The job of the phonological component is to specify the phonetic form of sentences generated by the syntactic rules. It does this by means of rules applying in a stated order to the items, which will be represented in an *underlying form*. This is composed of abstract segments referred to as 'systematic phonemes'[4] which are set up to express a relationship between two phonemes such as /eɪ/ and /a/ e.g. *grateful - gratitude* , or /i:/ and /e/ e.g. *serene - serenity*. To give a grossly simplified example: an underlying form might be say /dɪvIn/, and a relevant rule

$$I \rightarrow \left\{ \begin{array}{l} aɪ/-C\# \text{ etc} \\ ɪ \end{array} \right\}$$

This means: 'the underlying segment /I/ will be realized as [aɪ] in the environment of a consonant occurring before a word-boundary e.g. [dɪvaɪn] *divine* (and also in certain other environments which will not be detailed here); elsewhere, it will be realized as [ɪ]' e.g. [dɪvɪnɪtɪ] *divinity*.

Where do dialects come into this? The essential fact about dialects is that they are forms of a language which are in many respects similar to each other, but which differ in some respects. How is this fact expressed within the various approaches to dialectology?

The approach of traditional dialectology is to record the data in each dialect, and then essentially to take the similarities for granted and to concentrate on describing the differences between dialects.

Structural dialectology also examines the data of different dialects and describes the systems of elements within each. It then faces a problem: the main tenet of structural linguistics is that elements are defined by their relations to other elements within the system, and therefore it is impossible to equate elements in separate systems. For example, the existence in a dialect of a phoneme labelled /a/ is determined by its contrasts with other phonemes, not just by the fact that it sounds like [a]; if another dialect has a different set of phonemic contrasts, a phoneme labelled /a/ is not comparable to that in the first dialect, even though it too may sound like [a]. Perhaps recognizing that such a strict structural view is untenable in relation to dialects - for in effect it treats two dialects of say, English, as if they were no more similar than one of English and one of Chinese - dialectologists tacitly ignored it. They drew up dia-systems, which aimed to express both the similarities and the differences between the systems of different dialects.

What traditional and structural dialectology have in common is the fact that they both concentrate mainly on the *data* of the different dialects. This is where the approach of generative dialectology is claimed to differ: it focuses not so much on the data, the actual forms, as on the grammars of dialects - the *rules* which generate these forms. (As a related point here, it should be noted that generative grammar is a means only of expressing the facts about a language: it is not concerned with how these facts are discovered. Similarly, generative dialectology is only a way of describing dialect differences: it is not concerned with the 'earlier' major task of dialectology - surveys designed to collect the data to be described.)

If a generative description of phonology consists of a set of ordered rules applying to underlying forms, then clearly two or more such grammars may differ in having different underlying forms *and/or* a different set of rules *and/or* a different order of rules. But linguists of this school hold that when the grammars of different dialects are compared, it is normally the case that they will have the same underlying forms and a majority of the same rules. These two properties will explain one of the essential points about dialects: that they are forms of language similar in many respects. The other point, that though similar they differ in some ways, is explained by the fact that, beside the set of rules common to all dialects, some forms will be generated by:

A. the addition of one or more rules in the grammars of some dialects;

B. the deletion of one or more rules in the grammars of some dialects;

C. a different ordering of the rules in the grammars of different dialects;

D. a 'simplified' form in some dialects of a rule applying in others.

Several works provide detailed exemplification of this approach. An early one is an article by E. Vasiliu, 'Towards a generative phonology of Daco-Rumanian dialects' (1966). Vasiliu set up underlying forms and the rules necessary to generate the actual forms in various dialects; he was then able to classify Rumanian dialects on the basis of which of the set of rules they have, and how these are ordered. His resulting classification into dialects, varieties, and subvarieties is in fact very similar to that proposed by traditional dialectologists working on Rumanian, but its basis is held to be more explicit.

B. Newton's *The Generative Interpretation of Dialect* (1972) tackles the situation of the Greek dialects. He states that it is his intention to interpret dialects not as 'a conglomeration of static self-contained systems' (the extreme structuralist position), but as 'the outcome of historical changes acting on an originally uniform language'. So he starts with a set of underlying forms which he sets up as common to all dialects: dialectalization is then introduced by the phonological rules which operate on these: some do not apply in some dialects, some differ in character from one to another; some apply in different orders in the different dialects. As a result, though Greece is a linguistic continuum criss-crossed in all directions by a vast number of isoglosses, it is possible to see five basic groups of dialects emerging, established on the basis of which of nine important phonological rules apply to them, and in which order.

The situation in Greece is unusual in that there is historical documentation of the language and its dialects extending back over two and a half thousand years; we have therefore evidence of many of the actual historical changes which have produced the present-day dialects. But the underlying forms and the rules set up by a generative phonologist like Newton are such as can be established on the basis of internal present-day evidence - such as the phonological alterations within a dialect between different forms of the same word (e.g. [dIvaIn] - [dIvIn-ItI]), or cross-dialectal comparisons - rather than on the basis of historical documentation. Thus, though the rules often reflect historical changes, and their ordering often recapitulates the actual temporal sequence of these changes, there may well be some discrepancies between historical fact and synchronic description. But it is the latter which more nearly reflects what the native speaker is aware of: he may know nothing of the history of his language, but he 'knows' in some sense that there is a relation between [dɪvaɪn] and [dɪvɪnɪtɪ], or that Northerners in Britain 'merge' /ʌ/ and /u/.[5]

A book published in the same year as Newton's illustrates the point that a generative description with underlying forms and an ordered set of rules has in principle no connection with a historical study: Gillian Brown's *Phonological Rules and Dialect Variation* (1972) has the subtitle *A Study of the Phonology of Lumasaaba*. This is a language on which there is virtually no historical documentation, but nevertheless Brown was able to relate the dialects through a common set of underlying forms and a set of phonological rules: the correct phonetic realizations for each dialect are generated by specifying which of the rules apply and in what order. The underlying forms are closer to those of the Northern dialects (the three main ones are differentiated by whether or not two particular rules apply); the three Southern dialects all share a set of rules which do not apply in the Northern (and are then differentiated from each other by the order in which a further set of rules apply).

Let us consider some examples of the ways listed above by which different dialectal realizations can be generated from the same underlying forms.

A. Additional Rules

Let us suppose that words in English such as *cat*, *fact*, etc etc have underlying forms like /kat/, /fakt/ and so on. One way of generating the phonetic forms in British dialects[6] would be by means of a rule such as

$$/a/ \rightarrow \begin{cases} [æ] \text{ in RP and dialects} \\ A, B, C \ldots \\ [a] \text{ in other dialects} \end{cases}$$

This rule is in fact an abbreviation of two separate rules for generating two different phonetic forms, so essentially this method of derivation is using different rules for different dialects, and treating these as 'descriptively equal'.

Usually, however, there is good reason for assuming that one dialect form is more basic, and that others can most simply be described as a further step in derivation from this. So for example we might decide that the simplest grammar will contain a rule /a/→[a]. This will be the actually-occurring form in many dialects; but for others a further rule is added which simply makes this a slightly closer vowel: [a]→[æ].[7] The fact that this is a 'late' rule in the grammar would accord with one's intuition that the difference in question is only a matter of detail; to derive [a] and [æ] by means of different underlying segments (which no-one would suggest) would for example run entirely counter to this intuition.

Another example of where an additional rule might be employed in deriving some English dialect forms concerns the set of words including *grass*, *laugh*, *bath*, *dance* etc. From underlying forms such as /gras/, /laf/ etc our rules above will derive [gras], [græs] and so on, forms which do occur in some dialects. But for RP and certain other dialects we would want to add a rule, to be applied at some time *before* that for [a]→[æ], which will lengthen the vowel in certain environments:

$$[a] → [ɑ:]/ - [s,f,\theta,ns] \text{ etc}$$

Here the fact that this is a somewhat 'earlier' rule in the derivation accords with our intuition that the [a/ɑ:] difference is a rather more important one between English dialects than [a/æ].

A particular example of a treatment of dialect differences in terms of 'additional rules' is to be seen in the work of Brown referred to above: the Southern dialects of Lumasaaba all undergo the same basic set of rules as the Northern but they are also subject to an additional three rules.

B. Deletion of a Rule

It is a well-known fact about German that though the con- sonants [p,t,k,b,d,g] occur at the beginning and in the middle of words, only [p,t,k] occur at the end. Moreover, it happens that there are alternations between voiced [b] and voiceless [p], and similarly between [d] and [t], and [g] and [k] among forms of the 'same' word: thus [tak] 'day' occurs alongside [tagə] 'days', for example. On the other hand there are pairs of forms such as [dek] 'deck' and [dekə] 'decks', where [k] does not alternate with [g]; and so on. Linguists have suggested that the final consonants of [tak] and [tag] have different underlying forms, /tag/ and /dek/ and that there are phonological rules such as the following:

$$/k/ \rightarrow [k]$$

$$/g/ \rightarrow \begin{Bmatrix} [k]/ - \# \\ [g] \end{Bmatrix}$$

This means that underlying /k/ is always realized as [k], whereas underlying /g/ is [k] in word-final position ([tak]), but [g] otherwise ([tagə]).

The above situation applies with most varieties of German, but in some dialects in Northern Switzerland and in Yiddish, this is not the case. In those varieties, [b,d,g] *can* occur at the end of words, so that instead of alternations such as [bunt] 'band'/[bundə] 'bands' as in most dialects, in Northern Switzerland [bund]/[bundə] occurs; instead of [tak]/[tagə], Yiddish has [tog]/[teg], and so on.[8] Now it is reasonable to say that the grammars of these varieties simply do not contain the rule(s) that devoice /b,d,g/ to [p,t,k] at the end of words. But there is evidence that this rule did exist at an earlier period: the evidence is both external (texts from earlier centuries) and internal (forms in Yiddish such as [avek] 'away', [hant] 'hand', [gelt] 'money', for instance).

Historical evidence is not in itself a reason for including a rule that does not apply at the present time; but it is quite possible that the simplest grammar for German which seeks to generate all the present-day dialect forms will be one which has the devoicing rule applying generally, but then has a relatively 'late' rule applying in the case of certain dialects which deletes most of the effects of the devoicing rule.

C. Different Ordering of Rules

It should be noted that when 'order' is used in this context, it refers to descriptive not historical order. In other words, the order of the rules is that which results in the most natural and economical description of the dialects in question; it does not necessarily correspond to the historical sequence of the appearance of these rules, though it may do (see below).

In his treatment of Greek dialects, Newton has numerous examples of dialects where the data suggests that the same phonological rules exist in their grammars, but that these have different effects because they do not apply in the same order relative to one another. For example,[9] on the island of Rhodes he finds two different forms for the word meaning 'horse-dealer': [alvás] in the South-West, and [aloás] elsewhere. He suggests that the underlying form common to all Greek dialects is /aloɣas/, and that in Rhodes four rules (for which there is ample evidence elsewhere) may apply. In the South-West the order is:

Underlying form	aloɣás
A. Voiced fricative deletion	aloás
B. Height dissimilation	aluás

C. Glide formation   alwás
D. Consonantality   alvás

In the other Rhodes dialects, which have [aloás] it is *not* the case that rules B-D do not apply: the evidence of other items makes clear that they do, but they apply before rather than after the rule for voiced fricative deletion.

The effect in the case of this example is:

Underlying form   aloɣás
B. Height dissimilation   – (affects only contiguous vowels)
C. Glide formation   – (affects only contiguous vowels)
D. Consonantality   – (affects only 'glide' consonants)
A. Voiced fricative
    deletion   aloás

Different ordering of the same rules has been found to be an important aspect of dialect difference by others who have produced detailed exemplifications of generative dialectology. Vasiliu in his study of Rumanian found that the tradional major division of the dialects into 'Muntenian' and 'Moldavian' can be explained in terms of the different position of his 'Rule C' which, if it applies at all in Moldavian dialects, occurs in a different order.[10]

In Muntenian dialects the order of rules is ABCDEF...

In Moldavian dialects the order of rules is ABEF(C)...

Obviously the effect of Rule C will be different if E and F have already applied and thus changed the possible 'inputs' to this rule. Further examples can readily be found in Brown's description of Lumasaaba, where the Southern dialects are differentiated by the order in which a particular set of rules apply.[11]

D. Simpler Form of a Rule

From a synchronic point of view, this is strictly a matter of different rules applying in different dialects - held to be a relatively uncommon phenomenon as compared to those of additional rules or different ordering of the same rules. But these different rules are closely related historically *and* descriptively. A rule applying under specific conditions may either (a) have existed fairly generally at one time, but at a later date have been extended to apply in more contexts in some dialects; or (b) have arisen in one dialect but been reproduced in a less specific form when adopted by another. In either case, the rules as they apply in different dialects at the present time are not unrelated.

Consider the following example. Some English speakers may pronounce word-final /t/ as a glottal stop before another word beginning with a vowel. We could say that they have an (optional) rule of the form:

$$/t/ \rightarrow [\text{ʔ}] / -\#V$$

Use of [ʔ] for /t/ is becoming commoner in British English, so we could say that more and more speakers have rules such as the above in their grammar. But possibly some of them will misinterpret the data they hear containing glottal stops, and will assume that the rule is: /t/→[ʔ]/-V. Comparing the two forms of the rule, we see that the latter is 'simpler' i.e. less detailed than the former: the effect of this is that it is applied in a wider range of environments - before vowels *whether or not* a word boundary intervenes. The result is that while the first group may say [ə betə bɪʔ ə bʌtə] 'a better bit of butter', the latter could say [ə beʔə bɪʔə bʌʔə]. As noted earlier in this book, evidence from recent British studies suggests that the use of the glottal stop is less common (though increasing) in word-internal position than where a boundary intervenes, and this could be explained by saying that more people at present have the more specific form of the rule, but others are adopting the simpler form.

As has been made clear by the discussion so far, many of the 'rules' formulated by scholars producing generative descriptions of dialect variation look remarkably like the 'laws' a philologist might have deduced as being linguistic changes that have occurred in the historical development of the language.[12] But it must be emphasized that the rules are not established on the basis of historical evidence: this is not available anyway, in the case of most languages, and even where it is, the historical rules and their order are not *assumed* to be 'correct' for a synchronic grammar. (Nor indeed is the general organization, in terms of a common set of underlying forms and many common rules, but with dialect variations handled by differences among the remaining rules, *assumed* to be correct). The grammar is written on the basis of the internal evidence of the language as it is at the present time, and the preferred grammar will be the set of underlying forms and rules which in terms of criteria of 'generality' and 'naturalness' best handles the present-day alternations and dialect variations. It is held by generativists that the grammar emerging when criteria such as generality and naturalness are adopted will indeed be one which has much of its material common to all dialects and whose rules will largely reflect actual historical changes; in this case, the coincidence of the synchronic with the diachronic, and the way dialect variation is naturally explained as minor differences among a majority of common features, is held to be confirmation of the appropriateness of the grammar.

Adherents of this school of linguistics hold that an important property of any generative grammar is that its *formalization* ensures that it is entirely explicit: it sets out quite clearly all the facts, without leaving anything for the reader to have to deduce for himself. In relation to dialectology, a generative treatment will formalize the essential fact about dialects: that they have much in common but some differences. This is made

explicit by deriving different dialects from a common set of underlying forms, applying many rules to all or most of the dialects,
and accounting for their differences in terms of one or more
rules that are peculiar to them.

Another advantage claimed for generative grammar is that it
is more *powerful* - that it 'explains' more than other types of
grammar. A generative treatment of dialects is held to be more
powerful than both traditional and structural dialectology. The
traditional 'historical' approach revealed at the most the sequence
of particular linguistic changes which has resulted in the present-
day dialect differences; the generative approach formalizes not
only this but also all the consequences for linguistic structure
resulting from the different ordering in time of the various
changes. The structural approach to dialectology was of course
concerned primarily with such differences of linguistic structure,
but it is held that generative dialectology is more powerful here
too. For instance, (a) it makes it possible to set up a hierarchy
among the various dialect differences, in terms of whether the
rules concerned are 'early' ones that affect major structural
changes and apply to many dialects, or 'late' ones that make
relatively superficial changes in just one or two dialects; (b)
this in turn makes possible a classification of dialects which groups
together those with 'deeper' similarities (produced by later rules)
as secondary criteria; (c) the generative description will make
clear that identical superficial structures may sometimes result
from different rules (reflecting different linguistic changes); and
(d) differences of the 'incidence' type may be handled quite
naturally in a generative treatment. Structural dialectology ran
into problems with differences of the type where dialects had the
same phonemes in their systems but employed different ones in
certain particular words (e.g. both RP and Yorkshire dialects
have /aɪ/ and /i:/ in their systems, but in, say, *night* RP uses
/aɪ/ but rural West Yorkshire has /i:/).[13] An article by A. R.
Thomas (1967) shows with an example from Welsh how a situation
of this type can be handled quite naturally within a generative
description. Three Welsh dialects all have /oːɨ/, /oː/ and /uːe/,
but select differently in a particular word: thus D_1 [oːɨ], D_2
[oː], D_3 [uːe]. This can be handled by having all three dialects
undergo the rules which derive the D_1 form [oːɨ]; the D_2 form
[oː] is derived from this by a 'monophthongization' rule, and the
D_3 form [uːe] by rules which raise the [oː] element and lower
the [ɨ]. These D_2 and D_3 rules are phonologically quite plausible,
and moreover they are not set up specifically for these word-sets
but are parts of rules which are of more general application.

Though generative dialectology may have some advantages over
other methods of description, there remain a number of points on
which there is not complete agreement among members of the
school, and others where the 'outsider' is far from convinced by
the arguments presented.

The underlying forms are one area where different approaches
have been adopted by generativists. Some descriptions have set

up underlying forms which are either identical with or at least much closer to those of one dialect, with others derived by a sequence of rules that are not required for the 'basic' dialect. For example, in her description of Lumasaaba, Brown has underlying forms which are very close to those of the Northern dialects; Southern dialects are derived by a sequence of rules that are not required for the 'basic' dialect. The criteria generally adopted for choosing the basic dialect are 'generality', 'economy', and 'naturalness' in terms of the number and form of the rules required to generate all the dialect forms. Brown says that she also attempted (a) 'to construct a common Lumasaaba that would be neutral between Northern and Southern realizations', and (b) 'to derive Northern from Southern forms'. The former was rejected because 'parity of derivational difficulty between the two realizations could only be achieved by neutral forms that did not resemble any known phonological system, and by long and difficult derivations for both North and South', and the latter because it 'turned out that fewer rules were needed if a Northern form was taken as basic, and that these rules were much more general'. So the decision to derive Southern from Northern forms is justified by the more economical and 'revealing' statement which this method allows.

But as Thomas [14] points out, such criteria could lead one to adopt as basic forms sometimes those of one dialect, sometimes those of another. For example (see above), in deriving the pronunciations in English of words such as *grass*, *laugh*, *bath*, *dance* etc. it may be found simplest to take the short vowel form as basic and to have a rule '[a]→[ɑ:]/-[s,f,θ,ns] etc'. In deriving the pronunciations of *cup*, *love*, *flood* etc it will almost certainly be simpler to treat the [ʌ] form as basic, and to have the rule '[ʌ]→[ʊ]' in Northern dialects (the reverse would need a statement of environments and many exceptions). But to do this would be to take the Northern dialect as basic in the first case, and the Southern in the second.[15]

The alternative approach to adopting the forms of one dialect as more basic is to set up some more abstract underlying form which is not the same as that of any particular dialect. Again the form in question is held to be arrived at by adopting criteria such as those referred to above: the simplest set of rules for deriving all the dialect forms is possible if we set up this particular underlying form.

The whole idea of a common underlying form for all dialects is one which is superficially attractive, but it leads to considerable problems in certain cases. Perhaps such a form can be set up which does not seem too far-fetched if one is dealing with a language such as Brown was describing, which is spoken by a comparatively small number of people who do not reveal a large range of dialect variation when compared to some European languages. But the suggestion has been made that even with English the underlying forms are common to all dialects, and moreover that these underlying forms persist over long periods of time; [16] the actual forms are produced by a long sequence of rules, which may change from time to time in the various dialects. This proposal was originally made by American linguists; and since American dialects of English generally do not show extreme differences, it may be feasible to set up an underlying form from which they all may be derived without too complicated a set of rules. But if one attempts to do this for British dialects, where there are differences like those referred to in Chapter One between RP and West Yorkshire (e.g. [naɪt]/[niːt] *night* , [faɪt]/[fɛɪt] *fight*, [faɪnd]/[fɪnd] *find*, [naɪðə]/[nɔːðə] *neither* , etc etc), it would be necessary to have underlying forms which are so artificial from a synchronic viewpoint (however closely they and the rules may reflect diachronic developments) that it is difficult to believe they could be anything other than a linguist's plaything.

And the problem is that orthodox generativists maintain that the underlying forms and the rules to derive the actual dialects *are* much more than a linguist's invention: they believe that they have a certain 'reality' in that they are part of the native speaker's *competence* , his intuitive knowledge of the language; and it is this 'knowledge' of the common underlying forms and the rules which enables him to understand speakers of other dialects.

An attempt to produce a description along generative lines for British English is to be found in Trudgill's book on Norwich (1974a). He tried to account for the differences within Norwich English in terms of a common set of underlying forms and various rules to derive the actually occurring forms – but he admitted that it would be very difficult to produce a 'meaningful' description of this sort for more widely differing British varieties. He claimed that his system 'exists' in the sense that it is part of the native Norwich speaker's competence, and enables him to produce and understand utterances of different varieties within Norwich English (and also to recognize the varieties in question and so 'place' their speakers). If one discounts the claim that a speaker can *produce* examples of all other varieties – the evidence for which appears to be largely anecdotal, and which could be countered by contrary examples – the grounds for supposing that there is a psychologically real shared system are the ability of speakers to understand and 'recognize' those of other varieties. This is a main reason for other generativists wanting a common system for *all* English varieties. But if Trudgill believes the latter is unrealistic (and also, presumably, unnecessary) he must believe that speakers of say RP and West Yorkshire dialects understand each other without sharing a common system – presumably because of familiarity and because there is sufficient similarity between their two different systems (just as speakers of some different languages can understand each other to a certain degree – without sharing a common system). But if it is unnecessary to postulate a common system for two very different dialects of English, is it necessary to believe that all Norwich speakers share the same system?

A final doubt about generative dialectology also concerns the question of dialects having in common the set of underlying forms and a number of the rules. As was noted above, generativists hold that their approach focuses on the grammars of dialects rather than on the data: the starting-point is supposed to be a comparison of the grammars of individual dialects, from which it will appear that they have a great deal in common. This similarity is not simply *assumed* to exist, but it is claimed that grammars of the individual dialects produced independently according to the criteria of economy, naturalness, or whatever, will turn out to be so similar that a common grammar can then be set up. But as A. R. Thomas makes clear,[17] no one has ever done generative dialectology this 'long way round' – they have always started not by writing separate grammars for the dialects and then comparing them, but by producing a grammar with the common set of underlying forms, certain rules common to some dialects, and others peculiar to individual ones, and so on. So in this respect (like several others), the theory of generative grammar must be regarded as 'not proven'.

II.   A 'CONTINUUM' OF VARIETIES: THE 'DYNAMIC MODEL'

Until around 1960 the problem of variation had been neglected in general linguistics. The usual approach of the 'modern' era of the subject (i.e. the present century) had been to view language as something essentially homogeneous. Linguistics was structural: 'a language is a system where everything holds together', said Saussure – and linguists assumed that 'structure' must be equated with 'homogeneity'. They therefore shut their eyes to the differences within a language, and concentrated on an artifically homogeneous object – an individual speaker.[18] Linguists were aware that heterogeneity did exist, but they treated it as if it were merely an uncomfortable but theoretically unimportant fact, which could be left to stylisticians, dialectologists, and other such 'scavengers', whose job was to tidy up the trivial matters on the periphery of linguistics proper.[19]

But since the mid-1960s another viewpoint has been gaining ground. Heterogeneity within a language is so pervasive that linguists have come to accept that this situation is in fact the norm, and that variation should therefore be seen as central rather than peripheral to linguistics. More important, from the work of Labov and his followers it appeared that heterogeneity is not incompatible with regularity and structure: there is 'structured heterogeneity', or patterned variation - within the individual to some extent, but more importantly, within the community. In fact, Labov (a pupil of Weinreich, who had emphasized the importance of structure in the study of dialects) suggested that true regularity of linguistic patterns was to be found not in the individual speaker, but in the speech community as a whole. Furthermore, it was realized that this view not only fits the facts 'synchronically' (i.e. for a language at any one point in time), but also makes it possible to relate this to a theory of language change. Ever since Saussure had distinguished between the 'synchronic' and 'diachronic' aspects of language, most linguists had concentrated on the former, and had abstracted an artificial 'static' situation from the variation and on-going change inherent in all languages. It was time now to bring the two axes together again, and variation was seen to be a key issue here.

As variation moved into the centre of linguistics, it was soon realized that such frameworks as had previously been proposed for describing heterogeneity were inadequate. For instance, the idea that there may be 'co-existent systems' within a community (two or more discrete and self-consistent grammatical systems, whose random mutual interference might produce a range of inter-mediate varieties) was quickly rejected as simplistic, and various more sophisticated models were proposed. That of Labov and his followers was in terms of variable rules: rules with different probabilities of application according to the various linguistic environments and non-linguistic factors such as class, sex, age, and style. [20] This model has been referred to as 'quantitative': it attempts to state the relative quantities of different variants in different situations.

The main alternative viewpoint, called 'dynamic' (as opposed to 'quantitative' or 'static') by its adherents because it proposes that variation is simply an aspect of on-going linguistic change, is the subject of this section. Its relevance to dialectology may initially seem obscure - but dialect differences are of course a matter of variation within a language, and dialectalization is an important aspect of the inter-relation of linguistic variation and change. So this model must be considered in a study of the development of thought about dialect, such as the present volume.

The 'dynamic model' grew out of studies on *creole* languages (languages which have developed from *pidgins*- 'simplified' varieties adopted as means of communication between speakers of two mutual-ly unintelligible languages. Pidgins have no native speakers; but gradually they may develop into creoles: they are adopted as the native languages of various groups, and consequently expanded and acquire all the necessary functions of a natural language). In a situation where a creole is used in the same area as a standard form of the language on which it is based - for example, Krio and English in Sierra Leone; Haitian Creole and French in Haiti; Sranan and English in Surinam; and so on - it has often been found that there are 'intermediate dialects'. Scholars have used the term *basilect* to refer to the 'broadest' form of creole, and *acrolect* for the standard variety; the term *mesolect* has been proposed for a form somewhere between the two. It was suggested that a mesolect results from the mutual interference of the basilect and the acrolect.

In an important paper published in 1971, De Camp[21] argued that the picture was much more complicated than this in a 'post-creole situation' i.e. where there had been an extension of education and some breaking down of a formerly rigid social stratification. Using evidence drawn from his experience with Caribbean creoles, De Camp showed that it was unrealistic to divide varieties into creole and standard (or even into basilect, mesolect, and acrolect): there is no sharp cleavage between these forms - rather, there is a *continuum* of varieties between the extreme form of the creole and the standard language. A series of studies by Derek Bickerton on aspects of Guyanese creole developed this view in more detail, and C.-J. N. Bailey embodied these ideas in a wider theory of linguistic variation and change.[22]

There are two essential differences between the 'continuum' view and that of the basilect-mesolect-acrolect. First, it is held to be impossible to divide varieties into three discrete systems - or any number, for that matter. Some of the variable features show more than three variants, some less, and there is no 'bundling of isoglosses', as it were, in respect of these differences. The result is that it is unrealistic to divide varieties into any number of dialects with their own systems - there is simply a continuum of linguistic differences.[23] Second, it is *not* the case that the mesolect varieties (however many) result from the random mutual interference of the varieties at the ends of this continuum. Rather, it is held that the varieties are related 'dynamically', in that they represent successive stages of development from creole to standard. This is where the synchronic and diachronic axes of linguistics meet: Bickerton has claimed that a synchronic cut across the Guyanese community of today (with individuals ranged between creole and standard) reflects a diachronic cut through 150-200 years of its linguistic history (with progressive development by some speakers towards the standard, while others made less or virtually no 'progress').

Its proponents hold that this model is appropriate not only to post-creole situations, but to any language community. All other approaches to differences within a language have been in terms of *dialects*, which are essentially forms of language shared by a *group* of speakers - whether this is defined geographically, or in terms of social class, sex, age-group or whatever. But this approach puts much greater emphasis on the *individual* - and the term *lect* has been coined for an individual variety of language. Speaking is done by individuals, and probably anyone who has been engaged in detailed fieldwork on any scale - or even anyone who has simply observed the use of language around him - will agree that individuals who have the same sociological characteristics (e.g. sex, age, education, occupation, income etc etc) may nevertheless differ in speech-patterns. Whether this is because of differences in personality, experience, aspirations, or whatever is unimportant for our purposes: the point is that individuals do not all conform to a 'group norm'.[24]

It is when we examine the speech of the individuals in a speech community that we find that there is indeed a continuum of differences. But a Labov-type approach obscures this because it produces *average* scores for speakers in certain (non-linguistic) categories: the result is to give a false impression of discrete 'dialects' rather than a more or less smooth continuum of 'lects'. De Camp pointed out that it would be ridiculous if, when examining socio-economic characteristics which vary gradually within a society, one were to take, say, state-boundaries as natural divisions and then average the socio-economic 'scores' of individuals within each state. But sociolinguists have been doing something very like this when correlating continuously-varying linguistic data to pre-conceived categories of age, education, income etc (instead of correlating such non-linguistic variables to linguistic data, which would be justifiable).

My own research leads me to agree with this point. When investigating urban speech in West Yorkshire, one variable examined was the pronunciation or 'dropping' of h in contexts where it would occur in RP. With over a hundred informants altogether, I worked out percentage scores for class, style, and so on. For conversational speech (i.e. 'casual' plus 'formal' styles), there was apparently a clear stratification by social class in the amount of h-pronunciation:

I	II	III	IV	V
96	64	43	21	17

But (a) if we examine individuals rather than the group averages, we find that there were the following numbers of informants in each percentage 'band':

0	1–10	11–20	21–30	31–40	41–50	51–60	61–70	71–80	81–90	91–99	100
7	28	13	8	9	4	2	10	6	6	8	5

(b) it is not the case that this continuum can be divided in such a way that the members of each social class fall within a certain range, and members of other classes fall outside this. In fact, the range of individual scores in each class was as follows:

I	II	III	IV	V
81–100	7–100 (40–100)	2–100	0–86	0–80 (0–37)

In the case of Classes II and V the bracketed figures indicate what the range would have been had there not in each case been one individual whose speech was markedly 'status incongruent'.[25]

If these two individuals had not formed part of the sample the figures would look more 'regular', but there would still not be 'discrete groups which are relatively unified in their linguistic behaviour'.[26]

On grounds such as these, the whole notion of 'dialect' as a group phenomenon is rejected by Bailey and Bickerton.[27] A dialect is supposed to be a variety shared by a number of speakers, and delimited from other varieties by a bundle of isoglosses of some sort. But in actual fact such a situation is rarely found; instead, there is a continuum of lects (individual varieties). A 'grid' of all possible *isolects* (varieties differing from each other by just a single feature) could be established, covering the whole range of variation within a language. Many of these isolects will be realized by one or more individual speakers using a certain style; some may be (in theory, temporarily) unoccupied.[28]

The various lects are held to be 'implicationally related'. Since the notion of *implicational relations* is crucial to this school of thought, let us start with one or two simple examples of the sort of things that may be implicationally related. In my observation, if a Yorkshireman uses the /ɑ:/ variant in words like *grass*, he will certainly use the /ʌ/ variant in words such as *cut*; but the reverse may not be true - in other words, [kut grɑ:s] is most unlikely to occur, but [kʌt gras] is quite possible. So the use of /ɑ:/ in a certain set of words *implies* the use of /ʌ/, but not vice versa. Such implicational relations may hold not only between different variables, as in the above example, but also between different categories of words within the same variable. For example, with the variable incidence of /ɑ:/ and /a:/ if one uses /ɑ:/ in *trans-* or *plastic* , one will certainly use it in *grass* (but the reverse need not hold); if one uses /ɑ:/ in *grass*, one will certainly have it in *father* (but not necessarily the reverse); and so on.[29] Even more delicate differences of environment within a variable can be implicationally related: for example, Bailey uses some of the findings of Labov and his colleagues concerning the 'dropping' of word-final [t] from the consonant group [st]: if this occurs in *missed out* i.e. the environment [s+t# V], it will certainly occur in *missed catches* [s+t# C]; if in the latter, then in *mist in the valley* [st# V]; if in this, then in *mist cover* [st# C] - but in no case does the reverse implication hold.

The various lects in a *panlectal grid* (i.e. an array of all the possible lects in a language) are implicationally related to each other: each is essentially an individual grammar - a set of rules - and (since each isolect differs from those 'on either side' in respect of just one rule-difference) any lect implies the set of rules of the lect 'before' it on the continuum. But an essential point about this model is that the lects are held to be related not only synchronically but also historically. This is the 'dynamic' aspect of the model, as contrasted with the 'static' viewpoint of other schools of linguistics.[30]

Essentially, Bailey has proposed a new version of an old theory. The old theory in question is the 'Wave Theory' of Johannes Schmidt, put forward in 1872 to account for resemblances between separate but geographically adjacent branches of the Indo-European family of languages.[31] Schmidt's idea was that a linguistic change spreads outwards from some starting-point like waves on a pond into which a pebble has been tossed. Waves may be of various strengths, and may start at different points – depending on the size of the pebbles and where they were thrown in. The result is that different areas of the pond are affected by different combinations of waves. Similarly, a geographical area is affected by different combinations of isoglosses, and so ends up with various languages and dialects with varying degrees of similarity.

Bailey's modern version of this is that waves of change move, over a period of time, either through geographical space (as Schmidt had suggested) or through *social* space – or both; and they may be slowed down by barriers of either kind i.e. those of age, sex, class, etc, as well as physical geographical features. Changes are of course transmitted by individuals, and at any one time a particular change will have 'passed' certain speakers, but will not yet have reached others. Thus, for example, speaker C (whom a particular change has not yet reached) will differ from speaker A (whom the same change has passed) – and from speaker B (whom the change is just reaching, and who consequently sometimes produces the same output as A, sometimes the same as C). So the model accounts for both interpersonal variation (between A and C) and intrapersonal variation (within B).

Changes such as these are often implicationally related in the sense that a particular wave, say that affecting feature x, will gradually spread to cover the area already affected by the wave relevant to feature w. The result will be that a change in x will imply a prior change in w but a change in w does not necessarily mean that x will have changed. These implicational relations may again hold either between quite different changes (as in an earlier example it was suggested that a person who changes from saying [gras] to [grɑːs] will already have changed from [kʊt] to [kʌt], but his saying [kʌt] does *not* imply that he also says [grɑːs]), or between different environments of change within the same variable. In fact, it is held that linguistic changes do not affect all examples of a variable at once, but proceed environment by environment; and a change in a particular environment will imply a change in 'heavier-weighted' environments. Thus, for example, it has been seen that my own observations of the spread of the glottal stop in West Yorkshire suggest that it affects word-final environments before word-medial ones – so if a person says [bɪʔə] *bitter*, this implies that he says [bɪʔ ə stuf] *bit of stuff*, but someone may say the latter but not the former.

Diagrammatically, a simplified picture of the progress of a change is as follows (the symbol '+' is used to indicate that the change has occurred i.e. a 'new' rules applied; 'x' that sometimes the old rule operates, sometimes the new one i.e. there is variation: a speaker sometimes says [gras] and sometimes [grɑ:s], for example; and '-' that the change has not yet occurred):

Environments		a	b	c	d
	0	-	-	-	-
Stages of	1	X	-	-	-
change	2	+	X	-	-
	3	+	+	X	-

The 'stages' of change referred to here may be stages of time, but also they may be represented at any one time by different individuals or locations. If it is a matter of locations, these may not always occur in a contiguous area on a map, since changes do not always proceed so regularly.

A more graphic representation of the social or geographical spread of the waves of change is provided by the figure of the idealized representation of Bailey's 'Wave Model'.[32]

From the above table the implicational relations between the environments of change can be seen quite clearly: a 'categorical' change in any environment implies a categorical change in heavier-weighted environments (e.g. at stage 3, + in environment b implies + in environment a), and a variable change in one environment implies a categorical change in heavier-weighted ones (e.g. at stage 3, x in environment c implies + in environments a and b and - in environment d). If a change continues long enough it will eventually become generalized, i.e. it will not be limited to certain environments but will apply categorically in all.[33]

The ideas of Bailey and Bickerton in fact constitute a quite different view of the nature of variation, and of the relation between variation and change, from that which had previously been accepted. Labov and his followers had suggested that variation is 'inherent' within any speech community, and that while a linguistic change necessarily involves variation for some time between the old and the new features, the fact that there is variation does *not* necessarily mean that a change is in progress.[34] Bailey and Bickerton on the other hand hold that variation is simply a stage in linguistic change. A change begins by affecting some feature in some restricted environment: what happens is that the old and the new rules alternate for a time, then the new rule becomes categorical. But by this stage the change is affecting another environment at the point of origin, and also the more restricted change has spread 'outwards' from this point; and so on (see the wave diagram above). The earliest and least general changes have time to spread furthest, and at any one point there is, with time, increasing generatization of the rule; eventually the change may become categorical at all points, or it may cease to operate before this happens.

Essentially then there are three stages in a change as it affects any environment at any point: 1. old rule categorical, 2. alternation between old and new rules, 3. new rule categorical.

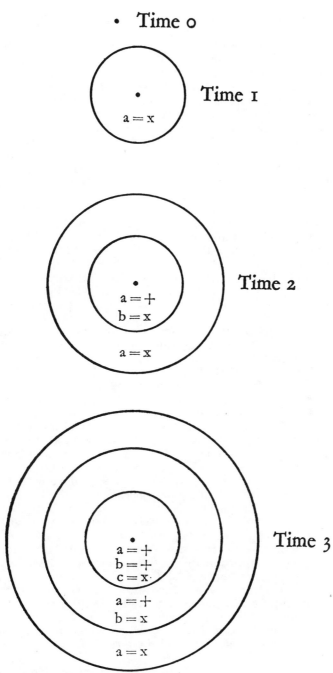

Idealized representation of Bailey's 'Wave Model'.   (Based on Bailey, 1973b.)

The second stage, 'variation', is simply a developmental phase between two categorical stages, and there is no need for any elaborate device such as 'variable rules' (with attendant difficulties concerning how much the actual speaker is believed to 'know' about the relative probabilities of the rule applying, according to different environments, different social categories, and so on). So what appears, with a 'synchronic cut' across a community to be a situation of inherent variation is in fact the equivalent of a 'diachronic cut' through history, when the variation will be seen as simply a phase in the change from one feature or rule to another.

Variation is thus held to be less of a problem than had been believed. Moreover, it is claimed that there is actually much *less* variation in a community than appears to be the case from the Labovian method of averaging scores for groups of speakers. If *individuals* are examined, and the different linguistic environments are carefully distinguished, it will emerge that most features are categorical, and that alternation between old and new categorical rules (i.e. variation) is much less than had been thought. Bickerton (1973b), discussing a feature of Montreal French, shows that when data is examined for individual speakers and specific environments, the amount of variation is 22 per cent; but if environments are lumped together variation appears to be 57 percent; and if individuals were grouped together the figure would be even higher. So a lot of the 'variation' found in Labov-type studies is in fact an artefact of the method of analysis. Bailey and Bickerton claim that if the percentage of use of a particular variable feature by individual speakers is plotted on a graph, the typical pattern will be an 'S-curve' (see diagram below). A curve such as this can be taken as representing a change passing fairly quickly through a population. Speakers with low percentages are those who are just acquiring the new feature; those with high percentages have almost fully acquired it and are getting rid of the old feature. Only relatively few speakers at any one time have middle percentages, i.e. appear to vary between two features without either being dominant.

The 'dynamic model' has not escaped criticism, but this is not the place to enter detailed discussion of the arguments on each side;[35] suffice it to say that while many people find its claims interesting, they feel that further detailed testing is called for. Nor is it appropriate to be concerned here with other questions that have been tackled by the proponents of this model - such as just how much 'knowledge' resides in the 'competence' of native speakers about the various lects in their language (should this be represented by 'polylectal' or 'panlectal' grammars?). To become involved with such matters would take us too far from dialectology into general linguistics. It is time to stop.

Indeed, some readers will feel that we have already gone too far. This article has dealt with ideas put forward mainly by linguists rather than dialectologists; those arguing for the 'dynamic

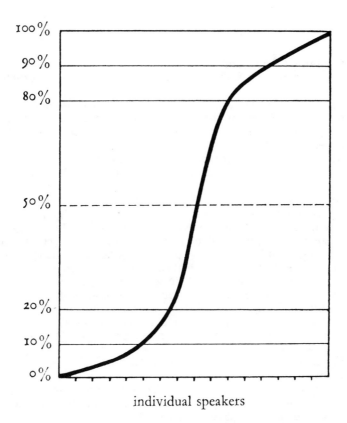

The S-curve of linguistic change.   (Based on Bailey, 1973b and Bickerton, 1975a.)

model' even reject the notion of 'dialect' entirely! But we started out with the broad definition that dialects are 'different forms of the same language', and both generative dialectology and the dynamic model are concerned with such.   Moreover, the most 'traditional' dialectology has concentrated on the historical develop-ment of differences within a language – and both these recent approaches have largely collapsed the synchronic/diachronic dichotomy upheld so fervently by modern linguistics this century, and have related linguistic differentiation to its historical context. Though some dialectologists still shy away from linguistics, a *rapprochement* between the two subjects is more possible than at any time this century, because linguistic variation – which is essentially what dialectology is concerned with – is now seen by many scholars as central rather than peripheral to linguistics.

FOOTNOTES

[1] See Halle (1959) and (1962).

[2] See Chomsky (1964), and Chomsky and Halle (1965) and (1968).

[3] See Klima (1964) and O'Neil (1968) for examples of papers concerned with generating grammatical differences among dialects.

[4] This corresponds to the term 'morphophoneme' earlier used by structural linguists.

[5] This is of course *historically* untrue: the North reflects the earlier situation;   in the South /r/ has 'split' into /ʌ/ and /ʊ/.

[6] I am using 'dialect' throughout this article, though we could of course treat some differences as merely 'accent'.

[7] Throughout this outline of generative dialectology I am, for the benefit of those with less technical background in linguistics, using familiar symbols for phonetic and phonemic segments rather than introducing the additional complication of *distinctive features*,   as usually employed in generative phonology.   Using the latter, the example under discussion would look even simpler, since it would merely be a matter of changing one feature, the degree of 'closeness' of the vowel e.g. [close 4]→[close 3].

[8] This example is discussed in Kiparsky (1968) p. 177 and King (1969) p. 46.

[9] Newton (op. cit.) p. 65.

[10] Vasiliu (op. cit.) pp. 85-8.

[11] Brown (op. cit.) p. 156.   On ordered rules in general, see also S. Saporta 'Ordered Rules, Dialect Differences, and Historical Processes' (1965).

[12] This is the case with generative phonology in general: for example Chomsky and Halle (1968) set up a velar fricative and a Great Vowel Shift rule in their supposedly synchronic description of modern English!

[13] Generative phonology does not in fact recognize the relevance of a unit at the level of the phoneme of structural linguistics, but it is not necessary to go into this question here.

[14] (op. cit.) p. 190.

[15] The objection could also be made that the first case reflects the actual historical development, while the second is counter-historical - though this is strictly irrelevant in a synchronic description.

[16] See Chomsky and Halle (1968) pp. x, 54 etc.

[17] (op. cit.).

[18] This approach is best illustrated in the era of structural linguistics by an important article on phonology by Bernard Bloch (1948):   he said that the object of study had to be *a single speaker in a single style on a single occasion*.   In the succeeding 'generative' period, Chomsky (1965) said that 'linguistic theory is concerned primarily with an ideal speaker-listener in a completely homogeneous speech-community'.

[19] Saussure's 'parole' and Chomsky's 'performance' (though these notions are not exactly alike) both allowed for matters that did not belong to the essential 'langue' or 'competence' respectively.

[20] A more developed framework for variable rules was proposed by Sankoff and Cedergren (1976).

[21] A scholar who had earlier produced one of the first studies of an American urban dialect: that of San Francisco.

[22] See especially Bickerton (1971), (1973a), and (1975a); and Bailey (1973a) and (1973b).

[23] Note that this notion differs from that of the 'dialect continuum' (e.g. that extending from Northern France to Southern Italy) in that (a) the continuum in this case may be social instead of, or as well as, geographical in its extent; and (b) the continuum is not one of 'dialects', but of individual varieties or 'lects' (see below).

[24] Extreme departures from the group 'average' have been termed 'status incongruence' by Labov and his followers. But the present approach would hold that probably *all* individuals within a group exhibit differences.

[25] In Class II the individual concerned was a former managing-director and an ex-mayor of Halifax, whose normal speech was more or less that of the stereotype blunt Yorkshireman; he told me that his wife [ple:z amlət əba:t ɪʔ]. The Class V individual was one of the few cases where the composite social class score concealed certain 'higher' ratings: he was a former clerk who had had grammar school education, but in terms of income, housing, and standard of living he scored very low. Apparently in his case the occupation and education categories were more closely related to his speech.

[26] See Trudgill (1974a) p. 59, where he says this was the intention of his division of the social class continuum. As evidence contrary to my own, it may be noted that Macauley in his work on Glasgow (see his 1978 paper, p. 137ff) examined individual as well as group scores, with the views of Bickerton and Bailey in mind. He found that there was indeed a continuum of linguistic variation, but that (using his rather crude total scores for a combination of four variables) there was evidence for believing that there *were* three discrete groups with their social dialects (though note that he had started out with the idea that there were *four* social classes).

[27] See Bailey (1973a) p. 161, (1973b) p. 11, and Bickerton (1973a) p. 643, for example.

[28] The positions on the isolect continuum are really abstract levels, not the fixed locations of actual speakers; and note that it is held that the same individual may on different occasions represent different lects within the 'panlectal grid' (see Bickerton, 1975a pp. 116, 203, etc).

[29] This example is given in extended form in Bailey (1973a) p. 173, but I would not agree that some of his relations hold for British English.

[30] The two views are contrasted point by point in Bickerton (1973b) and Bailey (1973b).

[31] See Pulgram (1953) for a useful summary.

[32] See Bickerton (1973b) p. 43 for a non-hypothetical wave diagram.

[33] Obviously the above picture is oversimplified in that it suggests that not only does change affect one environment at a time, but also that variation is only heard in one environment at once. Some of Bickerton's examples (e.g. 1971, p. 476ff) seem to lend support to this view, but in Bailey's fuller work (1973b) he suggests that all environments of a rule *may* become variable before the oldest becomes categorical. My own work, say for the change [t]→[ʔ] (if that is indeed the correct interpretation), certainly suggests that there may be variation in several environments at once, though the change may have progressed further in some environments than others.

[34] See Weinreich, Labov, and Herzog (1968): 'Not all variability and heterogeneity of language structure involves change, but all change involves variability and heterogeneity.'

[35] Several scholars have drawn attention to the problem of 'stagnant' variable rules (see Fasold, 1973): cases where we know that variation has existed for many years, without there being any clear evidence that a change from an old to a new feature is still in progress e.g. the variation between [θ] and [t] in *th-* words in some American varieties of English, or the '*h*-dropping' in many parts of Britain. A review of Bickerton's book by G. Sankoff (1977), while acknowledging the importance of the work, criticizes him for using his data selectively and illustratively rather than checking each of his hypotheses exhaustively against all his material, and also for not making clear *how* changes occur - do people go through change as individuals, or is it successive age-groups who progress to 'higher' lects? Other scholars feel that Bickerton and Bailey go too far in denying the validity of dialect-groupings (see Macauley, 1978).

REFERENCES

Bailey, C.-J. N. (1973a). "The patterning of language variation." In: R. W. Bailey & J. L. Robinson (eds.): *Varieties of Present-Day English*. New York: Macmillan.

Bailey, C.-J. N. (1971). *Variation and Linguistic Theory*. Arlington: Center for Applied Linguistics.

Bickerton, D. (1971). "Inherent variability and variable rules." *Foundations of Language*, 7.

Bickerton, D. (1973a). "The nature of a creole continuum." *Language*, 49.

Bickerton, D. (1973b). "Quantitative versus dynamic para-
digms: the case of Montreal 'que.'" In C.-J. N. Bailey &
R. W. Shuy (eds.): *New Ways of Analyzing Variation in
English*. Washington: Georgetown University Press.

Bickerton, D. (1975a). *The Dynamics of a Creole System*. London: Cambridge University Press.

Bickerton, D. (1975b). Review of Trudgill (1974), in *Journal
of Linguistics*, 11.

Bloch, Bernard. (1948). "A set of postulates for phonemic
analysis," *Language*, 24.

Brown, Gillian. (1972). *Phonological Rules and Dialect Variation*. London: Cambridge University Press.

Chomsky, Noam. (1957). *Syntactic Structures*. The Hague:
Mouton.

Chomsky, Noam. (1964). *Current Issues in Linguistic Theory*.
The Hague: Mouton.

Chomsky, Noam. (1965). *Aspects of the Theory of Syntax*.
Cambridge, MA: MIT Press.

Chomsky, N. & Morris Halle. (1965). "Some controversial
questions in phonological theory," *Journal of Linguistics*,
1.

Chomsky, N. & Morris Halle. (1968). *The Sound Pattern of
English*. New York: Harper & Row.

DeCamp, David. (1971). "Towards a generative analysis
of a post-creol continuum." In D. Hymes (ed.): *Pidginization and Creolization of Languages*. London: Cambridge
University Press.

Fasold, Ralph W. (1973). "The concept of 'earlier-later';
more or less correct." In C.-J. N. Bailey & R. W. Shuy
(eds.): *New Ways of Analysing Variation in English*. Washington: Georgetown University Press.

King, R. D. (1969). *Historical Linguistics and Generative
Grammar*. Englewood Cliffs: Prentice-Hall.

Kiparsky, Paul. (1968). "Linguistic universals and linguistic
change." In Emmon Bach & R. T. Harms (eds.): *Universals
and Linguistic Theory*. New York: Holt, Rinehart & Winston.

Klima, Edward S. (1964). "Relatedness between grammatical
systems." *Language*, 40.

Labov, William. (1963). "The social motivation of a sound
change." *Word*, 19.

Labov, William. (1966a). *The Social Stratification of English
in New York City*. Washington: Center for Applied Linguistics.

Labov, William. (1966b). "Hypercorrection in the lower middle
class as a factor in linguistic change." In William Bright
(ed.): *Sociolinguistics*. The Hague: Mouton.

Labov, William. (1967). "The effect of social mobility on linguistic behavior." In S. Lieberson (ed.): *Explorations in
Sociolinguistics* (=*International Journal of American Linguistics*, 33.4.2).

Labov, William. (1968). "The reflection of social processes in linguistic structures. In: Joshua A. Fishman (ed.): *Readings in the Sociology of Language*. The Hague: Mouton.

Labov, William. (1969). "Contraction, deletion, and inherent variability of the English copula." *Language* , 45.

Macauley, R. K. S. (1977). *Language, Social Class, and Education: A Glasgow Study*. Edinburgh: Edinburgh University Press.

Macauley, R. K. S. (1978). "Variation and consistency in Glaswegian English." In P. J. Trudgill (ed.): *Sociolinguistic Patterns in British English*. London: Arnold.

Newton, Brian E. (1972). *The Generative Interpretation of Dialect*. London: Cambridge University Press.

O'Neil, W. A. (1968). "Transformational dialectology: phonology and syntax." *Zeitschrift für Mundartforschung*, 35.

Pulgram, Ernst. (1953). "Family tree, wave theory, and dialectology." *Orbis* , 2.

Pulgram, Ernst. (1964). "Structural comparison, diasystems, and dialectology." *Linguistics* , 4.

Sankoff, D., & H. J. Cedergren (1976). "The dimensionality of grammatical variation." *Language*, 52.

Sankoff, Gillian (1977). Review of Bickerton (1975a). *Journal of Linguistics*, 13.

Saporta, Sol. (1965). "Ordered rules, dialect differences, and historical processes." *Language* , 41.

Saussure, F. de. (1916). *Course de Linguistique Générale*. Lausanne: Payot.

Thomas, A. R. (1964). "Generative phonology in dialectology." *Transactions of the Philological Society*.

Trudgill, P. J. (1974). *The Social Differentiation of English in Norwich*. London: Cambridge University Press.

Vasiliu, E. (1966). "Towards a generative phonology of Daco-Rumanian dialects." *Journal of Linguistics* , 2.

Weinreich, Uriel. (1954). "Is a structural dialectology possible?" *Word*, 10. [Ed. note: Reprinted in this anthology.]

Weinreich, Uriel, William Labov, & M. I. Herzog. (1968). "Empirical foundations for a theory of language change." In W. P. Lehmann & Y. Malkiel (eds): *Directions for Historical Linguistics*. Austin: University of Texas Press.

REGIONAL DIALECTS

Although Atwood's conspectus describes American dialectology up to only 1962, it is indispensable as the opener for the section. But his exposition should be supplemented by the more comprehensive and updating articles, too long for inclusion here, constituting the Fall-Winter issue of *American Speech* 52 (1977):163-327, by Harold B. Allen, "Regional dialects, 1945-1974," and Lee Pederson, "Studies of American pronunciation since 1945," and by the several articles in *Publication of the American Dialect Society* No. 71 (1984), an issue devoted to needed research in American English.

Principal current projects are Pederson's nearly complete Linguistic Atlas of the Gulf States and two projects for which Raven I. McDavid had assumed responsibility, the Linguistic Atlas of the North Central States and the Linguistic Atlas of the Middle and South Atlantic States. McDavid's death in late 1984 led the American Dialect Society, sponsor of both projects, to appoint William Kretzschmar to replace him as editor-in-chief. At present writing the ultimate location of the two projects has not been determined.

Overshadowing work in linguistic geography is the long-awaited *Dictionary of American Regional English* edited by Frederic Cassidy at the University of Wisconsin for the American Dialect Society. The Belknap Press of Harvard University will have published Volume I of DARE, as the dictionary is called, by the time this book appears. Its content will purport to include all American regional terms, gathered by fieldworkers and readers of dialect literature, newspapers, and personal letters. The first volume will explain research procedures, describe the communities and informants, list the questionnaire items, provide basic maps, and give the text of letters A, B, and C. Subsequent volumes will carry on through Z.

Atwood's article is supplemented here by the two best-known American dialect geographers, the late Raven McDavid, who offers a background piece, and Hans Kurath, who adds to such raw data as appear in his *Linguistic Atlas of New England* an interpretation of dialect boundaries in terms of their seminal sociocultural features.

Useful now is the late W. R. Van Riper's thorough-going study of the used and mis-used "General American," a designation still often found--and often rejected.

The remaining articles in this section concern the activity of the many researchers participating in what has become a revival of emphasis upon regional variation. The first four relate to four major dialect projects in the eastern half of the nation. Audrey Duckert reports on the effort to follow up the original investigations for the New England atlas. Timothy Frazer, exploring the range of South Midland speech in the North Central states, compares the findings of DARE and those of the Atlas of the North Central States. Because it is not likely to be found in many libraries, *The Linguistic Atlas of the Upper Midwest* is represented by an article defining its regional patterns. Lee Pederson next explains how his extensive recording of free conversation in the Gulf States provides rare material for making a folk grammar.

That dialect researchers may themselves sharply disagree in method and interpretation as well as in preparation is suggested when Ronald Butters compares an independent study of Appalachian English with its treatment in the research for the Linguistic Atlas of the Middle and South Atlantic States. His article deserves attention.

Besides the surveys already referred to only one other project is in process, the Oklahoma study here described by the wife of its director, the late W. R. Van Riper. It will be published independently. Such publication had once been expected of the then joint Pacific Coast and Pacific Northwest projects, but no plans exist for further work. These three have appeared.

Unfortunately, a conference at Boulder, Colorado, in 1952, intended to seed a Rocky Mountain dialect project, did not attain fruition. One dissertation emerged from Colorado, but the Colorado materials as a whole await editing. Some action is currently proposed for Utah, but there is no over-all approach to the area needs.

Cassidy's article is relevant as a case study of the unusual regional proliferation of the meanings and forms of a single word. The study is based on DARE evidence.

Finally, although the editors reluctantly had to omit attention to English elsewhere, they could not ignore the English of Canada. The late Walter Avis treats it in terms of a central norm, "General Canadian." But that Canadian English cannot be studied like American English is the theme of Ian Pringle, who insists that the historical distribution of language variants in Canada prevents such traditional regional studies as those that characterize work in the United States.

THE METHODS OF AMERICAN DIALECTOLOGY

E. Bagby Atwood

LEXICOGRAPHY

The earliest observations of what would nowadays be called "dialect" covered a variety of linguistic categories but tended to concentrate on lexical and grammatical peculiarities. They were, moreover, largely prescriptive, at least by implication, and observers usually regarded the collected material as something to be avoided. Probably the first collection that could be called in any sense systematic was that of the Rev. John Witherspoon, who published a series of papers on usage in the *Pennsylvania Journal and Weekly Advertiser* during the year 1781.[1] He is credited with having coined the term *Americanism* to designate "ways of speaking peculiar to this country".[2] Some of his examples, however, were neither American in origin nor "peculiar" to the United States; for example, *fellow countrymen* for *countrymen* and *notify* with its modern meaning of "inform". Witherspoon also collected a number of "vulgarisms", which were undoubtedly genuine and which are common even today: *knowed* for *knew*, *this here* for *this*, *drownded* for *drowned*, *attacted* for *attacked*, and others.[3]

The most famous of American lexicographers, Noah Webster, need not be treated in detail, since a vast body of material has been published concerning him. However, as far as I know, the effect of the regional American dialects, particularly those of New England, on his recordings of words and meanings remains to be determined. Certainly his first dictionary, that of 1806,[4] was attacked for seeming to sanction "Americanisms and vulgarisms", and Webster felt need to defend himself for having included such terms as *docket, decedent, dutiable*, and even *lot* (of land) --as well as such "cant words" as *caucus*.[5] In his *American Dictionary* of 1828[6] he recorded a considerable number of Americanisms, or at least new terms observable in America, including such controversial verb usages as *to notice, to advocate*, and *to progress*, all of which had been condemned by Benjamin Franklin.[7] We can only wish that Webster had recorded more "cant" terms.

The numerous glossaries of Americanisms that appeared during the course of the nineteenth century are to a great extent the work of amateurs whose observation tended to be somewhat random and impressionistic. Among the compilers of such lists were David Humphries (1815),[8] John Pickering (1816),[9] Robley Dunglison (1829-30),[10] John R. Bartlett (1848),[11] and John S. Farmer (1889).[12] None of these was primarily concerned with folk speech, yet occasionally items of considerable dialectal interest are entered and commented on; for example *be* (for *am*, *are*--Be you ready?), *clapboard* (siding), *poke* (bag), *run* (small stream), and *tote* (carry).[13] All of these appear as early as Pickering, and most are recorded in Webster's first dictionary.

By far the greatest of the early collectors of American usages was Richard H. Thornton, an Englishman who migrated to the New World in the 1870s.[14] Toward the end of the century he began to accumulate a carefully documented body of material, in which the source and the date of every usage were on record. His *American Glossary* was published in 1912 and later years;[15] although it is not primarily a dialect dictionary[16] it still serves as a model of lexicographic procedure.

The idea that popular (in the sense of uneducated) speech is worthy of serious scholarly study arrived perhaps somewhat later in America than in Western Europe. The first public manifestation of interest on the part of scholars was the organization of the American Dialect Society (ADS), which took place at Harvard University in 1889. Evidently the idea was first suggested by Charles H. Grandgent, and the organization meeting was attended by twenty-eight persons, including Edward S. Sheldon, Francis J. Child, J. B. Greenough, George L. Kittredge, and others of their stature--men who were or were to be, among the leading philological scholars of their time.[17] The avowed object of the Society was "the investigation of the spoken English of the United States and Canada, and incidentally of other non-aboriginal dialects spoken in the same countries".[18] By January of 1890 there were 158 members,[19] and the official organ of the Society, *Dialect Notes*, began publication in that year.

As Louise Pound has pointed out, the early dialect scholars must have been strongly influenced by German thought and method. The first four presidents of the ADS had all studied in Germany, and George Hempl, the eighth, took his doctorate at Jena.[20] The Wenker methodology, however, seems not to have been adopted as a basis for dialect collection, except to a limited extent and in a modified form. Hempl prepared a standard questionnaire of something over 90 items which he published in 1894,[21] requesting the collaboration of his colleagues in its circulation. Hempl's questions were awkward and unwieldy,[22] and it is difficult to see how most of them could have produced useful results. I believe that the only publication based on this material was Hempl's article on the pronunciation of *grease* (verb) and *greasy*, which appeared in 1896.[23]

From an early date, the ADS took the position that the great majority of members could make their most valuable contribution in the field of vocabulary. In various circulars, instructions were given as to the kinds of usages to be collected and the methods to be followed.[24]   It was the hope, obviously a rather naive one, that there might be assembled "*a complete record of American speechforms in our day*, say in 1900", and that in the following years there might be published "an authoritative dictionary of American usage, which would supersede all other work in that line".[25] Indeed, the idea of a dialect dictionary has always been prominent among the membership of the ADS; many have hoped that we might have a work comparable to Joseph Wright's monumental *English Dialect Dictionary*.[26]

Unfortunately the contributions to *Dialect Notes* were extremely uneven, both in completeness and in reliability. Even after some 40 years of collection, only a few names stood out for thoroughness of work--names such as L. W. Payne,[27] H. Tallichet,[28] Louise Pound,[29] and Vance Randolph.[30]   Most reports were pitifully meager, and the total mass fell far short of original expectations.

During the period when Louise Pound was president of the ADS (1938-41) she arranged, "as a private person, not as president of the society",[31] for the publication of the available dialect materials by the Crowell Company. On her recommendation, Harold Wentworth was chosen as editor. Within a relatively short time his *American Dialect Dictionary* had been prepared and published,[32] although without the official sanction of the ADS.   In answer to criticisms of her arrangements, Miss Pound replied that "a standstill of more than half a century seemed long enough. When an opportunity offered, why not seize it?"[33]

Wentworth's *Dictionary* must be regarded as an abridged one, whether so planned or not. It is very doubtful that all available material was included; and, in any case, the project was unfortunate in its timing.   At least three important collections were being made during this period, of which publication was under way or would shortly begin. These were the materials of the *Dictionary of American English*,[34] the *Linguistic Atlas of New England*,[35] and the Mencken Supplements to *The American Language*.[36] Moreover, the G. & C. Merriam Company must have had in its files a great deal of valuable dialectal material which would ultimately see publication.

In recent studies of the vocabulary of the Southwest and other areas I have had occasion to refer to Wentworth many times.   Although I frequently find valuable material, I am often annoyed by the absence of terms that are of considerable dialectal significance.   I cite 40 such instances (out of a considerably larger number): *acequia* (irrigation ditch), *angledog* (earthworm), *banquette* (sidewalk), *belly band* (saddle girth), (*blue*) *norther* (sharp north wind), *burro* (donkey), *buttonwood* (sycamore tree), *Cajun* (Acadian), *chaparral* (bushy country), *charivari* (serenade), *clearseed peach* (freestone peach, *coon* (Negro), *cope!* (horse call), *corral* (horse pen), *devil's darning needle* (dragonfly), *dogie* (lone calf), *dog irons* (andirons), *eaves troughs* (gutters), *evener* (doubletree), *fatcake* (doughnut or cruller), *firedogs* (andirons), *hogshead cheese* (pork mixture), *hoosegow* (jail), *jackleg* (untrained person), *lead horse* (horse on the left), *llano* (prairie), *lumber room* (store room), *mesa* (plateau), *middling*(*s*) (salt pork), *milk gap* (cow pen), *mosquito hawk* (dragonfly), *nigger shooter* (boy's weapon), *olla* (water jar), *pilón* (something extra), *pirogue* (canoe), *rainworm* (earthworm), *redbug* (chigger), *snake feeder* (dragonfly), *toot* (paper bag), and *worm fence* (rail fence). That these are common usages is attested by the fact that 31 of them are entered in the *Dictionary of American English*, while no less than 38 of them are treated in *Webster's Third New International Dictionary*,[37] usually with some indication of their geographical distribution.

It is clear that there has never been assembled an American dialect lexicon to compare with that of England.[38]   In fact, it is hardly possible that such a collection can ever be made, since "dialect" in the European sense is much less common in America than in England.   The American population has always been more fluid than that of Europe, both geographically and socially. Conditions were simply not right for the development of extensive local patois.   There is often little distinction between dialect and standard speech; regional terms are frequently found in the usage of the educated, and even "illiterate" features are common in the works of novelists who deal with "local color".   Most general dictionaries have taken cognizance of these facts and have included a great many terms of regional and even local currency.   The *Century Dictionary*, first published in 1889,[39] in successive editions entered and documented large numbers of American words of a "dialectal" nature.[40]   The same may be said of the *Dictionary of American English* (as exemplified on the preceding page), as well as of Mathews's *Dictionary of Americanisms*.[41] *Webster's Third New International* includes most of the words that are mapped in the *Linguistic Atlas of New England* and in Hans Kurath's *Word Geography*--even down to such Northern localisms as *belly bump*(*er*), *belly bunt*, *belly bust*(*er*), *belly flop*(*per*), *belly gut*(*ter*), and *belly whop*(*per*), all of which denote the act of coasting down a hill on one's belly.

In spite of the limitations that are apparent, and in spite of the overlapping that must of necessity take place, most members of the ADS, including myself, are hopeful that a truly systematic and comprehensive dictionary of American dialect terms may be prepared.   It is, however, only realistic to recognize that such a project must have a single leading spirit as director, who must have adequate time, adequate financing, and an adequate organization to carry the task to completion.   No dictionary has ever compiled itself.

Since 1944 the ADS has evidenced a considerable broadening of interests; its new series of *Publications*[42] has by no means restricted itself to the amassing of a dialect lexicon, but has on the other hand served as a medium for the circulation of important monographs on many subjects.[43]

As has been mentioned, new sources of lexical usage are now available.   Moreover, more systematic methods are being developed for the collection of vocabulary. One such method, devised largely by Frederic G. Cassidy, involves the circulation of extensive questionnaires to individual informants so that at least a nucleus of items may be compared on a nationwide scale.[44] The similarity of this procedure to that of many linguistic atlases is apparent, and other methods of the same sort will be discussed later.

In summary we may say that, although American words of a "dialectal" nature have been rather fully treated in separate studies and in general dictionaries, we still lack a comprehensive and fully documented dialect dictionary for the country as a whole.

LINGUISTIC GEOGRAPHY

Atlases of the Atlantic States

The idea of preparing a linguistic atlas of the United States must have been current for a good many years before any actual work was undertaken.[45] It was, however, in the years 1928 and 1929 that concrete proposals and plans were made. In December of 1928 the Present-Day English Group of the Modern Language Association approved the appointment of a committee to study the possibility of preparing an American atlas. At about the same time (independently, it seems), Edgar H. Sturtevant of Yale University, Director of the Linguistic Institute, had arranged for a conference of linguistic scholars to consider the same project.[46] The two groups were very shortly acting jointly, and proposals were soon submitted to the American Council of Learned Societies with a view to financial support. In August of 1929 the Executive Committee of this body authorized the appointment of a committee, headed by Hans Kurath, to prepare a somewhat detailed plan and an estimated budget. In view of the magnitude of the project, it was agreed that a relatively small area should first be surveyed, and the choice of the New England States[47] seemed the most feasible one.

The methodology of the American *Atlas* has been essentially that of Gilliéron,[48] as refined and modified for Italy by Karl Jaberg and Jakob Jud.[49] During the summer of 1930, Kurath engaged in extended conferences with these scholars, as well as with Paul Scheuermeier, the leading fieldworker for the Italian *Atlas*.[50]

The staff for the New England *Atlas* was shortly set up with Kurath as Director, Miles L. Hanley as Associate Director, and Marcus L. Hansen as Historian. Since it was desirable to complete the survey in a minimum of time, several fieldworkers were employed; the number was ultimately augmented to nine. Headquarters were established at Yale University, which also provided a Sterling Fellowship for one of the fieldworkers as well as half the salary of the Associate Director.[51] Other universities and colleges likewise shared in financial support of the *Atlas*; these included Dartmouth, Brown, Mt. Holyoke, and the University of Vermont.

The staff of the *Atlas* underwent a short but concentrated training period during the summer of 1931, when Jakob Jud and Paul Scheuermeier were present as instructors and advisers. There followed the actual fieldwork, which occupied a period of 25 months, ending in September of 1933.

The editing of the New England materials required several years, during which Kurath, with the able collaboration of Bernard and Julia Bloch, prepared 713 maps for publication. Between 1939 and 1943 the three volumes (bound in six parts)[52] were off the press, along with a *Handbook*[53] which explained the methodology, provided historical data, and summarized some of the most important dialectal features of the area.

Beginning in 1933, fieldwork was continued in the Middle Atlantic and South Atlantic States.[54] Guy S. Lowman, the ablest of the New England fieldworkers, gathered material more or less continuously until his death in an automobile accident in 1941. By this time he had completed work in all of the Atlantic States[55] except South Carolina, Georgia, and New York. In the years following the Second World War, this work was brought to completion by Raven I. McDavid, Jr. As yet these raw materials have not been prepared for publication.

The procedures which were used in the New England survey, and which were essentially followed in the other Atlantic states, may be described under a number of headings.

Communities. Ultimately 213 New England communities[56] were chosen for investigation. Of these a considerable majority were small towns or semi-rural communities; but the principal cities of the area were also included. The oldest settlements were given preference, and most of them were investigated; however, a fair selection was also made of secondary settlements and even of newer industrial areas. A brief history of each community was compiled, including its original settlement, subsequent changes in population, principal industries, and other pertinent characteristics.[57] Communities tended to be more or less equidistant save in northern Maine, where population was sparse. In the Middle Atlantic and South Atlantic States the same principles were followed, with possibly greater attention given to the larger cities. There are, for example, 22 records from the adjoining boroughs of Manhattan and Brooklyn, and McDavid gathered at least 10 in Charleston, South Carolina.

Informants. It is in the choice of informants that the American *Atlas* differs most strikingly from its European predecessors. Rather than restrict the investigation to rustic, or "folk", speech, Kurath required the inclusion of three principal types, which he describes as follows:

Type I: Little formal education, little reading, and restricted social contacts.

Type II: Better formal education (usually high school) and/or wider reading and social contacts.

Type III: Superior education (usually college), cultured background, wide readings, and/or extensive social contacts.

Each of these types is divided into two sub-classes: A, aged or old-fashioned, and B, middle-aged or younger, hence presumably more modern in usage.[58] The idea of the divisions, of course, is to provide a means of determining the extent to which "dialect" characteristics appear in the speech of better-educated members of the various communities. Of the 413 informants actually represented in the New England *Atlas*, 148 fall in Type I, 214 in Type II, and 51 in Type III.[59] In the remainder of the Atlantic States the proportions were about the same, except that in some areas Type I informants were proportionally more numerous than in New England. This would depend, of course, on the nature of the areas themselves. For example, during the 1930s in the Southern mountains it was not difficult to find illiterate or semi-literate informants of sufficient intelligence to answer the questions. In the whole of the Atlantic States there are 157 informants designated as "cultured."[60]

Actual choice of the informants was left to the individual fieldworkers, but certain general requirements were laid down. Every effort was made to secure truly native representatives, usually those born and reared in the area and descended from local families. No informant should have spent an extended period away from the area which he represented. Both men and women were accepted on equal terms and in about equal numbers. Fieldworkers were expected to provide material for a brief biography and character sketch of each informant.

Fieldworkers. The fieldworkers who did the interviewing in the Atlantic States are as follows: Hans Kurath, Bernard Bloch, Martin Joos, Guy S. Lowman, Miles L. Hanley, Lee S. Hultzén, Rachel S. Harris, Cassil Reynard, Marguerite Chapallaz, and Raven I. McDavid, Jr. All of these worked in New England except McDavid; in the other Atlantic states, as has been mentioned, Lowman and McDavid made all of the field records. All of the *Atlas* fieldworkers were highly trained. Several of them held the doctor's degree and were well grounded in the type of linguistic discipline that was current at that time. Moreover, they all underwent intensive training in phonetic transcription as part of their preparation for *Atlas* work. The idea of using several fieldworkers in New England has been justified by the relatively rapid completion of the *Atlas*. There are, however, certain unavoidable disadvantages. For one thing, most of the pronunciation features must be interpreted by someone who is thoroughly familiar

with the materials.[61]   Moreover, some fieldworkers were more
inclined than others to elicit archaisms in vocabulary and grammar.
It is my opinion that where multiple fieldworkers are used their
work should be spread over the same areas rather than confined
to respective "territories".   Otherwise there will appear what
seem to be geographical cleavages in usage which must be discount-
ed as merely fieldworker differences.

The Work Sheets.   The actual questions that were posed to
the informants were chosen after much research in previously
published materials.[62] Actually, the final form was not determined
until after a certain amount of preliminary fieldwork had been
completed.   In general, the items on the list represented everyday
concepts, and sought to elicit usages that would ordinarily be
transmitted orally within the family rather than in schools.
Questions were arranged topically in order to avoid incoherence
and to provide a more conversational atmosphere for the informant.
Some of the topics were: the weather, the dwelling, utensils
and implements, topography, domestic animals, and foods.   The
work sheets contained a sampling of pronunciation features, lexical
peculiarities, morphological variants, and occasionally syntactic
characteristics.   Some pronunciation items sought to determine
whether a phonemic distinction existed or not, or whether it
existed in a certain environment (*mourning* as against *morning*);
others were concerned with the incidence of a given phoneme
(/s/ as against /z/ in *greasy*) or with the exact phonetic quality
of a phoneme or sequence of phonemes (e.g., the vowel nucleus
in *five*).   Vocabulary items were concerned mainly with the currency of various synonyms for the same concept (*angleworm,
angledog, eaceworm, mudworm, earthworm*).   Very few, if any,
were directly aimed at the recording of variant meanings, although
most fieldworkers took note of deviant ideas or reactions on the
part of the informants.   The greater number of morphological
items were concerned with verb forms, such as *clum* for *climbed,
sot* for *sat,* or *hain't* for *haven't*.   The total number of items
(of all categories) used in New England was 711;[63] this was
augmented to 772 in the South Atlantic States.   An interview was
expected to occupy from eight hours to a good many more, depending on the personality of the informant.

Conducting the interviews. Gilliéron's method of merely asking
the informant to translate a term into his dialect would have
little value in the United States, since no one wants to admit
that he speaks a dialect.   The desired response had to be elicited
indirectly, if possible without using a word or phrase that might
be part of the answer.   No standard form was ever adopted for
the questions themselves;[64] each fieldworker was expected to use
his ingenuity in producing a response.   In the case of a concrete
object, a brief description might be given.   For example, Bloch
would usually secure a term for *seesaw* by asking: "What do you
call a plank laid across a trestle for children to play on?"[65]

McDavid's form for this question was somewhat fuller: ". . . you'd have a plank laying across--maybe a section of rail fence or a sawhorse or something like that, and a kid gets on one end and another gets on the other and they go up and down, what do you call that?"[66] Sometimes, particularly in the case of a verb form or a phrase, a question might be of the completion type. McDavid builds up this imaginary situation in order to bring out *new suit*: "Say somebody's about to get married, and his mother or his sister will look him over and say, 'You can't get married in those old clothes--you better go round to the store and get you a . . . .'" Sometimes, in order to encourage the use of a synonmy, a question might take the form: "Do you ever call it anything else?" Actual suggestion--that is, using what might be the response and asking the informant whether or not it is his usage--might be resorted to occasionally, but usually only if all other means of securing an answer had failed.[67]

Fieldworkers were instructed to keep careful notations regarding the types of responses. Besides occurring normally in answer to a question, a word or phrase might come out in conversation without a question having been asked at all; or it might have been directly suggested; or it might have been "forced" by undue insistence on the part of the fieldworker. The informant might label the usage as old-fashioned or obsolescent; or he might obviously be using a term humorously; or he might (rightly or wrongly) state that a feature is often heard in the community but that he himself never employs it. It is doubtful that fieldworkers' practice in these matters was uniform, particularly with regard to old-fashioned usage. Indeed, McDavid often asked his original question in the form: "What did you call so-and-so in the old days?"[68]

Phonetic transcription. The system of phonetic notation used in the American *Atlas* must be regarded as highly complicated by any standard. The editors take 20 pages in the *Handbook*[69] to explain it, and it seems to me that the reader would need a rather good grounding in phonetics in order to understand the explanation. Thirty-two basic vowel symbols are provided, and each of these may be used to indicate length or shortness, nasalization, labialization, retroflection, or devoicing. Over 50 consonant symbols are given, and many of these may also be marked so as to indicate special qualities such as aspiration, palatalization, velarization, dentalization, labialization, voicing, devoicing, retroflection, length, or syllabic quality. Stress marks were supposed to be used in polysyllabic words, and in some instances indications of intonation were required. The most skilled of the fieldworkers could manipulate the entire system accurately only in rather short utterances, and even then phonetic features were often overlooked or taken for granted.[70] Different practices by the individual fieldworkers can frequently be detected; these are most noticeable in the case of the low back vowels.[71] In view of the complexity of the system of transcription, we must say that the American

Atlas is firmly committed to the idea of using "professional", or highly trained, fieldworkers; others can make little contribution, at least in the field or pronunciation.

Mechanical recording. Although the desirability of a permanent aural record was recognized early,[72] none of the actual *Atlas* interviews were mechanically recorded. In the early days this was partially attributable to the awkwardness of the mechanisms themselves. However, shortly after the completion of the New England fieldwork, arrangements were made which permitted Miles L. Hanley to begin a collection of phonograph records in the area. In the years 1933 and 1934 he completed 657 double-faced 12-inch records which contained natural conversation and narrative materials from a variety of informants and communities. Many of the speakers were the same informants who had previously been interviewed for the *Atlas.*[73]

In the Middle and South Atlantic States no financial provision was made for the making of discs or tapes of informants' speech; hence mechanical recording in these areas has been very sporadic. I know of no comprehensive collection covering any large portion of the Atlantic States outside of New England.

Editing and Publication. The New England *Atlas* was prepared for publication according to Gilliéron's idea of entering each response in phonetic notation at its appropriate point on the face of a map. The mechanics of editing, important as they are, need be sketched only briefly. The first step was to stamp a positive identification on every page of every "work book" or field record. Then the books were disassembled so that all the page 1's, all the page 2's, and so on might be placed together. After this all the responses to a single "item", or question, were copied in the form of a list, with each response given the number which had been assigned to the informant who uttered it and to his community. The entering of the data on the faces of the maps required a good deal of planning and experimentation. Kurath's original hope was that a font of phonetic type might be cast, but various practical difficulties led to the decision to have the transcriptions drafted by hand.[74] The drafting was done (under the close supervision of Bernard Bloch) on a transparent overlay, and the base map was photographed through the overlay. The result was that the community numbers and the important geographical features (rivers, mountains, State boundaries, etc.) appeared in a light brown shade whereas the linguistic data came out in a clearcut black. A portion of one of the maps is reproduced (in black and white) in Figure 1.

The size chosen for the maps was 20 by 24 inches (about 51 by 62 centimeters). This permitted the entering of all actual responses at the proper point--even responses that were suggested, or heard from others, or regarded as obsolete, or used humorously, and so on. Entries of the latter types are preceded by an arbitrary symbol. However, a good deal of non-linguistic

Figure 1:   Portion of a map (Map 236) from the Linguistic Atlas
of New England, *showing variant terms for the earthworm.   Reprinted by permission.*

or semi-linguistic material usually remained: deviant meanings,
expressions of attitude toward a word and/or its referent, and
similar data.   The most important portion of this material was
entered in the "commentaries" which appeared by the side of the
maps.   Some of these commentaries are very full, and contain
observations of great interest to folklorists as well as to linguists.[75]
        The method used in publishing the New England records was
obviously an expensive one and would be much more expensive
at the present time.   The published price of the New England
Atlas was $180--a price which severely limited its circulation,
yet one which today would cover only a fraction of the cost.   We
can hardly hope that the field records of the Middle and South
Atlantic States will see publication in such a sumptuous format.
If the complete raw materials of these areas are to appear, the
most likely presentation seems to be in the form of lists of columns
of responses, from which individual researchers may prepare maps
to suit their purposes.

        Interpretive presentations.   Both the published and the un-
published field records have been scanned by the *Atlas* staff
and others, and various methods have been used for the carto-

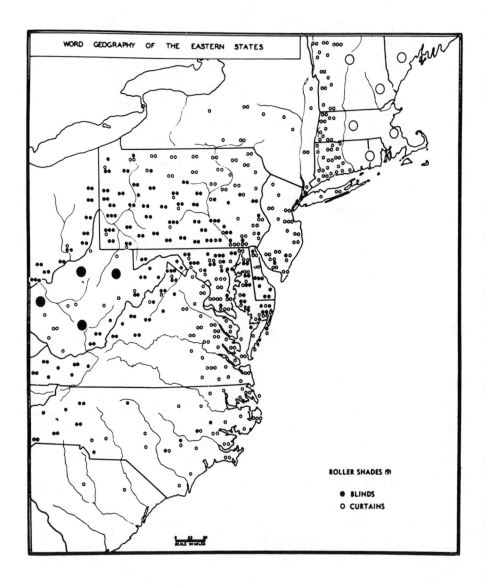

*Figure 2:   Map showing lexical variants by means of symbols,
from Hans Kurath,* A Word Geography of the Eastern United States.
Dots indicate the currency of blinds *and* curtains, *for roller
shades.   Reprinted by permission.*

graphic presentation of linguistic data in summary form. In the case of lexical variation, it is usually sufficient to assign a symbol to each "word"[76] and to enter this symbol at its appropriate point on a much reduced map. The New England *Handbook* (pp. 27ff.) contains a number of such presentations, where the principal lexical variants are entered on maps measuring only 3 3/4 by 4 3/4 inches (9 1/2 by 12 centimeters). This type of cartography was used by Kurath in his *Word Geography of the Eastern United States*,[77] which was based on the *Atlas* field records of all of the Atlantic States.   The maps on which the data is entered measure about 7 1/2 inches by 9 inches (19 by 22 1/2 centimeters); the portion occupied by New England is only about 2 3/4 by 3 inches, a space only one-eighth the diameter of the *Atlas* maps. In order to avoid overcrowding, Kurath sometimes used more than one map to present all the responses to a particular question. Another device which he developed was that of using oversized symbols at intervals in order to indicate universality of usage within a given area. (See Figure 2.)

The method of *isoglosses* has also been used for the carto-graphic presentation of lexical features.   What must be realized is that an isogloss based on the American materials can seldom, if ever, be more than approximate, since usages do not as a rule terminate abruptly.   Moreover, since responses from more than one informant are normally entered at each "point", an isogloss should never be regarded as a dividing line between two usages; rather it is an indication of the approximate outer limit of a single feature.   Many usages are not amenable to presentation by this method, since they appear in such scattered fashion that a large number of lines would have to be drawn in order to encircle them accurately.   No presentation by isoglosses is very convincing unless these are drawn by a competent scholar, and even then we need to know the individual distributions on which the lines are based, so that we may judge the extent to which the materials have been simplified.

The New England *Handbook* (p. 29) presents one map of lexical isoglosses, but it contains so many lines that it has a maze-like and bewildering appearance. Kurath, in his *Word Geography*, gives no less than 119 isoglosses, distributed over 41 maps.[78]   His use of these lines to determine the lexical speech areas, as well as the focal areas, of the Atlantic States[79] is one of the major contributions of his book; his segmentation of the region into North, Midland, and South (with various sub-areas) is now well known to scholars and is finding its way into general use as well.[80]   His correlation of these areas with the settlement and cultural history of the Atlantic Seaboard must be regarded as a thorough and brilliant work of scholarship.

In my *Survey of Verb Forms in the Eastern United States*[81] I largely followed Kurath's methods of cartographical representation. Ordinarily a separate symbol would be assigned to each verb form that was phonemically distinguishable from another. Problems of decision were relatively few, and pertained mainly to such

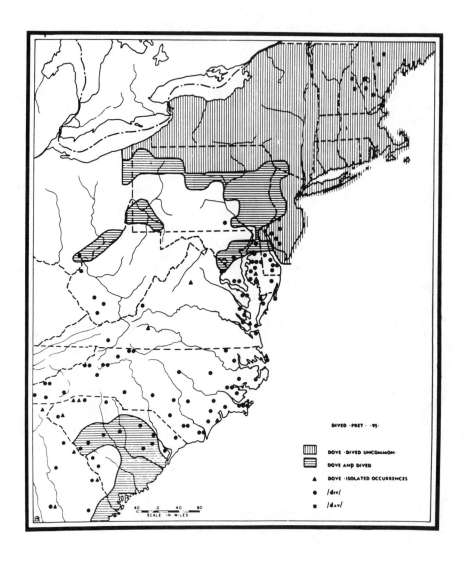

Figure 3: Map showing morphological variation by the use of shading and symbols, from E. Bagby Atwood, A Survey of Verb Forms in the Eastern United States. *Shading and dots indicate the currency of variant preterit forms of the verb* dive. *Reprinted by permission.*

matters as whether or not to group *taken* and *takened* together. I also experimented with the use of shading on some maps in order to indicate universality or near-universality of usage (see Figure 3), particularly when interesting minority usages needed to be entered on the same map. I have never been very satisfied with this device, and feel that it should be used only sparingly.[82]

It is with regard to pronunciation features that interpretive presentations are most difficult. Kurath and McDavid, in their *Pronunciation of English in the Atlantic States*,[83] have solved a great many of the problems in a logical way, although not within the framework used by many structural linguists. First of all, the idea (sometimes followed in Europe)[84] of entering all variant pronunciations of the same "word" on the same map was rejected, if it was ever considered. To take an example, the word *father* in various dialects of England and America may show variation in the initial consonant ([f] as against [v]); it may also show a considerable number of vowel qualities for the *a*; the medial consonant may be [ð] or [d]; and the final syllable may show not only variant vowel qualities but also different types of /r/: retroflex, tongue-tap, tongue-trill, and even uvular. At least 100 combinations of these features are possible, and the chances are that most of them would actually be used somewhere in the English-speaking world. The Kurath-McDavid principle, which is rigidly adhered to, is to observe one feature at a time, and to map only that feature on a particular map. Thus, in the case of *father*, the qualities of the first vowel are plotted on Map 32, those of the final syllable on Map 151. This method demands an early decision as to what features are to be observed. It also requires an understanding of what types of variation are possible; that is, whether we are dealing with a phonemic distinction (in certain environments), as in *four* and *forty* (Map 44), or with the incidence of a phoneme, as the /v/ in *nephew* (Map 169), or with the phonetic quality of a phoneme, as in the first vowel of *oxen* (Map 15--a portion of which is reproduced in Figure 4). With regard to the last type of variation, Kurath has revived the term *diaphone*, but with a meaning somewhat different from that assigned to it by Daniel Jones.[85] As I understand Kurath's use of the term, it would denote the sort of variation that occurs in the word *nine* (Map 26), where most informants have the same phonemic arrangement, but where readily observable differences in quality exist. That is, *diaphones* are sub-phonemic differences that occur between one speaker and another, or between one area and another, as opposed to *allophones*, which occur in the speech of a single individual and which are determined by the environment of the phoneme. Kurath and McDavid have adopted the "unitary" system of interpreting English vowels; that is, for example, everything that comes between the /t/ and the /k/ in *take* is interpreted as a single entity /e/, as opposed to the two entities /ey/ required by the "binary" system of Trager and

Smith.[86]   Thus, maps in *The Pronunciation of English* present a
great many vowel diaphones, since both monophthongal and diph-
thongal pronunciations may often be grouped together.

An interesting feature of Kurath and McDavid's presentation
is the inclusion of a series of 70 vowel "synopses" indicating the
differences in vowel quality observed in the records of cultured
informants. From these tabular chartings one can usually perceive
at a glance the phonemic and sub-phonemic variations that occur
in educated speech as one moves from region to region.

Obviously the Kurath-McDavid presentation could not be complete.[87]   Moreover, the huge mass and infinite variety of phonetic
transcriptions had to be greatly simplified, so that sometimes a
single symbol on a map covers a multitude of phonetic sins.[88]
Useful as the work is as a summary, it is not a substitute for
the raw material itself, which we can only hope will soon be
made available.

It is not possible in the present paper to do justice to the
numerous doctoral dissertations that have been based on the *Atlas*
field records.[89]   One of the earliest of these was Bernard Bloch's
study of the post-vocalic /r/.[90]   Others have been prepared by
Rachel S. H. Kilpatrick,[91] Yakira H. Frank,[92] Sumner Ives,[93]
T. H. Wetmore, Jr.,[94] Walter S. Avis,[95] and several others.[96]
Most of these are detailed studies of individual problems of pronunciation or of small areas, and the methodology is too complex and
varied for compact summary.

Extensions of Atlas Work

The originally planned "Linguistic Atlas of the United States
and Canada," directed by Kurath and at least partially sponsored
by the American Council of Learned Societies, will, it seems certain, be confined to the States of the Atlantic Seaboard. For
some time, however, a framework has existed within which scholars
in other areas could gather material comparable with that collected
in the original *Atlas* survey, whether or not such material might
result in a published atlas. An abridgement of the *Atlas* questionnaire consisting of about 500 items was prepared by Kurath in
1939; this has been the basis of most investigations to the westward. The "Short Work Sheets," as they are called, have usually
been augmented by items which might elicit usages of a regional
nature not current in the Atlantic States. A compilation of the
regional work sheets was prepared by David W. Reed and David
DeCamp.[97]

The progress of linguistic geography in the United States as
a whole since the Second World War has been slow and uneven.
This fact is usually attributable to lack of financial support rather
than to lack of scholarly interest. Since the 1940s, particularly

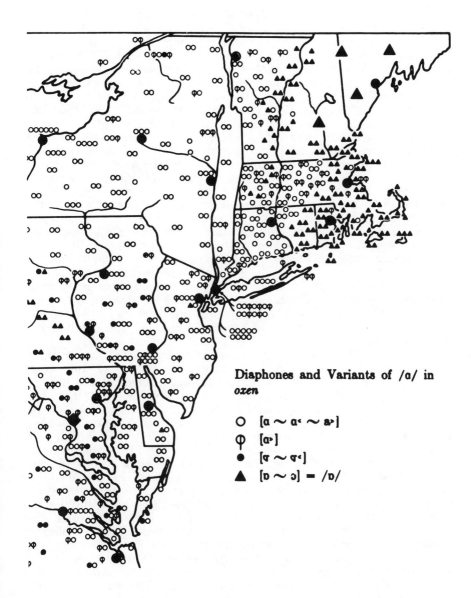

Diaphones and Variants of /ɑ/ in *oxen*

○ [ɑ ~ ɑ˂ ~ ɐ˃]

φ [ɑ˃]

● [ɐ ~ ɐ˂]

▲ [ɒ ~ ɔ] = /ɒ/

Figure 4: *Map showing pronunciation variants by means of symbols, from Kurath and McDavid,* The Pronunciation of English in the Atlantic States. *Dots indicate the vowel variants in the word* oxen. *Reprinted by permission.* Copyright © 1961 The University of Alabama Press.

since the emergence of the Cold War, both Federal and foundation support, as well as that of the American Council of Learned Societies, has gone chiefly to such "strategic" fields as the study of exotic languages and the teaching of English as a foreign language. Most dialect scholars have not been good beggars for private funds to carry on their research. Along with lack of money has gone lack of manpower, which, of course, is only another way of saying that times have changed. The fieldwork for the Atlantic States was mostly done in a time of depression and unemployment, when the services of competent and even brilliant young scholars could be obtained for a bare living, if that. The stipend of Lowman's fellowship for the academic year 1935-36 was $533.[98] If he were available at the present time, there is not the slightest doubt that he would receive many offers of over 10 times that amount to teach in one of our swollen colleges or universities.

In view of these difficulties, the use of multiple fieldworkers has become the rule rather than the exception. Most people engaged for this work can, or will, spend only a limited period of time at the task, usually as part of their work for an advanced degree. The use of tape recorders has varied from none at all to the taping of every interview complete. Publication of results will probably take many forms; and the various collections of data, particularly in the field of pronunciation, are not likely to be fully comparable.

I believe that (aside from the Atlantic States) the regional atlas that has been longest in progress is that of the North Central States,[99] directed by Albert H. Marckwardt of the University of Michigan.[100] Some records in this area were gathered as early as 1933,[101] but it was in 1938 that the main body of the work was begun. The "Short Work Sheets," with a few modifications, were used, and interviewing practices were essentially the same as those used in the Atlantic States. Up to the present time, with the interviewing almost complete, work has been done by 15 different fieldworkers, whose abilities have varied considerably.[102] Among them they have gathered something like 460 field records. Tape recordings were sometimes made during the later years of the survey; in some cases the entire interview was recorded and transcribed later from the tapes. No concrete arrangements have been made for the publication of the raw materials themselves; and presentations of results have so far been of the interpretive sort. Toward the beginning of the survey, Marckwardt mapped a number of distributions by the use of symbols on maps;[103] more recently he published some isoglosses (both lexical and phonological) based on a fuller coverage of the area.[104] These isoglosses are apparently only approximate, and are not accompanied by indications of exceptional usages[105] (see Figure 5). Nevertheless, Marckwardt's publications provide reasonably convincing evidence that Kurath's previously demonstrated cleavage between Northern and Midland continues through the North Central States. Raven I. and Virginia G. McDavid

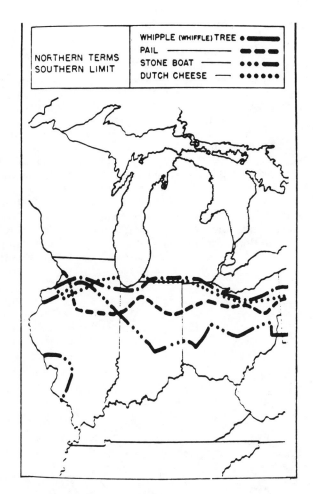

Figure 5: Map showing lexical limits by means of simplified isoglosses, from A. H. Marckwardt, Principal and Subsidiary Dialect Areas in the North-Central States. The lines show the southward extent of certain Northern words. Reprinted by permission.

have published grammatical materials from the same area.[106] Their maps provide both isoglosses and symbols for individual occurrences. It is doubtful that some of the lines should have been drawn; for example, one can see on the map which is reproduced (Figure 6) some 13 occurrences of the form *clum* that lie beyond the isogloss that purports to indicate its limits.

In the North Central States we were given our first convincing demonstration that lexical (as against phonological) features may be collected separately by quicker and less costly methods than

the employment of trained fieldworkers.   Toward the end of the
1940s Alva L. Davis prepared a lexical questionnaire (now called
a "checklist") of 100 items and sent copies of it by mail to
various more-or-less academic people (usually teachers of history
or some subject other than English) at many points in the area.
These checklists were to be placed directly in the hands of suitable
informants and ultimately mailed back.   The items on the list
were in the form of brief definitions followed by a number of
synonyms; the informants were supposed to encircle the usage
which they regarded as natural to them, or to write it down if
they did not find it listed.   A typical example would be Item 45:
"BEANS EATEN IN PODS: green beans, string beans, snap
beans".   The results of this survey were presented in Davis's
doctoral dissertation. [107]   The maps which Davis prepared indicated
the actual incidence of the lexical variants in the different local-
ities; but he was also able to draw isoglosses which corresponded
remarkably well to those based on fieldwork for the North Central
Atlas.   Other uses of checklists have been made in the area, but

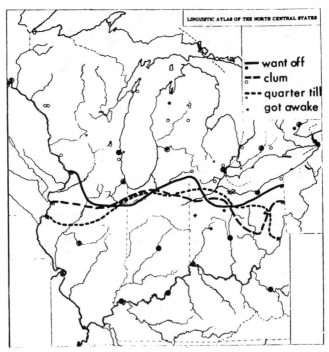

*Figure 6:   Map showing grammatical variants by the use of iso-
glosses and symbols, from Raven I. and Virginia G. McDavid,*
Grammatical Differences in the North Central States.   *The lines
show the approximate northward extent of the preterites* clum
(climbed) and got awake *(woke up), as well as the idioms* want off
(want to get off) and quarter till *(quarter to).   Reprinted
by permission.*

they are in the hands of different investigators, and I believe that they have not been incorporated into the atlas.

Another regional atlas in the northern part of the country is that of the Upper Midwest, [108] directed by Harold B. Allen of the University of Minnesota. Allen's basic procedure was very similar to Marckwardt's with regard to questionnaire, methods of interviewing, and so on; and he seems to have chosen about the same proportion of the different types of informants.[109] Allen himself did a large part of the interviewing, working mainly in the summers with the support of the University of Minnesota. Six other fieldworkers contributed records from time to time. All together, 208 field records are on file, and I believe that the survey is regarded as complete. In addition to conventional fieldwork, Allen made use of a checklist of 137 items; he was the first to definitely incorporate such materials into a regional atlas. Over 1000 of the checklists have been returned and are in the files. Since both field interviews and checklists were used through the same geographical areas, and since the latter were confined to vocabulary, there will be no possibility of methodological iso-glosses [110] to mislead a user of the atlas.

As in other areas, it is hoped that the raw materials from this region may be published, although no definite arrangements have been made. A presentation of the Gilliéron type (all transcriptions entered on maps) does not seem feasible, and Allen's present plan is the listing of responses in tables, with some of the distributions indicated by means of symbols on maps. Allen has already published some of his findings in the form of isoglosses of a simplified type. [111]

Students in the Midwestern states (North Central and Upper Midwest) have produced a number of doctoral dissertations dealing with a variety of topics. Two of these, by Virginia G. McDavid [112] and Jean Malmstrom, [113] have dealt with grammatical usage through-out the area. Dissertations by Edward E. Potter,[114] Robert R. Howren,[115] and several others have embodied complete studies of small areas or individual communities.

Investigators in the westerly portions of the country are faced with extremely serious problems arising chiefly from settle-ment history. In many of these areas, original settlement came relatively late, and population is still very sparse in many places. Recent sizable increases in population have come about largely through wholesale migration from many portions of the country. The most striking illustration of this state of affairs is California, which has been doubling its population about every 20 years. Between 1900 and 1960 the population of the United States as a whole increased by a proportion of about 2.4 to 1. Not many Eastern states have exceeded that rate, and the states of the Upper Midwest have fallen short of it. The population of Cali-fornia, however, has increased by a proportion of about 10.5 to 1, [116] and the influx is continuing with phenomenal rapidity.

Fully aware of the difficulties, David W. Reed has nevertheless undertaken an atlas-type investigation of California and Nevada.

Eleven fieldworkers have gathered some 300 records, and this phase of the work is regarded as complete. About 1500 checklists, of the type previously described, have also been returned and are now in the files. All geographical areas have been covered, but obviously many more records were collected in the centers of population than in the mountainous and semi-desert areas. Tape recordings were not used as a regular feature of the survey.

Reed hopes ultimately to publish his raw materials in the form of lists. However, as yet the only publications based on the California-Nevada survey have largely taken the form of statistical summaries. Reed's study of Eastern dialect words in the region provides percentages of occurrence of various lexical features characteristic of the North, the Midland, the South, and various subdivisions and combinations of these areas.[117] In David DeCamp's dissertation on the speech of San Francisco, [118] mathematical methods were devised to compare usage with that of the Atlantic States in matters of pronunciation as well. It seems to me that mathematical analysis will be a highly important tool in the presentation of material from such newly settled and lin-guistically mixed regions as the Pacific Coast. Moreover, although Reed's survey will determine some of the older and newer layers of usage, it would be highly desirable that similar work should be repeated a generation later, in order to bring to light the processes of selection and change that operate in such a situation.

Another atlas-type survey being conducted on the West Coast is that of the Pacific Northwest,[119] directed by Carroll E. Reed of the University of Washington. This project has made use of the "Short Work Sheets", with a good many additions; six field-workers have collected something like 50 records. Over 1000 checklists are also on file. Both tape and disc recordings have been made in connection with many of the interviews. As in the case of California, a great deal of attention was paid to urban areas, and records from such communities outnumber those from rural districts.

It is the hope of Carroll Reed that his materials may be published in map form, although probably not in the large format of the New England *Atlas*. He has already published a short "Word Geography" based very largely on the lexical checklists. [120] In addition to tabulations of the relative frequency of Eastern usages, he includes a series of maps on which individual usages are entered by means of symbols. He has used the half-serious term "scattergram" to describe this type of presentation. Although no clearcut isoglosses are likely to emerge, he feels (rightly, I think) that individual usages should be presented cartographically, regardless of whether or not they show concentrations or cleavages.

Another westerly area for which atlas plans have been made is the Rocky Mountain region, in which two statewide surveys have so far been made. One of these, by T. M. Pearce, covers the state of New Mexico, in which 50 interviews have been con-ducted. In addition to Pearce himself, who did about half the interviews, some 19 graduate students contributed from one to seven field records each. Some use was made of disc recordings. Informants were more highly educated than in other areas; something over half of them are of Type III (with college education). About 500 lexical checklists are also on hand. Pearce's plan for publication envisages small maps with symbols for individual usages. [121]

In the state of Colorado, a survey has been undertaken by Marjorie Kimmerle of the University of Colorado. Besides Miss Kimmerle, five fieldworkers were used, including McDavid, who conducted a summer course in field methods at the University of Colorado in 1950. Sixty-eight field records have been collected from 29 communities; the majority of these were made by Miss Kimmerle herself. The "Short Work Sheets" were used and it is clear that these had been augmented by items peculiarly adapted to the regional culture and topography.[122] Tape recordings were made of brief passages (5 to 20 minutes) of connected material from about half the informants. Checklists were used in a preliminary survey, but it is my impression that these will not be incorporated into the atlas.

A survey of the Colorado lexical materials has been published by Clyde T. Hankey,[123] who used a variety of methods in presenting the results. Tables of relative frequencies of the Eastern words are, of course, indispensable. These indicate, for the state as a whole, a Northern-Midland mixture, with a rather low proportion of southern usages. Clearcut isoglosses, as might be expected, are not numerous, and cannot be grouped in a convincing way. A more fruitful approach is the setting off of areas within which specific numbers of regional terms occur;[124] from this presentation, for example, it can be observed that Southern usages as a group are largely limited to the eastern and southeastern extremities of the state, although any one individual usage might seem to show a scattered distribution. Another similar device is that of demarcating "participation areas"; that is, subdivisions of the state which share relatively high proportions of usages that are less frequent in other areas.[125] It is unfortunate that individual word distributions are not given by the use of symbols on maps rather than by a presentation that involves somewhat wandering lines [126] and shaded areas. Chaotic as they might seem on the surface, the "scattergrams" would have been welcome, if only as a means of judging the nature and validity of the isoglosses.

Another statewide survey which is well under way is that of Oklahoma, directed by W. R. Van Riper. Work sheets are rather full (over 900 questions) and include items of regional and local interest with regard to both pronunciation and vocabulary. Van Riper himself has done all the field work, and he has now completed about 40 records. His interviewing of informants has been largely by means of "directed conversation", with specific questions only if necessary. Every interview has been recorded in its entirety on magnetic tape.   In addition to this type of fieldwork, Van Riper has used special vocabulary questionnaires or checklists.[127]

Undoubtedly a great deal of valuable material has been collected in other portions of the Western and Midwestern states, but, because of my lack of direct information on these projects, I am unable to describe them in any detail.   McDavid[128] reports field-work in progress in Utah, Wyoming, and Montana; and certainly there have been other dialect studies that have received little publicity or recognition.

In the states of the Gulf Coast and adjoining portions of the South, [129] the preparation of linguistic atlases in the traditional sense has not progressed rapidly, chiefly because of the lack of financial support.   This is unfortunate, since these states offer an excellent field for investigation.   With the exception of Texas, they have had a relatively slow population growth; and the lack of extensive industrialization has tended to preserve a greater stability of population and hence, presumably, of dialect features.

The oldest collection of atlas materials in the South Central part of the country is that of C. M. Wise of Louisiana State University.   Between 1935 and 1945, Wise's advanced students gathered 68 field records from various parts of Louisiana,[130] and work of this sort has been continuing to the present time.   The "Short Work Sheets" have been augmented by a rather large number of lexical items of regional interest.   In recent years tape recordings of the interviews have been made.   Under Wise's direction, a very considerable number of dissertations and theses have been prepared. [131]   Most of these pertain to pronunciation features, often those observed in a single community.

In other portions of the South and Southwest, there have developed certain departures from traditional atlas methodology. In my own investigations, which have centered in Texas, I have been able to assemble only a very limited number of satisfactory atlas field records of the conventional type; the best of these were collected by Arthur M. Z. Norman [132] and Janet B. Sawyer. [133] I came to the decision some time ago that fieldwork in vocabulary and in pronunciation might well be conducted separately.   This idea developed from a number of considerations.   In the first place, I was highly dissatisfied with the practice of using consider-able numbers of partially trained fieldworkers for the making of phonetic transcriptions.   I could hardly believe that in regions where this procedure was used the results would be satisfactory; yet there seemed to be no possibility of financing the work of a real expert for two or three years.   On the other hand, experi-mental investigations had shown that it was relatively easy to teach advanced students to collect vocabulary features, especially if they worked in communities where they had friends or relatives. Accordingly I extracted from the *Atlas* work sheets those vocabu-lary items which had proved to be most productive in the Atlantic States, and added to them a fairly large number of items designed to elicit words of Southwestern origin or currency.[134]   The total number of vocabulary questions was about 270.   Being addicted to the idea of field investigation *sur place*, I placed the vocabulary work sheets in the hands of fieldworkers rather than mail them out to be filled in by informants. Most of the interviewing was done by advanced students, originally those in my own classes, but later also students from other institutions under the direction of colleagues who were interested in linguistics.[135] This type of work went on for several years; at the present time there are on hand about 470 vocabulary field records gathered in Texas and portions of adjoining states.

In order to expedite editing and publication of the vocabulary materials, I made use of mechanical sorting and listing processes.[136] Every occurrence of every word was punched on a separate IBM card, together with coded data on the locality of its use and the characteristics of its user--age, education, sex, and so on. The tabulating machine was thus able to provide a running count not only of the total occurrences of a given usage, but also the occurrences in each geographical sub-area and each age and education group.

These lexical materials have recently been published in my volume entitled *The Regional Vocabulary of Texas*.[137] As might be supposed, I gave considerable attention to actual frequencies of occurrence, not only of individual words, but also of groups of words from the different dialect areas of the East, before ultimately concluding that the region is basically Southern. The editing methods also permitted a fairly precise examination of social distributions, as well as such matters as obsolescence and replacement. Geographical data was presented mainly in the form of individual "scattergrams"; but a fair number of isoglosses also emerged, notably a bundle separating Texas from Southern Louisiana.[138]

Other lexical studies based on similar methods have been made in both Texas and Louisiana. These include doctoral dissertations by Fred A. Tarpley[139] and Lucille P. Folk,[140] both of whom made use of mechanical processing methods under the direction of Nathan M. Caffee of Louisiana State University. Another lexical survey was that of the late Mima Babington, whose materials on southern Louisiana were to have been presented as a doctoral dissertation at The University of Texas.[141]

In other states of the Gulf Coast and interior South, a strictly lexical survey is being conducted by Gordon R. Wood of the University of Chattanooga (Tennessee). This is based on a postal checklist of 147 items, which is placed directly in the hands of informants. Out of a considerably larger number, Wood has selected about 1000 of the checklists for processing.[142] His methods of mechanical sorting and editing would seem to be similar to those used in Texas, although I am sure that he has made some significant advances. His reports have indicated an extensive use of arithmetical frequencies for terms used in the different portions of his territory. It seems that there will also emerge some very interesting concentrations and cleavages in lexical usage.

It is to be strongly hoped that the cartographical presentation of these features will take some form other than the simplified lines and shaded areas that have appeared so far. [143]

The concentration on vocabulary study in some of the major areas should not be interpreted to mean that the hope of recording pronunciation features has been abandoned. On the contrary, it is my own feeling that such work will be facilitated, in that the work sheets for pronunciation may be disencumbered of many items of purely lexical interest. Thus more samples may be taken in the same amount of time. Possibly in the future more attention may be paid to such features of suprasegmental structure as stress, intonation, and juncture. [144] It seems clear that tape recording will be almost obligatory in future pronunciation surveys. Earlier difficulties, such as poor fidelity of the mechanisms and the lack of rural electrification, have been so nearly eliminated that there remain no reasons other than financial for neglecting the permanent preservation of speech itself. The newly developed science of sound spectography [145] will almost certainly prove to be of use in the examination of speech differences; for such an application to be made we will need high fidelity recordings of actual utterances.

The present paper has so far omitted mention of a great deal of important dialect work, particularly that which does not fit readily into the usual categories. For example, John S. Kenyon's observations of American pronunciation through the years have resulted in his very useful *Pronouncing Dictionary,* [146] which takes full account of differences in standards from one region to another. Charles K. Thomas had also assembled a great deal of recorded data on pronunciation, which forms the basis of several publications on regional and social variation. [147] His studies have been based to some extent on the reading and recording of standard texts by literate informants. Other investigators--for example Katherine E. Wheatley and Oma Stanley [148]--have applied this method in studies of particular areas.

In other English-speaking areas of the Western Hemisphere there has also been progress in dialectology. Fieldwork in Canada, although not extensive, has been conducted by competent scholars. [149] In Jamaica, extremely sound work in lexicography has been accomplished by Frederic G. Cassidy; his forthcoming dialect dictionary is a model of thoroughness. Robert B. Le Page and David DeCamp have examined other aspects of usage by the use of atlas methodology. [150] DeCamp's successful application of the word-and-thing method [151] in his fieldwork should result in important publications concerning the relations of language and culture.

In summary we may say that dialect investigations of one sort or another have been carried on in almost all parts of the United States. The multiplicity of fieldworkers, the unevenness of their training, and the variations in their methodology will make much of their work very difficult to analyze and evaluate. This is particularly true of the recording of pronunciation, some of which in the long run may have to be done over again. We seem closest to achieving an overall picture of dialect vocabulary, and indeed this accomplishment will not be a trifling one. What is needed in all aspects of the work is support, financial and moral; for a full measure of this we may need to await a change in climate. The history of scholarship is to a considerable degree a history of patience, and of this quality the dialect scholar has need of more than his share.[152]

FOOTNOTES

[1] See M. M. Mathews, *The Beginnings of American English* (Chicago, 1931), p. 14.

[2] *Ibid.*, p. 16; H. L. Mencken, *The American Language*, 4th ed. (New York, 1938), pp. 4-7; G. P. Krapp, *The English Language in America*, 2 vols. (New York, 1925), I, 46-47; 72.

[3] Mathews, *Beginnings*, pp. 20-23.

[4] Noah Webster, *Compendious Dictionary of the English Language* (Hartford and New Haven, Conn., 1806).

[5] Mathews, *Beginnings*, pp. 49-50; Krapp, *English Language*, I, 360.

[6] *An American Dictionary of the English Language*, 2 vols. (New York, 1828).

[7] Mathews, *Beginnings*, pp. 52-54; Mencken, *American Language*, p. 7.

[8] Humphries attached a glossary to one of his plays, *The Yankey in England*. See Mathews, *Beginnings*, pp. 56-63.

[9] *A Vocabulary, or Collection of Words and Phrases Which have been Supposed to be peculiar to the United States of America . . . (Boston, 1816).

[10] In a series of articles appearing in the *Virginia Literary Museum* beginning in December, 1829. Reprinted in Mathews, *Beginnings*, pp. 99-112.

[11] *A Dictionary of Americanisms* (New York, 1848). Subsequently re-edited a number of times.

[12] *Americanisms Old and New* (London, 1889).

[13] All of these have been shown by the Linguistic Atlas materials to have clear geographical limits. See the discussion of linguistic geography, below.

[14] For further biographical information see *Dialect Notes* (*DN*), VI, Part XVIII (1939), 715-718 [American Dialect Society, University, Alabama].

[15] R. H. Thornton, *An American Glossary*, 2 vols. (London, 1912). The third volume was published piecemeal in *DN*, VI (1928-39).

[16] Of course, it contains many words of regional currency; for example, *bayou, chaparral, snake doctor, you-uns.*

[17]*DN*, I, Part I (1890), 1-2.   See also Louise Pound, "The American Dialect Society: A Historical Sketch," *Publication of the American Dialect Society (PADS)*, No. 17 (1952), 4-5. [American Dialect Society, University, Alabama.]

[18]"Constitution," *DN*, I, Part I (1890), 3.

[19]*DN*, I, Part I (1890), 30-32.

[20]Pound, "The ADS," pp. 7-9.

[21]George Hempl, "American Speech-Maps," *DN*, I, Part VII (1894), 315-318.

[22]For example, "Is *'a bunch of cattle'* familiar to you?" "What does the word *'to squint'* first suggest to you?   Mention other meanings in the order of their familiarity." "Which of the following words usually have *a* as in 'cat', or nearly that?" *Ibid* ., pp. 316-317.

[23]George Hempl, *"Grease* and *Greasy* ," *DN*, I, Part IX (1896), 438-444.

[24]Pound, "The ADS," pp. 4-5; see also "The 1895 Circular," *DN*, I, Part VIII (1895), 360-367.

[25]*Ibid.*, p. 360.

[26]Joseph Wright, *English Dialect Dictionary*, 6 vols. (London, 1898-1905). The English Dialect Society, founded in 1873, regarded its work as complete when Wright's material was ready for publication; accordingly the Society disbanded toward the end of 1896.

[27]L. W. Payne, "A Word-List from East Alabama," *DN*, III, Part IV (1908), 279-328, and III, Part V (1909), 343-391).

[28]H. Tallichet, "A Contribution towards a Vocabulary of Spanish and Mexican Words Used in Texas," *DN*, I, Part IV (1892), 185-195. Augmented in later issues.

[29]I believe the first of a considerable series of Miss Pound's dialect publications was "Dialect Speech in Nebraska," *DN* , III, Part I (1905), 55-67.

[30]Vance Randolph's publications on the Ozark area (Arkansas) are well known to folklorists as well as to dialectologists. Among many others, see "A Word-List from the Ozarks," *DN*, V, Part IX (1926), 397-405.

[31]Pound, "The ADS," p. 25.

[32]Harold Wentworth, *American Dialect Dictionary* (New York, 1944).

[33]Pound, "The ADS," p. 26.

[34]William A. Craigie and James R. Hulbert, *A Dictionary of American English*, 4 vols. (Chicago, 1938-44).

[35]For a discussion and citation, see the section on linguistic geography, below.

[36]H. L. Mencken, *The American Language, Supplement I* (New York, 1945); *Supplement II* (New York, 1948).

[37]Philip B. Gove, ed., *Webster's Third New International Dictionary* (Springfield, Mass., 1961).

[38]Wentworth's dictionary contains a little over 15,000 entries; Wright's includes 19,767 in the letters A to C only.   Wright, Vol. I, p. vii.

[39] William D. Whitney, *The Century Dictionary*, 6 vols. (New York, 1889-91).

[40] For example, the edition in my possession (that of 1906) includes *devil's darning needle*, *snake feeder*, *snake doctor*, and *mosquito hawk*, as well as the literary equivalent *dragon fly*.

[41] M. M. Mathews, *A Dictionary of Americanisms on Historical Principles* (Chicago, 1951).

[42] After a brief lapse during the Second World War, *Dialect Notes* was discontinued and the official series became *Publication of the American Dialect Society* (*PADS*) beginning in 1944.

[43] For example, D. W. Maurer, "White Mob," No. 24 (1955); Einar Haugen, "Bilingualism in the Americas," No. 26 (1956); Dwight I. Bolinger, "Interrogative Structures of American English," No. 28 (1957)--in addition to works on linguistic geography, some of which will be mentioned later.

[44] Cassidy is now "Custodian of Collections" for the ADS. His distinguished dialect studies, in the United States as well as in Jamaica, qualify him superbly to be the "leading spirit" in a nationwide lexical survey. [With the joint support of the University of Wisconsin and several governmental grants Cassidy is now engaged in collecting and editing data for the Dictionary of American Regional English, which will realize the American Dialect Society's long-cherished hope of a comprehensive lexicon of American dialects.-Eds.]

[45] The project of George Hempl has already been described. Many others had shown a keen interest in a speech survey: for example, Harry M. Ayres, Charles C. Fries, W. Cabell Greet, John S. Kenyon, and George P. Krapp. See Hans Kurath and others, *Handbook of the Linguistic Geography of New England* (Providence, R.I., 1939), pp. x-xi.

[46] *Ibid.*, p. xi. See also "Plans for a Survey of the dialects of New England," *DN*, VI, Part II (1930), 65-66, and "The Conference on a Linguistic Atlas of the United States and Canada," *Bulletin No. 4* of the Linguistic Society of America (Baltimore, Md., 1929), pp. 20-47.

[47] These states are Maine, New Hampshire, Vermont, Massachusetts, Rhode Island, and Connecticut.

[48] Jules Gilliéron and Edmond Edmont, *Atlas linguistique de la France* (Paris, 1902-12).

[49] Karl Jaberg and Jakob Jud, *Sprach und Sachatlas Italiens und der Südschweiz*, 8 vols. (Zofingen, 1928-40).

[50] Hans Kurath, "Report of Interviews with European Scholars . . .," *DN*, VI, Part II (1930), 73-74.

[51] "Progress of the Linguistic Atlas" ("Progress"--a series of reports), *DN*, VI, Part III (1931), 91-92.

[52] Hans Kurath, Miles L. Hanley, Bernard Bloch, and others, *Linguistic Atlas of New England* , 3 vols. in 6 parts (Providence, R.I., 1939-43).

[53] Hans Kurath and others, *Handbook of the Linguistic Geography of New England* (*Handbook*) (Providence, R.I., 1939).

[54] The Middle Atlantic States consist of New York, New Jersey, Pennsylvania, and West Virginia. The South Atlantic States are

made up of Delaware, Maryland, Virginia, North Carolina, South
Carolina, Georgia, and Florida.
[55] Only portions of Georgia and Florida were surveyed. In
addition to the states mentioned above, several field records were
made in the easternmost section of Ohio. A few were also made
in parts of Canada that adjoin the United States--chiefly in New
Brunswick and Ontario.
[56] "Communities" as here used means points, or numbers, on
the map. Occasionally two adjoining towns are treated as the
same community.
[57] For a full account of the New England communities, see
Handbook, pp. 159-240.
[58] *Ibid.*, p. 44.
[59] *Ibid.*, pp. 42-43.
[60] H. Kurath and Raven I. McDavid, Jr., *The Pronunciation
of English in the Atlantic States* (Ann Arbor, Michigan, 1961),
pp. 23-27.
[61] For example, as Kurath points out, the symbols [ɒ] and
[ɔ] might represent the same sound in the transcriptions of different fieldworkers. *Handbook*, pp. 126-127.
[62] McDavid cites in particular the following: C. S. Grandgent,
J. S. Kenyon, G. P. Krapp, and George Hempl. See "The
Linguistic Atlas of New England," *Orbis*, I (1952), 95-103; esp.
p. 98. [Centre International de Dialectologie Générale, Louvain.]
[63] *Handbook*, pp. 147-158.
[64] By contrast, The Linguistic Atlas of England requires that
all fieldworkers ask the same question in the same words. See
Harold Orton, "An English Dialect Survey: Linguistic Atlas of
England," *Orbis*, IX (1960), 331-348.
[65] Bernard Bloch, "Interviewing for the Linguistic Atlas,"
American Speech, X (1935), 3-9; p. 7. [Columbia University
Press, New York.]
[66] From a tape recording of a sample interview made by Mc-
David.
[67] Clearly this method would be less objectionable if several
alternate terms were suggested together, as *fish worm, fishing
worm, angleworm, mudworm, red worm*, etc., from which the informant
might make a choice.
[68] Lowman left behind a considerable number of abbreviated
labels for different types of usage; for example, *asach*, meaning
used as a child; *snat*, suggested, and regarded by the informant
as natural, and so on.
[69] *Handbook*, pp. 122-143.
[70] For example, the aspiration of the initial consonant in *two*
and *twice* is marked only sporadically (Map 53); the same may be
said of the nasalization of the vowel in *broom* (Map 155) and
mumps (Map 507).
[71] *Handbook*, pp. 126-127.
[72] "Progress," *DN*, VI, Part V (1932), 281).
[73] "Progress," *DN*, VI, Part IX (1934), 419.

[74] "Progress," *DN*, VI, Part X (1935), 449-450; *DN*, VI, Part XI (1935), 481.

[75] For example, details in the observance of the mockserenade (charivari, Katzenmusik) after a wedding (Map 409).

[76] Obviously, *word* is immensely difficult to define; yet practical problems in the American materials are not extremely serious. Usually phonological variants (such as *troughs* and *troths*) can be grouped together as the same "word."

[77] Hans Kurath, *A Word Geography of the Eastern United States* (Ann Arbor, Michigan, 1949).

[78] *Ibid.*, Figures 4-43.

[79] Kurath's methods of counting lines have never been explained in print. Presumably he estimated the numbers of lines in the larger and smaller bundles.

[80] *Webster's Third New International Dictionary* frequently assigns a term to one or another of Kurath's divisions; for example, *snake feeder* is labeled as *Midland*, *lightwood* as *Southern*.

[81] E. Bagby Atwood, *A Survey of Verb Forms in the Eastern United States* (Ann Arbor, Michigan, 1953).

[82] Others, however, have used shading quite freely. See, for example, Raven I. McDavid, Jr., and Virginia G. McDavid, "Regional Linguistic Atlases in the United States," *Orbis*, V (1956), 349-386; and Sumner Ives, "Pronunciation of 'Can't' in the Eastern States," *American Speech*, XXVIII (1953), 149-157.

[83] For citation see above.

[84] For example, in the Walloon *Atlas*, twenty-one pronunciations of the word *maison* are entered on the same map by means of symbols. See Louis Remacle, *Atlas linguistique de la Wallonie*, Vol. I (Liège, 1953), Map 56.

[85] Daniel Jones, *An Outline of English Phonetics*, 6th ed. (New York, 1940), pp. 52-53.

[86] George L. Trager and Henry L. Smith, Jr., *An Outline of English Structure* (Norman, Oklahoma, 1951).

[87] Very little material is found on variation in consonants.

[88] For example, on the map showing the vowel diaphones in *nine* (Map 26), diphthongs with their beginnings in low front, low central, and low back position are all represented by the same symbol.

[89] That is, some dissertations have not been mentioned at all; moreover, some of those that are mentioned are familiar to me only through *Dissertation Abstracts* (University Microfilms, Inc., Ann Arbor, Michigan).

[90] The Treatment of Middle English Final and Preconsonantal *R* in the Present-Day Speech of New England (Brown University, 1935).

[91] The Speech of Rhode Island: the Stressed Vowels and Diphthongs (Brown University, 1937).

[92] The Speech of New York City (University of Michigan, 1949).

[93]The Negro Dialect of the Uncle Remus Stories (University of Texas, 1950). Revised as "The Phonology of the Uncle Remus Stories," *PADS*, No. 22 (1954).

[94]The Low-Central and Low-Back Vowels of the Eastern United States (University of Michigan, 1957). *Diss. Abstracts*, XVIII, 1423. Revised as "The Low-Central and Low-Back Vowels in the English of the Eastern United States," *PADS*, No. 32 (1959).

[95]The Mid-Back Vowels in the English of the Eastern United States (University of Michigan, 1956). *Diss. Abstracts*, XVII, 140.

[96]For a further listing see Raven I. McDavid, Jr., and Virginia G. McDavid, "Regional Linguistic Atlases in the United States," *Orbis*, V (1956), 353.

[97]This is, I believe, still available in mineographed form. See also Sever Pop, *Bibliographie des Questionnaires Linguistiques* (Louvain, 1955).

[98]"Progress," *DN*, VI, Part XI (1935), 482.

[99]These are the states of Ohio, Indiana, Illinois, Michigan, Wisconsin, and Kentucky.

[100]Marckwardt has recently accepted a position at Princeton University (New Jersey). I do not know what effect this will have on the progress of the Atlas.

[101]"Progress," *DN*, VI, Part VII (1933), 365.

[102]We would expect the best results to have been achieved by Guy S. Lowman, Raven I. McDavid, Jr., Cassil Reynard, Harold Allen, and Frederic G. Cassidy, all of whom have made field records in the area.

[103]"Folk Speech in Indiana and Adjacent States," *Indiana History Bulletin*, XVII (1940), 120-140. [Department of Education, Indianapolis.]

[104]"Principal and Subsidiary Dialect Areas in the North-Central States," *PADS*, No. 27 (1957), 3-15.

[105]For example, Kurath's *Word Geography* (cited above) shows several occurrences of both *stone boat* and *Dutch cheese* to the southward of Marckwardt's lines. Kurath, Figures 78 and 125.

[106]"Grammatical Differences in the North Central States," *American Speech*, XXXV (1960), 5-19.

[107]A Word Atlas of the Great Lakes Region (University of Michigan, 1949).

[108]These are the States of Minnesota, Iowa, North Dakota, South Dakota, and Nebraska.

[109]The approximate proportions are 45 percent Type I, 45 percent Type II, and 10 percent Type III.

[110]This is my own phrase, by which I mean that in some instances different methods might produce different results. In a field interview there might be elicited certain "illiterate" usages which would seldom if ever be written by an informant in answer to a question.

[111]"Minor Dialect Areas of the Upper Midwest, *PADS*," No. 30 (1958), 3-16.

[112] Verb Forms of the North Central States and Upper Midwest (University of Minnesota, 1956). *Diss. Abstracts*, XVII, 1954.

[113] A Study of the Validity of Textbook Statements About Certain Controversial Grammatical Items in the Light of Evidence from the Linguistic Atlas (University of Minnesota, 1958). *Diss. Abstracts*, XIX, 1306.

[114] The dialect of Northwestern Ohio: A Study of a Transition Area (University of Michigan, 1955).

[115] The Speech of Louisville, Kentucky (Indiana University, 1958). *Diss. Abstracts*, XIX, 527.

[116] The proportions have been worked out from raw population figures given in *The World Almanac for 1961* (New York, 1961), pp. 80-81; 463.

[117] David W. Reed, "Eastern Dialect Words in California", *PADS*, No. 21 (1954), 3-15.

[118] The Pronunciation of English in San Francisco (University of California, Berkeley, 1954). Summarized under the same title in *Orbis*, VII (1958), 372-391; VIII (1959), 54-77.

[119] This includes thee states of Washington, Oregon, and Idaho. [Before Carroll Reed joined the faculty of the University of Massachusetts in 1969 he merged his atlas project with the California study directed by David Reed, who since then has become a member of the faculty at Northwestern University.-Eds.]

[120] "Word Geography of the Pacific Northwest", *Orbis*, VI (1957), 86-93. See also, by the same author, "Washington Words", *PADS*, No. 25 (1956), 3-11.

[121] Pearce believes that scholars might well adopt symbols of a specific shape or appearance to designate words from specific dialect areas of the East. He terms these symbols *grapholexes*.

[122] See Marjorie M. Kimmerle, "The Influence of Locale and Human Activity on Some Words in Colorado", *American Speech*, XXV (1950), 161-167.

[123] "A Colorado Word Geography", *PADS*, No. 34 (1960).

[124] *Ibid.*, pp. 20-23.

[125] *Ibid.*, pp. 36-50.

[126] Some of the lines seem to be improperly drawn, in that they connect two communities that are not adjacent by actual measurement; for example, figure 4 (Walden and Mecker), Figure 8 (Castle Rock and Akron), Figure 14 (Salida and Lake City), Figure 18 (Salida and Silverton), and Figure 19 (Saguache and Lamar).

[127] Some of these were of the same type as those used in Texas (see below). For a preliminary report on Oklahoma, see W. R. Van Riper, "Oklahoma Words", *The Round Table of the South-Central College English Association*, Vol. 2 (May, 1961), p. [3].

[128] "Regional Linguistic Atlases", pp. 377-378.

[129] These are the states of Georgia, Alabama, Mississippi, Tennessee, Louisiana, Arkansas, and Texas. [In May, 1968, with the support of the Southeastern Regional Educational Labora-

tory, Lee Pederson of Emory University held in Atlanta, Georgia, a conference of nine dialect specialists for considering plans for a proposed dialect atlas of the Gulf States and Inner South.-Eds.]

[130] C. M. Wise, "The Dialect Atlas of Louisiana--A Report of Progress", *Studies in Linguistics*, III (1945), 37-42. (University of Buffalo, New York.)

[131] For a list of these see *ibid.*, pp. 41-42.

[132] A Southeast Texas Dialect Study (diss., University of Texas, 1955). A summary, under the same title, is found in *Orbis*, V (1956), 61-79.

[133] A Dialect Study of San Antonio, Texas: A Bilingual Community (diss., University of Texas, 1957). A partial summary is found in the article "Aloofness from Spanish Influence in Texas English", *Word*, XV (1959), 270-281.

[134] For example, items that were used to demonstrate the currency of *burro* (donkey), *mott* (clump of trees), *draw* (dry creek), *remuda* (band of horses), *pilon* (extra gift), and many others.

[135] These included Robert N. Burrows, N. M. Caffee, Earnest Clifton, J. L. Dillard, Rudolph Fiehler, Alan M. F. Gunn, Sumner Ives, Charles B. Martin, Elton Miles, Ray Past, W. R. Van Riper, Harold White, and L. N. Wright.

[136] I claim no credit for having originated this idea, and I have no certain knowledge that I was the first to put it into practice. The Texas materials were processed between the years 1957 and 1959.

[137] University of Texas Press, 1962.

[138] *The Regional Vocabulary of Texas*, pp. 95-98.

[139] A Word Atlas of Northeast Texas (Lousiana State University, 1960). *Diss. Abstracts*, XXI, 2289.

[140] A Word Atlas of North Louisiana (Louisiana State University, 1961). *Diss. Abstracts*, XXII, 3653.

[141] For a summary of this work, see Mima Babington and E. Babgy Atwood, "Lexical Usage in Southern Lousiana", *PADS*, No. 36 (1961), 1-24.

[142] For non-linguistic reasons, a good many of the returned checklists were rejected. The most common reason for rejection was insufficient length of residence in a specific locality. See Gordon R. Wood, "Word Distribution in the Interior South", *PADS*, No. 35 (1961), 1-16.

[143] *Ibid.*, pp. 7-12.

[144] The problem of the application of structural linguistics to dialectology is a rather vexed one and has not been completely solved. For a recent discussion, see Pavle Ivić, "On the Structure of Dialectal Differentiation", *Word*, XVIII (1962), 33-53. (Linguistic Circle of New York.)

[145] For general discussions of this type of research, see Martin Joos, *Acoustic Phonetics,* Supplement to *Language* (Baltimore, 1948); and Ernest Pulgram, *Introduction to the Spectography of Speech*, *Janua Linguarum*, No. 7 (The Hague, 1959).

[146] John S. Kenyon and Thomas A. Knott, *A Pronouncing Dictionary of American English* (Springfield, Mass., 1944).

[147] A summary of Thomas's work is found in his *Introduction to the Phonetics of American English*, 2nd ed. (New York, 1958).

[148] The latest of their publications is "Three Generations of East Texas Speech", *American Speech*, XXXIV (1959), 83-94).

[149] For a summary of this work, see McDavid and McDavid, "Regional Linguistic Atlases", *Orbis*, V (1956), 380-381.

[150] See Le Page, "General Outlines of Creole English Dialects in the British Caribbean", *Orbis*, VI (1957), 373-391, and VII (1958), 54-64; also Le Page and DeCamp, *Jamaican Creole* (London, 1960).

[151] For example, he gathered data on many styles of baskets, machetes, and other artifacts.

[152] I am much indebted to colleagues in various parts of the country for having supplied me with recent information regarding their work, in personal conversations and in correspondence.

THE SOCIOCULTURAL BACKGROUND

OF DIALECT AREAS IN

AMERICAN ENGLISH

Hans Kurath

INTRODUCTION

A brief description of several attempts to achieve insight into the dialectal structure of an area on the basis of known heteroglossic lines, or to provide at least a tentative orientation, should throw light on some of the problems that must be faced.

In order to characterize and to evaluate the proposed schemes, the following factors must be taken into consideration:

(1) The character and fullness of the available data as determined by the content of the questionnaire, the choice of communities, and the method of gathering the data.

(2) The method of establishing boundaries within the area: (a) on the basis of congruent bundles of lexical, phonological, and morphological heteroglosses; (b) on the basis of bundles of any of the three types taken separately; or (c) on the basis of representative or diagnostic heteroglosses. (d) A boundary can also be suggested "intuitively" by a "convenient" heterogloss.

(3) Whether a diagnostic heterogloss is structural or non-structural is another point that must be taken into account.

THE DIALECTAL STRUCTURE OF NEW ENGLAND

Phonological and lexical heteroglosses form loose bundles running northward from Long Island Sound to Canada. These bundles divide New England into an Eastern and a Western dialect area (see Figure 1).

The course of these strands of heteroglosses exhibits no congruence with the boundaries of the New England states. Connecti-

From *Studies in Area Linguistics*, Indiana University Press, 1972, pp 39-53. Reprinted with permission.

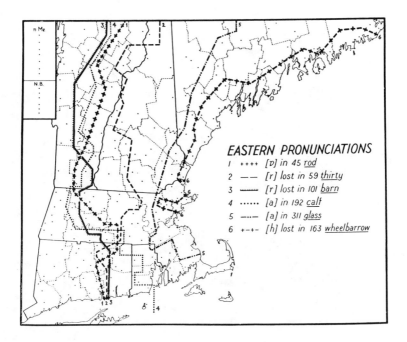

Figure 1:   New England: Eastern Pronunciations.   From Kurath,
Handbook of the Linguistic Geography of New England.

cut, Massachusetts, and Vermont are cut in half, while New Hampshire and Maine lie well within the Eastern area.   Political
boundaries have evidently not seriously interfered with communication between the inhabitants of the several states.

When we turn to a map showing the distribution of the population in New England (1930), we discover that of the two areas of
concentration one lies to the east of the bundles of heteroglosses
and the other to the west (see Figure 2).   From this demographic
fact we anticipate that the development of these two major dialect
areas of New England is somehow connected with these two population centers and their history.

We also observe that most of the heteroglosses run through
sparsely settled areas--along the Green Mountains of Vermont
and through the hill country of central Massachusetts and eastern
Connecticut.   Such areas impede communication and thus tend to
create and to stabilize existing dialect boundaries.

The Eastern concentration area extends from Narragansett
Bay (Providence, R.I.) to Casco Bay (Portland, Me.).   Its dominant center is Massachusetts Bay (Boston).   The Western area of
concentration extends from Long Island Sound (New Haven) to
Hartford and Springfield on the Connecticut River.   Both of

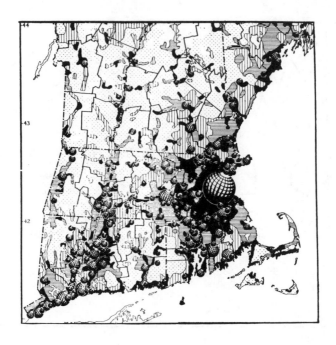

Figure 2:   New England: Population Distribution, 1930.   From
J. K. Wright, editor, New England's Prospect: 1933, page 23.
New York, 1933.

these centers date from early Colonial times and have continuously,
and increasingly, influenced the speech of their back county.
     The chronology of the settlement of New England has fortunate-
ly been worked out in considerable detail.   Between 1630 and
1645 colonies were planted along the open Atlantic and on the
lower Connecticut River.   Expanding slowly, they did not establish
contact with each other for about half a century (see Figure 3),
a period during which some regional differences in usage must
have become established.   Half a century later (1725) these two
settlement areas were in contact with each other in Connecticut
and in parts of Massachusetts, but the sparsely settled hill country
connecting them interfered with communication.
     Even more important is the fact that each of these areas
developed a transportation system radiating from the old centers
outward to the peripheral settlements, which served to consolidate
them economically, socially, and culturally.   This process of integration continued with increasing force in the nineteenth century
when turnpikes and railroads were built.   The network of railroads
in operation in 1930 effectively portrays this situation (see Figure
4).   Add to this the prestige enjoyed by Boston-Cambridge-Concord
from the middle of the nineteenth century onward in the fields of

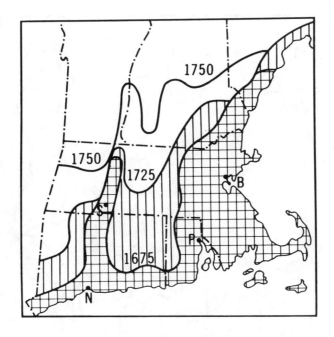

Figure 3: New England: Chronology of Settlement.

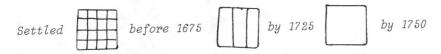

Settled ▦ *before 1675* ▥ *by 1725* ☐ *by 1750*

Cities: B(oston, N(ew Haven, P(rovidence, S(pringfield

Based upon Kurath, Handbook of the Linguistic Geography of New England (foldout map).

literature and scholarship, and you have a picture of the socio-cultural forces that have preserved Eastern New England as a highly distinctive dialect area.

Eastern New England is of course not a wholly uniform speech area. Settlement history is reflected for instance, in the survival of *tempest* "storm" and *cade* "pet lamb" from Narragansett Bay to Cape Cod, i.e., in the colonies established in Rhode Island and the Plymouth area [Kurath 1949: Figure 4]. Recession of the highly distinctive checked vowel /ǝ/, as in *coat*, *road*, *home*, is

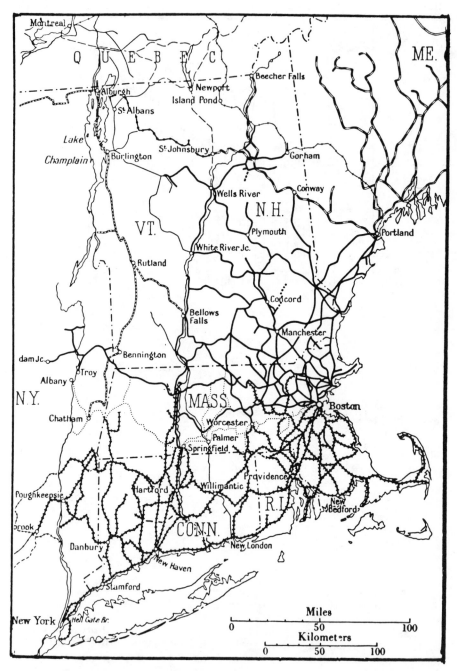

Figure 4: New England: Railroads. From J. K. Wright, editor,
New England's Prospect: *1933, page 345. New York, 1933.*

in progress, as shown by its regional, social, and age distribution [Avis 1961].

This brief account of the sociocultural background of the two major speech areas of New England must suffice. Its present purpose is to illustrate the method by which the discovery of congruences between dialect boundaries and the areas set off by them and sociocultural boundaries and domains leads to more or less plausible historical interpretations of areal linguistic phenomena.

THE BOUNDARY BETWEEN THE NORTHERN AND THE MIDLAND DIALECT AREAS

A close-knit bundle of lexical, phonological, and morphological heteroglosses runs through northern Pennsylvania, some thirty miles south of the state line, and continues westward into Ohio. At the eastern end (near Scranton) the heteroglosses fan out, some of them swerving southeastward through New Jersey, others continuing eastward to pass north of New York City (see Figure 5).

The prominent dialect boundary in northern Pennsylvania clearly reflects settlement history, channeled and reinforced by the topography. While the Pennsylvania settlements expanded up the Susquehanna Valley to the forested area in the northern part of the state, westward across the Alleghenies to the upper Ohio and its tributaries (Pittsburgh), and southwestward into the valleys of the Appalachians, New Englanders migrated westward into the basin of the Great Lakes, skirting the Dutch settlements in the Hudson Valley. New Englanders also moved southward into eastern New Jersey. From Upstate New York, some of them pushed southward into the wooded hill country of northern Pennsylvania. These lines of expansion are suggested in Figure 6. The chronology of the settlement is shown in Paullin-Wright 1933: Plate 76A–E.

In the Hudson Valley and in New Jersey the transition area between the North and the Midland reflects partly the complicated history of the settlement--English over Dutch--and partly the later effects of the chief communication route (New York-Philadelphia) that intersects the settlement boundary between East Jersey and West Jersey.

The speech of Upstate New York is obviously derived from that of New England. Features peculiar to eastern New England, such as the loss of postvocalic /r/ in *beard*, *hard*, *board*, or the low front vowel /a/ in *half*, *pass*, *aunt*, survive only sporadically. The chief reason for this is the fact that the majority of the settlers came from rural western New England at a time when the increasing population of eastern New England was absorbed into the developing industries and engaged in seafaring.

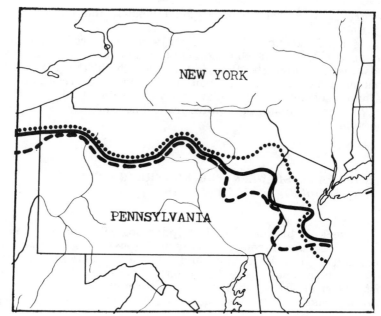

Figure 5:   *The Southern Boundary of Three Northern Words.*
　　　───────── *Whiffletree, Whippletree 'swingletree'*
　　　─── ─── *Pail*
　　　..... ..... *Darning Needle 'dragonfly'*

From H. Kurath, A Word Geography of the Eastern States.

　　In Pennsylvania the dialect boundary between the North and the Midland, created by the population movements outlined above, was supported in later years by the sparsely settled belt in the heavily forested section of northern Pennsylvania.

　　The westward extension of this boundary has been established on the basis of the sampling survey of the Great Lakes area directed by A. H. Marckwardt (see Figure 7). On lexical evidence, the dividing line between the North and the Midland runs through northern Ohio, Indiana, and Illinois to the Mississippi River (near Burlington, Iowa). To the north of it, New England regionalisms are current, of which many can be traced all the way to the North Pacific Coast, as C. E. Reed [1956, 1957] has shown.

THE STRUCTURE OF THE UPPER SOUTH

　　The Upper South, focused on eastern Virginia, constitutes a rather well defined subdivision of the Southern dialect area. Its northern boundary runs in an arc from the Atlantic Ocean through

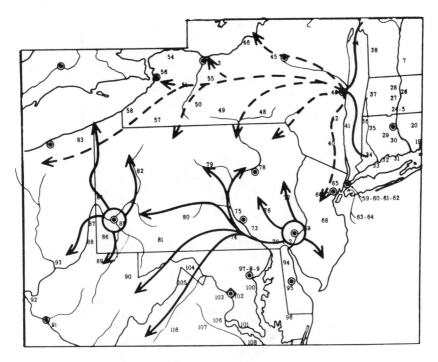

*Figure 6:   The Boundary between the Northern and the Midland
Dialect Areas.*

*The arrows suggest the westward expansion of the settlements
from New England and from eastern Pennsylvania in the latter
part of the eighteenth and the first two decades of the nineteenth century.*

Delaware (north of Dover) and Maryland (north of Baltimore) to
the Blue Ridge Mountains of Virginia.   From there the dividing
line follows the Blue Ridge southwestward to the upper reaches
of the Roanoke River.   To the north of this boundary lies the
North Midland area, to the west of it the South Midland area.
The southern limit of this area is less clearly defined.   It has
the character of a transition belt formed by spaced heteroglosses,
some of which dip into north central North Carolina, while others
follow the tidal inlet of the James River.

The focal area of the Upper South is suggested by three
concentric lexical isoglosses shown in Figure 16 and by an
important phonological feature in Figure 9.

The search for extralinguistic factors that might be responsible
for the prominent dialect boundary that sets the Upper South off
from the Midland reveals immediately that there is no congruence

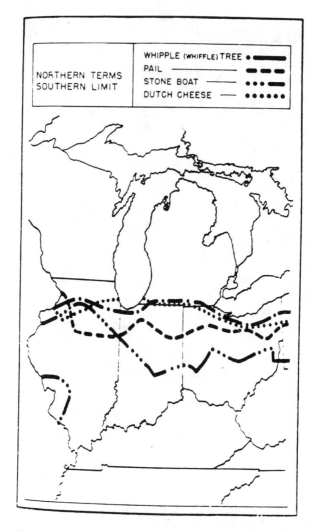

Figure 7:   The Great Lakes Area: Northern Words.
From A. H. Marckwardt, Principal and Subsidiary Dialect Areas in
the North-Central States.

whatever with major political boundaries, i.e., with state lines:
the linguistic boundary cuts right through Delaware, Maryland,
·and Virginia.   Secondly, although this boundary rests upon the
Blue Ridge Mountains in Virginia, which rise steeply out of the
coastal plain to form a rather formidable natural barrier to communi-

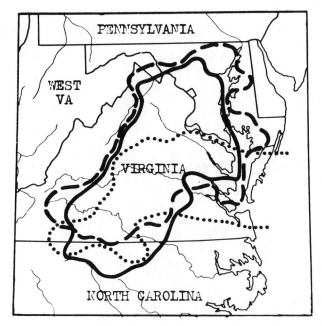

Figure 8:   The Virginia Piedmont: Word Boundaries

——————————   *Cuppin 'cowpen'*
——— ———   *Corn House 'corncrib'*
. . . .   *Cow House 'cow barn'*

From H. Kurath, A Word Geography of the Eastern States.

cation, it runs right through the coastal plain in Maryland and Delaware. An investigation of settlement history, the character of the economy, and the social organization of the Upper South readily leads to the discovery of forces that have shaped this dialect area.

The Upper South was settled by gradual expansion from the colonies planted on Chesapeake Bay in the seventeenth century. These movements up the river valleys were controlled to a large extent by the plantation aristocracy engaged in the cultivation of tobacco for the European market. As the fertility of the "old fields" was exhausted, new land suitable for growing tobacco was cleared. The heart of this plantation country is strikingly reflected in the concentration of Negro slaves in the Piedmont of Virginia from 1790 to 1860 [Paullin-Wright 1932:   plates 67B and 68B].

From the colonial seaports of this area--Richmond on the James River, Fredericksburg on the Rappahannock, and Alexandria on the Potomac--the tobacco was shipped to England, and in return manufactured goods were imported. The common interest of the dominant plantation aristocracy consolidated the area both economically and socioculturally. The linguistic integration of this area clearly emerged from this situation.

The areas north and west of the Upper South were settled largely from, and by way of, Pennsylvania. Northern Maryland and the Valley of Virginia (west of the Blue Ridge) never were plantation country. The settlers, many of them Ulster Scots and Germans, engaged in general farming; wheat fields and orchards characterized the landscape. In Virginia, the conflicting economic interests between the coastal plain and the Valley of Virginia, and consequently the divergent attitudes toward slavery, created a regional antagonism that tended to keep the two dialect areas apart.

In Figure 10 the settlement paths of the South and of the South Midland, and the dialect boundary separating them, are presented schematically.

Although set off from the Midland Dialect area by a well defined boundary, especially in its northern sector, the Upper South is still rather far from uniform in its linguistic usage. The Eastern Shore of Chesapeake Bay has preserved a considerable

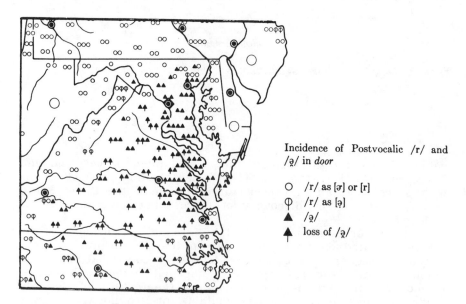

Incidence of Postvocalic /r/ and /ə̣/ in *door*

○ /r/ as [ɚ] or [r]
φ /r/ as [ə]
▲ /ə̣/
⬆ loss of /ə̣/

Figure 9: The Virginia Piedmont: Postvocalic /ə̣/
From H. Kurath and R. I. McDavid, Jr., The Pronunciation of English in the Atlantic States.

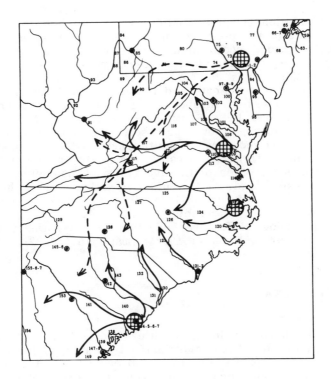

Figure 10:   Settlement Paths of the Coastal South and of the South Midland.

number of old local features.   Even the points of land between
the tidal inlets of the rivers on the western shore have not yet
been brought fully into line with the dominant focal area of the
Upper South--the Piedmont of Virginia.   Diffusion from this center
is still in progress, as evidenced by the social dissemination of
variants on its periphery [Kurath 1964:   135-44].

THE LOWER SOUTH

The sociocultural factors underlying the dialect situation of
the Lower South, of which South Carolina is the focus, resemble
those of the Upper South in many ways.   There are, however,
some rather marked differences.

The plantation economy (indigo, rice, and later cotton) controlled the life of the people from the very beginning and created the steeply graded social structure of the Lowcountry. Even more than in Virginia, the planter class dominated economic, political, and social affairs and in time largely submerged the Upcountry, where Ulster Scots and Germans from Pennsylvania had settled in considerable numbers. This development has been admirably described by a South Carolinian, R. I. McDavid, Jr. [1948]. The author shows how some linguistic features once peculiar to the Lowcountry of South Carolina have been diffused to the Upcountry from the prestige dialect of the planter class. To be sure, some other distinctive traits of Lowcountry speech have not spread inland, as the ingliding articulation of the vowels /e, o/ of *eight* [eət], *coat* [koət] in the Charleston dialect, a feature that seems to be receding even there.

Some phonological features peculiar to the Lower South are displayed in Kurath-McDavid 1961:   maps 16, 19, 21, 25, 156.

THE PACIFIC STATES

The English spoken in the Pacific States--California, Oregon, and Washington--has been investigated by David W. Reed and by Carroll E. Reed, partly by direct observation in the field and partly by correspondence. Their questionnaire includes a fair number of lexical items for which regional synonyms had been established in the Eastern States [Kurath 1949] and in the derivative North Central States [Davis 1948].

The evidence secured by correspondence in response to a "check list" of words whose currency is regionally restricted in the Eastern States is presented and analysed by D. Reed [1954] for California and by C. Reed [1956, 1957] for Oregon, Washington, and Idaho.

The chief findings are: (1) In this vast area, extending some eleven hundred miles from Mexico to Canada, the dissemination of regional Eastern words differs little from state to state, although San Francisco Bay, the Willamette Valley of Oregon, and the Puget Sound area of Washington were separate "growing points." (2) Regional synonyms of the East are current side by side without any marked differences in their relative frequency from state to state.   (3) Words used in large sections of the Atlantic Slope and/or the North Central States appear with greater frequency than synonyms restricted to subareas of the East. (4) Regional words derived from the Northern dialect area (New England and the basin of the Great Lakes) and from the North Midland (Pennsylvania and the Ohio Valley) appear with similar frequency, whereas words peculiar to the South Atlantic States are rare.   (5) The distribution by age groups shows that regional words are receding sharply all the way from California to Washington.

The authors point out some of the sociocultural factors underlying the behavior of the words investigated. Other factors can easily be adduced, since the settlement history of the Pacific Coast and later developments are so well known.

The salient facts can be briefly stated. Beginning with the 1840's, California, Oregon, and Washington received their rapidly growing English-speaking population largely from the same sources: New England, the Middle Atlantic States, and the Midwest. Immigrants from abroad poured into all of the Pacific States, though California had the largest share. In time the foreigners learned the language of the dominant English stock. These sociocultural factors account for the striking similarity in word usage throughout the Pacific States.

As in other sections of the United States, the recession of the largely rural regional words reflects the mechanization of farming and the rapid urbanization since the turn of the century. Nearly three-fourths of the population of the Pacific States now live in urban areas and are quite unfamiliar with life on the farm, where regional words brought in from the East survive as valuable evidence for the provenience of the native American stock of the Far West.

Among the words that clearly establish the Northern provenience of large elements among the English-speaking settlers in the Pacific States are the following: *co boss*! a call to cows; *angleworm* "earthworm"; *darning needle* "dragon fly." Confined to the Northern dialect area on the Atlantic Slope [Kurath 1949: Figures 99, 140, 141] and to the basin of the Great Lakes [Davis 1948: Maps 163, 165, 239], these lexical items unmistakably reflect the westward migration of New Englanders and their descendants in the basin of the Great Lakes to the Pacific Coast.

The westward trek from Pennsylvania and the Ohio Valley--the North Midland speech area--is shown with equal clarity by the currency of regional Midland words in the Pacific States, among them *blinds* "roller shade," *greenbeans* "string beans," *sook*! a call to cows, for which see Kurath 1949: figures 49, 133, 99 and Davis 148: Maps 178, 210, 163.

The relative frequency of these Northern and Midland words appears to be much the same in California and in Washington, which suggests that the proportion of "Northerners" and "Midlanders" in these two states as a whole differs little.

The behavior of regional words common to the North and the North Midland of the Eastern States supports this inference. In addition, it confirms the rule that the frequency with which such words appear in the "derivative area" of the Pacific States depends upon the extent of their currency in the "mother area." Thus *whinny* [Kurath 1949: Figure 97; Davis 1948: Map 161] and *skunk* [Kurath 1949: figure 137], shared by the North and the North Midland, are much more widely disseminated in California and Washington than the Northern and the Midland words illustrated above. In conformity with this rule, words confined to subareas of the North or the Midland survive only in scattered instances or not at all. See the lists in D. Reed 1954: 13-14 and C. Reed 1956: 7.

The calculation of the frequency with which regional words imported from the East occur in the Pacific States is an important contribution of the Reeds to the method of area linguistics, which has been applied with significant results to the regional vocabulary of Texas by E. B. Atwood [1962]. This device has special importance for dealing with derivative speech areas in which usage reflects recent mixture without any clear regional dissemination of the variants.

TEXAS

E. B. Atwood's book on *The Regional Vocabulary of Texas* [1962] is a well planned and circumspect treatment of one aspect of the linguistic situation in the state of Texas and its neighbors-- Louisiana, Arkansas, Oklahoma, and New Mexico. Most of his data were gathered between 1950 and 1960 by his friends and students with the help of a questionnaire. For Oklahoma, W. R. Van Riper contributed his field materials, for Louisiana, M. Babington.

For his questionnaire Atwood selected (1) items referring to farming and to life in the countryside for which regionally restricted (varying) terms are current in the eastern United States [Kurath 1949]; (2) designations referring to the range cattle industry and the topography of the western part of the state; and (3) some expressions that seemed to be peculiar to Texas or to southern Louisiana. The last two groups enabled him to show the Spanish and the French contributions to the vocabulary of Texas and to set off the areas in which they are current. The stock of regional terms brought in from the "mother" area of American English along the Atlantic during the westward movement, and recent trends in their currency, naturally are his primary concern.

The author found that most of the English regional terms used (or formerly used) by Texans are derived from the South Atlantic States--the Southern and the South Midland dialect areas [Kurath 1949: figure 3], and that the extent to which they are current in Texas stands in a fairly clear relation to the size of the areas they occupied in the Eastern States around 1940.

Thus *bucket* "pail," *Christmas gift* "merry Christmas," (*corn*) *shucks* "husks," *dog irons* ~ *fire dogs* "andirons," *paling* "picket" (of a fence), *pullybone* "wishbone," which are common to the South and the South Midland on the Atlantic slope, are widely used in Texas; and so are *nicker* "whinny" and *clabber cheese* "cottage cheese," although the former is not current in the

Carolinas and the latter is restricted to the South Midland and North Carolina.

Some terms that in the East are confined to the Southern speech area (the plantation country of the coastal plain), as *snap beans* "greenbeans," *carry home* "take (somebody) home," and *low* "moo" have (or had until recently) considerable currency in Texas and adjoining areas; so do *sook!* a call to cows, (*quarter*) *till* (*eleven*) "to," and the phrase (*I*) *want off* "want to get off," which are peculiar to Pennsylvania and the South Midland (West Virginia to the Upcountry of the Carolinas). See Figure 11.

Words that have limited currency in the East are infrequent in Texas or not used at all: Virginia *batter-bread* "soft corn cake"; coastal Carolinian *spider* "frying pan," *press peach* "cling-stone peach," *whicker* "whinny"; and *fire-board* "mantle shelf," *red-worm* "earth worm" of the southern Appalachians.

There are some exceptions to the rule that expressions current in large sections of the Atlantic states are more widely used in Texas than those confined to smaller areas. Thus general southern *light-wood* "kindling" is infrequent in Texas, whereas North Carolinians *tow sack* "burlap sack" has general currency. The

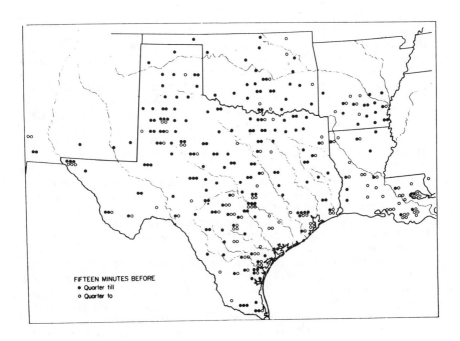

Figure 11: Texas: Quarter till *and* quarter to.
From E. B. Atwood, The Regional Vocabulary of Texas.

history of the "thing-meant" obviously has a bearing upon the frequency with which a term is used, and hence upon its dissemination.

The fact that words confined to different speech areas of the Atlantic States are current side by side in Texas leads to the inference--on purely linguistic grounds--that some of the early settlers, or their forebears, ultimately came from the Southern dialect area (the coastal plain) and others from the South Midland speech area (the Appalachians and the piedmont of the Carolinas). Since the English settlements in Texas lag only one or two decades behind those in the intervening areas--Trans-Appalachia and the Gulf States--the connection with the Eastern "homeland" is very close: Tennessee and Arkansas settlers who moved into Texas had only recently crossed the Appalachians, and the cotton belt in Alabama and Mississippi was not taken up until 1820-30 [Paullin-Wright: plates 76E, F]. Data concerning the provenience of the early and the later Texas settlers, though rather fragmentary, agree with the linguistic evidence [Atwood 1962: 7-10].

Atwood is inclined to attribute greater influence upon the regional vocabulary of Texas to the South Midland dialect than to Coastal Southern, but the evidence is far from conclusive. Until phonological and morphological data become available, the question should in my opinion be kept open.

The author finds no lexical evidence for drawing a linguistic boundary along the Brazos River, which on sociocultural grounds --the concentration of slaves in 1860--had previously been suggested as the probable western limit of the Southern dialect area [Kurath 1949: 37]. Nor is there any clear division between the north central and the southeastern section of the state, although some South Midland words have more extensive currency in the former and some Southern words in the latter [Atwood 1962: 82].

In his analysis of the currency of regional words, Atwood introduced two procedures hitherto not employed in this country or abroad: (1) A statistical determination of the frequency of the regional terms with the total area investigated; and (2) a statistical treatment of trends in word usage as inferred from the dissemination by age groups. These calculations were carried out with the aid of an electronic computer.

As to trends in usage, it is important to remember that many of the regional words brought in from the East fall within the semantic domain of farm and home life. Their currency has declined sharply in the nineteenth century, what with urbanization, merchandising of food stuffs, mechanization of the farm, extended schooling, and changes in fashion. Atwood effectively chronicles their decline generation by generation and convincingly points out specific sociocultural factors that underly their recession. His findings are significant not only for Texas and its neighbors; they are symptomatic of trends in word usage throughout the United States.

Atwood's investigation of this aspect of regional vocabulary demonstrates the effectiveness of combining geographic dissemination with age distribution in tracing linguistic change, a method equally applicable to phonological and to morphological data. A further dimension--the social dissemination of the variants--can be added to achieve the full potential of area linguistics in its effort to deal with language in its sociocultural context.

For the Spanish contributions to the vocabulary of Texas and their regional behavior see below.

In preparation for the sociocultural interpretation, Atwood outlines the history of the population of Texas. The salient facts are briefly mentioned below.

English settlement began in 1821 on the lower Brazos River and grew so rapidly that by 1835 the Spanish settlers were outnumbered two to one in a total population of about 35,000. The rout of the Mexican military forces in the battle of San Jacinto (near Houston) led to the formation of the Republic of Texas (1836) and its admission to the United States in 1845. During the days of the Republic the population had risen to more than 100,000; by 1861--when Texas joined the Confederacy--it was 600,000, concentrated in the eastern third of the state. As late as 1900 only the eastern half of the state had more than 6 inhabitants per square mile, although the population had increased to about 3,500,000. Between 1900 and 1930 the High Plains of northwest Texas were occupied, largely from the older parts of the state. Meanwhile urban centers grew apace. Whereas in a population of 4,500,000 two-thirds were classified as rural in 1920, by 1960 three-fourths of the 9,500,000 inhabitants of Texas lived in cities.

The expansion of the English settlements from east to west leads to the expectation that linguistic usage became established to some extent in the eastern section by 1861, where the planter class dominated economically and politically to such an extent that Texas joined the Confederacy. This raises the question of the provenience of this social class: Did the majority of the planters come via the cotton belt from the Atlantic coast and the Gulf plain or from the southern Upland via Tennessee?

The increase in population from 1845 to 1860 and again from 1870 onward is so phenomenal that continued influx from the outside clearly overshadows the growth of the indigenous population. Hence the question is to what extent the newcomers adopted the usage of the indigenous families when it differed from theirs.

The rather late development of important cities is a significant fact. They can hardly be expected to have had much influence upon the speech of their rural surroundings. Their phenomenal growth from 1920 onward implies that country folk flocked into them. What happened, and is happening, as a consequence can only be revealed by rather thorough future investigations of the speech of these centers and their hinterland.

REFERENCES

Atwood, E. B., *The Regional Vocabulary of Texas*.   Austin, Texas, 1962.

Avis, W. F., *The Mid-back Vowels in the English of the Eastern United States*. U. of Mich. diss., 1955.

Davis, A. L., *A Word Atlas of the Great Lakes Region*.   U. of Michigan diss., 1948.

Kurath, H., *A Word Geography of the Eastern United States*. Ann Arbor, Mich., 1949 [reprint 1966].

Kurath, H., "Interrelation between regional and social dialects." *Ninth International Congress of Linguists*, ed. H. G. Lunt, pp. 135-44. The Hague, 1964.

Kurath, H. and B. Bloch, *Handbook of the Linguistic Geography of New England*.   ACLS and Brown University, Providence, R.I., 1939.

Kurath, H. and R. I. McDavid, Jr., *The Pronunciation of English in the Atlantic States*. Ann Arbor, Mich., 1961.

Marckwardt, A. H., "Principal and subsidiary dialect areas in the north-central states." *PADS* 27.3-15 (1957).

McDavid, R. I., "Postvocalic /r/ in South Carolina: A social analysis." *AS* 23.149-203 (1948).

Paullin, C. O. and J. K. Wright, *Atlas of the Historical Geography of the United States*. Washington, 1932.

Reed, C. E., "Washington words." *PADS* 25 (1956).

Reed, C. E., "Word geography of the Pacific Northwest." 6.86-93 (1957).

Reed, D. W., "Eastern dialect words in California." *PADS* 21 (1954).

Wright, J. K., *New England's Prospect: 1933*. New York, 1933.

LINGUISTIC GEOGRAPHY

Raven I. McDavid, Jr.

Recently a federal judge ordered the Ann Arbor schools to show greater sensitivity to the dialect used outside the classroom by a group of students from a housing project. Accepting the obligation of the schools to teach standard written English, but recognizing that the speech of the students in their homes is a viable linguistic system, the court undercut a view too prevalent: that any speech diverging from local middle-class norms is a form of speech pathology. How the schools will execute the order remains to be seen. The families are Black; but others in Ann Arbor have speech unlike what was brought to Washtenaw County by rural New Englanders through Upstate New York, and later modified by Schwabians. That others than Blacks have problems in Ann Arbor is proved by my own experience: in 1937, two years after my Ph.D., and from a home where nonstandard forms were never used except in jest, I found my Up Country South Carolina pronunciation often the butt of wisecracks by the head of the Speech Department (on the national scene, we recall, Texans and Georgians of prominence have had similar experience).

While courts are urging linguistic sensitivity, scholars are providing evidence on linguistic variety. These scholars are of two kinds--complementing rather than competing--linguistic geographers and sociolinguists. Chiefly a linguistic geographer, I will deal mostly with that field.

Informal awareness of language variety goes back at least to the *shibboleth* episode (Judges 12:4-6), and has been used for various literary effects, chiefly comic, by Aristophanes, Catullus, Chaucer, and Shakespeare, to name a few. It became a systematic study toward the end of the last century, for testing the assumptions of comparative and historical linguists that pronunciation differences between related languages and dialects (English *pound, water, make*/German *pfund, wasser, machen*) have no exceptions. Evidence accumulated in Germany, France, and Italy revealed that in Europe regional speech differences are related to social and historical forces: original settlements, routes of migration, older political boundaries, and centers of cultural diffusion. For

From *CEA Critic* 42(3):17-23, 1980. Reprinted with permission.

gathering data, rigorous methods were developed: selection of identified communities; selection of identifiable speakers to be interviewed (natives of the community, of well rooted local families, with a minimum of outside influence on their speech); questionnaires on specific items of grammar and pronunciation and vocabulary; interviews by trained investigators in a natural setting; records of the data in finely graded phonetic notation.

In North America, a Linguistic Atlas of the United States and Canada was organized in 1929 by Hans Kurath, following the principles of European linguistic geography with two important modifications:

1. The atlases of Germany and France had studied only village speech; that of Italy touched only a few urban areas. The American surveys have investigated urban usage in every region.

2. In Germany, France, Italy, and England, one assumes a dichotomy between a uniform educated spoken language and a diversity of local dialects; consequently, investigators limited themselves to a single interview, with a folk speaker, in each community (again, the Italian survey is an exception, with two interviews in several large communities). The North American situation is different: educated speech of Charleston, South Carolina, is not that of Pittsburgh or Chicago, and all of these differ from the educated speech of Boston. Moreover, in every community there is a common speech between the folk and the cultivated. Consequently, Kurath planned to investigate folk and common speech in every community, cultivated speech in about one community of five.

The plans for a single Linguistic Atlas of the United States and Canada, under Kurath's direction, were dissipated as the Depression, World War II, and the Cold War restricted funds and diverted field workers and editors. As early as 1937, Kurath recommended autonomous regional surveys, with his personal supervision restricted to the Atlantic Seaboard. The accompanying map indicates the progress of these surveys.

Although the basic methods have been followed in all regions, there have been some differences. In recently settled areas, such as the Rockies and the Pacific Coast, length of family residence in the community is inevitably less than along the Atlantic Seaboard, where informants often trace their local roots back to the seventeenth century. There have also been two modifications of method: (1) many interviews (all of those for the Gulf States) are recorded on tape and later transcribed phonetically; (2) several surveys supplement the interviews with vocabulary questionnaires distributed by mail. The amount of data gathered so far is awesome.

Regrettably, consulting the data has not been as easy as the editors would like. Only the New England Atlas has been published in traditional cartographic form; its volumes are large and expensive, and the finely graded phonetics are beyond the competence of most classroom teachers. The more popular presentation in

Allen's *Atlas of the Upper Midwest* is still rather expensive, and difficult for the laity to follow. Interpretive studies, published or pending, will make the general picture more accessible, while microfilms of the original records give skeptics an opportunity to analyze the basic data for themselves.

Nevertheless, the surveys already provide better understanding of language variety in the United States. Clearest are the major regional patterns along the Atlantic Seaboard, extending into the Mississippi Valley: a Northern region of New England, the Hudson Valley, and their western derivatives; a Midland region of Pennsylvania and derivative areas to the west and southwest; and a Southern region of the South Atlantic coastal plantation area and its Gulf Coast derivatives. These major regions have subdivisions, again most clearly delineated along the Atlantic Coast. Two changes from an older classification are apparent: the uniform "General American," supposedly characteristic of the Middle West, is shown to be split by east-west lines setting off New York State from Pennsylvania, Michigan from Indiana, in vocabulary (*cherry pit/seed*), grammar (*dove/dived*) and pronunciation (the vowels of *fog* and *hog*). Furthermore, much of the historical South is shown to be basically Midland, the uplands reflecting early settlement by Germans and Ulster Scots from Pennsylvania. Here the Atlases provide the first serious response to the 1904 suggestion of Frederick Jackson Turner that the most urgent topic for historians of the South was the changing relationships between the coastal plantation areas and the upland region of small farms.

The records also show the contrast between FOCAL and RELIC areas. A number of areas, and the cities at their center, have expanded their influence: eastern New England (Boston), the Hudson Valley, the Delaware Valley (Philadelphia), the upper Ohio Valley (Pittsburgh), the Virginia Piedmont (Richmond), and the South Carolina Low Country (Charleston). The New York metropolitan area, however, does not seem to have influenced its hinterland, except through disseminating forms common throughout the Hudson Valley. In contrast are such relatively isolated areas, often declining in population and economic influence, as northeastern New England, the Delmarva Peninsula, the Albemarle Sound area of Northeastern North Carolina. Much of the quaint and picturesque speech in which casual observers delight is found in these areas, especially among older uneducated speakers.

The surveys also find patterns reflecting early settlement by speakers of other languages than English. The greatest number come from the Germans, whose colonies are scattered from the Mohawk Valley to the Savannah, and throughout the Middle West--*smearcase* "cottage cheese," *rainworm* "earthworm," *got awake* "woke up," and *the oranges are all* "all gone." But there are also Hudson Valley Dutch terms like *pot cheese* "cottage cheese," French-Canadian ones like *shivaree* "mock serenade," and the host of Spanish terms associated with the hacienda culture of the Southwest--*ranch, corral, bronco*, and *cinch*. Before the recent interest in West African survivals in American Black (and White) speech,

the Atlas records revealed a clustering of such survivals in South
Carolina as *pinder* "peanut" and *cooter* "turtle." The patterning
of these words in the early Atlas records led Lorenzo Turner to
study Sea Island Black speech, first with Atlas techniques and
then more intensively--giving us *Africanisms in the Gullah Dialect* (1949), still the most impressive study of Black speech in
North America.

Turner's work illustrates the way in which the American Atlases
may be used for the study of social as well as regional variation.
Even with their limited sample, the older European Atlases suggest
the spread of socially prestigious forms. For the areas investigated
in the United States we have fairly good ideas of the social
differences in usage and the indicated direction of change at the
time the field work was conducted.

To be sure, this is only a beginning. The smallest community
has more than three social levels (sociologists like the Warners
assume six or seven); if we include variables of age and sex and
ethnicity, the number is greatly multiplied for natives of the
community alone. Furthermore, the practical applications of sociolinguistics, as in the schools, involve the linguistic assimilation
of groups not native to the community--Latin Americans, Blacks,
Southern rural Whites, Italians, and Slavs. To appraise the
usage of a community, especially on a statistical basis, demands
a wider range of interviews than the Atlas plan permits and
probably shorter interviews, concentrating on a limited number
of frequently occurring variables of grammar and pronunciation--
features whose social significance is suggested in the older studies.
No linguistic geographer denies the need for these new studies.

But new studies do not invalidate old ones. Social differences
in language are not static; the usage of a community changes,
and the kinds of changes can be assessed only if we have a
framework, such as the regional surveys supply. William Labov
has frequently remarked that his study of social stratification in
the speech of the Lower East Side would have been meaningless
without the Atlas records made by Guy Lowman in 1941.

The American regional surveys and their English analogues
are providing a very useful framework for assessing social differ-
ences--not merely changes within a community *per se* but those
involving new arrivals. By now, for almost every urban area we
have evidence both on the speech of the host community and on
that of the source communities (such as West Virginia and Mississippi) from which these new arrivals have come. Moreover, the
traditional surveys also record the usage of important groups,
small but highly prestigious, who would hardly be caught by
random sampling, especially in a limited area like the Lower East
Side of Manhattan.

Taking the Atlas investigations and the more intensive local
studies, we can draw new and interesting conclusions about sociolinguistic patterns and the direction of change in various communities. A few examples:

1.   In the 1930s, the "New England short *o*"--a sound ap-
proaching the vowel of *cut*--in *coat, road, home* was already rare
and old-fashioned and rural. In urban areas it has now practically
disappeared.
2.   Natives of Cleveland interviewed in the 1940s kept a
contrast between such words as *cot* and *caught*. In the 1950s a
third of the college students in the Cleveland area lacked that
distinction, but in the 1960s the distinction was still normal in
Akron.   Why should this homonym, characteristic of Pittsburgh
speech, spread to one city (the one more insistent on its cultural
prestige) and not the other?
3.   For a long time, speakers in the Charleston area contrasted *pen* and *pin* but not *ear* and *air*, in both instances differing from the Carolina uplands.   Now, with the population of
Charleston growing by migration from the uplands, both local
patterns have changed, except for the usage of the more sophisticated Whites and the least sophisticated Blacks (In New York,
too, the old upper classes seem to be immune to changes affecting
other groups).
4.   Although educated Southerners traditionally do not pronounce the /-r/ in *beard, bard, bored*, recent studies show the
/-r/ flourishing among younger educated speakers. Various explanations have been offered, including the effect of the radio.
More likely, the change in linguistic values is due to social changes
brought about by the New Deal.   The extension of economic and
social advantages in the South meant that many /r/ speakers--here-
tofore the less fortunate group--could stand on all fours with
the older cultivated group, who may still do without the /r/ but
are now a minority among the educated, even like their New
York City counterparts.
5.   Familiarity with the framework of the regional surveys
would, finally, lead to a better understanding of the relationship
between the speech of Blacks and that of Whites. In the 1960s,
after studies in Northern and Western cities revealed striking
differences between middle-class White speech in the suburbs and
lower-class Black speech in the central cities, it became fashionable
to label the latter as "Black English," with some fifty stigmata.
But most of these features have been investigated in the regional
surveys, which show them not limited to Blacks but found in
old-fashioned speech in various regions where Black influence is
improbable: rural England, Ireland, Newfoundland, northeastern
New England, the Appalachians--*e.g., he do, I be tired, they's
lots* (=*there's*), disyllabic plurals of *post, fish, ghost*, and various types of multiple negation, such as *ain't nobody never makes
no pound cake no more*. To balance this, the a- participle (*he come
a-runnin*), often labeled as peculiar to Appalachia, is frequent
in New England.
Those of us intimately involved in the regional surveys have
had to acquire a veneer of patience as we find ourselves labeled
dull cataloguers of data, outmoded by exciting theoretical innovations.   But our discipline demands allegiance to data--recording,

classifying, analyzing. Theory can come later; it is our business
to set out the data so clearly and explicitly that it will be useful
whenever consulted, as every decennial census remains valuable
in interpreting the changes in our population.

REFERENCES

A. Regional Surveys: Primary Data

Kurath, Hans, Raven I. McDavid, Jr., and Raymond K. O'Cain.
Linguistic Atlas of the Middle and South Atlantic States. In
progress.

Kurath, Hans, et al. *Linguistic Atlas of New England*. 3 vol.
bound as 6, Providence, 1939-43. Second edition, 3 vol.,
New York, 1972.

Marckwardt, Albert H., Raven I. McDavid, Jr., et al. *Linguistic Atlas of the North Central States*. In progress.

Pederson, Lee, et al. *Linguistic Atlas of the Gulf States*.
Microfiche. Athens, Georgia, 1980.

Reed, David W., and Allan Metcalf. *Linguistic Atlas of California and Nevada*. Microfilm. Berkeley, California, 1979.

Van Riper, William R., Raven I. McDavid, Jr., et al. *Linguistic
Atlas of Oklahoma*. Microfilm. Chicago, 1980.

B. Interpretative Works

Allen, Harold B. *Linguistic Atlas of the Upper Midwest*. 3
vol., Minneapolis, 1973-76.

Atwood, E. Bagby. *The Regional Vocabulary of Texas*. Austin,
Texas, 1962.

Atwood, E. Bagby. *A Survey of Verb Forms in the Eastern
United States*. Ann Arbor, 1953.

Bright, Elizabeth. *A Word Geography of California and Nevada*.
Berkeley and Los Angeles, 1971.

Kurath, Hans. *A Word Geography of the Eastern United States*.
Ann Arbor, 1949.

Kurath, Hans, and Raven I. McDavid, Jr. *The Pronunciation of
English in the Atlantic States*. Ann Arbor, 1961.

Kurath, Hans, et al. *Handbook of the Linguistic Geography of
New England*. Providence, 1939. Second edition, enlarged,
New York, 1973.

GENERAL AMERICAN: AN AMBIGUITY

William R. Van Riper

Various labels have been applied to various types of American English, both factual and hypothetical, but no label and the hypotheses behind it have engendered as much controversy as General American, and none has shown such a confusing array of meanings. General American has been used to designate a regional type of American English, a type of American English which transcends all American regional boundaries, a variously constituted body of speech features of American English found in the speech of the great majority of Americans, and a set of American dialects which, perhaps by definition, share certain features under discussion, but which are represented by the speech of one person, a small number of persons, or by a generalized study. As a term for a regional variety of American English, its domain at various times has been thought to extend westward to the Rocky Mountains or the Pacific Coast from the Connecticut River, from the Hudson River, from New England, from parts of New York City, from New Jersey, or from Ohio. It has even been given territory as far northeast as Maine.

How did such a term get its start, and how did it spread?

Before the early years of the 1930s, the usual terms for the major dialects of American English, as they were recognized, were Eastern or New England, Southern, and Northern or Western.

In the mid and late 1920's, two works dealing with the mass of American English were published, George Philip Krapp's *The English Language in America* in 1925 and Hans Kurath's *American Pronunciation* in 1928.[1] These works dealt not with a local or regional variety of American English, but with the collected varieties as they were then understood. Kurath's work dealt with pronunciation, listing features for the major dialect areas as scholars thought them to be at that time, and defining the boundaries of these areas. Krapp's work, appearing earlier, dealt with a wider spectrum of American English and offered new terms along with the old for the regional types of speech, but it did not set geographical boundaries as such. Among the new terms offered by Krapp was General American.

From *Lexicography and Dialect Geography: Festgabe für Hans Kurath*, edited by H. Schaller and J. Reidy. Franz Steiner Verlag, 1973, pp 232-242. Reprinted with permission.

Although he may not have been the originator of the term General American, Krapp is certainly responsible for its early dissemination.[2] Krapp offered not only General American English as a label for that type of American speech which was neither Eastern nor Southern, but others as well: "a general or Western speech," "This general speech," "the Eastern, the Southern, and the Western, or General types," "General American English," "the General type," "General American," "the Western or General type of pronunciation," "the Western General type", and "Western or General American English" were all used by him in *The English Language in America*.[3] The use of general with a lower case g would appear to be confusing, since one would expect General if this designated a "third" type of speech and not merely a common, widespread, or supraregional type.[4] Krapp apparently meant each of these things.

When Krapp used general in his new designation, he referred to a type of speech which he considered not distinctively Eastern or Southern, and which transcended regional boundaries. It thus occupied the third area, and at the same time occurred in the other two. Krapp said, "One may say that in America three main types of speech have come to be recognized, a New England local type, a Southern local type, and a general or Western speech covering the rest of the country, and all speakers in New England and the South at the moments when their speech is not local in character."[5] Thus, he had discovered the standard for which he had searched, if the case were true. But this seemed to some scholars too great an assumption to make and they attacked it.[6]

If Krapp was the first to use these terms in addition to Western, John S. Kenyon was the moving force who popularized General American as the term to represent the type of speech with which Krapp was concerned. As an editor of the journal *American Speech*, Kenyon used General American in the "Usage Department" of the publication as early as 1928 to refer to the third type of American speech.[7] In the Preface to the First Edition of his enormously successful *American Pronunciation*, reprinted in subsequent editions, he declared that he had used the cultivated pronunciation of the Western Reserve of Ohio as the basis for his observations on cultivated speech.[8] In 1930 in the Preface to the Fourth Edition of the book, Kenyon asserted that Krapp's term General American applied to the type of pronunciation which was recorded in *American Pronunciation*, and went on to state that ninety million speakers used the General American type.[9] The employment of the term in the Fourth Edition was not complete, however. Here General American was substituted for the North and for Northern American in several places, but Northern American still remained.[10] In following editions, Kenyon repeatedly used General American and its abbreviation, GA. Thus the term came to be applied specifically to forms used in the cultivated speech of the Western Reserve of Ohio, a type of speech which Kenyon believed "virtually uniform in its most noticeable features

from New York state west, in the region north of a line drawn
west from Philadelphia."[11]   The term suggested a standard, and
now there was a printed body of forms to illustrate it.

In the 1930's the term General American was advanced by
writers and scholars who had both general and special interests
in the regional varieties of American English.   It was used as
both General American and general American by Kenyon in the
Guide to Pronunciation of the Second Edition of *Webster's New International Dictionary* .   Here General American was used in reference to one of "three main types of cultivated speech," equating
it to Western and Midwestern and contrasting it with the Eastern
and the Southern.   "The general American type" was used to
refer to a type of cultivated regional speech which, like Southern
British, had spread beyond its earlier limits.[12]

The term appeared in 1934 in *Dialect Notes* in a committee
report from A. A. Hill to the American Dialect Society suggesting
that the speech of a single speaker of Southern American English
be compared phonemically with General American.[13]   Stuart Robertson used it in his *Development of Modern English* (1934), along with
the General or Western type and General, to refer to the speech
of a particular area and to a type of American speech which
exhibited features of pronunciation which could be compared with
British pronunciation.[14]   Arthur G. Kennedy in *Current English*
(1935) favored Western or Western American, but on occasion he
also used General in conjunction with it, as "General, or Western,
American dialect," and "the Western, or General, type" to refer
to illustrative passages in phonetic characters, to particular pronunciations, and to a type of speech which was encroaching on
the "New England and Southern dialects."[15]   Albert C. Baugh
not only adopted the term General American, called by him "the
dialect of the Middle States and the West" in his *History of the
English Language* (1935), but he also provided a map of the three
speech areas as they were then understood and included a list of
distinguishing features for the speech of these areas.[16]   H. L.
Mencken in the Fourth Edition of *The American Language* (1936) used
the term to refer to "the speech with which the present volume
mainly deals."   In the Index to this edition, however, it was
Western American and not General American which was entered.
But it was General American which was widely used and discussed
in Supplement II (1948) and which appeared there as the main
entry in the Index with cross references at competing entries to
direct the reader to General American.[17]

The investigations of American speech in the 1930's and 1940's
provided scholars with evidence that American speech was not as
homogeneous as had been thought earlier, and that the dialect
areas and speech types, as they had been proposed, would require
more rigorous definition.[18]   By 1940 it was possible to sketch the
boundary separating the Northern and Midland areas in the Great
Lakes and Ohio Valley regions, a zone running across the area
which had been thought of as showing a uniformity which entitled
General American to be called the third and largest major regional

linguistic entity in the United States.[19] In 1949, the appearance
of Hans Kurath's *A Word Geography of the Eastern United States*
presented a mass of factual lexical data from the investigations
of the Linguistic Atlas of the United States and Canada which
showed that the supposedly unified General American area in the
Eastern United States did not exist, but that in reality a bundle
of isoglosses cut through it from east to west to mark the boundary
between a Northern and a Midland area.[20] E. Bagby Atwood's *A Survey of Verb Forms in the Eastern United States*, published in
1953, demonstrated that morphological features showed the same
patterning.[21] Thus, by the early 1950's the concept of General
American as the third regional variety of American English had
been tested and proven to be false. Analyses of Linguistic Atlas
data such as that presented by Albert H. Marckwardt in his
"Principal and Subsidiary Dialect Areas in the North-Central
States," by Raven I. McDavid, Jr., in W. Nelson Francis' *The
Structure of American English* and by the independent study of
C. K. Thomas continued to drive home the point.[22]

Some scholars responded to these facts by redefining the
General American area, others by abandoning the concept of General American entirely. Still others ignored them, some maintaining
that the data and the analyses of them did not represent or
apply to cultivated usage, or that the analyses had only a marginal
application as far as pronunciation was concerned. Baugh responded by redefining the dialect area and, although retaining the
term General American, took recognition of the work which had
been done in the Eastern states.[23] For the territory beyond the
Eastern states, however, he still used the term General American.
This was essentially the position taken by C. M. Wise.[24] On the
other hand, Frederic G. Cassidy, revising Robertson's *The Development of Modern English*, abandoned both the term and its regional
orientation, adopting instead the regional organization suggested
by and included in the newer studies.[25] By 1947, C. K. Thomas,
who collected data by interview and tape recording for his analyses
of pronunciation, had cut the lower eastern portion of the old
General American domain into two areas, "Middle Atlantic" and
"Western Pennsylvania." He had abandoned the idea of General
American as a regional type of speech by 1958, having concluded
on the basis of his continuing investigation that the area which
he had earlier classified as General American in fact contained
four different types of speech and four separate areas.[26] Some
of those with different purposes who retained General American
as the term for a type of speech or pronunciation which was
neither Eastern nor Southern relied in part upon such works as
Kenyon's *American Pronunciation*, which in editions after the Fourth
used the term with greater and greater frequency, upon Kenyon
and Knott's *A Pronouncing Dictionary of American English*, and
upon other studies made when or where the term General American
was either in wider favor or in looser use.[27] Such works, for
the most part, set General American as a point of departure, a
standard for a comparison, or else they suggested it as a model,

with examples, to be copied. Herman and Herman's *Manual of American Dialects for Radio, Stage, Screen and Television*, for example, used General-American, a hyphenated form of the label, with Middle Western pronunciation as the model for comparison. The authors commented to the effect that the speech of the Middle West "comes as close to being General-American speech" as any American dialect.[28]   Clifford Prator, Jr., in his *Manual of American Pronunciation* referred to the type of English upon which the book was based as General American, the authority being Kenyon and Knott's *A Pronouncing Dictionary of American English*.[29]   The *NBC Handbook of Pronunciation* also used General American as its basis of pronunciation, although the model for actual pronunciations was the speech of certain eminent radio announcers, since it was thought that the speech of these men resembled General American more than it did Southern or Eastern.[30]

The interest in American English in Germany after the Second World War saw the term also used there in treatises on American speech.   Sometimes General American was borrowed directly and used as such abroad, but it also appeared as a loan translation in several forms in German works - "Allgemein-Amerikanisch," "Gemein-Amerikanisch," and "Gemeinamerikanisch." General American was sometimes added after the loan translation to insure the meaning of the term, and sometimes the loan translation was added after another regional designation.[31]   The term "Common American" also appears.   Probably a new coinage based on General American, it is used at least once by Brunner in the First Edition of *Die Englische Sprache*, but the Second Edition makes use of newer studies and presents more modern findings on the regional structure of the major American dialects, and the term apparently has disappeared.[32]

In some American publications of the 1960s, the term continues to appear.   It is used in two encyclopedias early in the decade as the title for one of the major dialects of American English, it appears in general treatises on phonetics and American pronunciation, it is employed in at least one study of an American dialect to represent a body of features with which another body of features can be compared, it is attacked by dialect scholars, and it gains entry status in an increasing number of dictionaries.[33]

American dictionaries, in fact, provide some interesting insights into the status and meanings of the term, although dictionaries by the very mechanics involved in their undertaking may sometimes represent matters as they were a decade or more before their publication.   When General American first appeared in a dictionary, the term apparently was used only in the introductory pages, where it referred to a very widespread regional variety of American English.   In *Webster's New International Dictionary*, Second Edition, of course, it represented some kind of a standard, supraregional type as well.   Next, the term appeared in both the introductory pages and in the body of the dictionary.   In dictionary practice today it appears to be unusual in the introductory pages, rather common as an entry.[34]

Although the Second Edition of *Webster's New Internation-al Dictionary* used the term in its Guide to Pronunciation both with and without a capital g̲ throughout the course of its numerous printings, the term apparently was never given an entry form in the body of that edition. In 1951, it was entered in *Webster's New World Dictionary* as General American, the form most dictionaries now use. The *New World* used the term in the introductory pages to refer to the type of American English, specifically the "Central variety of General American English," which provided most of the pronunciations recorded in this dictionary.[35]   In another section, it was realistically explained that General American, as it was used, really represented a body of dialects rather than a single dialect and that further study might lead to the abandoning of the term.[36]   Between the appearance of this dictionary in 1951 and that of the 1957 College Edition, the editors made an interesting change in terminology in the introduction. When the dictionary appeared in 1951, part 1.15 of the introductory section titled The English Language read, "The pronunciation recorded in this dictionary is largely that of the Western Reserve of Ohio, especially as used by literate speakers in the city of Cleveland. It represents a type of American English used, with relatively minor variations, in the whole of the Central, the Middle Western, the Northwestern Middle Western, the Western New England, and the Middle Atlantic States,"   By 1957, the first sentence had become, "The pronunciation recorded in this dictionary is largely that of General American, especially as used by literate speakers in the central part of the country," and the narrow regional basis of the pronunciation entries was obscured, since the central part of the country includes such cities as Chicago, St. Louis, and Wichita.[37]   The term is entered in the body of this dictionary as General American and defined as "the English language as conversationally spoken by most people in the greater part of the United States, exclusive of much of New England and most of the South."   Since the term is defined as "the English language as conversationally spoken," it encompasses morphology, syntax, lexicon, and pronunciation.

The dictionaries which have appeared in the 1960's have taken differing attitudes toward the term, most defining it in the body of the work, but usually leaving it out of the introductory discussion. *Webster's Third New International Dictionary* does a turn-about from the *Second* in this respect.[38]   The term is entered in the body, but not in the introductory material. The main entry is "general american <u>n, sometimes cap G and cap A</u>." It is noteworthy that this entry recognizes the form with an initial lower-case g̲, strange that enough instances with a lower-case a̲ have been found to warrant mention. The definition, "the native speech of natives of the U.S. whose speech is not that of the South or of the r-dropping Northeast; <u>specif</u>: such speech exclud-ing that of the Middle Atlantic states and western Pennsylvania," shows in its qualification the restrictions imposed upon the old concept of a General American area by some of the scholarly studies which appeared in the late 1940's and the 1950's. Some definitions offered by dictionaries of the 1960's define the term only in the frame of the older concept of a third area, speech type, or pronunciation type which is not that of New England or the South, and some also add New York City. These dictionaries in addition usually qualify the main definition or the term itself in some way, restricting it, equating it with another term, or commenting on its status. *Funk and Wagnalls Standard College Dictionary* (1963) defines General American as "American English as spoken in the United States with the exception of the South, a large part of New England, and the New York City area," and then goes on to say "a term now rejected by many linguists."[39] The qualification is true as far as it goes, but it does not make the important point that many linguists not only reject the term, but also reject the hypothesis that the speech of this area is of a uniform type.

Still another type of definition in its qualification equates General American with a more current term and supposes some sort of identity between the two. *The World Book Encyclopedia Dictionary* of 1963 gives the main entry General American and defines this as "the variety of English spoken in most of the United States, exclusive of New York City, the South, and New England. As a regional dialect, it is currently called Midland by most language scholars."[40] Equating General American with Midland, of course, further confuses the issue. The geographical boundaries which have been determined for the Midland area are not those various ones which have been set forth for General American. The North Midland and the South Midland together constitute the Midland, and the Inland North dialect area stretches westward from the Northeastern New England and the Hudson Valley areas. Upstate New York is not Midland, and the elastic boundaries of the traditional General American domains have not extended into the South Midland. It is highly unlikely that scholars seriously concerned with the study of the dialects of the United States would equate these two terms.

There is yet another type of qualification which is used in defining the term, one which restricts by example. This is illustrated in the entry of the unabridged *Random House Dictionary of the English Language* , which appeared in 1966.[41] A precursor of this work at Random House, *The American College Dictionary* , used as the main entry General American Speech.[42] In the First Printing (1947), the entry was defined as "the pattern of speech, including articulation, pronunciation, intonation, etc., characteristic of speakers native to the region west of the Hudson river and north of the Mason-Dixon line (except for eastern Texas)." By the printing of 1953, the definition had lost its strict geographical limits and had become "the pronunciation of English typical of American speakers not native to New England, New York City or the South."[43] In *The Random House Dictionary* (1966), the geographical limits have disappeared entirely from the definition and General American Speech is defined as "a pronunciation of American

English showing few regional peculiarities: <u>Most U.S. radio and television announcers use General American Speech.</u>" Thus, although General American may have lost the regional boundaries which it acquired after Krapp set it loose, it nonetheless has gained the supraregional status which he thought it to have, but now recognized in a professional dialect which is acquired through special schooling by many of its users, whereby they receive instruction and practice in how to talk alike.

When Krapp advanced the term with its multiple forms and several meanings it was quickly accepted and extended by other scholars, although not much actual field work had been undertaken to establish just what the distinctive speech areas were west of the states along the Eastern Seaboard. The term had the advantage of not being restricted by geographical connotations, a handicap for its chief competitors, Western and Northern. Since the type of speech was thought to extend westward from western New England, referring to the way people talked in New Mexico as Northern and in New Jersey as Western had obvious disadvantages. Kenyon, in adopting the term to describe the type of speech used in his *American Pronunciation*, gave it a printed body of pronunciations which grew with every new edition of his text, and those dictionaries which stated that General American was the basis for their pronunciation entries further increased the stock - to the extent of the inventory of words in the dictionary, even though these were recorded in a semi-phonemic alphabet.

A dialect, however, is a complex of speech features together with their regional and social distribution. At the first, the presence of postvocalic, tautosyllabic, prepausal, and preconsonantal <u>r</u> as such in the pronunciation of the area, together with the presence of [æ] as opposed to [ɑ:] in certain words, served as two of the chief distinguishing markers of the type of speech described as being neither Eastern nor Southern and called General American. Detailed examination of the speech of the Eastern Seaboard and New England has led to a redefinition of the significant features which mark the major speech regions there, however, and the results of similar investigations appear with increasing regularity for the area to the west. Scholars have called attention for some years now to the indications of major dialect boundaries or zones running through the Midwest, and other scholars have taken heed. Dictionaries have come to recognize General American with entry forms and with definitions. It is not especially surprising that some of those definitions are misleading, since the term was at first applied to the American English which was left after two major dialects were accounted for.

The term General American has been with us for a least forty-five years, and during this time both speech types and linguistic areas have been obscured by its title. The term, ambiguous when it was proposed, has become more ambiguous with each definition which has been attempted. Although perhaps General American served a need for a while by functioning as a term without narrow geographical connotations, nonetheless the

real contribution which it has made to dialect study may be quite
different. This contribution is simply the confirmation of a truth
long known to dialect scholars, that neither a linguistic type nor
a dialect area can be determined with any degree of validity
unless the investigator has comprehensive data with which to
work. A hypothesis is not enough. It is imperative to have the
facts even though an enormous amount of time, effort, and skill
may be required to recognize and collect them.

FOOTNOTES

[1] George Philip Krapp, *The English Language in America*. Two
volumes. New York, 1925; Hans Kurath, *American Pronunciation*
(Society for Pure English Tract XXX), Oxford and New York,
1928.
[2] C. M. Wise in his *Applied Phonetics*, Englewood Cliffs, 1957,
p. 172, footnote 3, comments that he first heard "general American"
used publicly in the early 1920's by Windsor P. Daggett at a
meeting of the National Association of Teachers of Speech. In
all probability others used the term as well, but in nothing as
prominent as *The English Language in America.*
[3] Krapp, Vol. I, pp. 35-40; Vol. II, pp. 29, 230, 289.
[4] J. S. Hall uses "general American" with a small g in his
discussion of pronunciation in the Smoky Mountains. Since he
also refers to "The usual American [ε]" (p. 18), "standard American" (p. 26), and "the normal American variety" (p. 27), it is
difficult to determine whether he intends the term to apply consistently to a dialect of American English. See Joseph S. Hall,
The Phonetics of Great Smoky Mountain Speech. (*American Speech*,
Reprints and Monographs no. 4), New York, 1942. The form
with a lower-case g also is used in the article headed "English",
in the *Golden Home and High School Encyclopedia*, Twenty volumes,
New York (1961), Vol. 6, p. 877, and by Allen Walker Read in
his discussion of the term in his article "The Labeling of National
and Regional Variation in Popular Dictionaries," *International Journal of American Linguistics* 28 (1962), pp. 217-227. Recognition
of this form also is given in the entry in *Webster's Third New International Dictionary*, unabridged, Springfield (1961).
[5] Krapp, Vol. I, p. 35. On Page 39, in discussing the use
of [ɑ ꞉] and [æ], he said, "The South thus tends toward the
pronunciation of the General type in these words, and New England
towards the Eastern type."
[6] Hans Kurath in his review of *The English Language in America*, in *Language* 3 (1927), p. 132, particularly took exception to
the statement. He pointed out that although the Western type of
American speech had made inroads on the others, nevertheless
there was no recognized standard for American English.

[7]J. S. K., "Usage Department." In: American Speech IV, 2 (1928), p. 153.   Also in IV, 4 (1929), p. 324, and V, 4 (1930), p. 322.

[8]John S. Kenyon, *American Pronunciation*, First Edition, Ann Arbor, 1924, p. iv.

[9]Kenyon, Fourth edition, Ann Arbor 1930, pp. v, 13.

[10]Kenyon, 1930, p. 62: ". . . the author's type of r-sound, which he believes fairly represents that of Northern American English west of New York City."

[11]Kenyon, 1924, p. v.

[12]*Webster's New International Dictionary of the English Language*. Second edition, unabridged. Springfield 1934, pp. xxvi, lii, xliv.   "It has been stated that there are certain extensive regional types of cultivated English speech that have spread far beyond the area of their local origin, as the southern British or the general American type." p. xxvi.

[13]A. A. Hill, "Proposed Investigations of Southern Speech." In: *Dialect Notes* VI, IX (1934), p. 421.

[14]Stuart Robertson, *The Development of Modern English* , New York 1934, pp. 221 ff.

[15]Arthur G. Kennedy, *Current English* , Boston (1935), pp. 89, 165, 168.

[16]Albert C. Baugh, *A History of the English Language*. New York (1935), pp. 446 ff.

[17]H. L. Mencken, *The American Language* , Fourth edition, New York 1936, p. 370; Supplement II, New York 1948.   In the 1963 abridged and revised edition of this work, the term General American appears only in historical reference. In this edition a bibliography of studies of American English of the Midwest, useful in understanding the linguistic geography of the area, appears in footnote 9, p. 463.   H. L. Mencken, *The American Language* , The Fourth Edition and the Two Supplements, Abridged, with Annotations and New Material by Raven I. McDavid, Jr., with the assistance of David W. Maurer. New York 1963.

[18]For a survey of linguistic atlas investigations of this period and beyond which led scholars to more accurate definitions of the speech areas of the United States, see Raven I. McDavid, Jr., and Virginia McDavid, "Regional Linguistic Atlases in the United States," In: *Orbis* 5 (1956), pp. 349-86.   Pages 354 ff., 372 ff. deal with the term General American and the region involved, and with contributions made by Allen, Davis, Eliason, Kurath, the McDavids, Marckwardt, Potter and others to our undertanding of the speech of the areas which had been regarded as General American.

[19]On the basis of westward migrations and the relationship between settlement areas and speech areas in the Atlantic States, Hans Kurath expected to find both a Northern and a Midland region here.   On the basis of data collected under the direction of Albert H. Marckwardt, Kurath presented a map of this zone in Ohio, Indiana, and Illinois. See Hans Kurath, "Dialect Areas, Settlement Areas, and Culture Areas in the United States." In:

The Cultural Approach to History, Caroline F. Ware editor, New York 1940, pp. 331-45. See especially chart 6, p. 341.

[20] Hans   Kurath, *A Word Geography of the Eastern United States*, Ann Arbor 1949.

[21] E. Bagby Atwood, *A Survey of Verb Forms in the Eastern United States* , Ann Arbor 1953.

[22] Albert H. Marckwardt, "Principal and Subsidiary Dialect Areas in the North-Central States." In: *Publication of the American Dialect Society* no. 27 (April, 1957), pp. 3-15. Reprinted in: *Readings in Applied English Linguistics* , Second edition, Harold B. Allen editor, New York (1964), pp. 220-230. Another important article on the linguistic geography of the Midwest, Harold Allen's article "The Primary Dialect Areas of the Upper Midwest," also appears in *Readings* , pp. 231-241; Raven I. McDavid, Jr., "The Dialects of American English." In: W. Nelson Francis, *The Structure of American English*, New York (1958), pp. 480-543, 579-585; Charles Kenneth Thomas, *An Introduction to the Phonetics of American English* , New York (1947); Second edition, New York (1958). In the Second edition, see especially chapter 22, "The Speech Areas."

[23] Baugh, Second edition, New York (1957), pp. 436 ff.

[24] Claude Merton Wise, *Applied Phonetics*, Englewood Cliffs (1957).

[25] Robertson, Second edition. Revised by Frederic G. Cassidy, Englewood Cliffs (1954).

[26] C. K. Thomas, (1947), pp. 144-5; (1958), pp. 216-241.

[27] Kenyon, Tenth edition, sixth printing, Ann Arbor 1966; John S. Kenyon and Thomas A. Knott, *A Pronouncing Dictionary of American English* , Springfield (1944), (1953). It is of interest that in this dictionary the speech regions are referred to as the East, the South, and the North (p. xxxii).

[28] Lewis H. Herman and Marguerite S. Herman, *A Manual of American Dialects for Radio, Stage, Screen, and Television*, New York (1947), pp. xi, 297.

[29] Clifford H. Prator, Jr., *Manual of American English Pronunciation*, Revised edition, New York (1957), pp. xi, xv.

[30] *NBC Handbook of Pronunciation*, compiled by James F. Bender, New York (1943), p. x; Second edition, New York (1951), pp. vi, viii; Third edition, New York (1964), revised by Thomas Lee Crowell, Jr.   In the Third edition, the book is presented as "the standard reference book on pronunciation in General American speech." p. vii.

[31] For example, see Kurt Wittig, *Phonetik des amerikanischen Englisch*, Heidelberg (1956), pp. 27, 63, and Hans Galinsky, *Die Sprache des Amerikaners*, 2 Bde. Heidelberg 1951-52, Bd. I, pp. 3, 138, 150; Bd. II, pp. 479, 486.   Galinsky also uses Gesamt-Amerikanisch (Bd. I, p. 47), perhaps in the sense of supraregional American English. In *Amerikanisches und britisches Englisch*, München 1957, he shifts to more modern terminology and orientation, commenting in footnote 168, p. 39, "Der Terminus General American ist heute umstritten."

[32] Karl Brunner, *Die englische Sprache*. 2 Bde. Halle (Saale) 1950-51; Zweite Auflage. Tübingen 1960-62. See 1951, Bd. II, p. 358.

[33] "English." In: *The Golden Home and High School Encyclopedia*, Vol. 6, p. 877. "American English," In: *The Encyclopedia International*, First edition, twenty volumes, New York (1963), Vol. 1, p. 345; Mark Twomey, "Attitudes of Americans toward Pronunciation." In: *The Speech Teacher* XII, 3 (1963), pp. 204-213. Twomey puts General American as far north as Maine (p. 206); Charles T. Brown and Charles Van Riper, *Speech and Man*, Englewood Cliffs (1966), p. 11; Börje Holmberg, "Noah Webster and American Pronunciation." In: *English Studies* XLVI, 2, Arngart anniversary number (1965), pp. 118-129, especially pp. 122-3; Ralph Vanderslice and Laura Shun Pierson, "Prosodic Features of Hawaiian English." In: *Quarterly Journal of Speech* LIII, 2 (1967), pp. 156-166. The "North Midland dialect" of one of the authors is used as representative of General American and contrasted to Pidgin; Allen Walker Read, 1962, p. 224. Read mentions some of the inadequacies of the term general American and suggests the term generalized American for the speech along the Northern-Midland boundary in the Middle West.

[34] Not all scholars are yet convinced that the old General American concept has lost its usefulness in the discussion of American dialects. Morton Bloomfield takes such a stand in the introductory pages of *The American Heritage Dictionary of the English Language*, William Morris editor, Boston (1969), p. xvii. However, this dictionary does not have an entry for General American. Bloomfield and Newmark argue elsewhere that the lexical evidence and phonological evidence seem to contradict each other in part in the classification of American dialects, but agree that lexical evidence suggests major horizontal divisions. Morton Bloomfield and Leonard Newmark, *A Linguistic Introduction to the History of English*, New York 1963, pp. 194-5.

[35] *Webster's New World Dictionary of the American Language*, Encyclopedic edition, Joseph H. Friend and David B. Guralnik general editors. Two volumes. Cleveland (1951), Vol. I, p. x.

[36] *New World Dictionary*, p. xvii.

[37] *Webster's New World Dictionary of the American Language*, College edition, Joseph H. Friend and David B. Guralnik general editors, Cleveland (1957), p. xvii.

[38] *Webster's Third New International Dictionary of the English Language*, Unabridged, Phil B. Gove editor in chief, Springfield (1961).

[39] *Funk and Wagnalls Standard College Dictionary*, Text edition, Ramona R. Michaelis supervising editor, New York (1963).

[40] *The World Book Encyclopedia Dictionary*, Clarence L. Barnhart editor in chief, Chicago (1963).

[41] *The Random House Dictionary of the English Language*,   Unabridged edition, Jess Stein editor in chief, New York (1966). The qualification does not appear in the entry in the College edition of this dictionary, edited by Laurence Urdang, New York (1968).

[42] *The American College Dictionary*, Clarence L. Barnhart editor, New York (1947).

[43] *The American College Dictionary*, Text edition, Clarence L. Barnhart editor, New York (1953).

THE SPEECH OF RURAL NEW ENGLAND

Audrey R. Duckert

A statement on the speech of rural New England in terms of
cultural pluralism means, I should guess, both a look and a
listening in an attempt to try to find out how people who have
grown up looking at life and talking about it in their own distinctive
ways manage to get along when they find themselves needing,
wanting, or having to be neighbors with people whose ways of
looking at life, living it, and talking about it are very different
indeed. The past fifteen years have seen a migration of city-dwell-
ers, many of them from other states, into rural areas of New
England that were characterized in the *Handbook of the Linguistic
Geography of New England* (Kurath et al, 1939) as, e.g. "Historic
shire town with decreasing population. Agriculture." (Newfane,
Vermont). The January, 1977, issue of Blair and Ketchum's *Country Journal*, a back-to-the-land magazine that has been thriving
in southern Vermont for four years now, printed this classified
advertisement on page 94: NEWFANE, VERMONT--Clever, contemporary cluster house, 3-car garage, 2 wooded acres. Three
complete units rented, or ideal for large family and home business.
. . .

In North Ferrisburg, Vermont--"entirely agricultural" says
the *Handbook*,--a 69-year old farmer-carpenter told the *Atlas* field
worker--a very young Bernard Bloch--"I only wish that God would
call this heaven and let me alone. I don't ask anything better
than this." It is perhaps as well that he could not have lived to
see the coming of the superhighway that now runs near his old
home. (Part of Bloch's description of his speech says "final
consonants weak"; the sound of the traffic would drown them out
entirely today.)

The speech and lifeways of the urban migrants to rural new
England should eventually be considered too; but for now it
would seem better and wiser to view and hear the linguistic
changes that seem to be connected with that migration from the
perspective of the old-dwellers.

How does, or how did, the country Yankee make out in
dealing with his city cousins; and more recently how with total
strangers or "outlanders" who have been moving relentlessly north

and sometimes east from the New York-New Jersey metropolitan area? The "gray-flannel-suit" commuters in southwestern Connecticut have been augmented by the A-Frame people who go to the ski areas and the music festivals further north. Unlike the summer visitors of years ago who came and then went away, these people--often more affluent than the locals--buy land and build on it. Sometimes they buy lots of land and develop it. Connecticut has no state income tax; neither does New Hampshire, and the property taxes in less populated areas in most of New England were fairly low when the migration began.

But let me not leave my own area and go out of my depth talking about sociology, regional planning, urban sprawl, and rural slums--all of which are nevertheless real factors to consider in rural New England today, and all of which in some way must indeed impinge upon the English language heard and spoken there. In another fifty years, the speech of the remaining A-Frame pioneers in Stowe, Vermont, and of their descendants must, in honesty, be considered representative of the speech of the region --even as Elder Brewster's English took over from the Wampanoags three and a half centuries ago.

And so we must keep track. It is a Yankee way of life, keeping track. The dates of the first snowfall ("enough to track a cat") must be recorded, whether on the barn wall, in a diary, or in a black loose-leaf book like the one Emma Bowen kept on top of the refrigerator (which she, of course, called the *ice chest*) so she'd always know where it was. It is important to continue keeping track of the language and the society that uses it, whose life and living it both reflects and shapes. The settlement history so carefully researched by Marcus Hansen for the *LANE* and neatly mapped in the *Handbook* , is by no means a static phenomenon. Religious dissent was often the reason for early population movements; the present shifts may differ in etiology, but they, too, will eventually have their effect on the language.

A number of communes were set up in rural New England in the late Sixties; some of them continue. Here, too, is an influence on speech, especially since it would tend to introduce a greater diversity. Rob Ripley lives on a farm on Chestnut Hill Road in Montague, Massachusetts, right on the Leverett town line, territory that has been more or less in his family for nearly 200 years. Among his neighbors are the members of a commune and also a young couple--both of them city children--who want to love the land and guard the wilderness with all the zeal that converts are known to exhibit. The commune residents, some of them college students or ex-students, seem to come and go. The young couple, Jim and Linda, bought their land from Rob, who even agreed to a jagged boundary so they could include part of the brook and some trees they particularly liked. Jim comes from an Irish-English background on the North [of Boston] shore; Linda's Polish forbears came to this country more recently, and she grew up in a mill town near Springfield. The commune may drift on or it may drift away; Linda and Jim appear to have a deeper, more private commitment.   Rob Ripley is friendly and helpful to them all, for that is his nature.   He gives them advice on when to plant potatoes and on basic matters such as how to fell a tree so it will land in the right place.   They occasionally lend a hand during the busy season in his sugar house where he makes maple syrup each spring in his wood-fired evaporator just as surely as the sap rises in the trees along his roadsides.   And so these new and old residents meet and help out, and in doing so, they talk.   Rob's speech is much like that of his neighbors in New Salem, who were recorded by Bernard Bloch in 1931-32 for *LANE*; his younger friends have all had exposure to other varieties of English--Jim and Linda met while they were students at the University of Massachusetts; Jim did a tour in Viet Nam, Linda taught in Connecticut; on the linguistic gallimaufry of the nearest commune I have no recent information.

This is a real situation in my own north forty, so to speak, but it is a microcosm of what has been happening in rural New England during the last fifteen years.   Only time and later surveys will or can tell what effects it may have or have had on the base line of the common speech of the area.   I know the old base fairly well by now, and enough about its speakers to doubt they will change their speech ways or that they really care very much about the difference.   They are not mobile and have little desire to be--if we use the word in its current cliche context of being "upwardly mobile", which seems to mean get a more prestigious job and move to a more expensive neighborhood.   They may be aware that their [e:ja?]s and [mɛbɪ]s get imitated by the outlanders, but their own lives are hardly threatened by this.   How the children and grandchildren of the older, surer group get on with the "new people" who are their age remains to be seen. I'm not sure how far we need to go in studying personal and community relationships.   Dignity and privacy and our right to both demand a line that need not, should not, be crossed in the name of research.   There are limits to the need to know.

The popular, public image of the speech of rural New England might also be examined.   Over the years it has run quite a course--from Sam Slick to Dr. Holmes's Deacon and on through Calvin Coolidge to the contemporary monologist Marshall Dodge, who was born in Brooklyn, N.Y., and whose popular "Bert and I" recordings supposedly give us electronically the pawky wit and wisdom of downeast Maine--Wiscasset, to be exact.   The speech and its speakers are often presented--for outside consumption--as quaint and comic, yet infinitely sage, even while sounding countrified and naive.   Speech ways and life ways are supposedly equatable, but this is only partly true.   The language of the urban newcomer is not *ipso facto* refined or cultured or mannered or high-falutin any more than the up-country New England talk is always plain, truthful, direct, and marked by great verbal economy.   Both descriptions may be partly true: the third-generation Yale man on the ski slopes might come by the use of the

imperfect subjunctive in a condition contrary to fact just as naturally as a hilltown sawmill operator uses [eːjaˀ] to register agreement or says quietly, "I don't tell everything I know," in response
to a nosy question.   Language differences are not noted by the
educated alone; indeed, country people may be less tolerant of
the differences, more put off by them, more uncomfortable with
citified or affected speech.   They may also keep silent rather
than risk a grammatical error in the presence of those with more
formal education. (*Some* country people might, that is. One thing
one learns from Yankees is to qualify every possible statement.)
The urban folk, conceivably with an element of condescension,
appear less troubled by speech differences and more likely
to savor country speech than to reject it.

The *LANE* had a predominance of rural and small-town informants, yet map 449 TOURIST, which gives the country word for
the city visitor, has only twelve items, and notes the frequent
pronunciation [tɑurist] of a word that apparently still had a
strange air about it.   The map and commentary at 450 A RUSTIC
have sixty-two terms.   The Commentary begins: "The map shows
a great variety of terms, largely derogatory and jocular, applied
to a person who lives in the country--specifically to an old farmer
who seldom visits the village or city."   (The informant from
North Ferrisburg, Vermont, quoted earlier, responded with *green -
horn* and *gawky* ; an informant a few miles to the east, in Northfield,
said *Vermont crocker.*)   One term, *coof*, appears in both commentaries, and may involve an interpretation of data: Nantucket
informant two says it is an old word, used of someone who is not
a native; his response is recorded at TOURIST; informant three
says a *coof* is a Cape-Codder, an *off-islander*, and her answer
appears at RUSTIC.

Dude and *city slicker* have been the common, almost standard
terms for an urban person in a rural setting, with *summer people* ,
summer visitor, or *summer complaint* heard in vacation areas.   But
even now there is a change--a social and psychological one that
is documented in the growing number of unflattering terms natives
or long-time residents apply to the newcomers.

To consider the local speech of Cape Cod or Martha's Vineyard
as rural might require a stretch of the definition of the word
today, yet there is no question that the dialect remains firmly
regional and that the people to whom it belongs continue to use
it naturally and to regard it--when they think about it--as a
part of the local identity.   (They used to say that if you asked
to rent a [bot] in Maine, it was two dollars a day, but if you
asked for a [bɐt] it was only a dollar.   The prices have probably
gone up, but the distinction may just abide.)

A recent, albeit limited survey, asking specifically for local
pejoratives applied to new residents produced these: *sea gull*
(usually preceded by at least two even more pejorative adjectives
or "delete-able adjectives" in political terminology), *dead cod*, and
off - Cape (all of these from Cape Cod), and *summer gink* from

Martha's Vineyard. *Turkey* as a term of opprobrium for an outsider is apparently common in ski areas outside New England as well; but the suggestion that it comes from *tourist* is dubious; anybody who knows how stupid and ungainly turkeys are would not require phonetic similarity. In addition, the word appears to have general currency in casual, unflattering speech, equated roughly with *klutz*, *nerd*, and *plonk*.

This recent evidence for what could be designated as "the locals strike back" represents an acceleration of the introduction of terms for the outsiders. Some of the earlier ones were not totally disparaging, since the "summer complaint" also brought money into communities where cash was often scarce. But the situation was different in the Swift River Valley in Western Massachusetts when, in the 1930s, four entire towns were being demolished and the woods around them leveled to make way for the Quabbin Reservoir, the chief water supply for metropolitan Boston. Naturally, there was bitterness among the people whose homes were taken by eminent domain, and it was not alleviated much by the arrival in the area of a considerable number of unemployed and unskilled men, mostly from the Boston area, who were sent to cut the trees. The tools then were axes and crosscut saws, and the men were inept. "Don't know one end of an axe from t'other," is the most charitable and printable description used by a former resident. Their official title may have been *woodcutters*, but almost by universal acclaim, the Valley people called these men *woodpeckers*, and the two groups had a distinctly "them-and-us" relationship in which little love was lost.

"Non-standard Variation in White Speech" is the rubric under which these remarks are to appear, and it is not an entirely easy one in terms of the speech of *up-country Yankees*, as they are called and as many of them call themselves. To call one variety of language non-standard assumes another variety to which the term standard can accurately and justly be applied. The tapes and written records of rural New England language in the *LANE* Revisited collection do indeed contain ample instance of things that would be frowned upon by many a purist, by the College Entrance Examination Board, or by the Dale Carnegie Course. They even hold examples of the finite *be*, ("You know where the blueberry bushes be, don't you?") that would qualify as Black English under some definitions.

To distinguish standard from non-standard here may be asking too much but it is certainly possible to note certain features that mark varieties of a language and that its speakers themselves use as markers in sorting each other out. Speakers may call the other varieties anything from quaint to crude to high-falutin, but they certainly recognize the fact of difference. That may or may not be a happy distinction.

In conclusion, then, an assortment of features observed in rural New England during the past decade that have been rarely or not at all observed in urban speech during the same period:

PHONOLOGICALLY:

diphthongization in words like *machine* and *drain*, i.e.
[maǐijan], [dreijan]
a glide before [u] in *new*
raising and fronting of [æ] in *sap*, *had*, *strap*
[æu] rather than [au] in *how*, *about*
[a] surviving in *father*, *palm*
[i] final in *pity*, *city*

LEXICALLY:

In addition to the social innovations noted above, the retention of some relics: *serenade*, *yelk* and *yulk* (of an egg),
tunnel (funnel), *clothespress*, and *thank-you-ma'am* (in a road).

STRESS PATTERNS:

Stress on the second element in compounds such as: *maple*
'*tree*, *band* '*concert*, *polar* '*bear*, *battle* '*field*.

SYNTAX AND IDIOM:

up attic (cf. *down cellar*, which appears to be common and
standard.)
be there for 7:30, which means to be there at or by 7:30,
usually in the context of going to work.
I went *to school to* her, i.e. she was my teacher--usually in
context of grade or, occasionally, high school.
'*Twouldn't* anything else fit . . .
Couldn't anything but an ox do it . . .
This small sampling shows usages that are predominantly rural
in New England, some of them relics, but apparently very durable
ones.   These distinctions, and some additional ones, are with us
yet.   It remains to be seen if the increase in terms for "outlanders"
represents a trend or an isolated instance in which rural speech,
traditionally assigned lower social status, ends up having the
last word.

ACKNOWLEDGMENTS

Much of the evidence cited here for New England country
speech in the time since the publication of the *Linguistic Atlas of
New England*, for which the field work was finished in 1933, is
unpublished material from tapes and collections made in connection
with the *Linguistic Atlas of New England* Revisited project.   Some
of the speakers cited also served as rural New England informants
for the *Dictionary of American Regional English* (*DARE*).   Thanks
are due the many students who have helped most generously
over the years.

SOUTH MIDLAND PRONUNCIATION

IN THE NORTH CENTRAL STATES

Timothy C. Frazer

The purpose of this study is to determine the northward extent of six South Midland pronunciation features in the North Central states. The six features are the fronted nucleus in the diphthong of words like *ground* [græund]; /u/ preceded by a glide in words like *due* [diu]; glide reduction in the diphthong /ai/ in words like *time* [taəm]; the diphthongization of the vowel of words like *cough*; the checked vowel of *him* as an ingliding diphthong; and similarly the checked vowel of *them* as an ingliding diphthong. Hans Kurath and Raven I. McDavid, Jr. (1961) report all of these variants to be common to the South Midland and Upland South in the eastern United States; they find none to be widely distributed in the North and North Midland, except the ingliding diphthongs of *him* and *them*, which are confined regionally to western Pennsylvania and positionally to syllables under full stress.

Phonological variation within the Midland dialect of the North Central states has received little attention. However, studies by Alva L. Davis (1951), Albert Marckwardt (1957), Raven I. and Virginia Glenn McDavid (1960), and Robert Dakin (1971)[1] have charted the distribution of lexical and grammatical features in this area, as have the more detailed doctoral dissertations by Davis (1948), V. McDavid (1955), and Dakin (1966, including an excellent settlement history of the Ohio valley). Davis's dissertation was the first to establish a Northern–Midland dialect boundary in the area. The Midland, according to his maps, includes roughly the lower four-fifths of Ohio, all of Indiana except the metropolitan area of the Northwest corner, and all of Illinois except the metropolitan area of the northwest corner, and all of Illinois except a northeastern quadrant bounded on the south by the westerly flow of the Illinois River and on the west by the southerly flow of the Rock River. These boundaries in Illinois were later refined by Roger Shuy (1962). Since this study is concerned only with variation within the Midland dialect, it is restricted to the appropriate areas of Ohio, Indiana, and Illinois, plus southern Iowa,

From *American Speech* 53:40-48, 1978. Reprinted with permission.

all of Missouri, and those parts of Kentucky adjoining the Ohio River to determine the western and southern extent of isoglosses. The term "North Central states" here refers specifically to this area.

Evidence was taken from 124 interviews taped for the Dictionary of American Regional English: 28 in Ohio, 16 in Indiana, 46 in Illinois, 7 in Kentucky, 20 in Missouri, and 7 in southern Iowa. At the time these interviews were conducted for DARE (1965-70), almost 70 percent of the informants were over the age of sixty, 16 percent were in their fifties, 10 percent were in their forties, and 7 percent were under the age of forty. Of the population sample, 71 percent had attended more than two years of high school, 31 percent of these high school-educated informants went on to college; 23 percent completed the tenth grade or less. No information was available for the remaining 6 percent. There is no apparent relationship between the phonological variants and either the education or age of the informants.

As part of each interview, the informants read a short passage designed to elicit specific phonological variables. The investigation reported here was limited to this reading passage, the loss of spontaneity being more than compensated for by the uniformity of elicitation. A few informants did not read, but recorded only free conversation. In such cases, I have tried to find an occurrence of each feature in a phonetic environment similar to that of the reading passage. All transcriptions are my own, taken directly from the tapes.

The settlement history of the North Central states and its relationship to speech variation presents a complex problem. It is well known that this part of the Midwest did not offer the physical barriers to migration that are characteristic of the eastern United States. Yet the physical geography of the region had a decided effect on early settlement patterns, as did cultural, economic, and political factors. Since earlier studies of the area-- especially the dissertations of Davis and Dakin--have treated the settlement history of the area extensively, their findings are only outlined here.[2]

Three areas of the eastern states provided the bulk of the English-speaking settlers for the North Central states: South Midlanders from the Upland South, especially from Virginia, West Virginia, Kentucky and Tennessee; North Midlanders from Pennsylvania and New Jersey; and Northerners from New England and New York State. They were later joined by large numbers of Germans.

During the early part of the nineteenth century, settlers from the South Midland were attracted to the North Central states' rivers and wooded bottom lands. Some South Midlanders first settled the southwestern and east central portions of Ohio, while others moved up the Wabash into southwestern Indiana. In Illinois, South Midland settlers first populated the Wabash and Mississippi valleys in the southern half of the state, then moved north to the Sangamon valley around Springfield, and finally scattered west from Springfield across the Illinois River toward Quincy, Illinois, and Hannibal, Missouri, on the Mississippi.   Meanwhile, even more settlers from south of the Ohio River were attracted to Missouri, probably because it was not affected by the antislavery prohibition of the Northwest Ordinance. By 1880 a Southern-born population predominated in most counties of Missouri.

North Midland settlers from Pennsylvania and New Jersey settled most heavily in Ohio. Pennsylvanians occupied the Seven Ranges area along the eastern state line, spreading in somewhat smaller numbers throughout the state. New Jerseyans concentrated on the Symmes Purchase, a small area west of the Little Miami. Elsewhere in the North Central states, however, North Midlanders (mostly Pennsylvanians) were found only in much smaller numbers, scattered throughout central Illinois and Indiana, and concentrating in the Lead Region of Northwestern Illinois.

Ohio itself played the greatest part in the settlement of the states farther west. By the time migration from Ohio began, the railroad and the steel plow made the prairies accessible and tillable so that a wave of Ohioans in the middle nineteenth century inundated northern indiana and a large area of Illinois. The Ohio settlement area of Illinois included the large prairies that cover much of eastern Illinois and the smaller prairies between Peoria and Rock Island.   In Missouri, Ohioans concentrated along the Iowa border in the northwest and in some counties adjoining Kansas.

New Englanders scattered throughout the North Central states but concentrated mainly in three areas: the Western Reserve of Ohio along Lake Erie, the Marietta area, and that part of northeastern Illinois adjoining the Chicago metropolitan area.

Germans settled in four areas: in the Cincinnati area of Ohio, in adjoining parts of southeastern Indiana, along both banks of the Mississippi from Saint Louis south to Kaskaskia, and along the Missouri River west almost to Jefferson City.

DISTRIBUTION OF SOUTHERN AND
SOUTH MIDLAND VARIANTS

THE VOWEL IN *ground*, *scouts*:   NUCLEAR FRONTING AND OTHER VARIANTS.   Kurath and McDavid report the diphthong /au/ to be rendered most frequently throughout the South and South Midland with a fronted nucleus before voiced consonants; the North and North Midland generally have the low central nucleus.   North of the isogloss appearing as a solid line on map 1, informants universally have the low central nucleus; approximately 90 percent of the informants south of the isogloss have the fronted nucleus in either *ground* or *scouts*.   The fronted nucleus is rare in Ohio except in two areas: an isolated area that includes the old U.S. Military District and the city of Chilli-

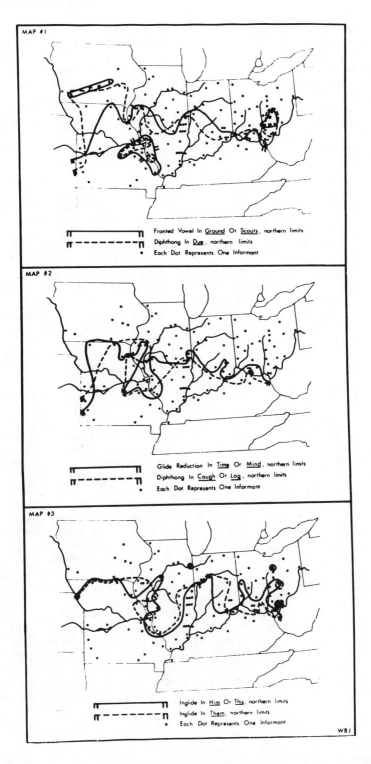

cothe, and a few communities along the Ohio that lie in the old
Virginia Military District.   The fronted nucleus predominates as
well in southwestern Indiana, its northernmost extent being found
along the Wabash valley.   In Illinois, the isogloss moves southward,
skirting the southern edge of the Grand Prairie, then rises again
to include the Sangamon country and the southern Military Tract.
All of Missouri except the Ohio settlements in the northwest and
west have the fronted nucleus.   This feature is given by two
informants, but is otherwise rare in Iowa.

There are, however, some striking exceptions to the regional
distribution of [æu].   A large speech island appears in the
German-settlement area of Missouri and Illinois.   The isogloss
also takes an unexpected southward dip in the Mississippi valley
just south of the Missouri-Iowa state line.   Both the informant in
Hannibal, Missouri, and the informant in Adams County, Illinois,
consistently used the low-central nucleus.

There is also some unexpected positional variation.   Kurath
and McDavid note a mid-central nucleus for /au/ before voiceless
consonants in much of Virginia and West Virginia, with a contrasting fronted nucleus before voiced consonants.   I did not, however,
find the final consonant to predict the fronting-centralization contrast anywhere in Ohio, Indiana, Illinois, or Missouri.   One would
expect fronting to occur more often, for example, in *loud* and
found, since they end in voiced consonants, than in *scouts*, which
ends in a voiceless cluster.   Nevertheless, only 8 informants
south of the *ground-scouts* isogloss had the fronted nucleus in
found, and only four in *loud*.   (The responses of the seven
Kentucky informants, on the other hand, were more predictable
in terms of Kurath and McDavid's data.   Four of them had the
fronted nucleus in *found*, three in *loud*.)   Since the reading
passage does not provide all possible environments for /au/, it
is impossible to formulate from my data a rule that will predict
"South Midland" midwestern vowel fronting according to phonetic
environment.   North of the Ohio, however, fronting occurs most
often in *ground* and *scouts*, least often in *loud* and *found*, with
much variation in *out.*   Because fronting appears most often in
the free-conversation occurrences of *around, county*, and *cow*,
the syllable-initial consonants /r/ and /k/ may condition it, but
the lack of a full range of phonetic environments for analysis
precludes anything more than the crudest speculation.

There is another variant of /au/ in the North Central states
that Kurath and McDavid do not discuss.   Informants throughout
the area with fronting in *ground* and *scouts*, but not in *loud* and
found, frequently have in the latter a low-central nucleus with a
greatly reduced glide--not a well-rounded /u/ or /U/, but [ə],
[ɤ], or length.   Such speakers would virtually rhyme *found* and
fond, the only difference, if any, being a slightly lengthened
vowel in the former.   This reduced glide appeared in the speech
of 4 Ohio informants, 4 Indiana informants, 9 Illinois informants,
and 5 Missouri informants, and does not appear to be common in

the German-settlement areas. None of the Kentucky informants had this feature in *loud* or *found*.

THE VOWEL IN *due*: DIPHTHONGIZATION AND OTHER VARIANTS. Kurath and McDavid report a diphthong [diu] or /dju/ after apical consonants throughout the South and South Midland. This feature is recessive in the North, which has monophthongal /u/, as does the North Midland. In drawing the isogloss that appears as a broken line on map 1, I counted occasional tokens of [ʉ], with a high central vowel, as South Midland. As the map shows, the isogloss for this Southern and South Midland feature usually bundles with that for *ground* and *scouts*. In Indiana and Illinois, the northward distribution of /dju/ is slightly more limited, whereas the variant predominates in southern Iowa. Elsewhere, the contours on map 1 are virtually identical. Once more, the German-settlement areas in Illinois and Missouri are set off as speech islands where South Midland variants are rare, and the U.S. Military District in Ohio is set off as a South Midland speech area in the midst of Yankees and North Midlanders.

THE DIPHTHONG IN *time*, *mind*: GLIDE REDUCTION. In the North Midland, Kurath and McDavid describe this diphthong as a low central nucleus followed by a high front or high central glide. Throughout the South Midland and most areas of the South, the glide is much reduced (except before voiceless consonants), becoming a mid-central or mid-front vowel, or simply vowel length. The solid isogloss on map 2 indicates the northern limits of the area in which this glide reduction is heard in the North Central states, although its frequency and distribution vary from speaker to speaker. North of this isogloss, a high front or high central glide is universal.

The northern limits of this glide reduction are much the same as those for the other South Midland features discussed so far, with some minor variation. In west central Illinois, for example, glide reduction is less common than are other South Midland features, while in Ohio it does not appear in the U.S. Military District. Elsewhere, however, this isogloss follows the same contours as those in map 1. Again, German-settlement areas in Illinois and Missouri appear as speech islands.

THE VOWEL IN *loft*, *cough*, *log*: DIPHTHONGIZATION. Kurath and McDavid find that words like *dog* have a monophthongal pronunciation in the North Midland, either with "open *o*" in eastern Pennsylvania or a lowered vowel in western Pennsylvania. In parts of the south and South Midland this vowel is diphthongized, with considerable variation in the articulation of both the nucleus and the glide. The broken line on map 2 has roughly the same contour as that for the reduced glide of /ai/, except that the South Midland pronunciation of words like *loft* is much more common in west central Illinois. The speech islands from which south Midland features are excluded appear once more.

THE CHECKED VOWELS IN *him*, *them*: INGLIDING DIPHTHONGS. Kurath and McDavid find monophthongal variants for these vowels in the North, ingliding diphthongs in the South and

South Midland. Pennsylvania is a transitional area, with ingliding diphthongs more common in the west. Most Pennsylvanians have monophthongal pronunciations, however, under half stress. Map 3 shows the northern limits of the ingliding diphthongs in *him* (also recorded in *this*) and *them*, which most informants read under half stress. Although these isoglosses have about the same contours as those discussed previously, the northernernmost distribution of the features is greater, perhaps because of west Midland influence. The ingliding diphthongs have made some inroads into the German-settlement areas, although these areas are still set apart.

CONCLUSIONS

The isogloss contours in this study are largely predictable from information about the settlement history of the North Central states. South Midland pronunciation is predominant in southwestern Indiana; in the Wabash, Mississippi, and Sangamon valleys of Illinois; and in all of Missouri except the Ohio settlements of the northwestern parts of the state. Only a small area in southern Ohio--once part of the Virginia Military District--exhibits these South Midland features consistently; in the U.S. Military District of east central Ohio, South Midland variants in *ground* and *due* may still be heard, but not the other features investigated. An intriguing question is raised by the appearance of the German-settlement areas as speech islands lacking South Midland features; the German-settlement area of southeastern Indiana, moreover, corresponds to the southward dip of all isoglosses there. Why do these areas exhibit pronunciation features of the North and North Midland?[3]

Still other questions are raised by the variant pronunciations of /au/ in the North Central states. Are the rules governing nuclear fronting indeed different from those suggested by Kurath and McDavid? And is the pronunciation with a reduced or schwa glide--apparently originating in the South Midland areas of the North Central states--a phenomenon that is spreading? We can answer these questions as soon as the material for the Linguistic Atlas of the North Central States is published. Fieldwork for the Atlas preceded the 1965-70 Dictionary fieldwork by fifteen to thirty years. If this feature is rare or absent in the Atlas field records, it will be clear that the North Central states have a new--and spreading--regional variant.[4]

FOOTNOTES

[1] Dakin is puzzled by the fact that his isoglosses for five Southern or South Midland lexical items (figure 2) do not bundle, but rather crisscross, loop, and whorl. I suspect their pattern is due to the fact that lexical features are individually subject to cultural and economic change that is independent of dialect. *Light bread*, for example, is likely to disappear with home baking, as more and more people go to the supermarket for what is simply labeled *bread*. Pronunciation is not subject to the same kinds of force (Frazer 1973, ch. 5).

[2] I consulted some additional sources for information about the migration of Ohioans and Germans into the North Central states. *The Compendium of the Ninth Census of the United States* (Washington, D.C., 1872) and the *Statistics of the Population of the United States* (Washington, D.C., 1883) both give nativity figures for each county. Perry McCandless, *A History of Missouri* (Columbia, Mo.: Univ. of Missouri Press, 1972), 2: 37, treats the Southern element in Missouri settlement.

[3] The diphthongs [au] and [ai] also occur in standard High German. Although it is possible to posit interference from German, I have elsewhere noted the appearance of a number of Northern and North Midland lexical features in the German-settlement areas of southern Illinois (Frazer 1973). A convincing body of circumstantial evidence indicates that the German settlers accepted the Northern or North Midland dialect as standard, rather than the predominantly south Midland speech of their neighbors. Yankees regarded Southern speech as inferior, and evidently the Germans --observing that the Yankee frequently held the economic power in the small towns and supplied the teachers for the schoolroom-- adopted this attitude as well (Frazer, 1979). Thomas E. Murray of Ohio State University has found a preference for northern forms in the city of St. Louis itself. Aside from the German question, a comparison of the south Midland feature distributions described in this paper with those in LANCS will require further examination. Outside of extreme southern Illinois, for example, LANCS informants rarely have the fronted nucleus of /au/ in *mountain*. An intensive study of McDonough County, Illinois, fronted nucleus *increased* in frequency, despite a "non-standard" designation among normative educators, possibly due to upheavals in rural life during the Depression and postwar era (Frazer, 1983). See also Habick (1980) on the way small-town teenagers use "southern" forms as small-group markers.

[4] This project was partially funded by Western Illinois University Research Grant no. 0610. I am grateful to Frederic G. Cassidy for permission to use the DARE materials.

REFERENCES

Dakin, Robert.   1966.   "The dialect vocabulary of the Ohio
    River Valley: A survey of the distribution of selected
    vocabulary forms in an area of complex settlement history."
    Ph.D. dissertation, Univ. of Michigan.
Dakin, Robert.   1971.   "South Midland speech in the Old North-
    west," *Journal of English Linguistics* 5: 31-48.
Davis, Alva L.   1948.   "A Word Atlas of the Great Lakes re-
    gion." Ph.D. dissertation, Univ. of Michigan.
Davis, Alva L.   1951.   "Dialect distribution and settlement
    patterns in the Great Lakes region." *The Ohio State Archaeo-
    logical and Historical Quarterly* 60: 48-56.
Frazer, Timothy C.   1973.   "The dialect subareas of the Illinois
    Midland." Ph.D. dissertation, Univ. of Chicago.
Frazer, Timothy C.   1979.   "The speech island of the American
    Bottoms: A problem in social history." *American Speech*
    54: 185-193.
Frazer, Timothy C.   1983.   "Sound change and social structure
    in a rural community." *Language in Society* 12: 313-328.
Habick, Timothy.   1980.   "Sound change in Farmer City:
    A sociolinguistic study based on acoustic data."   Ph.D.
    dissertation, Univ. of Illinois-Urbana.
Kurath, Hans, and McDavid, Raven I., Jr.   1961.   *The Pronun-
    ciation of English in the Atlantic States*.   Ann   Arbor:
    Univ. of Michigan Press.
McDavid, Raven I., Jr., and McDavid, Virginia Glenn.   1960.
    "Grammatical differences in the North Central states,"
    American Speech 35: 5-19.
McDavid, Virginia Glenn.   1955.   "Verb forms of the North
    Central States and Upper Midwest."   Ph.D. dissertation,
    Univ. of Minnesota.
Marckwardt, Albert.   1957.   "Principal and subsidiary dialect
    areas in the North-Central States." *Publication of the
    American Dialect Society*, no. 27, pp. 3-15.
Shuy, Roger.   1962.   "The Northern-Midland dialect boundary
    in Illinois." *Publication of the American Dialect Society*,
    no. 38, pp. 1-79.

THE PRIMARY DIALECT AREAS

OF THE UPPER MIDWEST

Harold B. Allen

In 1949 Hans Kurath, drawing upon the materials of the three Atlantic coast atlases for his *Word Geography of the Eastern United States*, made obsolete the traditional tripartite division of American English into Eastern, Southern, and General America. Four years later his overwhelming lexical evidence for the existence of what is now called the Midland dialect between the Northern and the Southern areas was supplemented by E. Bagby Atwood's *Survey of Verb Forms in the Eastern United States* with its showing that many non-standard forms are distributed according to the dialect divisions outlined in Kurath's study.

By implication both works raised the question: How far do the principal Atlantic coast dialect boundaries extend west of the Appalachians? For the immediately contiguous area in the northern part of the country an answer has now appeared in a preliminary review of the data collected under the direction of Albert H. Marckwardt for the Linguistic Atlas of the North Central States. These data suggest that the principal dialect areas in the North Central States are reflexes of the Midland-Northern areas along the Atlantic coast. The major bundle of Midland-Northern isoglosses stretches west to the Mississippi so that roughly the northern third of Ohio, the northern fourth of Indiana, and the northern third of Illinois lie north of the bundle, that is, in a territory settled largely by people who had moved westward from the Northern speech areas of northern Pennsylvania, New York State, and western New England. South of the bundle lies derivative Midland and South Midland speech territory.

The recent completion of fieldwork for the Linguistic Atlas of the Upper Midwest now makes possible for the first time a definitive demonstration of the Midland-Northern relationship in the region immediately west of the North Central States. It is the function of this paper to delineate that relationship rather than to establish a correlation between dialect patterns and population history, but a brief covering statement may provide a framework for the language information.

From *Studies in Language and Linguistics in Honor of Charles C. Fries,* English Institute of the University of Michigan, 1964, pp 303-314. Reprinted with permission.

Settlement in the five states designated as the Upper Midwest --Minnesota, Iowa, North and South Dakota, and Nebraska[1]--began with the first inrush of English-speaking families shortly before the Civil War. Into northern Iowa and southeastern Minnesota came settlers from western New England and New York State and from their secondary settlements in Ohio, Michigan and northern Illinois, and even Wisconsin. Into central and southern Iowa--but with a large overflow into Minnesota--came settlers from the mid-Atlantic area, principally Pennsylvania, and from the derivative settlements in Ohio, Indiana, and Illinois. And also into southern Iowa came a third group, smaller but distinctive, with its source in the earlier movement westward through the Cumberland Gap into Kentucky and thence into southern Indiana and southern Illinois. Gradually, though with waves roughly corresponding to economic cycles, population spread after the Civil War into western and northern Minnesota, the Dakotas, and Nebraska, reaching some parts of the extreme western sections as late as 1910[2]. This later spreading was caused by an influx of newcomers having the same three origins, by a second westward move on the part of families who already had settled in Minnesota or Iowa, and to a very large measure by the massive advent of thousands of immigrants directly from non-English-speaking countries in western, and later, in eastern Europe. For all these except the last, the following delineation of the principal Upper Midwest dialect divisions will permit reasonable inferences about the population distribution even though fully detailed treatment of the settlement history must await the future publication of the Upper Midwest Atlas. That in this area such inferences can be drawn safely without regard for any influence of the non-English-speaking immigrants has already been ascertained.[3]

Evidence for the dialect divisions described here is almost entirely that provided in the field records of 208 informants interviewed by fieldworkers between 1947 and 1956. Of this number, 103 are classed as Type I (older and uneducated or old-fashioned), 89 as Type II (middle-aged with high school education), and 16 as Type III (younger with college education). Except for about 25 additions the questionnaire used is essentially that of the short work sheets of the New England Atlas and of the work sheets of the North Central Atlas. The additions were of some general items thought to be productive, such as *slick* and *boulevard*, and of other items intended to probe lexical differences in the vocabulary of the cattle-country west of the Missouri River. Besides the general body of data there is available a supplementary resource in the marking of 136 lexical items on checklists returned by 1069 mail informants in the five states. For these particular 136 items, therefore, there actually is evidence from 1275 informants. Although it is statistically unsound to add the returns from the two groups together in light of the lower validity of the mailed responses, the later often turn out to have a strong confirming value.

Even though full analysis of the data is only now underway, the preliminary analysis of replies to more than 125 items in the full questionnaire offers clear evidence for the establishment of the primary isogloss patterns shown on the accompanying map. Replies to some two dozen others indicate a gradual dialect variation corresponding to these primary divisions, one so gradual that it can more effectively be shown by percentage comparisons. By "primary" is meant "reflecting Midland-Northern differentiation as carried west by population movement." Secondary patterns, those reflecting ecological, commercial, or other influences peculiar to the Upper Midwest, will be treated in another article for publication elsewhere.

Of the primary patterns revealing Midland-Northern differentiation the major isogloss bundle is shown on the map by the 1-1 line, with certain deviations represented by the a-1 line. (All references to the symbols on the map will read from right to left in conformity with population movement.)

The 1-1 boundary represents generally the northern limit of the following lexical items: *rick*, *scum* (of ice), *fire dogs*, *bucket* (of metal), *slop* (*-pail* or *-bucket*), *coal oil*, *nicker*, *piece* (a distance), *piece* (a lunch), (*died*) *with*, *slick* (of a pavement), and *taw* of *taw-line*. Of these items *fire dogs*, *bucket*, *slop-*, *coal oil*, *nicker*, *piece* (distance), and *piece* (lunch) are shown in the *Word Geography* (*WG*) as typical Midland or South Midland forms. Inferentially, the other items may be considered as having at least a typical Midland distribution pattern in the Upper Midwest, although *slick* cannot be checked with materials of the other atlases since it is one of the added items.

Phonological matters occurring largely in this Midland area are [m ɪniz] *minnows* , [ɛ] in *since*, and [k] in *spigot*.

The a-1 boundary, which presumably indicates the presence of a strong Northern population element in the Iowa triangle set off by Davenport, Cedar Rapids, and Dubuque, is the northern limit for Midland *draw* "shallow valley," *light bread*, *snake feeder*, and *belly-buster*, as well as for the non-standard morphological item *clum*, the preterit of *climb*. Of these *light bread*, *snake feeder*, and *belly-buster* are attested as Midland in the *WG*; and *clum* is similarly classified by Atwood.

The 1-1 boundary is also the southern limit in the Upper Midwest for the common *slough* [slu] "swamp," *griddle cake*, and the infrequent *quite* (cold), and for the phonological items [ɑn] *on* stressed, [ɛ] in *scarce*, [ɔ] in *caught*, [hj] in *humor*, and [ɑ] in *nothing*. Of these *griddle cake* is dominantly Northern in the *WG*, and [ɑ] for *o* in *on* is revealed as Northern (though not Eastern New England) in the Linguistic Atlas of New England and in an unpublished summary by Atwood.

The a-1 boundary appears as the southern limit of Northern lexical features such as *devil's darning-needle* "dragonfly" and *belly-flop*, but of no phonological items. Both of these are of frequent occurrence despite competition with a considerable number of other Northern regionalisms.

Study of the lesser areas within the principal Midland zone reveals at least three isogloss bundles which may represent successive waves of Northern and Midland population, although the first bundle may well indicate also the extension of South Midland features into this area.

The Midland lesser area included within a-1-b or 1-b, southern Iowa, is marked by the occurrence of *spouting* "eavestrough," *branch* "stream," *dogbit*, *pullybone* "wishbone," *sook!* "call to cows," *corn pone*, *sick in* and *sick on* (one's stomach), *drying cloth*, *-towel*, or *-rag* "dishtowel," *french harp* "harmonica," and *rack* "sawbuck," within the lexical evidence, and by fronted beginning of the [au] diphthong as in [kæu] *cow* and by the [e] in *Mary*, within the phonological evidence. South Midland origins are likely for the infrequent *dogbit* and *pully-bone*; the others presumably are Midland.

The second Midland lesser area includes southern Iowa and the eastern half of Nebraska below the isogloss line 1-c. Like the first lesser area, it is marked by the appearance of exclusively Midland forms, although the boundary marks also the southern extension of two Northern pronunciation features. Lexical inclusions are *weather-boarding*, *barn)lot*, *plumb across*, *fice(t* "small dog," [pui] and [hoi] as calls to pigs, *chickie!*, *clabber cheese* and *smearcase*, *barn owl*, *polecat*, and *babycab*. Phonological matters include [rɛnts] for *rents*, [kæg] *keg*, *tushes* for *tusks*. [ʌ] in *rather*, and [u] in *Cooper*. At the same time the 1-c bundle includes one isophone and one isomorph limiting two expanding Northern forms, [æ] in *married* and *dove* as the preterit of *dive*. *Dove*, incidentally, is significantly dominant with all types of speakers despite repeated pedagogical injunctions against it.

The third Midland lesser area, 1-d, includes the southern two-thirds of Iowa and all of Nebraska. Its main lexical features are *till* (in time expressions), *blinds*, *dust up* (a room), *comfort* "bedcovering," *pallet*, *paving* "rural concrete highway," *dip* "sauce for pudding," *hull* (of a walnut), *butter beans*, *snake-feeder*, and *sick at* (one's stomach). *Sick at*, which competes with two other Midland regionalisms, interestingly enough is often listed in textbooks as standard in contrast to the dominant Northern form *sick to*. A conspicuous non-standard phonological characteristic in this area is the excrescent [-t] on *trough* and *eavestrough*.

At the same time the 1-d bundle serves to set off a fourth area between 1-d and 1-1, southwestern South Dakota, in which is found the maximum extension of a few Northern forms, *parlor match*, *haycock*, and *tarvy* or *tarvia* for a macadamized road. Of these only *parlor match* was reported as used in Iowa. The *tarvy* item may require further study, as its incidence could be related to variables not related to population distribution.

Although detailed invesitgation of the Type distribution of each of the terms in these three lesser areas would be needed before accurate classification of each as expanding or receding, a reasonable inference would seem to be that, in general, Midland forms limited to these areas are receding or at least checked and that Northern forms found here are expanding.

The converse, then, may with equal reason be inferred with respect to the Midland and Northern forms whose distribution is marked by the isogloss bundles setting off the lesser areas north of the main dialect boundary, 1-1. There appear to be four such lesser isogloss bundles, 1-e, 1-f, 1-g, and 1-h, designating the limits of expanding Midland or checked or receding Northern forms.

Isogloss bundle 1-e, for example, clearly represents the northern limits of the Midland *armload* and *seed* (as in both *cherry-seed* and *peach-seed*), which are found in nearly all of South Dakota. They compete with Northern *armful* and *stone*. On the other hand, it appears to represent also the limit of the rather infrequent Northern expression *pothole*. This last term was not recorded in Minnesota or Iowa during fieldwork, but checklist returns show a spotty frequency in Minnesota in addition to the recorded uses in North Dakota.

Similarly, the boundary 1-f is chiefly comprised of isoglosses showing the northern expansion of Midland terms. Here in northwestern South Dakota and western North Dakota the Midland *hay - cock* and *haydoodle* have successfully competed with the receding Northern *haycock*. Midland *mouth harp* likewise is found here as far north as the Canadian border; so are Midland *bottoms* or *bottomland*, *roasting-ears*, *firebug* (firefly), and the locution *want off/in*. Only one apparently Northern word has so far been found to be limited by 1-f, *boulevard*. This term was not included in any eastern atlas study, so that no comparative data are available except some isolated occurrences reported in private correspondence from northern and central Ohio. However, in the sense "strip of grass between sidewalk and street," this term patterns exactly like a typical Northern word, and strong confirmation of this patterning is found in the responses on the checklists.

Although the line 1-e,g, setting off the eastern Dakotas, does indicate the full northern expansion of several Midland terms, it largely denotes the limited western extension of Northern forms which probably are receding or checked. Midland forms which have spread widely, if sparsely, as far as Canada are: *evening* "time before supper," *cling peach*, *took sick*, *come back* and *come back again*, and *the baby) crawls*. Northern words rarely found beyond this boundary are *the wind) is calming* (*down* (mostly in Minnesota), *curtains* (on rollers), *red up* and *rid up*, *whipple-* or *whiffle-tree*, *cluck* (*hen* "brooding hen," *fried cakes* "doughnuts," and *skip school*. Even in the North Central States the Midland *singletree* was unaccountably well on its way to supplant *whipple- tree* before the advent of the tractor. The Northern term now appears on the road to obsolescence. In addition several Northern pronunciation items are seldom recorded beyond this boundary: [ɑ] in *fog* and *foggy*, [gul] *goal*, [draut] "drouth," [sut] *soot*, and [bɑrǝl] "*barrel*." The last three of these apparently are old-fashioned, used almost exclusively by Type I speakers. The receding and infrequent Northern [kl ɪm], non-standard preterit of *climb*, also occurs only within this lesser area. [ɑ] in *fog*, it is curious, is obviously receding while the [ɑ] in stressed *on*, contrariwise, is expanding with vigor.

Boundary 1-e,h, enclosing principally northern Iowa and southern Minnesota with a small margin of South Dakota, chiefly sets off the extreme extension of receding Northern forms. Among them appear to be *spider* "frying pan," *fills* or *thills*, *brook* "fishing stream" (only in Minnesota), *feeding time*, [ho] "call to a horse," [kə'de] "call to sheep," *lobbered milk*, and *sugar bush*. Also apparently receding Northern forms are the pronunciations with [Os] or [ɔ̊z] in *troughs* and *eavestroughs* and [e] in *dairy*, and the morphological feature *see* as the preterit of *see*. This limited area also represents a last-ditch stand against at least two Midland forms which have spread throughout the rest of the Upper Midwest, possibly because of reinforcement by Midland population influx through Duluth. One is *rock*, as in *He threw a rock at the dog*; the other is *bawl*, to describe the noise made by a cow.

The regional patterns which have been outlined above are slightly complicated by the presence of at least one enclave and perhaps another. The area marked X on the map contains a number of Northern forms not reported generally in Southern Iowa or elsewhere in Nebraska. Its existence probably is to be correlated with the migration of a number of New York and Ohio families into the Eastern Platte River Valley after the Civil War. Within or marginal to this enclave, for example, both parents of each of two informants came from New York and the mother of another was born there. One informant reported both parents born in Ohio; another reported his mother's birthplace in the state. Besides, one informant's father came from Illinois and both parents of another came from Wisconsin. All other informants are of foreign-born parentage. Among the hence presumably Northern forms which appear in the Platte River Valley are *parlor match*, *haycock*, [ho], [kə'de], *fried cake*, *boulevard* and *quite* (*cold*), in addition to the pronunciations [ɑ] in *fog* and *foggy*, [ɔ] in *caught*, and [hj] in *humor*.

The putative second enclave is designated by Y on the map. It includes Duluth, Minnesota, and the communities along the Mesabi Iron Range. Considerable investigation is called for by the appearance in this area of a number of Midland forms. Although no one informant has consistent Midland speech (not one of them has a Midland background), the frequency with which Midland items occur points to a possible Midland influence because of the contacts between Duluth, a major port, and the Lake Erie ports of Sandusky, Cleveland, and Erie, which are not far from the Midland territory of southern Ohio and Pennsylvania. Lexical items with usual Midland distribution which turn up in this enclave are *cling* (*peach*, *blinds*, *lot*, *bucket* (of metal), *spigot* "faucet," *bag* (of cloth), *armload*, *coalbucket*, *bawl*, *chickie!*, *dip* "sauce", *hull* (of walnut), *butter bean* , *come back again* , *died with* , and *took sick*. Phonological forms recorded here include [e] in *chair* and *Mary*, [u] in *spoons* , [ɔ] in *on*, [u] in *Cooper* , and [wo] "call to horse."

But the description of the Midland-Northern differentiation in the Upper Midwest is by no means complete in terms of isogloss boundaries. As the existence of the various "lesser areas" reveals, a number of Northern terms have been recorded in various parts of that principal Midland-speaking territory which is set off by the main isogloss bundle 1-1; and, correspondingly, a number of Midland terms have been recorded north of that bundle, Clearly the Midland-Northern distinction becomes less sharp as the dialect boundary is followed westward. The distinction is clearest in Iowa; it has so far broken down in South Dakota that that state might as well be designated a transition area. Actually the degree of the breakdown is much greater than the map would suggest, for the diffusion of many a dialect feature is so gradual that an isogloss cannot be drawn for it. Rather, recourse must be had to percentage of frequency.

For nearly all forms already cited the distribution patterns are so clear that isoglosses may be drawn with some certainty. For example, a quick glance at a map bearing symbols marking the occurrence of *comfort* , *comforter*, and *comfortable* is adequate for one to be able to draw the isogloss of *comfort* , which is clearly limited to the Midland 1-d area. To establish its distribution pattern there is no need to resort to a study of the percentages. The statistics merely confirm the obvious. How percentages are related to a clear pattern may be seen in the figures for *comfort*:

$$
\begin{array}{cc}
0 & 2 \\
0 & \\
25 & 35
\end{array}
$$

This table, in which the figures are arranged so as to correspond spatially with the relative positions of the Upper Midwest states, is to be read like this: 2 percent of the Minnesota field informants replying to this particular question use the lexical variant *comfort*, 35 percent of those in Iowa, none in either of the two Dakotas, and 25 percent of those in Nebraska.

Such a table should now be compared with the following, which shows the percentage of frequency of occurrence of *poison* in the locution "Some berries are poison" (in which it contrasts with *poisonous*):

$$
\begin{array}{cc}
31 & 29.5 \\
50 & \\
54 & 39
\end{array}
$$

Reference to a map bearing symbols for the occurrences of *poison* would indicate no possibility of drawing an isogloss. Even the slight differences in percentage at first appear to be insignificant,

easily due to the variables that operate when informants are
interviewed by different fieldworkers. But when a corresponding
differential appears with item after item, and when each variation
correlates consistently with the Midland-Northern contrast, then
the gradation must be recognized as significant and not accidental.
Examination of numerous tabulations now makes clear that, regularly, some attested Midland forms not susceptible of delimitation by
isoglosses occur with greatest frequency in Iowa and Nebraska,
less in South Dakota, still less in Minnesota, and, usually, least
in North Dakota. Conversely, some attested Northern forms appear
regularly with highest percentages in Minnesota and North Dakota,
less in Iowa and South Dakota, and least in Nebraska. Since
the percentages have been calculated on the artificial basis of
the political boundaries, actually the figures are more significant
than at first sight, for the Midland percentage for Iowa would be
still higher if the informants in the Northern-speech territory of
the two upper tiers of counties had been counted in Minnesota
rather than in Iowa. The reverse, of course, would hold true
for a Northern form, which would have a lower frequency in
Iowa if the northern third had been counted in with Minnesota.

Now even though the spread in the percentages for *poison* is
not great--between 29.5 and 54--the spread clearly indicates a
higher rate of occurrence in Midland territory. Similar spread
appears in the percentages ascertained for these words:

the sun)	*came up*	*skillet*		*paper)*	*sack*
11.5	10.5	27	49.5	70	55
27		65		85	
40.5	22	81	90	81	73

Of these, *skillet* is shown in the *WG* to be the dominant Midland
term, with only a scattered handful of instances reported along
Long Island Sound. It would seem to be expanding with some
vigor in the Upper Midwest, and the checklist replies confirm
this expansion. The figures for *sack* may be questioned, but
they conversely match those for *paper bag*, which appears to have
a slight Northern dominance.

With the phonological items recourse to percentage analysis is
particularly productive, for matters of pronunciation seem much
less likely than vocabulary items to be characterized by fairly
distinct regional patterns. Yet regional variation on a graduated
scale appears when the statistics are examined for such as these:

[sʌt] *soot*		[æ] in *razor-strap*		[ɑ] in *wheelbarrow*	
19	25	46	37	10	22
24		48		8	
30	31	47	49	22	39

[-o] final in *wheelbarrow* [-wain] in *genuine*   [θ] in *with milk*

19	22	56	66	36	34
27		59		42	
30	50	62	73	41	52

[u] in *root*

38	23
25	
40	46

A Midland emphasis appears also in the distribution of a few morphological items which do not have sharp isoglossal patterning. With each of these items variation is heard from only Type I and Type II informants:

bushel (pl.   *begun*
after numeral)   *who-all?*   (pret.)   *drownded*

36	40	51	57	0	6	19	19
52		57		0		43	
50	72	78	66	11	19.4	14	35

At least two lexical items exhibit Northern weighting in their distribution:

paper) bag   *warmed up*

73	74	62.5	62.5
56		61.5	
40	58	38	28

Phonological responses revealing Northern emphasis are:

                                                    [Iŋ] in plurals
[bɑb] *wire*   [ɑ] in *harrow*   and gerunds

23	16	16	33	59	82
19		7		47	
11	10	6	12	48	46

Two morphological items may have Northern weighting also, the nonstandard adverbial genitive *anywheres* (contrasting with *anywhere* and *anyplace*) and the preterit *fitted*:

anywheres   *fitted*

23	19	28.5	22
16		17	
13	11.7	8	14

Although certainly most of the Upper Midwest worksheet items classed in the eastern atlases as either Midland or Northern reveal, to some extent at least, the same correlation, there are a few for which the evidence is puzzling and will require some special investigation if not supplementary collecting. *Clean across*, for instance, is reported in the *WG* as a "regional phrase" current along the

South Atlantic Coast; but in the Upper Midwest it turns up only twice in Midland Iowa and Nebraska, four times in South Dakota, and five times in North Dakota. *Mosquito hawk* "dragonfly" is reported in the *WG* only along the South Atlantic Coast for southern New Jersey to South Carolina (although Raven I. McDavid, Jr., has additionally recorded a few scattered occurrences in Upper New York); in the Upper Midwest this variant shows distinct Northern distribution with its seven occurrences in Minnesota and four in North Dakota but none in either Iowa or Nebraska. *Buttery*, according to Kurath, "is unknown in the Hudson Valley and in the entire Midland and South." Yet as a relic term it appears not only in Minnesota but also in the Midland speech area of Iowa and Nebraska. *Lead-horse*, according to the *WG*, is limited to Midland and South Midland areas; as a relic in the Upper Midwest it has fairly even distribution in the five states. *Fishworm* was recorded frequently in both New England and New York as well as in South Midland territory; in the Upper Midwest it is exclusively Midland. Both the field records and the checklists show that *angleworm* is the overwhelmingly dominant form in the Northern speech regions of the Upper Midwest. *Firebug* is reported in the *WG* as Pennsylvania vocabulary variant for *firefly*, with only a solitary instance in New York. But in the Upper Midwest the percentage distribution surely is not Midland:

15.4	9.5
16	
2.7	1

Furthermore, the checklist responses number 45 in Minnesota and North Dakota with only 10 in Iowa and 9 in Nebraska. *Raised* in "The sun raised at six o'clock" Atwood calls Middle Atlantic, but in the Upper Midwest it occurs as a rare non-standard form seven times north of the 1-1 boundary and only four times in Midland territory south of it.

In summary:

1. The primary Midland-Northern dialect contrast of the Atlantic coast States is maintained in the Upper Midwest.

2. The distinction is particularly clear in the eastern half of the Upper Midwest, that is, between the lower two-thirds of Iowa and the upper third of Iowa.

3. The distinction is less clear in the western half, that is, west of the Missouri River, where splitting of the major isogloss bundle reveals several lesser dialect areas delimiting expanding or receding forms.

4. In general, Northern speech forms seem to be yielding to Midland.

    a. The principal isoglosses bend northward, even to the point of indicating a complete blocking of some Northern terms.

    b. Most of the expanding forms are Midland; most of the receding forms are Northern.

      c. Diffusion appears to be more intensive for Midland forms in Northern territory, especially in Minnesota, than for Northern forms in Midland territory, especially southern Iowa.

      5. One Northern enclave occurs in Midland territory; a probable Midland enclave occurs in Northern territory.

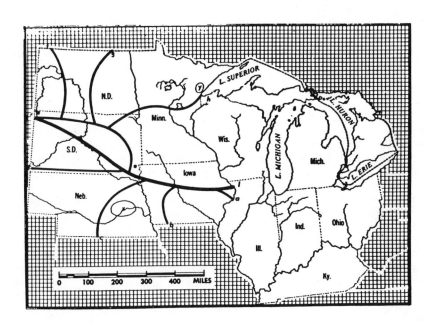

Map 1: Upper Midwest Dialect patterns.

FOOTNOTES

[1] These states have an area of 365,297 square miles and, in the 1950 census, a population of 7,931,298.

[2] The region adjacent to the extreme western boundary between the Dakotas had no significant permanent settlement, for example, until the Milwaukee railroad extended its line west to the Pacific coast in the late 1900s. Previously, of course, a sparse handful of cattle ranchers had occupied the region for three or four decades.

[3] Support for this statement was offered by the writer in a paper, "The validity of the use of informants with non-English-speaking parentage," read before the Linguistic Society of America in Chicago, December 29, 1955.

GRASSROOTS GRAMMAR IN THE GULF STATES

Lee Pederson

Sixty-seven years after Mencken's call for a descriptive grammar of American common speech,[1] more echoes than answers have
been heard. To be sure, shelves are filled with useful information
about American speech, but all of that together makes no national
grammar. Although Mencken's enthusiastic charge--like the
onomastic chutzpa in the title of his best book--reflects an imperfect understanding of a large problem, the idea of a grammar of
Spoken American English endures as a worthwhile task to be
completed. This demands individual and collective efforts: native
competence that is operational in every region and among every
significant social organization to provide the information and understanding needed to determine the ranges of dialectical variation,
the rules of grammar, and the standards of correctness, and
long-term projects that extend local studies across dialect areas
and explore every aspect of the communication process. Nothing
less will suffice to produce the kind of work that Mencken had
in mind, a description of the linguistic habits of the most socially
complicated people in the history of civilization.
    Within the Southern states, the work of James B. McMillan is
a classic individual effort of just that kind.   His description of
phonology and morphophonemics is an authoritative reference for
the speech of the Interior South, and his *Annotated Bibliography
of Southern American English* is a model regional index. The current
Linguistic Atlas of the Gulf States (LAGS) Project responds to
questions implicitly raised in the pioneering work of McMillan and
others.   His latter work, for example, is a discriminating guide
to more than 1400 titles, but only 62 of these directly concern
morphology and syntax, with nearly half of those involving personal pronouns in the second person--*you all*, *you-uns*, and *youse*.
When similar, if not comparable, bibliographies are compiled for
other regions of the United States, the problem can be stated
with elegance at a national level of concern.   Students will know
the kinds of information needed for a morphology and syntax of
the spontaneous speech of the American people, a grassroots
grammar.   Meanwhile, following McMillan's lead, the LAGS Project

From *James B. McMillan: Essays in Linguistics by his Friends and Colleagues,* edited by J. C. Raymond and
I. W. Russell. University of Alabama Press, 1977, pp 91-112. Reprinted with permission.

approaches the investigation in the Interior South to suggest some possibilities in an area where a substantial foundation has been laid.

Atlas data from most sections of the country provide baseline evidence for the inductive study of regional phonology, morphology, and vocabulary. Lightweight, sensitive, and dependable reel-to-reel tape recorders now offer a means to complement atlas collections with as much syntactic data as a regional grammarian might need for transcription and study through replays that are virtually instantaneous and limitless. Indeed, it is the tape recorder, more than innovative sampling, analytical, or descriptive procedures, that has advanced current sociolinguistic investigation. [2]

Conventional dialectology today with its emphasis on conversational discourse records and preserves every word spoken in the interview to provide a rich corpus of thoroughly verifiable data. Such material can be treated as cursorily or elaborately as the grammarian chooses, but the evidence stands and must be ultimately accounted for in a comprehensive fashion. Broad generalizations of phrase structure and overview of syntactic patterns must at some time be substantiated with context sensitive interpretations of grammatical forms based on microlinguistic analyses of all elements in the communication process.

The LAGS Project is designed to give the descriptive grammarian some of that information by organizing and indexing a corpus of regional American English--approximately 4,000 hours of tape-recorded conversational speech--in a survey of native usage in Florida, Georgia, Alabama, Mississippi, Tennessee, Louisiana, Arkansas, and East Texas. The present report identifies the sources and the substance of the grammatical data gathered in the LAGS Project to suggest some of the information available to a grassroots grammarian: (1) the evidence sought directly in the standard interview procedure, (2) the range of incidental material transcribed in a single protocol, (3) the contents of a brief passage from a field record summarized in the protocol, and (4) the probable format of the data that will be organized as a regional contribution to an inductive grammar of American common speech.

I

Because massive grammatical evidence occurs in spontaneous conversation, it is easy to overlook the valuable data elicited through items in the work sheets. These forms are the systematically contrastive features that have been surveyed in other regional atlas projects, thereby providing information of an indispensable sort. Although a comprehensive grammar must do more than characterize the formal properties of a selected set of morphological and syntactic features, few complete, skeletal, or even partial paradigms of inflectional morphology can be expected in an unstructured interview. Atlas material provides a core of comparable data, and every survey aims to enlarge and improve upon the work from which it has emerged.

For the sake of efficiency, atlas projects survey morphology and syntax through the investigation of features observed in earlier research and exploratory fieldwork. In the LAGS Project, for example, a number of grammatical items came from a variety of sources.[3] Combined with the items used in earlier atlas surveys, this material comprises a wide range of grammatical evidence--the morphology and syntax of verbs, substantives, and modifiers, as well as the alternation and deletion of function words and some grammatical operations of contrastive stress.

Verbs. Forms and functions surveyed in LAGS include the principal parts of 33 verbs from several historical classes, preterit and participial variation among 26 other finite verbs, and 27 auxiliary verb forms. In addition to these, 29 forms in the syntax of verb negation are sampled. Person, tense, mood, voice, status, and aspect are included incidentally, as well as special instances of durative and perfective constructions.[4]

Nouns and Pronouns. Investigation of substantive forms (i.e., nouns, nominals, and pronouns) and constructions in the work sheets include singular and plural forms of 15 nouns, five plurals of nouns of measure, and three variable plurals. The possessive case was surveyed in the preliminary work sheets--"John's book" versus "John's own book" and "He buried his son" versus "He buried him a son"--but such reflexive genitives were unproductive. They are, however, included in the protocol when occurring in conversation. As the most fully inflected set of English substantives, the pronouns are closely covered.[5]

Modifiers. Adjectival and the adverbial modifiers itemized in the work sheets are morphological, phrasal, and clause structures. Adjectives in the comparative degree are represented by the disyllabic form *pretty* (*prettier/more pretty*) and the present participle *loving* (*more loving/lovinger*) and in the superlative degree by past participle *grownup* (*most grown-up/grown-uppest*). The redundant *onliest* ("He was the onliest one to get sick") and superlatives of deprecation ("That was the sorriest dog of the bunch") are most effectively investigated incidentally. Free form alternation among adjectivals include *almost/nearly nigh on to*, *gone/all gone*, *none/not a one/ne'er a one*, and *many/many a one*.

Adverbial modifiers include the alternation of bound forms and free forms,[6] as well as syntactic features of tense, aspect, and phase: *anymore/nowadays*, *by and by/soon*, *in the past/used to*, *a week ago Sunday/Sunday week*, *a week from Sunday/last Sunday week*. Inchoative aspect is marked at the clause level by *during the night/of a night*; durative aspect, by *right on/steadily*.

Function Words and Idioms. Several prepositions and conjunctions are targeted in phrasal items,[7] but the most complicated of these occur in idiomatic constructions that must be evaluated in

terms of both grammatical and semantic distinctiveness.[8]   The
interpretation of semantic data requires close attention, and this
is the most demanding sort of analytical work, involving an open-
ended set of forms and constructions. Without close attention to
word and phrase structure, however, the grammatical system cannot be effectively described.

Closely related to function words in the interpretation of
grammatical and idiomatic constructions are the structural signals
of prosody--stress, pitch, and juncture as they combine in the
basic contours of intonation.   These include substantive/verbal
pairs *áddress/ăddréss, brúsh/brûsh, fréeze/frêeze,* and *whíp/whîp,*
a verbal/adjectival pair *hàs grôwn úp/môst gròwnúp,* a substantive/
adjectival pair ˌ *bóil /bôiled éggs,* a prepositional/adverbial pair
òn púrpŏse/pût it ón,   an   adverbial/verbal   pair *ràthĕr cóld/
wôuld ráthĕr,* and a substantive/verbal pair with morphophonemic
alternation *cálf/cǎlve.*   Other prosodic features influencing the
phonological structure of grammatical forms are the deliberately /
rapidly   articulated   utterances   *gîve mé/gîmmè* and *Mrš. Cóopĕr/
Mǐz Cóopĕr* (both as titles of a married woman.

II

In addition to the items covered in the work sheets, other
grammatical forms are recorded in every protocol transcribed in
the LAGS Project. Most of this morphological and syntactic information will not be immediately useful in the demarcation of regional
and social dialects, but all of it is necessary in the composition
of a regional grammar.   The following examples are limited to the
incidental protocol notation from a single field record.[9]   These
forms include base-form and inflectional morphology and syntactic
structures at the phrase, clause, and sentence levels.

Morphology. The combinations of morphemes recorded in free
conversation provide not only examples of lexical, semantic, and
grammatical variation but also outline processes of word formation
observable in the idiolect.   These include combinations of free
forms--nouns, verbs, modifiers, and function words--in the creation of nominal, verbal, and modificational constructions, as well
as composition by analogy and phrasal simplification (the deletion
of free forms): [10]

Nominal Constructions:
  Noun + Noun: dúskdàrk (late evening), *hóglàrd, pónd cătfìsh,*
    vélvĕt bèan; [11]
  Verb + Noun: bóilĭng meàt (sidemeat), *kíssĭng kinfòlks,*
    spréadĭng oùtĕr; [12]
  Modifier + Noun: hígh shèrĭff, [13] *scáredў càt, tráshў pèrsŏn;*
  Analogous Compounds: déerdòg (after *birddog*), *cătfìsh stêak*
    (after *beef steak*);

Reduced Compounds: chúckwàgŏn [steak] (small beef steak),
   [electric] lǐghtpòle, ráil[road] lǐght (kerosene lantern);
Reduced structure of modification: nòndáirў̆ (a nondairy
   from *nondairy product*);
Infixed Intensifier: tee-niny peas [tì:ná:nʏ̆ pl̀iz];[14]

Verbal Constructions:
   Analogous Constructions: lighten up (after brighten up),
      pooch out and *punch out* (both after *bulge out*);
   Blend: scweaming [skwíəmə̀n] (of a baby, *squirming and scream-
      ing*);

Modificational Constructions of Various Categories:
   Adjectival: trough-like (of gutters, *trough-like things*);
      swively [swíəvə̀lɨ] (from *shrivel* with derivational suffix,
      after *sticky*); *worlds of them* (many); *protracted meetings*
      [pə̀trǽktɨ̂d mí:tɨŋz] (extended meetings, i.e., *revivals*).[15]

   Supplementary evidence of inflectional forms in the protocol
includes these constructions: [brɛ́kfəsɨz] (*breakfast*, pl.),
[mɛ́:ngɑ̀ətɨz] (*men's garters*), [wɒ́əspnɛ̀əst] (*wasps' nest*), [hæ̃ɛv
stóʉld] (*steal*, pp.), and [ɒ́ɔ flɨ̃st] (*awful*, super.)
   Phrase Structure. Variation here includes contraction, deletion, and lexical selection in nominal, verbal, and modificational
structures. In this idiolect, the most frequently recurring of
these variant features is contraction and deletion in the auxiliary
construction *be* (*am*/*are*/*is*/*was*) *going* + infinitive marker *to*. In
these sometimes catenative phrasal units, the inflectional suffix
-*ing* is reduced to vowel nasality and the infinitive marker is
deleted, resulting in the forms [go u ~ gɔo] followed by the unmarked infinitives:

   I think I'm)going to try to learn [gõ̀ʊ trá↓ tə̀llʏ́ə̀n];
   They are going to stay [ðɛə gɔ̃̂õ stéɨ];
   . . . I can assure you it's going to be sore [gõ̂ʊbí:lsóə];
   I was afraid that fish)was going to eat he [wə̀z gõ̂ʊ í:t mì];
   *Daddy would have selected ones [watermelons], you know, that
   he would have picked out for different people that he was
   going to give to* [wə̀z gɔ̃̂õ gívtùu] *. . . and we'd always get
   one of those*

All of these contrast with the recorded finite form of *going*:

   . . . if she's not going[.] [ɪ̀f ʃî:z nɑ̀t góʉə̀n].

   Other instances of deletion include an inflectional suffix
(*it melt[s]*), a verb auxiliary (*they [have] run some tests*), and
a preposition (*You could smell them from here [to] yonder*). A
more complicated problem of deletion concerns article *the* preceding
only, recorded three times in the protocol:

*That's only land that I've really had experience with, sandy
  land;
Just this one time is only time we had to carry water;
That's only place*

In these instances the phonological and syntactic environments
are virtually identical, with the article position occurring between
fricatives (s/z) and the back vowel of *only* and following a linking
verb in an ostensible predicate adjective construction. The article
is also deleted before *onliest* in the same environment:

*That's onliest woman that I've ever seen smoke a pipe, but
  she did.*

In the uninflected forms above there is an adverbial sense: *only*
[*kind of*] *land*, *only* [*when*] *we had to carry water*, and *only place*
[*where it was found*]; but *onliest woman* is an explicit structure
of modification, i.e., adjective + noun.

A semantic consideration at the level of phrase structure
grammar involves the uses of the modifier *old*. In the work-sheet
phrase *good old days*, the sense of the remote past is clear, as
is the notion of approbation. Eight other phrases recorded in
the protocol are more complicated:

Indicating age, without emotional overtones:
  an old Negro woman [ə̆n ô̵l níg̈ə̈ wùmn̩];
Implying affection in recollections from the past:
  our little old porch [lî̈əl ô̵l póətʃ];
  a great old big pile (of sand) [grɛet ò̵ bîg pátl];[16]
  big old cans (of lard) [bîg ô̵l kǽɛnz];
  a little old thing (a cigarette roller used by her late
     husband during World War II) [lî̈əl ò̵l θín̩];
Implying playful disapprobation without reference to time:
  old moonshine whiskey [ò̵l mú̵ᵾnʃà:ɪn hwî̈əskî̵];
  old badman [ðə o̵l bæɛd mæɛn] (a haunt, the boogerman);
  old peckerwood [ou pɛkəwuəd] (a joking term of abuse);

The affectionate and playfully disparaging use of *old* is quite
common in Southern folk speech, as, for example, *sweet little old
thing* or *little old peckerwood* for a child and *good old boy* for
one of the boys or any misunderstood reprobate. The grammatical
interpretation of the form *old*, however, will require a delicate
interpretation of semantic structure in southern folk speech.
    Clause Structure. Examples here from the Aimwell protocol
include copula deletion, subject-verb agreement, word order, and
functional shift, specifically, the adverbial usage of verbs and
adjectives as phrase and clause modifiers. The lone instance of
a deleted copula occurred in a discussion of the use of whips in
urging horses on, but never with mules:

Oh, mules slow anyway [ó:ʉ‖mjʉʉlz│slôʉ ɛ́nɪ̵wèɪ̵].

In addition to the work-sheet items concerning subject-verb agreement, these structures of predication were recorded:

There was four other men.   [ðɛ̀ə wə̆z fôə ʌ̂ðə̆ mɛ́ən]
Don't that sound stupid?   [dòʉn ðæ̀ɛt sâon stʉ̆ʉpɪ̵d]
That don't go way back.   [ðæ̀ɛt dôʉn góʉ‖wêɪ bǽɛk]
The harnesses was hooked to that.   [ðə̆ hɑ́ənɪ̵sɪ̵z│wə̀z hʉ́kt tə̆ ðæ̀ɛt]

Also, a single occurrence of altered word order indicates an effort at emphasis: *Nevĕr dîd wé hàve ă ráil fènce* (after telling of various local rail fences).

Several instances of adjunctive structures are these:

He'd drink his [coffee] *black* (of coffee);
You had to cook that egg done, but not brown
   [of fried eggs for her son];
They would just come up volunteer [of crops not
   planted].

None of those is particularly distinctive in American English syntax, but a related utterance is considerably more complicated:

There used to just be bollweevils, real, real bad.
[ðɛ̀ə jʉ̂ʉstə̆ dʒʌs bî bóoʉ wĭ:vɪ̵z│rí:ʉɾí:ʉbæ̆ɛd]

In this idiolect, the immediate underlying sentence, *the bollwee-vils here used to be real[ly] bad,* must be evaluated with an eye to the habitual use of *used to* as a sentence modifier with the grammatical and semantic meaning of *years ago*.[17] A grammarian of either the armchair or ivory-tower variety can readily point to the split infinitive, the colloquial adverbial use of *just*, and the uninflected adverbs (*real*, *real*) modifying *bad*, but only a dialect speaker with native competence can explain the relationship of this commonplace verb phrase to its adverbial usage in Southern folk speech.

Other sentences in this protocol that combine phrase and clause structure peculiarities are these:

Does lobsters do that? (i.e., crawl backward as
   crawfish do);
The tadpoles make the frogs (i.e., grow to become
   frogs as seeds make plants).

Sentence Structure. In addition to instances of eccentric syntax already cited, relationships among clauses show several other kinds of variation. These include deletion, contraction, rearrangement, and substitution among elements of the clauses and their subordinators, as well as verb agreement in successive clauses. Contraction (of the verb phrase *was supposed to come*

true), deletion (of the subordinate adverbial-conjunction *for*) and
the rearrangement of clauses are all illustrated in the following
sentence describing the folklore of the *pully bone*: *The one that got
the short piece of the bone, the wish was supposed to come
true* [ðə wʌ̂n   ðət gɑ̂t ðə ʃɔːət] pí:s|ə̄ ðə̄ bɔ̃ũn‖ðə̄ wíə]| wə̄z
spóstə̄| kʌ̂m trʉ̂u], i.e., *the wish was supposed to come true
for the one that got the short piece of the bone.*

Substitution among subordinate conjunctions includes instances
of *that* for *when*:

> *You didn't ever see her that she didn't have that pipe
>   in her mouth;*
> *that* for *of which*:
> *Nobody ever killed a hog that you didn't get a piece;*
> *until* for *that* (with excrescent repetition of the form):
> *He didn't get to go hunting very much this year because
>   there's been so much crime until--the crime is increasing--
>   until they don't have time* (concerning the curtailment of
> of her son's deerhunting).

Examples of shifting reference in the succession of clauses
are these:

> *singular to plural:*
> *If you don't hem a snake up, they('re) not go(ing) to bother
>   you*
>   [ɪf jʉu dô:hə̂əm ə snêɪk ʌəp ðèɪ nɑ̀t gɔ̃ə bá:ðə̄ ɹə];
> *plural to singular:*
> *We have the great big black grasshoppers that eats things up.*

III

As most of the examples listed in the preceding summary
suggest, the best evidence for a comprehensive inductive grammar
will be conversational data, whether gathered by linguistic
geographers, sociolinguists, or descriptive grammarians. It should
be just as obvious, however, that such material is difficult to
organize. Even when roughly edited, none of the information is
systematically contrastive because sentences are not, like phonemes
or inflectional morphemes, members of clearly delineated and narrowly restricted sets. At the same time, sentences and their
constituents provide information that covers the full grammatical
range of an idiolect under investigation, and, although no atlas
field record can possibly cover every element, the available sketch
offers a step in that direction. To suggest how much information
is gathered in a single interview, a short conversational passage
is presented here from the Aimwell field record.

At Item #6, p. 24 of the LAGS work sheets (four hours and 42 minutes into the interview), the fieldworker, Gene Shaffer, asks:

F[ield worker]:   What types of boats do people usually use to go fishing?

I[nformant]:   Now, I'm just lost there.   I don't know too much about boats.   I really don't.   Skiffs, they used to call 'em skiffs, you know.

F: Um hm.

I: Way back then, you know, when they were first begun having these little things to fish in, you know, and they call 'em skiffs, And rowboats, and now they just, eh, just boats is all I ju--.

F: Can you remember what the skifts and the rowboats looked like?   How they were shaped?

I: Well, just like they are now.

F: um hm.

I: Cause they, you know, they been those, this shape boat has been in for as as long as I can remember.   Course, I remember what the, I remember seeing pictures of these boats, you know, way back when they used to make 'em.   The Indians used, but.

F: Um hm.

I: But these shaped boats go back as far as I do.

F: do they have flat bottoms or square fronts?

I: Yes, square, eh, eh, flat bottoms, but pointed on the end, you know, just like they do now.

F: Yeh, o.k.

I: My husband made, he and a friend of his made an aluminum boat one time.

F: Really?   Aluminum?   How did he do that?

I: They welded it together.   And, oh, we fished a lot when Billy was small; before we moved away from here, we fished a lot.   We'd go down on the Tombigbee River--that's the river down here.

F: Oh, yes.

I: Camp out at night.

F: Oh, that'd be great.

I: Yeh, that's a lot of fun.   It really is.   We caught--we went one time when Billy was five years old.   We went one Saturday night, spent the night.   We got up on Sunday morning, and one of their lines--you put out what you call trotlines.

F: What's that?

I: That's lines that you bait, and you go all the way across the river and have that line.

F: Oh.

I: There'd be one long line and then there's about, like, say every six feet, there would be a little short line down here with a hook on it, baited.   And you go across the river and take that thing across the river and tie it to something on the other side.   And it would be, it would be stretched all the way across the river.

So we had, one Saturday night, we went, and we had, and there was just a little willow tree that had, had grown up out of the river about this far, and it was just about as far as from here to that heater, from the bank. And they had finished with all the other lines--we just had a boat full of fish--so they got to this line and they could not pull the fish up. It had a fĭftў-síx póund cátfìsh on that little line, on that little willow tree! This man's wife and I had to wade out--it was shallow enough that we had to wade out--to take a trace chain for them to put on that fish to get this fish back in the boat.

F: Wow!

I: And we sold that. They brought that fish to town and dressed it and sold it to a market--to one of the markets here in town. Fĭftў-síx póund! It was larger than either, either one of them. They were both--my husband was--well, he was tall. He was really tall. Well, he was about as high as Billy, but he was--he never weighed over 135 pounds. Real skinny. And this man was a small man, too. So, we had to help them get that fish in that boat. And, of course, he was cutting up so bad. I was just--I thought sure I was go(ing to) drown. Fish was go(ing to) eat me. And I've always been so afraid of those fins, you know. They will just, oh, kill you.

F: Stick you.

I: They sure will, and it's very poisonous.

F: Oh, really? I didn't know it was poisonous.

I: I mean as far as infection is concerned. Yes, it will always become infected, nearly, most always.

F: What would you put on something like that?

I: Well, methylate or mercurochrome or something like that. First aid if you have anything at home. But usually, if you, if you, if it's very bad, you go to the doctor with it.

F: Really? I'll have to remember that next time I catch one of those things.

I: Yes, you do. If they fin you--and I can assure you it's go(ing to) be sore, réal, réal sòre. They just make a bad place, if it's very bad.

This passage--including the remarks of the fieldworker--span only four minutes and 50 seconds of a 485 minute field record. To summarize all of its grammatical constructions would require a text considerably longer than the present report. The verb forms alone offer a substantial corpus of data.

At the morphological level, the passage includes 117 verb forms--verbals (gerunds, participles, and infinitives functioning as other parts of speech), auxiliary, marked, and unmarked forms of 44 different verbs: *assure, bait, be, become, begin, bring, call, camp, can, catch, concern, cut, do, dress, drown, eat, fin, finish, fish, get, go, grow, have, help, kill, know, make, mean, move, point, pull, put, remember, see, sell, spend, take, think, tie, use, wade, weigh, weld,* and *will.*

The syntax of these verbs is most fully represented with seven of the eight forms of *be* attested in the passage: *am, are, be, been, is, was,* and *were*. With no occurrence of *being* in the text, the 41 instances of *be* exemplify (with the infinitive) 19 discrete elements of the verb paradigm:

As a finite verb:

present tense: *am, are, is;*

modal marked present tense: *is going to be, might be, would be;*

past tense: *was, were;*

phase marked past tense; ∅ *been, has been, have been;*

As an auxiliary verb:

as a present tense marker: *is going to be;*

as a past tense marker with an intransitive verb: *was going to drown;*

as a past tense marker with a transitive verb: *was going to eat me;*

as an aspect marker with an *-ing* verb base: *was cutting up;*

As an aspect marker with an *-en* verb base: *is concerned;*

as a voice marker in a verb phrase: *would be stretched;*

as a voice marker in a catenative construction: *were begun having*

As in some of those examples--∅ *been, were begun having,* and *that's lines*--the syntax of the verb phrase must be interpreted within the context of the situation, the structure of both the narrative and the communication process. The first two of these occur in halting syntax at the outset of the passage, where unfamiliarity with the topic, boats, is mirrored in several other syntactic aberrations as well:

> *they call 'em skiffs for they used to call 'em . . . or called 'em skiffs; now they just, eh, just boats is all I ju--for now they are just called boats; that is all I call them, just boats;*
>
> *I remember what the, I remember seeing . . . . The Indians used but for*
>
> *I remember seeing pictures of the boats that the Indians used, way back when they used to make them.*

None of those citations could rightfully include in a statement concerning morphological or phrasal deletion or in a description of clause patterns unless the context of the situation was identified. similarly, the apparent lapse of subject-verb agreement in the clause *that's lines* preserves the concord of the discourse at the expense of the clause. The fieldworker placed the plural *trotlines* in the singular with his question *What's that?* The informant replies *That's lines that you bait.* Elsewhere, the fieldworker's remark interrupts a compound verb phrase to replace the conjunction:

I: *We'd go down on the Tombigbee--*
F: *Oh, yes.*
I:--[And] *camp out at night.*

Later, the informant interrupts herself to preserve the suspense
of her story *We caught* [a 56 pound catfish once], to clarify
details *Well, he* [her husband] *was about as high* [tall] *as Billy*
[her son], *but he was--he never weighed over 135 pounds*.   *Real*
skinny [but he was real skinny],[18] and to express her excitement
in the situation, *I thought sure I was go(ing to) drown* [*and the*]
fish was going to eat me.
    All of this suggests not only the necessity of identifying
situational styles but also of characterizing both the subject matter
of the discourse and the informant's ability and willingness to
discuss the topic.   Attitude is difficult to define, but to ignore
the psycholinguistic implications of a situation invariably leads to
an imperfect representation of grammatical forms.   The problem
is not easily resolved, but a grassroots grammarian must always
be willing to sacrifice elegant description for accurate explanation. [19]

IV

    In the composition of a national grammar, the role of LAGS
and other regional surveys is predetermined by the division of
labor   within   the   field   of   descriptive   linguistics.   Linguistic
geography gathers the data, describes the regional and social
patterns, and indexes a corpus for other kinds of analysis and
description.   To   produce   a   complete   and   coherent   statement,
descriptive grammar must provide integrated rules to refine and
codify   the   discursive   and   nontechnical   summaries   of   linguistic
geography, as, for example, the substance of the present report.
    The LAGS Project was organized to develop summary descrip-
tions of 750-800 native idiolects in the Interior South and to find
social   and   historical   correlations   among   those   idiolects   in   the
identification of dominant and recessive forms, features, and patterns.   The passage from the Aimwell record, for example, comprises less than one per cent of the retrievable information, the
field   record of that single idiolect.   Consistent with its primary
goals, the LAGS Project will produce two collections and three
documents.   The basic collection is the complete set of tape-recorded interviews, from which will be derived the Linguistic Atlas of
the Gulf States.   The atlas will be published in the format of
1000 fiche of microphotography, including a reproduction of all
protocols (in narrow phonetic notation with substantial marginalia)
and as much connected discourse (in broad phonic and conventional
orthographic   notation)   as   time   and   space   permit.   The LAGS

handbook will follow the second edition of Kurath et al., *A Hand-book for the Linguistic Geography of New England* (1972), in form and content.

The three descriptive documents will follow the models of Kurath, Atwood, and Kurath and McDavid,[20] with the order of publication reversed and the contents reflecting the advantages of the tape-recorded corpus. Rather than a morphological state-ment limited to verb forms, it should be possible to identify all inflectional patterns investigated in the work sheets for nominals and modifiers and to note the recorded processes of contraction, deletion, rearrangement, and substitution. The word geography should reflect both the phonological and grammatical analyses that precede it, separating differences of phonology (e.g., *spigot/ spicket*) and differences of function words (e.g., *quarter of/to/ till/until*) from the proper study of the subject, i.e. lexical and semantic forms.

All of that material should provide useful information for a regional component in a national grammar, but more will be needed to complete the work, even within the province of Southern speech. The ultimate baseline contribution of a regional survey would be an encyclopedic description of morphological and syntactic con-structions in the conversational passages of the interview, as well as the systematically elicited items. This would give substance to a Grassroots Grammar of the Gulf States, a modern extension of Joseph Wright's *The English Dialect Grammar.* Whereas that work provided the historical backgrounds of English grammar from its Indo-European sources through the Nineteenth Century, a volume today could begin with Wright and place the regional speech within the context of the English language of the Twentieth Cen-tury. By means of the descriptive methodology developed during the past three decades,[21] an exhaustive index of morphological and syntactic structures could offer the very information that Mencken sought.

With all of that completed, data gatherers in the Gulf States will yield to the rule writers of descriptive grammar. That work properly done will carry LAGS research into the next century, and, perhaps, the grammarians can celebrate the centennial of Mencken's call with the publication of the comprehensive inductive grammar of the common speech of the United States. Looking to the immediate and distant future, a prudent seeker of information, assistance, and wise counsel heartily wishes James McMillan a happy birthday and many more of them.[22]

FOOTNOTES

[1] "My call for a comprehensive inductive grammar of the common speech of the United States, first made in a newspaper article in 1910, has never been answered by anyone learned in the tongues,

though in the meantime philologists have given us searching studies
of such esoteric Indian languages as Cuna, Chitamacha, Yuma,
and Klamath-Modoc, not to mention Eskimo." H. L. Mencken,
*The American Language/An Inquiry into the Development of English
in the United States*, the Fourth Edition and the Two Supplements, abridged, with annotations and new material, by Raven I.
McDavid, Jr. With the assistance of David W. Maurer (New
York: A. A. Knopf, 1963), 509.

[2] See "Tape/Text and Analogues," *American Speech* 49 (1974):
5-23, for some of the implications of the tape recorder in conventional linguistic geography. The tape-recorded interview is
designated *field record* and the narrow phonetic transcription of
forms elicited from the work sheets is designated *protocol* in the
LAGS Project. For a summary of progress through 1974, see
"The Linguistic Atlas of the Gulf States: Interim Report Two,"
American Speech 49 (1974): 216-24. Interim Report Three will
summarize the work completed through 1976, the termination of
field work and the plans for editing the atlas.

[3] The principal sources are these: E. B. Atwood, *The Regional Vocabulary of Texas* (Austin: University of Texas Press, 1962),
Raven I. McDavid, Jr., and Virginia McDavid, "Grammatical Differences in the North Central States," *American Speech* 35 (1960):
5-19, J. LeComte's "A Vocabulary Study of Lafourche Parish and
Grand Isle Louisiana," and William R. Van Riper's "Linguistic
Atlas of Oklahoma," as reported by A. L. Davis, Raven I. McDavid,
and Virginia G. McDavid, *A Compilation of the Work Sheets of
the Linguistic Atlas of the United States and Canada and Associated
Projects*, 2nd ed. (Chicago: University of Chicago Press, 1969),
for finite verbs, adjectives, and adverbs; James B. McMillan,
"Vowel Nasality as a Sandhi-Form of the Morphemes *-nt* and *-ing*
in Southern America," *American Speech* 14 (1939): 120-3, and
"Phonology of the Standard English of East Central Albama,"
University of Chicago diss., 1946, for items concerning morphophonemic alternation, consonant vowel assimilation, simplification
of final consonant clusters, and vowel nasality in sandhi forms;
and the Dialect Survey of Rural Georgia for items concerning
deleted articles, auxiliaries, and prepositions, as well as the habitual investigation of verbs in all three principal parts. For information on the plan and progress of the Dialect Survey of Rural
Georgia, see Lee Pederson, Grace Rueter, and Joan Hall, "Biracial
Dialectology: Six Years into the Georgia Survey," *Journal of English Linguistics* 9 (1975): 18-25; Pederson, "The Plan for a Dialect
Survey of Rural Georgia," *Orbis* 24 (1975): 38-44, Pederson, Dunlap, and Rueter, "Questionnaire for a Dialect Survey of Rural
Georgia," *Orbis* 24 (1975): 45-71.

[4] These include (1) the principal parts of *ask, begin, bit,
blow, break, bring, catch, climb, come, dive, do, drag, dream,
drink, drive, drown, eat, fight, freeze, give, grow, hear, help,
ride, rise, run, see, shrink, sit, swell, swim,* and *write*; (2)
finite forms of *be, borrow, burst, cost, do, draw, grease, hang,
kneel, know, launch, lie, make, shrivel, stab, sweat, teach, throw,*

tear, *wake*, and *want*; (3) the auxiliaries *be* /*am*/*is* /*was* /*were*, *can*/ *could*, *do*/*does*/*did*/*done*, *get* /*gets* /*got*, *go*/*goes*/*going*, *has* / *have*/ *had*, *may*/ *might*/ *might could!maybe could*, *shall*/*should*, *take*/*took*/ *taken*, *will* / *would*, *dare*, *ought*, and *used*; (4) verbal phrases of negation, the full and contracted forms of *aint*, *am not*, *are not*, *aren't*, *cannot*, *can't dare not*, *dassn't*, *does not*, *doesn't*, *do not*, *don't*, *haint*, *has not*, *hasn't*, *have not*, *haven't*, *ought not*, *oughtn't*, *should not*, *shouldn't*, *used not*, *usen't*, *didn't used*, *was not*, *wasn't*, *will not*, *won't*, and *would not*; (5) besides the inceptives listed above (*go* and *take*, as in "goes to drinking" or "takes to gambling"), the durative aspect (marked by the prefix a- to present participles) and the perfective aspect (marked by auxiliary *done*, as in "I done told you," as opposed to adverbial use in "He was done dead").

⁵ These include *as he is*/*as he be*/*as him*, *as I am*/*as I be*/*as me*, *he and I*/*him and me*, *it is I*/ *me*, *it is he*/ *him*, *it is her*/*she*, *it is them* / *they*, *you and I*/*me and you*, and *you*/*you-all* (singular and plural), *who*/*who-all* (*who-all* *is*/*who-all's*); *hers* /*hern*, *his*/ *hisn*, *ours*/*ourn*, *theirs* /*theirn*, *whose* /*who-all's*, *you-all's* /*your*, and *yours* /*yourn*; *those*/*them* (boys), *what* /*what-all*, *himself* / *hisself*, *themselves*/*theirselves*, and the relatives *that*/*which*/*who*/ *what* /ø.

⁶ These include *backward* /*backwards*, *forward* /*forwards*, *real*/ *really*, *almost*/ *like to*/*like to have*, *anyplace*/*anywhere*/*anywheres*, *apt as not*/*probably*/ *like as not*, *at home*/*home*/*to home*, *kind of* / *kindly*/*rather*/*sort of*.

⁷ These include *all at once*/*all to once*, *down*/*in*/*over*/*out*/*up in* (a given place), *fall off*/ *off of*, *fall off*/ *out of* (bed), (the wind is) *out of* /*from*/*to* (a direction), (put wood) *in*/ *into* (the stove), (it has buttons) *on* /*on to it*, *quarter of* /*till*, *to*/*until* (the hour), *half past*/ *after* (the hour), *toward* /*towards*, *sick to*/ *at*/*on*/*in*/*of* (*the*/*one's*) *stomach*.

⁸In addition to those listed above are *for to*/*to*/*in order to* (tell me), *as if*/*as though*/*like*, *because*/*since*, *by the time*/*time*, *as far as*/*all the farther*/*the farthest*/*all the fartherest*/*all the furthest*, *unless*/*without* (you go too), and *whether*/*as*.

⁹This 485 minute tape recorded interview was conducted by Gene Shaffer, May 5-6, 1976, in the community of Linden in Marengo County, Alabama. Forty miles due south of Tuscaloosa County, Marengo is bound on the west by the Tombigbee River, scarcely 20 miles from the Mississippi border, 90 miles due north of Mobile, and 75 miles to the south and west. She is a 56-year-old widowed housewife, a fourth generation native of the county. She completed two years of high school, married a lumber inspector, and several years later gave birth to a son, who is presently the sheriff of Marengo County.

With her husband having worked in the principal local industry (pulp wood), family travel in the Interior South, and her son's current position of authority, the informant is a good representative of Type II (common speaker) B (worldly, i.e., nonrustic or provincial within the context of Marengo County). According to her position in the community, the fieldworker assigned a heuristic social classification of upper middleclass; from the referents of Hollingshead's Two Factor Index of Social Position, middle to lower-middle class status should be assigned at a national level of ranking.

Phonologically, her speech is clearly a modernized, western extension of the East Central Alabama dialect described by McMillan (1946), including 19 of the 20 distinctive dialect features summarized in his conclusion. Only the unconstricted diphthong [3ɪ], as an allophone of /3/, as in *bird*, is unattested in the protocol. Although the substitution of /d/ for /z/ before the alveolar nasal /n/, as in *wasn't*, was not recorded, her pronunciation of *clumsy* [klʌ̈mᵈð̥ɪ̈ʌ] suggests the pervasive influence of nasal consonants on contiguous fricatives in West Central Alabama as well.

[10] The notation here is broad phonic, one of five transcriptional forms used in the LAGS Project, identified in "Tape/Text and Analogues," *American Speech* 49 (1974): 5-23.

Broad phonetic transcription is a system of notation that records all distinctive vowel and consonant units with various diacritical marks. These include the 32 vowels and 98 consonants identified for the *Linguistic Atlas of New England* and reproduced for the LAGS Project in Lee Pederson, Raven I. McDavid, Jr., Charles W. Foster, and Charles E. Billiard, *A Manual for Dialect Research in the Southern States* 2nd ed. (University: University of Alabama Press, 1974), pp. 243-4. This provides not only binary notation of all glides (diphthongs and triphongs), but also variation in the articulation of consonants. Only the diacritics of length, voicing, devoicing, nasality, and syllabification (i.e., syllabic consonants) are presently used. Thus, a narrow phonetic transcription of the word *mountain* [mã̈˞ö˞‹ntˀn̩] would be represented in broad phonic transcription as [mã̈öntˀn̩]. Such a system can be refined or simplified according to the idiolect or dialect in question, so long as the distinctive features are identified.

[11] These are described as black beans that "stung you" when you picked them; they were prickly (like okra) and were fed to cows to improve milk production.

[12] Among the snakes identified by the informant--*rattlesnake*, *chickensnake*, *ratsnake*, *water moccasin*, *black moccasin*, and *kingsnake*--was the cobra-like reptile that raises and spreads its head when threatened. Two different pronunciations were recorded [sprɛ́dn̩à̈ə˞l̩] and [sprɛ́dn̩à̈ət̬ə̃], both of which share phonological features of the phrases recorded in Mathews (DA), *spreading adder* and *spreading viper*: the alveolar stops [r~t] in the final syllable of each after *adder*) and preceding syllabic [aə] of each (after *viper*). The first form, if not misspoken, might be interpreted *spreading idol*, but the second seems a popular etymology, a *spreading outer.* Varieties of snakes were not, but should have been, systematically investigated in LAGS fieldwork.

[13] The informant notes that local blacks call the county sheriff the high sheriff, another relic form that endures in black folk

speech. As in one of the few authentic indigenous ballads from the Gulf States, *Stackerlee* (*Stagolee*, *Stackolee*), "The high sheriff told his deputies/'Get your guns and come with me; we go' go to town right now/Get that Stackerlee/He's a bad man;/That mean old Stackerlee.'"

[14] As an intensifier, i.e., *t-in-iny*, it seems to be an instance of infixing with [-i:n-] having the reduplicative morphological function of *bitty* in *little bitty*, perhaps derived from *teeny* in *teeny weenie* or *teeny tiny*, as in the popular tune of a decade or so back concerning, "Teeny-weenie, Yellow-Polka-Dot Bikini." If so, this is another instance of the process described by James B. McMillan in his paper, "Infixing and Interposition in English," presented at the ADS annual meeting, December 29, 1975.

[15] See Mary Celestia Parler, "'Lay-by Time' and 'Protracted Meetings'," *American Speech* 10 (1945): 306-7. Here is an instance of a word rarely occurring in LAGS interviews because the item was not included in the work sheets. Other constructions in this interview, rarely investigated in general surveys also were recorded: *honky tonk* [hɔ̃õ̯ŋkɨ̈ tɔ̃õ̯ŋk] (which was identified as a *Negro joint* [nɪ́grə̃ dʒɔ̃ənt] located on the county line), *an iron stab* [ə̃n ậɨ̯ən stɑ́ɔb] (i.e., an iron stake), *rolly pollies* (small gray armored insects variously called milk bugs, doodle bugs, or pill bugs, which when threatened roll themselves into balls), *keep it clean* (of cotton plants, i.e., free of weeds), and other morphological forms related to rural life. At the same time, this middle-aged informant reflects the contemporary vocabulary in a number of phrases that were elicited from the basic work sheets, e.g., *Georgia Cracker* (as a friendly term for all Georgians), *hoosier* (only in the phrase *Hoosier Hot Shots*, who were the rural counterparts of Spike Jones and his City Slickers in the 1940s and 50s), *instant grits*, *leisure suit*, *pants suit*, *piglet* (for a newborn pig), *run some tests* (in the hospital), and *sweet corn* (yellow corn imported from Florida, as opposed to locally raised *corn on the cob* and *yellow field corn*).

[16] I.e., *big old* → *old big*.

[17] Instances of *used to* as sentence modifier in the protocol include these: *We, used to, when we lived out in the country, we had neighbors*; *Used to, when there were trains around* . . . . At a "deeper level," no doubt, this sentence modifier is derived from *used to be*, but such speculation requires the native competence of the dialect speaker to reduce the observation to credible rules.

[18] The problem of pronominal reference here might be more ambiguous outside the rural South. The ensuing comment *he was cutting up so bad* --after references to the son, the father, and the other small man, as well as the fish identified earlier in the neuter gender--is here only superficially vague. In several LAGS records, the intimate use of the masculine pronoun is commonly used, whether the antecedent is a fish, a plant, or a bean: *Oh, the pinto bean, he's a spotted little feller*.

[19] Current investigators of urban speech, for example, would be much more convincing if they provided texts.

[20] Hans Kurath, *A Word Geography of the Eastern United States* (Ann Arbor: University of Michigan Press, 1949); E. Bagby Atwood, *A Survey of Verb Forms of the Eastern United States* (Ann Arbor: University of Michigan Press, 1953); Hans Kurath and Raven I. McDavid, Jr., *The Pronunciation of English in the Atlantic States* (Ann Arbor: University of Michigan Press, 1961).

[21] In addition to the aforementioned descriptive work of Atwood, Kurath, McDavid, and McMillan, other useful models include Eugene A. Nida, *A Synopsis of English Syntax* (Norman, Okla.: Summer Institute of Linguistics, 1960), George L. Trager and Henry L. Smith, Jr., *An Outline of English Structure* (Norman, Okla.: Studies in Linguistics, Occasional Papers, 3, 1951), and W. Freeman Twaddell, *The English Verb Auxiliaries* (Providence: Brown University Press, 1960), as well as several secondary sources, such as W. Nelson Francis, *The Structure of Modern English* (New York: Ronald Press, 1958) for phrase structure taxonomy, Archibald A. Hill, *Introduction to Linguistic Structures: From Sound to Sentence in English* (New York: Harcourt, Brace and World, 1958) for a taxonomy of phonological syntax, and Roderick A. Jacobs and Peter S. Rosenbaum, *English Transformational Grammar* (Waltham, Mass.: Blaisdell, 1968) for transformational taxonomic structures.

[22] Afterword: the composition of this essay, in the summer of 1976, led to the revision of LAGS plans to organize the atlas legend and index in a dictionary format, after the microfiche publication. When McMillan was asked about the proposed presentation, he said, "I have always thought that was the best way to publish linguistic atlas material."

THE SPEECH OF THE AMERICAN

HEARTLAND: OKLAHOMA

Bobbé Lou Van Riper

I'm here today to talk to you about Oklahoma speech . . . not because I'm an Okie, which I am . . . but because I married William Van Riper, the man who was the Director of the Linguistic Atlas of Oklahoma.[1] I helped him with this project, but my role was only that of "helper" . . . I was the extra "hands." My talk to you today will be filled with good information because it has been taken directly from my husband's notes . . . and, in most cases, will be presented in his own words.

Let me start by giving some background about the Linguistic Atlas of Oklahoma for those of you who may not be familiar with it already.

This Atlas is a part of the Linguistic Atlas of the United States and Canada and will present significant synchronic and diachronic perspectives of the speech of Oklahoma, using the format of a linguistic atlas.

Work on the Linguistic Atlas of Oklahoma began in the summer of 1959 after William Van Riper had spent two years listening to Okies and collecting checklists of Oklahoma speech. In 1959 and 1960, letters were sent to others directing atlas projects or regional surveys, asking about items which pointed toward Oklahoma. Following this, worksheets for *personal* interviews were compiled from McDavid's *Compilation of the Worksheets*, from the suggestions given in reply to letters, and from other items overheard or otherwise observed. Some 925 items--lexical, syntactical and pho-nological--were to be investigated. Most of the usual, primary items of the New England and eastern seaboard worksheets were included, together with some others not so usual. Among these latter are some for syntax, such as *in the morning/of a morning/ mornings*; *it rained/there was a rain/it came up a rain*; and *any-more*, used declaratively in an affirmative construction, such as "Anymore, we watch television." Some other items were to investi-gate word choice. For example, among other forms, *pond* or *tank?--horned toad*, *horned frog*, or *horney toad?--let go* or *turn*

From *Journal of English Linguistics* 3:65-71, 1979. Reprinted with permission.

loose?--stake or *stob*, and is there a difference in meaning?--was the usual, relaxed term for a man *fellow*, *guy* or *old boy*?--was something *rather good*, *kinda good*, or *kindly good*?

Still other items were added to check variant pronunciations, or to provide phonetic or phonemic contrasts. Some of these are:

shrivel/swivel, as of a withered peach or kernel of grain
trot line/trout line
Staple/steeple, for securing wire to a post
great big [gret/grɛt]
pin [pɪn/plɪən/pɛn]
thing [θiŋ /θɛŋ /θæŋ]

It should go without saying, of course, that these are merely some of the variants, and that the informant's normal form is discovered by leading him into a context where he will use his normal term and pronunciation and not by asking, "Do you say [θɪŋ] or [θæŋ]?"

Following compilation, the worksheets were revised for continuity so that one item would suggest the next to the informant and he would interview himself, so to speak, and the items could be recorded from conversation. This technique, admirably used by Raven McDavid, yielded good results. Occasionally, however, the technique had to be revised: In eastern Oklahoma, the early settlers burned wood, carried out the *ashes*, put them in an ash hopper, wet them, collected the *lye water*, poured it into a *barrel* of shelled *corn*, and thus made *hominy*. This sequence yielded the terms *ashes*, *lye*, *water*, *corn*, and *hominy*. In northwestern Oklahoma, the early settlers had no wood but burned cow chips. Needless to say, this sequence didn't work there.

Following the revision of the worksheets, the informant net for the state was drawn. The state was divided into 44 blocks with each to be represented by one informant. One additional informant was to be chosen from each of the five largest cities. Considering the population distribution, the settlement history, and the geography of the state, such a plan appeared feasible.

The informants for The Linguistic Atlas of Oklahoma were chosen carefully. Each was selected because he fitted the age/educational/occupational requirements to represent his particular place, because he had been born there and, except for college education, had been educated there, and had spent his life in this particular vicinity, except perhaps for military service or brief residence elsewhere. The oldest informants--one was 93--are an exception to this, since they were among the very first white settlers in their locality.

The informants were sought out and interviewed on their home ground so that their linguistic responses were as natural and unforced as possible. Van Riper recorded the responses manually, using phonetic script, and mechanically, using a tape recorder. Thus, the interviewer had an on-the-spot record for immediate examination, and also a mechanical reproduction of the interview for re-examination, cross-checking, and examination of pitch and stress patterns. The interviewing techniques which were used are described in "Shortening the Long Conversational Interview," *Studies in Linguistics in Honor of Raven I. McDavid, Jr.*

Field interviewing was carried out between 1960 and 1963, with over fifty personal interviews, each of between eight and twenty hours' duration, being completed, and each being tape-recorded in its entirety on 1/4 x 1800-foot reels of magnetic recording tape. William Van Riper's work, as Director of the Linguistic Atlas of Oklahoma, was supported by grants from the Oklahoma State University Research Foundation.

This Atlas is unique in that all interviews were conducted by a single interviewer, William Van Riper, so that there is a single interviewing style.

The people of Oklahoma have come from diverse places, and the pattern of settlement has been as diverse as the origins of these people. The Five Civilized Tribes and lesser tribes once "owned" the Indian Territory, but their surplus lands were eventually made available to the whites for settlement. White settlers from adjoining and distant states were quick to take advantage of a good thing. There have been nine major land openings in Oklahoma, openings in which the land was made available by "*Run*"--run for it, stake 160 acres of it, file for it, improve it, and it's yours; "*Squatters' Rights*"; *Land Lottery* --fill out the blank and we'll draw--if you're lucky, you win 160 acres; by *sealed bids* and finally, by *public auction*. These various openings are shown on this map. ONE, opened in 1889, was claimed by Run; TWO, then called NoMan's Land, opened in 1890, was by Squatters' Rights, since through some error this had not been part of any state or territory prior to this time; THREE, opened in 1891; FOUR, opened in 1892; FIVE, opened in 1893; and SIX opened in 1895, were all settled by Run. SEVEN, part of old Greer County, Texas, was determined to be actually part of the Territory, so in 1901, the settlers already there were allowed to file for 160 acres, and then buy 160 more at $1.00 an acre. EIGHT was purchased by settlers who submitted sealed bids; NINE, some of the old military lands, was sold at public auction. In 1906, it was decided that the Indians in the eastern part of the state could sell their land--they had "head-rights," by which each person was entitled to an equal share of the tribal holdings, 110 acres each in the case of the Cherokees--so this area, too, was opened for white settlement. There are still Indian reservations within the state.

After the initial openings, many people came to the state, and many left. Some came to buy the homesteaders' farms, some to work in the mines or in other industries, some from other oil-producing regions were drawn by the oil booms of the teens and the twenties, while yet others were blown out of the state by the dry winds of the drought years.

The method of settlement has encouraged speech diversity. Oklahoma's settling between 1889 and the early years of the twentieth century was directed toward the democratic ideal of equality, and equality does not generally promote a quick re-alignment of speech features. If everyone is equal, who is to be the model? Each participant in the runs and in the lottery was supposed to have an equal chance, each farm seeker who was fortunate enough to claim land received the same amount, 160 acres, and each person could make or break himself according to his luck, energy, intelligence, and desires. The family was the unit of settlement, and neighboring families generally had come from different places, not infrequently from different major dialect areas.

The linguistic sorting which gives a dialect distinctive features, or rather which makes a dialect, is obviously taking place in Oklahoma today, just as it is taking place everywhere else; but in Oklahoma, where most of the English-speaking population has arrived within the last 89 years, the situation is unusual. As a result of the runs and of the uniform size of the tracts offered, a county with no permanent population one day could have a family on every 160 acres and a liberal sprinkling of towns the very next day. A farmer from Texas might have a former Missourian as his neighbor, and this neighbor might call a *bucket* a *pail*, or a *cup towel* a *dish towel*, or for that matter, he might even use the uncouth word *bull* for a *surly*. If he used the former term, of course, he was using a four-letter word. Such situations were not uncommon, as the present distribution of terms clearly shows.

For example, *surly* as the polite term in Oklahoma for a bull is very uncommon today, but it can be found in the speech of a few old people. One of the informants showed considerable concern about the propriety of using the word *bull* in a coeducational university, and suggested that *surly* was the only possible word to use. It could have been pointed out that in parts of the Virginia Tidewater one of the polite terms is *top-cow*, but this would only have served to show that one man's euphemism may be another man's taboo.

Other words have spread into Oklahoma from the Southwest and still others have come from the more general areas where ranching is a common occupation or perhaps even a way of life. Although these words were brought in by the homesteaders, they had also passed through the Territory earlier, carried in by the cowboys who lived there and by the drovers who took herds along the four cattle trails from Texas through Indian Territory for delivery to the early railhead at Kansas City or later to the cattle towns which grew up on the railroad as it passed through Kansas.

Certain cow-country terms have lived their active lives in Oklahoma and have become mere relics. Such a one is *soogan*, which refers to a heavy bed cover used on or in a bedroll. This word was evidently quite common at one time in northwestern Oklahoma, but now it is fast disappearing, even though it is still found to some extent in neighboring western and northwestern Texas. Another expression which is dying fast is that for an old type of cowboy stew. The cowboys called this dish *son of a bitch*. Since the connotation was likely to be objectionable to those who were not fond of the dish or who thought of the expression only as one of abuse, the variant for the term of abuse was applied to the dish, and it became known politely as *son of a gun*. This, of course, did not at all do justice to the stew, which I have heard was excellent--and still is, if a cook can be found who knows how to make it.

Ranching terms, of course, make up only a minute portion of Oklahoma's linguistic stock. The regional dialects used here are predominantly South Midland and Midland, with a dash of southern and a spot of Northern mixed in. In Oklahoma, the thing a boy may throw at a rabbit, for example, is mostly called a *rock*, the term common in the South Midland and the South, but it may also be called a *stone*. In combination with *wall* or *fence*, *stone* is uncommon. Most Oklahomans would refer to *rock walls* and *stone fences*, although the things themselves are scarce. On the other hand, few Oklahomans would call the large grinding wheel for use around the farm a *grint rock*; the term used for this is usually *grindstone*. In the southeastern part of the state, *rock* is used as a combining form in *sand rock* and *lime rock*.

After a move to Louisiana State University, Van Riper continued with the organization and analysis of his data for the Linguistic Atlas of Oklahoma, with some research supported from LSU. He felt that computerized sorting of data would likely be necessary, so he audited a course in FORTRAN at LSU in the mid 60s and also organized a Modern Language Association seminar on Computers and Dialectology to learn more about this aspect of the project.

Although he made a running, manually-transcribed account in phonetic notation during most of the interviews, the on-the-spot transcriptions will require further checking against the correspond-ing taped interview, with a new alphabetic transcription accompany-ing the check.

The diversity of speech which existed in the early days in Oklahoma is still apparent, but it is considerably less today than it was at the time of settling. With the formation of towns and cities and the resultant opportunity for frequent conversation that was present in the densely settled areas, speech forms were exchanged rapidly. The stratification of society which took place also favored the sorting out of certain features.

In the country, the situation was somewhat different. There was less opportunity for conversation with a neighbor or a trades-man, and consequently a much less frequent exchange of speech. However, Oklahoma has had universal schooling from the time of statehood, and the schoolhouse, together with the church, fre-quently has served as the social center for the rural community. The rural schools were at first small and each served a limited area, but with the development of motorized transportation and the coming of the school bus, the small rural school has given way to the large consolidated school. As a result of this consolidation, young people from various neighborhoods instead of a single one are brought together to be educated, and of course, to talk to each other. Their speech community has grown. Whereas their grandparents may have gone to a rural school attended by children who lived as far as five miles away, the young people today in the "rural" schools may live twenty miles distant and may have as close friends other young people who live an equal distance off in the other direction. Such a shrinking of distance and consequent enlarging of the neighborhood cannot help having a homogenizing influence on speech.   Then, too, many of the high school graduates in the state go on to college.   In the grain belt of the northwestern part of the state, my husband was unable to locate a home-grown high school graduate between the ages of 25 and 35 who had not been to college for at least a semester.   The county agent, who served as his field contact there, pointed out that since nearly all of the young people around there went to college, the search would be understandably difficult.   The percentage of high school graduates going on to college is not this high in other parts of the state, of course, but for those who do go on there are two large state universities and nine state colleges, in addition to denominational and metropolitan institutions.   (The number at the time the interviewing took place.)   The young people who live at school or who commute are in close contact with others from different parts of the state, and again are probably hearing dialects besides their own.

The shrinking and enlarging of the neighborhood is also brought about by the automobile, but here the neighborhood becomes even larger. The Saturday night trip to town has frequently become the daily trip, and the yearly trip to the city may have become the weekly one. Again, this travel simply gives people a greater opportunity to talk with other people, people who may talk "different," and who may be regarded either consciously or unconsciously as models, social and linguistic.

These are not the only forces which are at work levelling the differences, but they are among the most important.   No single dialect will emerge from this sorting, at least none within the near future, but at least the family by family differences will disappear, as they have already, in many instances, and then the resulting uniformity will probably give way to more widespread uniformity.   Three areas may emerge, an eastern, a northern, and a southern-southwestern, but this may prove to be only a wild guess.   The facts of the matter will be apparent only when the analysis has been completed--and by then, as now for that matter, the speech will have changed still more and the Linguistic Atlas of Oklahoma will be only a historic account.   But after all, that is what a linguistic atlas is supposed to be . . . a record of a particular facet of the culture and a more-or-less unified group of people--a historical slice of a very fundamental and dynamic part of our culture.

William Van Riper's death in October of 1977 prevented the completion of the editing of the Linguistic Atlas of Oklahoma.

My husband had corresponded with the Library of Congress in the early 60s and arrangements were made then for the records of this atlas--all taped interviews and other materials--to be kept there after the completion of the editing.   I could have sent these records to the Library of Congress when my husband died. Instead, I called Dr. Raven McDavid and asked if he would assume responsibility for the completion of this work.   Dr. McDavid is more than editor-in-chief of two linguistic atlases, more than one of the more distinguished of our dialectologists.   Through the years, he was Van Riper's teacher, his colleague, and a close personal friend.   I knew that he could be trusted to see that the Linguistic Atlas of Oklahoma would be completed in a manner which would preserve the integrity of my husband's work.

I am happy to report that Dr. McDavid has agreed to accept this project, and it is largely due to his efforts, since my request for his assistance, that this atlas is a healthy and on-going project. We've also had encouragement and support from colleagues at LSU and Oklahoma State University.

Last month, the mayor of Baton Rouge planted a live oak tree and dedicated it to William Van Riper.   That seemed a fitting tribute.   It will seem an even more fitting tribute to see that his linguistic atlas is completed as he envisioned it.

It also seems especially fitting that the scholar who in 1947 envisioned the possibility of initiating linguistic atlas work in Oklahoma and adjacent territory be the one to now supervise the completion of this work.

NOTES

[1]This paper was read at the National Council of Teachers of English convention held 23-25 November 1978 in Kansas City.

[Ed. Note: Bruce   Southard   of   Oklahoma   State   University has accepted the responsibility of editing the Linguistic Atlas of Oklahoma.]

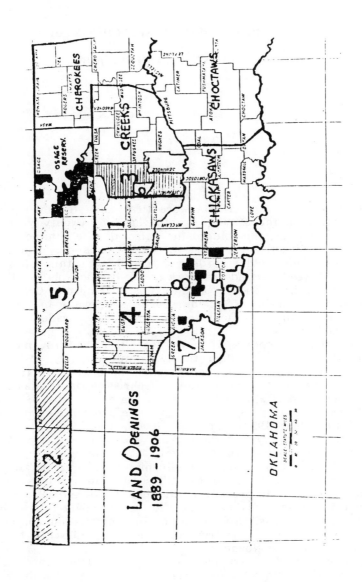

LAND OPENINGS
1889 - 1906

OKLAHOMA

PROBLEMS OF ENGLISH SPEECH MIXTURE

IN CALIFORNIA AND NEVADA

Carroll E. Reed

David W. Reed

Twenty years ago efforts were first made to develop a Linguistic Atlas of the Pacific Coast (that was twenty years after the beginning of the Linguistic Atlas of the United States). David Reed directed the work in California and Nevada, where check sheets and field records were completed within a few years, and Carroll Reed started the work in the Pacific Northwest, where check sheets were soon completed for Washington, Oregon, and Idaho, and a number of field records were made in Washington and Idaho. Only two field records have been made in Oregon, one by each of us.

In previous reports we have described the provenience and distribution of certain dialectically significant vocabulary items. In addition to this, the pronunciation of English in the Pacific Northwest has also been treated. Three doctoral dissertations have been written, based on Atlas material: David DeCamp, *The Pronunciation of English in San Francisco* (University of California, Berkeley, 1953); Fred H. Brengelman, *The Native American English Spoken in the Puget Sound Area* (University of Washington, 1957); and Elizabeth S. Bright, *A Word Geography of California and Nevada* (University of California, Berkeley, 1967).

Since so much of the work still remains in archives, it seems appropriate for us to present at this time at least a brief description of what these archives have to offer. Especially interesting, of course, is the possibility of comparing information contained in both sets of data, one from the Pacific Northwest, the other from California and Nevada.

It has been observed that the English of Idaho and Washington is characterized, to a high degree, as "Northern" speech, whereas Oregon shows more "Midland" features. California seems to have more Midland traits than Washington or Idaho, but less than Oregon. While such a statement reflects the general nature of settlement on the Pacific Coast, it fails to account sufficiently

From *Studies in Linguistics in Honor of Raven I. McDavid, Jr.*, edited by L. M. Davis. University of Alabama Press, 1972, pp135-143. Reprinted with permission.

for the transplanting and specific distribution of eastern dialect features; moreover, it does not take into consideration those dialect elements that are purely of local origin.

The westward migration of people in the 19th century and the early 20th century took similar paths: the Oregon Trail, the California Trail, and even the Butterfield Overland Mail originated in Iowa and Missouri. Most of the early settlers who came overland were born in these and nearby states, notably Illinois and Ohio. By far the largest single group of people were the New Yorkers who, along with residents of Maine and Massachusetts, made their way westward by sea.

In the Pacific Northwest there was a lively trade in furs; agriculture flourished; lumbering and fishing became profitable industries; supplies and facilities were provided for the transient hordes impelled by Alaska gold fever, and various local mining operations were established (in silver, coal, and lead, for example). Water was plentiful, both from rivers and from rain, and settlements were extended progressively along lines of access from urban centers to rural resources. This general pattern was disturbed only by massive industrialization in a few port areas after World War I.

While California and Nevada were largely agricultural states, it was the recurrent impetus of mineral discoveries that was responsible for the changing tides of early settlement. Until the beginning of the 20th century, the bulk of California's population was centered in San Francisco, which was the hub of civilization for settlers in the Sacramento and San Joaquin Valleys, and for would-be gold miners on the way to Nevada or Alaska. In the 20th century, however, southern California began to accelerate in growth, following the increasing availability of water, and the Los Angeles area soon became one of the world's most populated centers. As the railroads and highways developed, routes of access were shifted, sometimes rather radically. The tide of people seeking pay-dirt receded; and, where population pressure changed its directions, residual sectors lapsed into obscurity. All these factors constituting the ebb and flow of California settlement were then enormously complicated by the concentrated development of certain agricultural products, such as oranges, apples, avocados, walnuts, olives, cattle, and cotton.

Throughout all the Pacific Coast areas, natural facilities and natural barriers influenced the development of population and the incumbent speech patterns. Non-English elements came into the language most notably in the Spanish of southern California, but also, to some degree, in the French of the Pacific Northwest. The heavy German settlements in early days left few linguistic traces, and the influence of Scandinavian appears to have been equally light.

In connection with the maps that follow, it will be noted first that the Pacific Northwest is separated from California and Nevada by rugged terrain. Chains of mountains constituting the Coast Range and, further inland, the Cascades-Sierra Nevadas regulate the moisture fall, and widely different latitudes are related, from north to south, to increasing temperatures, evaporation, and dryness. The Sacramento and San Joaquin Valleys are flat, fertile, and moistened by small rivers and irrigation canals; they enjoy mild temperatures and a long growing season.

The land east of the Cascades-Sierra Nevadas is dry, frequently desert. In the Pacific Northwest it can be suitable for grazing or the raising of fruit and hard wheat. Most of eastern Oregon is sparsely populated. The same is true of Nevada, and much of eastern California is wasteland.

Southern California, cut off by mountains to the north, is much dryer and warmer than most of the valley in northern California, and is especially suitable for winter crops. Northern and southern California have their focal centers in the cities of San Francisco and Los Angeles, respectively.

In Linguistic Atlas check sheets and field records, a relatively high number of informants were polled in these important urban centers; otherwise, the gathering of data has been more or less uniform throughout all areas.

Maps 1-4 below illustrate the distribution of northern trace forms in the Pacific States, and it will be noted that previous observations are here confirmed. Folk terms for the dragonfly are more accurately depicted in moist areas, although definitions may also be adjusted in those places where the insect is rare. Nevertheless, this "Northern" term has its greatest relative concentration in northern Washington and Idaho, in eastern Idaho, in the San Francisco Bay Area, and in the Sacramento Valley.

A much more limited, but similar distribution is to be seen for the word *stoop* on Map 2, and again for the term *Dutch cheese* on Map 3, as well as for *johnny cake* on Map 4. The participation of California and Nevada in the use of such forms is relatively feeble, and distributions there are less predictable than in the Northwest because of the complicated settlement patterns described above. While San Francisco and its derivative sectors throughout the Sacramento Valley were settled in the early days by people from Northern dialect areas, various Midland groups soon followed, and clusters of divergent dialect speakers came to be located next to one another.

Nevada has been settled largely from California, first in response to gold discoveries, later as an extension of agricultural interests in the Sacramento Valley. The early seeding of Northern forms in Nevada is less significant than the initial planting in adjacent sections of California and is thus frequently obscured by the Midland influence of a later era.

Southern California shows a curious overlay of Northern and Midland forms, a situation occasioned also by successive waves of settlement involving the simultaneous arrival of diverse elements by sea as well as by land routes. Both San Bernardino and Riverside were founded by Northern speakers, and the descendants of these pioneers seem to have perpetuated their Northern characteristics up to the present day. In the course of time, other

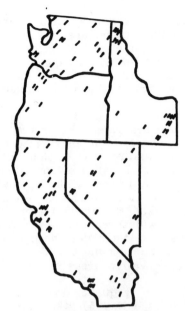

1. *(devil's) darning needle*
'dragonfly'

2. *stoop 'back porch'*

Northern terms (/).

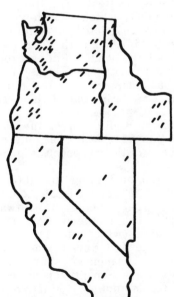

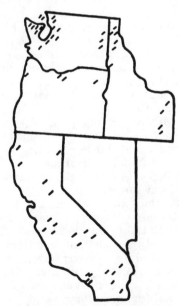

3. *Dutch cheese 'cottage cheese'*

4. *johnny cake 'corn bread'*

Northern terms (/).

groups came from both Midland and Southern areas (including Oklahoma, Arkansas, and Texas), and their traces are also unmistakable in the speech of this area. Los Angeles itself is heavily represented by people from New York and its neighboring States, as well as by those from areas further south, so that it shares too in the retention of trace forms from both Northern and Midland areas.

The Midland folk words for the dragonfly, *snake feeder* and *snake doctor*, see on Map 11, reflect most accurately the prominent areas of early Midland settlement. These are supported also by occurrences of the term *dog irons* for andirons (see Map 10), and (*barn*) *lot* for barnyard (see Map 9). Because of conditions peculiar to stock raising in the dry lands, however, the Spanish term *corral* has replaced other synonyms for barnyard, especially in California, Nevada, and Idaho, so that the trace forms are diminished accordingly. Similarly, the widespread use of a fire grate has all but eliminated andirons and their designations in approximately the same areas; hence, the diminution of (*barn*) *lot* here in contrast to the more conservative areas of western Oregon and southwestern Washington.

Other Midland terms of relatively high frequency in all areas are *roasting ears* for corn-on-the-cob (see Map 5) *piece* (*meal*) (or *piecing*) for a snack between meals (see Map 6), and *smearcase* for cottage cheese (see Map 7). The fact that the word *piece* (*meal*) follows regular Midland patterns is remarkable in view of its low prevalence in the eastern United States. On the other hand, the expression *quarter till* (eleven), which is widely used in the eastern Midlands, is drastically restricted in California and Nevada, even though well represented in the Pacific Northwest. The high occurrence of *quarter to* in all the Pacific States except Oregon reflects the strong use of this form in most areas of the East Coast: it is nearly as common as *quarter of* in the North, and is the only alternative to *quarter till* in the Midland and the South.

Of surprisingly strong occurrence in California is the word *mosquito hawk* for the dragonfly (see Map 12), which is generally known as a Southern term. Otherwise, Southern speech is poorly represented in all areas.

Maps 13 through 20 have information pertaining to California and Nevada alone. Isoglosses on Maps 13 and 14 are adapted from the work of Elizabeth Bright.[1] They show the outward limitations of usage for certain terms in Northern California. The distribution of *chesterfield* for sofa (which stops short of the northern tier of counties in California and Nevada) has been attributed to the commercial thrust of San Francisco, some enterprising dealers, and the effective delivery of San Francisco newspapers. The provenance of *shiners* for minnows, *burial/burying ground* for cemetery, and *public school* for grammar school, is still unknown, but their isoglosses here illustrate something of the speech continuity in Northern California and Nevada.

5. *roasting ear 'corn on the cob'*

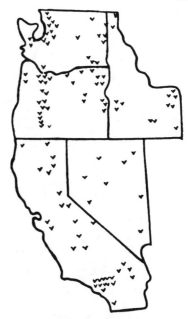

6. *piece(meal), piecing 'snack'*

Midland terms (v)

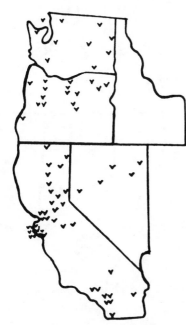

7. *smearcase 'cottage cheese'*

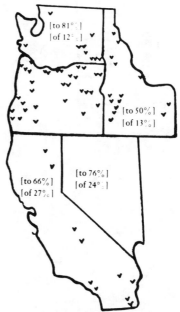

8. *quarter till 'quarter of'*

Midland terms (v)

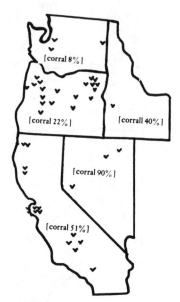

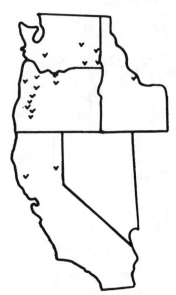

9. (barn) lot 'barnyard'   **10. dogirons 'andirons'**

Midland terms (v)

11. v snake doctor 'dragonfly'   **12. mosquito hawk 'dragon fly'**

∧ snake feeder

Midland terms (v   ∧).   *Southern term (o).*

Maps 15-18 show some of the unique contours of urban areas. A commercial term for flat, spirally formed sweet rolls is *butter-horns* in San Francisco and *snails* in Los Angeles as well as in other areas (*butterhorns* are most common in Washington, *snails* in Oregon).

In the matter of pronunciation, certain items are common to both cities: the use of a low unrounded vowel in the words *wash* or *on* (see Maps 16 and 17), and the use of a simple open [ɛ] in words like egg, rather than a higher mid-front vowel or a diphthong (see Map 18).

The localization of certain common phenomena and the application of different terms for the same is illustrated by words for a warm dry/moist wind, called a *chinook* in the Northwest and in Nevada, and a *Santa Ana* (or *Santana*) in southern California. Adoption of the Spanish terms is typical in the latter area, particularly with items of topography, ranching, or food. Map 20 indicates the area where *arroyo* is used in reference to a large dry gully. Although many Spanish loans are widely current throughout the West, the use of this term corresponds to the primary area of Spanish influence in California. Continued use of the Spanish language, particularly in southern California, adds a special dimension to the speech patterns of the Southwest. At the same time it promises to complicate once more the developing historical effects of what has here been described as an ebbing and flowing of diverse populations with consequent mixtures of English in California and Nevada.

FOOTNOTE

[1]All items have been checked carefully in the archives of the Linguistic Atlas of California and Nevada, located at the University of California in Berkeley.

13. -o-o-shiners 'minnows'
-----chesterfield 'sofa'
(northern limits)

14. -----burial/burying ground
-o-o-public school

15. butterhorns 'sweet rolls'

(otherwise: snails)

16. [wăs]

(otherwise: [wɒš])

17. put it on! [an]
(otherwise: [ɒn])

18. eggs [ɛ]
(otherwise: [eɪ/ɛɪ/e])

(dry) warm wind

I chinook

II Santa Ana

arroyo 'dry wash gully'

(Spanish loan-word)

UNSTRESSED VOWELS IN

APPALACHIAN ENGLISH

Ronald R. Butters

Despite recent attempts at "bridging the gap" between "atlas dialectologists" and those interested in "language in society," there persists today something of a split between the two groups.[1] Thus Wolfram (1978) points out in a sharp review of Shores and Hines (1977) a lamentable degree of imperviousness on the part of dialect geographers to the recent findings of sociolinguists. One might likewise cite McDavid and O'Cain (1977, p. 39), who bemoan "the frequent assertion by sociolinguists of the restricted ethnic status of [existential] *it*" - when the established position of sociolinguists has been just the opposite: that *it* for *there* is widespread in both black and white speech in the American South, though the variable-rule frequency may be greatest among some black subgroups (Wolfram and Fasold 1974, p. 171; Wolfram and Christian 1976, p. 126).

The imperviousness, however, is present on both sides. Social dialectologists (for example, Wolfram and Christian 1976) have also neglected important work of the area linguists. The purpose of this paper is thus twofold: (1) to discuss the final unstressed schwa in Appalachian speech and (2) to further the spirit of unified effort between the two schools by interpreting the Wolfram and Christian analysis (pp. 66-67) in the light of such "area" materials as Kurath and McDavid (1961).

Wolfram and Christian maintain that final unstressed schwa, as in *soda*, *extra*, and *sofa*, is variably raised and fronted in Appalachian speech to the high front vowel [i], spelled either *y* or *ee* in literary dialect (*soda* becoming *sodee* or *sody*); they find no such variant, however, for other final reduced-stressed vowels, for example, the [ə] (from /o/) of *tomato*.[2] While theirs is the best discussion of the phenomenon so far, atlas dialectology illuminates their thesis in at least three different ways.

First, there is a basic question: Is schwa-raising peculiar to Appalachian speech? Wolfram and Christian's study is based upon lengthy taped interviews with 165 natives of two counties in southeastern West Virginia during 1974-75. Kurath and McDavid

From *American Speech* 56:104-110, 1971. Reprinted with permission.

cover a much wider area and their data is several decades older; it is instructive to note (though Wolfram and Christian do not) that the earlier study does in fact find a final raised vowel for *sofa* and *china* in West Virginia, though also "with some frequency in northern New England, . . . and in the upper South, and relics of it appear elsewhere" (pp. 168-69). If final schwa-raising, then, is not exclusively Appalachian, it is nonetheless clearly Appalachian speech, and not something peculiar to the small area studied by Wolfram and Christian. Here (and everywhere) a look at *The Pronunciation of English in the Atlantic States* puts their observation in a far better geographical perspective.

Second, Wolfram and Christian are clearly wrong in the assertion that the phonetic character of "raised schwa" is the high front (tense) vowel [i]. The symbol used in Kurath and McDavid (pp. 168-69) is [ɨ], a central, lax vowel slightly lower and more retarded than [i], with little or no offglide, and alternating with the fully fronted counterpart [I] - or rather, as Lee Pederson points out (personal communication), there is a continuum between the central and front vowels. Of course, it is well-known that lax vowels, not tense ones, are the rule in unstressed syllables in English; the real question is why Wolfram and Christian say what they say. Perhaps the fact that their book is intended to be used by nonlinguists as well as linguists led them to what could be viewed as too great a simplification. Moreover, in their defense, it is also the case that the vowel in question may sometimes be fronted, tensed, and raised in the DIRECTION of [i], to some variant of the intermediate vowel [ɨ] (see the discussion of the Asheville, N.C., data below). Still, an examination of Kurath and McDavid might have suggested to Wolfram and Christian how inadequate their statement was. In sum: Appalachian schwa-raising varies from a higher mid central vowel to a high front diphthong and includes the intermediate positions.

Finally, and most important, there is the distribution of schwa-raising. Is the phenomenon limited solely to "words that actually end in a schwa-type sound"? In particular, is it true that "the process is not observed to apply to items which alternate a schwa with a final *ow*" (p. 67)?

The generalization proposed by Wolfram and Christian is vulnerable from two sides. First, there is clear evidence from dialect geography that at least two words in American English, *minnow* and *borrow*, have schwa-raising; furthermore, data collected in 1974 in North Carolina show [ɨ] fromm underlying final /o/ in several other words as well. Second, various considerations suggest [ɨ] ~ [ə] in some words ending in neither /ə/ nor /o/.

The case for the raising of final /o/ is clear. Allen (1977, p. 14) reports a high unrounded vowel finally in *minnow* in 25 percent of his Type I speakers and 12 percent of Type II.[3] Of course, Allen's study deals with the upper Midwest, not Appalachia, and his findings were perhaps published too late for Wolfram and Christian to have seen them. Moreover, Allen reports no fronting at all among his subjects in *meadow* , *tomato* , and *widow* (though variably *meadow* and *widow* suspiciously raise to what Allen writes as /u/). Still, his *minnow* is intriguing; one wishes that Wolfram and Christian had tried to elicit it from their subjects. Far more compelling, however, is *borrow*: Kurath and McDavid (pp. 169-70, maps 152-53) list /i/ (pronounced [ɨ] for *borrow* almost categorically in the folk speech of not only Appalachia, but also the entire South and South Midland area - including, of course, the very Mercer and Monroe counties in which Wolfram and Christian claim the phenomenon does not exist.

To be fair, *borrow* is the only final-/o/ word that Kurath and McDavid list with final /i/ in the Atlantic states. *Tomato* ending in [ə] or [ɚ] is reported in Appalachian folk speech (p. 179); similar are *widow*, *meadow*, and *yellow*. Still, one doubts that *borree* (and perhaps *minnee*) has passed totally out of existence in Mercer and Monroe counties in the thirty or so years between the two studies. If so, the disappearance itself would be of interest. Unfortunately, Wolfram and Christian were apparently unaware of the possibility, and so the question remains unanswered in their analysis.

My own data, however, indicates that [ɨ] from /o/ is still found in Appalachia particularly and in the Southern states generally, in *borrow* and other words as well.

The case of *borrow* is again especially clear. M.E. is a white female who has lived in rural Appalachian communities near Asheville, North Carolina, all her life (37 years when interviewed in May 1974). In her speech, *borrow* seems to have been relexified to [barɨ]; seven instances of *borrow* occur in the transcript, all with raised, centralized, and unrounded final vowels: *a borrowed ram*, *a borreed one*, *I borreed 'im*, *borree money* (twice), *borree some*, and *borree a suitcase*. All seven are clearly [ɨ] and not [ʊ], [ɫ], [ə], or [i].[4]

Borrow is, however, the only word in M.E.'s interview that shows [ɨ] from /o/. (It is interesting to note that she does not raise any of the final underlying schwas found in her sample, all of which occur in place-names: *Guatemala*, *Cuba*, *Bermuda*, *Virginia*, and *Oklahoma*.)[5] Other informants add further counterexamples to the Wolfram and Christian thesis. A semiliterate retired black domestic (aged 80 in August 1974) produced *someone to play the pianee* [piyæni], *he* . . . , though she also said [piyænə] in the phrase *piano player* in the next sentence. Another black informant (age 73) pronounced raised unstressed vowels variably at the end of two words with final underlying /o/: *Shiloh and* was [ša:ɫæn] but also [šaɫouænd]; *radio* was [rediow] once in sentence-final position, while *radio on* appeared as both [rediowon] (once) and [redɨon] (three times). Of course, both of these speakers are black, whereas Appalachian is usually viewed as a white dialect; moreover, while the second was from Appalachia (Asheville), the first was from Wilmington, on the coast. Still, it seems safe to conclude that /o/ is in fact raised to [ɨ] in Appalachian folk speech - in *borrow*, perhaps in *minnow*, perhaps sporadically in other /o/ words (*piano*, *radio*, *Shiloh*) as well.

At the very least, the sociolinguists' conclusion must be tested (if not modified) in light of the earlier scholarship.

And what about other vowels under reduced stress in final position - are any of them reduced to [ɨ] or [ɨ]? Wolfram and Christian say no, but are otherwise mute on the topic; Kurath and McDavid mention only the obvious reduction of final /i/ (*thirty*, *Cincinnati*). This reduction - a further (if minor) exception to the Wolfram and Christian dictum that only "underlying schwa" ends up as an *ee*-like vowel - is worth a brief digression, however. First, one of the items treated as ending in phonemic /i/ by Kurath and McDavid seems better treated as ending in underlying /e/ (*Thursday*); if so, it is a further exception to the Wolfram and Christian view. Second, words such as *belly* and *Sophie* show dialect variation, [ɨ] being more common in the South, [ɨ] in the North, though "many speakers in Eastern New England and New York City" use the former rather than the latter (Bronstein 1960, p. 147). Dialects such as Appalachian therefore blur a contrast which in other areas of the South is, in Sledd's words (1966), p. 31), of "great importance" structurally - *sofa*, *Stella*, *mister*, *comma*, *Bella* contrasting with *Sophie*, *telly*, *misty*, *Commie*, *belly*. This loss of contrast could be one reason that schwa-raising may be dying out.

Third, as Sturtevant noted as early as 1917 (pp. 79-80) some words ending in underlying final /i/ (for example, *Missouri*) are reduced all the way to [ə] by a process that seems to be the reverse of the schwa-raising in *sofa*. Sturtevant, in fact, connected the two processes, seeing hypercorrection as accounting for /i/-lowering: speakers who were told that *Nevada* is not "Nevady" decided that *Missouri* must be "Missoura." The trouble with this line of reasoning is that some speakers who favor "Missoura" go right on saying "Nevady." If they are hypercorrecting, they are unaccountably failing to correct the pronunciations that are actually "wrong." Among such speakers, according to Kurath and McDavid (map 150), are the Appalachian ancestors of Wolfram and Christian's informants, who prefer [ə] in both *Missouri* and *Cincinnati*, but [ɨ] in *thirty* and *happy*. The explanation of Pace (1960) is a rather persuasive one. Noting that, for the most part, the words with /i/ > [ə] all end in -*i*, Pace suggests that what we are observing is the result of a spelling pronunciation. Nineteenth century spelling manuals prescribed /ay/ as the preferred pronunciation for final-*i* - an Anglicized pronunciation still preferred by many today in such loan words as *alumni* and *quasi* (and obligatorily in *rabbi*). According to Pace, [ə] is the logical phonetic reduction for /ay/.[6]

Dialect geography thus offers several modifications of Wolfram and Christian's assertion that schwa-raising affects only "underlying schwa"; /o/, /e/, and /i/ are to some extent involved as well. Finally, here are a pair of observations for further investigation. First, the final vowels of the following do not seem likely candidates for [ɨ] ~ [ɨ] realization: *Dachau*, *rabbi*, *Tolstoy*, *Arkansas*. These are loanwords, not common in schwa-raising dialects and never pronounced with light enough stress on the final vowel to allow its reduction to any central vowel (including schwa). Second, /u/ certainly does reduce to [ɨ] sometimes; at least it does so in many dialects in unstressed monosyllables (*you know   y'know* [yɨnow]; *to use* [tɨyuwz]), and *menu* also seems likely, [mɛnyu] unrounding to [mɛnyɨ]. M.E. (the *borree* speaker above) in one instance clearly unrounds and fronts *value* to something very close to [vælyɨ].

FOOTNOTES

[1]Attempts at bridge building were, for example, the Third International Conference on Methods in dialectology (University of Western Ontario, London, Ontario, 1-9 August 1978) and the joint meeting of NWAVE and the American Dialect Society at Georgetown University (Washington, D.C., 2-4 November 1978).

[2]It is perhaps worth pointing out that, in Chomsky-Halle transformational phonology, there is no underlying schwa; in *The Sound Pattern of English* (p. 75), such words as *agenda* have underlying final /æ/. The Chomsky-Halle analysis seems to accord well with Pace's ideas (1960) on alternative pronunciations of *Cincinnati* (see below), but otherwise does not affect my discussion in any way that I can see. It should also be noted that words ending in /o/ may develop *r*-coloring in various dialects. Wolfram and Christian (p. 66) find it in *hollow, tobacco, yellow, potatoes, windows, Narrows* (a place-name), and internally at morpheme boundaries (*following, swallowing*). Wolfram and Christian agree with Kurath and McDavid (p. 170) that this phenomenon is "sporadic . . . in West Virginia" but assert that it is "more sporadic in the speech of the current generation than it apparently was at one time."

[3]Type I speakers are relatively uneducated (not high-school graduates) and are generally older; Type II speakers are high-school graduates but not college educated, and are generally middle-aged.

[4]Tape A7A, feet 408-30, recorded in notebook 12, pp. 15-16. In the text that follows, note the use of [ɚ] for *ow* in *yellow*, as well as the fact that the sociolinguist interviewer - far from anticipating [ɨ] from final /o/ - does not even understand the term *borreed* until it is explained to him:

M.E.: I've got three cows and three calves in the front pasture, and got five ol' horses down yonder, and one of 'em don't belong to us, and we're gonna sell one, and then I've got two, two ewes and a 1-, a *borreed* [barɨd] ram.

R.B.: Oh really?

M.E.: (laughs)

R.B.: (laughs)

M.E.:   And got - let's see, I got the dog on the hill and one that's loose, and I got a tomcat and another *yeller* [yɛlə] cat . . . and the husband and the daughter's got a rabbit project on the hill (laughs). How many's up there I don't know, I don't bother, I don't go up there, that's theirs (laughs).   I got enough to feed and take care of.

R.B.:   What kind of a ram did you say it was?

M.E.:   They're Hampshires. (Pause.) They're Hampshires. A *borreed* [barɨd] one.

R.B.:   A "borreed" one?

M.E.:   A *borreed* [barɨd] one.

R.B.:   What does that mean?

M.E.:   I *borreed* '*im* [barɨd ɨm]!

R.B.:   Oh, I see (laughs). I see (laughs).

[6]Place-names are, of course, apt to be unpredictable. Karl Nicholas (personal communication) reports that the natives of the Appalachian town of *Sylva* , *N.C.*, regularly pronounce it [sIlvɨ] and *Junaluska* [ǰunəlʌskɨ]. Nearby *Nantahala Gorge* and *Culasaja Gorge* regularly end in [ə], however.

The pronunciation of *Iowa* as [ayowe] (as opposed to the natives' [ayowə]) is probably a similar spelling pronunciation.

[Ed. note: That the final vowel of *borrow* manifests raising outside the Appalachian area, as Butters insists, is supported by further evidence in the *Linguistic Atlas of the Upper Midwest*. Seven of the 208 informants, all of them in the oldest and least educated class, have retained a raised final vowel. Six of the seven are in Midland speech territory.   Butters might well have noted also that the reduction of final /i/ to schwa is not inevitably linked to a spelling with final *i*, as Pace asserts, since in the Upper Midwest 18 of the 208 informants have schwa as the final vowel in *prairie*.]

REFERENCES

Allen, Harold B. 1977. "The linguistic atlas of the Upper Midwest as a source of sociolinguistic information." In *James B. McMillan: Essays in Linguistics by His Friends and Colleagues*, ed. J. C. Raymond and I. W. Russell, pp. 3-20. University, Ala.: Univ. of Alabama Press.

Bronstein, Arthur J.   1960. *The Pronunciation of American English*. Englewood Cliffs, J.N.: Prentice-Hall.

Chomsky, Noam, and Halle, Morris. 1968. *The Sound Pattern of English*. New York: Harper and Row.

Kurath, Hans, and McDavid, Raven, I., Jr. 1961. *The Pronunciation of English in the Atlantic States*. Ann Arbor: Univ. of Michigan Press.

McDavid, Raven I., Jr. and O'Cain, Raymond. 1977. "'Existential' *there* and *it*: an essay on method and interpretation of data." In *James B. McMillan: Essays in Linguistics by His Friends and Colleagues*, ed. J. C. Raymond and I. W. Russell, pp. 20-40. University, Ala.: Univ. of Alabama Press.

Pace, George B. 1960. "Linguistic geography and names ending in i ." *American Speech* 35:175-87.

Shores, David L., and Hines, Carole P., eds. 1977. *Papers in Language Variation: SAMLA-ADS Collection*. University, Ala.: Univ. of Alabama Press.

Sledd, James H. 1966. "Breaking, umlaut, and the southern drawl." *Language* 42: 18-41.

Sturtevant, Edgar H. 1917. *Linguistic Change*. Chicago: Univ. of Chicago Press.

Wolfram, Walt. 1978. Review of *Papers in Language Variation*, ed. D. L. Shores and C. P. Hines. *Language* 54: 679-81.

Wolfram, Walt, and Christian, Donna. 1976. *Appalachian Speech*. Arlington, Va.: Center for Applied Linguistics.

Wolfram, Walt, and Fasold, Ralph. 1974. *The Study of Social Dialects in American English*. Englewood Cliffs, N.J.: Prentice-Hall.

LANGUAGE VARIATION -- SOME REALITIES

Frederic G. Cassidy

For broad theorizing about language, language itself has to be seen broadly. So Chomsky describes the primary concern of linguistic theory as limited to an "ideal speaker-listener, in a completely homogeneous speech-community."[1] While this statement tacitly recognizes the fact of linguistic variation within actual speech-communities, it yet leaves out of consideration the "unideal" data. However necessary this approach may be to the theorist, it may make him feel safer than he is: the data he leaves aside are quite as real as the part he chooses to utilize. Variation is intrinsic to language. The simplifying theorist takes the risk of remaining unaware of the extent of variation, its causes or correlates, and its use as a tool for analysis and classification. His approach can be justified only as an initial one; ultimately he must admit the realities of unidealized language--not language as he chooses to see it, but language as it is.

In the past few years a reaction to such disembodied theory has set in. A number of scholars have insisted that variation has to be dealt with, and that methods for dealing with it must be devised.[2] One of the chief forces behind this reaction has been the continuing work of linguistic geographers,[3] whose findings had forced variation into the open as a fact of linguistic life. The following short presentation is an example of the degree to which variation and elaboration can go--has actually gone--in respect to a single word in a limited area of the United States within the past few generations, such that no less than forty phonemically different forms have developed (to say nothing of subphonemic variants); and further, of the fact that more than half of these forms are due to the "capture" of a formerly separate word, with its variants, all in current use in this century. The word under consideration is *catalpa*.[4]

The common catalpa is an American tree (*Catalpa bignonioides* and *C. speciosa*) native to the lower Mississippi basin, whence it was brought east around 1730 and naturalized thereafter throughout the settled area of the southern and midland states. The tree is not only well known for its handsome racemes of fragrant white flowers and as a shade and lumber tree, but as the source

of a favorite fish-bait, the *catalpa worm* (*Ceratomia catalpae*) which
infests the leaves, appropriately, in early summer.

The word which was "captured" by *catalpa* is *Catawba*, an
Indian tribal name (Choctaw *katapa*) applied also to the Catawba
River of North Carolina, along which these Indians dwelt, and to
a native grape from which a favorite wine is made. *Catawba*,
identified in the popular mind with *catalpa*, was therefore transferred to the tree and the worm. While it is true that *catawba* could
have developed as a phonetic variant of *catalpa* by simple vocalization of the /l/ (a fact which no doubt made the appearance of
identity easier) it is far more likely, since the Indians were
known earlier in the area than the tree, that when the tree was
brought in its similar name, *catalpa*, was understood as a form
of *Catawba*. Indeed, in an early source we find the statement
that "In the Carolinas and in Georgia the catalpa is called Catawbaw
Tree, from a tribe of Indians by that name who inhabited that
part of the country."[5]

The standard spelling of *catalpa* was arrived at at once.
Creek *kutuhlpa* was latinized as the genus name with three *a*'s,
and this remained as the English spelling, though the first-syllable
[ʊ] and the last-syllable [ɑ] became [ə] in English, responding
normally to the word's second-syllable stress. The earliest recorded spelling of catawba is *cattaba*,[6] the stressed *a*, like that in
catalpa, being of uncertain quality; but the history of these
spellings[7] makes /ɑ/ or /ɔ/ equally possible. For both words,
significantly, the stress is without exception on the middle syllable,
and the consonantal framework is /k-t-(1)p/. While this basic
similarity makes it understandable that *catalpa* could "capture"
catawba and its forms, it gives no hint why so surprising a
series of variants should have developed. But let us look at the
variants.

In the following tabulations, each variant is given with the
personal code of the informant[8] whose response it was to any
one of three interview questions: P5: What do you call the
common worm used as bait? P6: Other kinds of worms also
used as bait? and T9: The common shade tree with large heart-
shaped leaves, clusters of white blossoms, and long thin seed
pods or 'beans'? From *DARE*'s 1002 communities, putting the worm
and tree responses together, we received 541 examples of *catalpa*,
143 of *catawba*, and forty forms varying in one or more phonemes
from either of these. To P5 there were only four responses,
all *catawba* (FL26, MP1, NC6, OK23).

Variant names for the worm were twenty-three, reported from
five states; those for the tree were thirty-one, reported from
the same five states and ten others, many of which are beyond
the natural range of the worm, though the tree grows there.

An analysis of biographical or "social" facts (age, education,
sex, race, type of community, occupation) about the thirty-five
DARE informants who used these variants shows:

Table I

Forms (*DARE* spellings)		Resp. to P6 (worm)	Resp. to T9 (tree)
1.	batawfel	IL4	--	/bə'tɔfəl
2.	batawga	NC1	--	bə'tɔga
3.	bitawby	LA7	--	b 'tɔbɪ
4.	catabla	LA10	/kə'tɑblə	kə'tɑblə
5.	catabla	LA15	kə'tɑblə	kə'tɑblə
6.	catabla	LA31	--	kə'tɑblə
7.	catabla	LA34	kə'tɑblə	--
8.	cataca	seGA	kə'tɑkə	--
9.	cataga	seGA	kə'tɑgə	--
10.	catalba	TN67	--	kə'tɑlb ə
11.	catalca	MR5	--	kə'tælk ə
12.	catalfa	KY11	kə'tælfə	--
13.	catalfa	csKY	--	kə'tælfə
14.	catalfy	IL96	--	kə'tælfɪ
15.	catalpy	IL96	--	kə'tælp ɪ
16.	catapa	KA12	--	kə'tap ə
17.	catapwa	DL3	--	kə'tɑpw ə
18.	catawfa	MD13	--	kə'tɔfə
19.	catawpa	FL20	--	kə'tɔpə
20.	catawpa	IL50	--	kə'tɔpə
21.	catawpa	WI71	--	kə'tɔpə
22.	catowba	seGA	kə'taʊbə	--
23.	fataga	GA72	f ɘtɑgə	--
24.	kitaber	seGA	kɾ'tɑbər	--
25.	kitarber	seGA	kɾ'tɑrbər	--
26.	kitarby	MD42	--	kɾ'tɑrbɾ
27.	kitawber	seGA	kɾ'tɔbər	--
28.	macaltha	csKY	mə'kælθə	--
29.	patalca	IA22	--	pə'tælkə
30.	patalca	MR15	--	pə'tælkə
31.	patalfy	TN26	--	pə'tælf ɾ
32.	patalpa	KY43	pə'tælpə	--
33.	patawber	GA25	--	pə'tɔbər
34.	patawca	DL5	--	pə'tɔkə
35.	patorber	GA25	pə'tɔrbər	--
36.	taba	LA7	'tɑbə	--
37.	taber	seGA	'tɑbər	--
38.	taipa	seGA	'taɾpə	--
39.	talfa	KY23	'tælfə	--
40.	talfy	TN26	'tælfɾ	--
41.	talky	IN35	--	'tælkɾ

(continued)

TABLE I (continued)

Forms (*DARE* spellings)		Resp. to P6 (worm)	Resp. to T9 (tree)
42.	talpa KY21	--	'tælpə
43.	talpa KY43	--	'tælpə
44.	talpin csKY	'tælpɪn	--
45.	talpy csKY	'tælpɪ	--
46.	tataba seGA	tæ'tɑbə	--
47.	toby IL97	--	'tobi
48.	toby PA70	--	'tobi
49.	toby PA74	--	'tobi
50.	toby PA95	--	'tobi
51.	toby PA134	--	'tobi/
52.	topple IL67	tɑpl/	--
			(metathesis)

(1) that they were chiefly from rural communities: only three were urban; sixteen were of the most rural type, ten of the next most rural, six from small cities within a rural area independent of any metropolis.

(2) that twenty-seven were old (sixty years and over), six middle-aged, two young. (Sixty-six percent of *DARE* informants were old; these twenty-seven old are seventy-seven percent.)

(3) that most (nineteen) had no more than grade school education, though eight had high school and eight at least two years at college. (Twenty-seven percent of *DARE* informants had grade school education; these nineteen are fifty-four percent.)

(4) that only one black informant gave a variant--probably a matter of accident.

(5) that twenty-six were men, nine women, which may mean merely that more men go fishing or have to do with trees. As to occupations, there were thirteen farmers, six skilled workers (welder, blacksmith, carpenter, paperhanger, painter, fisherman), five housekeepers, two teachers, a motel operator and a storekeeper, a mailman and a policeman, a clerical worker, a journalist, a swamp guide and a salesman, and finally an administrator. Again, most of these occupations would not require a high degree of book-learning but would keep the speakers outdoors and dispose them to be aware of catalpa trees and worms.

What of the conditions contributing to produce this very large number of variant forms? Certain points can be made:

(1) The "capture" of *catawba* and its variants by *catalpa* more than doubled the number of variants. As already noted, these could have developed by direct phonetic change, but probably

did not. *Catawba* was earlier and better known than *catalpa*, was identified with it in sound, and then the sense was transferred from the Indians, the river, and the grape to the tree and the worm. The identification, already made in the early eighteenth century, was confirmed in the nineteenth, and in this century no less than forty variants have been found in use for the word *catalpa.*

(2) The stress on both words is without exception on the second syllable; there is no evidence it was ever anywhere else, not even in the Indian etyma. This has produced the two-syllable aphetic forms, *talpa*, *toby*, and so on--twelve variants.

(3) Though a botanical Latin form was produced early, and English spelling quickly settled down to *catalpa* and *catawba* , these written forms would have had little influence. The words were chiefly spoken--the variants developed under phonetic conditions hardly limited by reference to a spelled or standard form. One learns about good fish bait not from school books or newspapers, but from fishermen. In the oral tradition variation occurs more easily and frequently than under the literate tradition.

(4) Sound changes, while not obviously systematic and in individual cases not predictable, follow certain expectable patterns:

(a) Substitution of Consonants:

Initially: for /k/, /p/ patalka, etc.

/b/ batawga, etc.

/t/ tatawba

/f/ fataga

/m/ macaltha

Medially: for /t/, /k/ macaltha

Finally: for /lp/, /lk/ catalca, etc.

/lb/ catalba

/bl/ catabla (metathesis)

/lf/ catalfy

/fl/ batawfel (metathesis)

/lθ/ macaltha

(b) Intrusion of Consonants:

Medially: /r/ catarby, etc.

Finally: /r/ patawber, etc.

/l/ batawfel

/n/ talpin

/w/ catapwa

(c)   Variation of Vowels:

Initially: for /ə/, /ɪ/ kitarber

Medially: for /a/ or /ɑ/, /æ/ catalca, etc.

, /ɔ/ patawber

, /o/ toby, etc.

, /aʊ/ catowba

, /aɪ/ taipa

Finally: for /ə/, /ɪ/   catalfy, etc.

There are examples of metathesis, voicing and devoicing, the
possible vocalization of /l/ already mentioned, perhaps assimilation,
and even some folk-etymology (i.e., unetymological association
with more familiar words whose form is therefore wholly or partly
adopted).   While these and other phonetic alterations are always
latent, the structure of these two basic words, *catalpa* and
catawba, made them especially susceptible.   This unusual array
of variants was the result.

(5) Certain clearly regional or local forms developed: *catabla* in Louisiana (5); *toby* (for the tree) in Pennsylvania (4),
with one example in Illinois (the informants' parents from Maryland).

(6) Some informants had dual forms: IL96 said both *catalpy*
and *catalfy*; GA25 said both *patorber* and *patawber*; LA7 said *taba*
for the worm but *bitawby* for the tree.   This may have several
possible causes--individual vacillation, influence of local variantion,
or possibly increasing influence from the written form.   Though
education encourages conformity, new variants are still possible
in speech: the phase of elaboration and dispersion may not yet
be over.

Summing up, it seems necessary to repeat that, however useful
it may be in its own way, the idealization of any language hides
some realities of that language, one of which is that variation is
intrinsic, that conscious or unconscious creation of new forms is
always *in potentia*.   No "grammar" or linguistic system can be
complete unless it includes the means of dealing with these variants.

FOOTNOTES

[1]Chomsky, Noam. 1965. *Aspects of the Theory of Syntax*. Cambridge, Mass.: M.I.T. Press, p. 3.
[2]See especially Labov, William. 1966. *The Social Stratification of English in New York City*. Washington: Center for Applied Linguistics; Fasold, R. W. 1970. "Two models of socially significant variation", *Language* 25:29-50; Bickerton, Derek. 1971. "Inherent variability and variable rules". In *Foundations of Language* 7:457-92; Bailey, C. J. and R. Shuy, eds. 1973. *New Ways of Analyzing Variation in English* . Washington: Georgetown University Press; Bailey, C. J. 1974. *Variation and Linguistic Theory*. Washington: Georgetown University Press.
[3]The atlases of New England and the Atlantic Coast are now well known. Most recent to be published is Harold B. Allen's *The Linguistic Atlas of the Upper Midwest*, Vol. 1, 1973; Vol. 2, 1975; Vol. 3, 1976.
[4]Our evidence was gathered 1965-70 in oral interviews by fieldworkers for the *Dictionary of American Regional English*: 1002 communities covered in 50 states, the same questions being asked in each. To this are added four examples collected by Gordon Wilson in the Mammoth Cave area of Kentucky (1930-1965), and nine examples from the Dialect Survey of Rural Georgia (1968-75) kindly furnished by Dr. Joan Hall of the *DARE* staff. Wilson's examples are coded as csKY, Hall's as seGA.
[5]Browne, D. J. 1832. "Sylva 126". (From M. M. Mathews, *Dictionary of Americanisms*. Chicago: University of Chicago Press 1947).
[6]"1716 North Carolina Colonial Records" II:252 (From Mathews, ibid.)
[7]Compare "1721 Arkansias", "1770 Arcansas", "Arkansa", "1772 Arkansaws" (From Mathews, ibid.) By 1825 the present spelling had become pretty firmly established.
[8]*DARE* informant codes consist of two letters for the State plus the individual's own number. Thus DL3 is the third Delaware informant, representing Smyrna; PA134 is the 134th Pennsylvania informant, representing Hopwood.

THE CONTEMPORARY CONTEXT

OF CANADIAN ENGLISH

Walter S. Avis

About thirteen years ago, Randolph Quirk and the late Albert H. Marckwardt aired a public dialogue entitled *A Common Language*: *British and American English*, the gist of which was that xenophobes and chauvinists had long been exaggerating the differences between the two types and were thus guilty of oversimplification. At one point, this exchange took place:

QUIRK. When you speak of 'American English', do you include the English of Canada . . . as well as the English of the United States?

MARCKWARDT. The word 'American' is always giving Americans trouble. You see, it's the only word we have, really, to apply to people and things of the United States; but at the same time, it can apply to the entire continent as well, so that although there are some differences between the English of Canada and that of the United States, there aren't very many of them. And to use the term 'American English' for both . . . seems entirely satisfactory.

As a native speaker of Canadian English, I felt then that Al was himself guilty of oversimplification, especially since I had been holding forth on the subject for a dozen years beforehand; in fact, by that time I had co-edited two dictionaries in the Gage Dictionary of Canadian English series and was hard at work on two more. I can only hope that at this stage the existence of Canadian English--as distinct from British and American English-- has been established. Nevertheless, in view of the title of this conference and, indeed, of this particular panel, my contribution may be interpreted as somewhat eccentric; for I propose to talk about the present context of Canadian English, which I consider to be something more than some kind of regional variety of the English spoken in the United States.

It should be made clear at once that Canada is not now and never has been a monolingual nation of English speakers. Indeed,

Dialect and
Language Variation

during the seventeenth and a good part of the eighteenth centuries, Canada was in name and in fact a colony of France and the first European colonists were French-speaking, that is, francophones. Following the British conquests of the eighteenth century, the country attracted increasingly large numbers of English-speaking settlers from both the British Isles and the American Colonies to the south. From that day to this, the United Kingdom and the United States have been the principal source of immigrants to Canada. When the great influx of continental Europeans began at the close of the last century, English had become established as the dominant language in Canada. As a result, English was adopted by the non-anglophone newcomers, most of whom settled in English-speaking parts of Canada, from Ontario westward to the Prairies. Furthermore, the continuing stream of immigrants from the U.K. and, to a lesser extent, from the U.S. and the constant cultural influence exerted by these two countries reinforced the ascendency of the English language.

Yet the French Fact remained, particularly in Quebec, where French continues to be the mother tongue of the great majority. Yet every province has some French Canadians, many of whom are bilingual, and the English-French duality of Canada has been built in from the beginning. The British North American Act, which established Confederation on July 1, 1867, guaranteed the French Canadians the right to their religion and law within Quebec and to their language both there and in the federal Parliament. The Official Languages Act of July 1969 took further steps to protect French-Canadian rights, legalizing bilingualism by this stipulation, among others: "the English and French languages are the official languages of Canada" and "they possess and enjoy equality of status and equal rights and privileges as to their use in all the institutions of the Parliament and Government of Canada."

Canada, then, is legally a bilingual country in the sense that both English and French are the official languages; on the other hand, fewer than 14% of the population have knowledge of both languages. The fact is, however, that Canada is remarkably heterogeneous with respect to birthplace, ethnicity, religion, and language. According to the 1971 census, for example, 15.3% of the population were born outside Canada and 26.7% indicated that they belonged to an ethnic group other than British (44.6%) or French (28.7%). As to linguistic groups, the census supplies information under three headings: mother tongue, home language, and official language. Although 60.2% gave English as their mother tongue, 67% gave English as the language most used in the home; 26.9% gave French as their mother tongue, but only 7.3% used these languages most often in the home. The predominence of English becomes even more apparent in the statistics for the official-language situation: English only, 67.1%; French only, 18%; both, 13.4%, neither, 1.5%. These figures indicate that of all Canadians (some 23 million), 80.5% speak English and 31.4% speak French.

It should be pointed out that among bilinguals French Canadians far outnumber English Canadians, a clear consequence of
the former group being so long subject to economic and other
pressures that forced many of them to learn the language of the
majority.   Furthermore, over the past century or so, thousands
of ethnic French Canadians have been completely absorbed into
the anglophone community, especially in regions distant from the
Quebec heartland.   Thus, the Québécois, jealous of their cultural
heritage and surrounded by a sea of anglophones, not only on
the Canadian side of the border but to the south of it, came to
realize their peril; as their awareness of the threat grew, the
stronger their resistance to it became.

Although French-Canadian nationalism has had its advocates
from a time long before Confederation, the movement has been
strongly articulated during the past twenty years.   Out of the
"Quiet Revolution" of the 1960s grew the Separatist Movement,
which gained wide credence amongst those Québécois, the young
and the educated, who feared cultural and linguistic assimilation
and sought to offset it by becoming masters in their own home
("maîtres chez nous").   The extreme expression of this sentiment
was the terrorism perpetrated by the *Front de Libération du Qué-
bec* during the late 60s.   In the meantime, the non-violent but
no less dedicated *Parti Québécois* took up the cause of separation
under the leadership of René Lévesque.   This party, which is
committed to withdrawing Quebec from the Canadian Confederation,
was elected to the National Assembly, the provincial parliament
of Quebec, on November 15, 1976, with a substantial majority of
members and a significant plurality of the popular vote.   This
development, then, with the attendant prospect of what has been
called "deconfederation" is an important part of the background
against which the present position of Canadian English must be
considered.

Furthermore, as a relatively new country, Canada has attracted
immigrants of many origins, a multi-ethnic mixture augmented by
a substantial number of native people, both Amerindian and Inuit.
This great diversity, nurtured by Canada's preference for the
patchwork quilt of multiculturism as opposed to the melting-pot
policy, has set up additional stresses and strains which have
acted as a brake on the realization of a sense of national identity.

To these obstacles must be added the physical fact that 23
million Canadians occupy 3.8 million square miles of land, much
of it inhospitable and difficult of access; communication is both
costly and inconvenient and topographical differences extreme.
As a result, regional disagreements are frequent because of diverse
economic interests, ethnic origins, cultural aspirations, and political objectives.   All in all, the odds have been against the attainment of that spirit of common purpose that is a prerequisite of
healthy nationhood.

In name, Canada has become an independent country; in fact,
she is culturally divided and economically dependent.   For one
thing, the British connection dominated Canadian life for a century

and a half and carries some weight still, England's queen being Queen of Canada too; for another, the United States has made its presence felt since early colonial times. As the influence of John Bull became less, that of Uncle Sam became greater, with the result that its mighty tentacles now reach into every sphere of Canadian life. Indeed, the reasons for the intransigence of the Québécois lie much deeper than their differences with their Canadian compatriots, for they see Americanization as the ultimate threat to their way of life, that is, to their language and their cultural identity. On the other hand, most English-speaking Canadians would doubtless make substantial concessions to keep Quebec within Confederation because the alternative of having an independent Quebec isolate the Atlantic Provinces from the rest of Canada is unthinkable, especially since such a situation might lead to balkanization and eventual "statehood." All these matters, too, are relevant to the present context and therefore to the future of Canadian English.

This intensely pro-Canadian attitude is too often wrongly interpreted as anti-American. It should, on the contrary, be interpreted as indicative of a sense of national identity which is felt by most anglophones and perhaps still by most francophones; for Canada grew into nationhood under the stresses of this duality, in the awareness of two solitudes, and it is impossible to conceive of Canada otherwise. I am not saying that some other arrangement is inconceivable; it may even be inevitable. But the result will not be Canada. At the moment, however, Canada does exist, and it enjoys two official languages--French and English. Each has developed its own special Canadian character, an important ingredient of each being constant enrichment through cross-borrowing during many years of close association in North America. The result is two special varieties of these two languages--Canadian French and Canadian English, each with its own regional variants. My commitment, as you may know, has long been to the latter.

In its broad sense, the term Canadian English refers to the several regional varieties of English spoken in Canada. For historical reasons, the type of English associated with Southern Ontario, formerly Upper Canada, has become the basis for a national norm, an imperfectly described but recognized standard across Canada. This type, which may be designated "General Canadian," has a phonemic system and a number of subphonemic features which, along with certain distributional characteristics, give General Canadian much of its special character. These phonological features and numerous Canadianisms of vocabulary are summarized and illustrated in my article "The English Language in Canada," *Current Trends in Linguistics*, 10 (1973), pages 40-74, where the historical background and settlement history are also given.

General Canadian meets the requirements of a standard language in that it is the type of English used in the conduct of educational, cultural, governmental, and commercial affairs by leaders of the English-speaking community. It is, moreover, the type of English used in national radio and television broadcasting and, for the most part, by local stations as well. Furthermore, it is the type of English aspired to by those who wish to take part in the country's affairs above the local level. And, perhaps most significantly, it is the type that, with minor variations, marks the educated, non-regionalized Canadian. As such, it is the only type that has spread widely across the country, to be heard with increasing frequency among the young in every province, including Newfoundland, where the several dialects have become deeply entrenched over several centuries of relative isolation; for Newfoundland, although the newest province, is the oldest English-speaking colony in North America.

It seems clear that this wide acceptance of General Canadian by the native born has played its part in the twentieth-century thrust toward a sense of national identity. This movement reached its greatest momentum during the sixties and its high point during the centennial of Confederation and the tremendous success of Expo 67. An almost euphoric sense of oneness lasted for another five years and was accompanied by an acknowledged maturity and Canadianness (both English and French) in literature, theatre, ballet, art, and scholarship. Commerce and industry were flourishing; and distinctive accomplishments in motion pictures, television, and publishing were evident both to those at home and those abroad. It seemed that Canada was at last united and that the future was bright indeed.

The future does not look so bright nowadays and the turning point may well have been the so-called October Crisis in 1970, when the War Measures Act was applied to put down an outbreak of terrorism by the FLQ in Montreal. This drastic action, with its awesome military activity and its wholesale arresting of suspected subversives, undermined French-Canadian confidence in Confederation and badly frayed the fragile bond linking the two founding peoples of Canada. The subsequent economic recession and stagflation acerbated the deterioration of amity so that the future of Canada is in great jeopardy. The situation was momentarily relieved by the modest success of the Montreal Olympics in the summer of 1976; but it was, in the end, aggravated by the political controversy that marred the Games and the substantial financial losses that were incurred by the promoters. In any event, the voters of Quebec have spoken at the polls; they have replaced what they thought to be a tired and incompetent federalist government with one that promises to withdraw the Québécois from Canada.

Under such distressing circumstances, such matters as Canadian English seem very much less important than was the case ten, even five, years ago. While there can be little doubt that General Canadian is well established and thriving, its future may well be in doubt; for its well-being and continued development are entirely dependent on the future of the country itself.

THE CONCEPT OF DIALECT AND THE STUDY

OF CANADIAN ENGLISH

Ian Pringle

The amount of scholarship devoted to Canadian English is amazingly small. An annotated bibliography covering everything between 1792 and 1975 which makes any statement at all about Canadian English lists 723 items.[1] Compared to what one might expect to see in a bibliography of Canadian geography, Canadian literature or even Canadian entomology, that is little enough. But it is actually less: the great bulk of what is listed in that bibliography is of interest only as primary evidence for a study of language attitudes in Canada, rather than for real information about the English language in Canada. For example, what Sir Andrew MacPhail had to say about Canadian speech writing in *Saturday Night* in 1935 (item 414) can be used to represent a certain point of view about Canadian English, but as a scholarly statement about Canadian English it has no validity whatsoever. Of the 723 items listed--plus, perhaps, twenty which could be added since 1975--fewer than 100 are articles written by professional linguists or grammarians, and of those, most are only small comments on minor points--valid, to be sure, but not the result of comprehensive, major studies. In the whole field, there are fewer than a dozen major studies which have been brought to a successful completion: a dictionary, three or four Ph.D. dissertations, a few Master's theses, a "national" survey of questionable design. A number of ongoing studies--in Newfoundland, New Brunswick, the Ottawa Valley, Vancouver, promise to extend this list to more than double its present size. But it will still be a small list: on the whole, it is not an impressive record.

And yet, it is not hard to understand why this should be so. On the one hand, the nature of dialectology as a field of study, the way it developed in Europe to respond to European concerns, the way it was adapted in North America to respond to American concerns, has encouraged a kind of study which may be of dubious relevance to the geographical realities of Canadian English. For the English-speaking settlement of Canada, and the kind of English that developed in Canada as a result, is for

From *Queen's Quarterly* 90:100-121, 1983. Reprinted with permission.

the most part, quite different from what happened elsewhere in the English-speaking world.

Most of the linguists who study the English language in Canada would call what they do dialectology. Of course, that does not necessarily mean that they consider Canadian English to be a dialect. It depends in the first place on what one takes "dialect" to mean. At least four senses are potentially relevant.

The first sense underlies the idea that a language for which there exists no written form, a language which has not yet been alphabetized, is for that reason intrinsically inferior, not a real language, but a mere dialect. It is an attitude which we find quite commonly in incidental references to Amerindian languages in the writings of early explorers and missionaries; Father Charles D'Alemant, for example, writing to the General of the Jesuits in Rome in 1626, comments, "Our labours this year have had no further fruit than a knowledge of the country, of the natives, and of the *dialects* of two tribes."[2]

It is an attitude which is ultimately of classical origin - it is to the Greeks, after all, that we owe the tradition that all those who do not speak our language are--necessarily--barbarous. And, like many language attitudes ultimately of classical origin, including modern puristic attitudes, it survives not because it is of classical origin, but probably merely because it is fundamentally silly, and thus in the mainstream of western popular thinking about language.

A second definition of *dialect* that is somewhat less irrelevant, is the exact converse: all languages, whether they are written or not, are merely *dialects*; *dialect* equals *language*. It is an attitude that we find expressed, for example, in *The Master's Wife* by Sir Andrew MacPhail. Discussing the relations between Scots Gaelic and English in Prince Edward Island in the nineteenth century, he makes the familiar Scottish claim that because the Islanders were bilingual and literate in both languages, their English was less subject to change, therefore less subject to corruption, and therefore *better* than that of English monolinguals. He expands this into a general claim that in bilingual situations, the more distant the relationships between the languages, the more powerful and therefore the more beneficial is the conservative effect: "an allied *dialect* is only a means of further debasement."[3]

The same idea is sometimes expressed by the term *jargon*: Lionel Groulx, for example, in his address before the Monument National in Montreal in 1918, warned, "One of these days we shall find ourselves speaking the horrible *jargon* of Toronto."[4] This notion also has its etymon in Greek *dialektos* in one of its senses, but it owes its modern existence to the realization in the late eighteenth century by Sir William Jones that Sanskrit, the classical language of India, must be related to the European classical languages, Latin and Greek, and that the relationship must have been that they had had a common ancestor. This is a realization that must have been quite horrifying to any classically educated European of the eighteenth century, and certainly its implications were far too radical ever to have filtered down into popular thought.   It implied that all three of those venerated classical languages, regarded in India and Europe as the epitome of all that is perfect and unchanging, must have had their origin as mere dialects of some older language.   This, of course, implies that linguistic change is not necessarily corruption: a fact that has never been able to make any headway against the older puristic attitudes.

The third sense of *dialect* is the first that is directly relevant to what it is that dialectologists claim they do.   This is the definition that you can expect to find represented in introductory textbooks in linguists.   A *dialect*, to quote Ruth McConnell, is "A sub-variety of a language, either regional or social.   It is distinguished from other sub-varieties of the same language by a unique combination of language features: pronunciation (including stress and intonation); grammatical forms; words and expressions; meanings of words and expressions."[5]   In more popular terms, this means that if two people who would like to talk to each other cannot understand each other, they must speak different languages.   If they *can* understand each other, they must be speaking the same language; if they nevertheless don't sound quite the same or don't always use the same word for the same concept, then they must be speaking different *dialects*.   The sources of this definition are complex, but one of the most important of them is the American structuralists' naive but egalitarian assertion that all languages and all varieties of languages are equally good.

Note, first of all, that dialects are said to be either regional or social: two speakers of the same language can differ from one another because they come from different areas; or they can differ from one another because they come from different social classes.   Their speech can differ slightly (merely in accent, or in word choice), or massively.   Consequently everybody has his or her own dialect: I have mine, you have yours, Susanna Moodie had hers, and our Queen has hers.   It is a notion that would probably horrify our Queen; it would certainly have horrified Susanna Moodie.   Moodie, like most people of her class, then and since, had a quite different attitude to dialect.   For her, the English language was what *she* spoke; every form of English which deviated from this was a mere dialect.   Thus in the memorable scene near the beginning of *Roughing It in the Bush* where she is describing the first landfall at Grosse Isle:

> A crowd of many hundred Irish emigrants had been landed during the present and former day and all this motley crew - men, women and children, who were not confined by sickness to the sheds (which greatly resembled cattle-pens) - were employed in washing clothes or spreading them out on the rocks and bushes to dry.   The men and boys were *in* the water, while the women, with their scanty garments tucked about their

knees, were tramping their bedding in tubs or
holes in the rocks, which the retiring tide had
left half full of water. Those who did not possess
washing tubs, pails, or iron pots, or could not
obtain access to a hole in the rocks, were running
to and fro, screaming and scolding in no measured
terms. The confusion of Babel was among them.
All talkers and no hearers - each shouting and
yelling in his or her uncouth *dialect* . . . .[6]

This represents perfectly the popular idea of dialect and
most of the connotations that surround the idea: a dialect is
uncouth--an ugly, imperfect, corrupt version of a language which
I myself speak perfectly.   On one level this sense is merely a
survival of the same classical attitude which reduced unwritten
languages to the status of mere dialects.   But on another it is
closely related to the last definition that is important, the idea
that a *dialect* is something like a *patois* , in the French sense, a
distinctive and honorable but rural and moribund by-form of a
language.

This is the most complex of all the senses of *dialect*, and it
draws on all the senses mentioned so far.   It is also closest to
the heart of language; for that reason it is best discussed in
relation to the two opposed forces which are at work in linguistic
change.   One is the principle of imitation: two people who are
speaking to each other as equals both adapt their speech slightly
so that each is more like the other's than would otherwise be the
case.   On an individual level, this is something that most of us
catch ourselves doing from time to time: speaking to someone
whose English is slightly different from ours, we modify our own
speech so that it is a little more like theirs, and they, in replying,
do the same.   Spread out onto a societal level, maintained over
centuries, this phenomenon means--or meant - that every village,
town, region had its own dialect.

The second force is the impulse to differentiate: to exaggerate
the difference between your speech and the speech of the person
you are talking to, especially if you do not particularly like the
person you are talking to.   On an individual level this principle
of differentiation can often be observed particularly clearly when
a native speaker of English is speaking to someone for whom
English is a second language: the native speaker, instead of
helping the non-native speaker by speaking as *normally* as possible, makes things as difficult as possible, either by adopting an
artificially elegant variety of the language, or perhaps by shouting,
or by exaggerating every vowel so that it represents the written
language as fully as possible, and is thus as far removed as
possible from everyday speech.   This ensures that the non-native
speaker has even greater difficulty understanding what is being
said, and also provides false models so that, if non-native speakers
do try to imitate what they hear, they will get it wrong. (Decent
social distances are thus maintained.)   On the societal level, this
force to differentiate creates and maintains class dialects.

From a linguistic point of view, the essence of a *patois* is that it could have become a national standard language, but didn't. The situation is perhaps clearest if we think not of Canadian English, but of a language like French in the Middle Ages. At that time there were a number of regional varieties of French, many of them vehicles of a high culture. In principle, all of them might have survived, so that instead of one language, French, there would today be what would seem like a whole group of closely related languages: as similar, say, as Portuguese and Spanish, which are recognized as two languages but came into existence in precisely this way; or as Dutch and German, which are the two standard languages which happened to develop out of the continental West Germanic dialect continuum. Or some variety might have survived as the sole national standard other than the one that did: Burgundian, for example, or Gascon, or Franco-Provençal. But for various reasons (reasons which have almost nothing to do with language, but a lot to do with political and economic power), the *patois* spoken around Paris gained the political and thus the linguistic ascendancy, and developed to become what we think of as standard modern French.

When one single *patois* comes to dominate in this way, a number of things happen. One is that the newly established standard, because it is spoken by the group which sets all standards--of dress, of culture, of elegance, of education--comes to be thought of as beautiful and elegant. The relics of the other *patois*, by contrast, come to be thought of as either charming but quaint, or else as corrupt and ugly. (In the British context, for example, rural dialects such as Somerset, West Country, Yorkshire, are charmingly quaint, but lower-class urban dialects--Cockney, Birmingham, Manchester, Newcastle--are corrupt and ugly.)

Secondly, the winning *patois* begins to change fairly quickly, and especially in the area that is least subject to the restraining influence of the written form of the language: its pronunciation. This phenomenon is a direct consequence of the principles of imitation and differentiation in their urban manifestations. To oversimplify, the middle classes want to seem to be like the upper classes, and so they strive to talk more like them. The upper classes, however, have no desire to sound like the middle classes and so, quite unconsciously, they change their pronunciation in order to keep a decent distance between them. Consequently, although most of those who speak upper-class dialects invariably think they speak the purest and therefore the most conservative variety of the language, in reality they typically speak the newest and most innovative.[7]

The third phenomenon is that once *patois* has won out in this way, the other regional languages gradually lose their status, including their literary status, and come to be languages that are merely spoken. This is particularly likely to happen as education spreads (and note that this usually happens in the name of egalitarianism). Again the situation in France is particularly revealing. It ought to strike a modern Canadian observer as ironic that France is so assiduous in its concern for one minority language in North America, since of all the countries of Europe, only Spain has been more repressive traditionally of its minority languages than France is, and since the recent liberalization in Spain, France is now clearly Europe's most repressive country so far as minority languages are concerned. And for closely related reasons, one of the paradoxes of European intellectual history is that the French Old Order, before the Revolution, although it depended on acceptance of the idea of a social hierarchy and was absolutely opposed to social equality, in fact supported linguistic equality, by leaving both the minority languages and the *patois* to continue their development more or less unimpeded, whereas the revolutionary authorities, in the name of freedom and equality, set in motion the forces which eventually would destroy the *patois*, and are still trying to destroy the minority languages.[8]

Dialectology as a serious field of study came into existence in Europe in the late nineteenth century. Part of the motivation was a consequence of the discovery, then a century old, that Latin, Greek, and Sanskrit were descended from dialects of Indo-European. From that came the great philological enterprise to which linguistics was primarily devoted in the nineteenth century: the attempt to classify the languages of the world genetically, to work out their relationships and how they had changed. In that study, the collection of the data from the *patois* was considered to be extremely important, by the late nineteenth century, because the *patois* often retained the kind of evidence needed for genetic classifications and historical study that could not be found in the more innovative standard languages. This motivation was reinforced by another: the essentially romantic idea that in the language of the common folk can be found something purer, older, and more authentic than the sophisticated standard language of the cities, so that folk language is worth collecting for its own sake. These motives worked together to give European dialectology both its characteristic concerns and also its typical methodology. A third factor strongly reinforced the trend: the feeling of urgency, the feeling that if something was not done as soon as possible to collect and record all the relics of the *patois*, then the growing centralization of government and the spread of mass education would completely destroy these precious shreds of evidence of earlier stages of language and culture.

Consequently, the approach of European dialectology is typically like this. The investigator starts with a questionnaire, and it is as long a questionnaire as he feels he can possibly handle: some of them have taken up to a week to administer. He chooses the places in which sampling is to be done. For the most part, this means locating places out of the mainstream of culture, and away from all main transport routes. Thus, for example Bartoli, in his planning for the *Linguistic Atlas of Italy*, required that his *centri minimi* be villages with no railway station, no high school, no higher ecclesiastical status than that of a simple parish; that they not be vacation areas, or sports centers, or have skiing or skating facilities. In this way the risk of

what is typically called "contamination" from the standard language
is minimized.   And then, having arrived in one of these tiny
little out-of-the-way villages, he locates his subjects.   The great
Rumanian dialectologist Sever Pop, in choosing his subjects for
the *Linguistic Atlas of Rumania,* required that each subject be a
native of the place he or she was chosen to represent; that his
or her spouse also be a native of the area; that the families of
both always have lived in the same area, so far as is known;
that the subjects be farmers; that, as far as possible, they have
never left their native village; that if possible they be illiterate
and otherwise that they have had as little education as possible;
that they not be people recommended as knowledgeable about
things local; that if possible they have done no military service;
and so on.   The only more or less positive criteria are that they
be more or less intelligent, and that they have good teeth.   So
in this European kind of dialectology, the field worker is up in
the hills somewhere with such a person, and still can't ask exactly
what he wants to know, because one of the most annoying facts
about eliciting natural, unmonitored language is that most people,
when they are asked what they say, will tell you not what they
say, but what they think you think they ought to say.   Sometimes
they want to be helpful; sometimes they misrepresent what they
do, for fear they will seem to be provincial or ill-educated (even
though, in Europe, that may be precisely why they have been
selected).   So, instead of asking them what they say, the field
worker has to try to get them to say it by disguising his real
purpose in some way: by pretending to be engaged in a real
conversation, by pretending to be investigating something other
than language.   The following dialogue is transcribed from part
of such an interview conducted in the Ottawa Valley.   The aim
was to elicit the word for *teeter-totter*; the field worker led up
to it by asking a more general question about the kinds of games
the subject's children played when they were small.

> "When they were small he got them, he made
> a, from boards, you know, kind of a square box,
> got some gravel in: I told him, I says, 'Get
> some gravel that they have something to play',
> you know, 'cause around the house they couldn't,
> it was all grass and we had no lawn-mower; 'twas
> all. . . . So they played in that thing there when
> they were small and the sand and amused them-
> selves till they were tired."
>
> *"Uh huh.   Did you ever have one of those
> things where you'd put a plank over a log or
> something, you'd have . . ."*
>
> "A wippel-woppel."

Because of this orientation towards the archaic, the data
that are gathered through this kind of enquiry typically represent
a very ancient stage of the language: Harold Orton, the director
of the Survey of English Dialects, apparently seriously thought
that through the study of the geographical distribution of linguistic

features in the English of the extremely conservative stratum of
society that he interviewed in the middle of the twentieth century,
he would reveal something about the pattern of English dialects
in the Middle Ages.

Note that because the techniques of dialectology were developed
in Europe to respond to a particular cultural and linguistic circumstance there, they are biased away from the notion that any
sub-variety of a language is a dialect, worthy of study for that
reason, and towards the notion that dialects are quaint, rural,
archaic, queer.   That is, traditional dialectology carries at the
center of its methodology a concept of dialect which is not the
concept commonly ascribed to by linguists, but something narrower,
and in fact something a great deal closer to the popular concept
of dialect as a non-standard form of the language that I myself
speak almost perfectly.   And that bias has persisted in North
American dialectology through the unfortunate coincidence that
similar techniques for similar reasons happened to be relevant in
the first region of North America to be studied dialectologically:
New England.

Broadly speaking, we can talk about two kinds of dialect
patterns.   The first is the classical kind, the kind that clearly
existed in Europe until the nineteenth century and still persists
in most of the world.   In this kind of pattern, the linguistic
patterns are the reflection of ancient settlements: most of Europe
was settled by the ancestors of the speakers of the present
languages at least two thousand years ago.   In most of the
intervening centuries, the vast majority of people did not ever
move more than a few miles from the village or town where they
were born, and of course were illiterate.   As a result, in Europe
there exists relics of ancient, persistent and above all variegated
patterns that can be seen in many European linguistic atlases,
with an amazing amount of variation within a very small area.
The *Linguistic Atlas of Scotland*, for example, shows the distribution of thirty-six different words currently in use in that small
country for *earwig*.[9]

The other kind of pattern is the kind of pattern that one
would expect to find in a colonial situation.   What happens in
colonies is a result of the breakdown of the principle of differentiation.   In most colonizations, the majority of the people who come
are not speakers of the standard language of the source country,
of course.   Rather, they bring with them a haphazard mix of
local regional dialects, different class dialects and so on, and in
the mix the likelihood that the standard language of the source
country will be predominant is in reality very slight.

The adults who come as colonizers continue to speak more or
less the language they brought with them; beyond a certain point,
adults are not very successful at modifying their speech towards
the speech of those they talk to.   With children, however, imitation
is dramatically successful.   This is something observable these
days in the typical differences between the speech of immigrants
and their children.   So long as children remain at home, they

continue to speak as their parents do. But as soon as they get out of the home, they begin to speak as other children do, and by the time they are teenagers, especially if they are boys, they may well refuse to speak as their parents do. In a mixed community with no clear standard, what must have happened in the first generation or two of settlement is a homogenization produced by peer-group pressure among children, above all.

That the effects of his homogenization persist is due to the breakdown of the rigorous hierarchical structure of the source society in colonial situations. Socially, among the immigrants to Canada, the Susanna Moodies were to be the mind, the taste, and the voice of the nascent society. But as R. L. McDougall has noted, the Moodies themselves had to come to terms with the fact that life in the bush, and later in the clearings, undermined old-world conceptions of class.[10] Linguistically, it is always the majority that wins out; in Canada this meant the poor and ill-educated, the Yankees and Irish and Scots and Yorkshiremen whose "dialects" so offended Moodie.

This phenomenon was observed repeatedly in Canadian French in the eighteenth century by visitors from France. Since only a very small proportion of the population of France even at the end of the eighteenth century actually spoke French, almost all the colonizers who came to New France must have spoken a *patois*. But (and this is the important point) they all spoke *different patois*. Within a very short time, their children had created Canadian French, a variety of French which, as it happened, was not strikingly different from the standard French of the period. De Bacqueville de la Potherie, writing in 1721, notes of Canadian French "*On parle ici parfaitement bien sans mauvais accent.*" Jean-Baptiste d'Aleyrac, a French officer who lived in Canada between 1755 and 1760, noted in his diary that "*les Canadiens parlent un francais pareil au nôtre.*" And the Marquis de Montcalm himself, who, as a native of the southwest of France had often had occasion to travel to Paris and thus to note that hardly anyone spoke French who did not live in Paris and was neither a member of the aristocracy nor of the administrative class, noted with surprise that in Canada, when the *paysans* spoke to him he could understand them.[11] The surprise was linguistic, not social: not that the *paysans* spoke to him, but that when they did, he could understand them. That would not have been the case in France.

Together, these two forces of homogenization and social breakdown create the dialect pattern of linguistic colonies. Obviously, they account for the great linguistic uniformity which is characteristic of linguistic colonies as compared to the source countries. This is strikingly clear in New Zealand, where the colonization did not begin until 1840, and was for all practical purposes complete by 1890, where the attempt to create a neat little replica of English society broke down completely, leaving to come into existence in its place one of the most aggressively egalitarian societies known, and where the language is amazingly uniform. Something similar must also have happened in Australia, and in French Canada.

This new, homogenized, and typically highly standard variety of the source language then becomes the model which the children of all subsequent settlers adopt. Thus, the massive immigrations into Australia since the Second World War have had very considerable effects on many aspects of Australian life, changing Australia, for example, from a country with one of the world's highest per capita consumptions of beer to a country with one of the world's highest per capita consumptions of wine. But it has had barely any effect on the English spoken in Australia.

Finally, once the linguistic determinant in the new settlement has been established, it then remains remarkably stable. It can be upset only by massive new migrations which bring settlers in such numbers that they completely outnumber those who are already there, or by the development over time of a new, highly stratified society. But if there are no new migrations then the colonial language remains pretty much what it was when it was first established in its homogenized form. What is surprising today in the comments on Canadian French made by French aristocrats in the eighteenth century is that they found Canadian French so good. It is a different discovery from the one made by recent French immigrants and visitors, who typically find Canadian French bad. What they do not know (and often cannot be brought to believe) is that the colonial language has not changed as much as they suppose; rather it is their own which reflects the much greater rate of linguistic change in Europe, which is still so much more highly stratified, and where the principle of differentiation therefore continues to have its full effect.

What happened in the English of Australia and New Zealand and the French of New France must have happened initially in the English-speaking settlements of North America. In New England, various people, from various parts of England, speaking various accents and dialects, came together through the fact of migration in various settlements. In these, the mixed dialects homogenized. But for two reasons, the English of New England proved to be closer to a classical European kind of dialect pattern than any of the other colonial languages I have mentioned. The first was simply that the settlements occurred such a long time ago. In principle, if a settlement is old enough, and the social situation is stable enough, then the kind of pattern typical of Europe will grow in a colonial situation. The second is that the settlements were sufficiently isolated not only from the source country but from each other that the somewhat different mixes which were implanted in different parts of New England came to form slightly different dialects. As a result, it was possible to apply in New England techniques very much like the techniques used in Europe, to reconstruct a comprehensive and plausible picture of what New England's rural dialects were like, before the larger demographic movements of the nineteenth century and the onset of industrialization began to upset them. The results of that investigation are recorded in the *Linguistic Atlas of New England*, originally published in 1939, and widely regarded as one of the best linguistic atlases from a technical standpoint.[12] In terms of what it tries to do, it is triumphantly successful.

Unfortunately, it was the first atlas project in what was conceived of as a continent-wide study of the English of North America, a project known as the Linguistic Atlas of the United States and Canada. As such, it set the model for almost all the investigations of regional variation in North American English which have been attempted since. Yet the social realities of the situation of English in Canada have always been such that the intrinsic bias in this kind of linguistic investigation may make it irrelevant in almost all of Canada. There is a clear exception to that generalization in the coastal dialects of Newfoundland. The thin line of settlement around the coast is old enough, and until recent times has been stable enough, for genuine regional dialects to have developed out of the various mixes of Irish, Western, and South-Western English dialects that the settlers brought with them, and to have stabilized subsequently into the distinctive dialects which so clearly do exist there. Because the rural settlement of the Maritimes is so old, and has been so stable, traditional techniques can be justified there too. It is possible that the same could be said of the areas originally settled by Loyalists in southwestern Ontario, though the preliminary field work needed to test such an assumption has not been undertaken. But outside of these two or perhaps three areas, the situation has been such that it has simply defied investigation.

Like all kinds of English outside of Britain, Canadian English has its beginnings in the English brought by the first English-speaking explorers and settlers. In the literary records of those first encounters with Canada, what we see most clearly is the shock--the perception that, to quote the poet Allen Curnow writing of another settlement, "It was something different, something/Nobody counted on."[13] As an experience, it looks forward to Bob Edwards' encounter with Winnipeg two hundred years later. It is a double realization: it is perfectly clear what it is not; it's not so clear what it is. "So this is Winnipeg," he said. "I can tell it's not Paris."

That sort of failed epiphany is very much a part of modern experience. T. S. Eliot notes it in "East Coker": "It was not (to start again) what one had expected."[14] Still more is it part of colonial experience; it is perhaps the common kernel from which every colonial and post-colonial sense of national identity grows. Joshua Marsden, writing his *Narrative of a Mission to Nova Scotia, New Brunswick and the Somers Island, with a Tour to Lake Ontario* (1816) said: "There is, sir, a solitary loneliness in the woods of America to which no language can do adequate justice. It seems a shutting out of the whole moral creation."[15]

What this shock points to is the mismatch between the language such people brought with them and the realities they encountered. Modern linguistics has often repeated a claim that all languages can be made to communicate whatever seems worth communicating to those who use them: at the societal or general level, we say, language is necessarily "adequate to culture." The language the first explorers and settlers brought with them reflected and embodied a particular culture and the range of experiences possible within the culture. In Canada, it simply did not fit. Hence the shock recorded by the literate minority: Northrop Frye has said that "the outstanding achievement of [early] Canadian writing is in the evocation of stark terror," a phenomenon which he attributes to "the frightening loneliness of a huge and thinly settled country." [16]

The echoes of that shock continue to reverberate in Canadian literature, just as the same feeling of linguistic anomie can be heard in so much modern literature of whatever source. But in Canada there was also among some writers an adaptive reaction, an attempt to come to terms with the new environment, both linguistically and emotionally. This growth towards a positive adaptation was also to become a major trend in Canadian poetry, perhaps receiving its fullest expression before the twentieth century in the nature poetry of the late nineteenth century. The same process of linguistic adaptation was taking place in the language of the semi-literate and illiterate majority of the settlers --a process of linguistic adaptation by which the English language was stretched, trimmed, reshaped, moulded, until it did fit the reality. The *Dictionary of Canadianisms on Historical Principles* [17] reveals the details of what happened: the flood of borrowing from the indigenous languages for names of animals and plants and topographic features unknown in Britain; the French terms borrowed, like the technology they label, for the fur trade and water transport and lumbering; the stretching of the meanings of extant English words and the borrowing of words from other immigrant languages for new cultural and political realities as they developed and grew. This stage of shock and adaptation is the first stage of the development of Canadian English. So far, it is the only stage which Canadian linguistic scholarship has been able to handle confidently on a large scale; and it has in fact done so with distinction. Canadian English as a whole has one dictionary, the *Dictionary of Canadianisms on Historical Principles*, which is in some respects the best dictionary of any national variety of English; the new regional dictionary, the *Dictionary of Newfoundland English*, [18] is just as important an achievement.

The second stage of Canadian cultural history that is relevant to the development of Canadian English is the stage of the first large-scale settlements. It is at this stage that the model of what happened elsewhere in the English-speaking world begins to fail.

It is important to stress that so far as the linguistic development of English Canada is concerned, the first massive settlement outside of Newfoundland came from the United States. The Loyalists did not bring with them a uniform "American" variety of English, already conveniently homogenized into something that we would all recognize today as an "American" rather than a Canadian or British accent. They must have come, rather, with a variety of dialects and accents, ranging from pure coastal New England and pure inland Pennsylvanian to the various accents and dialects of recent British migrants and, as a matter of fact, the Gaelic and German accents, among others, of non-English-speaking Loyalists. Still, to judge by what happened later, if the accents were not already homogenized, they had the makings of homogenization which, in Nova Scotia, proved to be very similar to the English of New England, and in southwestern Ontario, to the English of Pennsylvania: that is, to American varieties.

Canadians have never been able to decide how to handle that cruel reality. For two centuries it has plagued children learning to spell in Canada: some teachers are probably so convinced that the non-*U* spellings of words like *honour* are totally dishonorable that they use *U* spellings even when they are writing Latin (*honour omnia vincit*, one hopes); but Canadian children have always read non-*U* spellings in what they read, not least in their school books. As early as 1835, a prototype of the Canadian Nationalist was growling:

> It is really melancholy to traverse the Province and go into many of the common schools; you will find a herd of children instructed by some anti-British adventurer, instilling into the young and tender minds sentiments hostile to the parent state, . . . and American spelling books, dictionaries and grammar, teaching them an anti-British dialect and idiom.[19]

For much of the history of Canadian English, the same kind of divided linguistic consciousness affected attitudes to the pronunciation of English in Canada. On the one hand, there is the attitude represented by Sir Andrew MacPhail, once again:

> All speech may be beautified. The speaking voice can be trained in beauty by the same process that is applied to the singing voice. The human ear detects and detests a flat note in singing. The flat vowels in our Canadian speech are equally unpleasant. We can remedy that by taking thought, by listening acutely to beautiful speech, and listening with equal acuteness to our own. Any form of beauty is an asset in the struggle of life. I am not saying . . . that we should sedulously ape some imported accent, English or other. . . . But in England there is a standard

of beauty and an established correctness of speech
which the wise ones strive to achieve if it is not
theirs by rights. [20]

It is a point of view for which there has always been some
sympathy in Canada, even in points east of the tearooms of
Victoria. True Brit seems to be the received standard of the
Stratford stage, and it is not unknown among academics, in certain
areas of the federal civil service and elsewhere.

The converse is the resigned realism of Stephen Leacock: "I
myself talk Ontario English. I don't admire it, but it's all I can
do: anything is better than affectation."[21]

The same divided consciousness probably gave rise to, and
has certainly sustained, one of the most characteristic activities
among linguists studying Canadian English: the usage survey.
So characteristic is this activity that a recent essay by a well-
known University of Toronto linguist starts by criticizing the
methodological weaknesses of most such studies, and then proceeds
to illustrate them by reporting the results of the writer's own
informal usage surveys. [22] Typically, the usage survey consists
of asking respondents whether for example they rhyme *lever*
with *beaver* (the "British" variant) or with *ever* (the "American"
variant); how they pronounce such words as *vase*, *tomato* and
schedule; and so on. This is a far cry indeed from the *Linguistic Atlas of Scotland*, with its thirty-six different words for *earwig*. Indeed, on the surface it sometimes appears to be a mere
fascination with the trivial--a fascination that is hardly likely to
tell us more about Canadian English. In reality there is a certain
point to it: in urban Canadian English, differences are so subtle,
and the range of discernible variability so restricted, that almost
everything to be discovered has to be discovered within the
narrow range. When such superficial and apparently trivial differences were examined in the English of a carefully selected group
of Ottawans, all sorts of correlations between linguistic choices
and such factors as sex, age, and socio-economic status became
apparent: Ottawans do in fact use such subtle and apparently
trivial linguistic variability to mark their similarity to and difference from other people.[23] Consequently, the much larger study
of this kind of variability in the English of Vancouver, carried
out under the direction of Professor R. J. Gregg, promises to
make a truly significant contribution to our understanding of the
dynamics of the uses of English in urban Canada, for this study
is still more careful in its design and much larger in scope.

However with the exception of these studies and a few related
ones (all associated with the Department of Linguistics at the
University of British Columbia), there is a major methodological
weakness in Canadian usage surveys: they do not attempt the
rigor of a normal sociological survey; indeed, most of them look
as though they were devised by fund-raisers for some political
party. The difficulty is then to know whether we can extrapolate
from the haphazard group of people who happen to be in some
professor's first year classes to any larger population. That

91.2 percent of such a group of Torontonians pronounced *lever* to rhyme with *beaver* rather than with *ever* tells us nothing at all about Canadian English in Toronto.

There is a linguistic fallacy in many of these discussions which is still more serious: the assumption that one form is unambiguously American or British. The truth of the matter is that not all Americans say *tomehdo*, and not all Brits say *tomahto*, and most Canadians do not think of whatever form they themselves use (and it might well be another) as anything other than Canadian. Nor is it anything other than Canadian.

If Canadian English has developed in accordance with what American English, Australian English, and New Zealand English would lead us to expect, then the Loyalist settlements which caused the divided linguistic loyalty celebrated in the usage surveys would have determined the course of Canadian English thereafter, except where it was overwhelmed by waves of later settlement. One of the peculiarities of Canadian English west of the Maritimes is that the Loyalist settlement *was* overwhelmed, at least numerically, and nonetheless determined what Canadian English was to be. Or at least it did in the cities. The ten thousand or so Loyalists who settled in Upper Canada after the American Rebellion had been overtaken, by 1848, by almost one million native speakers of English, of whom only 4.5 percent were American natives. That is to say, the vast majority of the English-speaking population by 1850 was not of Loyalist or "late Loyalist" origin. Nonetheless, despite the wavering over *tomato*, *lever*, *schedule*, etc., Canadian English is clearly an American type of English, and, at least in the cities, remarkably uniform: indeed, English Canada has been described as the most uniform speech area of any world language.[24] Thus there is usually no possible way to localize a Canadian urban speaker within Canada. A Canadian Higgins lurking on the portico of the Timothy Eaton Memorial Church not only would not be able to tell the parishioners what part of Toronto they came from; he probably could not even tell whether they came from Toronto, Vancouver, or Winnipeg. Not by their English anyway.

Tentatively, what seems to have happened is something like this. The Loyalists already had almost all the best land, and had already started to form the towns that would become the major cities of southern Ontario. The British immigrants who followed them were themselves mixed; that is, they came from all parts of Britain. (This was not the case in Australia and New Zealand, where the majority of settlers came from the southeastern quadrant of England.) Consequently their children assimilated linguistically to what was already there, because in most places there were not enough speakers of any one variety of British English to form a new majority. And since southern Ontario was the source of so much of the English-speaking settlement of northwestern Ontario and the Prairies, it was still this predominantly American kind of English which became the linguistic model for the other major cities of Canada as well.

Yet that too is an enormous oversimplification. It is not just that urban Canadian English is not absolutely uniform (although, thanks to Howard Wood's important study of Ottawa, it has now beween demonstrated that that is the case), but rather that, once you get out of the cities, Canadian English proves to be enormously varied - perhaps in fact the most varied national variety of English anywhere in the world. The extent of this variability can be gauged by the terms elicited by field workers of the Linguistic Survey of the Ottawa Valley in just two counties (Renfrew and Lanark) in eastern Ontario. They include not only the predictable *teeter-totter* and *see-saw* and the highly unpredictable *wippel-woppel* already mentioned, but also three related forms of Scottish provenance, *shuggie*, *shuggie-shoe*, and *shuggie-shook*, and four related forms of Irish provenance, *weighdy*, *weighdy-bucky*, *weighdy-bucket*, and *weighdy-buckety*. (*Wippel-woppel* is of German origin, related to the standard German *Wippe*.)

This astonishing complexity in rural Canadian English is in part a consequence of the nature of settlement outside of the areas taken by the Loyalists. The first point is that the proportion of native speakers of other languages among the settlers was very high. Speakers of other languages came to the United States in much greater numbers, of course, but in most places there they were assimilated into the already huge English-speaking population. The linguistic aspect of the Canadian mosaic owes something to the fact that the pressure on newcomers to "adjust" has always been less forceful in Canada than in the United States. But it owes more to the realtively high *proportion* of speakers of other languages.

A second factor, however, and one of still greater importance is the condition of life in the settlements. For many immigrants, the conditions in which they came were appalling, and the conditions in the settlements were often just as bad. For most settlers, the first winter must have been a desperate shock; only the Americans and later the Russians and Ukrainians could have had any realistic idea of what they were in for. And as they established their farms, many of them had to come to terms with the realization that they were not farming on ten feet of rich topsoil, as some misleading advertisements in Britain and Europe suggested would be the case. Instead, they found themselves scratching at the surface of the Canadian Shield, picking stones. Trying to maintain enough land for subsistence farming meant constant, back-breaking labor. And that was the case even when things were going fairly well: the normal round of yearly activities was such that most people could not often move very far away from their own farms.

Such factors conspired to limit the social contacts of the settlers who lived on farms (and in 1850, that meant 75 percent of the population of Ontario). Overall, the picture one has of the typical radius of social contact of a farming family in the nineteenth century is something like this:

One can imagine a family ten to fifteen years on
the land with children up to the teenage years,
going to church most weeks, or making neighbourly
social calls on many occasions, especially in winter
or at times of lull in the farming activities.
Individual family members might be called down
the road to assist in a building project or the
harvest, to attend a sick neighbour on the next
farm, undertake the occasional shopping trip for
tools, cloth or salt, or simply check for mail at
the post office.   Children hiked a mile or more
to school, where such was available. All of these
purposes suggest a weekly average of three or
four short expeditions by one or more members
of the family.   There were fewer trips for those
more recently arrived in the neighbourhood, and
a higher proportion of those were made by foot.[25]

There are two points to be made. The first is that although
this is ostensibly about the nineteenth century, much the same
conditions applied in parts of Ontario and the West as late as the
1930s.   The second is that this is probably not enough social
contact for the principle of imitation to apply. Thus, the social
conditions have created a situation which on the face of it seems
impossible to describe: every household could have its own dialect
--and to some extent does.

And even this is an oversimplification. The historical aspect
of dialectology is further baffled by the fact that so many of
these settlers, having tasted roughing it in the bush long enough
to realize that the glaciers had deposited their topsoil elsewhere,
moved on.   At times the rate of turn-over is phonemenal: 50
percent in Toronto Gore between 1837 and 1881, an estimated 80
percent in Chinguacousy Township in Peel County in one decade
between 1840 and 1850.   Moreover it has continued non-stop ever
since.   In the Prairie provinces between 1951 and 1961, the
greatest source of Canadian in-migration into Manitoba was from
Sasketchewan.   In Saskatchewan, however, the greatest single
source of Canadian in-migration was Prince Edward Island.   As
for out-migration, people from Sasketchewan went in their largest
numbers to Alberta, with British Columbia as a second choice;
Manitobans chose British Columbia, Alberta, and Ontario, in that
order. [26] This incessant movement not only slows down the process
of homogenization; it also means that the few people one can find
who do satisfy the normal European criterion of long, stable
residence are often the least representative of the population.

Moreover, even in areas where, on the basis of census data,
we can point to what appears to be fairly stable settlement of a
particular kind (e.g. Scots), there is usually no earthly reason
to imagine that when they came they would all have spoken the
same way.   In Eastern Ontario today, a speaker who grew up
and is still living in an area of Lowland Scottish settlement that
was adjacent to Irish settlements sounds quite different from a

representative of the English-speaking Highland Scots settlement
of McNab Township, which was partly intermingled with Irish
settlement, and both sound quite different from representatives
of the Glengarry settlement, originally predominantly a Gaelic-
speaking settlement, which was adjacent to a Loyalist settlement
of predominantly central and western New York origins. Some of
the differences are due to the variable admixture of other English
dialects, but some is due to what the original settlers brought
with them: if Canada is not the English-speaking world's most
varied speech area, then Scotland certainly is.

Thus the concepts of "dialect" which North American dialectology inherited, despite itself, from Europe have done the study
of Canadian English a double disservice. The notion that Canadian
English is itself a "dialect," as a national variety of English, has
focused attention on trivial questions about what is predominantly
English and what is predominantly American in the make-up of
its urban variety, without doing anything to explain how the
invariable parts of this urban variety could possibly have come
to be so remarkably uniform across so huge a country. Conversely, the concept that a "dialect" is first and foremost an
archaic rural variety of a language has focused attention on what
is most strange in non-urban varieties of Canadian English while
ignoring the fact that those who speak in such ways are the
least representative members of the rural population. In Eastern
Ontario, and probably in many other parts of Canada, it is surprisingly easy to find a fifth-generation Canadian who speaks a good
Ulster dialect. Good, but not perfect. But there is really little
interest in trying to find a perfect Ulster dialect in Canada: if
you want to record a really good Ulster accent, the sensible
thing to do is to go to Ulster. If one wants to study Canadian
English, however, one has no choice but to look not only at the
strikingly odd, but also at the fully standard, and also at everything in between: the proper field of study is the whole ecology
of English in Canada.

For Canadian English doesn't really exist: it is still coming
into existence. Or rather, there are an undetermined number of
Canadian Englishes - and perhaps thousands of them. They are
linked by the fact that, in their different ways, they are all
reflections and embodiments of aspects of a shared, if complex
and subtle, cultural unity (whose existence, however much insiders
may doubt it, has always been perfectly clear to outsiders).
They can be distinguished by the different accommodations and
compromises they represent between what they started from and
what they are becoming. The study of these Canadian Englishes
is going to be enormously complex. But is promises to be richly
rewarding. And those of us who have the privilege of undertaking
it can also attest that it is fascinating.[27]

FOOTNOTES

[1] Walter S. Avis and A. M. Kinloch, *Writings on Canadian English 1792-1975: An Annotated Bibliography* (Toronto: Fitzhenry & Whiteside, 1978).

[2] R. G. Thwaites, ed., *The Jesuit Relations and Allied Documents*, Vol. IV: *Acadia and Quebec: 1616-1629* (New York: Pageant, 1959), Letter XVII, pp. 178-79. The original Latin has *"Nullus ergo alius hoc anno fructus quam loci, personarum et idiomatis duarum nationum cognitio,"* which admittedly does not illustrate the meaning of *dialect* as well as the translation.

[3] Sir Andrew Macphail, *The Master's Wife* (New Canadian Library No 138) (Toronto: McClelland & Stewart, 1977), p. 4.

[4] Abbe Lionel Groulx, "Pour l'Action francaise," in *Dix ans d'Action francaise* (Montreal: Bibliotheque de l'Action francaise, 1918), p. 50: *"L'un de ces jours nous nous reveillerons parlant l'affreux jargon des 'Parisiens' de Toronto. . . ."* The quotation in the text is from the mistranslation in John Robert Colombo, ed., *Colombo's Canadian Quotations* (Edmonton: Hurtig, 1974), p. 236, col. 2, s.n. *Groulx*.

[5] R. E. McConnell, *Our Own Voice : Canadian English and How It is Studied* (Toronto: Gage Educational, 1979), pp. 96f.

[6] Susanna Moodie, *Roughing It in the Bush* (New Canadian Library No 31) (Toronto: McClelland & Stewart, 1962), pp. 24f.

[7] The role of what I have called the principles of imitation and differentiation in such linguistic change is discussed in Uriel Weinreich, William Labov and Marvin I. Herzog, "Empirical Foundations for a Theory of Language Change," in W. P. Lehmann and Yakov Malkiel, eds., *Directions for Historical Linguistics: A Symposium* (Austin: University of Texas Press, 1968), pp. 95-195.

[8] For a brief sketch of official French repression at the time of the Revolution and subsequently, see Sever Pop, *La Dialectologie* (Université de Louvain, Recueil de Travaux d'histoire et de philologie, 3e série, fascicule 39; Louvain, 1950), tome 1, pp. 9-14. A clear example of recent attempts at suppression, the situation of Alsatian German since the Second World War, is documented by Frédéric Hartweg, "La situation linguistique en Alsace: un bilan," *Carleton Germanic Papers*, 2 (1974), 1-30.

[9] J. H. Mather and W. Speitel, *Linguistic Atlas of Scotland*, Vol 1 (London: Croom Helm, 1975), Maps 82, 82A, pp. 128f.

[10] Robert L. McDougall, "Editor's Introduction" to Susanna Moodie, *Life in the Clearings* (Toronto: Macmillan, 1959), pp. xiii, xv.

[11] Quotations taken from G. Dulong, "Historie du français en Amérique du Nord," in T. A. Sebeok, ed., *Current Trends in Linguistics*, Vol 10: *Linguistics in North America* (The Hague: Mouton, 1973), Part 1, p. 412. See also Douglas C. Walker, "Canadian French," in J. K. Chambers, ed., *The Languages of Canada* (Montreal: Didier, 1979), pp. 13437.

[12] Hans Kurath, director and ed., *Linguistic Atlas of New England* (3 vols) (Providence: American Council of Learned Societies and Brown Univ., 1939-43).

[13] Allen Curnow, "The Unhistoric Story," in A. Curnow, ed., *The Penguin Book of New Zealand Verse* (Harmondsworth, Middlesex: Penguin, 1960), pp. 203-4.

[14] T. S. Eliot, *Collected Poems 1909-1962* (London: Faber and Faber, 1963), p. 198.

[15] Quoted from *Colombo's Canadian Quotations*, p. 407, col. 1. I have not been able to verify this quotation.

[16] Northrop Frye, "Canada and Its Poetry," *The Bush Garden* (Toronto: Anansi, 1971), p. 138. (Originally published in *Canadian Forum*, 23 [275], December 1943, 207-10.)

[17] W. S. Avis, ed.-in-chief, *A Dictionary of Canadianisms on Historical Principles* (Toronto: Gage, 1967).

[18] G. M. Story, W. J. Kirwin, and J. D. A. Widdowson, eds., *Dictionary of Newfoundland English* (Toronto: University of Toronto Press, 1982).

[19] Thomas Rolph, *Observations Made During a Visit in the West Indies and a Tour Through the United States of America, in Parts of the Years 1832-3; Together with a Statistical Account of Upper Canada* (Dundas, U.C.: G. Heyworth Hackstaff, 1836), p. 262.

[20] Sir Andrew MacPhail, "Our Canadian Speech," *Saturday Night*, 25 June 1935, 1-2.

[21] Stephen Leacock, "Good and Bad Language," *How to Write* (New York: Dodd, Mead, 1943), p. 121.

[22] J. K. Chambers, "Canadian English," in Chambers, ed., *The Languages of Canada* (Montreal: Didier, 1979), p. 168-77.

[23] Howard B. Woods, "A Socio-Dialectology Survey of the English Spoken in Ottawa: A Study of Sociological and Stylistic Variation in Canadian English." Unpublished Ph.D. dissertation, University of British Columbia, 1979.

[24] Woods, "Socio-Dialectology Survey," p. 33: "A uniform Canadian dialect covers a larger land-mass than any other one dialect in the world."

[25] Thomas F. McIlwraith, "Transportation in the Landscape of Early Canada," in J. David Wood, ed., *Perspectives on Landscape and Settlement in Nineteenth Century Ontario* (The Carleton Library No 91) (Toronto: Macmillan, 1978), p. 56.

[26] David Wood, "Introduction: A Context for Upper Canada and Its Settlement," in Wood, ed., *Perspectives*, p. xxvi; Thomas R. Weir, "The Population," in P. J. Smith, ed., *The Prairie Provinces* (Toronto: University of Toronto Press, 1972), pp. 93-8.

[27] This paper was originally delivered as the Marston LaFrance Fellowship Lecture at Carleton University, 19 February 1981. I should like to acknowledge my gratitude to the University for granting me a one year's full-time leave to pursue my studies of English in the Ottawa Valley as the 1980 Marston LaFrance Fellow. The paper also draws on the research of the Linguistic Survey of the Ottawa Valley, which is supported by the social Sciences and Humanities Research Council of Canada.

SOCIAL DIALECTS AND LANGUAGE VARIATION

Just as regional dialects are the result of regional or geographical distance, social dialects are the result of social distance. Each social group, no matter how small, that identifies itself as a social group develops speech patterns that set it apart from every other social unit. Obviously the greater the social distance between groups, the greater the difference one can expect to find between their speech patterns.

However, it should not be forgotten that regional dialects and social dialects and social dialects complement each other, as demonstrated by Harold B. Allen's and Virginia McDavid's articles. McDavid draws upon the files of the Linguistic Atlas of the North Central States and shows the distribution of verb forms by type of informant. Allen similarly utilizes the Linguistic Atlas of the Upper Midwest to show how grammatical and phonological items reflect class usage. The next article by Crawford Feagin serves as a transition between traditional regional dialect geography and sociolinguistics. She combines methods from both regional and social dialectology as she describes the continuum that exists between southern and other American dialects, as well as the continuum that exists between the speech of black and white Americans.

The remaining articles in this section, while they are concerned with language variation, are not concerned with dialects *per se*. Ohmann demonstrates that Bernstein's model of restricted and elaborated speech codes, as used by lower and middle class speakers respectively, badly misrepresents the social forces at work in social class language patterns. Instead of the static class difference in speech, hypothesized by Bernstein, Ohmann finds that the dynamic and changing power relations occurring in class structure are reflected in language use. The next article, by Labov, is an updated version of part of his dissertation, *Social Stratification of English in New York City*, which pioneered in the field of modern sociolinguistics. Sharon Ash, a one-time graduate student of Labov, next applies his research approach in describing a specific situation in which an incipient sound change seems to be spreading normally until altered social conditions block it. Anthony Kroch argues (1) that the public prestige dialect of the elite in a stratified community differs from the dialect of the non-elite strata in at least one phonologically systematic way and (2) that sound change begins in the working class.

Leslie Milroy, continuing her work on social networks reported in her seminal book, *Language and Social Networks* (University Park Press, 1980), draws upon her work in Belfast to address the problem: what is a linguistic norm, specifically a non-standard vernacular, as opposed to a fully codified standard norm? In addition, she discusses focusing, as yielding a variety of language perceived by its speakers as a distinct entity. Further, her article demonstrates a relationship between social network and sex on the one hand and linguistic choice on the other. Next, Roger Shuy demonstrates the application of sociolinguistics as he illustrates its usefulness in analyzing literature and conducting medical interviews.

The following two articles concern the difference between the speech of men and that of women. In the first, Peter Trudgill, after summarizing much of the current discussion, details several reasons for expecting differences to exist. In the other article, Robin Lakoff also concludes that there is a woman's language, but warns that there is a danger in opposing "woman's" language to the standard, just as there is of opposing any group's behavior to a hypothetical standard. In the last article in this section, Wolfgang Viereck discusses the conflict between intuitive vs. data-oriented linguistics, insisting that more data are needed to settle such sociolinguistic debates as that over the existence of black English, one that he feels is rich in theory but poor in data.

Beginning students who want to investigate this topic further might start with Peter Trudgill's *Sociolinguistics: An Introduction* (London: Penguin Books, 1983). For the more advanced student Labov's *Sociolinguistic Patterns* (Philadelphia: University of Pennsylvania Press, 1972) is highly recommended. Although primarily a textbook, Walt Wolfram and Ralph Fasold's *The Study of Social Dialects in American English* (Englewood Cliffs: Prentice Hall, 1974) should not be ignored. Those interested in the relationship between language and sex should consult *Language and Sex: Difference and Dominance* edited by Barrie Thoren and Nancy Henley (Rowley, Mass.: Newbury House, 1975) or *Language, Gender, and Society* edited by Barrie Thoren and Cheris Koramarae.

THE SOCIAL DISTRIBUTION OF SELECTED

VERB FORMS IN THE LINGUISTIC ATLAS

OF THE NORTH CENTRAL STATES

Virginia McDavid

The decade of the 1970s is a bright one in American dialectology. The *Dictionary of American Regional English*, long the major project of the American Dialect Society, is nearing completion under the editorship of Frederic G. Cassidy, and some portions of it should appear by 1980. The *Linguistic Atlas of New England* was reprinted in 1972 and its *Handbook* in 1973, the latter with the addition of a Word Index and Map Inventory by Audrey Duckert. Under Raven I. McDavid, Jr. editing has been completed for the Linguistic Atlas of the Middle and South Atlantic States, and final copy is being prepared for printing by the University of Chicago Press. The first fascicles will appear in 1978. Fieldwork for the Gulf States has been completed, and editing has begun, with Lee Pederson directing the project. The *Linguistic Atlas of the Upper Midwest* has appeared (1973, 1975, 1976), the culmination of a project begun in 1947 by Harold B. Allen.

The last two years have also seen the resumption of active editing of the materials of the Linguistic Atlas of the North Central States, which comprises Wisconsin, Michigan, Illinois, Indiana, Kentucky, Ohio, and southern Ontario. This area is a crucial one and tantalizing for dialect study because dialect patterns reflect settlement patterns, patterns which generally reflect a movement from east to west. Just as the material from New England and the Middle and South Atlantic States can help explain what is found in the North Central area, so the North Central data can provide a foundation for understanding what is found in areas further west.

The Linguistic Atlas of the North Central States was begun by Albert H. Marckwardt in 1938 as one of the regional atlases into which the originally planned Linguistic Atlas of the United States and Canada was to be divided. Most of the field work was completed between 1938 and 1957, some before this period

From *James B. McMillan: Essays in Linguistics by his Friends and Colleagues,* edited by J. C. Raymond and I. W. Russell. University of Alabama Press, 1977, pp 41-50. Reprinted with permission.

and more after it.   Until 1975 these materials had largely lain
fallow with little active editing or use of them.

In June 1975 a small conference with Marckwardt as chairman
was held at the University of Chicago to discuss plans for editing
and interpreting the material.   The Linguistic Atlas of the North
Central States will not present the data in list manuscript form,
as in the Linguistic Atlas of the Middle and South Atlantic States,
but rather in summary volumes, closer in format to those of the
Linguistic Atlas of the Upper Midwest.   These under their separate
editors will describe the phonology, grammar, and lexicon of the
area and be accompanied by a handbook.   After Marckwardt's
death later in 1975, Raven I. McDavid, Jr., the principal fieldworker in the North Central area, became editor.

Much has been accomplished since the 1975 conference.   The
final inventory of the records is nearly finished.   The Atlas will
include nearly 500 complete records and 50 partial ones, some
44,000 pages.   All records have been renumbered, a procedure
made necessary by the inclusion of substantial amounts of new
material, especially in Illinois.   The most important development
has been the publication of each record in the original forms in
which the fieldworker transcribed it.   These *Basic Materials*, as
they are now known, are part of the University of Chicago *Microfilm Collection of Manuscripts on Cultural Anthropology*, edited by
Norman McQuown, and are available either in microfilm or on
Xerox prints.   Editing of the grammatical materials has now begun.

While the preliminary work was continuing, some studies were
made of verb forms.   The conclusions are admittedly tentative.
The Ontario materials have been omitted because it had been
thought that additional Ontario records would shortly be added,
an incorrect assumption.   The Indiana materials are now being
retranscribed from the original tapes with the resultant emergence
of much new grammatical material.   Some changes in the conclusions
presented here are therefore likely after the materials in their
final form have been studied.   The average number of responses
per item in this group of ten verbs was 444.   Of these 49
percent, an average of 218 responses, are from Type I informants;
42 percent, an average of 185 responses, are from Type II informants; and 9 percent, an average of 41 responses, are from
Type III informants.

The data for the preterit or past participle form of ten verbs--
bite, *come*, *do*, *drive*, *give*, *run*, *shrink*, *tear*, *throw*, and *write*--
are presented here.   These ten were selected because the use of
the "correct" or "standard" preterit or past participle form is
regarded, both popularly and in usage guides, as a reflection of
social and educational status.   For these ten a clear pattern of
distribution appears: the standard forms are used least commonly
by the oldest and least educated informants and most commonly
by the youngest and most highly educated informants. Statistically
these differences are overwhelming (See Tables 1, 2, 3, and 4).

TABLE I. Average number of responses per item: 444. The number of responses is given in parentheses following the percentages. Type I, 49% (218); Type II, 42% (185); Type III 9% (41).

	Ave.		I		II		III	
bitten, ppl.	34%	(152)	27%	(61)	38%	(72)	51	(19)
bit	66	(296)	73	(163)	62	(115)	49	(18)
came, pret.	46	(251)	35	(98)	52	(116)	84	(37)
come	54	(294)	65	(182)	48	(105)	16	(7)
did, pret.	48	(223)	32	(76)	55	(98)	92	(49)
done	52	(244)	68	(159)	45	(81)	8	(4)
driven, ppl.	55	(238)	41	(83)	62	(115)	93	(40)
drove	45	(194)	59	(121)	38	(70)	7	(3)
gave, pret.	51	(228)	40	(91)	57	(106)	97	(31)
give	49	(217)	60	(135)	43	(81)	3	(1)
ran, pret.	40	(194)	27	(64)	45	(94)	82	(36)
run	60	(294)	73	(172)	55	(114)	18	(8)
shrank, pret.	16	(50)	15	(20)	10	(14)	40	(16)
shrunk	84	(258)	85	(109)	90	(125)	60	(24)
torn, ppl.	59	(243)	42	(85)	74	(125)	87	(33)
tore	41	(166)	58	(116)	26	(45)	13	(5)
threw, pret.	63	(302)	51	(118)	69	(143)	98	(41)
throwed	37	(179)	49	(114)	31	(64)	2	(1)
written, ppl.	71	(300)	59	(124)	84	(142)	87	(34)
wrote	29	(120)	41	(87)	16	(28)	13	(5)

There are regional patterns for these verbs as well (see Table 5), but they are not considered here. Kentucky, for example, has a generally lower use of standard forms, and other studies with North Central materials reveal a higher use of relic forms there.

Consideration of the past participle of *bite* (*bitten* or *bit*) and the preterit of *shrink* (*shrank* or *shrunk*) should be separated from that of the forms of the other eight verbs because with these two the traditional standard forms are used with strikingly less frequency. *Bitten* is used by one-fourth of the Type I informants, 40 percent of the Type II informants and 51 percent (statistically nonsignificant) of the Type III informants. The forms *dog-bit* and *snake-bit*, found in Kentucky and southern Indiana and Ohio, were not included here.

TABLE II.   Use of Standard Forms by Types of Informants

	I	II	III
0–10%		shrank	
11–20%	shrank		
21–30%	bitten ran		
31–40%	came did gave	bitten	shrank
41–50%	driven torn	ran	
51–60%	threw written	came did gave	bitten
61–70%		driven threw	
71–80%		torn	
81–90%		written	came ran torn written
91–100%			did driven gave threw

Shrunk is the most common preterit for all informants of all types. *Shrank* is used by 40 percent of the Type III informants, but again no conclusion can be drawn from this figure. Current dictionaries recognize divided standard usage for the forms of these two verbs, giving both *bitten* and *bit* and *shrank* and *shrunk*. These data support that decision, but if the first form listed in dictionaries is intended to be the more common one, the order should be reversed to read *bit* and *bitten* and *shrunk* and *shrank*.

The other eight verbs may also be grouped together because of the similarity of the data. In all, the standard forms--*came*, *did*, *driven*, *gave*, *ran*, *torn*, *threw*, and *written*--are much more common in the speech of the more highly educated informants.

Came: About one-third of the Type I informants use *came*, one-half of the Type II informants, and 84 percent of the Type III informants.

Did: One-third of the Type I informants use *did*, a little more than half of the Type II informants, and more than 90 percent of the Type II informants.

Table III.   Binomial Test of Significance, Assuming the Null
              Hypothesis

The statistics for all items *not* marked with an asterisk (*) are
significant at the a = .05 level. In other words, for items not
marked there is one chance in twenty or less that the result
would occur under the null hypothesis. Under the entry *bitten*,
bit, .0001 means that there is less chance than one in 10,000,
and .0016 means that there are less than sixteen changes in
10,000, that these results would occur by chance.

	I	II	III
bitten, bit	.0001	.0016	*.9268
came, come	.0001	*.4592	.0001
did, done	.0001	*.2040	.0001
driven, drove	.0078	.0010	.0001
gave, give	.0034	*.0672	.0001
ran, run	.0001	*.1646	.0001
shrank, shrunk	.0001	.0001	*.2058
torn, tore	.0286	.0001	.0001
threw, throwed	*.7948	.0001	.0001
written, wrote	.0108	.0001	.0001

Driven: Two-fifths of the Type I informants use *driven*,
three-fifths of the Type II informants, and 98 percent of the
Type III informants.
  Gave: Two-fifths of the Type I informants use *gave* and 97
percent of the Type III informants. The statistics for the Type
II informants are nonsignificant.
  Ran: Fewer than one-third of the Type I informants use *ran*
and 82 percent of the Type III informants. The statistics for
the Type II informants are nonsignificant. A lower percentage
of all types of informants use the standard form of this verb
than of any other.
  Torn: Two-fifths of the Type I informants use *torn*, three-
fourths of the Type II informants, and nearly 90 percent of the
Type III informants.
  Threw: About one-half of the Type I informants use *threw*,
70 percent of the Type II informants, and nearly all the Type
III informants.
  Written: Nearly 60 percent of the Type I informants use
written, a higher percentage of use of the standard form among
Type I informants than for any other of the eight verbs. About
85 percent of the Type II and Type III informants use *written*.
  Table 2 reveals the increasing use of the standard forms as
one progresses from Type I to Type III informants. If *bitten* and
shrank are excluded, more than 80 percent of all Type III speakers
use the standard forms *came*, *did*, *driven*, *gave*, *ran*, *torn*, *threw*,

TABLE IV. Results of Chi-Square Test

This table gives the result of a chi-square test for the significance of the variation in the use of standard as opposed to
nonstandard forms as a function of information type.   In each
of the columns I, II, and III the left figures are the number
of responses actually heard, while the right figures are the
number of responses which would be expected under the hypothesis
that there is no relation between response and information
type (the null hypothesis).   In the rightmost column are the
chi-square statistics for each item.   All are significant at
the 0.005 level, which means that there is one chance in 200
of the observed results occurring under the null hypothesis.
All except *bitten-bit* are significant at the 0.001 level, which
means that there is one chance in 1000 of the observed results
occurring under the null hypothesis.   Under the null hypothesis
the smallest expected number of responses is 6.494, so the
chi-square test is appropriate here.

	I		II		III		Total	
bitten	61	76.000	72	63.446	19	12.554	152	
bit	163	148.000	115	123.554	18	24.446	296	
	224		187		37		448	$X^2 = 11.236$
came	98	128.954	116	101.782	37	20.264	251	
come	182	151.046	105	119.218	7	23.736	294	
	280		221		44		545	$X^2 = 43.078$
did	76	112.216	98	85.475	49	25.308	223	
done	159	122.784	81	83.525	4	27.692	244	
	235		179		53		467	$X^2 = 45.030$
driven	83	112.389	115	101.921	40	23.690	238	
drove	121	91.611	70	83.079	3	19.310	194	
	204		185		43		432	$X^2 = 45.855$
gave	91	115.793	106	95.811	31	16.396	228	
give	135	110.207	81	91.189	1	15.604	217	
	226		187		32		445	$X^2 = 39.784$
ran	64	93.820	94	82.689	36	17.492	194	
run	172	142.180	114	125.311	8	26.508	294	
	236		208		44		488	$X^2 = 50.806$
shrank	20	20.942	14	22.565	16	6.494	50	
shrunk	109	108.058	125	116.435	24	33.506	258	
	129		139		40		308	$X^2 = 20.544$
torn	85	119.421	125	101.002	33	22.579	243	
tore	116	81.579	45	68.998	5	15.423	166	
	201		170		38		409	$X^2 = 50.349$

(continued)

TABLE IV. (*continued*)

	I		II		III		Total	
threw	118	145.663	143	129.967	41	26.370	302	
throwed	114	86.337	64	77.033	1	15.630	179	
	232		207		42		481	X^2 = 36.613
written	124	150.714	142	121.429	34	27.857	300	
wrote	87	60.286	28	48.571	5	11.143	120	
	211		170		39		420	X^2 = 33.511

and *written*. More than 61 percent of the Type II speakers use *driven*, *threw*, *torn*, and *written*; between 41 and 60 percent *came*, *did*, *gave*, and *ran*. Between 41 and 60 percent of the Type I speakers use *driven*, *threw*, *torn*, and *written*, and between 21 and 40 percent use *came*, *did*, *gave*, and *ran*.

Phrased somewhat differently, between 21 and 40 percent of the Type I informants use *came*, *did*, *gave*, and *ran*, and between 41 and 60 percent of the Type II informants. Between 41 and 60 percent of the Type I informants use *driven*, *threw*, *torn*, and *written*, and between 61 and 90 percent of the Type II informants. More than 90 percent of the Type III informants use all eight forms.

What general conclusions can be drawn from this small study based on the North Central data? One conclusion never doubted but here confirmed is that these materials can and do contribute significantly to our knowledge of social variation in American English. A further conclusion is that dialectology, and specifically the findings of the linguistic atlases, have real and serious implications for education, especially the study of English usage, which has too long been a record of prejudice rather than of fact.

ACKNOWLEDGMENT

The author wishes to acknowledge her indebtedness to Glenn T. McDavid, programmer/analyst, First National Bank of Chicago, for his assistance in the preparation and interpretation of the statistical data and tables.

TABLE V. Percentages of Responses by States

	WI	MI	IL	IN	KY	OH
bitten, ppl.	47% (24)	37% (27)	40% (49)	15% (7)	25% (21)	34% (24)
bit	53 (27)	63 (46)	60 (74)	85 (41)	75 (62)	66 (46)
came, pret.	38 (25)	42 (39)	57 (87)	43 (19)	33 (34)	54 (47)
come	62 (41)	58 (54)	43 (65)	57 (25)	67 (69)	46 (40)
did, pret.	29 (17)	54 (42)	56 (74)	34 (13)	39 (33)	57 (44)
done	71 (41)	46 (36)	44 (57)	66 (25)	61 (52)	43 (33)
driven, ppl.	51 (27)	53 (33)	65 (82)	59 (30)	36 (26)	61 (40)
drove	49 (26)	47 (29)	35 (45)	41 (21)	64 (47)	39 (26)
gave, pret.	55 (31)	47 (33)	63 (84)	25 (7)	35 (29)	59 (44)
give	45 (25)	53 (37)	37 (50)	75 (21)	65 (54)	41 (30)
ran, pret.	32 (19)	27 (20)	53 (70)	40 (21)	31 (31)	46 (33)
run	68 (41)	73 (53)	47 (62)	60 (31)	69 (68)	54 (39)
shrank, pret.		10 (6)	21 (23)	5 (2)	20 (9)	17 (10)
shrunk		90 (52)	79 (85)	95 (36)	80 (35)	83 (50)
torn, ppl.	55 (23)	64 (38)	71 (84)	50 (24)	46 (36)	59 (38)
tore	45 (19)	36 (21)	29 (34)	50 (24)	54 (42)	41 (26)
threw, pret.	67 (34)	65 (50)	70 (92)	62 (32)	49 (48)	64 (46)
throwed	33 (17)	35 (27)	30 (40)	38 (20)	51 (49)	36 (26)
written, ppl.	79 (41)	83 (53)	78 (88)	64 (32)	47 (33)	75 (53)
wrote	21 (11)	17 (11)	22 (25)	36 (18)	53 (37)	25 (18)

The number of responses is given in parentheses following the
  percentages.
The preterit of *shrink* was not recorded in Wisconsin.

THE *LINGUISTIC ATLAS OF THE UPPER MIDWEST*

AS A SOURCE OF SOCIOLINGUISTIC INFORMATION[1]

Harold B. Allen

When, nearly fifty years ago, Hans Kurath included a three-point social dimension in the selection of field informants for the Linguistic Atlas of New England, he provided a precedent that increasingly has brought to light significant social variation in American English.[2]   The phonological analysis prepared for the third and final volume of the *Linguistic Atlas of the Upper Midwest*,[3]   along with the treatment of the lexicon and the grammar in the first two volumes, now adds measurably to the sociolinguistic data available not only to dialectologists but also to students and teachers of usage, to textbook writers, and to sociolinguists themselves.

The *Linguistic Atlas of the Upper Midwest* (*LAUM*) covers the states of Minnesota, Iowa, North and South Dakota, and Nebraska. Its primary function, like that of other American regional dialect atlases now in process, is of course the presentation of regional differences in American English.   But, also like the other atlases, it follows Kurath's lead in giving information about ascertained social differences as well.   It specifies the social range and sometimes even the register of many linguistic items: lexical, grammatical, and phonological.   The use of the term "range" must not be overlooked.   Although the data are presented as summarized frequencies with each of the three informant classes, they are not to be interpreted as absolute frequencies for the classes as such.   A frequency distribution of, say, 72% for the relatively uneducated speakers in Type I, of 22% for the better educated high school group of speakers in Type II, and 6% for the cultivated college group in Type III means simply that there is a fairly sharp decline in the use of a given item or form as one looks at people along the educational ladder, a ladder which at the time of the field work could in the Upper Midwest be reasonably equated with the social ladder.

Two important limitations, then, restrict the interpretation of the data.   First, the information is for a particular region, the Upper Midwest, and hence is suggestive and not definitive with

From *James B. McMillian: Essays in Linguistics by his Friends and Colleagues*, edited by J. C. Raymond and I. W. Russell. University of Alabama Press, 1977, pp 3-19. Reprinted with permission.

respect to other sections of the country, where the distribution might be quite different. It demonstrates principles and procedures only so far as other areas are concerned. Second, the information was gathered at the midcentury point and hence for at least certain items is not to be taken as reflecting the current situation, more than a quarter of a century later. It may be noted, furthermore, that the information is derived from interviews that in themselves offer variation ranging from an occasional fairly formal register to the usual informal and sometimes even casual style. But the language reported is always living English, never the edited variety analyzed in studies of the printed page.

Although within the 800-item corpus of the Upper Midwest worksheets more attention is given specifically to the vocabulary, the lexicon is not very significant in exhibiting social contrast. The selection of vocabulary items was made primarily to reveal differences in everyday words, not levels of personal lexical choice. Yet even with this limitation some vocabulary matters do manifest social range. For example, only a handful of the Type I and Type II informants use bus or railroad *station* exclusively, but 25% of those in Type III use only the word. Its prestige is suggested by the informant who calls *depot* "improper," and by another informant who during the interview corrected himself by saying "station" after he had first replied with "depot," and then commented, "That's the right word." "The sun *rose*" is preferred by all the college graduates and by 83% of the high school group but by a smaller 70% of the Type I informants, with the others choosing *came up*. A slightly higher proportion of the cultivated speakers select *dishcloth* (58%) and a corresponding proportion of the Type I's prefer *dishrag*. Of the 18 informants out of 208 who offer *widow woman* instead of simple *widow*, fourteen are in Type I, four in Type II, and none at all in the college-trained group III. *Relations* instead of *relatives* is preferred by 37% of the least educated, 18% of the high school group, and none of the Type III informants. More than one-third of the Type I speakers use *learn* in the sense of *teach*, but only a few Type II informants do, and none at all in Type III. It may be additionally noted that of the many colorful equivalents of *tired*, *vomit*, and *jilt*, nearly all are offered by Type I and Type II speakers and only a meager few by those in Type III.

But it is with respect to grammar and pronunciation that the field records are most revelatory of social contrast. Specifically, for more than half a century repeated educational research has found the irregular verbs to be the source of most of the so-called grammatical errors in the writing of school children. It is not surprising that they reveal the greatest social differences in the actual field investigations in the Upper Midwest. Nor is it surprising that, as the not infrequent total of more than 100% indicates, some informants are so insecure that they shift back and forth from one form to another.

Although textbooks and usage manuals usually posit a rather sharp division between the correct and incorrect, the acceptable and the inacceptable, in actual practice the contrast is rather one of varying frequency on a sliding scale or range. Three points on the range can be taken as summaries of sections of the range as a whole. Of the thirty-seven worksheet verb forms listed below, for example, only five are not used by at least one college graduate. Thirty-two of them are in use throughout the complete social range, though of course with increasing or decreasing frequency between one end of the range and the other. As social markers, they can be held significant, then, only insofar as they occur with other social markers. Neither the presence nor absence of a given form in the speech of one informant is sufficient evidence to categorize him as a Type I, II, or III speaker.

"He *come* yesterday," for example, though clearly the dominant choice of Type I informants with 75% frequency, still is used in the speech of nearly one-half of the high school group, and by a perhaps surprising 19% of the college-trained informants. Similarly with "He *run* into me." in which the base form *run* appears as a preterit in the speech of 65% of those in Type I, 36% in Type II, and even with 19% again in Type III. Likewise, *give* occurs in a past time context in "He *give* it to me yesterday" for most of the Type I informants but also with decreased incidence in the speech of those in Types II and III. The converse, a preterit form used as past participle, exhibits a similar range in the 59% frequency of "I've never *drove* a horse" among Type I speakers but only 19% among the college informants.

Even "He *done* it" does not turn out to be an entirely illiterate expression if language itself is not used as the criterion. One-fourth of the high school group has it along with one college-trained speaker.

Lie and *lay* are even less inclined to fit into the rigid dichotomy implied in textbook prescriptivism. The distant loss of any *Sprachgefuhl* for the special sense and function of preterit causative verbs long ago led to such confusion that today it is a fifty-fifty chance whether an Upper Midwest college graduate will say "She *lay* in bed all morning" or "She *laid* in bed all morning." But Type I speakers are not in doubt as to which is the right form. Eighty-five percent of them are confident that it is *laid*. The infinitive is only slightly less a problem to the Type III informants, 81% of whom have the orthodox "I'm going to *lie* down." Of greater value as a social marker is the preterit of the simplex of the analogous verb pair, *sit* and *set*. Although more than one-third of the least educated speakers have *set* as the preterit on "Then they all *set* down," all but one of the Type III group have the standard "They *sat* down." The remaining verbs in the following list likewise offer evidence supporting the existence of a continuous range or continuum along which social contrast is to be measured.

Several of the miscellaneous grammatical items recorded during the interviews provide more positive social markers than do the strong verbs. Concord with *be*, for example, is rigorously ob-

Table I: Irregular Verbs

	Type I %	Type II %	Type III %
bitten	45	81	68
climbed, *pret.*	73	86	100
clum	25	12	0
clim	9	1	0
come, *pret.*	75	41	19
did	57	81	94
done, *pret.*	63	27	6
drank, *ppl.*	92	78	47
drunk	8	27	60
driven	65	80	94
drove, *ppl.*	41	13	6
drownded, *ppl.*	29	8	0
give, *pret.*	52	19	13
gave	66	94	94
lie, *infin.*	60	70	81
lay = lie, *infin.*	52	40	19
laid, *pret.*	77	69	47
lay, *pret.*	15	28	53
ridden	48	82	81
rode, *ppl.*	59	21	19
ran	63	90	100
run, *pret.*	65	36	19
saw	73	82	87
see, *pret.*	42	27	13
sat	60	88	94
set = sat	37	15	6
swam	85	97	100
swum, *pret.*	18	5	0
tore, *ppl.*	42	26	7
torn	60	75	93
threw	77	94	100
throwed, *pret.*	31	9	6
awoke	6	20	19
wakened	6	6	25
woke (up)	84	73	56
written	79	92	100
wrote, *ppl.*	22	9	0

served by the college informants. Not one of them favors the
construction accepted by a majority of the Type I speakers, *we
was* or *they was*.   Nor did any of the college informants use
Here's followed by a plural subject, such as *your clothes*, although most of the Type I speakers and more than one-half of
the Type II's apparently treat *Here's* as an unchangeable formula
to be used before either a singular or a plural noun in the
predicate.

"I *ain't* going to" is likewise missing in the speech of the
college group, although it is in the speech of one-fourth of the
Type II's and of one-half of the least educated informants.
"I *ain't* done it" is even more clearly a social marker, as it is
not only abjured by informants in Type III and used by only
nine percent of the high school Type II but is accepted as normal
by more than one third of the Type II's.

The controversial inverted negative interrogative of *be* offers
a different picture. The historically normal phonetic development
of *Am not I?* is *Ain't I?*, but the latter has acquired such a pejorative aura that in the Upper Midwest only nine percent of the
Type III speakers will use it occasionally in contrast with 45% of
the Type II informants and 63% of the Type I's.   Conversely,
two-thirds of the Type III informants use the stilted *Am I not?* in
contrast with only 29% of the Type I speakers, while a surprising
27% of the college group take refuge in the bizarre and illogical
Aren't I? --although none would seek such consistency as would
exist if they should say "I was going too, aren't I?"

Third person *don't* is not so distinctive a social marker as
usage manuals would imply. *He don't* is the customary locution
not only for almost all the Type I informants and more than
one-half of the Type II's but also for nearly one-half of the
college-trained group.   A similar social gradation appears in the
distribution of *way* and *ways*.   While *a long way* is preferred by
twice as high a proportion of educated informants as by the least
educated, the seeming plural *ways* (historically the adverbial gene-
tive in *-es*) is the majority choice of all three types.

Still greater inconsistency appears in the contrast between
two locutions in which a numeral precedes a modified noun.
Only 15% of the Type I informants and a bare seven percent of
the Type II's accept the locution *two pound*, as of flour or sugar;
not one college graduate has it.   But with the historically parallel
two bushel the incidence in Type I rises to 62%.   Nearly one-half
of the Type II speakers have it, as do even 13% of the Type
III's.   The former is clearly a sharp though minor social marker;
the latter, despite its being analogous, is only suggestively so.

Although in the somewhat unusual interview situation nearly
one-half of the cultivated informants use the formal *It wasn't I*
(preponderantly the female speakers), only 20% of the Type II
informants have it, and only four percent of the Type I's.   In
all three types the majority say simply *It wasn't me*.   When all
three types are examined it appears that 80% of those who say *It*

wasn't I are women.   The relation of this fact to the current concern with sexism in language remains to be studied.

Two syntactic constructions with relative clauses yield variants providing rather sharp social contrast.   In the non-restrictive relative clause modifying a noun with the + human feature, as "He's the man REL PRO . . .", more than three-fourths of the Type I speakers select *that*, as do nearly that many of the Type II's; but only one-fourth of the cultivated speakers choose it. Conversely, only one-fifth of Type I select *who*, but three-fourths of those in Type III have it.   A minor social marker is the zero or omitted relative as subject, castigated in usage manuals, as in "he's the man brought the furniture."   One-tenth of the least educated informants have this construction, as do two percent of the high school group, but none in Type III.   The genitive relative pronoun bemuses one-half of the Type I informants.   In the possible context "he's the boy whose father . . ." they replace *whose* with *that his* (30%) or *that the* (9%), or with simple *his* and no relative pronoun (9%).   Each of the three minor variants is a clear social marker.

A well-known social contrast between *those* and *them* as adjectivals before a plural noun is expectedly attested in the Upper Midwest.   *Those boys* is the only locution reported for the college group; *them boys* is used by 60% of the Type I informants and by 22% of the Type II's.   Several additional social markers are listed in the following chart, where it is shown that these language matters as well occur with greater frequency in the speech of the least educated: *poison* as a predicate modifier in "Some berries are poison;" *sick at the stomach* and *sick in the stomach*; *in back of* (the door); *died with* rather than *died from*, and *towards* and *toward*.   When in the following chart percentages total more than 100, the indication is simply that an informant uses more than one form.

Although certain gross matters of pronunciation have sometimes been labeled "incorrect" in the schools, the three-point social range investigated in dialect research provides a sounder description of the social contrasts discernible in phonological variation. While most of the phonological differences revealed in the field records of the Upper Midwest survey are only regionally significant, a number manifest social contrast as well.   They occur in several categories.

Stress variation exhibits social correlation in a few words. Among Type I and Type II informants, for instance, the proportion favoring initial stress in the verb *address* is twice as high as among those in Type III.   Nearly one-half of the least educated speakers have initial stress in *umbrella*, but only one-fifth of the college group do.   One-fourth of the Type I's have primary or secondary stress on the second syllable of *theater*, but only 6% of the Type III's.   A conspicuous example is the pronunciation of *genuine*.   The least educated speakers strongly favor heavy stress on the final syllable; the cultivated speakers favor zero stress, with corresponding reduction of the vowel to /I/.   A

Table II: Grammar Miscellany

	Type I	Type II	Type III
We/they was	60%	30%	0
We/they were	53	76	100
Here are N PL	24	48	100
Here's N PL	81	59	0
I ain't going to	46	26	0
I'm not going to	58	83	100
Ain't I?	63	45	9
Am I not?	29	45	64
Aren't I?	5	15	27
I haven't done it	72	97	100
I ain't done it	38	9	0
He doesn't	26	51	77
He don't	88	60	46
a long) way	24	30	47
a long) ways	86	82	73
two) bushel	62	49	13
two) bushels	43	52	87
two) pound	15	7	0
two) pounds	89	94	100
He's the man that...	77	65	27
He's the man who...	19	42	73
He's the man Ø	10	2	0
He's a boy whose father...	49	79	87
He's a boy that his father...	30	11	7
He's a boy that the father...	9	5	0
He's a boy his father...	9	5	7
Some berries are poisonous	47	67	93
Some berries are poison	55	32	7
those boys	61	90	100
them boys	60	22	0
sick at the stomach	32	26	13
sick in the stomach	13	3	0
sick to the stomach	52	68	94
back of (the door	26	27	31
in back of (the door	8	7	0
behind	71	73	75
toward	40	54	100
towards	63	48	0
died from	31	33	44
died of	45	59	63
died with	29	8	0

Table III: Stress Variation

		Type I	Type II	Type III
address, *vb*.	/ǽdrès/	26%	25%	11%
genuine	/jɛ́nyuɪn/	17	47	86
	/jɛ́nyuwàɪn/	83	54	14
guardian	/gàrdín/	34	15	0
theater	/θí-êtə̀/	23	8	6
	/θíə tə̀/	64	78	63
	/θɪə tə̀/	13	14	31
umbrella	/ə́mbrɛ̀l ə/	44	24	19

similar contrast occurs with *guardian*, with 34% of the Type I
informants favoring /gɑrdín/ while all the cultivated speakers have
/gárdɪən/.

Vowel variation may create social markers. *LAUM* reports that
the pronunciation of *root* as /rut/, although accepted by one-third
of the Type I and Type II speakers, is preferred over /rʊt/ by
only 13% of the college group. The same checked vowel /ʊ/
in *soot* is the choice of one-half of the least educated speakers
but by nine out of ten of the Type III's. None of the latter
group has the pronunciation /sət/, the choice of one-third of the
Type I speakers. A few of the Type I's have adopted what
must be a spelling pronunciation, /sut/. Two variants of *yolk*,
/yɛlk/ and /yulk/, are favored by Type I speakers over the
customary /yok/. The pronunciation /rɛdɪš/ is normal for one-
third of the least educated but rare among college-trained speakers. The form /kæg/ for *keg* is a minor social marker, with 15%
preference in Type I and no use at all by Type III's.   In
Minnesota and North Dakota /ɑnt/ and /ænt/ have become social

Table IV: Vowel Variation

		Type I	Type II	Type III
aunt	/ɑnt/	15%	21%	32%
keg	/kæg/	16	5	0
radish	/rɛdɪś/	33	22	6
root	/rut/	33	35	13
	/rʊt/	76	66	87
soot	/sut/	18	8	13
	/sʊt/	51	73	88
	/sət/	34	18	0
yolk	/yɛlk/	31	19	6
	/yulk/			

Table V: Terminal Reduction Vowel

		Type I	Type II	Type III
meadow	/mɛdo/	78%	93%	92%
	/mɛdə/	14	2	0
	/mɛdu/	9	8	8
minnow	/mɪni	25	12	0
	/mɪno/	67	83	100
	/mɪnu/	10	12	6
tomato	/təméto/	46	62	73
	/t@métə/	54	38	27
widow	/wɪdo/	55	71	82
	/wɪdə/	14	4	0
	/wɪdu/	30	25	18

markers, with the former pronunciation of *aunt* preferred by 32% of the Type III speakers and even by 15% of those in Type I. And for speakers stressing the first syllable in *theater* there is a choice of free and checked vowels. More common is /i/, but twice as high a proportion of Type III's selected checked /ɪ/, a pronunciation apparently associated by these informants with the French and British spelling *theater*.

Even an unstressed vowel in terminal position manifests socially correlated variations. All the college-educated informants have final /o/ in *minnow* (excepting one with /u/), but the folk speech /mɪni/ is found in the speech of one-fourth of the Type I's. A few of them also have the variant with final /u/. For *meadow* and *widow* a pronunciation with final /ə/ is a minor social marker; for *tomato* it is much more significant, with its use by more than one-half of the Type I speakers.

An apparent epenthetic or anaptyctic vowel exhibits social contrast. It seems to be induced by initial stress in *umbrella*, for the same speakers have both, nearly always in Type I. A similar vowel in *mushroom*, however, is actually historical, as the French etymon is *mousseron* and orthographic variants with medial *e* have persisted since the early 15th century. It is preserved in the speech of one-fourth of the least educated informants, but is rare in the speech of the others. Incidentally, a final *n* instead of *m*, likewise historical, is also preserved largely by Type I speakers, 55% of whom have it beside only 20% of the college group. Another example of the epenthetic schwa may actually be a reduced form of the pronoun *it*. For the injunction *Look here!* 42% of the Type I speakers have either /lʊkəhir/ or /lʊkəthir/, with the incidence dropping to one-third in Type II and only 14% in Type III.

A nonhistorical excrescent /t/ is a sharp social feature. It occurs after /n/, with 26% of the Type I informants and 14% of the Type II's adding it to *once* and *across* (but no college graduates), and after /f/, with 18% of the Type I informants and

Table VI: Addition and replacement

		Type I	Type II	Type III
Look here!	/lʊkəhɪr/			
	/lʊkɪhɪr/	42%	33%	14%
	/lukɪthɪr/			
mushroom	/mə̃ʃrum/	46	75	87
	/mə̃ʃrun/	55	23	20
	/mə̃ʃərun/	23	9	6
nothing	/nə̃θɪn/	35	17	6
something	/sə̃mθɪn, sə̃mpʔm/	25	20	13
umbrella	/ə̃mbərɛ̃lə/	44	24	10

eight percent of the Type II's adding it to *skiff*, *cliff*, or
trough (but no college graduates).

Although replacement of terminal velar /ŋ/ by alveolar /n/ is
common in the verbal ending *ing*, its presence in the words *nothing* and *something* is much more definitely of social significance.
More than one-third of the Type I's say /nə̃θɪn/ but only 6% of
the Type III's.   One-fourth of the Type I's say /sə̃mθɪn/ or the
assimilated form /səmpʔm/, but only 13% of the Type III's.

The historical tendency toward the reduction or simplification
of consonant clusters manifests itself with greater strength among
the uneducated, except perhaps for the initial cluster /hw/.
There the unaspirated variant /w/ is becoming more acceptable
to many speakers in Types II and III, as in *wheel*, *whetstone*,
white,   and *whip*, though apparently not in *wheat*.   Generally
Upper Midwest speakers seem to retain initial /h/, especially in
Minnesota and North Dakota.   But the initial cluster /hy/ has
been reduced to simple /y/ for more than one-half of the Type I
informants, largely in Iowa and Nebraska, and for one-fifth of
the college group.

The final *sts* cluster in several words tends to be retained
by cultivated speakers.   *Fists*, for instance, is /fɪs·/ or /fɪs·t/
for 75% of the Type I speakers but for only 44% of the Type
III's.   In two words, *library* and *secretary*, simplification may
have been reinforced by the tendency toward dissimilation.   *Library* is simply /laibɛri/ for 28% of the Type I informants but for
only 12% of the Type III's; and *secretary* is /sɛkɪtɛri/ for 57% of
the Type I speakers, and for more than one-fourth of the Type
II's, but for only six percent of the Type III's.   The cluster
/nd/ in *hundred* is reduced to /n/ in the pronunciation /hənɚd/
recorded in the speech of 18% of the Type I and 15% of the Type
II informants.   No Type III informant was heard to use it.

Spelling pronunciation, the use of the visual form as a guide
to the oral form, does not always result from the same factors in
yielding a social contrast.   The school emphasis upon spelling as
the criterion may cause a change in the pronunciation of a familiar
word, or sudden encounter with an unfamiliar word may lead to

Table VII: Cluster Simplification

		Type I	Type II	Type III
fists	/fɪsts/	28	44	56
	/fɪs·t/	19	5	13
	/fɪs·/	56	13	31
humor	/yumə/	54	29	20
	/hyumə/	43	70	80
hundred	/hə́nəd/	18	15	0
library	/laibrɛri/	70	75	94
	/laibɛri/	28	21	12
secretary	/sɛkrɪtɛri/	39	74	94
	/sɛk tɛri/	57	27	6

word, or sudden encounter with an unfamiliar word may lead to a plausible but nonhistorical pronunciation.

Of the several notable instances in *LAUM*, one, the pronunciation of *mongrel* with visually-suggested /ɑ/ rather than the historical /ə/ otherwise accepted unquestioningly in such words as *money*, *monkey*, and *wonder*, is usual among college graduates but chosen by but not much more than one-half of the less educated informants. But other examples of spelling pronunciation illustrate a readier acceptance of spelling as a guide by folk speakers. Although one-half of the college informants are sufficiently bemused by the *phth* combination in *diphtheria* to pronounce the obvious first letter and overlook the second, 95% of the Type I informants accept the same solution to the problem with the pronunciation of the first syllable as simple /dɪp/. Nearly one-half of the least educated follow analogous *earth* in their pronunciation of *hearth*; only seven percent of Type III do. One-fourth of the Type I informants have a spelling pronunciation of *palm* with the voiced /l/; only seven percent of the college speakers do. Nearly one-fourth of the Type I's have /s/ in *raspberries* instead of /z/; none of the college informants does.

Although too sporadic to be relied upon as social markers, a number of aberrant pronunciations appear almost exclusively in the speech of Type I informants and hence do have some value

Table VIII: Spelling Pronunciation

		Type I	Type II	Type III
diphtheria	/dɪfθɪryə/	5	18	50
	/dɪpθɪryə/	95	82	50
hearth	/haθ/	44	26	7
mongrel	/məngrəl/	43	31	18
	/mɑngrəl/	57	69	82
palm	/pɑlm/	25	29	7

in supporting social categorization.   One is the pronunciation
/čimbli/ for *chimney*; another is the use of the affricate in either
/rinč/ or /rɛnč/ for *rinse*.   Two lisped pronunciations of /θ/
occur as /f/ in /drauf/ for *drouth* and in /mæfyu/ for *Matthew*.
And the Midland preterit or participial ending /t/ rather than
/d/ is preserved almost entirely by Type I informants in their
versions of *boiled, spoiled,* and *scared*.

Sociologists have quite ignored such data as this article presents in their various attempts to define social classes and sub-
classes by means of educational and socioeconomic criterions.
Sociolinguists have neglected the rich source of relevant data in
linguistic atlas field records.   In the teaching of English little
attention has been placed upon this kind of information.   But
perhaps now the more readily accessible facts in *LAUM* will be
found useful by them in their studies of social mobility and their
sometimes imperfect recognition of a range or dimension rather
than neatly tiered social classes and usage levels.

FOOTNOTES

[1]This is a revised version of a paper orally presented at the
regional meeting of the American Dialect Society in St. Louis,
Missouri, November 4, 1976.

[2]Although Jakob Jud and Karl Jaberg had incidentally included a few informants from different social classes in their
Sprach und Sachatlas Italiens und der Südschweiss   (1928-1940).
Kurath was the first dialectologist to build social range into
a systematically surveyed population of a dialect project.
As early as 1948 Raven I. McDavid, Jr., drew attention to
the significance of the resulting social data for the social scientist.   Observation of social contrast appeared in Kurath's *Word
Geography of the Eastern United States* (1949) and in his and
McDavid's *Pronunciation of English in the Atlantic States*
(1961), although it was not detailed and quantified.   More
detailed statements are in E. Bagby Atwood's *Survey of Verb
Forms in the Eastern United States* (1958), a study subsequently
extended in two University of Minnesota dissertations by Virginia
Glenn McDavid in 1954 (Verb Forms of the North Central States
and Upper Midwest) and Jean Malmstrom in 1958 (A Study
of the Validity of Textbook Statements about Certain Controversial Grammatical Items in the Light of Evidence from the
Linguistic Atlas).

[3]Harold B. Allen.   *The Linguistic Atlas of the Upper Midwest.*
Volume I: *Handbook and Lexicon,* 1973.   Volume 2: *Grammar,*
1975.   Volume 3: *Pronunciation ,* 1976.   Minneapolis, Minnesota:
University of Minnesota Press.

SOUTHERN WHITE IN THE ENGLISH
LANGUAGE COMMUNITY

Crawford Feagin

INTRODUCTION

This study has examined the verb system of Southern White English--tense, aspect, modality, agreement, and negation. It has shown how social class, locale, age, and sex can affect the grammar; and the various forms found in Anniston have been compared with what has been found in other varieties of English. These diverse elements can be pulled together to show how they interact. First the concepts of language, dialect, and variety are summarized. Then the relationship, from the perspective of the verb phrase, between White Southern and other varieties of English is explored--Black English, Northern and Upper Midwestern American English, Regional British and archaic English, and Atlantic Creoles. A discussion of the specific regional origins of these grammatical features in the British Isles is also in order. Finally, the position of southern White in relation to pan-English is assessed.

Throughout the article Anniston White English is compared with the English of other groups. For these comparisons there are two kinds of information which are called 'quantitative' and 'qualitative'. Quantitative data states the frequency of occurrence of a form as against its expected occurrences. In the figures it is shown as a percentage of nonstandard forms out of all occurrences, a weighted mean. A qualitative comparison contrasts the occurrence or nonoccurrence of a particular form in two or more groups. In qualitative comparison, a three valued scale will be used: X indicates that examples were found in the source, ? that there was no information available in the literature, 0 that there was contrary evidence or circumstantial evidence against occurrence of the form.

"Southern White in the English Language Community" originally appeared as "Southern Whites in the English Language Community," in Feagin, Crawford, *Variation and Change in Alabama English*, 1979. Georgetown University Press. Used by permission of the publisher.

LANGUAGE, DIALECT, AND VARIETY

While there is no doubt that the English of Southern Whites is one variety among many in the English-speaking world, the question arises of the amount of difference between that variety and the others. Various comparisons have been made concerning Southern White with varying degrees of accuracy. Among the more notable are claims that Southern White is the same as Black English or that the speech of mountain whites is pure Elizabethan English. Too often these observations have been supported by examples selected to prove the hypothesis in an 'all-or-nothing' manner. The result has been an understandable confusion.

Some definitions of 'language', 'dialect', and 'variety' would be useful at this point. The definitions established by Ferguson and Gumperz (1960) have not been improved upon, and they are used here. A 'variety' is defined as

> any body of human speech patterns which is suf-
> ficiently homogeneous to be analyzed by available
> techniques of synchronic description and which
> has a sufficiently large repertory of elements and
> their arrangements or processes with broad enough
> semantic scope to function in all normal contexts
> of communication (1963:3).

'Variety' in this sense has been called 'lect' by C.-J. Bailey. He defines this as

> a completely non-committal term for any bundling
> together   of   linguistic   phenomena   (1973:11).

A 'language', then,

> consists of all varieties . . . which share a single
> superposed variety (such as a literary standard)
> having substantial similarity in phonology and
> grammar with the included varieties or which are
> either mutually intelligible or are connected by a
> series of mutually intelligible varieties (Ferguson
> and Gumperz 1960:5).

Finally, a 'dialect' is

> any set of one or more varieties of a language
> which share at least one feature or combination
> of features setting them apart from other varieties
> of the language, and which may appropriately be
> treated as a unit on linguistic or nonlinguistic
> grounds   (Ferguson   and   Gumperz   1960:7).

Dialects may be either geographical or social. Density of communication determines the nature and degree of differentiation of geographical dialects; interspeaker attitudes are the determining factor for the differentiation of social dialects. In regard to geographical dialects, Ferguson and Gumperz propose:

> Other things being equal, the more frequently
> speakers A and B of language X communicate
> with each other, by means of X, the more

> the varieties of X spoken by them will tend to
> become identical (1960:8).

(This has also been observed in regard to social dialects.) As for interspeaker attitudes, they emphasize group solidarity as an important feature.

> Any group of speakers of language X which
> regards itself as a close social unit will tend
> to express its group solidarity by favoring
> those linguistic innovations which set it apart
> from other speakers of X who are not part
> of the group (Ferguson and Gumperz 1960:9).

Using these definitions, Anniston White English can then be placed in the following context: Anniston English consists of at least two varieties (Standard and Nonstandard) of Southern White English which in itself is a separate dialect of English on both geographical and social (group solidarity) grounds. Wood (1971) has shown that, for whites, on the basis of word geography, there is a distinct geographical Southern dialect area which can be further divided into several subregions such as Mid Southern and Gulf Southern. Although there has been no formal study of social attitudes, my observation is that white Southerners see themselves as separate from non-Southerners. This is evidenced by the creation of the Confederacy and the resulting War Between the States. Until recently, 'Dixie' was played at most Southern (white) sports events along with the national anthem and the school song. The speech of non-Southerners is perceived by Southerners as 'harsh' and 'ugly'. Moreover, the material folk culture[1] of the South, both Upland and Lowland, sets the South apart from the North, the Mid-Atlantic, and the Midwest (Glassie 1968:39). So, informally, for the purposes of this article, it can be said that White Southern is both a geographical and a social dialect. The evidence from Anniston is used in this article as an example of White Southern.

WHITE SOUTHERN AND BLACK ENGLISH

The variety of English most often compared with White southern is Black English. The work of Dillard, Wolfram, and Dunlap is among the more recent of these comparisons. The issues most often raised are whether or not southern White and Black English are the same, and if they differ, how they differ.

In an attempt to deal with the question of divergence between White Southern and Black English, the Anniston data has been compared throughout this study to previous work in Black English. However, a summary of those comparisons seems appropriate at this point; both quantitative and qualitative comparisons are possible.

Quantitative Comparison

In six cases it is possible to compare black and white groups. The groups to be compared are the working-class teenage blacks in Harlem studied by Labov's team (Labov et al. 1968) and the urban and rural whites of the Anniston area. The Harlem teenagers are the Club members, the Oscar Brothers, and the Lames. The 31 Club members belong to named gangs: the Jets, the Cobras, the Aces, and the Thunderbirds. The three Oscar Brothers are an older black teen group (age 16-20) who are in the process of leaving Black English and leaning toward Standard English. The 10 Lames are isolated individuals who do not participate in the street culture.

First to be compared are invariable *was*, invariable *don't*, third person singular + Ø, and negative concord within the clause. (See Figure I.) It is especially interesting that, of these four features, only third person singular + Ø (e.g. *he go*) demonstrates a real distinction between the black and white groups. This distinction, however, lies at the heart of subject-verb agreement, so it is a crucial difference. The negative concord rate seems to be generally higher for the blacks than for the whites. The other two features, invariable *was* and *don't*, show perhaps surprisingly similar scores.

Second, there is the case of copula deletion in regard to *is* and *are*, again showing a large discrepancy between the black and white groups.

The Copula

One of the important points of comparison between black and white vernacular English is the copula. At one time it was claimed that Black English had no copula, an assertion disproven by Labov (1969) who showed that the variable absence of copula in Black English is a result of normal English contraction but with an additional innovative deletion of final s. Wolfram (1974) compared Labov's findings in Harlem Black English to his own research on white English in Mississippi, and showed that deletion of the copula exists in the English of Mississippi whites, but that while it is qualitatively the same, it is quantitatively quite different. Wolfram's paper deals with *are* deletion, *is* deletion, and invariant *be*.

It seemed useful to replicate Wolfram's Mississippi study with the Anniston data in order to see how it would compare, especially since Anniston is quite different from Meadville, the locale of Wolfram's study. Meadville is more isolated, being 75 miles south of Jackson, in the middle of a national forest; Anniston is 60 miles east of Birmingham and 100 miles west of Atlanta on the main highway between those two cities. Franklin County is one of the poorest in Mississippi; Calhoun County is one of the richest (top 20%) in Alabama. The main industries of Franklin County are logging and farming; the main industry of Calhoun County is

Figure I: Black/white quantitative comparison: Four features. Harlem male teenagers and Anniston working class. Percent nonstandard forms. [Source: Labov et al. 1968: 161, 247, 177.]

| | Harlem Teen Males | | | Anniston White Working Class | | | | | |
| | Club | Oscar | Lames | Teen | | Older | Urban | Older | Rural |
	members	Brothers		Girls	Boys	Women	Men	Women	Men
3rd per. singular + Ø									
A	64	67	-	-	-	-	-	-	-
B	71	61	59	1	4	3	3	5	1
Negative concord within clause									
A	99	96	-	80	-	-	-	-	-
B	97	97	90	60	70	84	69	75	88
Invariable *was*	86	27	29	48	79	77	74	98	96
Invariable *don't*	97	61	64	98	94	91	69	100	100

A = group style; B = interview style. Club members = Jets, Cobras, Aces, Thunderbirds.

the manufacture of metals, textiles, and apparel, mainly in and around Anniston. The informants for Wolfram's analysis were 44 whites in three age levels--8-10 years, 11-13 years, and 16-17 years--representing a typical distribution of the population, the majority in the lower socioeconomic levels, and a number of adults, mainly middle class.

Are Deletion

Wolfram shows that his informants deleted *are* from 10 to 100% of the time, with the larger amount of deletion correlating to a lower socioeconomic status. He then subdivides the data into preceding and following environments, showing that at one end of the continuum there is a lect in which there is categorical deletion of *are* following pronouns and at the other end of the continuum there is a lect in which the deletion of *are* may take place only before *gonna*. These extremes represent speakers from the lowest and highest socioeconomic levels respectively. The constraints examined were the following environments of noun phrase, predicate adjective or locative (including adverbs), verb + *ing*, and *gonna*. The preceding environments were divided into pronoun and noun phrase.

Altogether, the Anniston working class showed about half as much *are* deletion as Wolfram's informants. One explanation is that the Anniston working-class informants probably have a more 'r-ful' speech, that is, they may have more r-construction in word final position than the Mississippi informants. After all, Anniston is in the foothills of the Blue Ridge, so it is not surprising that r-construction would be more prevalent than in the more 'Southern' area of southern Mississippi. A second possible explanation is the difficulty of perceiving [ə] or [ɝ] as an off-glide. Perhaps as an r-less speaker myself and as a native of Anniston, I heard such an off-glide more often than Wolfram did, since he is neither a Southerner nor an r-less speaker. This possibility raises the question of my unconscious bias toward counting what I heard as /r/ and Wolfram's unconscious bias against counting what he heard as /r/. A summary of the Anniston and Meadville data is presented in Figure II.

Is Deletion

In contrast to the high percentage and socially widespread deletion of *are*, Wolfram found a much smaller amount of *is* deletion, checking the same environments as he did for *are*. His informants deleted *is* between 0% and 33.3% of the time. Out of 45 informants, only 15 deleted *is* at all, though all age groups were included among those that did. The patterning follows the constraints for *are* deletion.

The Anniston data does not differ from Wolfram's Mississippi data to any great extent; details are presented in Figure III.

Figure II: Are deletion in Alabama and Mississippi whites.   [Source for Mississippi data: Wolfram 1974.]

UPPER CLASS

Teenage girls	N=6	Teenage boys	N=6
Occurrences	22/168	Occurrences	15/140
% deletion	15.4	% deletion	10.7
Older women	N=6	Older men	N=6
Occurrences	19/127	Occurrences	23/82
% deletion	22.8	% deletion	28.0
Total	93/517 17.9% N=24		

WORKING CLASS:
URBAN

Teenage girls	N=7	Teenage boys	N=7
Occurrences	33/147	Occurrences	21/52
% deletion	22.4	% deletion	40.3
Older women	N=6	Older men	N=6
Occurrences	47/119	Occurrences	48/104
% deletion	39.4	% deletion	46.1
Total	149/422 35.3% N=26		

WORKING CLASS:
RURAL

Older women	N=8	Older men	N=7
Occurrences	20/44	Occurrences	38/59
% deletion	45.4	% deletion	64.4
Total	58/103 56.3% N=15		

WOLFRAM'S MISSISSIPPI
INFORMANTS

Teenage girls	N=5	Teenage boys	N=6
Occurrences	29/37	Occurrences	39/53
% deletion	78.3	% deletion	73.5
Adult women	N=5	Adult men	N=3
Occurrences	17/53	Occurrences	11/30
% deletion	32.0	% deletion	36.6

Teen total: 68/90   75.5%
Teen & adult total: 96/173   55.4%
Complete total (including children): 238/371   64.1%

Qualitative Comparison

Although White Southern and Black English are quantitatively quite different in regard to three out of the six forms just discussed, they seem to be qualitatively the same in many respects. To begin with, third person singular + $\emptyset$, deletion of *are*, and deletion of *is*, while rare in Southern White English, nevertheless do occur. Figure IV takes 19 items and shows whether or not

Figure III: Is deletion in Alabama and Mississippi whites; Harlem Black
teen boys. [Sources: Wolfram 1974; Labov et al. 1968.]

UPPER CLASS
  Teenage girls   N=6   Teenage boys   N=6
   Occurrences   0/185   Occurrences   3/145
   % deletion   0   % deletion   2.0
  Older women   N=6   Older men   N=6
   Occurrences   5/212   Occurrences   4/126
   % deletion   2.3   % deletion   3.1
   Total   12/668   1.7%   N=24

WORKING CLASS:
URBAN
  Teenage girls   N=7   Teenage boys   N=7
   Occurrences   7/323   Occurrences   21/118
   % deletion   2.1   % deletion   17.7
  Older women   N=6   Older men   N=6
   Occurrences   16/315   Occurrences   14/231
   % deletion   5.0   % deletion   6.0
   Total   58/987   5.8%   N=26

WORKING CLASS:
RURAL
  Older women   N=8   Older men   N=7
   Occurrences   4/101   Occurrences   9/90
   % deletion   3.9   % deletion   10.0
   Total   13/191   6.8%   N=15

WOLFRAM'S MISSISSIPPI
INFORMANTS
  Teenage girls   N=6   Teenage boys   N=4
   Occurrences   3/61   Occurrences   3/35
   % deletion   4.9   % deletion   8.5
  Adult women   N=7   Adult men   N=4
   Occurrences   0/59   Occurrences   1/38
   % deletion   0   % deletion   2.6

  Teen total: 6/96 6.2%
  Teen & adult total: 7/193 3.6%
  Complete total (including children): 34/520 6.5%

LABOV'S HARLEM
TEEN BOYS
  Club members   Oscar Brothers
   Occurrences   341/811   Occurrences   9/92
   % deletion   42.0   % deletion   9.7

Figure IV: Black/white qualitative comparison: 19 features.   Black English
from Harlem male teenage gangs (Labov et al. 1968); Southern White from Anniston working class (urban, rural), and Anniston upper class in both interviews
and anonymous observations.

	BLACK ENGLISH Harlem club members	SOUTHERN WHITE Anniston working class	Anniston upper class
Done	X	X	(X)
Future gon	X	X	X
Ain't	X	X	(X)
Liketa	X	X	X
A- + verb + -ing	?	X	X
Double modal	X	X	X
Negative inversion	X	X	X
Neg attrac same clause			
Indefinite	X	X	X
Verb	X	X	X
Neg attrac across clause			
Indefinite	X	X	0
Verb	X	X	X
Invariable don't	X	X	(X)
Invariable was	X	X	(X)
Nonstandard preterit	X	X	0
Nonstandard past part	X	X	(X)
There's + NP plural	?	X	X
NP [-they] pl + -s	?	X	0
I + -s	X	X	0
3rd p sing + $\emptyset$	X	X	0

X = form noted; ? = not in the literature; 0 = contrary evidence or circumstantial evidence against occurrence; (X) = special style (jocular, baby
talk).

they exist in the Black English studied by the Labov team in
Harlem or in the Southern White English of the working class or
the upper class in Anniston.   In the case of the upper class,
anonymous observations were included as a basis for establishing
whether or not a form exists in that lect.   The items cover
tense, aspect, agreement, quasi-verbs, and negation.   Of the
features discussed, the White Nonstandard English of Anniston
and the Black English of New York City share at least 15 of the
19 items.   This is certainly a large amount of agreement between
the two lects.   However, there are two items not on the chart
which raise problems, invariant *be* and *bin*.

Invariant Be

Although examples of invariant *be* have been found in the
South among whites, most of the cases can be explained as examples
of the contraction and deletion of *will* and *would* as in the following
examples:

(1) Reckon it be cheaper at the other store?   (Edwina H.
     60's).
(2) I be through here just a minute (Myrtice J. R62).

Wolfram found such deletions in his Mississippi data also. Since
he found no clear-cut examples of the distributive *be* in the
interviews, he devised a test to determine whether adolescent
whites had it in their grammar.   The test consisted of three
positive sentences which the subjects were asked to negate.
Two of the three sentences called for *don't be* negation if their
positive *be* could be interpreted as distributive *be*. Not surprisingly, he found that 34 out of 53 black adolescents but only 11 of
the 55 white adolescents provided *don't be* to negate the following:

(3) Sometime Joseph be up here.

A more extreme example is the following:

(4) Sometime his ears be itching.

For sentence (4), only 3 whites as against 32 blacks gave *don't
be*.   As a result, Wolfram concludes, 'Both blacks and whites
have *be* derived from *will* or *would be*, but only blacks typically
use "distributive *be*"' (1974:522).   However, it seems to me that,
like the deletion of *is*, the point is not that the whites have so
few responses indicating a competence which includes distributive
be, but that 20% of the white adolescents demonstrated their use
and knowledge of the form in one case and 5.4% in the other.
Dunlap (1973, 1974), like Wolfram, found no examples of invariant *be* in the 48 interviews he taped with white native Atlanta
fifth graders from the upper middle, lower middle, and lower
classes.
Although I had not been attempting to collect data on distributive *be*, I found in my anonymous observations four examples, all
from the same informant, Myrtice Jordan (R62), of invariant *be*.
The meanings, however, are not 'subject or event distributed
intermittently in time', as defined by Fasold (1969:775).

(5) I put her up till I be sure.
(6) It caught up with you after you be here a little bit.
(7) After you be there so long, you're ready to get up and
     go again!
(8) Or if I be out there, I'll . . .

Examples (6) and (7) seem to mean 'had been' or 'have been'. Example (8) could possibly be a deletion of *should*, though it seems unlikely that Mrs. Jordan would use such formal language.

While those five examples may not be at all similar to invariant *be* in Black English, at least, as it has been reported, *don't be* is considered the negation of invariable *be*, and as such, was used by Wolfram in his diagnostic test (Fasold 1969:773; Wolfram 1974:520). Myrtice Jordan who produced (5) through (8) in natural conversation, also gave two examples of *don't be*:

> (9) You hope she calls you, you don't be here.
> (10) It's a wonder they don't be sick.

Thus it appears that invariant or distributive *be* may form part of the grammar for some southern Whites.

Another four examples from the interviews use contracted *would* + *be* in an unusual manner. Three of them occur with the progressive and another with an adjective. The speakers are all women, but from both age groups, both urban and rural, and from both the upper and working classes:

> (11) An' he'd be plowin' and I'd be walkin' (Carrie R. W72:52.I.227).
> (12) Papa seen that dog. He seen it lots of times when he'd be walkin' to work (Myra T. W74:46.II.315).
> (13) But I'd be missin' everybody, though. I'd still come home, you know (Sandra M. W16:38.II.262).
> (14) This poor ol' man, he had this ol' awful wife, you know, and she'd always be sick (Ellen K. U17:9.II.440).

In (11) and (13) *would plow*, *would walk*, and *would miss* would be more normal, while in (12) and (14), *was* would seem more appropriate than *would be*. Perhaps this strange use of *would be* is connected to 'invariant *be*'. But only in (12) and perhaps (14) is 'intermittent' intended.

A possible explanation for the occasional occurrence of invariant or distributive *be* does not necessarily involve a transfer of the feature from Black English to Southern White, though that is probably what has happened, at least in recent years. Although a great deal of attention has been paid to the use of invariant *be* in Black English recently, apparently the information available in the dialect dictionaries has not been noticed. (However, see Rickford 1974.) Unfortunately there are too few full citations to check for meaning, but Wright (1898:I,197) reports the use of invariant *be* in Northern Ireland (Antrim), Wales (Pembroke), and England, especially from the Midlands south: Northumberland, Yorkshire, Nottingham, Lincoln, Rutland, Northhampton, Worcester, Shropshire, Hereford, Gloucester, Oxford, Berks., Bucks., Bedford, Hertford, Cambridge, Suffolk, Essex, Kent, Surrey, Sussex, Hampshire, Isle of Wight, Wiltshire, Dorset,

Somerset, Devon, and Cornwall. Often he cites its use in two
or more parts of each county, as in north, east and south Hertford,
and north and south Wiltshire, altogether 44 locations. *Be* is not
used either exclusively or necessarily with all (grammatical) persons in these locations, although that seems to be the case in
south Worcester, north Bucks., west Bedford, and some other
places. Rather, it is often one of several variants, as in west
Worcester, where Wright reports 'I be or bin, thee bist; 'e or
'er be, or 'e's; us be or bin, you be thaay be or bin' (1898:I,197).
Sentences using   cited by Wright are reproduced in (15) through
(18).

> (15) I be very sadly. (Rutland)
> (16) That be the new man as belongs to Velder Verm.
>   (Berkshire)
> (17) I be for more fat pigs and less fat parsons. (Sussex)
> (18) My beloved uz mine, an' I be his'n. (north Wilts.)

Wright also reports the phrase *to do be* which he defines as
'to do habitually, be accustomed or in the habit of doing' (1900:
II,99) and gives four examples each from Ireland and southern
England, some of which are listed in (19)-(24).

> (19) Your cow does be threspassin' an my fields. (Ireland)
> (20) And you do be always with the hounds, sir? (Ireland)
> (21) He does be shavin' de naybours dere every Sunday
>   mornin'. (Wexford)
> (22) She do be so strict with us gals. (S. Oxford)
> (23) The childer do be laffen at me. (Cornwall)
> (24) They do be getting all their bad ways again. (Sussex)

Thus the claim that invariant *be* is necessarily peculiar to Black
English does not seem to be entirely correct. It is difficult to
say what the connection might be between the *be* in British dialect,
and the *be* in Black English, and the *be* in the Anniston data.
It is not clear that they are equivalent; nor is it clear that they
are so different that they are altogether unconnected. (Labov
suggests [1976:personal communication] that, despite striking
parallels, the difference between the Anglo-Irish and Black English
be centers around the semantics; that Anglo-Irish *be* often applies
to a 'steady state' rather than to an 'intermittent state'.) The
easiest explanation for its infrequent occurrence in Southern White
and its frequency in Black English is that the whites, having
more access to education, dropped it for some reason so that
now it is quite rare, whereas the blacks, deprived of education,
maintained the form. But then why were other nonstandard
features maintained by the whites in the face of education?
Also, since invariant *be* does not exist in any form in basilect
Creole, where does it originate and how does it get into acrolect
Creole and ultimately Black English? Rickford (1974) has a good
explanation, though he assumes that *be*, while occurring in Irish

English, does not exist in Southern White. This, however, leads into a discussion of the decreolization of Black English, which is not pertinent to the topic at hand.

Remote Present Perfect Been

One last Black English feature that must be compared with Southern White English is a special use of *been*. Labov refers to it as 'remote present perfect *been*' (1972b:53-55). Rickford has given the feature extensive treatment, explaining its meaning and use and showing 14 environments for it (1975b:178). Some of his diagnostic examples follow:

(25) ____ Ved   They BÍN ended that war.
(26) ____ Ving   I BÍN, knowing him.
(27) ____ NP   He BÍN the leader.
(28) ____ Adj   She BÍN nice.
(29) done ____   He done BÍN locked up.

Other environments he shows with BÍN are ____ knew; ____ have; ____ done; ____ bin; have ____ had; ____ Modal; ____ got Passive; ____ Passive; 've ____ had. Some environments, such as ____ Ved and ____ Ving are found more frequently than others.

Although I did not look for this form in Anniston, a few examples in the data--(30) through (37)--point in the direction of this Black English BIN, though nothing more forceful can be concluded.

(30) Well, I'd been knowin' him all his life (Milly B. W77: 36.I.391).
(31) I been knowin' your grandaddy for forty years (Henrietta S. 50's [wife of owner, small business]).
(32) I been knowin' John Sparkman ever since he was in the Senate (Sam C. W70:34.II.014).
(33) I come up here oncet a month to see Brother McDaniel. Been knowin' 'im, I don't know, fifty year, I guess. Naw, I ain't been knowin' 'im that long. I been knowin' 'im, I guess, forty years (George R. R75:57.426).
(34) I call her Josie and I always have ever since I been born (Kenneth F. U17:23.III.056).
(35) I was gon tell you a while ago 'bout I been up there one time to Sunday School, my aunt wanted to carry me and my brother [context: single event 60 years before] (Laura McH. W70:30.III.085).
(36) That was the last time I been (Tom G. W17:40.I.371).
(37) Well, I chewed tobacco some, and then I started smokin' --started smokin' cigarettes. Course I--I been quit about 15 years since I smoked (Homer B. R67:58.368).

The meanings of these examples are, for the first four, 'began in the past long ago and continued up to the present'; for the next three, 'once, long ago'.

Three more examples, all from anonymous observations, were found, two from Myrtice Jordan, and one from a dance band director. None of them quite fit Rickford's *done been* category as he has presented it in his paper. Here *been* seems to be used as in Standard English.

(38) They started it and then they stopped it. It shoulda done been gone (Myrtice J. R61).

(39) She said the soap had done been dumped and they have to be done by hand in the morning (Myrtice J. R61).

(40) I done *been* playin! (Jack W., middle-aged dance band director).

Eleven--or eight--examples do not prove that Southern White English has the same special *been* found in Black English. However, this special *been* is not common in New York City among blacks, either, according to Labov (1972b:53), although it is common among blacks in Philadelphia and other areas (Rickford 1975). (Rickford implies that the different methodology used in New York and Philadelphia would account for the difference in results.) It could be argued that *been* is not an important feature of Black English as is such a frequently encountered item as invariant *be*, and thus does not provide a good point of comparison for Southern White English. But Rickford's findings on *been* show that this is not the case; blacks and whites--at least in the Philadelphia area--do indeed react differently to certain uses and especially meanings of *been*. This would definitely be an interesting area for investigation in Southern White.

Wright and the Scottish National Dictionary both list *bin* or *been* as special dialect forms. Wright shows that it can occur as a variant of *am* or *are* in Lancaster, Stafford, Warwick, and Worcester (1898:I, 197); the Scottish National Dictionary says that it is 'used for a perfect or pluperfect, through omission of 'v, 'd, contractions, for *have*, *had*' (Grant and Murison 1931:I, 67).

Conclusion

Altogether, so far as the verb phrase is concerned, Southern White English, especially Nonstandard Southern White, and Black English remain quantitatively somewhat different, but qualitatively quite similar in their syntax, the main difference lying in the subject-verb agreement for finite verbs. This is not to say that they are exactly the same. The semantics of Black English verbs seems to be qualitatively different, despite striking parallels. Still, it does not seem at all farfetched to claim that two peoples of disparate origins, after 250 to 300 years of living together, now share a common language encompassing near-standard at one end and highly nonstandard at the other end, with individuals of either race scattered all the way from most standard to least standard, but with the whites as a group concentrated between the completely standard end and the second quartile and the blacks as a group concentrated at the nonstandard end up to the third quartile. The important point is that it is a single system. Parts of the system can be broken off, such as 'Standard Southern White English' or 'Black English' and given special treatment, but distortion results if it is forgotten that either end is today part of a continuum, despite the possible historical origins of the extreme parts.

I therefore conclude that, on the basis of the Anniston data as compared to the Harlem data, White Southern and Black English are very similar, though not identical. My position, then, is in the moderate camp of the divergence controversy, along with Labov, Wolfram, and Fasold.

WHITE SOUTHERN AND OTHER WHITE AMERICAN DIALECTS

If White Southern shares 16 of 19 features with Black English as shown in Figure IV, how many of these same features does it share with other white American dialects? After all, Linguistic Atlas material is available to the English of New England, the Middle Atlantic states, and the Upper Midwest.

Taking the same 19 features and comparing them to the findings of the Linguistic Atlas for New England and the Middle Atlantic states as presented in Atwood (1953), supplemented by Labov et al. (1968) for negative concord among New York City whites, it seems that 8 features are definitely shared with New England English, 2 are apparently not shared, and there is no information on 8; while 11 features are definitely shared with the Middle Atlantic states, 4 are not shared, and there is no information on 3 features. (Certain features were not reported in the New England Atlas which were reported in the Middle Atlantic Atlas. Moreover, aside from contraction, negation is not treated in At-wood.) As for the Upper Midwest as reported in H. B. Allen (1975), it seems that of those 19 features, 10 are shared with the Upper Midwest, 3 are not shared, with no information on 6. (See Figure V.)

It appears then, that despite the lack of comparable information, Southern White English differs from Northern and Midwestern White English (at least that of New England, the Middle Atlantic states, and the Upper Midwest) in only 5 features out of 19, perfective *done*, future *gon*, and three types of negative concord: negative attraction to verbs in the same clause and to indefinites and verbs across clauses. Moreover, the Upper Midwest definitely

Figure V: Qualitative comparison of White Southern with New England, Middle Atlantic, and Upper Midwest [Sources: Atwood 1953; Labov et al. 1968; H. B. Allen 1975.]

	White Southern	New England	Middle Atlantic	Upper Midwest
Done	X	0	0	0
future gon	X	0[1]	0[1]	0[1]
Ain't	X	X	X	X
Liketa	X	?	X	?
A- + verb + -ing	X	X	X	X
Double modals	X	?	X	X
Negative inversion	X	?	?	?
Neg attrac same clause				
Indefinites	X	?	X	X
Verbs	X	?	0	0
Neg attrac across clause				
Indefinites	X	?	0	0
Verbs	X	?	0	0
Invariable don't	X	X	X	X
Invariable was	X	X	X	X
Nonstandard preterit	X	X	X	X
Nonstandard past part	X	X	X	X
There's + NP plural	X	X	X	X
NP pl [-they] + -s	X	X	X	?
I + -s	X	X[2]	?	X
3rd p sing + ∅	X	?	X[3]	0

[1]Gonna, only; [2]I says, only; [3]What make, he do; isolated cases, only. X = examples found in source; ? = no mention; 0 = contrary evidence or circumstantial evidence against occurrence.

does not have third person singular + ∅. Information is lacking for one feature, negative inversion.

As for invariant *be*, H. B. Allen points out that

> As a finite form, *be*, not found at all in the Middle and South Atlantic states but occurring as a relic in New England, New York, Wisconsin, and Michigan, has only a ghostly existence in the Upper Midwest (1975:32).

Allen reports two instances of *be* from Type I informants (old people with less than an eighth grade education), one in Minnesota and one in northern Iowa:

(41) They be coming home about midnight [context: past].
(42) How be you?

Neither of these examples is a case of the invariant   discussed in the literature on Black English. Example (41) is another case of deleted *would be* + verb + *-ing* as in (11)-(13) in the Anniston

data.   Example (42) is not the sort of construction associated
with Black English invariant *be*.
    Remote present perfect *been* is not mentioned in the Linguistic
Atlas reports.

WHITE SOUTHERN AND ENGLISH
OUTSIDE THE UNITED STATES

    The next issue to be attacked is the historical problem in
regard to Southern White English, that is, the problem of its
relationship to regional British English, archaic English, and to
Atlantic Creole English.   Its relationship to older forms of Black
English involves the history of Black English and its decreolization;
this problem is too specialized to be dealt with here, except by
implication.

White Southern, Regional British
English, and Archaic English

    Leaving the American South, the first set of comparisons is
between White Southern and what I call 'Regional British English',
including   under   that   rubric   Scots,   Irish   English,   Yorkshire,
Cockney, and all the other varieties of English noted by Wright,
Grant, and the Oxford English Dictionary.   Although this is a
rather mixed bag, there seems to be no other reasonably succinct
way to deal with the nonstandard English of the British Isles.
Along the same lines, archaic, obsolete, or simply older forms of
English as found in either the OED or in Visser are also compared
with Southern White.   Figure VI shows what was found in each
source in regard to 16 features.
    The only features found in all four sources, as well as in
White Southern, are   *liketa*, *a-* + verb + *-ing*, double modals,
multiple negation, and nonstandard preterit and past participle.
The only feature which could not be found in any source is
negative inversion, although positive inversion and standard negative
inversion (*Scarcely had she arrived when* ..., *Never did I lack
for* ...) are shown.   *Ain't* and invariable *don't* are not as
widespread as one would think; *binna* and *dinna* seem to be Scots
and English dialect forms instead.   Future *going to* never occurs
in the Southern form of *gon*, but rather in such dialectal forms
as *ganna*, *gauna*, *ginnie*.
    Some of the discrepancies among reported data are due to
the nature of the data: single words or very short phrases, as
in double modals, were more likely to be cited than more complicated
syntax such as *there's NP plural*, negative inversion, or multiple
negation.   Examples of the latter were to be found only as illustrations of *no* or *never*, or, as in Visser, were included by chance

Figure VI: Qualitative comparison of White Southern with Regional British and older forms of English.   OED: Combines regional and archaic.   Visser: Older forms of English. Wright: Regional dialects of Great Britain.   Grant: Scots English.

	Southern White	OED	Visser	Wright	Grant
Done	X	X	X	0	0
Future gon	X	0	?	0[1]	0[1]
Ain't	X	X	?	X	0
Liketa	X	X	X	X	X
A- + verb + -ing	X	X	X	X	X
Double modals	X	X	X	X	X
Neg inversion	X	?	?	?	?
Multiple Neg	X	X	X	X	X
Inv. don't	X	X	X	0	0
Inv. was	X	X	X	X	?
NS preterit	X	X	X	X	X
NS past part	X	X	X	X	X
There's + NP pl	X	?	X	?	?
3rd p pl + -s	X	X	X	X	?
I + -s	X	0	0	X	?
3rd p sing + Ø	X	X	X	X	?

[1]ganna, gauna, ginnie, etc. only. X = exmaples found in source; ? = no mention; 0 = contrary evidence or circumstantial evidence against occurrence.

as examples of other features. So, considering the limitations of the sources, it is even more striking that there should be so much convergence.

In conclusion, it is obvious that all three systems, Southern White, Regional British English, and obsolete or archaic English share many features. While such sharing, devoid of phonological and lexical considerations, cannot be the basis of saying that the systems are the same, nevertheless it is undeniable that they are very similar.

Southern White and Atlantic Creoles

Lastly, Southern White will be compared with available data on two Atlantic Creoles, Jamaican and Guyanese. Because of the nature of the sources, the basilect and the mesolect of the creoles have not been separated. (The acrolect was excluded since it would overcomplicate the comparison.) For the sake of simplicity, upper-class and working-class Southern have been likewise collapsed into a single Southern White. (See Figure VII.)

In contrast to the strong similarities between Southern White and regional and archaic British English for the 16 features investigated, it is obvious that the Atlantic Creoles, as embodied in

Figure VII: Qualitative comparison of White Southern with Jamaican and Guyanese
Creoles. Sources: B. Bailey (1966); Bickerton (1975).

	Southern White	Jamaican Creole	Guyanese Creole
Done	X	X	X
Future gon	X	X	X
Ain't	X	0	0[1]
Laketa	X	?	?
A- + verb + -ing	X	0	0
Double modal	X	X	0[2]
Neg inversion	X	?	?
Multiple neg	X	X	X
Inv don't	X	0	0[1]
Inv. was	X	X	X
NS preterit	X	0	0
NS past part	X	0	0
There's + NP pl	X	?	?
3rd per pl + -s	X	0	0
I + -s	X	0	0
3rd per sing + Ø	X	X	X

[1]See discussion in text, [2]Bickerton (1973: personal communication). X =
examples found in source; ? = no mention; 0 = contrary evidence or circumstantial
evidence against occurrence.

basilectal and mesolectal Jamaican and Guyanese Creole, are rather
different from Southern White.   Very possibly this is because of
the lack of resources parallel to the 6 volumes of Wright, 9 (to
Vu-) of Grant, 4 (to Ny-) of Craigie, 12 of the OED, and 6 of
Visser available for checking British dialect and archaic forms.
Altogether, though, based on B. Bailey (1966) and Bickerton
(1975), Southern White has little in common with Atlantic Creole.
Only 6 features out of 16--*done,* double modals, invariable *was,*
future *gon,* multiple negation, and the third person singular +
Ø--are the same, and the last is certainly marginal to Southern
White.   *Ain't* and invariable *don't* present certain problems.
Guyanese Creole has negative markers *en* and *doon(t)* which could
be considered as equivalent to Southern White *ain't* and *don't.*
Bickerton says,

> It is unclear whether *en* stems from *ain't* or
> *haven't* or is the joint product of both (1975:
> 91).

However, concerning both *en* and *doon* (*t*), he goes on to explain,

> As regarding their meaning and function,
> there is certainly no systematic correspondence
> between these markers and their English equiva-
> lents, and apparently little consistency as

between different mesolectal speakers. This lack
of correspondence is connected with the fact
that, though these forms may derive *diachronically* from English negative forms, they do
not derive *synchronically* in the way that
English forms derive (Bickerton 1975:91).

Jamaican Creole *en* is a past marker according to B. Bailey
(1966:140).

One feature, *a-* + verb + *-ing*, has a similar form in Creole,
though the Creole form lacks the *-ing* and occurs rather as *a* +
verb. Four other features of Southern White Nonstandard, two
of them rather basic--nonstandard preterit, nonstandard past
participle, third person plural NP + -s, and *I* + *-s*--do not
occur in the Creoles of Jamaica and Guyana; it seems highly
unlikely that yet another feature, *there's* + NP plural, would
occur. No information was available for *liketa* and negative
inversion.

Invariant *be* and remote present perfect *been* are found in
Guyanese Creole as acrolectal *doz be* and basilectal and mesolectal
bin or *bina* (Bickerton 1975:120; 35-39; 82-83); remote present
perfect *been* also occurs in Jamaica as a variant of past marker
en (B. Bailey 1966:140). As shown, both forms are marginal at
the most in Southern White, though they are central to Black
English.

Thus, one can only conclude that, while the basilectal and
mesolectal Creoles and Southern White share some features, they
are rather distant from each other.

Conclusion

On the historical front it appears unquestionable that, on
the basis of the Anniston, Jamaican, and Guyanese data, Southern
White and Atlantic English Creoles share few grammatical features
in their verb systems, while many of the peculiar forms found in
Anniston can be found in the British Isles (or could have been
found during the last century) or in documents written in earlier
forms of English. Thus, dialectologists seem to be essentially
correct in attributing variations from Standard English in Southern
White to British dialect or to archaic or obsolete forms of English.

The relationship of Black English to these features of British
dialect or to older forms of English is a question to be dealt with
by those involved in the decreolization problem. (See Stewart
1970; Brewer 1974.) It must be emphasized, however, that Black
English has certain features which do not occur in Southern
White, British dialects, or older stages of English and which are
undoubtedly grammatical remnants of Creole: (1) remote present
perfect *been*; (2) lack of agreement; (3) lack of possessive s;
(4) *is* deletion.

ORIGINS OF SOUTHERN WHITE ENGLISH

One last question remains. Do the grammatical features discussed throughout this study have any specific regional basis in the British Isles, and if so, is it the same as that of the lexical and phonological features of the American South?

It was demonstrated that of 16 grammatical features, 13, that is, all but perfective *done*, future *gon*, and negative inversion also occur, or did occur, in the last two or three hundred years in the British Isles. However, a more careful examination of the occurrences of those 13 items shows no one section of Great Britain or Ireland predominating.

For example, the nonstandard preterits and past participles found in Anniston are also found throughout the British Isles. However, it is not worthwhile to discuss each variant here, although that would be necessary to give an accurate picture of the geographical distribution of those forms (Wright 1905:281-296). *A-* + verb + *-ing* is reported for Scotland, Ireland, but not north of Pembroke, Shropshire, Warwick, Northampton, Rutland, Cambridge, or Norfolk in England except for Lancaster, Lincoln, and Leicester (Wright 1898:I,3). Perfective *been* has not been recorded since 1581 when it occurs in Scots English. True double modals are found in Scotland, except in the northeast, and in Lincoln, England (Wright 1898:I,502). Double modals with quasi-modals such as *useta could* have been recorded in northern England, the Midlands, Hampshire, Essex, and Lancaster (Wright VI:332). *Liketa* occurs from Aberdeen in the north to Somerset in the south, Yorkshire and East Anglia in the east, and Cheshire in the west (Wright 1902:III,601). As for agreement, all persons, except when preceded or followed by the subject pronoun, take s, -z, or əz in the Shetland and Orkney Islands, Scotland, Ireland, the northern and most of the north Midland counties of England. All persons of the plural take -s, -z, or -əz in most of the south Midland, eastern, southern, and southwest areas of England. In some of the southern and southwestern dialects, the first person singular has the ending -s, -z, or -əz. The -s, -z, -əz ending is often dropped in the south Midlands, eastern, and southern dialects for the third person singular (Wright 1905:296-297).

Ain't/be is found in yorkshire, Nottingham, Lincoln, Leicester, Warwick, Hereford, Suffolk, Essex, Kent, Surrey, Hampshire, Devon, and Cornwall (Wright 1898:I,198), while *ain't/have* is found in roughly the same area: Yorkshire, Nottingham, Warwick, Oxford, Berkshire, Cumberland, Suffolk, Kent, Surrey, Sussex, and Hampshire (Wright 1902:III,88). Although negative concord is undoubtedly found all over the British Isles, no consistent data on that point is available. Information on negative inversion could not be located.

So assuming these grammatical forms were brought to America by immigrants from the British Isles, no single section can be

named as the source. The same can be said for both lexical and
phonological items.

Taking the five words used by Wood as a test vocabulary for
general Southern speech [2]-- *barn lot*, *corn shucks*, *light bread*,
pallet, *snack*--the OED, Wright, and the Scottish National Dictionary showed the following. *Pallet* and *snack* are clearly of British
origin. While the OED shows examples of *pallet* in Chaucer and
Milton (VII:397), Grant and Murrison say that it is 'Of Sc. origin,
entering Eng. in 18th ce.' (VII:22). Wright says *snack* extends
from Scotland to Devon and Kent. The other three--*light bread*,
corn shucks, and *barn lot* --present a problem. None of these
forms exists in Britain. *Corn shucks* certainly could not, since
corn in Britain is *wheat* in American English. *Shuck* refers to
'husk, shell or pod' (Wright V:415) in Britain. *Farm yard* is the
main British word for Southern *barn lot* (Orton and Dieth 1962
I,1:49); 1969 II,1:54; 1969 III,1:55; 1967 IV,1:79. [Response
I.1.3]), though Wright (I:169) and OED (I:675) also mention
barnyard. *Lot* has various dialect uses in Scotland, Ireland, and
England, according to Wright (VI:536), but none fits in here.
Lightening can mean 'yeast' or 'any substance to make dough or
pastry rise' in Yorkshire (Wright III:598). The OED adds that
it is obsolete, except for dialectal use, giving a 1720 citation
(VI:277). It is easy to see that *lightening bread* could have
become *light bread*, as it did in the American South. So, while
it can be concluded that the Southern test words are partly of
British origin, their exact geographical origins are unclear.

A brief investigation of two salient phonetic characteristics
of Southern speech, r-less (the realization of underlying r in
syllable final position as $\emptyset$ or [ə]) and monophthongal i ([$\overline{ə}$]),
results in a similar stalemate. Monophthongal i is found in Yorkshire, Lancashire, and Westmoreland of the northern counties of
England (Kolb 1966:224-237; C.-J. Bailey 1973:88). R-lessness
is found in all the northern counties investigated--Northumberland
(though rarely), Cumberland, Durham, Westmoreland, Lancashire,
Yorkshire, Lincoln, and the Isle of Man (Kolb 1966:84-119).
Discussion of other parts of Britain awaits the completion of the
Linguistic Atlas of England and the Linguistic Atlas of Scotland,
both in progress.

Thus none of the more striking phonological, lexical, or grammatical features which are often considered Southern can be traced
to any particular part of Great Britain. This should not be
surprising since Kurath (1949:10), Atwood, and McDavid had already concluded that

> . . . it is futile to seek the origins of American
> English, or any of its regional varieties, in
> any single folk dialect of the British Isles,
> or in the court speech of the seventeenth
> century . . . It is equally futile to see the
> origins of American English in what was the
> standard English of seventeenth-century London,
> though trade and other ties exposed all colonial

communities to London linguistic fashion in
greater or less degree (McDavid 1973b:7).
Discussing the origins of verb forms in particular, Atwood says,

> One is impressed by the small number of innova-
> tions and of [verb] forms that are demonstrably
> American in origin. By far the greater number
> of forms that are widely used in America are
> of Early Modern English origin, and are more
> or less fully attested . . . in the written
> language of the fifteenth to the eighteenth
> centuries, as well as in the modern British
> dialects . . . A good many other forms that
> are not recorded, or not unambiguously docu-
> mented, in Early Modern English have been
> observed in nineteenth- and twentieth-century
> British dialects, and may very well have been
> current in the British speech of our colonial
> period . . . [But] to argue from present-day
> distribution that a certain form must have
> been brought to an American colony from a
> certain area of England is risky and neglects
> the possibility that many forms may have become
> obsolete in certain areas in the course of two
> or three hundred years (1953:41-42).

At this time, then, the search for the origins of Southern White
English in particular regions of Great Britain must be considered
unsuccessful and it is not likely to be successful in the future.

WHITE SOUTHERN AS PART OF PAN-ENGLISH

The preceding sections of this article have shown that White
Southern participates in the same language system as Black
English, Northern and Upper Midwestern American English, Regional British English, and, to a much lesser extent, the American
Creoles. It is unfortunate that almost no quantitative studies
have been made of nonstandard English grammar, aside from Black
English. Because of this, it is quite difficult to compare the
variation from Standard in the Southern White data presented
here with other types of Nonstandard White English.

Apparently, many of the controversial items of Southern White
syntax do occur in the English of the rural Northeast and Upper
Midwest of the United States, in various regional dialects in Great
Britain, and have been found in documents dating to the era of
early colonization or perhaps before. However, the specific origins
of southern speech within the British Isles cannot be traced at
this time. Nevertheless, all the evidence seems to point to Southern
White, especially Nonstandard Southern White, as a relic variety
of English with the exception of the innovations perfective *done*,
future *gon*, and negative inversion, assuming that they were not
brought to the South by white immigrants from the British Isles.

In regard to the relation between Southern White and Black
English, I propose that there was an interchange between blacks
and whites in the South, a bidirectional interchange. The non-
standard/regional English of the whites picked up those items of
creole syntax which already existed in their own grammar, if
only marginally, while the acrolect toward which the creole was
decreolizing--the speech of those same whites--reinforced creole
items which were similar to items in nonstandard Southern White
English.   Cassidy has discussed this kind of convergence in
regard to the Jamaican creole lexicon.

> I use the term . . . 'multiple etymologies'
> to refer to only those words which seem to
> be derivable with equal plausibility from two or
> more of the languages known to have been
> in contact at the time of their formation.
> From this equal plausibility I argue that the
> word should not be assigned to either, or
> to any one, of the putative source languages--
> that on the contrary it must be assigned to
> them jointly.   This is not merely the result
> of the absence of historical evidence, which
> leaves the etymologist unable to decide a priority
> in favor of one of the languages concerned;
> rather, it implies the proposition that, in some
> instances at least, the words in question are
> due to literal combination or conflation (1966:
> 211).

Cassidy further notes that 'the English element [of Creole
English] includes a large amount of what is now dialectal,
archaic, or obsolete in Britain, and clear evidences of North
Country, West Country, Scots, and Irish influences' (1966:212).
Edwards, also dealing with the lexicon, calls this 'syncretism
and reinforcement' which he defines as

> . . . a lexeme from English [which] is fully
> adopted (borrowed) into pidgin.   Although lexical
> items of African heritage might play little or no
> role in sharping the form or function of the pidgin
> item, they often functioned as a stimulus for its
> selection.   It only need be the case that the
> reinforcing items share meaning, and a minimum
> of form, a simple CV or CVC cluster, with the
> item being borrowed (1974:6).

Traugott has discussed this from the grammatical point of
view:

> . . . although syntactic structures are practically
> never borrowed wholesale, they can be borrowed
> if they approximate, or can be naturally accommo-
> dated into, the linguistic system of the receiving
> language.   More often a structure in one language
> will reinforce a similar structure in another . . .
> It would be worthwhile to consider whether many

of the so-called creole forms remained in [Black English] precisely because they were reinforced by similar structures in English . . . [for instance] it is tempting to speculate . . . that invariant *be* was not borrowed from English but that perhaps it was reinforced by English dialects (1972:6).

While I am not saying that the language of blacks and Southern whites of the same class is identical, it is, however, very similar. The differences include certain uses of the verb *to be* such as aspectual *be* and *bin* and particular differences in verb agreement such as third person singular and NP plural, to mention two widely discussed topics.   Also, the occurrence of nonstandard forms seems to be greater for working-class blacks than for working-class whites for many features.   Partly, however, we are speaking of class differences.   When we refer to Southern White English, we include the whole range of the social structure. When we refer to Black English, we include only working-class blacks.   The Southern White of the upper class and upper middle class retains only a few of these features, rejecting others as shibboleths.

In conclusion, I see Black English and White Southern as ranging along a continuum, similar to the creole continuum in the Caribbean.   In most areas of syntax, Black English and working-class/rural White English overlap, but Black English extends farther in one direction, toward the Atlantic Creoles, and Southern White extends in the opposite direction, toward Metropolitan English.   More information, especially of a quantitative nature, concerning the syntax of both nonstandard and standard spoken English from other areas of the United States and Canada and of other parts of the English-speaking world is needed to form a better picture of where Southern White fits into the larger framework of English.   A study similar to this one of the syntax of a community of the same general size in an English-speaking region of Great Britain, Northern New England, Canada, Australia, or New Zealand would provide the kind of information needed to come closer to a resolution of some of the issues subsumed under the general rubric of variation in language, especially in regard to English.

FOOTNOTES

[1]Material folk culture includes furniture, crockery, spinning and weaving technology, and folk architecture--house and barn types, log construction methods, fence or wall types, plans for courthouse squares. See Marshall and Vlach (1973) for a discussion of the interrelation between dialect and material folk culture.

[2]A sixth word, *kerosene*, is irrelevant to this discussion since the word was coined in 1853, long after the ancestors of most Southerners had arrived in America.

REFLECTIONS ON CLASS AND LANGUAGE

Richard Ohmann

Two interviews are the starting point of this essay. I got them from a video project called "The Unemployment Tapes,"[1] designed to explore through talks with local people the human costs, the sources, and the possible cures of unemployment in an old industrial area of Connecticut. The Connecticut Council for the Humanities funded the project, and I was a consultant to it. At the time (fall, 1978) I was also reading and thinking about class and language, and it occurred to me that interviews like these might be helpful. No interview can ever be a "natural" context for the speech of the person interviewed, but at least these respondents had no reason to think that their language was being observed, except in the incidental ways that we all observe one another's language. The interviewers were not linguists, psychologists, or sociologists. They were friendly, casual, young, not personally intimidating. The interviews followed no fixed schedule; in this they were more like conversations than are many experiments and interviews in sociolinguistic research. Yet the subject and the goals of the questioning remained fairly constant throughout.

So here are the transcripts, with some names and places disguised.

I. A COUPLE AT A SHOPPING MALL

Interviewer: I'd like to ask you if you have jobs right now.
Respondents: Yes.
I: Have either of you ever been unemployed for any length of time?
R: No.
I: Well, would you say there was an unemployment problem in this area?

Man: Well, we're new in the area.   We just moved in a couple of months ago.   From what I've been reading there is unemployment in the area.

Woman: I would say so.   There are an awful lot of people going to Oakfield and Hill County to get jobs.   They're not staying in the valley.

I: Do you have any ideas about what causes that problem?

M: I have no idea.

W: Not enough industry up here.   A lot of industry is just leaving the area.

I: How come?

W: Taxes are too high?   There's no rebate or anything else for them.

I: So if we give a tax break and some other breaks to business, then--

W: I would say that there's no reason for businesses to stay in Connecticut.   They're not getting any benefits from it. It's cheaper to go down to the South and get cheap labor now.

I: What happens when labor in the South matches labor up North?

W: They're going to have a problem.

I: Go overseas?

W: Possibly, yeah.

I: Then when labor overseas matches labor in the United States--

M: A vicious cycle.

I: What's the solution?

M: I don't know.   If I knew I wouldn't be standing here.

I: Have you other thoughts on the subject?

W: I just wish they'd do something about it, that's all.

I: Who?

W: The government.

I: Could the government solve the problem?

M: I think they could make it a little easier.   I don't think they could solve it.   It's just going to - you're going to stop it here, it's going to start somewhere else.   You're not going to be able to stop it.   It's impossible.   Like trying to stop war.

I: So it's part of the system?

M: I think so, yeah.   I think it's part of life, but I think the government could make it easier.

I: Some people think a different system would solve the problem--

Both: I don't know.

I: A different economic system.

Both: I don't know.

II. THE MAYOR OF MILL TOWN

Interviewer: How do you think the high rate of unemployment
has affected this community as a whole, in terms of its self
image, in terms of its ability to deal with problems?

Respondent: Well, you know a very high percentage of unemployment is never a healthy condition, whether it's in Mill
Town or anywhere else, and this lower Mill Valley region here
has been pretty much plagued by high amounts of unemployment
for at least fifteen to twenty years, and probably the greatest
contributor to that would be the fact of how automation has
taken over so much of the factory process that was once the
main employer.

I: What are the other causes of unemployment, besides automation?

R: Well, I believe that automation is perhaps the chief cause
of unemployment.   Secondly, if we delve with other causes I
would say it would be the lack of opportunity for the number of
people that you have.   We have a very densely populated area
here, and like Mill Town with 6.2 square miles and you have
over 21,000 people cramped into them, doesn't leave much space
for industrial growth.   In other words, we need to put our
people to work.   We need more facilities.   We need more concerns
here operating, businesses operating here, and we don't have
the place to put them.

I: Whose responsibility is it to see that industry comes to,
like, stop the high rate of unemployment?   Do you see that as
the responsibility of the government?   Do you see it as the
responsibility of business?   Who puts pressure on business to do
that?   Whose responsibility is it?

R: Well, I don't think there is any one segment of society
which, you're trying to point out, that is responsible.   Like if it
isn't there, that this is part of the responsibility of this particular
segment.   I think that it is very conducive to government to
encourage industry in their area.   I know I myself, as Mayor,
am very anxious, and we have been working very hard, to fill
up these remaining parcels we do have because it serves basically
two purposes.   It expands our tax base which makes life a little
more comfortable for our citizens in terms of their tax bills, and
secondly, it also in some effect provides more jobs which lowers
that unemployment rate at least somewhat.

I: Do you think that the federal government should play a
major role in bad economic times, as it is doing with CETA?

R: Well, certainly, I think if you look at the entire history
of our country, that it has always been the federal government
that has come to the rescue.   Take the great depression and all
the federal programs that we used to bail it out.   What you are
really doing is, you stimulate the economy by priming up the
pump and throwing money into the economy.   That's - but by
giving these people salaries and positions and all, they are going

out and spending money, which gives business, the private sector, more of a stimulus, because they've got money coming in, they have the cash flow, and you hope for expansion.

I: Does that ever make you think about the economic system that we have, that it always has to be fed?

R: I think unfortunately it will always have to be fed. The government - the government - the federal government - the government in general are big partners in the private sector. I think they really prime a lot of money into them that, you know, makes things happen.

I: And you think that is the way it should be?

R: I don't think it's the way it should be. It would be wonderful to have private enterprise exist on their own, without any regulation or any help from government, but I don't feel that it is workable.

I: Why not?

R: Oh, for many, many reasons. I don't think first of all that private - well, you just take private enterprise as it is, and what if it wasn't regulated? I mean you take, again - going back historically, Standard Oil and all the great trusts that were brought together there in the early 1900s where a few people were making millions and millions of dollars - and which were like trillions today - and the majority of the people in the country, the standard of living was very, very low. It was when government came in and started to regulate the amount of profits that these people could make and to really decentralize the main business interest that people started to get a better standard of living. The unionism thing was all part of the entire movement, I believe, which created a better standard of living, and this was all done through government legislation.

******

Now I want to present in schematic form some rather sharp contrasts between the way the Mayor talks and the way the man and woman talk, leaving aside all judgments about effectiveness, clarity, and intelligence.

A. Length and Complexity

1. The responses are much shorter in interview I. So are the sentences: there is no independent syntactic unit of more than sixteen words in I; six of the sentences in II are longer than thirty words.

2. There is little coordination and almost no subordination in I, except in sentences beginning "I think," "I would say," etc. There is much of both in II. For instance, in the sentence beginning, "That's - but by giving. . . ," the main clause is preceded by a gerund phrase and followed by a relative clause with an embeded appositive, then an adverbial clause that contains another appositive-like structure ("they have the cash flow"); and there are several coordinate constructions along the way.

3.   There are few explicit causal or logical connections in I,
and many in II.

B. Modifiers

There are few adjectives and adverbs in I, and those mainly
of degree.   Modifiers are many and various in II, including
derived adjectives ("industrial") and nouns used as modifiers
"*unemployment* rate").

C. Abstraction

There are few abstract nouns in I, many in II. Those in I
appear mainly in simple constructions with the verb "be," and
are unrelated to one another: "There is *unemployment* in the
area"; "*Taxes* are too high"; "There's no *rebate*." The abstract
nouns in II appear in a variety of syntactic positions, and are
often related syntactically and conceptually to one another.   For
example, in his fourth answer the Mayor connects all the following
nouns within a single sentence: "economy," "salaries," "positions,"
"business," "sector," "stimulus," "cash flow," and "expansion."

D. Reference to Context

The man and woman refer only a few times to the context of
the discussion: "Oakfield," "Hill County," "down to the South,"
"Connecticut."   The Mayor not only anchors the discussion geographically to Mill Town with its 21,000 people in only six square
miles, but also gives it a context in the social system (the economy,
the government, etc.) and in history (the last fifteen to twenty
years, the depression, the early 1900s). Note also that interview
I includes one exophoric pronoun (a pronoun with no antecedent
in the discourse):   "I just wish *they's* do something. . . ."
There are none in II.

E. Reference to the Discourse Itself

There is virtually none in I, other than expressions of uncertainty, like "I think" and "I don't know." The Mayor uses such
constructions, and also refers to the discourse in at least four
other ways:

1.   He comments on the interviewer's question. For instance,
when he begins his first answer, "Well, you know a very high
percentage of unemployment is never a healthy condition," he in
effect says "That's a silly question," by stating a general principle
that covers the situation and that should be obvious to anyone.
Compare this to the beginning of his fourth answer.
2.   He implicitly rejects the question: when asked who is
responsible for reducing unemployment, he denies the presupposi-
tion that some *one* part of society is.   When asked if the need

for Keynesian measures makes him "think about the economic system," he simply reiterates the need for Keynesian measures, declining to answer the question (answer 5). When asked, next, if he thinks that is the way it should be, he does respond, but then goes on to show that the question is infelicitous - you cannot properly ask is X *should* be the case when X *must* be the case.

3. He comments reflexively on his own terms and statements: "In other words"; "I mean"; "like if it isn't there"; "business, the private sector"; "money . . . the cash flow"; "the government - the federal government - the government in general."

4. He makes new starts in the middle of a sentence, indicating that he has reconsidered and thought of a better way to proceed: "That's - but by giving these people salaries"; "I don't think first of all that private - well you just take private enterprise"; "I mean you take again - going back historically." (The man in I does this once: "It's just going to - you're going to stop it here, it's going to start somewhere else.")

Contrasts like these run through all the unemployment tapes that I have studied. People on the street, picked out as ordinary workers or perhaps unemployed people, were asked the same kinds of questions about unemployment as were officials, businessmen, and specialists. Speakers from the first group did not elaborate, rank, or expand their ideas much, did not make many distinctions, made few logical and casual connections, did not develop abstract ideas, did not relate their words very explicitly to context, and referred little to the discourse itself in a critical or metalinguistic way. Speakers from the second group rated high on all these measures.

In the last two decades, the sorts of contrast that emerge in these two interviews have drawn a lot of attention, especially in Britain. There a group of sociologists and linguists inspired and led by Basil Bernstein has done very extensive research on differences between working-class and middle-class speech. And Bernstein's concepts of "restricted" and "elaborated" codes[2] are now firmly planted in the center of this intellectual terrain - much respected and much criticized.

According to Bernstein and his colleagues, the elaborated code of the middle class runs more to subordination and modification than the restricted code of the working class. It includes more adjectives, adverbs, prepositions, complex verbs. It facilitates distinctions of all sorts, in particular logical ones. Elaborated code users distance themselves more from the immediate situation and from the content of their talk, through abstraction, through passives, through expressions of probability, through suppositions ("I think"), through questions and refusals to commit themselves quickly to definite interpretations of ambiguous experience. The elaborated code allows or encourages more individuation of response and more reflection on language itself. Restricted code users are more bound to the local, concrete situation. Much of their meaning is implicit - dependent on prior understandings of the context. (Hence they do not refer so explicitly   the context; exophoric pronouns are an extreme example.)   In Bernstein's own words, the restricted code emphasizes "the communal rather than the individual, the concrete rather than the abstract, substance rather than the elaboration of processes, the here and now rather than exploration of motives and intentions, and positional rather than personalized forms of social control."[3]   Again,

> elaborated codes orient their users toward uni-
> versalistic meanings, whereas restricted codes
> orient, sensitize, their users to particularistic
> meanings. . . . Restricted codes are more tied to
> a local social structure and have a reduced potential
> for change in principles. Where codes are
> elaborated, the socialized has more access to the
> grounds of his own socialization, and so can enter
> into a reflexive relationship to the social order he
> has taken over. (p. 176)

By now it should be clear that the analysis assigns profound social values to the two codes and that it has wide political implications.   Bernstein himself does not dwell on these, but does hint at the depressing circularity suggested by his findings.   For instance, "One of the effects of the class system is to limit access to elaborated codes" (p. 176).   In another article he argues that "the genes of social class may well be carried less through a genetic code but far more through a communication code that social class itself promotes" (p. 143).   Putting these statements together, we can derive this principle of social continuity: the class system sorts people into elaborated and restricted code users; the codes perpetuate the class system.

The moral is drawn more fully in *The Politics of Communication* (New York: Oxford University Press, 1975), by Claus Mueller, who draws on Bernstein's research as well as many other studies of class, child-rearing, language, and belief.   Mueller argues that in advanced capitalist societies, a social order marked by severe inequality and the powerlessness of most people is sustained and legitimated, not so much by coercion (the police and the army) or even by manipulation (propaganda, censorship), as by

> distortions of political communication which are
> related to the social structure insofar as it is
> expressed in class-specific language codes and
> socialization patterns, as well as to constraints on
> public communication. . . . Because of the re-
> stricted language code and rigid socialization pat-
> terns, the individual from the lower classes engages
> in arrested communication and tends to see the
> political universe as a static one and to abide by
> the prescriptions of external authorities. (p. 84)

He thinks this impasse especially intractable because the codes are passed on in the home to very young children. He agrees with Bernstein that class differences in child-rearing are decisive, and that working class parents block the development of linguistic autonomy in their children through strategies of teaching and discipline that call on authority more than on reasoning and ex- ploration. If this is so, neither school nor "Sesame Street" could easily undo the damage, even if school, for working-class kids, were an open and supportive institution. Mueller concludes that the only likely challenge to the legitimacy of the political system in countries like ours will come, not from the traditional working class, but from the intellectual and cultural "strata."[4]

Now I find myself in one of those strata and trying to challenge the legitimacy of power in the United States. For people in that position, Marxism has long been the richest source of political practice. A few Marxists would, even now, join with Mueller in giving up on the proletariat as the revolutionary class. A more common Marxian position is that, indeed, some intellectuals defect from the capitalist social order, but they do not become thereby a revolutionary class or group in themselves: on the contrary, their task is to work politically and educationally (the two are really the same) within the proletariat, which is the leading force for revolutionary change. Marxism itself is, in this view, the system of ideas that derives from the experience of the working class - no proletariat, no *Capital*. But intellectuals must help give it voice, as Marx did, and so play at least a small role in the articulation of working-class consciousness.

If Bernstein and Mueller are right, however, there is a barrier to this task higher even than those raised by bourgeois control of police, schools, and media. Marxism as a system of ideas abstracts a great deal from local contexts and immediate experience; it cannot be given voice in a restricted code. If I may exaggerate, a bit, the implications of Bernstein's and Mueller's position: the revolutionary class in advanced capitalist societies, the class with the experience of exploitation and powerlessness and with the motive for socialism, has been excluded from the concepts and the very linguistic structures that must be used to express that experience and develop the institutions that will lead toward social- ism. This would make the job of the revolutionary intellectual truly herculean. As I put it a while back, in the form of a question to myself and other radicals: "When we try to communicate to workers a socialist understanding of things, must we think of our task as, in part, making up a cognitive and linguistic deficit?"[5]

I couch this discussion in Marxian terms to make clear my own commitment. But Marxists are by no means the only ones who should be concerned about the social implications of Bernstein's research. Anyone who favors social equality, democracy, and a politically competent people, and does not see much of these in our society, should feel in these questions of class and language an urgency. For if Bernstein and Mueller are right, those who have available only a restricted code can do little more than passively observe the shaping of the future. Worse, there is probably as much potential for fascism as for democracy in the working class, since people raised by rule and nurtured in restricted codes tend "to abide by the prescriptions of external authorities."

I want now to turn a critical eye on the picture I have just drawn.[6] Bernstein and Mueller, whom I have allowed to stand for many others, advance an argument that has an hypnotic power. Once its underlying concepts and premises are allowed, the research leads inexorably to the conclusions I have sketched and to the political pessimism they sanction. But those concepts and premises are extremely problematic. It is my own belief that they are so defective as to invalidate the conclusions drawn from Bernstein's research, as well as the political interpretation of those conclusions that Mueller and others have offered. The trouble begins right at the beginning, with the concepts of "class" and "code."

Take class. The idea of class that both Bernstein and Mueller deploy is drawn from mainstream social science. It is basically an heuristic concept, obtained by calibrating one or more such factors as income, education, and occupation, and selecting a cluster of them as convenient or experimentally handy. They may then be correlated with other variables: speech patterns. IQ, lifespan, childrearing practices, beliefs, voting behavior, height, hair length, literally anything that can somehow be measured. Plainly there is no reason that any of these other factors might not be substituted for one of the original three, if doing so produced "better" correlations. Such a shift in definition would of course change the actual membership of each class, but that would not matter because the classes, within this framework, have no reality other than a heuristic one for the sociologist manipulating data. The unreality of this scheme is reflected in the fact that it can lead to three or six or any number (nine was the one in favor when I took sociology in college) of classes, which are no more than "strata situated along a continuum" (Mueller, p. 45), artifically segmented to the convenience - again - of the experimenter or theorist. Since their continuum of groups has no intrinsic relation to the structure of society or its historical evolution, correlations obtained within it do not much illuminate the way society works, but leave us within a closed explanatory circle where nothing has priority over anything else. There is no way to tell, for instance, whether occupational status explains speech patterns or vice versa - or both.[7]

A Marxian idea of class is a much better foundation for discussion of these issues. Without going into the complexities of this subject, let me note that when we ground class in basic relations of production, the difficulties I've just listed disappear, and there is at least a *chance* of connecting class to something like language in a way that explains how society works, how it reproduces itself, and how it changes.

Note first that from this perspective Bernstein and Mueller are not talking of two classes, but mainly of two parts of the working class. Almost everyone included in both domains must sell his or her labor power in order to live, having no significant capital. (The exceptions: some independent professionals and small business people, apparently included in Bernstein's and Mueller's middle class.) The main distinction between the two is that most of the people they call working class sell their power to execute routine tasks at someone else's command - physical labor power,[8] in effect - while those they call middle class sell their power of conception - mental labor power - as well. Bernstein's working class (let me use the shorthand, "physical workers," for the moment) is limited mainly to executing someone else's plan, while his middle class (I'll say "mental workers") has at least a small role in the planning itself.

Once the discussion is so grounded, and for all the immense complexities that remain, Bernstein's results make a good deal of initial sense. For instance, his account of restricted and elaborated codes:

- Restricted, *context bound*; elaborated, *context free*. At work the context is almost entirely provided *for* physical workers by their bosses; mental workers can do more to shape the context of their work.
- Restricted, *concrete*; elaborated, *abstract*. At work, physical workers manipulate things, while mental workers manipulate ideas, numbers, etc.
- Restricted code, *predictable*; elaborated, more *individuated*. Physical workers are not paid to vary from set routines; employers value to some extent the individuality and creativity of mental workers.
- Restricted code, few *hesitations*, *expressions of uncertainty*, or *"metalinguistic" references to the discourse*; elaborated code, high on all these dimensions. Physical workers are limited to executing someone else's plan; mental workers have some responsibility for planning - precision and critical awareness in speech are important to them.
- Restricted code, *simple in syntax*; elaborated code, *complex*, with much *subordination*, *logical tissue*, *modification*, etc. Physical workers are not asked to make many connections, see broad relationships, understand the larger processes in which their work is embedded; the reverse is true for many mental workers.

Of course, young children - the subjects of much of Bernstein's research - do not work in factories or law firms. For the hypothesis I am sketching out to have any plausibility, it would have to derive "socialization" practices from the total experience of classes and subclasses in production. Bernstein's findings do point to such a connection, as a few examples will suggest:

    - "Working-class" discipline of children stresses results, "middle-class" discipline, intentions.   This corresponds to the distinction between execution and conception at work.
    - "Working-class" parents teach skills; "middle-class" parents teach principles.   This corresponds to what will be expected of the children later in their jobs.
    - "Working-class" parents use "positional controls" (e.g., coercion: or, "Do it because your father says to do it"); "middle-class" parents favor "personal controls" (e.g., "If you don't clean up your room, your mother will have to do it, and she's very tired today").   Physical workers must learn to take orders without asking why.   Mental workers need to know something of the rationale for what they do on the job.

    From this pairing up of findings and causal hypotheses (overly schematic, to be sure),[9] a clear picture emerges.   A class builds its life on its role in production.   The social relations it experiences there may be embedded in its linguistic codes, and carried over into the kind of training it gives its children at home.[10]   Now this is a very simple hypothesis, and may or may not turn out to be right.   My point is that this approach to class at least permits us to work toward an explanation, in social structure and historical process, of the ways people talk, rather than leaving us enclosed in a limitless circle of measurable attributes, none with causal priority over the others.   It roots language and consciousness in material life.
    But within a Marxian framework, this is still insufficient.   I have been using a notion of class that is structural and static.   In this way of thinking, a class is defined by its relationship to the means of production and to other classes.   The concept is incomplete unless joined to one grounded in the continuous movement of history.   In this second view, I do not simply and eternally *belong* to the professional and intellectual portion of the working class.   Rather, in all my doings from day to day I and the people I mingle with and am affected by constantly *create* my class position.   As, for instance, I confirm it by writing in this way to this audience, by continuing to work with my mind and my mouth more than with my hands, by failing to get rich enough so that I might if I liked stop working altogether, by sending my children to college so that *they* can work with their minds and probably also not get rich, and so on.   From this perspective, class is not a permanent fact, but something that continually *happens*.[11]
    As soon as we look at it in this way, a still different relationship of class and language comes into focus.   My way of talking, whether "caused" by my class or not, is one of the important means by which I, in my relations with other people, recreate my class, confirm it, perhaps alter it.   When I talk I mark myself, for others, as some kind of intellectual worker.   Learning to talk that way was, of course one prerequisite to securing myself a place in intellectual work.   I might add that although

my father did similar work, I don't believe I learned my code at home so much as in various acculturating institutions along the way to professordom.

Just as my father did not talk like an intellectual in the nursery, neither do I talk to my children as I talk to my colleagues. And I speak differently again when I'm lecturing in class, when I'm trying to explain at the electrical supplies store what kind of switch I need, and when I am a witness in court. To follow this line of thought is to call into question the second main term - "code" - in Bernstein's equation. He does allow that speakers of the elaborated code also can use the restricted code. I think it's more complicated than that. I don't "have" a code the way I have my Ford Maverick out in the garage, to use whenever I go somewhere. If analogies are any use, a better one is probably to my wardrobe, from which I select in order to present myself in various ways on various occasions. Although there are clothes and way of talking in which I feel most at home, sometimes I am *not* "at home," and I can confidently dress and talk to be comfortable in a variety of situations (though not all). But even that analogy won't do. Unlike a car or a wardrobe, a code has no material existence in history, except as it is ceaselessly recreated when people speak. The same is true of a class, seen in the second Marxian perspective. And of course when we recreate a code by speaking, we almost always do so in collaboration with other people, and never in a setting that is socially neutral. Whenever we talk we do so within a nexus of power, status, intimacy or remoteness, family roles, institutional roles, designs on one another, and so on. It is hardly an exaggeration to say that the whole of society as I know it is present in or impinges on my every verbal transaction.

Now this position, which I have laid out very generally and will try to make more precise later, is a close neighbor to one of the cardinal principles of sociolinguistics. I mean the idea that for all of us speech is variable. Sociolinguists speak of "variable rules," meaning, for instance, the frequency with which a New Yorker will use or omit the postvocalic /r/, or with which a worker will say "he don't" as against "he doesn't," in various situations. Along with our grammatical abilities, we also tacitly know what counts as a timely and appropriate utterance at different stages of a speech situation, as well as how to relate through speaking to people of various sorts (bosses, priests, kids), for various purposes (to buy a hamburger or get a job), and in various genres (story-telling, arguing, answering questions). It begins to seem very hard to disentangle a single code from the dozens of ways that speech and society impinge on each other.[12] The way one speaks at any time is strongly influenced by the whole surrounding network of social circumstance, more than by relatively remote things like income, the job status of one's parents, or the number of years one spent in school.

This perspective applies not only to such constructs as "code" and "vernacular," but even to the individual word itself. To quote V. N. Volosinov:

> Every sign . . . is a construct between socially organized persons in the process of their inter-action. Therefore, THE FORMS OF SIGNS ARE CONDITIONED ABOVE ALL BY THE SOCIAL ORGANIZATION OF THE PARTICIPANTS INVOLVED AND ALSO BY THE IMMEDIATE CONDITIONS OF THEIR INTERACTION.[13]

The sign, both in its form and in its meaning, is in Volosinov's view "ideological": to simplify, it projects consciousness on reality, and consciousness, in turn, derives from the organization of society. Since different classes have different consciousness, and since for the most part they use the same signs in communication, in each sign different ideologies intersect. The sign itself is, in Volosinov's words, "an arena of the class struggle" (p. 23).

That is a rather dramatic way to put it, but I think the point is right. Many words have alternative pronunciations that carry a marker of prestige or class. There is Labov's example of postvocalic /r/ in New York; there is "dese" vs. "these"; in "My Fair Lady" there is "the /rayn/ in /spayn/" vs. "the /reyn/ in /speyn/." When teachers "correct" kids on such matters, they comment on the kids' class. When a speaker who normally drops the "r" or says "dese" or "/rayn/" talks with someone from a higher class or in a position of authority, he or she may shift to the more prestigious pronunciation or defiantly stand his or her linguistic and social ground. (I'm as good as you are, and I'll talk the way that's natural for me.) Such encounters may not be the heart of the class struggle, but they surely express conflict that is rooted in class.

As for meaning, consider the use of the word "industry" by the woman in interview I, and by the Mayor of Mill Town. For her, industry is concrete (factories and machines), but also a remote and uncontrollable condition like the weather: "Not enough industry up here." Hence, not enough jobs - a fact of life. When the Mayor says government should "encourage industry in their area," he speaks as a member of the government who has some modest influence over the movements of industry. For him, industry is real people with interests that he can address, and with whom he is involved as other than just a seller of his labor power. "Industry" is the same sign in both sentences, but used in ideologically contrasting ways. For her, industry is an alien force, for him a set of valuable if evasive allies whom he wishes to help in their project of development. Both agree that it is good to have industry in the Valley, but their political involvements in the matter are quite different. And they express their social situations in the ways they use the word.

It should be clear by this point, if you accept the argument, that Bernstein and Mueller ground their conclusions on a socio-linguistic method that in turn derives from damagingly static ideas of code and class, and of the links between code and class. In effect, Bernstein seeks to *correlate* two things, neither of which can be abstracted without distortion from the stream of social interaction, and both of which are incessantly re-created in every encounter.

In other words, we are dealing here with a phenomenon that is dialectical as well as dialectal. The power relations of a society permeate speech and shape it, while speech reproduces or challenges the power relations of the society. Please don't take me to be saying that class is only an artifact of the ways we talk to one another. But it would be equally wrong to say that the ways we talk are only an artifact of our class. The two are embedded in each other. Speech takes place in society and society also "takes place" in our verbal transactions with one another - which of course are inseparable from the economic and other transactions we enter. I have made this point a number of times now, insisting so much because it is important and, for social scientists at least, counter-intuitive.

But it is time to turn from theory back to the interviews and show how they may be seen afresh from this outlook. To begin with, both interviews explore the same subject, and the questions asked are quite similar in content. Nonetheless, the interview with the anonymous man and woman is in significant ways a quite different event from the interview with the Mayor. One takes place in the street outside a shopping mall; it is impromptu. The other takes place in the Mayor's office, by appointment. He has had time to prepare his thoughts. The Mayor is interviewed because he is who he is; the specific identities and positions of the man and woman are of no consequence. They are selected precisely because they are representative, part of a mass. Again, the Mayor is an expert on the economy of the Valley. That is part of his job, while the man and woman suddenly find themselves in an intellectual terrain that is unfamiliar. Finally, the Mayor is used to such encounters, and the man and woman are not. We may guess that the video equipment is at least a bit intimidating for them; it must make them feel that they are being observed, tested. Working with television is a more familiar challenge for the Mayor. In a way, television is an extension of his office and his power, something he can use to his own ends if he is skillful. The television people are there by his sufferance and on his timetable: he begins the interview as in some ways their superior. So although the issues remain almost constant through the two interviews, social relations do not.

As you might expect, the participants also create their relationships differently in the two interviews, through the ways they talk to each other. For instance, the interviewer in I begins with four yes-no questions. This is a way of getting out some basic information, but it also establishes a particular social relationship. A yes-no question strictly limits the form of its answer. The questioner sets up a tight cognitive paradigm, asking only for some information to complete it. Of course the respondent may decline to play the game this way, but to do so requires a breach of decorum. By contrast, a wh- question frequently gives the respondent a kind of carte blanche as to how detailed and lengthy the answer may be. The three wh- questions with which interview II begins all accord the Mayor that kind of freedom. On top of that, the first two questions to the man and woman request personal information. They do so in a respectful way; nonetheless, one condition for a felicitous question is that the questioner has the right to ask. If that right is not given by intimacy, it is usually given by virtue of some official purpose, as to bank officers considering loan applicants or to census workers. However gently, the sidewalk interviewer assumes such a prerogative. (Note that when he shifts to an impersonal question about unemployment, the man feels constrained to preface his answer with more personal information, by way of excuse.) The first question to the Mayor, on the other hand, is not only general and impersonal but assumes much knowledge on his part. It positions him as an expert, someone whose opinion is worth knowing, in detail and on a highly complex subject. It is an invitation to expatiate.

These differences arise from no bias of the interviewers. On the contrary, since I know them I am confident in saying what I believe is also implicit in the interviews: that their sympathies lay more with the workers and unemployed people they met than with the managers, officials, industrialists, and bureaucrats.   The differences stem from the speech situations themselves, and from moves that the participants make which accept and confirm those situations.   As a result of these moves the first interview proceeds somewhat like a quiz.   When the interviewer shifts to wh-questions after a bit, it seems as if he is testing the man and woman.   They respond like school children being drawn out against their will by an insistent teacher who is asking them to *have* opinions and ideas so that they may be judged. (Note especially the series of leading questions on cheap labor - a kind of catechism.)   In interview II, by contrast, when the interviewer shifts to yes-no questions, their aim is to challenge and explore views that the Mayor has already expressed. His position has itself become the subject of the discussion, and is in this way dignified.   The interviewer is pressing him, as a serious antagonist.

Perhaps that is enough to establish my claim about the social dynamics of the interviews.   One cannot know for sure how these people speak at other times, but the contrasts I have mentioned are certainly *sufficient* to have elicited a restricted code from the couple and an elaborated code from the Mayor. Let me return, somewhat speculatively, to my initial analysis of the interviews, looking at Bernstein's categories from this new perspective:

A. Length and Complexity

The short responses and short, simple sentences of the man and woman are obedient answers of unprepared people who feel themselves tested and perhaps judged. Why not, with the camera looking on, and the questioner who clearly knows more than they about the subject? Their task, as I see it, is to avoid exposure or humiliation, to avoid the risk of saying something purely foolish. They take their leads from the interviewer, and try to sense from his reaction whether they have said the right thing. For them "I don't know" is the ultimate defensive strategy, since it is at least not a wrong answer. The Mayor is invited to dilate upon his subject; he does so, and in the complex (though often vapid) sentences appropriate to that task.

B. Modifiers

The man and woman are not being asked to individuate their opinions, to shade, specify, quality. "Do you have any ideas about what causes that problem?" The interviewer is asking them to take a stab at it. A short, tentative answer is the natural response. But the Mayor is invited to discourse on the "community as a whole," its "self-image," "its ability to deal with problems." He could hardly take on this huge and complex subject without qualifying his answer along the way. Also, because of who he is, his words are important. They will go on record. They had better be measured and circumspect.

C. Abstraction

For the man and woman, terms like "industry," "taxes," "rebate," and "cheap labor," are hand-me-downs from TV, the newspapers, casual conversation about distant matters out of control. They produce these terms as part of their role in the quiz, but the terms are alienated. The man and woman have nothing to back them up with, no way to relate them conceptually to one another and to reality. For the Mayor, abstractions about the economy are rooted in his daily work: in technical reports bearing on decisions he must make, in talk with advisors, the Chamber of Commerce, state and federal bureaucrats. This is not to say that his account of unemployment is better than that of the man and woman. In my own view, automation is a shallow cause, and the lack of acreage in Mill Town an empty one, while the woman is right on target in pointing to the free flow of capital in pursuit of cheap labor. One may talk flaccid nonsense in elaborated codes, and hard truth in restricted ones; and as the Mayor's speech well illustrates, an elaborated code may serve as a bureaucratic smokescreen. At the same time, abstractions *are* a verbal medium the Mayor is used to and works within. He manipulates them freely and voluntarily, rather than tentatively and with an air of talking someone else's language, under pressure. They are an instrument of power for him in this situation, and a token of powerlessness for the man and woman.

D. Reference to Context

The subject of the interviewer's questions belongs to the Mayor's field of action.   They already have a context in his work and thought.   For the man and woman, government, the movements of corporations, unemployment, and history in the large sense are distant forces and events, not because of any cognitive or linguistic deficit, but just in that the couple are connected to such matters only through activities like drawing a wage, buying commodities, and voting, which relate them to the historical context only in fragmented and isolating ways--ways which the mass media reinforce.

E. Reference to the Discourse Itself

The Mayor's self-reflexive expressions, his comments on the interviewer's questions, his refusal to accept their premises, his new starts, all reflect the Mayor's sense that he is in charge of the conversation.   The questions are not, as he sees it, a form of power over him and a cage within which he must submissively remain.   He can establish the terms and set the ground rules, up to a point.   And what he says is important enough to warrant his taking pains, finding just the right formulation.   (It may also be relevant to mention that the questioner in this interview is a woman.)

In all these ways the interviews embed power relations and speech conventions that existed prior to the encounters.   But this is not to say that the speakers' codes reflect only the social relations that previously obtained.   Choice is available at every point: note, for instance, how the Mayor takes over leadership of the interview by volunteering the chief cause of unemployment without being asked, how he changes the terms of the questions, and so on.   No law prevents the man and woman from doing likewise (though the power relations they walk into have nearly the force of law).   The participants *create* the social relations of each encounter, in addition to inheriting them.   In so doing they reproduce society.   By such tiny increments is class made and remade.

If my argument is sound, then, a Bernsteinian explanation of these interviews badly misrepresents the social forces at work in them, assigning to static "class" differences in speech that express dynamic and changeable power relations.[14]   More broadly, I have argued that this mistake follows from serious misconceptions of class and code.   More the pity, because (1) Bernstein clearly meant it to serve the working class;   (2) it has been highly influential, especially in Britain; and (3) the pedagogical inference drawn from it has generally been that we should teach elaborate codes to working-class kids, within the customary social relations of the school. Instead, I think the educational moral is roughly that of the 1960s reform movements, now much condemned: students should have as much responsibility as possible for their own educations. The habits of expressive power come with actual shared power, not with computerized instruction in sentence-combining or with a back-to-basics movement that would freeze students' language into someone else's rules, imposed from without. Respect the linguistic resources students have; make language a vehicle for achievement of real political and personal aims.

Finally, Mueller's political pessimism is justified only if we assume, as many leftists do (myself included at the time I first addressed these questions), that political consciousness is fixed, either at home in infancy and childhood or, even more deeply than that, by gross structural features of the society--if we assume that workers cannot become equal communicators and political participants step by step, and through action, but only by understanding, in a kind of conversion experience, the fundamental concepts of Marxism. Movements toward worker self-management, coops, progressive credit unions, consumer movements, union organizing, populist movements of many kinds, are all fertile soil in which elaborated codes (better than that of the Mayor, I hope) may grow along with the habit of democracy.

FOOTNOTES

[1] Thanks to Gerry Lombardi and Jan Stackhouse, who carried out the project and gave me copies of some of the tapes.

[2] In this usage, a code is not a dialect or a language, but a way of mobilizing one's dialect in real situations. Bernstein also speaks of it as an "orientation."

[3] *Class, Codes and Control* (London: Routledge and Kegan Paul, 1971), I, 143. In characterizing the two codes I have also drawn from research published in volume 2 of this three-volume work, and in W. Brandis and D. Henderson, *Social Class, Language and Communication* (London: Routeledge and Kegan Paul, 1970) and P. R. Hawkins, *Social Class, The Nominal Group and Verbal Strategies* (London: Routledge and Kegan Paul, 1977). Altogether, there are more than ten books in this series, edited by Bernstein and consisting mainly of research grounded in his ideas. Note: "positional" control is authoritarian; "personalized" control is more flexible and interactive. This may also be the place to note that Bernstein never, to my knowledge, defines "class," but his references to the concept make it seem that he identifies class with the parents' educational level and job status. Brandis spells this out technically in Appendix I of *Social Class, Language and Communication*.

[4]Mueller notes that most of the studies he surveys define class "by education, occupation, and/or income" (p. 46). His own definition stresses education and occupation (p. 45).

[5]"Questions About Literacy and Political Education," *Radical Teacher*, 8 (May 1978), pp. 24-25.

[6]In doing so, I have learned much from Raymond Williams, "Language," in his *Marxism and Literature* (Oxford: Oxford University Press, 1977); Chris Sinha, "Class, Language and Education," *Ideology and Consciousness*, 1 (May 1977); William Labov, various articles, especially "The Study of Language in its Social Context," in Joshua Fishman, ed., *Advances in the Sociology of Language* (The Hague: Mouton, 1971); Dell Hymes, "Models of the Interaction of Language and Social Life," in John J. Gumperz and Dell Hymes, ed., *Directions in Sociolinguistics* (New York: Holt, Rinehart and Winston, 1972); Norbert Dittmar, *Sociolinguistics; A Critical Survey of Theory and Application*, tr. Peter Sand, Pieter A. M. Seuren, and Kevin Whiteley (London: Edward Arnold, 1976); Harold Rosen, *Language and Class: A Critical Look at the Theories of Basil Bernstein* (Bristol: Falling Wall Press, 1972); and from other works cited later. Thanks also to Wendy Melechen and Steve Ward, who explored these matters with me in a tutorial at Wesleyan University, to Johannes Fabian, who gave me helpful leads, and to Don Lazere, Wayne O'Neil, Barry Phillips, and Bob Rosen, who helpfully criticized a draft of this article (Lazere and Philips disagree with me in major ways). It may be unnecessary to add that very little in this essay is "original."

[7]In such an impasse, there is a tendency to look for causes in the *chronologically* prior years of childhood, hence in practices of "socialization." Aside from the theoretical arbitrariness of such a strategy, its political implications are obvious and rather nasty - e.g., the poor may be blamed for their own poverty; black parents may be held accountable for their children's failure in school; or, only a little more benignly, the liberals may set out to correct, in school, the cultural "damage" done at home.

[8]This is so whether they are blue- or white-collar, assembly-line workers, keypunch operators, or McDonalds' robots doing it all for us. See Harry Braverman, *Labor and Monopoly Capital* (New York: Monthly Review Press, 1974), chapters 15 and 16, for an account of how clerical and service jobs have been reduced to smaller and smaller actions, requiring little thought on the worker's part. In this section of my argument I am relying on some basic distinctions that Braverman makes in his invaluable book, following Marx.

[9]And of course I am omitting entirely some obvious differences in the kinds of schooling generally given to children of the two subclasses, not to mention different cultural environments at home (books, etc.), different relationships to television, and so on. Please excuse the drastic but necessary simplification.

[10] Bernstein briefly mentions such an explanation in a memorable paragraph in *Class, Codes and Control*, I, 143. But he does not develop it at all, nor can it be derived from his conception of class.

[11] The formulation is that of E. P. Thompson, in *The Making of the English Working Class* (New York: Vintage, 1963), which renders a persuasive account of the way a group of people made themselves into a class through institutions like church, union, and party, and through struggles over work and life, as well as through cultural production - song, oratory, writing, etc.

[12] Some sociolinguists - including Hymes and Labov - have even suggested that we drop the idea of grammatical competence and think instead of a flexible "communicative competence." This seems to me a damaging strategy, one which would forbid the abstraction from speech that is necessary for any systematic study of language.   See Noam Chomsky's remarks on this subject in *Language and Responsibility* (New York: Pantheon, 1977), pp. 53-58 and 189-192.   But the work of these sociolinguists surely does call into question the abstraction, *code* (and probably that of *language*, too).   Nor do I think it permits Labov's idea of the "vernacular," on which he settles in a kind of last ditch attempt to get at the way people *really* speak when they are completely at ease.   The vernacular he defines as "the style in which the minimum attention is given to the monitoring of speech" ("The Study of Language in its Social Context," p. 170; see footnote 6).   For any person, the vernacular is the most systematic of his or her codes, hence the most worth studying.   But studying it is nearly impossible, since people monitor and "correct" their speech when they think it's being observed, being noticed *as* speech.   What surprises me is that Labov singles out the encounter of linguist-observer and "ordinary" speaker as so unusual in its ability to interfere with the vernacular.   Speakers of one or another vernacular, unless completely isolated in rural valleys or perhaps prisons, are constantly in touch with bosses, officials, teachers, cops, and so on; and sociolinguists have documented well the "shift" of code that takes place in such encounters, mainly on the part of the subordinate person.   Likewise, all speakers but the most lowly derelict or infant speak at times with people subordinate to them.   Then there are also shifts from friend to stranger, from manipulation to just rapping, etc. The "vernacular" dissolves in real social contexts.   Unlike grammatical competence, it is not the kind of idealization that helps get at what is systematic in language.

[13] *Marxism and the Philosophy of Language*,   trans.   Ladislav Matejka and I. R. Titunik (New York: Seminar Press, 1973), p. 21.

[14] The Mayor, it is worth noting, came from the industrial working class, and was a high-school baseball coach before entering politics.

THE SOCIAL STRATIFICATION OF (r)

IN NEW YORK CITY DEPARTMENT STORES

William Labov

"As this letter is but a jar of the tongue, . . . it is the most imperfect of all the consonants."

John Walker,
Principles of English Pronunciation, 1791

Anyone who begins to study language in its social context immediately encounters the classic methodological problem: the means used to gather the data interfere with the data to be gathered. The primary means of obtaining a large body of reliable data on the speech of one person is the individual tape-recorded interview. Interview speech is formal speech - not by any absolute measure, but by comparison with the vernacular of everyday life. On the whole, the interview is public speech - monitored and controlled in response to the presence of an outside observer. But even within that definition, the investigator may wonder if the responses in a tape-recorded interview are not a special product of the interaction between the interviewer and the subject. One way of controlling for this is to study the subject in his own natural social context - interacting with his family or peer group (Labov, Cohen, Robins, and Lewis 1968). Another way is to observe the public use of language in everyday life apart from any interview situation - to see how people use language in context when there is no explicit observation. This article is an account of the systematic use of rapid and anonymous observations in a study of the sociolinguistic structure of the speech community. [1]

This article is the first of a series of six which deal primarily with the sociolinguistic study of New York City. The main base for that study (Labov 1966a) was a secondary random sample of the Lower East Side, and this data will be considered in the following chapters. But before the systematic study was carried out, there was an extensive series of preliminary investigations. These include 70 individual interviews and a great many anonymous observations in public places. These preliminary studies led to

From *Sociolinguistic Patterns* by William Labov. University of Pennsylvania Press, 1972, pp 43-69.

the definition of the major phonological variables which were to be studied, including (r): the presence or absence of consonantal [r] in postvocalic position in *car, card, four, fourth*, etc. This particular variable appeared to be extraordinarily sensitive to any measure of social or stylistic stratification. On the basis of the exploratory interviews, it seemed possible to carry out an empirical test of two general notions: first, that the linguistic variable (r) is a social differentiator in all levels of New York City speech, and second, that rapid and anonymous speech events could be used as the basis for a systematic study of language. The study of (r) in New York City department stores which I will report here was conducted in November 1962 as a test of these ideas.

We can hardly consider the social distribution of language in New York City without encountering the pattern of social stratification which pervades the life of the city. This concept is analyzed in some detail in the major study of the Lower East Side; here we may briefly consider the definition given by Bernard Barber: social stratification is the product of social differentiation and social evaluation (1957:1-3). The use of this term does not imply any specific type of class or caste, but simply that the normal workings of society have produced systematic differences between certain institutions or people, and that these differentiated forms have been ranked in status or prestige by general agreement.

We begin with the general hypothesis suggested by exploratory interviews: *if any two subgroups of New York City speakers are ranked in a scale of social stratification, they then will be ranked in the same order by their differential use of (r).*

It would be easy to test this hypothesis by comparing occupational groups, which are among the most important indexes of social stratification. We could, for example, take a group of lawyers, a group of file clerks, and a group of janitors. But this would hardly go beyond the indications of the exploratory interviews, and such an extreme example of differentiation would not provide a very exacting test of the hypothesis. It should be possible to show that the hypothesis is so general, and the differential use of (r) pervades New York City so thoroughly, that fine social differences will be reflected in the index as well as gross ones.

It therefore seemed best to construct a very severe test by finding a subtle case of stratification within a single occupational group: in this case, the sales people of large department stores in Manhattan. If we select three large department stores, from the top, middle, and bottom of the price and fashion scale, we can expect that the customers will be socially stratified. Would we expect the sales people to show a comparable stratification? Such a position would depend upon two correlations: Between the status ranking of the stores and the ranking of parallel jobs in the three stores; and between the jobs and the behavior of the persons who hold those jobs. These are not unreasonable assumptions. C. Wright Mills points out that salesgirls in large department stores tend to borrow prestige from their customers, or at least make an effort in that direction.[2] It appears that a person's own occupation is more closely correlated with his linguistic behavior - for those working actively - than any other single social characteristic. The evidence presented here indicates that the stores are objectively differentiated in a fixed order, and that jobs in these stores are evaluated by employees in that order. Since the production of social differentiation and evaluation, no matter how minor, is social stratification of the employees in the three stores, the hypothesis will predict the following result: salespeople in the highest-ranked store will have the highest values of (r); those in the middle-ranked store will have intermediate values of (r); and those in the lowest-ranked store will show the lowest values. If this result holds true, the hypothesis will have received confirmation in proportion to the severity of the test.

The three stores which were selected are Saks Fifth Avenue, Macy's, and S. Klein. The differential ranking of these stores may be illustrated in many ways. Their locations are one important point:

Highest-ranking: Saks Fifth Avenue
     at 50th St. and 5th Ave., near the center of the high fashion shopping district, along with other high-prestige stores such as Bonwit Teller, Henri Bendel, Lord and Taylor
Middle-ranking: Macy's
     Herald Square, 34th St. and Sixth Ave., near the garment district, along with Gimbels and Saks-34th St., other middle-range stores in price and prestige.
Lowest-ranking: S. Klein
     Union Square, 14th St. and Broadway, not far from the Lower East Side.

The advertising and price policies of the stores are very clearly stratified. Perhaps no other element of class behavior is so sharply differentiated in New York City as that of the newspaper which people read; many surveys have shown that the *Daily News* is the paper read first and foremost by working-class people, while the *New York Times* draws its readership from the middle class.[3] These two newspapers were examined for the advertising copy in October 24-27, 1962: Saks and Macy's advertised in the *New York Times*, where Kleins was represented by only a very small item; in the *News*, however, Saks does not appear at all, while both Macy's and Kleins are heavy advertisers.

No. of pages of advertising
October 24-27, 1962

	NY Times	*Daily News*
Saks	2	0
Macy's	6	15
S. Klein	1/4	10

We may also consider the prices of the goods advertised during those four days. Since Saks usually does not list prices, we can only compare prices for all three stores on one item: women's coats. Saks: $90.00, Macy's: $79.95, Kleins: $23.00. On four items, we can compare Kleins and Macy's:

	Macy's	S. Klein
dresses	$14.95	$ 5.00
girls' coats	26.99	12.00
stockings	0.89	0.45
men's suits	49.95–64.95	26.00–66.00

The emphasis on prices is also different. Saks either does not mention prices, or buries the figure in small type at the foot of the page. Macy's features the prices in large type, but often adds the slogan, "You get more than low prices." Kleins, on the other hand, is often content to let the prices speak for themselves. The form of the prices is also different: Saks gives prices in round figures, such as $120; Macy's always shows a few cents off the dollar: $49.95; Kleins usually prices its goods in round numbers, and adds the retail price which is always much higher, and shown in Macy's style: "$23.00, marked down from $49.95."

The physical plant of the stores also serves to differentiate them. Saks is the most spacious, especially on the upper floors, with the least amount of goods displayed. Many of the floors are carpeted, and on some of them, a receptionist is stationed to greet the customers. Kleins, at the other extreme, is a maze of annexes, sloping concrete floors, low ceilings; it has the maximum amount of goods displayed at the least possible expense.

The principal stratifying effect upon the employees is the prestige of the store, and the working conditions. Wages do not stratify the employees in the same order. On the contrary, there is every indication that high-prestige stores such as Saks pay lower wages than Macy's.

Saks is a nonunion store, and the general wage structure is not a matter of public record. However, conversations with a number of men and women who have worked in New York department stores, including Saks and Macy's, show general agreement on the direction of the wage differential.[4] Some of the incidents reflect a willingness of sales people to accept much lower wages from the store with greater prestige. The executives of the prestige stores pay a great deal of attention to employee relations, and take many unusual measures to ensure that the sales people feel that they share in the general prestige of the store.[5] One of the Lower East Side informants who worked at Saks was chiefly impressed with the fact that she could buy Saks clothes at a 25 percent discount. A similar concession from a lower-prestige store would have been of little interest to her.

From the point of view of Macy's employees, a job in Kleins is well below the horizon. Working conditions and wages are generally considered to be worse, and the prestige of Kleins is very low indeed. As we will see, the ethnic composition of the store employees reflects these differences quite accurately.

A socioeconomic index which ranked New Yorkers on occupation would show the employees of the three stores at the same level; an income scale would probably find Macy's employees somewhat higher than the others; education is the only objective scale which might differentiate the groups in the same order as the prestige of the stores, though there is no evidence on this point. However, the working conditions of sales jobs in the three stores stratify them in the order: Saks, Macy's, Kleins; the prestige of the stores leads to a social evaluation of these jobs in the same order. Thus the two aspects of social stratification - differentiation and evaluation - are to be seen in the relations of the three stores and their employees.

The normal approach to a survey of department store employees requires that one enumerate the sales people of each store, draw random samples in each store, make appointments to speak with each employee at home, interview the respondents, then segregate the native New Yorkers, analyze and resample the nonrespondents, and so on. This is an expensive and time-consuming procedure, but for most purposes there is no short cut which will give accurate and reliable results. In this case, a simpler method which relies upon the extreme generality of the linguistic behavior of the subjects was used to gather a very limited type of data. This method is dependent upon the systematic sampling of casual and anonymous speech events. Applied in a poorly defined environment, such a method is open to many biases and it would be difficult to say what population had been studied. In this case, our population is well defined as the sales people (or more generally, any employee whose speech might be heard by a customer) in three specific stores at a specific time. The result will be a view of the role that speech would play in the overall social imprint of the employees upon the customer. It is surprising that this simple and economical approach achieves results with a high degree of consistency and regularity, and allows us to test the original hypothesis in a number of subtle ways.

THE METHOD

The application of the study of casual and anonymous speech events to the department-store situation was relatively simple. The interviewer approached the informant in the role of a customer asking for directions to a particular department. The department was one which was located on the fourth floor. When the interviewer asked, "Excuse me, where are the women's shoes?" the answer would normally be, "Fourth floor."

The interviewer then leaned forward and said, "Excuse me?" He would usually then obtain another utterance, "*Fourth floor*," spoken in careful style under emphatic stress.[6]

The interviewer would then move along the aisle of the store to a point immediately beyond the informant's view, and make a written note of the data. The following independent variables were included:

the store
floor within the store [7]
sex
age (estimated in units of five years)
Occupation (floorwalker, sales, cashier, stockboy)
race
foreign or regional accent, if any

The dependent variable is the use of (r) in four occurrences:

casual: fourth floor
emphatic: *fourth floor*

Thus we have preconsonantal and final position, in both casual and emphatic styles of speech. In addition, all other uses of (r) by the informant were noted, from remarks overheard or contained in the interview. For each plainly constructed value of the variable, (r-1) was entered; for unconstricted schwa, lengthened vowel, or no representation, (r-0) was entered. Doubtful cases or partial constriction were symbolized *d* and were not used in the final tabulation.

Also noted were instances of affricates or stops used in the word *fourth* for the final consonant, and any other examples of nonstandard (th) variants used by the speaker.

This method of interviewing was applied in each aisle on the floor as many times as possible before the spacing of the informants became so close that it was noticed that the same question had been asked before. Each floor of the store was investigated in the same way. On the fourth floor, the form of the question was necessarily different:

"Excuse me, what floor is this?"

Following this method, 68 interviews were obtained in Saks, 125 in Macy's, and 71 in Kleins. Total interviewing time for the 264 subjects was approximately 6.5 hours.

At this point, we might consider the nature of these 264 interviews in more general terms. They were speech events which had entirely different social significance for the two participants. As far as the informant was concerned, the exchange was a normal salesman-customer interaction, almost below the level of conscious attention, in which relations of the speakers were so casual and anonymous that they may hardly have been said to have met.   This tenuous relationship was the minimum intrusion upon the behavior of the subject; language and the use of language never appeared at all.

From the point of view of the interviewer, the exchange was a systematic elicitation of the exact forms required, in the desired context, the desired order, and with the desired contrast of style.

Overall Stratification of (r)

The results of the study show clear and consistent stratification of (r) in the three stores.   In Figure 1, the use of (4) by employees of Saks, Macy's and Kleins is compared by means of a bar graph.   Since the data for most informants consist of only four items, we will not use a continuous numerical index for (r), but rather divide all informants into three categories.

all (r-1):   those whose records show only (r-1) and no (r-0)
some (r-1):   those whose records show at least one (r-1) and one (r-0)
no (r-1):   those whose records show only (r-0)

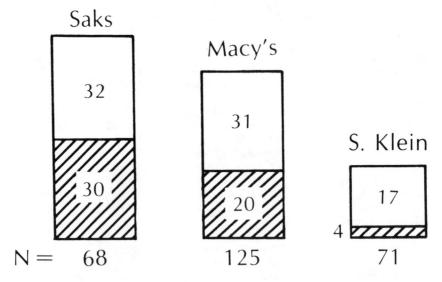

Figure 1:   Overall stratification of (r) by store.   Shaded area = % all (r-1); unshaded area = % some (r-1); % no (r-1) not shown.   N = total number of cases.

From Figure 1 we see that a total of 62 percent of Saks employees, 51 percent of Macy's, and 20 percent of Kleins used all or some (r-1). The stratification is even sharper for the percentages of all (r-1). As the hypothesis predicted, the groups are ranked by their differential use of (r-1) in the same order as their stratification by extralinguistic factors.

Next, we may wish to examine the distribution of (r) in each of the four standard positions. Figure 2 shows this type of display, where once again, the stores are differentiated in the same order, and for each position. There is a considerable difference between Macy's and Kleins at each position, but the difference between Macy's and Saks varies. In emphatic pronunciation of the final (r), Macy's employees come very close to the mark set by Saks. It would seem that r-pronunciation is the norm at which a majority of Macy employees aim, yet not the one they use most often. In Saks, we see a shift between casual and emphatic pronunciation, but it is much less marked. In other words, Saks employees have more *security* in a linguistic sense. [8]

The fact that the figures for (r-1) at Kleins are low should not obscure the fact that Kleins employees also participate in the same pattern of stylistic variation of (r) as the other stores. The percentage of r-pronunciation rises at Kleins from 5 to 18 percent as the context becomes more emphatic: a much greater rise in percentage than in the other stores, and a more regular increase as well. It will be important to bear in mind that this attitude - that (r-1) is the most appropriate pronunciation for emphatic speech - is shared by at least some speakers in all three stores.

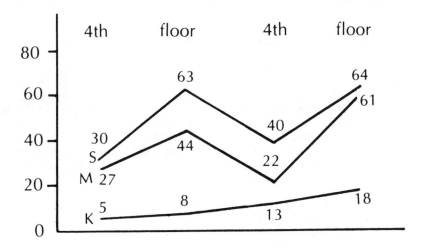

Figure 2: Percentage of all (r-1) by store for four positions. (S = Saks, M = Macy's, K = Kleins.)

TABLE I. Detailed Distribution Of (r) By Store And Word Position

(r)	Saks		Macy's		S. Klein	
	Casual 4th floor	Emphatic 4th floor	Casual 4th floor	Emphatic 4th floor	Casual 4th floor	Emphatic 4th floor
(r-1)	17 31	16 21	33 48	13 31	3 5	6 7
(r-0)	39 18	24 12	81 62	48 20	63 59	40 33
d	5 5	4 4	0 3	1 0	1 1	3 3
No data*	8 14	24 31	11 12	63 74	4 6	22 28
Total no.	68 68	68 68	125 125	125 125	71 71	71 71

*The "no data" category for Macy's shows relatively high values under the emphatic category. This discrepancy is due to the fact that the procedure for requesting repetition was not standardized in the investigation of the ground floor at Macy's, and values for emphatic response were not regularly obtained. The effects of this loss are checked in Table II, where only complete responses are compared.

Table I shows the data in detail, with the number of instances obtained for each of the four positions of (r), for each store. It may be noted that the number of occurrences in the second pronunciation of *floor* is considerably reduced, primarily as a result of some speakers' tendency to answer a second time, "Fourth."

Since the numbers in the fourth position are somewhat smaller than the second, it might be suspected that those who use [r] in Saks and Macy's tend to give fuller responses, thus giving rise to a spurious impression of increase in (r) values in those positions. We can check this point by comparing only those who gave a complete response. Their responses can be symbolized by a four-digit number, representing the pronunciation in each of the four positions respectively (see Table II).

Thus we see that the pattern of differential ranking in the use of (r) is preserved in this subgroup of complete responses, and omission of the final "floor" by some respondents was not a factor in this pattern.

The Effect of Other Independent Variables

Other factors, besides the stratification of the stores, may explain the regular pattern of r-pronunciation seen above, or this effect may be the contribution of a particular group in the population, rather than the behavior of the sales people as a

TABLE II. Distribution Of (r) For Complete Responses

						% of total responses in		
(r)						Saks	Macy's	S. Klein
All (r-1)	1	1	1	1		24	22	6
Some (r-1	0	1	1	1		46	37	12
	0	0	1	1				
	0	1	0	1	etc.			
No (r-1)	0	0	0	0		30	41	82
						100	100	100
N =						33	48	34

whole. The other independent variables recorded in the interviews enable us to check such possibilities.

Race

There are many more black employees in the Kleins sample than in Macy's, and more in Macy's than in Saks. Table 3 shows the percentages of black informants and their responses. When we compare these figures with those of Figure 1, for the entire population, it is evident that the presence of many black informants will contribute to a lower use of (r-1). The black subjects at Macy's used less (r-1) than the white informants, though only to a slight extent; the black subjects at Kleins were considerably more biased in the r-less direction.

The higher percentage of black sales people in the lower-ranking stores is consistent with the general pattern of social stratification, since in general, black workers have been assigned less desirable jobs. Therefore the contribution of black speakers to the overall pattern is consistent with the hypothesis.

TABLE III. Distribution Of (r) For Black Employees

	% of responses in		
(r)	Saks	Macy's	S. Klein
All (r-1)	50	12	0
Some (r-1)	0	35	6
No (r-1)	50	53	94
	100	100	100
N =	2	17	18
% of black informants:	03	14	25

Occupation

There are other differences in the populations of the stores.
The types of occupations among the employees who are accessible
to customers are quite different. In Macy's, the employees who
were interviewed could be identified as floorwalkers (by red and
white carnations), sales people, cashiers, stockboys, and elevator
operators. In Saks, the cashiers are not accessible to the
customer, working behind the sales counters, and stockboys are
not seen. The working operation of the store goes on behind
the scenes, and does not intrude upon the customer's notice.
On the other hand, at Kleins, all of the employees seem to be
operating on the same level: it is difficult to tell the difference
between sales people, managers, and stockboys.

Here again, the extralinguistic stratification of the stores is
reinforced by objective observations in the course of the interview.
We can question if these differences are not responsible for at
least a part of the stratification of (r). For the strongest possible
result, it would be desirable to show that the stratification of
(r) is a property of the most homogeneous subgroup in the three
stores: native New York, white sales women. Setting aside the
male employees, all occupations besides selling itself, the black
and Puerto Rican employees, and all those with a foreign accent,[9]
there are still a total of 141 informants to study.

Figure 3 shows the percentages of (r-1) used by the native
white sales women of the three stores, with the same type of

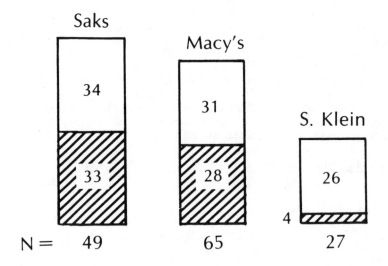

*Figure 3: Stratifications of (r) by store for native New York
white sales women. Shaded area = % all (r-1); unshaded area
= % some (r-1); % no (r-1) not shown. N = total number of
cases.*

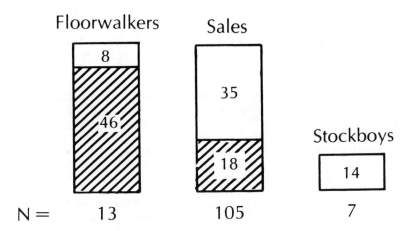

Figure 4: Stratification of (r) by occupational groups in Macy's. Shaded area = % all (r-1); unshaded area = % some (r-1); % no (r-1) not shown. N = total number of cases.

graph as in Figure 1.   The stratification is essentially the same in direction and outline, though somewhat smaller in magnitude. The greatly reduced Kleins sample still shows by far the lowest use of (r-1), and Saks is ahead of Macy's in this respect.   We can therefore conclude that the stratification of (r) is a process which affects every section of the sample.

We can now turn the heterogeneous nature of the Macy's sample to advantage.   Figure 4 shows the stratification of (r) according to occupational groups in Macy's: in line with our initial hypothesis, this is much sharper than the stratification of the employees in general.   The total percentage of those who use all or some (r-1) is almost the same for the floorwalkers and the sales people but a much higher percentage of floorwalkers consistently use (r-1).

Another interesting comparison may be made at Saks, where there is a great discrepancy between the ground floor and the

TABLE IV.   Distribution Of (r) By Floor in Saks

(r)	Ground floor	Upper floors
% all (r-1)	23	34
% some (r-1)	23	40
% no (r-1)	54	26
	100	100
N =	30	38

upper floors. The ground floor of Saks looks very much like Macy's: many crowded counters, salesgirls leaning over the counters, almost elbow to elbow, and a great deal of merchandise displayed. But the upper floors of Saks are far more spacious; there are long vistas of empty carpeting, and on the floors devoted to high fashion, there are models who display the individual garments to the customers. Receptionists are stationed at strategic points to screen out the casual spectators from the serious buyers.

It would seem logical then, to compare the ground floor of Saks with the upper floors. By the hypothesis, we should find a differential use of (r-1). Table IV shows that this is the case.

In the course of the interview, information was also collected on the (th) variable, particularly as it occurred in the word *fourth*. This is one of the major variables used in the study of social stratification in New York (Labov 1966a) and elsewhere (Wolfram 1969; Anshen 1969). The most strongly stigmatized variant is the use of the stop [t] in *fourth*, *through*, *think*, etc. The percentage of speakers who used stops in this position was fully in accord with the other measures of social stratification which we have seen:

Saks	00%
Macy's	04
S. Klein	15

Thus the hypothesis has received a number of semi-independent confirmations. Considering the economy with which the information was obtained, the survey appears to yield rich results. It is true that we do not know a great deal about the informants that we would like to know: their birthplace, language history, education, participation in New York culture, and so on. Nevertheless, the regularities of the underlying pattern are strong enough to overcome this lack of precision in the selection and identification of informants.

DIFFERENTIATION BY AGE OF THE INFORMANTS

The age of the informants was estimated within five-year intervals, and these figures cannot be considered reliable for any but the simplest kind of comparison. However, it should be possible to break down the age groups into three units, and detect any overall direction of change.

If, as we have indicated, (r-1) is one of the chief characteristics of a new prestige pattern which is being superimposed upon the native New York City pattern, we would expect to see a rise in r-pronunciation among the younger sales people. The overall

distribution by age shows no evidence of change, however in
Table V.

This lack of direction is surprising, in the light of other
evidence that the use of (r-1) as a prestige variant is increasing
among younger people in New York City.   There is clearcut
evidence for the absence of (r-1) in New York City in the 1930's
(Kurath and McDavid 1951) and a subsequent increase in the
records of Hubbell (1950) and Bronstein (1962).   When we examine
the distributions for the individual stores, we find that the even
distribution through age levels disappears.   Figure 5 shows that
the expected inverse correlation with age appears in Saks, but
not in Macy's or Kleins.   Instead, Macy's shows the reverse
direction at a lower level, with older subjects using more (r-1),
and Kleins no particular correlation with age.   This complex
pattern is even more puzzling, and one is tempted to dismiss it
as the absence of any pattern.   But although the numbers of the
subgroups may appear to be small, they are larger than many of
the subgroups used in the discussions of previous pages, and as
we will see, it is not possible to discount the results.

The conundrum represented by Figure 5 is one of the most
significant results of the procedures that have been followed to
this point.   Where all other findings confirm the original hypothesis, a single result which does not fit the expected pattern
may turn our attention in new and profitable directions.   From
the data in the department store survey alone, it was not possible
to account for Figure 5 except in speculative terms.   In the
original report on the department store survey, written shortly
after the work was completed, we commented:

> How can we account for the differences between
> Saks and Macy's?   I think we can say this: the
> shift from the influence of the New England pres-
> tige pattern (r-less) to the Midwestern prestige
> pattern (r-ful) is felt most completely at Saks.
> The younger people at Saks are under the influ-
> ence of the r-pronouncing pattern, and the older
> ones are not.   At Macy's, there is less sensitivity
> to the effect among a large number of younger
> speakers who are completely immersed in the New
> York City linguistic tradition.   The stockboys,

TABLE V.   Distribution Of (r) By Estimated Age

| | Age groups | | |
(r)	15–30	35–50	55–70
% of (r-1)	24	20	20
% some (r-1)	21	28	22
% no (r-1)	55	52	58

the young salesgirls, are not as yet fully aware
of the prestige attached to r-pronunciation.   On
the other hand, the older people at Macy's tend
to adopt this pronunciation: very few of them
rely upon the older pattern of prestige pronunciation which supports the r-less tendency of older
Saks sales people.   This is a rather complicated
argument, which would certainly have to be tested
very thoroughly by longer interviews in both
stores before it could be accepted.

   The complex pattern of Figure 5 offered a considerable challenge for interpretation and explanation, but one possibility that
always had to be considered was that it was the product of the
many sources of error inherent in rapid and anonymous surveys.
To confirm and explain the results of the department store survey
it will be necessary to look ahead to the results of the systematic
interviewing program.   When the results of the major study of
the Lower East Side were analyzed, it became clear that Figure 5
was not an artifact of the method but reflected real social patterns
(Labov 1966a:342 ff).   The Lower East Side data most comparable

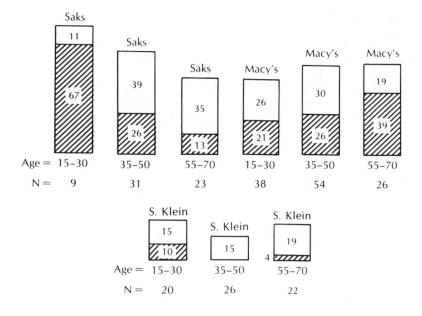

*Figure 5:   Stratification of (r) by store and age level.   Shaded
area = % all (r-1); unshaded area = % some (r-1); % no (r-1)
not shown.   N = total number of cases.*

to the department store study are the distribution of (r) by age
and class in Style B - the relatively careful speech which is the
main bulk of the individual interview.   To Saks, Macy's, Kleins,
we can compare upper middle class, lower middle class, and working
class as a whole.   The age ranges which are most comparable to
the department store ranges are 20-29, 30-39, and 40-.   (Since
the department store estimates are quite rough,   there would be
no gain in trying to match the figures exactly.)   Figure 6 is
then the age and class display for the Lower East Side use of
(r) most comparable to Figure 5.   Again, we see that the highest
status group shows the inverse correlation of (r-1) with age:
younger speakers use more (r-1); the second-highest status group
shows (r) at a lower level and the reverse correlation with age;
and the working-class groups at a still lower level with no particular correlation with age.

This is a very striking confirmation, since the two studies
have quite complementary sources of error.   The Lower East Side
survey was a secondary random sample, based on a Mobilization
for Youth survey, with complete demographic information on each
informant.   The interviews were tape-recorded, and a great deal
of data on (r) was obtained from each speaker in a wide variety
of styles.   On the other hand, the department-store study involved
a much greater likelihood of error on a number of counts: the
small amount of data per informant, the method of notation, the
absence of tape recording and reliance on short-term memory,
the method of sampling, the estimation of age of the informant,
and the lack of background data on the informants.   Most of
these sources of error are inherent in the method.   To compensate
for them, we had the uniformity of the interview procedure, the
location of the informants in their primary role as employees, the
larger number of cases within a single cell, the simplicity of the
data, and above all the absence of the biasing effect of the
formal linguistic interview.   The Lower East Side survey was
weak in just those areas where the department-store study was
strong, and strong where it was weak.   The methodological differences are summed up in Table VI.

The convergence of the Lower East Side survey and the
department-store survey therefore represents the ideal solution
to the Observer's Paradox: that our goal is to observe the way
people use language when they are not being observed.   All of
our methods involve an approximation to this goal: when we
approach from two different directions, and get the same result,
we can feel confident that we have reached past the Observer's
Paradox to the structure that exists independently of the analyst.

Given the pattern of Figure 5 as a social fact, how can we
explain it?   The suggestions advanced in our preliminary note
seem to be moving in the right direction, but at that time we
had not isolated the hypercorrect pattern of the lower middle
class nor identified the crossover pattern characteristic of change
in progress.   We must draw more material from the later research
to solve this problem.

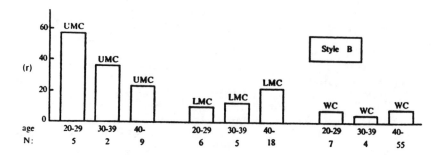

Figure 6:   Classification of (r) by age and class on the Lower East Side: in style B, careful speech.

Figures 5 and 6 are truncated views of the three-dimensional distribution of the new r-pronouncing norm by age, style, and social class.   Figure 7 shows two of the stylistic cross sections from the more detailed study of the Lower East Side population, with four subdivisions by age.   The dotted line shows us how the highest status group (Class 9) introduces the new r-pronouncing norm in casual speech.   In Style A only upper-middle-class speakers under 40 show any sizeable amount of (r-1).   None of

TABLE VI.

	Lower East Side study	Department-store study
LES > DS		
sampling	random	informants available at specific locations
recording of data	tape-recorded	short term memory & notes
demographic data	complete	minimal: by inspection & inference
amount of data	large	small
stylistic range	wide	narrow
DS > LES		
size of sample	moderate	large
location	home, alone	at work, with others
social context	interview	request for information
effect of observation	maximal	minimal
total time per subject (location and interview)	4-8 hours	5 minutes

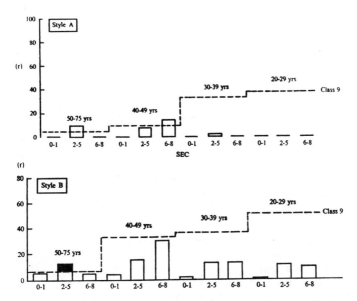

Figure 7:   Development of class stratification of (r) for casual speech (Style A) and careful speech (Style B) in apparent time. SEC = socioeconomic class scale.

the younger speakers in the other social groups show any response to this norm in Style A, though some effect can be seen in the middle-aged subjects, especially in the second-highest status group (Class 6-8, lower middle class). In Style B, this imitative effect is exaggerated, with the middle-aged lower-middle-class group coming very close to the upper-middle-class norm. In more formal styles, not shown here, this subgroup shows an even sharper increase in r-pronunciation, going beyond the upper-middle-class norm in the "hypercorrect" pattern that has appeared for this group in other studies (Levine and Crockett 1966; Shuy, Wolfram, and Riley 1967). Figure 7 is not a case of the reversal of the age distribution of (r-1); rather it is a one-generation lag in the peak of response to the new norm. The second-highest status group responds to the new norm with a weaker form of imitation in connected speech, with middle-aged speakers adopting the new norm of the younger high-status speakers; Figure 8 shows this schematically. Our studies do not give the exact profile of the use of (r) among younger upper-middle-class speakers, since we did not focus on that age range. In later observations, I have met some upper-middle-class youth who use 100 percent (r-1), but in most families, (r-1) is still a superposed pronunciation in adolescence and Figure 8 reflects this. If we wish to express the (r-1) distribution in a single function, we can say that it is inversely correlated with distance from the highest-status group (taking Class 9 as 1, Classes 6-8 as 2, Classes 2-5 as 3, and

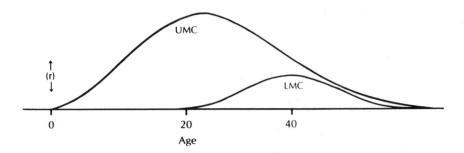

Figure 8: Hypothetical distribution of (r) as an incoming prestige feature.

Classes 0-1 as 4). It is also directly correlated with the formality of style and the amount of attention paid to speech (taking casual speech, style A, as 0, careful speech, style B, as 1, etc.). The slope of style shifting is modified by a function which may be called the "Index of Linguistic Insecurity" (ILI), which is maximized for the second-highest status group. The age distribution must be shown as greatest for the upper middle class at age 20 and at age 40 for the lower middle class. We can formalize these observations by writing

$$(r-1) = -a \text{ (Class)} + b \text{ (Style) (ILI)} - c |(\text{Class}) \cdot 20 - (\text{Age})| + d$$

The third term is minimized for the upper middle class at age 20, for the lower middle class at age 40, the working class at age 60, etc. Figure 7 supports this semiquantitative expression of a wave effect, which still has a number of unspecified constants.

There is a considerable difference between the behavior of the highest-status group and the others. The upper middle class develops the use of (r-1) early in life - as a variable expression of relative formality to be found at all stylistic levels. For the other groups in New York City, there is no solid basis for (r-1) in the vernacular style of casual speech; for them, (r-1) is a form which requires some attention paid to speech if it is realized at all. As in so many other formal marks of style-shifting, the lower middle class overdoes the process of correction. This is a process learned late in life. When speakers who are now 40-50 were growing up, the prestige norm was not (r-1) but (r-0). Before World War II, the New York City schools were dominated by an Anglophile tradition which taught that (r-1) was a provincial feature, an incorrect inversion of the consonant, and that the correct pronunciation of orthographic *r* in *car* was (r-0), [ka·], in accordance with "international English".[10] No adjustment in the pronunciation of this consonant was then necessary for New Yorkers who were trying to use the prestige norm

- it was only vowel quality which had to be corrected. This r-less norm can be seen in the formal speech of upper-middle-class speakers, over 40, and lower-middle-class speakers over 50. It also appears in subjective-reaction tests for older speakers. The lower-middle-class speakers who now shift to (r-1) in formal styles have abandoned their prestige norm and are responding to the form used by the younger high-status speakers that they come into contact with. On the other hand, many upper-middle-class speakers adhere to their original norm, in defiance of the prevailing trend. The pattern which we have observed in the department-store survey is therefore a reflection of the linguistic insecurity of the lower middle class, which has led the older generation to adopt the most recent norm of (r-1) in preference to the older norm. The process of linguistic socialization is slower for lower-middle-class groups who do not go to college than for upper-middle-class speakers, who begin adjusting to the new norm in the upper class tracks of the academic high schools. For those who do not follow this path, it takes 10 to 20 years to reach maximum sensitivity to the hierarchical organization of formal language in their community.

SOME METHODOLOGICAL DIRECTIONS

The most important conclusion of the department-store study is that rapid and anonymous studies can be a valuable source of information on the sociolinguistic structure of a speech community. There are a number of directions in which we can extend and improve such methods. While some sources of error are inherent in the method, others can be eliminated with sufficient attention.

In the department-store survey, the approach to sampling might have been more systematic. It would have been preferable to select every *nth* sales person, or to use some other method that would avoid the bias of selecting the most available subject in a given area. As long as such a method does not interfere with the unobtrusive character of the speech event, it would reduce sampling bias without decreasing efficiency. Another limitation is that the data were not tape-recorded. The transcriber, myself, knew what the object of the test was, and it is always possible that an unconscious bias in transcription would led to some doubtful cases being recorded as (r-1) in Saks, and as (r-0) in Kleins.[11] A third limitation is in the method used to elicit emphatic speech. Figure 2 indicates that the effect of stylistic variation may be slight as compared to the internal phonological constraint of preconsonantal vs. final position. The total percentages for all three stores bear this out.

% of all (r-1) for each position

Casual		Emphatic	
fourth	floor	fourth	floor
23	39	24	48

A simple request for repetition has only a limited effect in inducing more formal speech. The use of reading passages, word lists, and minimal pairs in the Lower East Side study gave a wider range of styles. It might be possible to enlarge the stylistic range in rapid and anonymous studies by emphasizing the difficulty in hearing by one technique or another.

The sources of error in the department-store study are offset by the comparability of the three subsections, the size of the sample, and the availability of the population for rechecking. Though the individual speakers can be relocated, the representative population can easily be reexamined for longitudinal studies of change in progress. There are limitations of such a "pseudo-panel" as compared to a true panel study of the same individuals; but the advantages in cost and efficiency are overwhelming.

With such promising results in hand, it should be possible to refine and improve the methods used, and apply them in a wider range of contexts. In large cities it is reasonable to select single large institutions like department stores, but there is no reason to limit rapid and anonymous surveys to sales people or to institutions of this character. We can turn to any large body of individuals located at fixed "social addresses" and accessible to interaction with the public: policemen, postal clerks, secretaries, ushers, guides, bus drivers, taxi drivers, street peddlers and demonstrators, beggars, construction workers, etc. The public groups which are most clearly identified tend to be concentrated towards the lower end of the social scale, with sales people at the upper end. But we can reach a more general public by considering shoppers, spectators at sports events, parades or construction sides, amateur gardeners, park strollers, and passersby in general; here the general character of the residential area can serve the same differentiating function as the three department stores mentioned above. Many professionals of relatively high social standing are available for public interaction: particularly teachers, doctors, and lawyers. Such public events as courtroom trials and public hearings allow us to monitor the speech of a wide range of socially located and highly differentiated individuals. [12]

There is in all such methods a bias towards those populations that are available to public interaction, and against those which are so located as to insure privacy: business and social leaders, or those engaged in aesthetic, scholarly, scientific, or illegal activities. Any of these groups can be studied with sufficient ingenuity: sociolinguistic research should certainly rise to the challenge to develop rapid and anonymous studies that will escape the limitations of convenience. But it should be emphasized that since those who are most available to public interaction may have the most direct effect upon linguistic change and the sociolinguistic system, the bias through missing the more extreme and obscure ends of the social spectrum is not as great as it may first appear.

Since the department-store survey was carried out in Manhattan, several parallel studies have been made. In Suffolk County, Long Island, rapid and anonymous observations of the use of (r) were made by Patricia Allen (1968). In three stratified stores, 156 employees were observed. In the highest-status store (Macy's), only 27 percent of the subjects used no (r-1); in the intermediate store (Grant City), 40 percent; and in the low-status store (Floyd's), 60 percent. We see that the general New York City pattern has moved outward from the city, producing a comparable stratification of (r) in three stores of a somewhat narrower range than those studied in Manhattan. Our own analysis of the New York City situation shows that rapid and anonymous surveys of this kind cannot be interpreted fully without detailed knowledge of the dialect history of the area, and a more systematic study of the distribution of linguistic variables and subjective norms. [13] In this case, rapid and anonymous surveys should be considered a supplement or preliminary to other methods, not substitutions for them. Yet there are cases where rapid methods can give solutions to problems that have never been circumnavigated by conventional techniques. We have used observations of the speech of telephone operators to construct a national map of the merger of the low back vowels in *hock* and *hawk*, and the merger of *i* and *e* before nasals in *pin* and *pen*. In our recent study of the Puerto Rican speech community in New York City, we utilized such natural experimentation to find out what percentage of those heard speaking Spanish on the street were raised in the United States, and what percentage were born in Puerto Rico (Labov and Pedraza 1971).

Future studies of language in its social context should rely more heavily on rapid and anonymous studies, as part of a general program of utilizing unobtrusive measures to control the interactive effect of the observer (Webb et al. 1966). But our rapid and anonymous studies are not passive indices of social use, like observations of wear and tear in public places. They represent a form of nonreactive experimentation in which we avoid the bias of the experimental context and the irregular interference of prestige norms but still control the behavior of subjects. We are just beginning to study speech events like *asking for directions*, isolating the invariant rules which govern them, and on this basis develop the ability to control a large body of socially located public speech in a natural setting. We see rapid and anonymous observations as the most important experimental method in a linguistic program which takes as its primary object the language used by ordinary people in their everyday affairs.

FOOTNOTES

[1] This article is based upon Chapters 3 and 9 of *The Social Stratification of English in New York City* (1966), revised in the light of further work with rapid and anonymous observations. I am indebted to Frank Anshen and Marvin Maverick Harris for reference to illuminating replications of this study (Allen 1968, Harris 1968).

[2] C. Wright Mills, *White Collar* (New York: Oxford University Press, 1956), p. 173. See also p. 243: "The tendency of white-collar people to borrow status from higher elements is so strong that it has carried over to all social contacts and features of the work-place. Salespeople in department stores . . . frequently attempt, although often unsuccessfully, to borrow prestige from their contact with customers, and to cash it in among work colleagues as well as friends off the job. In the big city the girl who works on 34th Street cannot successfully claim as much prestige as the one who works on Fifth Avenue or 57th Street."

[3] This statement is fully confirmed by answers to a question on newspaper readership in the Mobilization for Youth Survey of the Lower East Side. The readership of the *Daily News* and *Daily Mirror* (now defunct) on the one hand, and the *New York Times* and *Herald Tribune* (now defunct) on the other hand, is almost complementary in distribution by social class.

[4] Macy's sales employees are represented by a strong labor union, while Saks is not unionized. One former Macy's employee considered it a matter of common knowledge that Saks wages were lower than Macy's, and that the prestige of the store helped to maintain its nonunion position. Bonuses and other increments are said to enter into the picture. It appears that it is more difficult for a young girl to get a job at Saks than at Macy's. Thus Saks has more leeway in hiring policies, and the tendency of the store officials to select girls who speak in a certain way will pay a part in the stratification of language, as well as the adjustment made by the employees to their situation. Both influences converge to produce stratification.

[5] A former Macy's employee told me of an incident that occurred shortly before Christmas several years ago. As she was shopping in Lord and Taylor's, she saw the president of the company making the rounds of every aisle and shaking hands with every employee. When she told her fellow employees at Macy's about this scene, the most common remark was, "How else do you get someone to work for that kind of money?" One can say that not only do the employees of higher-status stores borrow prestige from their employer - it is also deliberately loaned to them.

[6] The interviewer in all cases was myself. I was dressed in middle-class style, with jacket, white shirt and tie, and used my normal pronunciation as a college-educated native of New Jersey (r-pronouncing).

[7] Notes were also made on the department in which the employee was located, but the numbers for individual departments are not large enough to allow comparison.

[8] The extreme style shifting of the second-highest status group appears throughout the New York City pattern, and is associated with an extreme sensitivity to the norms of an exterior reference group.

[9] In the sample as a whole, 17 informants with distinct foreign accents were found, and one with regional characteristics which were clearly not of New York City origin. The foreign language speakers in Saks had French, or other western European accents, while those in Kleins had Jewish and other eastern European accents. There were three Puerto Rican employees in the Kleins sample, one in Macy's, none in Saks. There were 70 men and 194 women. Men showed the following small differences from women in percentages of (r-1 usage:

	men	women
all (r-1)	22	30
some (r-1)	22	17
no (r-1)	57	54

[10] See for example *Voice and Speech Problems*, a text written for New York City schools in 1940 by Raubicheck, Davis, and Carll (1940:336):

> There are many people who feel that an effort should be made to make the pronunciation conform to the spelling, and for some strange reason, they are particularly concerned with *r*. We all pronounce *calm, psalm, almond, know, eight, night,* and *there* without worrying . . . Yet people who would not dream of saying kni: or psai' kɒlədʒi insist on attempting to sound the *r* in words like pɑ·k or fɑðə just because an *r* marks the spot where our ancestors used a trill . . . More often than not, people do not really say a third sound in a word like park but merely say the vowel : with the tongue tip curled back toward the throat. This type of vowel production is known as "Inversion."

Letitia Raubicheck was the head of the speech program in the New York City schools for many years and exerted a powerful influence on the teaching of English there. The norm of "international English" was maintained by William Tilly of Columbia and followed by Raubicheck and many others in the 1930's and 1940's. As far as I know, this norm has lost entirely its dominant position in the school system: a detailed study of its disappearance from the radio networks and the school system in the 1940's would tell us a great deal about the mechanism of such shifts in the prestige form.

[11] When the phonetic transcriptions were first made, doubtful cases were marked as *d* and were not included in the tabulations

made later.   There is however room for interviewer bias in the
decision between (r-0) and d and between d and (r-1).

[12] Hearings of the New York City Board of Education were
recorded during the study of New York City, and preliminary
analysis of the data shows that the pattern of social and stylistic
stratification of (r) can easily be recovered from the wide variety
of speakers who appear in these hearings.   Courtroom proceedings
at the New York Court of General Sessions are a natural focus
for such studies, but speakers often lower their voices to the
point that spectators cannot hear them clearly.   Only a small
beginning has been made on the systematic study of passerby.
Plakins (1969) approached a wide variety of pedestrians in a
Connecticut town with requests for directions to an incomprehen-
sible place, phrased at three levels of politeness.   She found
systematic differences in mode of response according to dress
(as an index of socioeconomic position) and mode of inquiry;
there were no "rude" responses [huh?] to polite inquiries.

[13] Allen's tables resemble the New York City patterns but
with one major difference; the number of speakers who use all
(r-1) is roughly constant in all three stores: 27 percent in
Floyd's; 27 percent in Grant City, 32 percent in Macy's.   Examination of the distribution in apparent time showed that this phenomenon was due to the presence of a bimodal split in the lower-store
adults (over 30 years old).   Eighty percent used no (r-1) and
20 percent used a consistent all (r-1):   there were none who
varied.   On the other hand, 50 percent of the adults were showing
variable (r) in the two other stores.   This points to the presence
of an older r-pronouncing vernacular which is now dominated by
the r-less New York City pattern (Kurath and McDavid 1961),
but survives among working-class speakers.   The disengagement
of such bimodal patterns is a challenging problem (Levine and
Crockett 1966), and certainly requires a more systematic survey.
Similar complexity is suggested in the results of rapid and anonymous survey of stores in Austin, Texas, by M. M. Harris (1969).
In this basically r-pronouncing   area, the prestige norms among
whites appear to be a   weak constricted [r], with a strongly
retroflex consonant gaining ground among younger speakers.
But for the few blacks and Mexican-Americans encountered, this
strong [r] seems to be the norm aimed at in careful articulation.
Although these results are only suggestive, they are the kind of
preliminary work which is required to orient a more systematic
investigation towards the crucial variables of the sociolinguistic
structure of that community.

REFERENCES

Allen, P. 1968. /r/ variable in the speech of New Yorkers in department stores. Unpublished research paper, SUNY, Stony Brook.

Barber, Bernard. 1957. *Social Stratification*. New York: Harcourt, Brace.

Bronstein, A. 1962. Lets take another look at New York City speech. *American Speech* 37: 13-26.

Hubbell, A. F. 1950. *The Pronunciation of English in New York City*. New York: Columbia University Press.

Kurath, H., and R. McDavid. 1951. *The Pronunciation of English in the Atlantic States*. Ann Arbor: University of Michigan Press.

Labov, W. 1966. *The Social Stratification of English in New York City*. Arlington, Virginia: Center for Applied Linguistics.

Labov, W., P. Cohen, C. Robins, and J. Lewis. 1968. A study of non-standard English of Negro and Puerto Rican speakers in New York City. Final report, Cooperative Research Project 3288. 2 vols. Philadelphia, Pa.: U.S. Regional Survey, 204 N. 35th Street., Philadelphia 19104.

Levine, L., and H. J. Crockett, Jr. 1966. Speech variation in a piedmont community: postvocalic *r*. In Lieberson 1966

Lieberson, S., ed. 1966. *Explorations in sociolinguistics*. Special issue of *Sociological Inquiry* 36 (2).

Shuy, R., W. Wolfram, and W. K. Riley. 1967. *A Study of Social Dialects in Detroit*. Final Report, Project 6-1347. Washington, D.C.: Office of Education.

THE VOCALIZATION OF INTERVOCALIC

/l/ IN PHILADELPHIA

Sharon Ash

The vocalization and deletion of liquids is a widespread phenomenon which has received much attention in the case of /r/ and has also been documented for various languages in the case of /l/, including French (Fox and Wood, 1968), Polish (Stieber, 1973), and various dialects of English (Hall, 1942; Labov, Cohen, Robins, and Lewis, 1968; Allen, 1976; and Wolfram and Christian, 1976). The variables reported almost, if not entirely, occur in preconsonantal position. In Philadelphia, word-final /l/ is vocalized with great frequency, and for some speakers the vocalization rule may be categorical. This appears to be a recent development in Philadelphia speech, as it is not mentioned at all in Tucker's observations on distinctive aspects of the Philadelphia dialect in 1944. He does remark on the constraining effect of final /l/ on the fronting of /ow/ and /uw/, but he writes nothing of any peculiarity in the /l/ itself. The tendency to vocalize /l/ has spread to every linguistic environment in Philadelphia. This paper is a first report of the /l/-vocalization that occurs variably in intervocalic position in Philadelphia speech.

Vocalization occurs when the tongue does not rise in the mouth far enough to contact the hard palate, either on the alveolar ridge, as is typical for syllable-initial and intervocalic /l/ in most dialects of American English, or with raising of the back of the tongue, giving the velarized /l/ of syllable-final position. Velarized /l/ is a frequent allophone of /l/ in Philadelphia, especially in syllable-final position, but it also occurs in intervocalic position. When contact with the roof of the mouth fails altogether, the result is a segment that resembles a voiced glide articulated far back in the mouth. It may also be accompanied by lip-rounding, which results in the sound of /w/, or it may be deleted entirely, resulting in two vowels in hiatus.

The sample examined for this report consists of interviews of 18 individual speakers and one group of eight children. All the speakers except two were born and raised in Philadelphia; of the two who were not from the city proper, one had been born in

From *The SECOL Review* 6:162-175, 1982. Reprinted with permission.

the city and lived there for eight years, then moved to a suburb
about a mile north of the city limits for twelve years, and finally
moved back to the city three years before the interview was
conducted. The other had lived until the age of 25 in another
suburb adjacent to the city and then moved to the city proper
two years before the interview was conducted. The speakers
were all interviewed for periods of time ranging from 45 minutes
to more than three hours, during which time three speech styles
were sought: (1) casual style, with minimum self-monitoring, that
is, the style that is used when the speaker is emotionally involved
in the content of his speech, as in the case of first-person
narratives for example; (2) careful style, the usual conversational
speaking style of a person being interviewed; and (3) word list
style. In most cases the speakers were asked to read a list of
words at the end of the interview to elicit fully stressed instances
of words of interest with attention of the speaker focused on
production of the given words.

Coding of the tapes yielded 2,978 occurrences of intervocalic
/l/. Each token was coded for six linguistic factors which were
thought possibly to affect vocalization; the stylistic factor just
described; and five speaker-dependent social factors: age, the
neighborhood in the city where the speaker grew up, ethnic
group, socioeconomic class, and sex.

The first linguistic factor to be considered is the vowel preceding the /l/. Preliminary examination of the data indicated
that preceding vowels could be classified as in table 1.

The probabilities in table 1 and subsequent tables are calculated
by the mathematical model originally advanced by Cedergren and
Sankoff (1974) and considerably refined since then. The version
currently in use is a logistic model which uses a maximum likelihood
algorithm for deriving the probabilities and provides a test of
the significance of factors. It is discussed in detail in Sankoff
and Labov (1979). The derived probabilities are interpreted as
the probability that occurrence of a given factor will result in
application of the rule, in this case, the vocalization of /l/,
when all other factors are held constant. The actual computer

TABLE I.   Intervocalic /l/ - Vocalization by Preceding Vowel

Vowel preceding IV /l/	% voc*	P(voc)**	Total N
nonlow front V's and glides	29	.39	1,091
low front	27	.65	265
low back	38	.68	413
nonlow back V's and glides	32	.59	279
reduced	5	.21	930

*percent of vocalization
**probability of vocalization

program used for the analysis has been modified over a period of time for use on the DEC PDP 11/10 at the University of Pennsylvania.

Calculation of the probabilities provides the benefit of being able to take into account the cooccurrence of factors with different effects on the rule. In the case of the data at hand, I suspect that nonlow front vowels show a relatively high percentage of vocalization because words in this category also fall into the category of marked lexeme, which favors application of the rule, and which is discussed in detail below. The suspicion of cooccurrence can be checked by determining the distribution of nonlow front vowels with respect to the category of marked lexeme. In this case, the suspicion proves to be correct: 62 percent of the cases of preceding nonlow front vowel occur in marked lexemes, and this group exhibits vocalization in 35 percent of the cases, while unmarked lexemes with nonlow front vowels preceding the /l/ show vocalization in only 20 percent of the cases. Therefore, the high cooccurrence of preceding nonlow front vowel with marked lexeme inflates the percentage of vocalization for tokens with preceding nonlow front vowel when it is considered alone. The probabilities give the more accurate picture of the effects of the different vowels.

The effects seen here can be readily explained as a function of the articulation of the vowel plus /l/ sequence. The articulation of a high or mid front vowel places the tongue precisely in position for articulating unvocalized /l/. It brings the tongue forward and up, so it is quite prepared to deflect up far enough to contact the alveolar ridge. In the case of low and back vowels, the opposite is the case; the tongue is not in a position to contact the alveolar ridge so easily; thus it is not surprising that those vowels are most likely to favor vocalization of a following /l/.

The low probability associated with reduced vowels preceding the /l/ indicates that schwa is high enough and front enough to facilitate articulation of unvocalized /l/, as are nonlow front vowels. In addition, the lack of stress may play an independent role in favoring the retention of unvocalized /l/.

The segment following the /l/ can also be expected to exert an effect on vocalization. The data initially seemed to suggest that a following unreduced vowel would inhibit vocalization, while a following reduced segment would favor it. The probabilities calculated by the variable rule program for the factors of following unreduced vowel, schwa, ɚ, and unstressed /iy/ (which was kept separate from other unreduced vowels because of its high frequency and because it is a high front vowel, which might have a distinct inhibiting effect on the rule) do not fit this set of expectations, however, as may be seen in table 2.

The percentages of vocalization are in line with what is predicted, but the probabilities, with the high value for unreduced vowels, are contrary to our expectations.

TABLE II.   Intervocalic /l/ - Vocalization by Following Segment

Segment following IV /l/	% voc	P(voc)	Total N
unreduced V*	8	.53	891
schwa	37	.60	771
unstressed /iy/	22	.33	996
ɚ	31	.55	320

*other than unstressed /iy/

The irregularity is resolved when this group of factors is redefined. The factor of unreduced vowels does not take into account the difference between unreduced unstressed vowels, as in *fellow*, and stressed vowels, as in *hello*. A stressed vowel following the /l/ causes the /l/ to resemble word-initial /l/, both in articulatory and in acoustical terms (Lehiste, 1964). A brief scan of the data on word-initial or syllable-initial /l/ reveals that those /l/'s are vocalized only rarely, in about two percent of the cases. Therefore, this group of segments following intervocalic /l/ should be redefined and the probabilities recalculated as shown in table 3.

Table 3 confirms that the vowel following intervocalic /l/ exerts an effect on the /l/ which depends primarily on the stress pattern of the word and secondarily on the nature of the following vowel. The strongest effect is the disfavoring of the rule associated with stress immediately following the /l/. A smaller negative effect on the rule is that exerted by following unstressed /iy/. The data confirm the prediction that anticipation of the high

TABLE III.   Intervocalic /l/ - Vocalization by Following Segment and Word Stress

Segment follow- ing IV /l/	% voc place of primary stress			P(voc)			Total N		
	P	E	F	P	E	F	P	E	F
unreduced V	26	6	1	.63	.42	.17	238	78	575
schwa	34	41		.61	.65	.65	535	234	
unstressed /iy/	25	11		.33	.58		811	185	
ɚ	36	14		.53	.62		240	78	

P = immediately preceding IV /l/
E = immediately following IV /l/
F = neither immediately preceding nor immediately following IV /l/

TABLE IV. Intervocalic /l/ - Vocalization by Word Stress

Place of primary word stress	% voc	P(voc)	Total N
immediately preceding IV /l/	29	.64	1,828
immediately following IV /l/	1	.22	575
elsewhere	23	.68	575

front vowel after the /l/ places the tongue in a position which favors articulation without vocalization, as happens also in the case of preceding high front vowel. A similar but much smaller inhibiting effect may be due to an unreduced vowel following the /l/ when the stress falls neither on the immediately preceding nor the immediately following vowel.

We may now examine the overall effects of word stress in table 4. The data in table 4 are as expected. Stress following the /l/ strongly inhibits vocalization, while stress preceding /l/ or elsewhere strongly favors vocalization. There appears to be a small difference between the latter two factors, but this difference is not statistically significant.

The effect of stress goes beyond the level of the word; it is also significant at the level of the phrase, as can be seen in table 5. There is a rather small, but again statistically significant correlation in table 5: lighter stress favors vocalization.

Word class, in terms of nouns, names of people and places, adjectives, and so on, was thought initially to have a possible effect on /l/-vocatization. The data in table 5, however, show that this is not the case. Judging from the percentages in table 6, proper names seem to have some effect favoring vocalization as compared to all other types of words. The probabilities, however, contradict this inference. Again, a cooccurrence of factors is the likely cause of the discrepancy between percentages and probabilities. In the second part of table 6, we see that a large number of the names in the sample fall in the category of marked lexeme, which favors vocalization and which was mentioned earlier in connection with the vowel preceding the /l/. In consideration of these results, I conclude that word class has no bearing on /l/-vocalization.

The category of marked lexeme was motivated by evidence that rules of linguistic change affect individual lexemes one at a

TABLE V. Intervocalic /l/ - Vocalization by Phrase Stress

Level of phrase stress	% voc	P(voc)	Level N
heavy	18	.42	1,731
medium	28	.50	880
weak	32	.58	367

TABLE VI.   Intervocalic /l/ - Vocalization by Word Class

Word Class	% voc	P(voc)	Total N	% voc (marked lex.)	%voc (un-marked)	Total N	Total N
noun	19	.47	1,218	8*	20	13	1,205
name	37	.51	287	47	24	172	115
adjective	22	.47	410	--	22	--	409
verb	21	.50	295	--	21	--	295
adverb & function word	25	.56	768	31	14	506	262

*These items are the occurrences of the word *really* in word lists.

time (Chen and Wang, 1975; Labov, 1981).   I chose three items
as candidates for being in the forefront of intervocalic /l/-vocaliza-
tion.   The items are the very high frequency adverb *really*, *Philadelphia*, and the common by-name of the city, *Philly*.   Table 7
gives the data for the effect of this category on vocatization.
    In table 7 the relationships between marked and unmarked
lexical items agree for the percentages and probabilities of vocalization.   The difference between the two classes is considerable.
The words to which marked lexical status were ascribed were
chosen essentially by pure speculation; it is gratifying to see
that this experiment produced positive results.   It also suggests
that a great deal more could be done to pursue this line of
inquiry.
    Overall, vocalization of intervocalic /l/ occurs in 23 percent
of the cases; thus clearly the first two of the marked items
favor vocalization substantially.   That the name of the city favors
the rule more than the adverb might be thought to be due in
part to the extremely weakened articulation of the syllables surrounding the intervocalic /l/.   This seems especially likely since
the name *Philly*, when considered separately, does not appear to

TABLE VII.   Intervocalic /l/ - Vocalization by Lexical Status

Lexical status	% voc	P(voc)	Total N
unmarked	20	.39	2,286
marked: overall	35	.61	692
by lexeme:			
really	31	.44	520
Philadelphia	60	.77	115
Philly	19	.34	57

TABLE VIII.   Intervocalic /1/ - Vocalization by Style and Phrase
              Stress

Style	all levels of stress			heavy stress only	
	% voc	P(voc)	Total N	% voc	Total N
casual	27	.57	341	20	163
careful	26	.54	1,994	24	926
word list	10	.38	643	10	643

share the special lexical status of the other two items. However,
for unmarked lexemes with a nonlow front vowel preceding the
/1/, vocalization occurs in 21 percent of the cases when stress
neither precedes nor immediately follows the /1/, as it does in
Philadelphia. .   This suggests that stress is not a significant
factor in the differing degrees of vocalization of *really* and *Philadelphia*, but rather that there is a difference inherent in the
words themselves.

To sum up the effects of the linguistic factors on /1/-vocaliza-
tion, we have seen that by and large the linguistic condition of
the rule is quite straightforward.   Stress is the single most
important factor governing vocalization, and it intersects with
the distribution of vowels in the interesting way we have seen in
the case of the segment following the /1/.   Special lexical status
also has a straightforward effect on vocalization which was predicted by means of fortunate speculation.

Style is also a constraining feature for /1/-vocalization.   The
data on the effect of style are to be found in table 8.

There is no significant difference between /1/-vocalization in
casual and careful style, but in word lists there is a great deal
of correction. Again, the question of stress arises: the reading
of a word list is such that each word is fully stressed, and it
might be questioned whether that feature contributes heavily to
the relatively low level of /1/-vocalization in word list items.
The general level of /1/-vocalization is so low that people in
general are not aware of it, and when it is brought to their
attention they do not make either a positive or negative judgment
about it.   Still, to resolve the question of whether it is the
heavy stress of the word list items or correction towards a norm
that constrains vocalization in word lists, we may compare the
vocalization of heavily stressed items in the three different styles
in the second part of table 8.   We can see that heavy stress
reduces the level of vocalization slightly, at least in the case of
casual speech, but the effect of word list style is still strong.

The social factors which might influence /1/-vocalization remain
to be considered.   Table 9 shows the data for /1/-vocalization as
a function of age.

The information in table 9 shows a clear increase in /1/-vocali-
zation with increasing age up to age 20, followed by a leveling

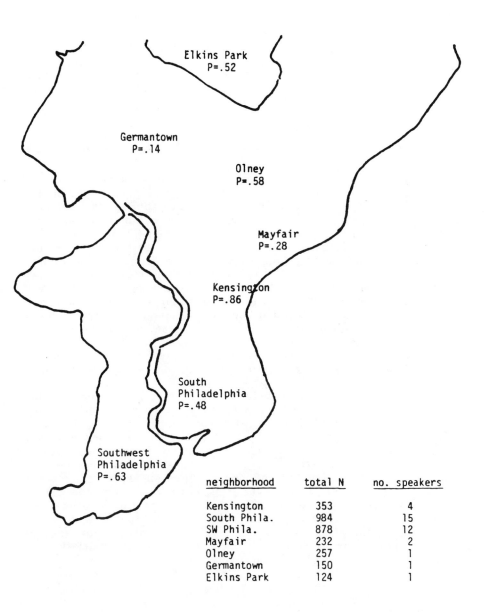

Fig. 1. Intervocalic /l/ - Vocalization by Neighborhood

TABLE IX.   Intervocalic /l/ - Vocalization by Age Group

Age group	% voc	P(voc)	Total N	Number of speakers
under 10	2	.16	103	3
10-19	11	.41	499	12
20-29	29	.78	576	6
30-39	25	.60	1,390	11
40-49	0	0	0	0
50-59	30	.80	380	3
60 and over	6	.27	30	1

off of the upward trend, and then an abrupt drop in use of vocalized /l/ after age 60. The trend is more pronounced in the percentage figures, but it follows the same course for both percentages and probabilities. This data suggests that /l/-vocalization originated when the people who are now in their 50s were acquiring their dialect, but it does not appear that young people now are advancing a change from unvocalized to vocalized intervocalic /l/.

Turning to the question of neighborhood within the city, we find a pattern which is illustrated in figure 1. The center of /l/-vocalization in Philadelphia is the large, long-established working-class neighborhood of Kensington, and one might deduce that /l/-vocalization has spread out from there, its influence falling off with increasing distance. The situation is further elaborated in figure 2, which shows the percentage of vocalization for the three neighborhoods represented by four or more speakers with respect to age.

Figure 2 supports the conclusion that /l/-vocalization originated in the area of Kensington, since the people who vocalized most there are about ten years older than the heaviest vocalizers in the other two neighborhoods. On the other hand, the pattern of change in progress is that the frequency of the incoming variant increases with decreasing age. Since in all cases here the frequency of vocalization falls off for younger speakers, some other process must be at work. Yet it is remarkable that the center of /l/-vocalization is Kensington, since this is the neighborhood that has originated other recent sound changes that are occurring in Philadelphia. It should come as no surprise that another sound change, or at least another case of phonetic variation, is strongest in that neighborhood.

Along with the question of neighborhood, the question of ethnicity must be considered. Table 10 shows the distribution of vocalized /l/ by ethnic group.

The typical pattern of sound change in Philadelphia is that innovations are introduced by the residents of the neighborhood of Kensington, which is heavily Irish. Since Kensington is the neighborhood where /l/-vocalization is strongest, we would expect

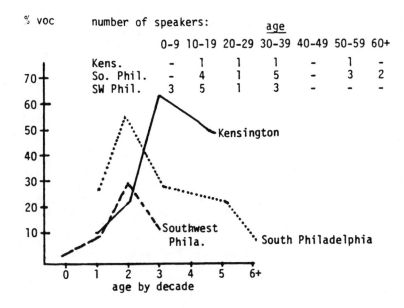

Fig. 2. Intervocalic /l/ - Vocalization by Neighborhood and Age

that the Irish would favor the vocalized variant the most. Examination of the data shows that this is not the case. Italian speakers, who are concentrated in South Philadelphia, usually are a little outside the mainstream of sound change in Philadelphia; the Italian language is still very much alive in South Philadelphia and plays a part in influencing the English of Italian Americans in the city. Since both Italian and Irish ethnics reside in Kensington and South Philadelphia, we are able to compare the two groups in the two neighborhoods in table 11.

TABLE X. Intervocalic /l/ - Vocalization by Ethnic Group

Ethnic group	% voc	P(voc)	Total N	Number of speakers
WASP	18	.63	179	2
Italian	29	.60	1,050	16
Irish	19	.27	602	7
German	37	.49	124	1
Jewish	34	.51	257	1
East European	12	.51	766	9

TABLE XI.   Intervocalic /l/ - Vocalization for Two Ethnic Groups
             in Two Neighborhoods

	% voc		Total N		No. of speakers	
	Kens.	S. Phila.	Kens.	S. Phila.	Kens.	S. Phila.
Italian	52	30	163	718	2	10
Irish	36	13	190	23	2	1

The data in table 11 are remarkably well ordered: Italians
in both neighborhoods vocalize more than the Irish in the respective
neighborhoods, and both ethnic groups in Kensington vocalize
more than the corresponding group in South Philadelphia. Thus
the overall picture of ethnicity as a determinant of vocalization is
anomalous, as is also the situation regarding age, for a case of
sound change in progress.

Social class, as determined by joint consideration of education
and occupation, is an additional factor which plays a part in
linguistic change. It has been found that change generally is
initiated by the upper working class (Labov, 1980). In this
sample, however, the middle class appears to be ahead in intervocalic /l/-vocalization, according to the data in table 12.

The difference in probabilities in table 12 is fairly small, but
it is statistically significant in showing that the middle class
leads in /l/-vocalization.

The final parameter to be considered is sex. The relevant
data are reported in table 13.

Again, the data contradict the usual prediction for a sound
change in progress. Most sound changes are led by women,
with a few exceptions. In this data, though, men are somewhat
in the lead, and again the difference between men and women is
statistically significant. To elaborate the picture further, we
may consider vocalization as a function of sex and style in figure
3.

In both casual and careful styles, men vocalize more than
women, although the difference is of doubtful significance in careful style ($x^2 = 3.77$; $.1 > P > .05$). There is no significant difference between casual and careful styles for each group, but for

TABLE XII.   Intervocalic /l/ - Vocalization by Social Class

Class	% voc	P(voc)	Total N	Number of speakers
working	21	.43	1,848	28
middle	27	.57	1,130	8

TABLE XIII. Intervocalic /l/ - Vocalization by Sex

Sex	% voc	P(voc)	Total N	Number of speakers
men	26	.60	1,658	18
women	19	.40	1,320	18

both sexes there is a higher significant difference between careful and word list styles. Furthermore, there is virtually no difference between the vocalization behavior of men and women in word list style. We conclude that men and women share the same overt norm for the (L) variable, but they show different behavior in actual speech.

What does all this odd data on social factors mean? The linguistic factors condition /l/-vocalization in natural, predictable ways. The data on neighborhood are consistent with our expectations for a new phonological variable in Philadelphia, but this is not the case for age, ethnicity, class, and sex.

The fundamental question posed by the data is whether the vocalization of /l/ is an advancing sound change or whether the new variant is receding. If it were advancing, we would expect

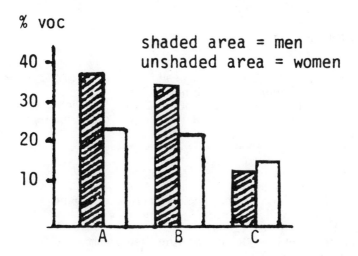

Fig. 3. Intervocalic /l/ - Vocalization by Style and Sex

to see the most vocalization by teenagers and younger children, especially by the Irish, and especially by women. In fact, the opposite of all these predictions has been found to be the case. We are forced to conclude that /l/-vocalization in intervocalic position has lost its thrust and is receding. This view provides a highly consistent picture. It predicts that teenagers will not show more extensive use of the variant than their elders and that young children under ten will show even less vocalization than speakers between the ages of 10 and 19. It also predicts that the Irish would have abandoned vocalized /l/ more than other ethnic groups and that women would have discarded it more than men. Finally, it predicts that the working class would be getting away from the new variant more than the middle class. In short, we find exactly the situation we would predict for sound change in progress, except that the rule which is being advanced is the discarding of vocalized /l/, rather than the spread of vocalized /l/. It is consistent to find the highest level of vocalized /l/ in the neighborhood of Kensington, since that is where the variant advanced the furthest before it began to lose ground.

The study of vocalized intervocalic /l/ in Philadelphia provides a unique case of an incipient sound change progressing normally and naturally in terms of linguistic parameters while being abruptly cut off by social considerations.

REFERENCES

Allen, H. B. 1976. *The Linguistic Atlas of the Upper Midwest.* Vol. 3. University of Minnesota Press.

Cedergren, H., and D. Sankoff. 1974. "Variable Rules: Performance as a Statistical Reflection of Competence." *Language*, 50:333-355.

Fox, J., and R. Wood. 1968. *A Concise History of the French Language.* Oxford University Press.

Hall, J. S. 1942. *The Phonetics of Great Smoky Mountain Speech.* King's Crown Press.

Labov, W. 1980. "The Social Origins of Sound Change." In W. Labov (ed). *Locating Language in Time and Space.* New York: Academic Press.

Labov, W. 1981. "Resolving the Neogrammarian Controversy." *Language*, 57:267-308.

Labov, W., P. Cohen, C. Robins, and J. Lewis. 1968. *A Study of the Non-Standard English of Negro and Puerto Rican Speakers in New York City.* Cooperative Research Project #3288 of the Office of Education, U.S. Dept. of HEW.

Lehiste, I. 1964. *Acoustical Characteristics of Selected English Consonants.* Indiana University Press.

Sankoff, D., and W. Labov. 1979. "On the Use of Variable Rules." *Language in Society*, 8:189-222.

Stieber, Z. 1973. *A Historical Phonology of the Polish Language*. Carl Winter Universitatsverlag.

Tucker, R. W. 1944. "Notes on the Philadelphia Dialect." *American Speech*, 19:37-42.

Wang, W. S.-Y., and M. Y. Chen. 1975. "Sound Change: Auctuation and Implementation." *Language*, 51:255-281.

Wolfram, W., and D. Christian. 1976. *Appalachian Speech*. Center for Applied Linguistics.

TOWARD A THEORY OF

SOCIAL DIALECT VARIATION

Anthony S. Kroch

INTRODUCTION

Over the past ten years the study of language in its social context has become a mature field with a substantial body of method and empirical results.[1]   As a result of this work we are arriving at new insights into such classical problems as the origin and diffusion of linguistic change, the nature of stylistic variation in language use, and the effect of class structure on linguistic variation within a speech community.   Advances in sociolinguistics have been most evident in the study of co-variation between social context and the sound pattern of speech.   The results reported in numerous monographs have laid the basis for substantial theoretical progress in our understanding of the factors that govern dialect variation in stratified communities, at least in its phonological aspect.[2]   The formulation of theories of the causes of phonological variation that go beyond guesswork and vague generalities appears at last to be possible.   Therefore, we offer the following discussion, based on the material that is now available, as a contribution to the development of an explanatory theory of the mechanisms underlying social dialect variation. Although we shall state our views strongly, we know that they are far from definitive.   We present them, not as positions to be defended at all costs, but as stimuli to further theoretical reflection in a field that has been, thus far, descriptively oriented.

The thrust of our proposal can be expressed in the form of the following two-part hypothesis that, while not exhaustive, covers a wide range of recently investigated cases: *First*, the public prestige dialect[3] of the elite in a stratified community differs from the dialect(s) of the non-elite strata (working class and other) in at least one phonologically systematic way.[4]   In particular, it characteristically resists normal processes of phonetic conditioning (both articulatory and perceptual) that the speech of non-elite strata regularly undergo.   This tendency holds both

Reprinted from *Language in Society*, 7:17-36, 1976, by Anthony S. Kroch by permission of Cambridge University Press.

for dynamic processes of linguistic change and for diachronically stable processes of inherent variation.[5] *Second*, the cause of stratified phonological differentiation within a speech community is to be sought not in purely linguistic factors but in ideology. Dominant social groups tend to mark themselves off symbolically as distinct from the groups they dominate and to interpret their symbols of distinctiveness as evidence of superior moral and intellectual qualities. This tendency shows itself not only in speech style but also in such other areas of social symbolism as dress, body carriage, and food. In all these areas dominant groups mark themselves off by introducing elaborated styles and by borrowing from external prestige groups; but in the case of pronunciation they also mark their distinctiveness in a negative way – that is by inhibiting many of the low level, variable processes of phonetic conditioning that characterize spoken language and that underlie regular phonological change. Because these processes are of variable application, they admit readily of non-linguistic influences. Of course, since the different social strata belong to the same speech community, their speech patterns influence one another profoundly. Processes that originate in the popular vernacular infiltrate the prestige dialect and processes of the prestige dialect extend to popular speech. The extent of these mutual influences is variable from case to case, depending on such social factors as the degree of linguistic self-consciousness of the prestige dialect speakers and the strength of their ideological influence on the population as a whole (see Barber 1964). It depends as well on a complex of linguistic, articulatory and perceptual factors.

In the discussion that follows we shall attempt to confirm this hypothesis by investigating, on the one hand, recent descriptions of the phonological differences among social dialects and, on the other hand, the evidence that has become available concerning the ideological motivation for these differences. We shall discover that popular dialects exhibit their greater susceptibility to phonetic conditioning in such features as simplified articulation, replacement or loss of perceptually weak segments, and a greater tendency to undergo 'natural' vowel shifts.[6] As far as ideology is concerned, we shall see that there is both experimental and historical evidence that prestige dialects require special attention to speech, attention motivated not by the needs of communication but by status consciousness.

CURRENT THEORY OF
DIALECT DIFFERENTIATION

Before we proceed with our argument, let us clarify the difference between our hypothesis and others' explanations for social dialect variation. In particular, we must state explicitly the relationship between our views and those of Labov, since his work provides so much of the empirical material available to theoretical reflection.   Labov's research has generated considerable evidence for the proposition that working-class speech is more susceptible to the processes of phonetic conditioning than is the prestige dialect.   Unfortunately, Labov and other contemporary sociolinguists neither state this principle explicitly nor attempt to provide an explanation for it.   Indeed, Labov is not willing to make a clear empirical claim on the linguistic character of social dialect variation.   His theoretical statements sometimes point towards our characterization of social dialect differences, but on other occasions he seems to take a position contrary to our proposal.

In the article 'The social setting of linguistic change,' Labov states that ordinary phonological change, what he calls 'change from below the level of conscious awareness,' generally does not originate in the highest status group in a speech community.   He says:

> It does sometimes happen that a feature will be introduced by the highest class in the social system, though as a rule this is not an innovating group.
>
> (Labov 1972: 295)

Changes which are introduced by the highest class tend to be conscious attempts to imitate an even more prestigious dialect outside the local area:

> Innovation by the highest-status group is normally a form of borrowing from outside sources, more or less conscious; with some exceptions these will be prestige forms.
>
> (Labov 1972: 290)

In a more recent article, however, he says:

> Dialect differentiation is not confined to uneducated lower-class people.   It is well known that some linguistic changes originate in the upper social groups.   Many of these represent the importation of forms from high-prestige foreign languages or classical standards. But some new developments seem to be pushed fa[r]ther and faster among educated speakers, at least until the change becomes noticed and subject to strong social correction.
>
> (Labov 1974: 224)

In his extensive study of vowel shifts currently in progress in English dialects (Labov, Yaeger & Steiner 1972) Labov does indicate that these shifts seem to originate in the popular vernacular, but elsewhere he explicitly denies that the vernacular differs from the prestige dialect in ease of articulation. In the 'Study of language in its social context,' he says:

> Why don't all people speak the prestige dialect?
> The usual response is to cite laziness, lack of
> concern, or isolation from the prestige norm.
> But there is no foundation for the notion that
> stigmatized   vernacular   forms   are   easier   to
> pronounce.   (Labov 1972: 249)

In this passage, Labov is clearly concerned with discrediting
the class-prejudiced notion that the working class vernacular is
an inferior or 'lazy' dialect.   He is, of course, correct to want
to defeat this prejudice; but the proper way to do so is not to
deny the fact, obvious from his own research, that non-prestige
dialects tend to be articulatorily more economical than the prestige
dialect.   Defeat of prejudice requeires rather that we give a
better explanation of this fact that the laziness 'theory' provides.
The only evidence Labov gives that vernacular forms are not
easier to pronounce is that the vowel shifts in progress in urban
working class vernaculars increase the muscular effort needed to
pronounce tense vowels over that required in standard English.
This point is, however, irrelevant to the existence of a tendency
toward ease of articulation because that tendency manifests itself
primarily in the consonant system, which Labov does not mention.
On another point, Labov's statement explicitly equates ease of
pronunciation with 'laziness' and lets the reader believe that if
the non-prestige dialect were easier to pronounce, then the charge
of laziness would be valid.   This is, of course, not so as we
shall see in our discussion of the motivation of social dialect
differences.

One of the reasons why Labov and other sociolinguists have
not seen the link between phonetic conditioning and social dialect
variation more clearly is that linguists' traditional attitudes toward
this variation are incompatible with the relationship that recent
studies have revealed.   Because these attitudes, in one form or
another, underlie most sociolinguistic theory, including the best
and most recent work, the implications of the empirical research
have been obscured.

The central assumption of linguists about the origin of dialect
variation has been that when sound changes arise in the speech
of individuals or small groups, the further spread of these changes
depends on the prestige of their users.   Under this assumption
there is no reason to expect the speech of non-elite groups to
be more susceptible to phonetic processes than that of the elite.
Indeed, it would lead one to expect either that social dialect
variation was phonologically unsystematic or that the speech of
the elite showed more phonetic conditioning than that of the common
people.   The first alternative results if one assumes that sound
change is not governed by substantive factors (as in Postal 1968),
the second if one assumes that sound change is so governed. A
position close to this latter is put forward in Joos (1952) and
argued for in Fischer (1964), although neither gives any empirical
findings to support his claim. Fisher says (quoting Joos's comment
in its entirety):

The clearest and most comprehensive statement
of social factors in linguistic change which
I have encountered is found in an article by
Martin Joos (1952). . . . He speaks of 'the
phonetic drift, which was kept going in the
usual way: that is, the dialects and idiolects
of higher prestige were more advanced in
this direction, and their speakers carried
the drift further along so as to maintain the
prestige-marking differences against their
pursuers.   The vanity factor is needed to
explain why phonetic drifts tend to continue
in the same direction; the "inertia" sometimes
invoked is a label and not an argument.'
This protracted pursuit of an elite by an envious
mass and the consequent 'flight' of the elite is in
my opinion the most important mechanism in
linguistic drift, not only in the phonetic drift
which Joos discusses, but in syntactic and
lexical drifting as well.

(Fischer 1964: 286)

Of course, our view, as put forward in the introduction to
this paper, contradicts all approaches that derive sound change
from innovation by a prestige group.   We are proposing instead
that:

1. ordinary unconscious phonological changes are definitely
   not arbitrary but are, in general, phonetically motivated
   processes;
2. prestige is a secondary factor in the propagation of
   phonetically motivated linguistic changes, whose linguistic character is the original basis of their diffusion;
3. the main force of social prestige is to inhibit phonetically
   conditioned processes, both of change in progress
   and of stable inherent variation, in the speech of high
   status groups and those whom they influence.

These three propositions immediately imply that social dialect
variation should be systematic and that popular speech should
be more 'advanced' than the standard.   The evidence which
we shall provide in this paper will make it clear that they provide a better basis for sociolinguistic theory than the traditional
view.

In view of his empirical work, it is surprising that Labov's
theoretical position on the causes of variation and change is
in some respects a version of the traditional view as we have
outlined it.   Labov does criticize Bloomfield and others for their
assertion that new forms originate among speakers with the
highest social status and are then borrowed by those of lesser
status.   He says:

> Oddly enough, a great deal of the speculative
> literature on dialect borrowing is based on
> the notion that all movement of linguistic forms is
> from the higher-prestige group to the lower.
>
> (Labov 1972: 286)

He then quotes a passage by Bloomfield that puts forward
this view and comments:

> This is simply a remark, with no more justifica-
> tion than any of the other general observations
> in Bloomfield's treatment of dialect borrowing.
> Studies of current sound changes show that
> a linguistic innovation can begin with any
> particular group and spread outward and that
> this is the normal development; that this one
> group can be the highest-status group, but
> not necessarily or even frequently so.
>
> (Labov 1972: 286)

But although he rejects the notion that new forms originate at
the top of the social hierarchy, he does not abandon the idea
that the spread of linguistic innovations depends on the social
prestige attached to them. Instead he proposes that popular
speech has its own prestige, perhaps as a marker of local identity.[7]
He suggests that a change often originates among individuals in
a non-elite stratum and is then adopted by their peers, becoming
a linguistic symbol of the group's solidarity. This view, which
Labov has adapted from Ferguson & Gumperz (1960), we might
call 'linguistic pluralism' because it maintains that different social
groups within a language community have different prestige norms,
much as pluralist social theory claims for those groups different
interests and values generally. In this view linguistic variation
in the speech of individuals when they switch between more and
less formal speech styles is due to the opposition of values between
the overall prestige value of the standard and the solidarity
value of the popular vernacular.

Labov's linguistic pluralism is certainly less objectionable than
earlier views of the popular vernacular as an imperfect imitation
of standard speech. Because it still relies on the notion that
arbitrary social values are the motive force behind phonological
innovation and social dialect variation, however, it cannot
adequately account for these phenomena. His theory still gives
one no reason to expect the speech of the common people to be
more open to phonetic conditioning than that of the elite. In
fact, his pluralistic conception of prestige leads one to expect
change to originate equally at all social levels and social dialect
variation to be, therefore, linguistically random. Thus, the result
of Labov's theoretical commitment is that where he notices the
greater susceptibility to phonetic conditioning of popular dialects
(i.e., in vowel shifting) he can give no explanation for it[8] and
that he fails to recognize some of the ways in which this susceptibility manifests itself.

PHONETIC CONDITIONING IN
SOCIAL DIALECTS

Having set out our theoretical perspective, we shall now present the evidence by which we justify it. We shall discuss the three main processes of change or inherent variation on which substantial empirical results are available, and we shall see that all three types more readily affect vernacular dialects than standard ones. The processes are: (1) consonantal simplifications, including both articulatory reductions and the loss or replacement of perceptually indistinct segments; (2) vocalic processes of chain shifting; and (3) assimilations of foreign phonemes to a native pattern. Of course, these processes do not exhaust the phonological differences between social dialects nor do they cover all possible kinds of phonetic conditioning in language.[9] Our purpose in presenting the material below is to provide evidence for our basic hypothesis, not to describe exhaustively the range of sociolinguistic phenomena.

Consonantal Simplification

In his study *The Social Stratification of English in New York City*, Labov described the variation of several phonological elements in the city. The consonantal elements were: (1) the initial consonant in words like *thing*, *theater*, *thought* (th); (2) the initial consonant in words like *then*, *the*, *there* (dh); (3) the final and preconsonantal /r/ in words like *car*, *bear*, *card*, *beard* (r).[10] He discovered that these elements were realized differently by different social classes and by the same social class in different situations. In particular, he found that in casual speech there was a regular correlation between a person's class position and his pronunciation of the elements listed. Lower position in the social hierarchy correlated with: (1) greater use of a lenis stop [t] or the affricate [tth] where standard pronunciation has the fricative [th]; (2) greater use of the voiced stop [d] or affricative [ddh] where standard pronunciation has the voiced affricate [dh]; (3) greater vocalization and dropping of final and preconsonantal /r/.

As far as stylistic variation was concerned, Labov found that in the most formal contexts speakers of all classes shifted their speech away from working class patterns and toward upper middle class norms. Figure 1 illustrates this stylistic and class variation in the dropping of final and preconsonantal /r/.

The data from Labov's study clearly exhibit the greater tendency toward simplification of consonant articulation that we have postulated for non-prestige dialects. The consonantal variables all exhibit articulatory simplification and all involve the loss or modification of perceptually indistinct segments. In the case of final and preconsonantal /r/ the vocalization or dropping of /r/ involves both an articulatory reduction that weakens or

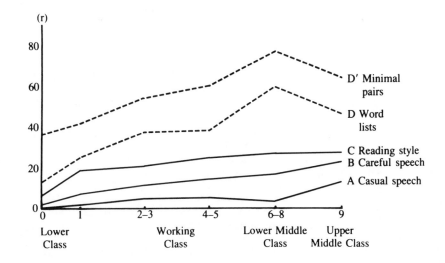

Figure 1: Simplified style stratification of (r): six class groups (Labov 1966: p. 240, fig. 10).

eliminates a tongue movement and the loss of a segment that is hard to distinguish from the preceding vowel. Also, the loss of /r/ before a consonant tends to create articulatorily more natural syllable structures in which consonant clusters are shortened or eliminated (Schane 1972). The substitution of stops for the fricatives [th] and [dh] eliminates segments that are at once difficult to articulate[11] and hard to distinguish from other fricatives.

Data comparable to Labov's have been collected on Panamanian Spanish by Henrietta Cedergren (1970), on Brazilian Portuguese by Gregory Guy & Maria Luiza Braga (1976) and on Montreal French by William Kemp & Paul Pupier (1976); and all of them confirm our hypothesis concerning consonant articulation. Cedergren's study involved the following five linguistic variables:

1. (R): the devoicing fricativization, pharyngealization, and deletion of syllable-final /r/, with values ranging from 1 to 6 in the direction of these processes.

2. (PARA): the alternation of the full form of the preposition *para* with *pa* with values of 1 and 2 respectively.

3. (ESTA): alternation of the full form *esta* with *ta*, assigned values of 1 and 2 respectively.

4. (S):   the syllable final alternation of [s], [h] and
               [∅] with values of 1, 2 and 3 respectively.
5. (CH):   palatal versus retroflex and reduced stop on-
               set of /č/, with values of 1 and 2 respective-
               ly.
                                   (Quoted in Labov 1972: 293-4.)
    The results of Cedergren's study are summarized in Table
I. Each of the five variables shows distinct social variation and
in each case the less prestigious social groups use the articulatorily reduced variants more often than does the most prestigious
group.   That the variants favored by the lower class groups
are articulatorily simplified is clear.   In the case of (R) and (S)
the non-prestige speaker tends to weaken or delete a syllable
final consonant.   In the case of (PARA) and (ESTA) the non-
prestige tendency is to drop an entire syllable.   With (CH) no
deletion is involved but the tendency is still to replace an
energetically pronounced consonant with a weaker one.
    Guy & Braga (1976) studied the loss of redundant plural
markers in Brazilian Portuguese noun phrases like the following:

         1. *aqueles rapazes* 'those boys'.
         2. *as minhas cadeiras* 'my chairs'.

They found a pronounced tendency for the plural morpheme to
be deleted from noninitial elements of the noun phrase, often
leaving only one marker of plurality per phrase. This articulatory simplification through the deletion of grammatically redundant consonantal segments was much more pronounced in 'lower
class' than in 'middle class' speakers.
    Kemp & Pupier (1976) studied consonant cluster reduction in
Montreal French and found that in environments where this
simplification was possible there was a regular and marked
stratification of simplification in the direction we would predict.
Figure 2 summarizes their results.
    Aside from the specific consonant changes documented
by Labov and others, there is a more general tendency towards

TABLE I.   Social Stratification of Five Spanish Variables in
Panama (Cedergren 1970)

| | Social groups | | | |
	I	II	III	IV
(R)	1.62	1.88	2.29	2.29
(PARA)	1.11	1.37	1.39	1.69
(ESTA)	1.26	1.56	1.62	1.71
(S)	2.03	2.24	2.31	2.36
(CH)	1.88	2.24	2.13	2.00

The highest social group is I, the lowest IV.

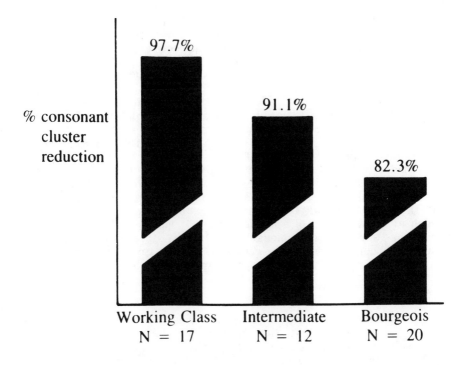

Figure 2: Consonant cluster reduction by class group in Montreal French (Kemp and Pupier 1976).

simplifying consonantal articulation that is favored by non-prestige dialects - that is, a tendency to favor the articulatory reductions of rapid speech. An informal pilot survey of eastern Connecticut speech patterns that we conducted indicates that working class casual speech favors some very marked articulatory reductions and assimilations. For example, we frequently found among working class speakers reduced forms like [n?əm] for 'and them' or [wəsəmaetə] for 'what's the matter?' and assimilations like the palatalized [laeseiyə] for 'last year' or [wəcə duwIn] for 'what are you doing'; such forms were rarer among middle class speakers.

The processes that go on in rapid or casual speech are perhaps the clearest examples of phonetically conditioned processes that linguists have discussed. Zwicky (1972) points out that:

> Casual speech processes seem to be constrained to be phonetically natural. In the extreme case they can be explained as the inevitable result of increasing speed of speech: the articulators simply cannot achieve their targets in the time available. This is the sort of

explanation suggested by Lindblom (1963) for certain vowel reductions in fast speech.

Even when such strong direct explanations are not available, casual speech processes are obviously 'euphonic', serving either ease – assimilation, neutralization, insertion of transitional sounds – or brevity – simplification of geminates, vowel contraction, deletion of weakly articulated segments, monophthongization.
(Zwicky 1972: 608)

He also points out that different speakers use rapid speech forms more or less readily at a given rate of speech. What seems to be true of our informants is not that working class speakers speak more rapidly than middle class speakers but rather that they are more likely to use the reduction processes of rapid speech at a given rate of speech. Indeed, many of the consonantal variations across social class and speech style that have been catalogued could simply be reflexes of the greater openness of non-prestige groups to the euphonic processes of rapid speech.

Vowel Shifts

In addition to its findings on consonantal variables, Labov's study of the Lower East Side also shows that working class and lower middle class speakers in New York City tend to tense and raise low front and back vowels. This raising is part of a general vowel shift currently in progress in a number of American English dialects. Although there are detailed descriptions of vowel shifts in many languages, little is known about their functional effect on phonological systems or the reasons for their widespread occurrence. As Labov points out, ease of articulation does not seem to be a factor in such shifts, and we know too little about how sounds are perceived to know whether perceptual prominence is involved. On the other hand, it seems apparent from the many vowel shifts that have been described that some regular forces are involved for these shifts tend to go in some directions rather than others. In particular, Miller (1972) and Stampe (1972) have pointed out that front and back vowels (which Miller calls 'chromatic' vowels) tend quite generally to raise. There are a number of examples of such raising, perhaps the best known of which is the Great Vowel Shift that occurred from late middle to early modern English.[12] Similar vowel shifts have occurred throughout the Indo-European language family and in other language families as well (see Wolfe 1972; Labov, Yaeger & Steiner 1972).

From the historical evidence Miller and Stampe concluded that the raising of front and back vowels, particularly tense ones, is a natural phonological change; and we can apply their conclusions, at least tentatively, to New York City vowel raising. Since this raising is most prevalent and extreme in working class and lower middle class speech, the New York City data suggest that non-prestige vowel systems may be more open to natural vowel shifting than prestige systems.

This conclusion is greatly strengthened by the empirical work on contemporary vowel shifts reported by Labov, Yaeger and Steiner. They report that the New York City vowel shift is merely one example of an extremely widespread kind of vowel shifting currently in progress in many urban dialects of American and British English. In the more than a score of cities represented in the study, the authors found: (1) that the vowel shifts obey general principles (not very different from the principles of naturalness proposed by Stampe and Miller) and (2) that the vernacular speech of the working class uniformly carries the shifts further than the prestige dialect does.

Phoneme Assimilation

When words are borrowed into one language from another, the phonologically simplest way for this borrowing to occur is for the words to be assimilated to the native sound pattern. This assimilation enables the speakers to use already learned articulations and rules on the borrowed words instead of having to learn new patterns for the sake of a few lexical items. Sometimes, if the borrowing is on a very large scale, features of the phonology of the source language may be borrowed along with the words, as happened with the Romance Stress Rule in English after the Norman Conquest. This is not, however, the usual case. When we look at social dialects, we discover that prestige dialects often preserve in borrowed words the pronunciation of the source language, or some approximation to it, after the vernacular has completely assimilated the words to the native pattern. The blocking of this assimilation is another example of how prestige dialects inhibit phonetic processes that go on in the vernaclar.

Examples of the difference between prestige and vernacular dialects in the assimilation of foreign words are easy to find. Thus, in English many words and phrases borrowed from the French are pronounced variably, with the more learned pronunciation being closer to the French original than is the vernacular one. An excellent example of this sort of variation is described by Bright & Ramanujan (1964) for Tamil, a Dravidian language of India. They compared the borrowing of foreign words into the Brahmin and non-Brahmin dialects of the language and found that the non-Brahmin dialect was more likely to assimilate the pronunciation to the native pattern.

PRESTIGE DIALECTS AND THE SUPPRESSION OF PHONETICALLY CONDITIONED PROCESSES

Linguists have long noticed that prestige dialects tend to preserve archaic forms that are changed or lost in the vernacular. Bloomfield states:

> . . . the standard language, closely tied up
> with the literary language, tends to become
> archaic (that is to ignore the changes of the
> last generations).

(Bloomfield 1964: 393-4)

This same position is put forward by Bright (1964) as regards
Tamil and another Dravidian language, Kannada. Bright points
out that in these languages the highest caste dialect often
preserves phonological characteristics that have undergone
change in the non-Brahmin dialect. Thus, he says:

> . . . the non-Brahmin dialect [of Kannada]
> shows more sound change within native vocabu-
> lary; cf. non-Brahmin *ālu* 'milk', Brahmin
> *hālu* (medieval *hāl*, Old Kannada *pāl*): non-
> Brahmin *gombe* 'doll', Brahmin *bombe* (Old Kan-
> nada *bombe*).

Bright, 1964: 470)

Some evidence is available of a similar pattern
[to that of Kannada] in the caste dialects
of Tamil. For instance Old Tamil has a retroflex
fricative which may be transcribed z; this
is preserved in Brahmin dialects but merges
with y, ḷ, l or zero in most non-Brahmin dialects.

(Bright 1964, 471)

A similar situation seems to exist in the Indonesian language
Javanese with its prestige and non-prestige speech levels (Krama
and Ngoko). There is evidence that some of the differences
between these levels is due to the retention of archaic phonological
features in Krama (White 1972: 26-7).

Facts like these fit quite well with Labov's results on present-
day English, as he himself has pointed out (Labov 1972: 297).
If we assume that systematic phonological changes resisted by
prestige dialects are phonetically conditioned, then the facts fit
our poisition as well. What is still lacking is a clear explanation
for the facts. Bloomfield and Bright both suggest that the central
factor retarding phonological change in prestige dialects is literacy.
They argue that prestige speakers, being the most educated stratum
of society, are more influenced by the literary tradition to resist
change. Bright & Ramanujan (1964) suggest that in the non-written
Dravidian language Tulu the Brahmin dialect is not phonologically
more conservative than the non-Brahmin dialect.

The literacy argument for the tendency of prestige dialects
to resist change undoubtedly has some merit. Thus, there are
numerous cases in English where the written language has influenced the spoken language, not only by resisting change but
also by altering pronunciation in the direction of spelling form
(see Barber 1964). We believe, however, that more than the
influence of the literary language is involved and also that this
influence cannot simply be pointed out but requires an explanation.

Our position, as stated earlier, is that prestige dialects resist phonetically motivated change and inherent variation because prestige speakers seek to mark themselves off as distinct from the obvious way to do this. Thus, we are claiming that there is another particular ideological motivation at the origin of social dialect variation. This ideology causes the prestige dialect user to expend more energy in speaking than does the user of the popular vernacular. In addition, there is another reason why prestige dialects would tend to resist phonological change. These dialects are maintained by social elites and such elites are by and large conservative. The use of conservative linguistic forms is for them a symbol of their whole value system. From this standpoint the conservation of the literary language has basically the same source as that of the spoken prestige dialect, since the standards of the literary language are set by the elite. The influence of the literary language on the spoken standard is one manifestation among others of a socially motivated inhibition of linguistic change. This conclusion is reinforced by the fact that prestige dialects not only inhibit changes that violate written forms but also resist changes in such features as vowel quality long before those changes would cause noticeable contradictions between the written and the spoken forms.

Evidence for our explanation of the tendency of prestige dialects to resist phonetic processes can be found in a number of sources. One source of evidence is Labov's documentation of the suppression of change by the upper middle class in New York City (Labov 1966). He found that changes originating in the working class and the lower middle class spread outwards from there to influence the speech of the upper middle class until at a certain point the change has advanced enough linguistically to be noticeable. Then a process of suppression begins in the upper middle class and slowly spreads downward through the social hierarchy. This suppression is associated with definite negative social evaluation of the suppressed feature as 'lower class' (Labov 1972). Thus, Labov's results indicate not only that the social elite suppresses change but also that the motivation for this suppression is a desire to maintain social distinctiveness in speech.

A second source of evidence for our position lies in the attitudes of intellectuals who set standards of usage for the prestige dialects. Such works as Fowler's *A dictionary of modern English usage* (1944) have as their express aim slowing down the rate of change in the language (see Barber 1964: 9). The French Academy is an even more obvious expression of the notion that the standard language should resist change. The guardians of usage view change as degeneration from a past epoch of linguistic and literary greatness; and for them the fact that an innovation arises in the popular vernacular is generally sufficient grounds for excluding it from the prestige dialect.

A third piece of evidence for our view can be found in an extremely interesting experiment conducted by the psychologist

George Mahl and analysed linguistically by Labov. Mahl studied the effects of two factors on the speech of 17 middle class college students: (1) blocking a subject's self-monitoring of speech with white noise and (2) blocking his view of the interviewer's face. He collected samples of the subjects' speech under the following four conditions:

(1) Facing the interviewer, without masking noise.
(2) Facing away (so as not to be able to see the interviewer's face), without masking noise.
(3) Facing the interviewer, with masking noise (i.e., wearing earphones through which white noise is administered at sufficient volume to prevent the subject from hearing his own voice).
(4) Facing away, with masking noise.

The two alternations of the normal conversational situation introduced by Mahl would both seem to make communication more difficult. Therefore, one would expect that under the abnormal conditions 2-4, subjects would speak more distinctly so as to overcome the interference with communication. Indeed, the masking noise did cause the subjects to speak more loudly, even though the interviewer was not hearing the noise and told the subjects that they need not raise their voices (Mahl 1972: 225).

Interestingly, however, Labov's linguistic analysis found that the subjects shifted toward the vernacular rather than towards prestige pronunciations under the abnormal conditions. Table 2 shows the shift toward replacing interdental fricatives with stops in the speech of one subject.

The results of Mahl's experiment must be treated as tentative because only a limited body of speech was carefully analysed, but they are nonetheless extremely suggestive. Only if we assume that the use of standard English pronunciation is motivated by social ideology can we explain them. The removal of auditory feedback through masking prevents the speaker from monitoring

TABLE II. Percentage of 'th' Variants in the Speech of Subject 13 in the 4 Conditions (Mahl 1972: 237)

	Facing No noise	Facing away No noise	Facing Noise	Facing Away Noise
θ ð (think, that)	86.5	75.9	74.5	68.8
t d (tink, dat)	13.5	24.1	25.5	31.7
	100.0	100.0	100.0	100.0
N (occurrences)	333	261	541	362

his speech and so it drops to a more natural level. This demonstrates, as Labov points out (Labov 1972: 97-8), that the prestige dialect requires special attention to be paid to speech. Even more significantly, however, removing the subject's view of the interviewer's face causes just as great a shift toward vernacular forms. This result can only be due to the absence of visual cues lessening the psychological impetus for maintaining an elevated style of speech. If such a small change in the circumstances of conversation causes so significant a shift toward vernacular forms, we can reasonably conclude that social status motivation plays a large part in maintaining the prestige dialect.

Finally, we want to point out that the results of Mahl's experiment are excellent evidence against the 'laziness' theory of vernacular speech. Indeed, under that theory the results would be inexplicable. The laziness theory would certainly predict that under conditions that make communication more difficult, speakers who control both vernacular and prestige forms would favor the latter. However, the results of Mahl's experiment are exactly the reverse: it is precisely under conditions that are less favorable for communication that vernacular features occur more readily. Thus, we can conclude from Mahl's experiment that concern for social status, not concern for communication, is what maintains the prestige dialect.

POSSIBLE COUNTER-EXAMPLES
TO THE THEORY

We shall conclude our discussion of social dialect variation with a discussion of some possible counter-examples to the theory we have proposed. The first such case is that of final and preconsonantal /r/ deletion in New York City and the rest of the East Coast (see Labov 1966). Labov says that at the turn of the century the speech of New York City was essentially /r/-less in final and preconsonantal position for all classes. In the 1930s a new prestige norm of /r/ pronunciation arose and this norm became dominant after World War II. This new prestige form (which may be related to the decision by radio and television to adopt a general mid-western pronunciation as the broadcast standard) appeared first in the speech of the upper middle class. Furthermore, even at the time of Labov's study, only the upper middle class used /r/ to any appreciable extent in casual speech. The form appears in working class speech only informal styles. From our point of view the reintroduction of final and preconsonantal /r/ is a phonetically unmotivated sound change since it revives a perceptually indistinct segment and increases articulatory effort. The change is an excellent example of the tendency, mentioned earlier, of prestige dialects to borrow prestige forms from outside the local area.

Thus far the case of /r/ is unproblematic; but when we turn
to the history of final /r/ pronunciation, a possible counter-example
to our theory emerges. It has long been known that the /r/-less
pronunciation of the eastern United States was originally due to
Anglophile sympathies of the upper class. In other words, this
consonantal simplification originated as a prestige form and filtered
down. Our theory, on the other hand, predicts that such a
change would be resisted by the prestige dialect. Further examination of the history of /r/ dropping, however, shows that the
case does not pose a real problem for our theory. First of all,
there is some evidence (Labov 1972: 287) that the loss of final
/r/ originated in England as a lower or lower middle class change
later adopted by the upper classes for unknown reasons. When
the change was adopted by the English upper classes, it became
for upper class eastern Americans, who admired the British
aristocracy, a symbol of refinement. Moreover, although the
/r/-less pronunciation was originally adopted by the upper classes
of the eastern United States, its spread to the other classes is
easy to explain. Not only would these groups tend to adopt the
pronunciation to the extent that they were influenced by the
norms of the dominant social groups, but also the pronunciation
would spread throughout the population because of its phonetic
motivation. Thus, our theory predicts that the /r/-less pronunciation in nineteenth-century America should be different from other
prestige forms. In particular, it should appear in all of the
speech styles of the lower and working classes and not be restricted
to the formal styles. Also, it should not reflect social stratification
due to preferential usage by the dominant class. All historical
data that we have on New York City confirm these predictions
(see Labov 1966:   342f., 564).

The second case that might be seen as a counter-example to
our theory is the case of the centralization of the syllabic element
in the diphthongs /ay/ and /aw/ on the island of Martha's
Vineyard, Massachusetts, as described in Labov's article, 'The
Social Motivation of a Sound Change' (see Labov 1972: chap. 1).
As Labov, Yaeger & Steiner put it:

> The centralization of (ay) and (aw) forms
> a striking reversal of a general drift in English.
> (Labov, Yaeger & Steiner 1972: 309)

In fact, the change violates the principles of vowel shifting that
the authors formulate and certainly seems an unnatural one.
Moreover, since the change seems to have originated with and is
most evident among the fishermen of the rural Chilmark section
of the island, one could argue that, according to our theory,
the change should have been in a natural direction.

Fortunately, Labov's work on the social context of this change
was extremely perceptive and the apparent contradiction with our
theory can be resolved. Labov points out that Martha's Vineyard
is an archaic dialect area that often preserved linguistic features
after they were lost in the rest of New England. Among these
features was a somewhat central pronunciation of the syllabic

element in /ay/. This pronunciation was characteristic of southern
England at the time that Martha's Vineyard was settled (the seventeenth century) but disappeared in one of the last changes of
the Great English Vowel Shift. Since the 1930s, Labov showed,
the centralization of /ay/ has increased and it has spread by
analogy to the parallel diphthong /aw/. The motivation for this
change and other strengthening of archaic features that are
occurring is an increasing desire on the part of local residents
to separate themselves symbolically from invading tourists and to
reaffirm local tradition (Labov 1972: 28-32). In other words,
the unnatural change in progress on Martha's Vineyard is an
attempt to preserve and extend an archaic feature of the local
dialect. The tourist economy has given native residents easily
understandable reasons for wanting to mark themselves off from
the rest of the population. Thus, the particular social situation
on Martha's Vineyard explains why a non-prestige group is be-
having linguistically in a way otherwise characteristic of elites
without invalidating our general position.

Perhaps the most significant problem for our theory in available
sociolinguistic studies is the fact, documented by Labov, that
the lowest stratum of a community does not initiate phonological
change. In his study of the Lower East Side, Labov found that
such change originated in the 'working class' and the 'lower
middle class' strata but not in the 'lower class'. Moreover, this
result has been confirmed in studies of Detroit, Panama City,
and Norwich, England (Labov, Yaeger & Steiner 1972: 16). On
the other hand, the lower class, while it does not initiate phonological change, is less influenced by the prestige norm than are the
working class and lower middle class strata. Thus, when a
phonological change that originated in one of these strata is represented by the upper middle class, the lower class ends up using
the stigmatized form more frequently than groups above it on the
social hierarchy (see, for example, Table 1).

These facts are troublesome to us since we would expect the
lower class, being the least influenced by the prestige norm, to
also be the most common source of phonological change. Labov
himself gives no detailed explanation for the phenomenon in print,
but he has suggested that the lower class may desire the local
identity marking that he thinks causes phonological change (Labov,
personal communication; also see footnote 5). We would suggest
that the explanation may lie rather in the degree to which the
lower class is socially and linguistically integrated into the local
speech community. For example, if the lower class contains a
higher proportion of relatively recent arrivals in the local area
or if it is geographically more mobile than working class strata
with more stable and better paid employment, then its tendency
not to originate sound changes would be explicable. Such changes,
while they occur everywhere and have similar linguistic characteristics, differ in detail from one local community to another and
would be less likely to arise in a less settled population. In any
case, more research is needed not only to resolve the question

of the linguistic behavior of the lower class but also to investigate any aspects of social dialect variation that have been as yet little explored.   We hope that, in proposing our theoretical model of social dialect variation, we will contribute to making future research in sociolinguistics as fruitful as recent investigations have been.

FOOTNOTES

[1] I want to thank the many people, too numerous to mention, who have read and commented on an earlier version of this paper. Special thanks must go to W. Labov, whose comments have been so helpful to me in revising the paper for publication.

[2] This paper directly concerns only the phonological aspect of social dialect variation and, therefore, it cannot hope to present a comprehensive theory of variation.   There may well be important parallels between variation and change at the phonological and at other levels; but claims about the one certainly cannot be extended to the others in any direct or automatic way.   In our opinion further empirical studies of syntactic and semantic variation will be necessary before it becomes possible to propose substantial theoretical hypotheses in these areas.

[3] The exact relationship between this dialect and the social elite is far from clear at present.   For one thing the dialect seems most characteristic not of an economic and/or political ruling class but of the professional representatives of the dominant culture; i.e. the elite in such professions as academia, the law, business management, medicine and the mass media.

[4] Our discussion of phonological differentiation must be limited to contexts where there are established prestige dialects.   Dialects which are in the process of becoming established, say as standard languages, may easily be less conservative phonetically than the local vernaculars they replace.   In the historical process whereby the standard languages of Europe, for example, arose the relationship between prestige and vernacular dialects was quite different from the one we shall be discussing between established prestige dialects and their vernaculars.

[5] This view is, of course, not original with us.   For example, H. G. Schogt (1961) says:

> Passant maintenant à l'examen des couches sociales d'un seul dialecte géographique, nous constatons deux forces opposées: la langue populaire riche en innovations, qui a pour elle le grand nombre, et la langue des classes aisées, qui est plus conservatrice et qui s'impose par son prestige (p. 91).
>
> [Passing now to the examination of the social strata of a single geographic dialect, we ascertain two opposed forces: the popular language,

> rich in innovations, which has numbers on its side, and the language of the well-to-do classes, which is more conservative and imposes itself by its prestige.]

The point of our paper is to show that the evidence made available by recent sociolinguistic research can be interpreted so as to support and elaborate this perspective.

[6] By '"natural" vowel shifts' we mean regular changes in vowel quality, especially chain shifts, which appear frequently in diverse languages and which seem to have a phonetic motivation, but for which there is as yet no adequate phonetic theory. Thus, we use the term 'natural' in an informal sense to indicate a faith in an eventual substantive (as opposed to formal) explanation of the phenomena, not out of adherence to any theory of naturalness. For systematic exposition of a substantive perspective on phonology see, among others, Lindblom (1971) and Chen & Wang (1975).

[7] In one place Labov puts his position as follows:

> A linguistic change begins as a local pattern characteristic of a particular social group, often the result of immigration from another region. It becomes generalized throughout the group, and becomes associated with the social values attributed to that group. It spreads to those neighboring populations which take the first group as a reference group in one way or another. The opposition of the two linguistic forms continues and often comes to symbolize an opposition of social values. These values may rise to the level of social consciousness and become *sterotypes*, subject to irregular social correction, or they may remain below that level as unconscious *markers*. Finally, one or the other of the two forms wins out. There follows a long period when the disappearing form is heard as archaic, a symbol of vanished prestige or stigma, and is used as a source of stereotyped humor until it is extinguished entirely.
>
> (Labov, Yaeger & Steiner 1972: 279)

For another statement of this position see Labov (1974: 250 ff.).

[8] Our analysis of Labov's views on the underlying causes of social dialect variation has the advantage of explaining one striking feature of his work: the contradiction between his empirical results and theoretical statements on sound change. The former universally point to the working class and lower middle class as the originators of sound change in contemporary American English; but the latter claim that sound change can originate in any social stratum.

[9] In particular it is not the case, nor are we claiming, that regular phonological processes can all be reduced to simplification of some sort. Simplified articulation is just one of the possible

manifestations of phonetic conditioning. It happens to be a very common one that covers much of the available data.

[10] The dropping of word final *r* was studied only when the following word began with a consonant. Among white New Yorkers *r* is rarely dropped in the environment r # # V.

[11] The assertion that interdental fricatives are difficult to articulate is supported by a number of facts. Firstly, the sounds are relatively rare to the world's languages. Secondly, children learning to speak English acquire these sounds late. Thirdly, adult speakers learning English as a second language generally have difficulty mastering these sounds.

[12] The effect of the Great Vowel Shift is illustrated in the following diagram:

(taken from Wolfe 1972: 1)

Thus we have the following correspondence between early modern English and middle English:

Middle English	Early Modern	Present Day	
[naːme]	[neim]	[neym]	name
[dɛːd]	[diːd]	[diyd]	deed
[geis]	[giːs]	[giys]	geese
[wiːn]	[weyn]	[wayn]	wine
[stɔːn]	[stoːn]	[stown]	stone
[goːs]	[guːs]	[guws]	goose
[huːs]	[hows]	[haws]	house

(taken from Bloomfield 1933: 387)

[13] The masking noise does not really interfere with communication acoustically since only the subject hears it. The subjects seem to have behaved, however, as though the interviewer was also hearing the noise. The loudness of their speech is one indication of this phenomenon.

REFERENCES

Barber, C. (1964). *Linguistic change in present-day English.* Birmingham, Alabama: University of Alabama Press.

Bloomfield, L. (1933). *Language*. London: Goerge Allen and Unwin.

Bloomfield, L. (1964). Literature and illiterate speech. in D. Hymes (ed.), *Language in culture and society*. New York: Harper and Row.

Bright, W. (1960). Linguistic change in some Indian caste dialects. In C. Ferguson and J. Gumperz (eds), *Linguistic diversity in South Asia*. (Publication of the Research Center in Anthropology, Folklore and Linguistics, No. 13.) Bloomington: Indiana University Press.

Bright, W. (1964). Social Dialect and Language History. In D. Hymes (ed.), *Language in culture and society*. New York: Harper and Row.

Bright, W. & Ramanujan, A. K. (1964). Socio-linguistic variation and language change. In H. Lunt (ed.), *Proceedings of the Ninth International Congress of Linguistics*. The Hague: Mouton.

Cedergren, H. (1970). Patterns of free variation: the language variable. Mimeo.

Chen, M. & Wang, W. (1975). Sound change: actuation and implementation. *Language* 51. 225-81.

Chomsky, N. & Halle, M. (1968). *The sound pattern of English*. New York: Harper and Row.

Ferguson, C. & Gumperz, J. (eds). (1960). *Linguistic diversity in South Asia*. (Publication of the Research Center in Anthropology, Folklore and Linguistics, No. 13). Bloomington: Indiana University Press.

Fischer, J. L. (1964). Social influence in the choice of a linguistic variant. In D. Hymes (ed.), *Language in culture and society*. New York: Harper and Row.

Fowler, H. W. (1944). *A dictionary of modern English usage*. Oxford University Press.

Guy, G. & Braga, M. L. (1976). Number concordance in Brazilian Portuguese. Paper presented at the fifth annual Conference on New Ways of Analyzing Variation in English at Georgetown University, Washington, D.C.

Hymes, D. (1964). *Language in culture and Society*. New York: Harper and Row.

Joos, M. (1952). The medieval sibilants. *Language* 28. 222-31.

Kemp, W. & Pupier, P. (1976). Socially based variability in consonant cluster reduction rules. Paper presented at the fifth annual Conference on New Ways of Analyzing Variation in English at Georgetown University, Washington, D.C.

Labov, W. (1966). *The social stratification of English in New York City*. Washington, D.C.: Center for Applied Linguistics.

Labov, W. (1972). *Sociolinguistic Patterns*. Philadelphia: University of Pennsylvania Press.

Labov, W. (1974). Language change as a form of communication. In M. Silverstein (ed.), *Human communication: theoretical explorations.* Hillsdale, N.J.: Lawrence Erlbaum Associates.

Labov, W., Yaeger, M. & Steiner, R. (1972). *A quantitative study of sound change in progress.* (Report on contract NSF-GS-3287). Philadelphia: University of Pennsylvania.

Lieberman, P. (1973). On the evolution of language: a unified view. *Cognition* 2. 59-94.

Lindblom, B. (1963). On vowel reduction. Report 29 of the Speech Transmission Laboratory. Stockholm: Royal Institute of Technology.

Lindblom, R. (1971). Phonetics and the description of language. Mimeo.

Mahl, G. (1972). People talking when they can't hear their voices. In P. Siegman and B. Pope (eds), *Studies in dyadic communication.* New York: Pergamon Press.

Miller, P. (1972). Vowel neutralization and vowel reduction. In P. Peranteau, J. Levi, and G. Phares (eds.) *Papers from the Eighth Regional Meeting of the Chicago Linguistic Society.* Chicago: Chicago Linguistic Society.

Postal, P. (1968). *Aspects of phonological theory.* New York: Harper and Row.

Schane, S. (1972). Natural rules in phonology. In R. Stockwell and J. Macaulay (eds). *Linguistic change and generative theory.* Bloomington: Indiana University Press.

Schogt, H. G. (1961). La notion de loi dans la phonétique historique. *Lingua* 10. 72-92.

Shuy, R., Wolfram, W. & Riley, W. (1967). *A study of social dialects in Detroit.* Washington, D.C.: Office of Education.

Stampe, D. (1972). On the natural history of diphthongs. In P. Peranteau, J. Levi, and G. Phares (eds). *Papers from the Eighth Regional Meeting of the Chicago Linguistic Society.* Chicago: Chicago Linguistic Society.

Trudgill, P. (1974). *The social differentiation of English in Norwich.* Cambridge University Press.

Weinreich, U., Labov, W. & Herzog, M. (1968). Empirical foundations for a theory of language change. In W. Lehmann and Y. Malkiel (eds), *Directions for historical linguistics.* Austin: University of Texas Press.

White, D. (1972). Social dialect formation. Unpublished ms.

Wolfe, P. (1972). *Linguistic change and the Great Vowel Shift in English.* Berkeley: University of California Press.

Zwicky, A. (1972). On casual speech. In P. Peranteau, J. Levi, and G. Phares (eds.). *Papers from the Eighth Regional Meeting of the Chicago Linguistic Society.* Chicago: Chicago Linguistic Society.

SOCIAL NETWORK AND LINGUISTIC FOCUSING

Lesley Milroy

INTRODUCTION

The general theoretical notion to which this paper addresses itself is that of a *linguistic norm*--specifically a non-standard or vernacular norm, as opposed to a fully codified standard norm. Questions concerning linguistic change and variation, which are commonly associated with the Labovian tradition, will not be considered here; for the moment, these phenomena will be taken for granted. On the other hand, it seems clear that some under-standing of the opposite phenomenon which is much less frequently discussed and which Le Page has described as 'focusing' is also crucial to sociolinguistic enquiry (cf. McEntegart and Le Page, 1982). A language variety is described as 'focused' when speakers perceive it in some sense as a distinct entity (Le Page 1975). Thus, in the context of the English language, accents such as those of Birmingham, Glasgow, Liverpool, and the others described by Hughes and Trudgill (1979), which are all popularly perceived as distinctive and discrete, could be described as rela-tively focused. On the other hand, the language patterns of geographically or socially mobile persons, which cannot be said to be characteristic of any particular namable accent, but rather a mixture of various social and regional accents, might be said to be relatively *diffuse* (also Le Page's term).

The notion of 'accent' appears to be psycho-social rather than strictly linguistic. Thus, although accents clearly have a psycho-social reality in the sense that speakers show an awareness of their importance as markers of various aspects of social identity, and react correspondingly strongly to them, it is not possible to produce strict 'phonological' definitions of accents any more than 'dialects' can be seen as clear linguistic entities (see Trudgill 1974 for a discussion of this last point and Giles and Scherer 1980 for a recent collection of papers on aspects of the social significance of speech). Nevertheless, the vagueness of the con-cept of accent should not prevent us from acknowledging that in

From *Sociolinguistic Variation in Speech Communities*, edited by S. Romaine. Edward Arnold (Publishers) Ltd., 1982, pp 141-152.

the relatively recent past the urban accents of many British (and other) industrial cities would not have been perceived as distinct entities meriting a label, far less the degree of codification conferred by the descriptions in a book such as that by Hughes and Trudgill. The characteristic structure of these accents has developed (i.e. linguistic focusing has taken place) along with the development of the industrial cities with which they are associated, many of which are not much more than a century old. Le Page in fact views linguistic focusing as the natural result of a more general cultural process involving the emergence of a distinct sense of group solidarity and identity (1979: 176).

Belfast is a city of relatively recent development, having undergone its major period of growth (1850-1900 approx.) some 50 years later than comparable English industrial cities. For that reason, Belfast offers an excellent vantage point for examining the phenomenon of focusing in urban speech. One aspect of focusing which we will examine here is the sociolinguistic patterning characteristic of an accent popularly perceived as a relatively homogeneous urban vernacular. In view of this theoretical orienta- tion, it will be clear that although many of the analytic procedures employed are Labovian, the general theoretical orientation is not at all characteristic of Labov.

THE DATA

The argument of this paper is based on data collected in the course of a recent study of Belfast vernacular speech and more fully reported elsewhere (Milroy and Milroy 1978; L. Milroy 1980).

The language of pre-existing social groups in three poor working-class communities--Ballymacarrett, the Clonard, and the Hammer--was studied. Although the communities were similar in terms of social status (predominantly unskilled working class) their internal social structure was by no means similar. Bally- macarrett, largely due to its location in the shipyard area, differed from the others in suffering very little from male unemployment. The Clonard and the Hammer suffered unemployment rates of around 35 per cent. This had a considerable effect on informal social relationships in the areas, as Ballymacarrett men tended to work locally and find their entertainment in local pubs and clubs, often interacting almost exclusively within narrow territorial boundaries. Women were much more inclined to look for work outside the locality, and men's and women's activities were sharply polarized. Although the same social patterns may once have prevailed in the Clonard and the Hammer at a time when the traditional linen industry provided local employment, men from these communities now customarily travel to different parts of the city in search of work, often share domestic and child-care duties, and do not contrast so markedly with women in their socialization habits as do their Ballymacarrett counterparts. Despite these local differences, the informal social strcuture of all three communities corresponded to the dense, multiplex, often kin-based network patterns described by many investigators as characteristic of working-class areas of cities (Young and Wilmott 1962; Fried 1973). This meant that people interacted mostly within a clearly defined territory, tended to know each others' social contacts, and were linked to each other in several capacities simultaneously--for example as kin, neighbours, and co-employees. Following Bott's arguments (Bott 1971), social anthropologists now generally agree that a social network of this type, which in effect constitutes a bounded group, has the capacity to impose general normative consensus on its members. This point is of great relevance to the argument here, which is fundamentally concerned with the whole notion of a norm. For the moment it is worth recalling Labov's remarks on the capacity of closeknit peer groups to impose consensus on specifically *linguistic* norms upon their members (Labov 1972: 257).

Although this network structure was generally evident in the Belfast communities, the extent to which *individuals* were linked to local networks varied considerably. Some people for example worked outside the area and had no local kin and no local ties of voluntary association, while others were linked to local networks in all these capacities. These differences in personal network structure, which appeared to be the result of many complex social and psychological factors, cut across categories of age, sex, and locality; the strongest vernacular speakers however appeared rather consistently to be those whose local network ties were strongest. This observation was treated as a hypothesis, and tested in the manner described in the following section.

LANGUAGE/NETWORK CORRELATIONS

An individual network score on a scale of 0-5 was calculated for each of the 46 informants. This scale took account of the character of the individual's network ties in the sectors of work, kin, neighbourhood, and voluntary association (see Cubitt 1973 for a discussion of the general importance of these particular network sectors). The score assigned to each individual provided a means of reflecting differences in multiplexity and density of personal networks without using corporate group constructs based on, for example, status as a means of differentiating individual speakers.

An informant's network score was calculated by assigning him one point for each of the following conditions he fulfilled:

1. Membership of a high density, territorially based cluster (i.e. any identifiable bounded group).

2. Having substantial ties of kinship in the neighbourhood. (More than one household, in addition to his own nuclear family).

3. Working at the same place as at least two others from the same area.

4. The same place of work as at least two others of the same sex from the area.

5. Voluntary association with workmates in leisure hours.

Condition one is designed as an indicator of density, and reflects Cubitt's (1973) insistence on the importance of taking account of the density of specific clusters in considering networks (as we are here) as norm enforcement mechanisms. (A cluster is defined as a portion of a personal network where relationships are denser internally than externally). The Jets, Cobras, and T-Birds described by Labov (1972) form clusters; many of the young men in the Belfast communities belong to similar clusters; some of the middle-aged women belong to clusters of six or seven individuals who meet frequently to drink tea, play cards, and chat. Some individuals on the other hand avoid association with any group of this kind.

Conditions two, three, four, and five are all indicators of multiplexity; if they are all satisfied, the proportion of the individual's interactions which are with members of the local community is very high. Three and four are intended to reflect the particular capacity of an area of homogeneous employment to encourage the development of dense, multiplex networks; four also reflects the fact that polarization of the sexes usually occurs when there is a large number of solidary relationships in a specific neighborhood.

It may appear at first sight that multiplex ties of the kind reflected in conditions three, four, and five are usually contracted by men, and that men would, therefore, automatically score higher on the network strength scale. In fact, since both the Hammer and the Clonard are areas of high *male* unemployment, individual women frequently score as high as or higher than men.

The scale is capable of differentiating individuals quite sharply. Scores range from zero for someone who fulfils none of the conditions, (although a zero score is rare) to five for several informants who fulfil them all. Such individuals must be considered extremely closely integrated into the community in the sense that their kin, work, and friendship ties are all contracted within it; additionally, they have formed particularly close ties with a corporate group (such as a football fans' club) or a less formal group based in the area. The defined territorial base associated with the kind of network structure which interests us here is reflected in conditions one and two. This is very important, for geographical mobility appears to have the capacity to destroy the structure of long established networks (Turner 1967; Wilmott and Young 1962).

It is important to emphasize that the network strength scale is designed fundamentally as a tool for measuring differences in an individual's level of integration into the local community. It is not claimed that this scale is the *only* means of doing so; for example attitudinal factors are likely also to be good indicators. However, the major advantage of the scale adopted here is that the indicators are *based on an explicit set of procedures* for analysing social relationships. Further, they can be observed directly and are subject to checking and verification (see Boissevain 1974 for a full account of network theory and Milroy 1980 for a discussion of its relevance to sociolinguistic method and theory).

Scores for each individual speaker on eight separate phonological variables were calculated (using the methods developed by Labov 1966) and a large number of rank order correlation tests carried out as a means of testing the hypothesis that network patterns were related to patterns of language use. When all subjects were considered together, significant results were obtained for five of the eight variables. This result appears to confirm the hypothesis that the strongest vernacular speakers are those whose network ties are strongest. Of those eight variables, only the significant ones are considered here.

Before proceeding further, it is necessary to explain the relevant phonological features associated with these variables. This account is necessarily brief and partial; a fuller description of the complexities of this urban vernacular phonology can be found in Milroy (1981) and to a more limited extent in L. Milroy (1980); and Hughes and Trudgill (1979).

1 (a)   Index scores are used, measuring degrees of retraction and back-raising in items of the /a/~/ɑ/ class (e.g. *hat, man, grass*). A five point scale is used, ranging from one for tokens with [æ] to five for tokens with [ɔə] with intermediate variants of [a], [ä], and [ɑ]. Scores are based on 60-80 tokens per speaker.

2 (th)   Percentage scores measure deletion of intervocalic [ð] in a small lexical set (e.g. *mother, brother*). Since the lexical distribution of this variable is limited, scores are based on only 856 tokens for all speakers--approximately 16-20 tokens per speaker.

3 (ʌ)   Percentage scores measure frequency of [ʌ] variant in a small lexical set which alternates between the /ʌ/ and /ʊ/ word classes: e.g. *pull, shook, foot.* Altogether, 1500 tokens are considered. An account of this word class and its importance for theories of lexical diffusion and linguistic change can be found in J. Milroy (1980).

4 (ε1) (ε)   Percentage scores measure frequency of low vowel [ä] (as opposed to a mid-vowel [εə] in items of the /ε/ class (*peck, bet, went*). This analysis is restricted to monosyllables closed by a voiceless obstruent or by a voiceless obstruent preceded by a liquid or nasal.

5 (ε^2)   *Percentage* scores measure frequency of the same
low vowel in di-and polysyllables.

The correlations between individual scores for these five variables
and individual network scores are presented in Table 1.   This
significant relationship between network structure and language
use was further explored by dividing the informants into subgroups based on sex, age, and area and again correlating linguistic
scores with network scores.   It is the results which emerged
when the sub-groups were divided according to area which are
of particular interest to us here.

In fact, it is only in Ballymacarrett that many phonological
variables correlate significantly with personal network structure.
Five of the eight give statistically significant results in Bally-
marcarrett, one in the Hammer and none in the Clonard (see
Table 2).

We may arrive at a plausible interpretation of these results
by referring back to the variant network patterns in the three
communities.   In Ballymacarrett *male* networks seemed more closeknit largely as a result of local employment patterns and contrasted
sharply with the relatively looseknit *female* network pattern.   This
contrast between the sexes was not apparent in other areas.   A
series of analysis of variance tests was carried out to check on
significant differences in the distribution of *network* scores by
age, sex, and area (see L. Milroy 1980 for details).   Although
many significant differences and interactions emerged, the
important result for our purpose here is that *only in Ballymacar-
ret* are male and female network scores significantly different
(means = 3.9583:1.3333).   These may be compared with the Hammer
(2.125:1.875) and the Clonard (2.750:2.875).   Considered overall,
network scores did not vary significantly simply according to
area; the variables of network and sex were apparently connected
in a subtle and complicated way.

The main points of the argument so far may be summarized
in the following way.   Of the three lower working-class areas
studied, only in Ballymacarrett do patterns of language use
correlate with personal network structure when individual scores

TABLE I.   Correlations between network scores and linguistic variable scores
for all subjects.   N refers to the number of subjects tested for a given
variable.

Variable	r	t	N	Level of significance
(a)	0.529	3.692	37	p<.01
(th)	0.485	3.591	44	p<.01
($\wedge^2$)	0.317	2.142	43	p<.05
(ε^1)	0.255	1.709	44	p<.05
(ε^2)	0.321	2.200	44	p<.05

Table II.* Correlations between network scores and linguistic variable scores calculated separately for three areas. B = Ballymacarrett, H = Hammer, C - Clonard.

Variable		r	t	N	Level of significance
(a)	B	0.930	8.360	13	p<.01
	C	0.345	2.287	15	p>.05
	H	-0.344	2.286	9	p>.05
(th)	B	0.816	4.679	13	p<.01
	C	0.011	0.039	15	p>.05
	H	0.346	1.379	16	p>.05
(Λ^2)	B	0.426	1.560	13	p>.05
	C	-0.042	0.151	15	p>.05
	H	0.247	0.920	15	p>.05
(ε^1)	B	0.771	4.016	13	p<.01
	C	-0.118	-0.429	15	p>.05
	H	0.053	-0.199	16	p>.05
(ε^2)	B	0.719	3.433	13	p<.01
	C	0.027	0.098	15	p>.05
	H	0.096	0.361	16	p>.05

*One further variable (I), showed a significant relationship to network scores
only in the Hammer.

on those two sets of variables are compared.   In the same area
the difference between the network structures of the two sexes
also emerges as very much sharper than in either the Clonard or
the Hammer.   We now move on to examine differences in *patterns
of language use* between the sexes.   This is of course quite a
different matter from the *correlations between the language scores
and the network scores* of individuals which have already been
discussed.

LINGUISTIC SEX GRADING IN THE COMMUNITIES

The simplest initial way of examining patterns of sex grading
in the communities is to refer to the graphic patterns presented
in Figures 1-4.   These represent scores on the four variables
(th) (ε^1) (a) and (Λ) calculated in accordance with the methods
outlined by Labov (1966).   All four of these phonological elements
have emerged as sharp sex-markers in working class Belfast (Milroy
and Milroy 1978; L. Milroy 1980) and in   Ballymacarrett the difference between male and female speech is in all cases much sharper
and more consistent across two generations of speakers than in
the other two areas.

TABLE III: Mean scores for ([1]) of both sexes in three areas

	Male	Female
Ballymarcarret	100.000	50.9421
Clonard	92.9763	78.8200
Hammer	93.5625	75.7138

Mean scores for (ε[1]) of both sexes in 3 areas.

    This is particularly clear if (ε[1]) is considered; there appears to be a tendency in *all* areas for this phonological element to function[1] as a sex marker; but the tendency is sharpest in Bally-macarrett. Some of the figures on which Figure 1 are based are given in Table 3. These reveal that in Ballymarcarrett the low centralized variant of (ε[1]) seems to be categorical amongst males, but used only just over half the time by females. Men and women in the other two areas differ less in respect of their use of (ε[1]), although men still use the low centralized variant much more than women.

    A similar pattern emerges with (th); sex differentiation patterns are *sharpest* in Ballymacarrett, although they are still very clear elsewhere. Mean differences between male and female scores for both (ε[1]) and (th) are in fact significant at 0.01 level when all areas are considered together.

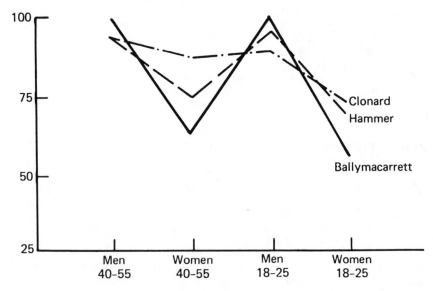

Figure 1. Percentage low vowel for (ε^1) in variable monosyllables and prefixed and inflected disyllables.

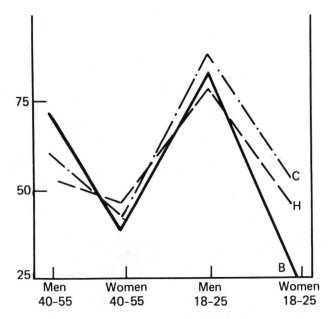

Figure 2.   Percentage zero form of [ð] in intervocalic positions.

The character of the contrast between the (a) and (ʌ) patterns in *Ballymacarrett* as opposed to the other areas is rather different. it is not simply a matter of the sex differentiation being *sharper* in Ballymacarrett; rather, only in Ballymacarrett are patterns of sex-differentiation with respect to these elements *stable over two generations*. In the case of (a) there is only a tiny and insignificant difference between the sexes in the Hammer while in the Clonard the *young women* (but not the older women) use backed variants of (a) at a particularly high level. In fact, this irregular pattern reflects statistically significant interaction effects (area by sex: $F = 5.7593$, $p < 0.01$; sex by age: $F = 6.0003$, $p < 0.05$). If we examine the (ʌ) graph, we see that in both the Hammer and the Clonard, but particularly in the Clonard, the older women use the unrounded variant at unexpectedly high levels. Again, this pattern reflects a statistically significant sex by age interaction effect: ($F = 16.8535$, $p < 0.001$). The notion of statistical interaction and the importance of taking interaction effects into account in interpreting sociolinguistic data are discussed in L. Milroy 1980.

One plausible conclusion to be drawn from these patterns however is that when we consider two important variables, (a) and (ʌ), only in Ballymacarrett does there seem to be clear agreement on their social function as sex markers across two generations. On the other hand there seems to be agreement across generations on the function of (th) and (ε[1]) in all three

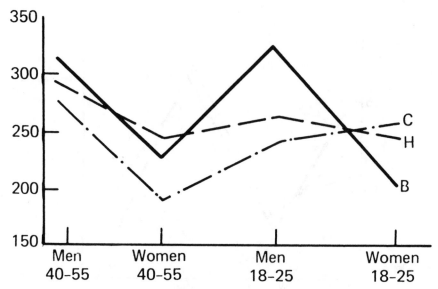

Figure 3.   Backing of /a/ in the three communities: (a) index score.

areas; but the patterns of sex differentiation are consistently sharpest in Ballymacarrett. Thus, it seems reasonable to suggest that in Ballymacarrett the linguistic norms of the community can be most clearly observed; there is apparently very consistent agreement on what constitutes appropriate speech for males and females. Moreover, as we would expect from other urban studies, females generally favour variants characteristic of high-status social groups. The subjective responses of males and females to these same variants are very sharply different, but as expected reflect the patterns of Figures 1–4. The subjective reaction tests on which these responses are based are discussed in O'Kane 1977.

Interestingly, sharp sex grading in Ballymacarrett appears to go along with this clear tendency of all speakers to use phonological variables extremely consistently. Thus, the fact that a norm appears to have emerged in Ballymacarrett by no means implies linguistic uniformity or denies the existence of the regular patterns of variability which we have come to expect in a real (as opposed to an imaginary) community. On the contrary, it is the very *regularity* of these patterns of variability (as opposed to their irregularity in the Clonard and the Hammer) which might be said to constitute the linguistic norm.

In fact, if we view variable language behaviour as parallel, in important respects, to other types of variable social behaviour we might predict a pattern rather like that revealed in Figures 1–4. For much of the literature on traditional closeknit working-class communities of this type has emphasized polarization of the

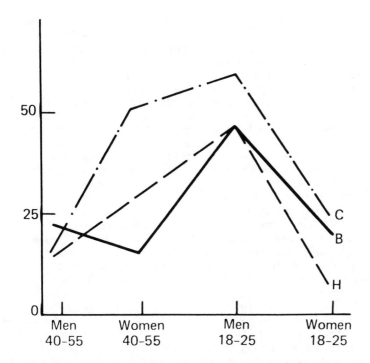

Figure 4. % [ʌ] variant in the three communities.

sexes as an important characteristic (see Bott 1971 for a review).
This seems to be generally true of low-status closeknit communities,
although on the whole only broad social reflexes of this polarization
(such as allocation of tasks and responsibilities) have been considered, rather than specifically linguistic reflexes.   However,
from our point of view, we may conclude that an important sociolinguistic reflex of *focusing* (or the emergence of an agreed norm)
may be the presence of clear linguistic sex-grading, without complications being introduced into the pattern by, for example, age
or area interaction effects.

CONCLUSION

A large amount of social and linguistic data has been adduced
in this paper, and the same set of data has been analysed in
more than one way.   It will be helpful at this point to pull the
main strands of the argument together, and relate them to the
central concern of the paper.
First, we saw that only in Ballymacarrett was there a clear
and consistent correspondence between a person's network structure and his (or her) degree of use of vernacular phonological

variants. It was further noted that social conditions in Ballymacarrett were favourable to the emergence of a closeknit network
structure of the type commonly found in traditional low-status
communities. It was suggested that these language/network correlations in Ballymacarrett were associated with the capacity of a
closeknit network to impose normative consensus on its members.
This point is not a new one; it has already been made by Labov
(1972a) in his discussion of the consistent relationship between a
speaker's place in the adolescent peer group structure and the
extent to which vernacular features are evident in his speech.

However, a second point is that the relationship between
group structure and language is not as simple as the correlations
shown in Tables 1 and 2 imply. A closeknit network structure
is not observable in Ballymacarrett independent of other social
variables. When individual *network* scores for all three areas are
considered, Ballymacarrett differs from the others in that males
and females have sharply different network patterns, with males
scoring high on the network strength scale and females scoring
low. It appears from the anthropological literature that in communities of this type the polarization of the sexes reflected by these
scores is rather general.

The third point may be related to the second. Sex grading
in language (as well as in network structure) is very much sharper
in Ballymacarrett than in the other two areas. Furthermore, in
Ballymacarrett more clearly than elsewhere, speakers reveal in
their patterns of language use the existence across two generations
of an agreed set of linguistic norms.[2] Paradoxically, this agreement on a set of norms does not involve a simple reduction in
variability, or in any sense a move towards linguistic uniformity,
since sex grading in Ballymacarrett is, as we have seen, particularly sharp. Rather, it involves the emergence of regularity in the
patterning of these variable elements and the development of a
clear social function to which that rgularity might be related.

Taking all these points together, I would suggest that if we
wish to examine the social mechanisms which encourage linguistic
focusing we must view the variables of sex and network structure
as working together in a particularly intimate way. At the moment
we are not able to characterize this relationship very precisely.

The relationship between group structure and the emergence
of a linguistic norm has already been discussed by Le Page (1979
et passim), who makes very similar points to some of those raised
here. In particular, he suggests that the emergence of a closeknit
group, a sense of solidarity and a feeling of shared territory are
all conditions favouring focusing (cf. also Cheshire, this volume).
However, he does not use the concept of social network as an
analytic procedure to examine the sociolinguistic reflexes of focusing, as I have tried to do in this paper. In fact, the set of
procedures which are used in social network analysis appears to
have very powerful implications for sociolinguistic research (cf.
also Russell, this volume). Network analysis is designed fundamentally to reflect the character of an individual's relationship to

the informally constituted groups with which he is associated. From the point of view of the linguist, the technique can be seen as a useful tool for the purpose of characterizing the manner in which persons adapt their language to the language of the various groups to which they may be said to belong. To describe, at a satisfying level of linguistic and social detail, the relationships between individual and collective linguistic behaviour must surely be the most important ultimate goal of those engaged in the study of language variation.

NOTES

[1] The term *function* is used here and elsewhere in much the same manner as the Prague School linguists: that is, a phonological element may be said to function within the sociolinguistic system, if it is possible to point to a job it does in relation to other elements. To say that an element functions as a sex marker, for example, does not then in any way imply that speakers are conscious of this function (although in fact, subjective reaction tests reveal their general awareness of sociolinguistic markers) any more than Mathesius's use of the term implies that speakers are conscious of the functional significance of theme and rheme (cf. O'Kane 1977). I am indebted to Suzanne Romaine and Philip Smith for drawing my attention to possible misunderstandings of the term *function*.

[2] I use the term 'sociolinguistic norm' here to refer to an element which displays regular distributional patterns in the community of the kind we have been discussing.

REFERENCES

Boissevain, J. 1974. *Friends of friends: networks, manipulators and coalitions*. Oxford: Blackwell.

Boissevain, J. and Mitchell, J. C., eds. 1973. *Network analysis: studies in human interaction*. The Hague: Mouton.

Bott, E. 1971. *Family and social network* (rev. edn.). London: Tavistock.

Cubitt, T. 1973. Network density among urban families. In Boissevain and Mitchell, eds. 67-82.

Fried, M. 1973. *The world of the urban working class*. Cambridge, Mass.: Harvard University Press.

Hughes, A. and Trudgill, P. 1979. *English accents and dialects*. London: Edward Arnold.

Labov, W. 1966. *The social stratification of English in New York City*. Washington, DC: Center for Applied Linguistics.

Labov, W. 1972. *Language in the inner city*. Philadelphia: Pennsylvania University Press.

Le Page, R. B. 1979. Review of Dell Hymes--*Foundations in sociolinguistics* and Norbert Dittmar--*Sociolinguistics*. *Journal of Linguistics* 15, 168-79.

McEntegart, D. and Le Page, R. B. 1982. An appraisal of the statistical techniques used in The Sociolinguistic Survey of Multilingual Communities. In Romaine, ed. 105-124.

Milroy, J. 1981. *Regional accents of English*. Belfast: Blackstaff.

Milroy, L. 1980. *Language and social networks*. Oxford: Blackwell.

Milroy, J. and Milroy, L. 1978. Belfast: change and variation in an urban vernacular. In Trudgill, ed. 19-37.

Trudgill, P. 1974. *Sociolinguistics*. Harmondsworth: Penguin.

Trudgill, P., ed. 1978. *Sociolinguistic patterns in British English*. London: Edward Arnold.

Turner, C. 1967. Conjugal roles and social networks. *Human relations* 20, 121-30.

Young, M. and Wilmot, P. 1962. *Family and kinship in East London*. London: Penguin.

ASPECTS OF LANGUAGE VARIABILITY

AND TWO AREAS OF APPLICATION

Roger Shuy

Although any effort to define a broad field of study such as language variety is subject to question and criticism by its practitioners, it will be useful to outline at least some aspects of its complexity. Three major characteristics tend to characterize the field:

1. A concern for viewing language *variation* rather than the sort of universals upon which grammars are usually based.
2. A concern for seeing language in real *social contexts* rather than as abstract representations.
3. A high potential for relationship and application to other fields such as education, sociology, anthropology, psychology, and many others.

In a sense, the third characteristic is really an outgrowth of the first two, but, for our purposes here, these three aspects will be treated equally.

Currently, those who study variation within a language or across languages are often referred to as sociolinguists. Their work is carried out with a view toward describing that variation or toward writing rules which incorporate it (rather than, as in the past, ignoring it), relating such variation to some aspects of the cultures which use it, doing large scale language surveys (macroanalysis), doing intensive studies of discourse (microanalysis), studying language functions (in addition to language forms), discovering the comparative values of different varieties of language or of different languages for the benefit of political or educational planning and decision making, studying language attitudes, values, and beliefs, and relating all the above to other fields which may make use of it (including education).

Although there has been a recent flurry of interest in language in real social settings, it would be foolish to claim that sociolinguistics is a new concept. It is quite likely, in fact, that man has been interested in the sorts of variation by which people set themselves off from each other since the very beginnings of speech. Humans have always lived with the cultural and linguistic paradox of needing to be like each other while, at the same time, needing to establish their individuality. These needs, coupled with the multitude of complexities involved in cultural and linguistic change, motivations, attitudes, values, and physiological and psychological differences, present a vast laboratory for sociolinguistic investigation.

In many ways, the current renewed interest in language variation involves a putting back together of a number of separations that have taken place over the years within the field of linguistics. For one thing, the separation of language universals from variability has proved very troublesome in recent years. The more traditional view of linguistics (common in the sixties) which excluded the variational and functional aspects of language from formal linguistic analysis and described such characteristics as mere trivial performance is currently out of favor. In a sense, the term *static* may be used to refer to the frameworks of both structural and transformational linguistics when such frameworks exclude variation of any sort, including time, function, socioeconomic status, sex, and ethnicity, from the purview of formal linguistic analysis.

The recent emphasis on social context is, of course, old hat to anthropologists, especially ethnographers of communication. Dell Hymes has been arguing for a realistic description of language for many years, observing that institutions, settings, scenes, activities, and various sociocultural realities give order to such analysis.[1]   An enthnographic approach to speech requires that the analyst have information about the relative statuses of the interlocutors, the setting of the speech act, the message, the code (including gestures), the situation, the topic, the focus, and the presuppositions that are paired with the sentences.   At long last, the ethnographers of communications are beginning to get some help from linguists with other primary specializations. The upshot of all this ferment within the past few years has been an almost entirely new set of attitudes within the field of linguistics.

This renewed concern for language variation arose out of a number of factors within the field of linguistics itself.   A convergence of different avenues away from orthodox generative theory took place among dialectologists, creolists, semantacticians and anthropologists.   Although the avenues were different, each shared a concern for variation, social reality, larger units of analysis (discourse), and a sense of continuum.

A focus of study which developed out of a diversity of interests the way sociolinguistics has is likely to have an equally diverse literature.   Yet there are some common threads which seem to help hold together the study of language variation.   One such characteristic is the concept of gradience.

I. GRADIENCE

As is often the case, personal experience provides a good first example. When I was in college I had a part-time job in a wholesale grocery warehouse loading and unloading trucks and boxcars. My fellow teamsters knew that I was a college kid but also expected me to be one of them in some sense of the word. As a native speaker of their local version of non-standard English, I found it possible to use the locally acceptable "I seen him when he done it" forms but their linguistic expectations of a college kid made them suspicious of me every time I tried. The following sentences may serve as illustrations of some of the points on such a continuum.

1. Hey!   Don't bring no more of dem crates over here!
2. Hey!   Don't bring no more a dose crates over here!
3. Hey!   Don't bring no more a those crates over here!
4. Hey!   Don't bring any more of those crates over here!
5. Hey!   Please don't bring any more of those crates over here!
6. Gentlemen, will you kindly desist from your conveying those containers in this general direction.

Number 6 is surely undesirable in most communications and it is included only to extend the limits of the continuum as far as can be imagined. Most of the adjustments that an educated speaker makes to his audience are found in various modifications of numbers 3, 4, and 5. Most certainly, there are few opportunities for him to go home to the non-standardness of numbers 1 and 2. Those who know him will think he is patronizing them or, worse yet, making fun of them. Consequently, what the speaker does is to make subtle adjustments to his vocabulary, grammar, and phonology depending on the informality of the situation, the audience, and the topic. One safe move is to standardize the grammar, since grammar is the most stigmatizing aspect of American social dialects, while occasionally preserving a few of the less stigmatizing pronounciations and leaving in some flavor of the lexicon. This is a highly subtle and complicated linguistic maneuver which can hardly be oversimplified or underestimated.

In no way should it be implied that the specific continuum given as example above is meant to be a right to wrong slide. Each item of the continuum has the potential for appropriateness and accuracy if the proper setting topic and person is discovered. But the schools would be likely to take it as a right-wrong series with a sharp line between numbers 3 and 4 with *wrong* facing one direction and *right* facing the other. Likewise, all of the *rights* would be considered good and all of the *wrongs* would be thought bad. What such an oversimplification denies, of course, are the following things:

1. That language use is more complex than a presuppossed context or pseudo-moral code will permit.

2. That users of language may intentionally select so-called stigmatized constructions.

3. That users of language may unintentionally select so-called constructions which, having been used, provide clear evidence of their having learned part of the pattern though not all of it.

II. FREQUENCY OF OCCURRENCE

In addition to the complexities growing out of gradience and general variability, another area of complexity to which linguists have only recently attended is quantitative variability. As odd as it now may sound, it has not been the practice of linguists to note the frequency of occurrence of a given variable feature until very, very recently. An amusing internal argument is still going on between linguists who understand this principle and those who do not. It is said, for example, that copula deletion is a characteristic of Vernacular Black English as it is spoken in New York, Washington, D.C., and Detroit. Certain linguists violently object to this idea, noting that Southern Whites also say "he here" or "you gonna do it." And, of course, they are quite correct. What they fail to see, however, is that those who posit copula deletion as a characteristic of Vernacular Black English are not comparing Southern Whites to Northern Blacks but are, quite the contrary, concerned about what is considered Vernacular Black English in those specific Northern contexts. But even there, we find that speakers of that dialect do not delete every copula. In fact, the frequency of occurrence of that deletion stratifies quite nicely according to socio-economic status. Likewise, not every standard English speaker produces a copula every time it might be expected in his speech, although the frequency of occurrence is probably very high. An even clearer case is that of multiple negation which is also said to characterize Vernacular Black English, even though it is quite clear that many Whites also use the form regularly. What, then, can it mean to call it Vernacular Black English? Simply, that it is consistently found to occur in the continuous, natural speech of Blacks at a much higher frequency than it occurs in the speech of Whites from the same communities and of the same socio-economic status. Strangely enough, this sort of finding is still rather new in linguistics and, to some linguists, quite heretical.

It is reasonably safe to assume that the extent of language variation is much broader than previous research methodologies ever revealed. If an informant is asked, for example, what he calls the stuff in the London air, he may respond only once, /fag/. If he should happen to use the /a/ vowel before a voiced velar stop only 50% of the time during all the occasions in which he was recorded, this fact is totally lost in this single representation in the interview. If he talks continuously for thirty minutes or so, he might use this pronunciation a dozen or more times, giving an increasingly more probable representation of his actual usage. Of course, such data gathering techniques work better for pronunciations in which the inventory of possible occurrences is very high than they do for lexicon. On the other hand, research in sociolinguistics indicates that pronunciation and grammar are more crucial indicators than vocabulary, a factor which certainly justifies highlighting them for research.

III. SELECTIONAL OPTIONS

Once we dispose of the notion of the right-wrong polarity evaluation and conceive of language as a continuum which operates in realistic contexts, the possibility of selectional options becomes meaningful. It is conceivable for example, that a speaker, out of a number of possible motivations, may select forms which, in some other context, would be considered stigmatized. Detailed studies of language variation have only begun to scratch the surface of such continua but several examples are suggestive of fruitful avenues of future research.

For example, I can clearly remember that as a child in a blue-collar industrial community, certain language restrictions were operational among pre-adolescent boys. To be an acceptable member of the peer group it was necessary to learn and to execute appropriate rules for making masculinity. If a boy happened to be the toughest boy in the class, he had few worries for whatever else he did would be offset by this fact. Those of us who were not the toughest could establish our masculinity in a number of ways, many of which are well recognized. For example, the use of tough language, especially swearing, and adult vices, such as smoking, were sometimes effective means of obtaining such status. Likewise, if a boy was a good athlete, he could easily establish himself as masculine (in our society this was true only for football, basketball, and baseball and not for sports such as swimming, soccer, or tennis). On the other hand, a boy could clearly obtain negative points by having a non-sex-object relationship with a girl, by liking his sister, by playing certain musical instruments (especially piano and violin), and by outwardly appearing to be intelligent in the classroom. It is the latter avenue which is of interest to us here since the major instrument for adjusting one's outward appearance of intelligence was his use of oral language. Interestingly enough, what one did with written language seemed less crucial, as long as it remained a private communication between teacher and student. That is, a boy could be as smart as he wanted to on a test or an essay as long

as the written document did not become public (i.e. become displayed on the bulletin board).

IV. PERCEPTUAL VIEWPOINT OF THE WHOLE

Still another characteristic of the study of language variation
involves the very viewpoint from which language phenomena are
perceived. It is logical to believe that once the basics of language
are understood, other less central features will fall into place.
It has been traditional in linguistics to follow this logic. Thus,
linguists of various theoretical persuasions have searched for the
core, the basics, and the universals of language and have paid
little attention to the peripheral, the surface, or the variables.
Sociolinguists do not decry an interest in universal or basics,
but feel that the peripheral variables are much more important
than have ever been imagined. In fact, sociolinguists tend to
treat peripheral and basic components on a par, and they believe
that to understand one, they must also know a great deal about
the other. Sociolinguists, therefore, stress variation, especially
as it is related to sex, age, race, socio-economic status, and
stylistic varieties. They feel that by paying attention to such
variables, they can better understand the exciting dynamics of
language and see it as a whole.

V. SUBJECTIVE REACTIONS

The development of sociolinguistics has also been paralleled
by an interest in the subjective reactions of speakers to language.
If speakers produce linguistic features with varying frequencies,
if they make use of complex selectional options and if they shift
back and forth along a base line continuum, they most certainly
also react to language produced by others. In recent years,
sociolinguists have become interested in three types of subjective
reactions to variation in spoken and written language:

1. Studies which compare subjective reactions to more
   than one language.
2. Studies which compare subjective reactions to
   variation within the same language.
3. Studies which compare accented speech, the production
   of a language by non-native speakers.

It is felt that such studies will enable linguists to get at the threshhold if not at the heart, of language values, beliefs, and attitudes. From there it is a relatively short step to relating such attitudes to actual language teaching and planning. For example, research by Wallace Lambert and his associates (1960) attempted to determine how bilingual Canadians really felt about both English and French in that area. Therefore, several bilinguals were tape recorded speaking first one language, then the other. The segments were scrambled and a group of bilingual Canadians were asked to listen to the tape and rate the speakers on fourteen traits such as height, leadership ability, ambition, sociability, character, and others. The listeners were not told that they were actually rating people twice--once in French and once in English. It was somewhat surprising to the researchers that the speakers were generally stigmatized when they spoke French and favored when they spoke English. This was interpreted as evidence of a community-wide stereotype of English-speaking Canadians as more powerful economically and socially.

An example of a study which compares listener reactions to variation within the same language was done in Detroit (Shuy, Baratz, and Wolfram 1969). An equal number of Black and White, male, adult Detroiters from four known socio-economic groups were tape recorded in a relatively free-conversation mode. These tapes were played to Detroiters of three age groups (sixth grade, eleventh grade, and adult). An equal number of males and females, Blacks and Whites listened to the tape. These judges represented the same four socio-economic groups as the speakers. The purpose of the study was to determine the effects which the race, sex, socio-economic status and age of the listener have on identifying the race and socio-economic status of the speaker. The results of the study showed that racial identity is quite accurate for every cell except for the upper middle-class Black speakers, who were judged as White by 90% of the listeners, regardless of their race, age or sex. It also showed that the lower the class of the speaker, the more accurately he was identified by listeners, regardless of all other variables. The significance of this lies in the fact that listeners apparently react negatively to language more than favorably to it. That is, stigmatizing features tend to count against a speaker more than favoring features tend to help him. Such information is, of course, useful in determining how to plan a language learning curriculum, among other things.

Language variation is a vast expanse of possibilities which should keep linguists busy for years to come. A very small dent has been made in the study of variation among certain minority groups. Through an accident of history, a great deal has been learned about Vernacular Black English but very little is known about the variation used by standard English speakers, regardless of race. Little is known about the sort of variation which establishes a speaker as a solid citizen, a good person, or an insider. Despite some intensive research in the area, little is known about how people shift from one register to another or, for that matter, from one dialect or language to another. Only the barest beginnings have been made in the study of special group characteristics related to language (i.e. language and religion, law, and medicine, etc.). A great deal of research needs to be done on language attitudes, values, and beliefs. Although language change has received attention in a number of recent studies, sociolinguistic research still lacks knowledge of a number of aspects of the exciting dynamics of language.

As an example of the richness of the applicational possibilities, we will cite two areas in which sociolinguistic theory and research have shown promise: literary analysis and medicine.

VI. LITERARY ANALYSIS

The systematic study of code-switching by linguists usually involves the following techniques: anonymous observations, individual informant interviews, and small-group elicitation or discussion sessions. As far as can be determined, little or no work has been done by linguists in studying the already written observation of code-switching by sensitive authors. One hypothesis of sociolinguistics is that a theory of code-switching can be applied not only to the examination of real conversational data, whether elicited surreptitiously or in interview contexts, but also to the written representation of such real conversational data by competent authors. By applying what is known about code-switching as a ruler governed behavior we should be able to determine the degree to which a given author consistently represents this rule-governed behavior and, to the extent which he is consistent or inconsistent, evaluate that author's innate sociolinguistic effectiveness.

For the sociolinguist, the information being examined (a novel, a short story, or a poem) may be little more than a new batch of data through which he can crank and test his sociolinguistic theory and machinery. To the literary critic, however, the results of recent research in communicative competence in general, and in this case, code-switching in particular offer a new and objective instrument for analyzing an author's consistency in representing reality, for examining a writer's subtle shifts of intention or indications of characterization.

In order to illustrate the usefulness of the knowledge of code-switching in a literary context, I have selected D. H. Lawrence's novel *Lady Chatterley's Lover*, which contains one of the classic literary instances of dialect shifting.[2] Mellors, the gameskeeper in the household of Lord and Lady Chatterley, speaks what Lawrence describes as broad Derbyshire dialect on many occasions. On the other hand, he is also known to speak a rather standard version of English, perhaps as a result of his being ". . . attached to some Indian colonel who took a liking to him" when he served as a Lieutenant in the British Army. We get a glimpse of this linguistic situation when Lady Chatterley asks her husband: "How could they make him an officer when he speaks broad Derbyshire?". To this Sir Clifford replies: "He doesn't . . . except by fits and starts. He can speak perfectly well, for him. I suppose he has the idea if he's come down to the ranks again, he'd better speak as the ranks speak". This speech certainly reflects the observations of sociolinguistic re- searchers on how social information is revealed by language switch- ing. It is also a strong indication that Lawrence was probably consciously aware of the complexity and importance of language variety. What remains is to observe how well he carried it out in his representations of the speech of his characters.

The codes involved in *Lady Chatterly's Lover* are assumed to be two homogeneous and clear-cut dialects of English. Lawrence is relatively clear in the instances in which he wishes his reader to perceive the dialogue as being in the latter dialect. The accuracy of his representation will not be at issue here but suffice it to say that the phonology of this dialect is represented in spellings (*yer* for *you*, *waitin'* for *waiting*, *'adn't* for *hadn't*, *Ah* for *I*, *pleece* for *place*, etc.). The grammar of the dialect is predictably non-standard, with double negatives (*Sir Clifford 'adn't got no other key then*?), non-standard verb usages (*Ah thowt it wor ordinary.*) and local syntactic forms ("*Appeh Sir Clifford'ud know*). The standard dialect is characterized primarily by a regularity of orthography and grammar but primarily by the absence of the marked forms of broad Derbyshire such as those noted above. In the minds of writers, as apparently, in the minds of most speakers, standard is primarily the absence of stigmatized forms.

In terms of the *settings* and *participants* involved in the switching, Mellors speaks only standard English to Sir Clifford, Sir Malcom, and Mrs. Bolton. He speaks standard English to Hilda until she insults him at which point he answers her in dialect. He also speaks to Hilda primarily when she is a visitor in his house. He speaks local dialect consistently to his dog and to his penis on the occasions which he addresses it as a person. It is only when Mellors switches in speaking to Lady Chatterley that clarification is required.

As noted above, *topic* also is an essential factor in code- switching. consistently throughout the novel certain topics are discussed by Mellors in standard English only. Whenever the topic of Lady Chatterley's proposed trip to Venice is introduced (three separate occasions) Mellors discusses it only in standard. The same can be said for the topics of sex (mutual orgasm, his libido, and any memories of their past sexual experiences), three discussions about their philosophies of life, Mellors' personal background, the topic of divorce (four times), and discussions about what constitutes good English. More personal topics, however, are generally discussed in dialect, including his relationship with his daughter, the general topic of children, and any philosophical discussions relating to the hardship of the life of a peasant.

In terms of *language situations* or functions, the consistent contrast between standard English and dialects in Mellors' speech is maintained. Introductions, conversational openings, conversational closings, insults, invitations to sex, and rejection of sexual overtures are in standard English, while all representations of meal-time conversation, talk during love-making, and post-intercourse afterglow conversations were in dialect.

It is not the purpose of this paper to detail all the ways in which Lawrence made use of code-switching in his novel but suffice it to say that he did it masterfully and, from what we know about code-switching in real-life research settings, realistically.

What this research suggests is that certain tasks of the literary critic will be aided by recent theoretical developments in sociolinguistics. Specifically, literary critics can be helped to ascertain how effectively and how consistently an author portrays the language of his fictional characters. Recent developments in conversational analysis can provide a scientific touchstone (in well-defined contexts) for literary comparison. One type of analysis might have been to match the orthographic representation of broad Derbyshire dialect with the linguistic atlas research which has been done in that area. In this case, we have chosen rather to make use of a measurement point which is less concerned with the surface manifestation of language representation (the phonology and grammar) and more concerned with the meaning, particularly the sort of meaning which may or may not be consciously controlled by the author. If we had analyzed the former question we could learn about how well the author knew the dialect he represented. The latter question gets at a much larger issue: How well does the author know how to make use of the uses of language?

It should be clear, then, that recent developments in sociolinguistic analysis can offer analytic assistance to the field of literary criticism. Unfortunately, the analysis summarized here tells us little that we did not already know about Lawrence's capturing and discussing that ability in measurable terms, perhaps as a point for comparing that same ability in other authors but at least a way of more concertely describing what it is that Lawrence did so well. Perhaps this is all that science can ever offer art.

VII. MEDICINE

Another area for application of sociolinguistic theory and research is the possibly unlikely field of medicine. The field of
medicine has been almost completely overlooked by linguistics as
a potential area in which to expand our work domain. To be
sure it is not easy to convince the profession which has perhaps
the greatest status in America that it needs help from anyone,
much less from linguistics, but there are signs that the armor is
beginning to crack. Part of our lack of success in convincing
medical doctors that we have anything to say to them stems from
the strategy we have taken. Typically we have begun with the
assumption that doctors want to know what linguistics is. Not
only is this a poor approach, but is is also probably wrong.
What the medical profession is usually interested in are solutions
to *their* problems. Most perceived problems relate to medical
technology. These we probably can't help much with. Others
relate to their relationships with their patients. Such relationships
are invariably carried out in language, either spoken or written.
The medical history is the first and usually the longest verbal
interaction in which doctors and patients participate. This event
is of critical importance for the patient, since all future treatment
hinges on its accuracy and breadth. Yet little or no training is
given the medical student in the "field methods" of his profession,
in the "ethnography of interrogation", in the language of minorities, in foreign language, or in any sort of cross-cultural understandings. No mention is made of the need for the medical
student to develop at least a receptive competence for the many
varieties of language which a non-suburban practice might produce
and no teaching packages have been developed to help accommodate
this possibility.

Only a few linguists in this country are in dialogue with the
medical profession on these matters but there is reason to be
optimistic about its future development, provided that the focus
of the relationship has integrity. That is, there needs to be a
genuine promise of help in solving a real problem and there
cannot be evidence of the overpromise of applied linguistics which
characterized the overzealous blunders of our earlier history.

One purpose of a set of recent studies at Georgetown University
was to examine the extent of this behavior, to examine how much
patients feel or are led to feel that they must communicate with
doctors in doctor language. Conversely, we were also interested
in those occasions in which doctors showed a need to try to
communicate with their patients in patient language. One might
hypothesize a continuum such as the following:

1. Doctors talking only doctor language.
2. Doctors talking doctor language but understanding
   patient language.

3. Doctors talking and speaking both doctor and patient language.
4. Patients talking and speaking both patient and doctor language.
5. Patients talking patient language but understanding doctor language.
6. Patients talking only patient language.

By far the largest part of the medical histories were conducted in doctor language and the patients tried very hard to operate in as close a version of doctor language as they could muster. Most serious breakdowns came when patients could (or would) not speak doctor language and doctors could (or would) not understand patient language. Our data, though still brief and fragmentary, display evidences of success and failure at all points on the continuum. Our data shows, for example, clear evidences of the patients' ability to acquire doctor talk during the interview. In some cases, the learning was purely social, the patient putting forth the best possible social dialect to meet the formality of the occasion. On other occasions, specific medical language was acquired during the interviews.

The research also reveals instances in which doctors begin to understand patient talk. It will take considerably more data than are now available for us to catalogue the types of misunderstandings doctors have of patient language, primarily because the patient says so little during the medical history, following a strategy so successfully used by minority school children who learn very early that the name of the game is to be right as often as possible and wrong as seldom as possible and that the best way to avoid being wrong is to keep one's mouth shut. Another reason why we have so few examples of doctor's misunderstanding of patient language stems from the social structure of the speech event. The doctor is simply not to be wrong. We have some recorded instances, however, in which clear acquisition of patient talk by a doctor seem to have taken place:

P: Oh, he did, uh, in last April he had a little touch of sugar when . . .
D: He has a little *what*?
P: You know, diabetic . . .
D: Oh, he had some sugar.

A more serious example occurred during an early observation during which the doctor asked the patient if she had ever had an abortion. She denied that she had, even though her chart clearly indicated two previous abortions. In the doctor's mind, the patient had chosen to tell a lie for the evidence was clearly before him. After the doctor had left, the patient was asked by a linguist whether or not she had ever lost a baby. She readily admitted to having lost two. In the ensuing conversation it was determined that the patient was defining abortion as self-induced while the doctor was using the term to refer to a wider range of possibilities. It seems obvious here that the doctor has not learned patient language either.

On the other hand, few doctors demonstrate ability to speak patient talk. If evidence from our research and from the accounts in medical journals is accurate, few doctors have mastered the ability to speak the language of the working-class, minority, or foreign-language-speaking patient. Severe problems can result from miscommunication on all levels, particularly for the non-English speaker. In fact, the clearest mandate seems to be for hospitals, clinics, and other medical facilities to gear up for medical services for speakers of foreign languages.

A more cautious note must be sounded, however, for the need for doctors to attempt to speak patient dialect, a practice which can lead to serious problems. For example, one conscientious doctor, sensitive to the fact that his patient was Black and poor, assumed that she would be more comfortable with "homey" expressions, despite the fact that she had already passed through such fine distinctions as flebitis, rheumatic fever, transfusions, and epilepsy. He was doing very well in his history taking, giving the appearance of casual yet professional ease. He was friendly and interested in the patient as a person. And then he blew it with his liberal enthusiasm, offending the patient with his very effort to sound like her.

In summary, on the general points on the doctor-patient, medical history language continuum the major breakdowns occur at the extremes. Some patients cannot or will not speak doctor language. Likewise, some doctors cannot or will not speak patient language. It has been suggested, in fact, that it is probably disastrous for them to try. The obvious area of hope lies in the central portions of the continuum. Historically, we have expected patients to carry all the burden here. Either they learn to understand doctors or they remain ignorant. Naturally this is a gross generalization but one which is generally supportable from our data. One would hope for considerably more from the medical profession.

At the very minimum one would hope that the medical profession would give some attention to the matters in the language of interrogation. It is strange that of all professions, both teaching and medicine rely so heavily on the answers of their clients but pay so little attention to the vast complexities of question-asking.

Secondly, one would hope that the medical profession would give some attention to the matter of receptive competence of patient language on the part of their practitioners. It is patently absurd to run the risk of getting inaccurate information in the medical interview simply because the patient does not want to admit ignorance of the question or because the question was indelicately asked. There is far too much at stake for such a situation to be maintained. Despite the extant crowding in the medical school curriculum this situation is serious enough to merit change. Focus and time must be given to the language and culture of minorities in medicine.

VII. CONCLUSIONS

The argument of this paper has been rather obvious. We have suggested that the major concerns of sociolinguistics (variability, social context, cross-disciplinary sensitivity, and the various internal distinctions including gradience, frequency of occurrence, selectional options, the perceptual viewpoint of the whole, and the importance of subjective reactions of language) are all components for analyzing the complexity of language. I have tried to illustrate the usefulness of these defining qualities of sociolinguistics in the areas of literary analysis and medicine. These are intended to be only suggestive of the broad areas in which the field might continue to develop. There is probably no academic field which intersects with so much of the rest of life as does linguistics. We have hardly begun to scratch the surface of its potential.

FOOTNOTES

[1]One might cite many references over a period of time. For an overview, however, see Dell Hymes, "The Scope of Sociolinguistics", in *Sociolinguistics: Current Trends and Prospects*, R. Shuy (ed.), Washington, D.C.:   Georgetown University Press (1973).

[2]Roger W. Shuy, "Code Switching in Lady Chatterley's Lover", *Working Papers* in Sociolinguistics, Number 22 (February, 1975).

SOCIAL IDENTITY AND LINGUISTIC

SEX DIFFERENTIATION

Peter Trudgill

It has been known for some considerable time that in some societies language is involved in covariation, not only with parameters such as social stratification, social context and age, but also with the parameter of sex. The fact that the speech of men and women may differ in interesting ways was initially noted in only a rather small number of linguistic articles and discussions, and research tended to concentrate either on non-urbanized communities or on relatively peripheral aspects of the subject (see Jespersen, 1922, chapter 13; Sapir, 1929; Haas, 1944, Hertzler, 1954; Fischer, 1958; and the summary of other work in Crystal, 1971). In the past two decades, however, a number of studies have appeared which present accurate, structured data illustrating the form that sex differentiation takes in the linguistic communities of complex urbanized societies. Early work of this type was based on sociolinguistic investigations into varieties of urban American English (see Labov, 1966a; Levine and Crockett, 1966; Shuy et al., 1967; Wolfram, 1969; Fasold, 1968). More recent studies of other varieties--and very many could be cited--include Trudgill (1974a), Milroy (1980), and Cheshire (1982); and see also chapter 10.

The results of all these sociolinguistic studies, and they are by now very numerous, have one very striking feature in common. They are all agreed that women, allowing for other variables such as age, education and social class, produce on average linguistic forms which more closely approach those of the standard language or have higher prestige than those produced by men.

It is important to stress the point that this type of differentiation is *on average* . All the studies that have been made of urbanized societies indicate that this aspect of sex differentiation in language is a matter of sex-preferential tendencies--the speech of men and women differs only in general and by degree. Differences are not sex-exclusive. (This point has sometimes been misunderstood. Spender (1980), for example, writes, with refer-

From *On Dialect: Social and Geographical Perspectives,* New York University Press, 1983, pp 161-168. Reprinted with permission.

ence to Trudgill (1974b), that 'Trudgill maintains that there is a feminine and a masculine linguistic variety'. This has actually never been maintained, of urbanized western societies, by anyone.)

Nevertheless, this phenomenon is one that requires explanation, and over the past several years a number of explanations have been advanced, some of them in print, some informally, many of them controversial, and most of them speculative. Amongst them we may include the following:

1. One explanation lies in suggesting that the phenomenon of sex differentiation in language actually does not exist (and therefore does not have to be explained). Spender (1980) writes that 'it might be possible that women do speak "better" than men, . . . but at the moment the available evidence is not convincing'. The evidence from sociolinguistic studies is, as we have seen, in fact utterly convincing and overwhelming. It is the single most consistent finding to emerge from sociolinguistic studies over the past 20 years. This phenomenon may be found by some people to be embarrassing and undesirable, but there can be absolutely no doubt that it does exist.

2. Another attempt to 'explain away' this finding involves the, on the face of it very reasonable, suggestion that the phenomenon is due to the fact that field-workers in sociolinguistic studies are male. (See , e.g., Smith, 1979: 117) Male informants, the argument goes, are more relaxed or more inclined to accommodate (Giles, 1973) in a same-sex situation than are female informants with a male interviewer, and thus produce more casual speech. This is in fact simply not the case, since studies employing female fieldworkers (see Romaine, 1978; Milroy, 1980; Cheshire, 1982) produce exactly the same results.

3. A further attempt to find an explanation lies in an appeal to the notion of 'appropriateness'. In Trudgill (1974b) I wrote that:

> geographical, ethnic group, and social-class varieties are, at least partly, the result of social *distance*, while sex varieties are the result of social *difference*. Different social attributes, and different behaviour, is expected from men and women, and sex varieties are a symbol of this fact. Using a female linguistic variety is as much a case of identifying oneself as female, and of behaving 'as a woman should', as is say, wearing a skirt. What would happen to a man who, in our society, wore a skirt? His fate would be the same as that of Carib men who attempted to use women's language: 'The women have words and phrases which the men never use, or *they would be laughed to scorn*'.

It is interesting to observe how analogies of this type are reacted to. For example, Spender (1980) takes the skirt analogy to imply that

> if a man wore a skirt . . . he would be identifying himself with all that is negative and undesirable in our society and would be open to ridicule or abuse. To Trudgill, linguistic variety helps to maintain the demarcation lines between the sexes, to prevent contamination--for men--and, implicitly then, is to be upheld.

There are a number of comments that can be made here. It will be apparent, I hope, that Spender's version is actually a caricature of what I wrote, and it is certainly a travesty of my actual feelings about this phenomenon. To describe a particular state of affairs does not, obviously, mean that one, implicitly or otherwise, wishes this state of affairs 'to be upheld'. A description is simply a description, and to report that men who wore skirts would be 'open to ridicule and abuse' is to report the truth. It does not, moreover, seem to be that this situation is a matter of 'contamination' or of men identifying themselves 'with all that is . . . undesirable in our society'. Rather, it is a matter of appropriateness. It is widely, and strongly, held in our society that it is inappropriate for men to wear skirts--and use certain vocabulary items--just as it is felt to be inappropriate, by many, for women to swear or wear a three-piece pin-stripe suit. A woman wearing such a suit would seem incongruous, not because she was contaminating herself or identifying herself with 'all that is undesirable', but simply because what she was doing was inappropriate and unusual.

The skirt analogy, it is true, may not be without its deficiencies, but the parallel with language is clear, and it is actually encouraging, for many people, to note that notions about appropriateness can change. A hundred years ago the wearing of trousers by women was highly inappropriate. This is no longer so. Similarly, the use of taboo vocabulary is now much more evenly distributed between the sexes than formerly.

A criticism of the appropriateness explanation that Spender ought to have made, but did not, is that it still begs the very large question of *why* different forms of linguistic behaviour are widely, if usually subconsciously, held to be appropriate for men and women. Explanations in terms of appropriateness, that is, are not really explanations at all.

4. A further set of discussions of sex differences in language rest on what I would argue is a mistaken attempt to equate the findings produced by sociolinguistic surveys of the kind discussed above with the results of other studies of a different type. The sociolinguistic surveys found evidence of sex differentiation in phonetics, phonology and morphology. The evidence, as we saw above, is very clear, but it concerns no more than the fact that on average, women say, for example, the less prestigious form [pæʔ] rather than the more prestigious form [pæt] *pat* less often than men; and that they also say, for example, the less 'correct' *I done it* rather than the more 'correct' *I did it* less often than

men.   These features, we can say, are matters of *dialect and accent*.   Other types of work have found linguistic sex differences of other--and, I would suggest, not necessarily comparable--kinds. These include linguistic phenomena such as the use of particular hesitation phenomena, particular syntactic devices (such as ellipsis and tag-questions), and particular communicative and conversational strategies.   These we can perhaps label collectively as *language use* differences.

As an example of work which attempts to make this equation, we can cite Brown (1980).   In a highly insightful paper on language use in a Mayan community, Brown attempts to interpret the *dialect and accent* findings of sociolinguists as an indication that women demonstrate greater linguistic *politeness* than men, and relates this 'politeness' to deference and subservience. (Spender (1980) also equates more prestigious speech with 'politeness or subservience'.)   However, it can very readily be argued that to equate the usage of more standard, 'correct' linguistic variants with 'politeness' is to confuse the issue.   In some cases, it is true, to speak in a more standard, formal, or prestigious manner may be to indicate politeness.   But in other cases it can certainly indicate the reverse.   In English the desire to convey an impression of politeness may well often lead to a greater usage of standard linguistic features, but the reverse is not true: the usage of more 'correct' language does not *necessarily* indicate politeness. It is perfectly possible to employ high-status pronunciations and standard grammatical forms together with impolite lexis and other signals of distance and dominance.   (Indeed, Giles' (1973) notion of 'accent divergence' suggests precisely this kind of phenomenon: in order to be impolite to an interlocutor who speaks a less standard variety, a speaker can employ more standard linguistic forms than normally.)

In fact, Brown's 'politeness' interpretation works mainly with *language use* sex differences, and it is for the most part these to which she devotes her paper.   (Features she cites include: emphatic particles, intonation, negative questions, repetition, rhetorical questions, and diminutives.)   These differences can indeed be used to signal greater or less politeness and/or deference and/or subservience.   Preisler, for example, has indicated (see Laver and Trudgill, 1979) that speakers playing a dominant role in a conversation make more suggestions, use more imperatives, and employ fewer interrogatives than people taking a subordinate role--and dominant speakers are more often male than female. *Dialect and accent* differences, on the other hand, are not, I would maintain, so widely employed in this way, and are not to be explained entirely in the same terms.

Brown (1980) also makes the interesting point that, when we are attempting to explain linguistic sex differences, we should consider the possibility that one reason for these differences may lie in the fact that women and men may be trying to achieve different things through language.   If this is so, then clearly it will be the *language use* level that will be a reflection of these differences, since *dialect and accent* variants must be held to be socially different (but linguistically equivalent) ways of doing the *same* thing (cf. the discussion in the literature on the nature of linguistic variables--see Lavandera, 1978; Labov, 1978; Romaine, 1981).

This distinction between the two types of linguistic sex differentiation is reinforced by Togeby (1978). He points to the finding (see Jorgensen, 1970) of the Lund project on spoken Swedish that women use fewer syntactic markers of prestige style (such as longer or more complete sentences) than men. Togeby in fact argues, with reference to discussions such as Trudgill (1974b), that 'all claims that women are more sensitive to prestige than men collapse in the face of counterevidence of this type' (my translation). He subsequently, however, gives a very clear explanation for these findings, and makes it plain that he is actually comparing two rather different types of phenomena--*language use* data from the Lund study, and the *dialect and accent* data discussed in Trudgill (1974b). Prestigious or stigmatized phonological and morphological variants, Togeby says, are readily perceived as such by speakers involved in conversational interaction, whereas syntactic features and devices typical of less or more formal styles are not directly perceived as low status or prestigious at all. One does not, for example, normally notice the fact that one's interlocutor is using more words per sentence than oneself. And even if one does, we can add, differences of this type are not generally perceived as being a matter of greater or lesser 'correctness'. It is therefore no surprise that women do not employ these devices as they do 'correct' pronunciations and standard morphological forms.

Language use differences, then, may indeed be due to differential expressions of politeness etc., which may in turn be due to subservience and deference--but we still remain without an entirely satisfactory explanation for the *dialect and accent* differences that have been so fully documented and with which this chapter is chiefly concerned.

5. Interestingly, both Brown and Togeby also attempt to provide explanations for linguistic sex differentiation in terms of social networks. This is obviously a very promising avenue for research, since Milroy (1980) has shown that the type of social network in which speakers participate, and the strength of their participation, can have a significant effect on their linguistic behaviour. If men and women in particular communities participate in different types of networks, then they will demonstrate different types of linguistic behaviour, as Milroy has shown for Belfast.

Brown's discussion of the role of social networks applies most pertinently in her own research to *language use* differences. She writes:

> Positive politeness prevails if and when social networks involve multiplex relationships, that is, members have many-sided relationships with each

> person they interact with regularly. . . . Where
> men dominate the public sphere of life and women
> stick largely to the domestic sphere, it seems
> likely that female relationships will be relatively
> multi-stranded, male ones relatively single-
> stranged, and where these conditions prevail,
> positive politeness should be strongly elaborated
> in women's speech.

It seems perfectly plausible, however, that networks can be appealed to also in explanations for *dialect and accent* sex differences. Togeby, for instance, attempts to relate both types of sex differentiation to differential responses by men and women to the 'authority norm' and the 'ambition norm'. These in turn stem from the fact that the two sexes are differentially involved with the 'intimate, family sphere' and the 'social and economic sphere' of social life. The family sphere, Togeby argues, is the only area in which the 'authority norm' can predominate (though he does not give a satisfactory explanation of why this is so). Since women are more closely connected with this sphere than men, they are more responsive to the 'authority norm', i.e. they are more susceptible to the linguistic influence of those members of society who wield the power - and therefore employ more prestigious pronunciations. (Men, correspondingly, are more involved with 'ambition', and therefore use more competitive, attacking conversational strategies.)

6. A further explanation, or series of explanations, that is frequently advanced is one that depends on the findings of sociologists (see Martin, 1954) that women in our society are generally speaking, more status-conscious than men, and are therefore more aware of the social significance of linguistic variables. There are three reasons which are, in turn, advanced for this greater linguistic/social awareness:

> (a) Women are more closely involved with child-rearing
> and the transmission of culture, and are therefore more aware
> of the importance, for their children, of the acquisition of
> (prestige) norms.

> (b) The social position of women in our society has traditionally been less secure than that of men. It may be,
> therefore, that it has been more necessary for women to
> secure and signal their social status linguistically and in other
> ways, and they may for this reason be more aware of the
> importance of this type of signal.

> (c) Men in our society have traditionally been rated
> socially by their occupation, their earning power, and perhaps
> by their other abilities - in other words, by that they *do*.
> Until recently, however, this has been much more difficult
> for women, and indeed women continue to suffer discimination
> against them in many occupations. It may be, therefore,
> that they have had to be rated instead, to a greater extent
> than men, on how they *appear*. Since they have not been
> rated, to the same extent that men have, by their occupation

or by their occupational success, other signals of status, including speech, have been correspondingly more important. (The fact that I have written the above should, once again, be taken to be a straightforward reportage of what I take to be the facts concerning our society's traditional evaluation and provision of occupations for women. It does not mean that I approve of occupational discrimination against women, and it most certainly does not mean 'that Trudgill does not take women's work into account and does not value it' (Spender, 1980). One should not, as Spender does, blame the messenger for bringing back news, however much one dislikes the news.)

7. A final, though not necessarily unrelated, explanation, lies in the claim that working-class speech appears in our society to have connotations of masculinity.

REFERENCES

Brown, P. (1980) "How and why women are more polite: some evidence from a Mayan community." In S. McConnell-Ginet et. al., *Women and Language in Culture and Society*. New York: Praeger.

Cheshire, J. (1982). *Variation in an English Dialect: A Sociolinguistic Study*. Cambridge: Cambridge University Press.

Crystal, D. (1971) "Prosodic and paralinguistic correlates of social categories." In E. Ardener (ed.), *Social Anthropology and Language*. London: Tavistock.

Fasold, R. W. (1968) "A Sociolinguistic study of the pronunciation of three vowels in Detroit speech. Unpublished mimeo: Center for Applied Linguistics.

Fischer, J. L. (1958) "Social influences on the choice of a linguistic variant." *Word* , 14.47-56.

Giles, H. (1973) "Accent mobility: a model and some data." *Anthropological Linguistics*, 15, 37-105.

Haas, M. (1944) "Men's and women's speech in Koasati." *Language*, 120, 42-9.

Hertzler, J. (1954) *A Sociology of Language* . New York: Random House.

Jespersen, O. (1922) *Language: Its Nature, DEvelopment, and Origin*. London: Allen & Unwin.

Jörgensen, N. (1960) *Om makrosyntagmer i informell och formell stil*. Lund: Lund University.

Labov, W. (1966) *The Social Stratification of English in New York City*. Washington, D.C.: Center for Applied Linguistics.

Labov, W. (1978) "Where does the sociolinguistic variable stop? A response to Beatriz Lavender." *Working Papers in Sociolinguistics*, 44. Austin, Texas: Southwest Educational Development Laboratory.

Lavender, B. (1978) "Where does the sociolinguistic variable stop?" *Language in Society*, 7, 171-83.

Laver, J. and Trudgill, P. (1979) "Phonetic and linguistic markers in speech." In K. Sherer and H. Giles (eds.) *Social Markers in Speech*. London: Cambridge University Press.

Levine, L. and Crockett, H. J. (1966) "Speech variation in a Piedmont community: postvocalic r." In S. Lieberson (ed.) *Explorations in Sociolinguistics*. The Hague: Mouton.

Martin, F. M. (1954) "Some subjective aspects of social stratification." In Glass, D. V. (ed.), *Social Mobility in Britain*. London: Routledge & Kegan Paul.

Milroy, L. (1980) *Language and Social Networks*. Oxford: Blackwell.

Romaine, S. (1978) "Postvocalic /r/ in Scottish English: sound change in progress?" in P. Trudgill (ed.) (1978a) *Sociolinguistic Patterns in British English*. London: Edward Arnold.

Romaine, S. (1981) "On the problem of syntactic variation: a reply to Beatriz Lavender and William Labov." *Working Papers in Sociolinguistics*. 82. Austin, Texas: Southwest Educational Development Laboratory.

Sapir, E. (1929) "Male and female forms of speech in Yana." Reprinted in D. Mandelbaum (ed.) (1949) *Selected Writings of Edward Sapir in Language, Culture and Personality*. Berkeley and Los Angeles: University of California Press.

Shuy, R. W., Wolfram, W. A., and Riley, W. L. (1967) *Linguistic Correlates of Social Stratification in Detroit Speech*. Cooperative Research Project 6-1347. East Lansing: U.S. Office of Education.

Smith, P. (1979) "Sex markers in speech." In K. Scherer and H. Giles (eds.) (1979) *Social Markers in Speech*. London: Cambridge University Press.

Spender, D. (1980) *Man Made Language* . London: Routledge & Kegan Paul.

Togeby, O. (1978) "Autoritets- og ambitionsnormer hos kvinder og maend." In K. Gregersen (ed.) *Papers from the 4th Scandivanian Conference of Linguists* . Odense: Odense University Press.

Trudgill, P. (1974a) *The Social Differentiation of English in Norwich*. London: Cambridge University Press.

Trudgill, P. (1974b) *Sociolinguistics: An Introduction*. Harmondsworth: Penguin Books.

Wolfram, W. A. (1969) *A Sociolinguistic Description of Detroit Negro Speech*. Washington, D.C.: Center for Applied Linguistics.

YOU SAY WHAT YOU ARE: ACCEPTABILITY
AND GENDER-RELATED LANGUAGE

Robin Lakoff

> Her voice was ever soft,
> Gentle and low, an excellent thing in woman.
> W. Shakespeare, *King Lear* 5.3, 272-3

Within the model of transformational generative grammar, questions of grammaticality at first were the ones deemed interesting, important and, indeed, answerable; to the extent that the question of acceptability was raised at all, it was felt to reflect 'performance' rather than 'competence' and therefore to be out of the range of interest of linguistic theory proper. Today, when our model is much more sophisticated and we are very much more demanding of our theory, we tend to be a bit bemused at our insensitivity to the data, a mere decade--nay, seven or eight years--ago; but there was good reason for it, and it is lucky for us today that we in the past were so blind to the facts.

Grammaticality implies an either/or (*/non*) distinction; assuming (an untenable assumption in reality, but the enterprising linguist should be able to believe six impossible things before breakfast) that one can divide all the sentences of a language according to such a criterion makes for a tolerably workable theory. Binary distinctions such as this are relatively simple to make, and there will likely be widespread agreement among linguists as to the assignment of asterisks; indeed, such a theory virtually entails such agreement, since questions of personal idiosyncrasy and imaginativeness are thereby ignored. In those far-off days, too, it will be recalled, binariness of various sorts of features was a feature of transformational theory: phonological distinctive features, syntactic selectional restrictions and semantic markers all were binary. It was tempting to believe that linguistic markers, like other animals, came in pairs, and it was therefore natural to assume that grammaticality was an either-or question.

Syntactic rules were formulated on this basis. Either a derivation was subject to a particular rule or it was not. If a phrase-marker underwent a rule in accordance with its structural descrip-

From *Acceptability in Language*, edited by S. Greenbaum. Mouton Publishers, 1977, pp 73-87.

tion and the conditions on the rule, the resultant derivation would prove grammatical; otherwise an asterisk would be assigned, and that was that. The validity of a particular formulation of a rule was checked this way, too: if sentences were, by this automatic procedure, assigned stars when the native speaker would declare them grammatical, or not assigned stars when he would not, the assumption was that something was the matter with the formulation of the rule; a better one had to be found. The least, in fact, that one could expect of a theory (one that was observationally adequate) was that it would allow all and only the sentences of a language to be generated - another way of saying what I said above.

Assuming, again, that this evaluation procedure approximated the facts of language, it was a simple, streamlined, and elegant procedure. It is obvious that only under such an assumption could rules of the type that were being written at that time have been written at all. Of course, we see with our 20-20 hindsight that this very fact - that binary grammaticality judgments necessitated as well as permitted the rules of classical transformational grammar - casts doubt on the entire set of assumptions we call classical transformational grammar; but at the time, this seemed to us the way things ought to be in a well-ordered universe, and we were still capable of believing, with our endearing childlike faith, that the linguistic universe was well-ordered.

It is further true that a new theory can arise only out of an old theory; it was out of transformational grammar with all its faults that we have constructed our present-day theory with its unnumbered virtues. The change in emphasis from grammaticality to acceptability was forced upon us, around 1967 or 1968, by our recognition of a whole new range of data and our consequent search for more sophisticated explanations for the occurrence and nonoccurrence of sentences. Where grammaticality judgments were determinable by purely linguistic criteria, acceptability judgments invaded the realms of psychology and sociology, greatly increasing the range of possible explanations. But we found we could no longer honestly restrict the concept of explanation to purely linguistic determinants; and inexorably at the same time we found that our judgments were no longer predicated on a binary system of grammaticality, but had to make use of a hierarchy of acceptability.

The necessity for this became clear to me when I was looking (1969) at the use of *some* and *any* in English. When Klima (1964) had examined the data, he had attempted to make grammaticality judgments about the use of these forms, to assign asterisks to sentences on the basis of purely linguistic data. (He managed to sneak psychological assumptions into his set of criteria by the use of his [+affect] marker, but he never openly acknowledged that this was the purpose, or the effect, of adopting his apparently linguistic and apparently binary marker.) When I started looking at sentences containing *some* and *any*, however, I found it impossible to declare many of them purely 'in' or purely 'out'; one could declare a sentence 'good if one made the following assumptions about the state of the speaker's mind' or 'generally out, but acceptable in case the speaker is in a particular and peculiar social situation'. And of course, social, psychological, and linguistic situations intersect and interact with one another, so that immediately it was clear we were dealing with a delicately shaded and rather interminable hierarchy of acceptability.

What also became clear with some more thought was that the hierarchical fuzziness was the form, the clear grammatical judgment rather the exception, an artificial construct useful for the facilitation of theory development rather than an accurate perception of how speakers spoke in the real world. Even those sentences that had previously been adjudged unexceptionably grammatical could now be seen for what they were - good *if* one were uttering the sentence in a particular social-psychological environment; and in fact, many of the sentences so insouciantly described as fully grammatical were now, in the clear light of day, seen to be rather bizarre, like Gleitman's well-known

(1) I wrote my grandmother a letter yesterday and six men can fit in the back seat of a Ford.

That is one obvious case of a sentence that is fully grammatical, that is, linguistically unexceptionable; and yet, if we are judging acceptability - that is, the probability of such a sentence being uttered, or the number of conceivable real-world circumstances or the normality of the real-world circumstances in which this sentence is apt to be used - we find a different judgment pertains, and we must rank this sentence low on an acceptability hierarchy.

On the other hand there are sentences which, taken out of context, are bizarre; some even violate selectional restrictions, such as Morgan's (1973) celebrated example:

(2) I think with a fork.   [Morgan's (106)]

As Morgan notes, 'fragments' such as (2) are intelligible when interpreted from the point of view of a larger context, discourse or social; sentence (2), for instance, is fully intelligible if uttered as a reply to (3):

(3) How does Nixon eat his tapioca?   [Morgan's (105)]

Sentences like (2) would have been asterisked in any classical transformational discussion, as it violates certain selectional restrictions. Yet sentences such as this are frequent in ordinary speech and hence would rank high on any rational acceptability hierarchy. So there are sentences that are ungrammatical but of relatively high acceptability *in context*. Thus, given the correct set of social, situational, and linguistic contexts, both (1) and (2) might be considered good sentences of English. The difference between the two in this regard is that, while one can imagine a reasonably high number of contexts - and 'plausible' contexts, too - in which (2) might be uttered, the same cannot be done for (1). So, defining acceptability in this way, the 'ungrammatical' (2) is a 'better' or more acceptable sentence than the 'grammatical' (1).

Another way to view the grammaticality/acceptability distinction is to say that grammaticality is a special case of acceptability. A sentence is grammatical if it is acceptable according to purely linguistic criteria. Grammaticality is acceptability shorn of social and psychological differentiations. Then it seems fairly apparent that grammaticality is a very highly specialized and not terribly useful concept, outside the realm of strictly autonomous syntax. As soon as we concur that autonomous syntax is not a viable level of analysis (as various works written in the last ten years have, I feel, conclusively proved), we see that a separate notion of grammaticality is neither necessary nor possible within a coherent linguistic theory. But if we discard grammaticality as a criterion, how are we to talk about cases of the kind discussed above, where, apparently, grammaticality and acceptability do not coincide? Here we must speak of normal extra-linguistic context. Although a sentence is judged by its appropriateness in its social, psychological, and linguistic contexts, we may assume that some of these contexts outrank others in determining whether a sentence is acceptable. Thus, (1) would have to be judged acceptable in terms of linguistic context, unacceptable in psychological context (that is, a participant in a discourse would be hard put to figure out what the two parts of the conjunct had to do with each other, and hence the conjunct as a whole is psychologically invalid). But (2) is unacceptable in terms of pure syntactic grammaticality (selectional restrictions between verb and adverbial phrase are violated) but psychologically viable (since participants are capable of figuring out from prior linguistic context what has to be supplied to make the sentence in this particular form intelligible). Further, we may say that in certain social situations - e.g., informal discourse - (2) is acceptable. But in others, though the participants have the psychological ability to make sense of the utterance, they are unwilling or unable to use it, and so we must confine the acceptability of (2) to certain social contexts. These examples serve to show that psychological acceptability outranks purely linguist acceptability.

In any case it is clear that using acceptability rather than grammaticality judgments forces us into a much more complex theory of syntax and one with many more variables, but one which, used correctly, makes for more accurate predictions - which is, after all, what a linguistic theory should do. It is a far more problematic theory, however; and the assignment of particular points on the hierarchy to particular sentences is not the hardest issue to be solved if one is to make good use of the notion of hierarchical acceptability. What I want to do for the remainder of this paper is examine one particularly vexing problem: the applicability of the concept of acceptability to one dialect of American English, and the question of when a judgment of acceptability ceases to be a linguistic judgment and becomes a political statement.

In earlier work (1975) I talked about differences between men's language, or rather the standard language, and 'women's' language. I catalogued a number of features that seem to charac-

terize women's language, in those segments of the American populace that, consciously or otherwise, make that distinction. (It is
useful to bear in mind, here and in succeeding discussion, that
a speaker's disavowal of the use of, or even the knowledge of,
women's language does not mean she does not or cannot use or
understand it. In socially and psychologically charged issues
such as whether or not one speaks women's language, one's judgments as to one's own speech patterns may easily be false; what
one says is by no means identical to what one wishes one says
or fears one says. This fact colors *all* intuitive observation, as
Labov has correctly noted; but it colors the most strongly those
observations where the observer has something to gain or lose
by his (or her) decision. And although some women will find it
necessary to believe that they *always* use women's language, and
others that they *never* do, it is probably true that all of us use
some of it some of the time, whether we want to or not, whether
we hear ourselves doing it or not.)

Let me recapitulate briefly what I consider characteristic of
women's language:

1. Special vocabulary - in particular, women seem to discriminate linguistically among colors with more precision than do men.

2. Use of adjectives that principally express the speaker's
feelings toward the subject under discussion: *charming*, *adorable*,
divine, and the like.

3. Use of empty intensifiers like *so*, *such*.

4. Greater adherence to standard 'correct' forms, avoidance
of slang and neologisms, both lexically and grammatically. For
example, psychological studies of kindergarten-age and nursery-
school children indicate that, even at this age, little girls are
guardians of 'correct' grammar: they 'drop their gs' in participial
endings (*runnin'*, *talkin'*) much less than boys, use fewer substandard forms (*ain't*, *snuck*), less double negation (*I didn't do
nothin'*), use fewer 'bad' words and in general articulate more
precisely. These traits become a part of traditional adult women's
language.

5. Use of lexical, grammatical or phonological devices to suggest hesitancy or deference. Examples:

a. Prefacing declarative utterances with *I guess*, questions
with *I wonder*, etc. In this way the speaker mitigates the force
of her speech act, creating an impression of hesitancy to impose
her opinions on other participants in a discourse and thereby
giving an impression of politeness, or deference. Of course
things are not necessarily what they seem, and the politeness,
or deference, may be conventional rather than real. But confusion
may easily arise, and the speaker's character be judged by her
superficial style - marking her as indecisive, inarticulate and
fuzzy-minded. On the other hand, if, in traditional American
culture, a female speaker habitually fails to employ these devices,
she is categorized as aggressive and unfeminine. Until recently,
most speakers have opted for the first of these uncomfortable
options.

    b.   Silences or interjections like *ah*, *um*. . .

    c.   Use of questions where a declarative would be more appropriate (i.e., where the speaker is in possession of the necessary information, if anyone is). In such cases, the question is not a request that the addressee supply *information* but rather that he supply *reassurance* that the speaker's speech-act is acceptable to him.

    d.   Lower vocal volume, sometimes a mere whisper.

    6.   Greater use of euphemism for topics that are considered to be taboo or unladylike, as well as greater tact in avoiding sensitive topics in the presence of people they are sensitive to. For this reason (also a part of non-linguistic behavior, of course) women have typically been considered the arbiters of etiquette as well as the mainstays of conservatism. This latter role is also illustrated in point 4. Otto Jespersen was perhaps the first to discuss the role of women in linguistic conservatism. More recently Labov has made the opposite claim: that women are linguistically more innovative than men. As with most cases of conflicting claims, both are probably partially valid, and each especially valid in the writer's contemporary society. It is also true that a group might be conservative in one aspect of language use, radical in another. Thus, if the behavioral role of a particular group were facilitated by an emergent linguistic form, the group to whose advantage it would be to adopt this form might well do so more quickly than other social groups and in this regard appear especially innovative. But in other aspects of language use, the same group might elect to be more conservative. For example (as discussed by Edwin Newman [1974] among many others) a relatively recent trend in American speech favors the use of speech-act hedges like *like, y'know, I mean* . . . (For some discussion of the role of these hedges in American English, see my review of Newman [to appear].) Now as I noted above, for reasons consonant with their traditional social role, women have a tendency to use hedges more profusely than do men. It might therefore be to their advantage to adopt these hedges more quickly and more profusely than men do. But they might still stoutly resist other changes, e.g., the use of *like* for *as*. Labov, I believe, was talking about phonological innovation. Often, nonstandard phonological forms sound 'cute', or nonserious, and mark the speech-act in which they occur as amusing, social rather than informative. For example, we can think of the shift to Black English among middle-class white academics when they are feeling linguistically playful or the use of baby-talk by one speaker to show that he isn't really in sympathy with someone else's complaints. The more serious the occasion, the more pompously conservative the style, and bombast seems in our culture to be more available to men than to women. Thus it would be to a woman's advantage to use phonological forms that made her sound 'cute' and nonserious - for the same reason that it is to her advantage to have in her lexicon adjectives like *charming*, *divine*, and *adorable*. In other times, women might be assumed to be

more innovative because they were less educated, were less in touch with a formal norm. And where women are seen as the arbiters of respectability, it is to be expected that they will resist any change that can be viewed as a lowering of standards, linguistic or moral.

7. Greater variation in pitch and intonation. This difference might be viewed in either of two ways: as a means of achieving indirectness or as a way of expressing emotion. By making use of pitch and intonation variation, one can express thoughts and feelings nonverbally which it might be difficult or uncomfortable to put into words. But if one has no intention of explicitly talking about one's feelings, more emotional warmth is conveyed by a speech style that allows these variations than one that does not. So to judge what such a trait connotes for an individual's speech-style, one must first examine the rest of her (or his) style.

Then we may say that three basic trends characterize women's language as a deviation from the standard:

1. Nondirectness: e.g., 5, 6, 7
2. Emotional expression: e.g., 2, 3, 6 and 7
3. Conservatism: e.g., 4 and 6

Point (1) does not figure in this summary, and indeed it is rather misleading to categorize 'special vocabulary' as idiosyncratic to women's language. The deeper point to be made here is that every subculture has its own vocabulary and that vocabulary will involve terms that are of specific use to the particular culture in question. Whorf, of course, was the first to raise this issue when he pointed out that Eskimo has six words for 'snow' where English has just one - presumably because snow is much more important in the Eskimos' lives than it is in ours, and minute differences in the quality and quantity of snow are for them of crucial importance, as they are not for us. So they need precise words to make these crucial distinctions, as we do not. As I have said elsewhere, this is undoubtedly the reason for the more precise color-discrimination vocabulary among women because it has traditionally been considered important for a woman to possess this sort of expertise, for fashion and interior decoration have both been women's work. Of course, men have their own special highly developed vocabularies, e.g., in regard to automobiles and sports, to which women traditionally have not been privy.

What we find, then, in looking at those traits that distinguish women's language from neutral language is that we can define them in terms that cover more purely linguistic behavior. In fact, the only distinction it seems reasonable to assert between the two forms of English, rather than arising directly out of differences in the learning of a linguistically relevant grammatical system, appear to stem from differences in what is socially and psychologically expected of women in terms of explicit behavior, both linguistic and nonlinguistic. Where women's speech differs syntactically from the standard it does not differ in containing more, fewer or differently stated rules. I know of no syntactic

rule present in one group's grammar and entirely absent from
the other: that is, I know of no case where a sentence utterable
by one group would be totally impossible in all contexts for the
other.   In this sense we are not even dealing with differences in
the linguistic conditions for the applicability of rules, or their
order, as is true of dialect differences in quantifier-crossing as
discussed by Carden and others.   It is not out of the question
that this *might* be so, and in other languages it would not be
overly surprising if it were so.   How would it look?   It might
mirror Carden's cases.   Thus, suppose that all English-speaking
men, when they encountered (4):

   (4)   All of the boys don't like some of the girls,
interpreted it as (5):

   (5)   None of the boys like certain girls: namely, Mary, Alice,
Nancy . . .
Whereas, faced with the same sentence, all English-speaking women
interpreted it as (6):

   (6)   Only some of the boys - Fred, John, Max . . . - like
some of the girls.
But, as I say, I know of no such cases.   Rather, even where
syntactic rules such as question-formation are involved, the difference between the dialects lies in the fact that in one a sentence
is usable in more social or psychological situations than in the
other.   So we cannot define the two dialects in terms of purély
linguistic autonomous-syntactic distinctions.   Additional reason for
this belief is the fact that even if a woman will not or cannot
use certain forms that are not parts of traditional women's language, she can certainly understand them and, if she is of a
certain personality type, when she encounters them in other people's speech, can correct them, i.e., indicate what forms in *her*
dialect are equivalent to the ones she has heard.

   All this suggests that linguistic deviation from the norm is
but one form of social deviation from the norm.   But here we
must raise another, and more troubling, question: what do we
mean when we talk about the norm?   Whose norm?   And to what
extent, when we talk about norms and standards and deviations,
are we invoking value judgments?   Psychological writers in particular often claim piously that they intend no reproof when they
speak of abnormality or aberration; but actually one typically
finds the implicit claim that the standard is better, and if you
know what's good form you'll adhere to it.   Of course, this then
constitutes a self-fulfilling prophecy.   The same has been true
too often in the past in linguistic dialectology, which tended to
be prescriptive and, more or less overtly, looked with disapproval
at 'substandard' forms.   But in the case of women's language the
question becomes a bit more complex: if a woman in our society
speaks traditional women's language, and more generally behaves
like a traditional woman, is she conforming to our cultural norm?
Or deviating from it?   And if we must be prescriptive, what
shall we punish as deviant?   More positively, for what kinds of
behavior shall a woman in our society be rewarded?   What, return-

ing to the theme of this essay, constitutes 'acceptability' for a woman in this culture - linguistically and behaviorally?

In fact it is less the bare notion of acceptability that causes difficulty than the fact that it is made into a prescription. In the same way we can talk about expectation being a two-edged concept. We *expect* women to talk a certain way, which is only partly damaging; but we also expect it of women that they will behave a certain way, and thereby we impose a value judgment, either that it's good for a woman to talk traditional women's language because it fits the stereotype, which is by definition good because it does not force us to readjust our perception of reality; or it's bad for women to speak women's language because it deviates from the norm, and the norm for society as a whole is viewed as a good thing to adhere to, and any deviation is to be criticized. And both linguistically and otherwise, when we say that a certain form of behavior is 'acceptable' for a woman, we tend to be prescribing - both for the woman, that she act this way to indicate she 'knows her place,' and for a man, that he *not* act this way, to show he knows *his*. This kind of prescriptivism is constraining and destructive. We should be able to think about acceptability in regard to linguistic gender distinctions without recourse to value judgments, just as linguists several generations ago pointed out that description did not imply prescription, that talking about a norm did not imply that deviation from that norm was censurable. I recall that Paul Goodman - no doubt in good company - made this mistake some years back in an article in the *New York Review of Books*, in which he criticized Chomsky's linguistic work on the grounds that - by distinguishing sentences that were grammatical from those which were not - he was squashing linguistic creativity and innovation. But the distinction between description and prescription is still blurrier, even among linguists, than we might like, particularly in areas where we have been brought up to make value judgments before we learned to be disinterested academic observers. The question of gender-related roles is one of these highly charged areas, and it therefore behooves us in discussing acceptability as a factor in understanding women's language to bear in mind that there is a danger that we will confuse linguistic norms with social values.

There are other confusions to be avoided. The notion of acceptability, I have said above, implies a standard against which a speech act may be judged. It has also been pointed out that, in talking about acceptability as opposed to grammaticality, that standard is grounded in social and psychological context: an act of speech or behavior is judged acceptable in a specific context. Now, it would seem at first glance that men and women, being these days participants in the same activities, similarly educated, at least superficially raised alike, would share this set of contexts. A male and a female, participating in a specific kind of behavior, linguistic or otherwise, would perceive the context in which the behavior was to take place similarly. But if acceptability implies appropriateness within a particular social-psychological setting, and as we have suggested men's and women's languages differ somewhat in terms of what is acceptable, then we are faced with a paradox.

We must, rather, assume, I think, that a given context is interpreted one way by a male speaker, another by a female. Actually, it will be recalled we are dealing with a complex hierarchy of acceptability, and it is in principle not at all unlikely that different speakers will arrange their worlds in quite different ways. It is not as though every male speaker of English defines Contexts A-L, let us say, as 'situations requiring directness' and M-Z as 'requiring nondirectness', while all women interpret situations A-P in the former way, Q-Z in the latter. We would prefer to say - continuing for the sake of clarity to look at the division of social contexts in this extremely simplistic way for the moment - that women would tend to interpret situations as requiring nondirectness until further down in the alphabet than men typically would. But all sorts of variations are conceivable. That is, what I mean by saying that traditionally women's language has tended toward nondirectness is that women will interpret a greater number of social contexts as being appropriate for nondirect expression than will men; and perhaps as well, that women will, in a situation in which both men and women would tend toward nondirectness, tend toward greater nondirectness. But this implies that a woman's social/psychological context is often, or perhaps always, different from that of a man. Whether innately, or through early education, a woman learns to perceive social situations, and interpret psychological events, one way, a man, another. Hence a setting that would evoke one set of linguistic responses in a man would be expected to evoke another in a woman.

It this is true, it seems reasonable to say that, if we want to even out the differences in linguistic behavior between men and women (a goal the utility not to say feasibility of which is in my mind very much open to question), linguistic behavior cannot be changed directly but only through somehow educating men and women so that they typically perceive the same situation in the same way. Of course, many questions are being begged here: it is also apparent that no two individuals, in all likelihood, perceive a single social or psychological setting precisely identically. But we are talking here about somewhat grosser differentiations; the problem is, how much grosser? Since we have been talking in terms of a complex, highly individualized hierarchy, at what point do we draw the line and stop speaking about individual idiosyncrasies and start recognizing broader sex-linked distinctions? Since it will, predictably, never be so that 100 percent of the men react in one way to a situation, 100 percent of the women a different way, at what point do we decide we are dealing with 'women's language'?

We tend to consider women's language as the aberration from the norm, the standard. To do so raises more problems.

First, there is the implication that to be a woman is to be a deviant. This has traditionally been true - people have looked at men's behavior as the norm, as rational, and men's language likewise. Hence it has been typical - to the extent that such a topic has even been considered worthy of discussion - to talk about women's language. Men's language is language and need not be further specified. But this is the case also as we would expect for other aspects of human behavior. Until recently no one has lifted an eyebrow at questions like, 'Was will das Weib?' suggesting that a woman was a thing apart, something *we* could analyze. But the question 'Was will der Mann?' would have been unthinkable. But if men's behavior is the standard, so normal that it is not even worth investigating in its own right, then a woman cannot expect equality with men. She simply is not parallel to a man, and thus cannot expect to be treated similarly.

Moreover, there is another danger in looking at women's language as having special and idiosyncratic standards for acceptability. What is a woman to do? If she adopts the frame of reference of a man - supposing she can - she will be ostracized by traditional society for not conforming to what is acceptable for a woman. If, on the other hand, she does adopt women's behavior, she will be treated nonseriously because her behavior is not commensurate with the standard, the behavior expected of men.

There is one corner of the real world where, interestingly, the distinction between men's and women's language seems to be blurred: the same set of social and psychological conditions, or very nearly so, are operative in determining the acceptability of utterances both of men and of women. This occurs in academia. The traits I listed earlier as characteristic of women's speech are frequent in academic men's speech, and academic women's speech tends at the same time to use these devices less than does the speech of traditional women. This is not, I think, to imply that academics are sexless or that academic men and women find themselves in social settings that cause them to perceive their roles differently less often than does the general populace. Rather, I think that this difference indicates that male and female professionals, in academia, regardless of gender, perceive their roles as similar and hence tend to have similar perceptions of the social and psychological settings in which they find themselves. It is interesting that the distinction is not erased in favor of the masculine form, but rather there is a neutralization toward the center. What is of interest in this is that in society generally, when there is pressure to blur sex distinctions in roles, usually women seek to adopt men's prerogatives, seldom the reverse. But in academia some of women's prerogatives - nondirectness and expression of emotions - are adopted by men. I have suggested elsewhere that these traits have less to do with anything inherent in the female character than they do with being at the periphery of power, or opting out of power. Academics, the British upper class men, and women all share this situation, for various reasons and in different ways, and hence, to a rather surprising extent, share their language.

My conclusions then are clear:

1.   There is a women's language in American English, if by that we mean that in a particular context, women and men may not express the same thing in the same way.

2.   This difference is not traceable to the purely linguistic grammar: the distinctions are not statable in terms of syntactically conditioned rules, nor are they statable as *either/or* pairs.   The differences involve hierarchical acceptability - some sentences are better for women to say in some circumstances.

3.   Acceptability in language is directly related to social and psychological perceptions; a sentence is defined as acceptable if it is fitting in the setting in which it is used.   Grammaticality, then, is a special case of acceptability, in which only the linguistic aspects of the social-psychological setting are taken into account.

4.   Therefore it seems likely that men and women learn to view similar social and psychological contexts diifferently and hence will find it appropriate to utter different sentences in the same setting.

5.   Women's language differs from the standard in being more nondirect, more capable of expressing emotion and more conservative.

6.   There is a danger in opposing 'women's language' to 'the standard', as there is of opposing any group's behavior to a hypothetical 'standard'; and it is by no means clear what is best for women or for society: to perpetuate the dual standards of acceptability or seek to merge them.

REFERENCES

Klima, E.   (1964), 'Negation in English', in J. A. Fodor and J. J. Katz, eds., *The Structure of Language: Readings in the Philosophy of Language*.   Englewood Cliffs, N.J., Prentice-Hall.

Lakoff, R.   (1969), 'Some reasons why there can't be any some-any rule', *Language*, 55, pp. 608-615.

Lakoff, R.   (1975), *Language and Woman's Place*.   New York, Harper and Row.

Lakoff, R.   (1976).   'Why you can't say what you mean,' review of E. Newman, *Strictly Speaking*, *Centrum* 4: 151-170.

Morgan, J. L.   (1973), 'Sentence fragments and the notion, "Sentence"', in B. Kachru et. al., eds., *Issues in Linguistics in Honor of Henry and Renee Kahane*.   Urbana, Ill., University of Illinois Press.

Newman, E.   (1974), *Strictly Speaking*.   New York, Bobbs-Merrill.

SOCIAL DIALECTOLOGY:

A PLEA FOR MORE DATA

Wolfgang Viereck

In the *Grammar* of his home dialect of Windhill in Yorkshire, published in 1892, Joseph Wright presented a vowel system that had developed "correctly" from the vowel systems of Old and Middle English. According to Wright, someone who was born in a certain area, had lived there all his life, and had been exposed only to the linguistic influences of this limited area had to mirror correctly this local speech pattern. If he deviated from this norm and used 'unexpected' forms - Wright noticed this (cf. his *English dialect grammar*, pp. IV and V); however, he suppressed it in his Windhill-*Grammar* - he was making "mistakes", for which there was no room in the description of a "pure, homogeneous" dialect. Wright was not aware of the fact that a speaker could make use of several linguistic registers and that his way of speaking could be influenced by a number of factors. Consequently, the result was an idealized description of a dialect in which every dialectal sound could be derived correctly from a Middle English predecessor. Quite a few descriptions of English dialects that followed used Wright's analysis as a model.

We meet idealizations in linguistics also later, even if different premises underlie them. With regard to linguistic theory certain idealizations are no doubt necessary. Ideally, linguistic data obtained on a sound basis should condition linguistic theories and models. This is self-evident to anyone working in the field of linguistic variation, one should think. Linguistic theory needs a strong empirical basis. "We will concede that it is desirable to have the most elegant theoretical analysis possible. Nevertheless, data must not be buried in an elegant symmetry. If the theory will not accommodate the data, then the theory must be modified in some way, or a new theory must be devised", as R. I. McDavid, Jr., has put it elsewhere. Symptomatic of the method, however, employed in several linguistic quarters nowadays seems, regrettably, to be a book by Burgschmidt and Götz, published in 1974, on contrastive linguistics: the first five chapters, i.e. almost three quarters of the book, are concerned with theoretical

From *Studia Anglica Posnaniensia* 7:12-25, 1979.

questions. Only at the end of the book does the reader get
some information on actual differences between German and English.
The arrangement and the weighting of both parts of the book
point in the same direction: Theories exist prior to linguistic
data!

Yet also in a theory-dominated time there existed the "dull
cataloguer of data", to use Robert B. Lees's 'famous' remark.
Even though today *data* is the most obscene of the four-letter
words for many linguists, we have witnessed in recent years a
significant change insofar as the "dull cataloguer of data" no
longer leads a shadowy existence now. In some linguistic areas
he even begins to dominate the scene. The analysis of the
"mistakes" in the sense of Joseph Wright has come of age. Even
in the area of formal grammar the study of language as a social
instrument does not remain without influence. Chomsky's theses
of the "well-formedness" of "grammatical" "sentences" were criticized increasingly in the light of linguistic reality, i.e. also linguistic variability. There is no way of talking about grammaticality
or well-formedness without getting involved in the intricate details
of social interaction by means of language.

In the area of linguistic variation in English it is, perhaps,
advantageous to differentiate with Aarts (1976) between two directions of present-day research - one that deals primarily with language *structure* and the other that is mainly concerned with the
investigation of *usage*. As regards the direction mentioned first,
we owe the most detailed synchronic description of English to the
collaborators of the London *Survey of English usage*. The *Grammar
of Contemporary English* by Quirk *et al* ., published in 1972, is
characteristically restricted to 'educated English'. It is a so-called
'common-core' grammar of "educated English current in the second
half of the twentieth century in the world's major English-speaking
communities" (p. V), i.e. it is made clear that *the* English language
does not exist. It is rather a heterogeneous formation; the
common core of all 'educated variants' is described here. On the
American side there is nothing comparable to this *Grammar*. Instead, American scholars are concerned above all with problems
of *usage* trying to cover the complete linguistic reality in concrete
situations. (It was, above all, Trudgill 1974 who introduced this
kind of research in Great Britain.) Most of these sociolinguistic
studies also claim to be structurally oriented. However, there is
an important difference between this type of study and the just
mentioned *Grammar* by Quirk and his associates - which, by the
way, is concerned almost exclusively with syntax - in that the
sociolinguistic studies investigate the social stratification of certain
elements which are not related with one another. In other words,
they are extremely taxonomic. The first survey of this school of
thought in the United States we owe to Wolfram and Fasold. In
their book *The study of social dialects in American English*, published in 1974, they provide in chapter 2, entitled "Social dialects
as a field of inquiry", an historically oriented overview - which
is rather unfair. They discuss Charles C. Fries's *American Eng-*

lish Grammar (1940) in half a page, the activities of the American
linguistic geographers in less than two pages and then describe
at great length the 'new type' of dialect studies under the heading
"Quantitative studies" - as if Fries's *Grammar* had not been quantitative.   However, he also quantified the results of his empirical
study; in fact, we owe a number of important insights to Fries.
But, it is true, only a few people listened to him and hardly
anybody in the schools, to whom he had mainly addressed himself.

As regards the criteria according to which Fries classified
his informants - they are almost identical with those of the *Linguistic atlas*.   Of course, they do not suit the taste of modern
sociolinguists - for them they lack objectivity.   Modern sociolinguists rather stick to objectively measurable factors, such as
income and house type, which they then multiply differently without giving any reasons for this.   This is the procedure followed,
among others, by Shuy, Wolfram, and Riley in their Detroit Dialect
Survey (1968).   Here as well as in similar studies of a more
recent date the procedure is binary: two races are distinguished,
two classes - a middle and a working class - and these two classes
are again subdivided each into an upper and a lower class.
Whether a division according to purely mechanical factors, as the
ones mentioned, is better than to ask - as the *Linguistic atlas*
does - for factors such as church membership, leisure-time activities and community organizations is at least an open question.
The latter-named factors may have a more direct bearing on social
class than a simple measurement of economic factors.

Still, there is not the slightest doubt about the importance
of the dialect studies of the new type.   Although quite a few of
them do not come up to their self-imposed standards - one should
not let oneself be deceived by the statistically ascertained results
which give a very reliable and exact impression - some of these
studies have affected linguistic theory a great deal - above all
the work carried out by William Labov.   Right from the beginning
he had the consequences of his research for linguistic theory in
mind.   In *The social stratification of English in New York City*
(1966) he says clearly: "In the past few years, there has been
considerable programmatic discussion of *sociolinguistics* at various
meetings and symposia.   If this term refers to the use of data
from the speech community to solve problems of linguistic theory,
then I would agree that it applies to the research described
here.   But *sociolinguistics* is more frequently used to suggest
a new interdisciplinary field - the comprehensive description of
the relations of language and society.   This seems to me an
unfortunate notion, foreshadowing a long series of purely descriptive studies with little bearing on the central theoretical problems
of linguistics or of sociology" (p. V).

Thus Labov's work must also be seen as a reaction against
those areas which had before been excluded from serious consideration by *many* authorities in US linguistics, such as the field of
language change or the problem whether linguistic variants are
really "free".

Labov and Chomsky hold completely opposite views. (We deliberately exclude the Prague school from our discussion here.) Chomsky is concerned with anti-sociolinguistic idealizations of the ideal speaker-listener and of the homogeneous speech of the speaker-listener. In his *Aspects of the theory of syntax* of 1965 Chomsky says: "A grammar of a language purports to be a description of the ideal speaker-hearer's intrinsic competence" (p.4). According to Chomsky, the grammar of *one* member of a homogeneous and static speech community is thus identical with that of every other member of the same speech community. Thus interpersonal (and intrapersonal) linguistic variation is completely ignored. On the other hand, Labov maintains that "the construction of complete grammars for 'idiolects', even one's own, is a fruitless and unrewarding task; we now know enough about language in its social context to realize that the grammar of the speech community is more regular and systematic than the behaviour of any one individual", as he puts it in his article "Contraction, deletion, and inherent variability of the English copula", published in *Language* in 1969. This, again, is an idealization, even if different from the one proposed by Chomsky, for Labov's grammars make far too great demands on the human memory. This becomes especially noticeable with Labov's variable rules. If, for example, a certain element is deleted in certain speakers in 75.2% of all cases, then a rule is postulated that deletes this element in these speakers in 75.2% of all possible applications. It has already been pointed out (e.g. by Bickerton 1971) that it is completely impossible to learn a language in this way as the numbers of different variability are far too great and unsystematic. Later Labov changed his variable rules: the percentage figures that originally appeared as index numbers were abandoned in favour of a hierarchical arrangement in which variability is taken into account in that way that some rules are more optional than others. Apart from the fact that the number of such relations is still enormously high, the question arises whether these variable rules are really capable of what they seem fit in their adherents' opinion, namely to predict precisely the linguistic behaviour of *any one* member of the group from which the speech data were drawn. Some scholars were, it is true, somewhat cautious with this far-reaching claim, while others postulated it bluntly. To the latter group belong Cedergren and Sankoff (1974), who declare that the variable rule "accurately predicts the behavior of each individual" (p. 335). It is exactly this precise predictability of linguistic behaviour which must be doubted very much in view of the fact that two speakers belonging to the *same social class* - however defined - show great differences with regard to the use of a certain variable. Wolfram in his analysis of Detroit Negro speech, published in 1969, provides significant examples of this. One must therefore ask with Butters 1973 (1975) whether Labov did not simply set a statistically idealized speaker-listener against Chomsky's idealized speaker-listener. In any case, linguistic variability of *individual* speakers deserves thorough investigation.

Another objection against Labov's approach - rightly pointed out already by Dressler (1976) - lies in the problem of the perception of the numerous, often only *fine-grained* frequencies and their immediate 'consumption' by the hearer. This asserted capability is the more surprising when Labov concludes from subjective reaction tests "that stigmatized features are not overtly perceived up to a certain frequency, and heard beyond a certain frequency, as occurring all the time" (1971:470). As Labov himself found out, the classification of a speaker according to various sociolinguistic criteria takes place so fast - in his subjective reaction tests Labov used only very short speech samples of every classifiable person - that no representative probabilities could have possibly been attained by the hearer (cf. also Dressler 1976:61).

Despite extensive empirical investigations carried out by Labov and his followers many questions, as we have seen, still remain unanswered. To this list also belong the following: how many styles have to be differentiated, how are they to be determined, and how are we to differentiate between stylistically conditioned and inherent variability. It is true that Labov explains linguistic variation within the same situation as inherent variability; on the other hand, he also takes dialect mixture into account without, however, stating the limits of the applicability of this principle.

Fries's *American English grammar* and the 'new type' of dialect studies have in spite of all the undeniable differences revealed as a common result the fact that speakers belonging to different social classes mostly differ from each other not by the rigorous use versus non-use of certain investigated linguistic features but only by differences in frequency. Linguistic features often found in the lower social class are also heard, although more rarely, in the middle and upper social classes. Thus Detroit Negroes of *all* social classes use, e.g. *he work* and *he works* and analogous forms, although with different frequencies. In other words, it is wrong to allot certain *closed* linguistic systems, which are so readily postulated by many linguists, to certain social classes. The boundaries - linguistic as well as social - are in reality not fixed. Such 'systems', whenever postulated, are nothing but abstractions from real life and allotting them to certain social classes shows an undue simplification.

In the foregoing remarks we referred once or twice briefly to the English spoken by Negroes in the United States. This Black English, so-called, has received increasing attention during the last ten or so years by dialectologists and sociolinguists, thus ignoring other underprivileged groups which outnumber the Afro-Americans by far. It is to be hoped that the linguistic research carried out in the area of the disadvantaged will soon give up this largely one-sided orientation in favour of the Americans of African descent. That Black English is so much discussed today by linguists and educationists alike is not so much justified numerically, but is rather politically motivated. This discussion is often led with more heat than reason and it is necessary to separate fact from fancy.

Mainly two opinions are put forward in this matter nowadays which are unreconcilable with one another. These had their advocates already in the 1930's. We refer in passing here only to the discriminations on the part of the Whites who attributed the English of the Negroes to their low intelligence, and to the 'fact', so-called, that their speech organs had not been properly developed. Consequently, Negroes spoke a corrupt English which resembled *baby talk*. Such views were expressed in the relevant literature rather early, i.e. already during the early years of the twentieth century. At that time "the assumption of the innate and inherited inferiority of non-Anglo-Saxon racial and ethnic groups permeated and dominated intellectual as well as popular thought" in the United States. "Social, scientific and historical thought both mirrored and reinforced this racism" (Yetman 1967:538). Unfortunately, the above-mentioned views can still be heard today. Of the two opinions referred to earlier, one, perhaps the older view, is advanced by American dialectologists who maintain that the English spoken by *lower* class Negroes - the Negroes of the middle and upper middle classes speak Standard English just as the Whites of a comparable social level do - does not differ *typologically* from that of the Whites of the same social and regional background. Black and white speech exhibit the same range of variants, differing at best in frequency. (See the publications of, among others, Juanita Williamson 1972 and 1973, herself a black scholar.) Further, the origin of this kind of English can be traced back to British English and British English dialects. Since for economic reasons Negroes migrated in considerable numbers from the *rural* Southern United States to the *urban* areas in the North and West (roughly within the last sixty years) and naturally took their modes of speech with them, it is possible to speak of a *de facto* Black English in the North of the United States - which in effect is Southern (white) American English. The linguistic geographers tolerate one exception: that is Gullah or Geechee, a creolized variety of English still spoken on the South Carolina and Georgia coasts and on the nearby Sea Islands. The creolists, on the other hand, scholars like William Stewart (1966-67, 1967, 1968) and Beryl L. Bailey (1965), maintain that Black English is a language altogether different from White English because its *deep structure* is different, having its origins in some proto-creole grammatical structure. This is asserted because of some structural similarities between Gullah and some creoles spoken in the Caribbean. Consequently, the British English/British dialect-based origin of Black English is strictly denied. According to the creolists, features of Black English can ultimately be derived from West African languages. Stewart believes that Black English in the rest of the United States, except Gullah that is, is now in a state of decreolization in which creole features are gradually lost. He tries to "prove" the different stages in the development of Black English by unearthing mainly 18th and 19th century attestations of Negro speech in works of literature - which of all the available evidence is the most unreliable source! It is, above all, in the diachronic area where intensive research is still needed before conclusions can be drawn. Apart from Negro speech attestations in works of literature, newspaper advertisements concerning runaway slaves were investigated (cf. Read 1916 and 1939). Of course, no direct conclusions on the nature of early Black English should be drawn from such studies. Furthermore, letters written by Negroes before the Civil War were analysed (cf. Eliason 1956), but these were letters written to their masters, not to fellow slaves. The best available diachronic evidence seems to have hardly been touched so far (an exception is Brewer 1973 [1975]). It consists of 2300 ex-slave narratives. In the 1930's interviews had been conducted in seventeen states with old, mainly rural Blacks who before emancipation had experienced slavery themselves. These vivid reminiscences from ex-slaves have several advantages for a study of Black English: the material "covers a time span extending back to the middle of the nineteenth century [and] it covers a wide geographical area . . . The narratives were written down in longhand as they were spoken" (Brewer 1973:7). Although the project director advised the interviewers that "all stories should be as nearly word-for-word as is possible" (quoted from Brewer 1973:7), a certain amount of editing of both the interviewers' longhand version and the published narratives cannot altogether be ruled out. However, since several interviewers were at work in every state (among them also Negroes), the possible bias of a single interviewer can fairly easily be discovered. Most of this valuable material has recently been published/reprinted (Rawick 1971-1972) and now awaits linguistic analysis.

Although the status of Gullah is undisputed, the relationship between Gullah and the Black English in the other parts of the United States is not; in fact this relationship is crucial also with regard to the origin of the features of Black English. Whereas the dialectologists believe with Turner (1949) that Gullah is an anomaly which developed in a culturally unique situation, it is for the creolists an important piece of evidence to prove an African creole substratum in *all* of Black English. However, their arguments remain unconvincing as long as the creolists fail to explain why certain features which they think characteristic of Black English - such as the habituative or durative *be* - have so far not been recorded in Gullah. They bring forward what serves their purpose and ignore all the other evidence. Thus, durative *be* is found in British English dialects, as is *gwine* 'going to' and related forms; they dominate in the whole south-west of England. Yet creolists trace its origin back to Akan language forms of the word *gwa*, *gwo*, which - according to them - syncretized early with the 'to go' verbs of the Germanic languages (cf. Viereck 1978). So much for this line of research.

From the purely descriptive point of view, Stewart's opinion was supported by Marvin Loflin. He notes: "Efforts to construct a grammar for Nonstandard Negro English suggest that the similarities between it and Standard English are superficial. There is every reason, at this state of research, to believe that a fuller description of Nonstandard Negro English will show a grammatical system which must be treated as a foreign language" (1967:1312). However, the evidence he brings forward is by no means convincing. Thus Loflin, e.g., overlooks the fact that the past tense marker of the verbs, the suffix *-ed*, is deleted in Black English for purely phonological reasons. Wolfram demonstrated this in his investigation of Detroit Negro speech, referred to earlier. This analysis no doubt has its merits, the principal one being to have shown that there exists a stratification of English also within the Black community. However, it sheds no light whatsoever on the problem of the relationship between black and white English. Only by using multiple correlations between black and white speech patterns within social status categories would it have been possible to prove with validity the existence of Black English. (The extent to which Wolfram's data give evidence of the existence of Black English specifically because his informants are black is rather doubtful.) Fragments of an adequate procedure are to be found in Wolfram's comparison of the speech behaviour of the upper-middle class black and white informants. There he had a reference group, although it only served the purpose of representing Standard English. Further shortcomings of Wolfram's procedure are that his sample is not representative of the black community of Detroit at all and that his results, conclusions, and statements are therefore only valid when referring to each individual informant of his sample. One final point deserves mention: Wolfram's analysis of final Z is noteworthy in several respects. With the possessive – which we will take as an example – Wolfram discovers a so-called sharp stratification, that is, there is a distinct difference in usage between the social classes. This is a useful descriptive statement. Deep-structurally, however, Wolfram *cannot* do with *one* deep structure for his *few working-class black informants*! He says: ". . . there are several individuals (among the working-class informants) for whom Z possessive is much more frequently absent than present. For these informants, it is difficult to postulate an underlying . . . Z as a part of their basic N[onstandard] N[egro] E[nglish] system" (1969:142). Apart from the fact that this so-called Black English feature – the absence of the possessive *s* – can also be found in Southern white speech (and in British English dialects), Wolfram encounters the same deep structure difficulties in his treatment of the simplification of consonant clusters (cf. 1969:82) and the post-vocalic /r/ where he says: "It may well be that *some* working-class informants have no underlying R [word-finally and before a consonant]" (1969:115; our italics). We can watch with close attention how many deep structures will be presented to us in the future! Recently, Luelsdorff (1975a, b, c) has added an 'interesting' tint in this respect. In his various contributions Luelsdorff postulates different deep structures for the dialects of Northern, Midland and Southern American English. He does this in using or rather misusing Black English where – in his opinion - there is no contrast between /ɛ/ and /ɪ/ before a nasal, so that e.g. *pen* and *pin* are pronounced the same, namely *pin*. Some reading would have indicated to Luelsdorff that his assertions are incorrect: the pronunciation feature mentioned is by no means characteristic of Black English!

It is, of course, possible to postulate a Black English as a hypothesis but then the results of the investigations must allow a verification or falsification of this hypothesis. As indicated above, Wolfram could do this only in a very insufficient way; it is altogether impossible for Luelsdorff to follow such a procedure, since he works with a *single* informant only: a 14-year old male adolescent! Methodological mistakes are thus perpetuated. One cannot possibly prove the existence of a Black English by comparing the linguistic behavior of blacks and whites of the same social and regional background in comparable speech situations, to say nothing of the problem of the origin of the linguistic forms. This, surely, is a long-term project and nothing for those who - instead of trying to collect all relevant data first - prefer to jump to far-reaching conclusions with little or not even a shred of evidence. Research on Black English has up to now been rather data-poor and theory-rich. The sooner this state is changed, the better it will be for a sensible discussion of the many problems involved.

APPENDIX

At the author's suggestion Edgar W. Schneider analysed a sizeable portion of the slave narratives and published his results in *Morphologische und syntaktische Variablen im amerikanischen Early Black English*. Bamberger Beiträge zur Englischen Sprach-wissenschaft 10.1981. Articles summarising his results in English appeared in *English World-Wide* 3 (1982), the *Journal of English Linguistics* 16 (1983), and *American Speech* 58 (1983).

REFERENCES

Aarts, F. G. 1976. "The description of linguistic variation in English: From Firth till the present day". *English Studies* 57. 239-251.
Bailey, B. L. 1965. "Toward a new perspective in Negro English dialectology". *American Speech* 40. 171-177.
Bickerton, D. 1971. "Inherent variability and variable rules". *Foundations of Language* 7. 457-492.
Brewer, J. 1973 (1975). "Subject concord of *Be* in Early Black English". *American Speech* 48. 5-21.

Burgschmidt, E. and D. Götz. 1974. *Kontrastive Linguistik: Deutsch/Englisch*. Hueber Hochschulreihe 23.

Butters, R. R. 1973 (1975). "Black English [-Z]. Some theoretical implications". *American Speech* 48. 37-45.

Cedergren, H. J. and D. Sankoff. 1974. "Variable rules: Performance as a statistical reflection of Competence". *Language* 50. 333-355.

Chomsky, N. 1965. *Aspects of the Theory of Syntax*. Cambridge, Mass.: The MIT Press.

Davis, L. M. (ed.). 1972. *Studies in Linguistics in Honor of Raven I. McDavid, Jr*. University, Ala.: The University of Alabama Press.

Dillard, J. L. (ed.). 1975. *Perspectives on Black English*. The Hague: Mouton.

Dingwall, W. O. (ed.). 1971. *A Survey of Linguistic Science*. College Park, Md.: University of Maryland.

Dressler, W. W. 1976. "Inhärente Variation und Variable Regel: zur Relativierung eines amerikanischen soziolinguistischen Konzepts". In Schaff, A. (ed.). 1976. 54-73.

Eliason, N. E. 1956. *Tarheel Talk: An Historical Study of the English Language in North Carolina to 1860*. Chapel Hill: The University of North Carolina Press.

Fries, C. C. 1940. *American English Grammar*. New York: Appleton-Century-Crofts.

Labov, W. 1966. *The Social Stratification of English in New York City*. Washington, D.C.: Center for Applied Linguistics.

Labov, W. 1969. "Contraction, deletion, and inherent variability of the English copula". *Language* 45. 715-762.

Labov, W. 1971. "Methodology". In Dingwall, W. O. (ed.). 1971. 413-497.

Lees, R. B. 1957. "Review of N. Chomsky, *Syntactic Structures*". *Language* 33. 375-408.

Loflin, M. D. 1967. "A teaching problem in Nonstandard Negro English". *English Journal* 56. 1312-1314.

Luelsdorff, Ph. 1975a. "Generative dialectology: A review and critique". *Linguistische Berichte* 37. 13-26.

Luelsdorff, Ph. 1975b. "Dialectology in generative grammar". In Dillard, J. L. (ed.). 1975. 74-85.

Luelsdorff, Ph. 1975c. *A Segmental Phonology of Black English*. The Hague: Mouton.

Quirk, R., Greenbaum, S., Leech, G. and J. Svartvik. 1972. *A Grammar of Contemporary English*. London: Longman.

Rawick, G. (ed.). 1971-1972. *The American Slave: A Composite Autobiography*. 19 vols. Westport, Conn.: Greenwood Publishing Co.

Read, A. W. 1916. "Enghteenth century slaves as advertised by their masters". *Journal of Negro History* 1. 163-216.

Read, W. W. 1939. "The speech of Negroes in colonial America". *Journal of Negro History* 24. 247-258.

Schaff, A. (ed.). 1976. *Soziolinguistik*. Wien: Europa-Verlag.
Scholler, H. and J. Reidy (ed.). 1973. *Lexicography and Dialect Geography. Festgabe for Hans Kurath* . ZDL. Beihefte N. F. 9.
Shuy, R. W., W. A. Wolfram, and W. K. Riley. 1968. *Field Techniques in an Urban Language Study*. Washington, D.C.: Center for Applied Linguistics.
Stewart, W. A. 1966-67. "Nonstandard speech patterns". *Baltimore Bulletin of Education* 43. 52-65.
Stewart, W. A. 1967. "Sociolinguistic factors in the history of American Negro dialects". *The Florida FL Reporter* 5. 11, 22, 24, 26.
Stewart, W. A. 1968. "Continuity and change in American Negro dialects". *The Florida FL Reporter* 6. 3-4, 14-16, 18.
Trudgill, P. 1974. *The Social Differentiation of English in Norwich*. Cambridge: Cambridge University Press.
Turner, L. D. 1949. *Africanisms in the Gullah Dialect*. Chicago: The University of Chicago Press. (Reprinted New York 1969 and Ann Arbor 1973).
Viereck, W. 1978. "Afro-Amerikanische Aspekte der Mobilität: 'Black English' - eine kritische Auseinandersetzung". *Amerikastudien/American Studies* 23. 330-340.
Williamson, J. V. 1972. "A look at the direct question". In Davis, L. M. (ed.). 1972. 207-214.
Williamson, J. V. 1973. "On the embedded question". In Scholler, H. and J. Reidy (eds). 1973. 260-267.
Wolfram, W. A. 1969. *A Sociolinguistic Description of Detroit Negro Speech*. Washington, D.C.: Center for Applied Linguistics.
Wolfram, W. A. and R. W. Fasold. 1974. *The Study of Social Dialects in American English*. Englewood Cliffs, N. J.: Prentice-Hall.
Wright, J. 1892. *A Grammar of the Dialect of Windhill, in the West Riding of Yorkshire*. London: English Dialect Society 67.
Wright, J. 1905. *The English Dialect Grammar* . Oxford: Clarendon.
Yetman, N. R. 1967. "The background of the slave narrative collection". *American Quarterly* 19. 534-553.

ETHNICITY AND DIALECTS

Although there can be a correlation between ethnicity and dialects, it does not necessarily exist. Because people identify with those around them, both the region in which they live and the social class to which they belong influence their speech. But because not everyone identifies himself or herself as a member of a particular ethnic group, not everyone speaks an ethnic dialect. Ethnic dialects are spoken only by those whose self-identity is primarily with their ethnic group. For these people, linguistic characteristics may be the most important defining criteria for group membership. When social and economic barriers exist, ethnic dialects are more easily maintained and some times even used to increase social distance. When social mobility and assimilation with the majority group are possible, ethnic dialects tend to atrophy and may even disappear.

Of course, not every member of any ethnic group is distinguishable as a member of that group by his speech. Thus the speech of many Italian Americans, German Americans, Black Americans and Irish Americans does not identify them as members of their respective groups. While not all members of any ethnic group speak the ethnic dialect and some non-ethnic members do speak it, the vast majority of those who do speak it do belong to that ethnic group. For example, not all American Blacks speak Black English Vernacular (BEV), but most people who do speak it are Black. When you hear someone speaking BEV on the telephone, you most likely assume that he or she is Black.

Here it should be mentioned that there is no inherent or necessary link between the spoken language and the ethnicity of the group. Ethnic dialects persist, not because of physical, psychological, or mental characteristics, but because speech patterns are used to signal ethnic and group membership.

In the first article in this section, Martha Laferriere demonstrates that ethnic identity is not of primary importance in determining language variation. Her three-stage model predicts the assimilation of ethnic dialects into Standard English. The variation of *or* among Irish, Italian, and Jewish ethnic groups in Boston suggests that family relationships are a more significant influence than peer group.

In the second article, Ralph Fasold summarizes much of the research on the origin of BEV and concludes that it must have developed as a creole. He provides evidence that some aspects of BEV distinguish its speakers from even the most sociologically comparable southern white speakers. Next John Baugh reviews the controversy surrounding the use of copula in BEV and then uses the Cedergren-Sankoff variable rules to substantiate that it has been influenced by West Indian creoles as well as by Standard English. In the final article, Roger M. Thompson discusses how different aspirations within the Chicano community affect dialect patterns.

The following readings will be helpful for those who want to pursue this topic further:

Baugh, John. *Black Street Speech: Its History, Structure and Survival.* Austin: The University of Texas Press, 1983.

Baugh, John. "A survey of Afro-American English," *American Review of Anthropology*, vol. 12, 335-54, 1983.

Haugen, Einar. *The Norwegian Language in America: A Study in Bilingualism.* 2 vols. Bloomington: Indiana University Press, 1969.

Heath, Shirley Brice. *Ways With Words: Language, Life, and Work in Communities and Classrooms.* New York: Cambridge University Press, 1983.

Labov, William. *Language in the Inner City.* Philadelphia, University of Pennsylvania Press, 1972.

Smitherman, Geneva. *Talkin and Testifyin: The Language of Black America.* New York: Houghton Mifflin, 1977.

Trudgill, Peter. *Sociolinguistics: An Introduction to Language and Society.* London: Penguin Books, 1983.

Wolfram, Walter A. *Sociolinguistic Aspects of Assimilation: Puerto Rican English in New York City.* Arlington, VA: Center for Applied Linguistics, 1974.

ETHNICITY IN PHONOLOGICAL

VARIATION AND CHANGE

Martha Laferriere

In the Boston dialect, the variable *or* as in *short*, *forty*, has two phonetic variants: dialectal [ɒə], and more standard [oə]. Speakers of three ethnic groups--Irish, Italian, and Jewish--showed systematic differences in stylistic and diachronic use of the variants, and in subjective evaluation of them. The observed differences are consistent with a three-stage model of variation and change based on ethnicity and, secondarily, on education. However, an additional factor of 'cultural force' is required to explain why the model may operate at different rates. The model has implications for the acquisition of dialectal vs. standard variants, and lends support to the view that the 'family' provides a stronger influence than the 'peer group' in the development of phonological systems.

'We were a cosmopolitan gang. There were Italians, Scotch, Irish, Bohemians, Jews, and nondescripts. . .' (Goldberg [1929] 1975:347).

Recent studies have documented the importance of age, occupation, sex, socioeconomic level, and social class in conditioning the use of linguistic variants (Fisher 1958, Haas 1944, Labov 1966, 1972, Trudgill 1974, Wolfram 1969). A social factor of equal importance, which has not received as much systematic study, is ethnicity. Like age, occupation, and economic level, ethnic identity is information directly available to the interviewer; but like social class, it contains implicit values which are subtle and accordingly more difficult to quantize. The standing of

From *Language* 66:603-617, 1979. Reprinted with permission.

one's ethnic group in a community may be more of a determinant of social class and self-image than one's income and education. Thus, in communities where the local lore acknowledges more than one ethnic group, we would expect ethnicity to be a factor in linguistic variation.

Boston is just such a community, and among the several factors which govern variation in the speech of Boston, ethnicity plays a major role. This paper will describe the ways in which the identities of three groups--Irish, Italian, and Jewish--correlate systematically with variation, yet cut across such well-established criteria as age, income, and occupational level. Ethnicity is, further, a factor in phonetic change. The importance of ethnic identity in Boston is probably not unique to the city, but may well characterize speech patterns in all areas where there are clearly-defined ethnic groups.

1. THE *OR* VARIABLE. A characteristic of the Boston dialect is the pronunciation of the orthographic sequence *orC*. A word containing this sequence falls into one of two phonetic classes, depending upon whether the word has a unique or a variant pronunciation, as shown in Table 1.

Words in the non-alternating Class I have invariant [o], as in *border* [bóɾə]; however, in monosyllables the vowel is diphthongized to [oə], as in *fort* [foət]. Words in the alternating Class II have two variants: [o], as in Class I, and [ɒ], the dialectal variant--a low, back, slightly rounded vowel, again with a [ə] off-glide in monosyllables: *forty* [fɒ́ɾiy], *short* [šɒət]. (The dialect pronunciation of *short* as [šɒət] would thus be homophonous with *shot*, since in this dialect short-*o* words, e.g. *shot*, *top*, *coffee*, also have the vowel [ɒ].)

The membership of an *or*-word in either the non-alternating or alternating class appears to be phonetically arbitrary, as may be seen from the shared phonetic environments of the two classes. Length and learnedness are also not factors: *orchestra*, *orthopedic*, *corporation*, *organization* are all in the alternating class. It thus appears that speakers of the Boston dialect learn *or* words as members of two separate phonetic classes.

The purpose of the present study was to determine whether the use of dialectal [ɒ] in alternating words, as opposed to more standard [o], could be systematically ascribed to non-linguistic factors. The variant *or* was chosen as a subject of investigation because it is a clear mark of regional speech, but not one which is consciously recognized as a New England shibboleth, like *ar* in *car*. An interview was designed to elicit several phonetic features of the Boston dialect, including *or*, in four stylistic contexts: casual (conversation), reading (light texts), formal (word lists), and minimal pairs, the last being used to elicit judgments of correctness.[1] Both the word lists and the reading passages included *or*-words from Classes I and II. Each Class II word was then judged by me to have either the dialectal [ɒ] or an

TABLE I.

	Class I		Class II	
NASALS	torn		form (-er, -al, -ula) normal storm dorm(itory)	horn(y) born corn thorn corner morning
VOICELESS STOPS	corpse fort port report court sports important	pork torque porch torch	short (-en, -age) sort quarter forty corporation	New York cork fork orchestra orchid orchard Dorchester
VOICED STOPS	board border ford cord afford	mortgage gorgeous gorge	orbit order Nordic Jordan (Marsh) (land)lord	organ organize organization George orgy
SPIRANTS	morphine force source course hoarse divorce	abortion portion Porsche	orphan horse yours	north(-ern) orthopedic orthodox

[o]. Judgments were made on the conservative side: any sound not unambiguously an [ɒ] was judged an [o].

The quality of the syllabic nucleus, [ɒ] or [o], was the classificatory criterion, rather than the presence or absence of an [ə] or [r] off-glide. This is consistent with the reactions of Boston speakers, who distinguish unequivocally between the two variants. To most speakers, pronouncing *short* as [sɒət] is called 'dropping the r', whereas *short* as [soət] is 'putting the r in'. That is, speakers are aware of the vocalic difference, though they label it inaccurately from a phonetic point of view.

Interviews were conducted with 29 speakers, all natives of the Boston area by the following criteria: (1) they had spent the first 18 and the last five years of their lives in the Boston area;[2] (2) they had attended its public or parochial, but not

TABLE II.

Name	Age	Education[a]	Occupation	Ethnicity[b]	Place Raised[c]
Ben S.	71	Tech	pharmacist	J	Chelsea
Sam G.	69	C	business-owner	J	West End (B)
Pat B. (f)	68	Tech	reg. nurse	Ir	Charlestown
Vera F.	68	GS	veg. vendor; recept.	It	North End (B)
Bim B.	67	Grad	business-owner	J	Roxbury (B)-Brookline
Stel B.	65	Tech	GS teacher	J	Cambridge
Jack Z.	61	HS	clerk	It	Brookline
Eli G.	53	HS	furniture salesman	J	Revere
John D.	52	C	computer analyst	Ir	Roslindale (B)
Marcello C.	51	Grad	C teacher	It	Revere
Ruth G.	46	C	secretary	J	Brookline
Charles W.	40	Grad	C teacher	Ir	Allston (B)
Jim N.	39	Grad	C teacher	Ir	Roslindale (B)
Stephan M.	37	Grad	C teacher	J	Brookline
Jimmy F.	31	HS	electrician	It	East Boston (B)
Bob C.	30	Grad	commod. exch. broker	It	Cambridge
Mike B.	30	Grad	linguistic researcher	Ir	Sommerville
Ellen B.	29	C	carpenter, folk musician	J	Brookline
John C.	28	Tech	hairdresser	Ir	Dorchester (B)
Pat W. (m)	27	C	welfare dept. superv.	Ir	South Boston (B)
Tom M.	26	C	writer; social worker	Ir	Brighton (B)
Fran G.	25	HS	receptionist	It	Jamaica Plain (B)
Mary P.	24	HS	receptionist	Ir	South Boston (B)
Debbie L.	24	C	secretary	It	East Boston (B)
John McC.	22	Grad	graduate student	Ir	Medford
Marc C.	22	Grad	graduate student	It	Revere
Lorraine R.	19	HS	secretary	It	Everett
Barry C.	15	----	HS student	Ir	Sommerville
Roberta C.	15	----	HS student	Ir	Sommerville

[a]GS = grammar school; HS = high school; Tech = high school plus technical training; C = 4 years of college; Grad = college plus M.A. and/or Ph.D.
[b]Ir = Irish, It = Italian, J = Jewish.
[c](B) after a name indicates that the location is a part of the city of Boston, rather than a neighboring town.

private, schools; (3) they had at least one other phonetic characteristic of the Boston dialect in their speech (*ar* as [a:], *o* as [ɒ], or [eə] as [iə]); and, most importantly, (4) they considered themselves Bostonians. An attempt was made to interview a wide range of ages, educational levels, and occupations, as shown in Table 2.

There were 12 Irish speakers (9 men, 3 women); 9 Italians (5 men, 4 women); and 8 Jewish speakers (5 men, 3 women). They ranged in age from 15 to 71, and comprised several levels of education (grammar school through graduate and professional school), occupation (blue and white collar), and income.

2. RESULTS. The values cited in each of the figures below represent the percentage of the dialect variant [ɒ] in Class II words. For example, the word lists contain 62 Class II words. A value of 88 for a given speaker means that speaker pronounced 55 of those words, or 88%, with dialectal [ɒ], and 7 words with [o]. The percentages of [o] in casual speech are based on different absolute occurrences of [ɒ], since some speakers employed Class II words more frequently than others during the interviews. The lowest number of Class II words used in casual speech by a speaker was 9; the highest, 53.

2.1. STYLISTIC VARIATION AND ETHNICITY. Figure 1 shows the percentages of [ɒ] used in Class II words by the three ethnic groups in three speech styles: casual, reading, and formal.

All groups use the dialect variant [ɒ] most frequently in casual speech, as expected, and least in formal speech; but the three groups contrast in the degree to which they use the variant. Jewish speakers have the lowest percentages of [ɒ] in all styles; Italians have the highest; and Irish speakers have values parallel to and between the other two. This finding is interesting in light of the fact that Jewish speakers tend to associate [ɒ] with an 'Irish accent', rather than with Italians, who in fact use [ɒ] more frequently. Irish and Italian speakers make no ethnic associations with [ɒ].

The reaction of Jewish speakers to [ɒ] probably lies in the social dynamics of the city. Boston's long political domination by the Irish, coupled with the existence of the term 'Boston Irish' but not 'Boston Italian', may explain the association of a linguistic feature with the dominant, high-profile group (cf. Labov 1963).

Italian, Irish, and Jewish speakers also have different patterns of stylistic variation for *or*, as shown in Table 3. This table, based on the values in fig. 1, displays the differences in percentage points between styles for each ethnic group. The higher a value, the greater the difference between two styles in percentage of [ɒ] used. A high value thus indicates a more marked difference in stylistic roles for [ɒ] and [o].

The differences in values between casual and formal styles (third column) distinguish Irish and Jewish speakers as a unit from Italians. Both Irish and Jewish speakers have large differences (26 and 28 percentage points respectively) between casual and formal styles, indicating a degree of stylistic delineation of usage for [ɒ] and [o] not present to such a degree in the Italian data. Thus, for Irish and Jewish speakers, the more formal the speech style, the more marked is the tendency to use [o], the variant closer to standard English--i.e. the variant associated with 'putting the r's in".

For Irish speakers, the reading of texts is more like casual speech (9-point difference) than it is like formal speech (17-point difference). Irish speakers' casual and reading styles thus con-

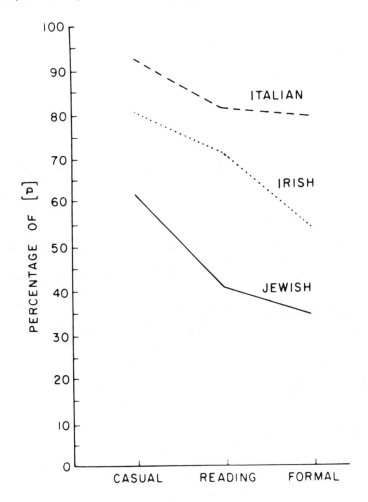

Figure 1. Use of [ɒ] in three speech styles for Italian, Irish, and Jewish speakers.

trast with their formal style, with its considerably lower percentage of [ɒ].   For Jewish speakers, reading style is much more like formal style (6-point difference) than it is like casual style (22-point difference).   It appears, then, that for Irish speakers, reading a passage aloud, especially a humorous text, is similar to talking informally; for Jewish speakers, reading a passage is a more conscious, self-monitored activity, since it elicits behavior almost identical to that of formal speech.

The Italian figures show the same trend as the Jewish figures: reading style is more like formal style (3-point difference) than it is like casual style (12-point difference).   However, all the

TABLE III.

	Casual/Reading	Reading/Formal	Casual/Formal
Italian	12	3	15
Irish	9	17	26
Jewish	22	6	28

Italian values are greater than 78%, so the stylistic behavior differential of this group is not as striking as that of the other two groups.

2.2. AGE, EDUCATION, AND ETHNICITY. When the factor of age is added to the behavior of the *or*-variable across ethnic groups, a more complex picture emerges. Figure 2 plots percentages of [ɒ] used in casual speech by individual speakers in each ethnic group as a function of age.

It can be seen here that the shapes of the three trajectories differ radically. Italian speakers have a consistently high percentage of [ɒ] (>85%) in casual speech for all ages. Jewish and Irish speakers, however, show great shifts along the age continuum in percentage of [ɒ] used. The nature of the shifting is, however, different for the two groups. For Jewish speakers, the shift

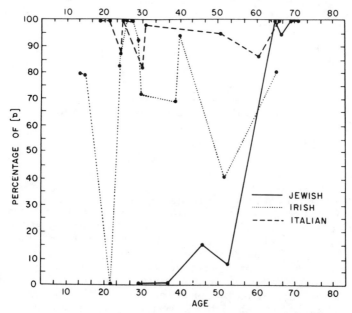

Figure 2. Use of [ɒ] in casual speech of individual speakers, by age, for three ethnic groups.

coincides with a sharp age division: those over 55 use dialectal
[ɒ], but younger speakers eschew [ɒ] in favor of [o].   For
Irish speakers, the percentage of [ɒ] shifts in a seemingly erratic
manner from speaker to speaker along the age continuum.
    The patterning of [ɒ] for the three groups does not change
radically under the formal style condition shown in Figure 3.
The shapes of the age trajectories for the three ethnic groups
are essentially the same as in casual speech--the major difference
being that, in formal speech, two of the Italian speakers have
values lower than 60%.
    The behavior of Jewish speakers is directly related to differ-
ences in age, or more probably in generation; but the behavior
of Irish speakers is clearly not analysable in terms of this single
factor.   To explain the seemingly erratic Irish pattern, two new
parameters--educational level and percentage-point difference
(PPD)--must be utilized. PPD, introduced in the discussion of
over-all ethnic differences (Table 3), is the value derived by
subtracting the percentage of [ɒ] used in an individual's formal
speech (Fig. 3) from that of his casual speech (Fig. 2).   It is
an indication of a speaker's utilization, and possible awareness,
of the stylistic distinctiveness of [ɒ] vs. [o].   Speakers with a
high PPD are sensitive, at a conscious or subconscious level, to
the pragmatics of the [ɒ] ≈ [o] alternation, in which [ɒ] is the
actual speech form, [o] the target of correctness.   Speakers

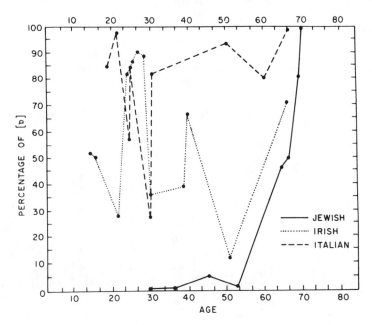

Figure 3.   Use of [ɒ] in formal speech of individual speakers, by
age, for three ethnic groups.

with low PPD's do not display the linguistic insecurity of the
former group.   They are comfortable using either [ɒ] or [o]
almost exclusively in all styles.

Figure 4 plots PPD as a function of years of education for
the three ethnic groups.   Solid black lines connect average PPD's
for each educational category.   Of the three groups, only Irish
speakers show a systematic pattern: the more years of education
an Irish speaker has, the greater the PPD between casual and
formal [ɒ] use.   Italian and Jewish speakers also show an average
PPD increase between the HS category and the next higher category
(C for Italians, Tech for Jews).   However, in the transition
from C to Grad for Italians, and Tech to C for Jews, the PPD's
fall; for Jewish speakers, the PPD rises again between C and
Grad.

Increased education, especially when it leads to a profession,
has represented for many a means of enhancing social and economic
status, in Boston (Thernstrom 1973) as elsewhere.   It often brings
with it a shifting of speech patterns away from the dialect, and
toward a standard of correctness.   For Irish speakers, then,
increased education brings with it an awareness that the [ɒ]
variant may be considered stigmatized for a certain audience,
and that the [o] variant is more acceptable to that same audience.
PPD's for Jewish and Italian speakers allow no such systematic
interpretation according to years of education, because of the
extremely high and low PPD's within each educational category.
In fact, the low PPD's of Italian speakers with the most education,
Marcello C. and Marc C., reflect the almost exclusive use of
dialectal [ɒ] rather than [o].   Among Jewish speakers, both
high and low PPD's occur in three out of four educational categories; but in contrast to Italians, extremely low PPD's in the C
and Grad categories reflect the more standard [o] variant rather
than [ɒ].

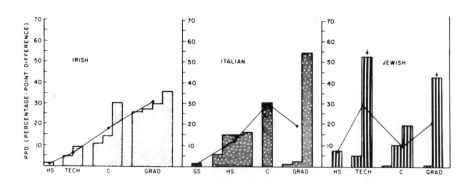

*Figure 4. Percentage-point differences as a function of educa-
tional level for three ethnic groups.*

3. HISTORICAL CHANGE AND PRAGMATIC COMPETENCE. To interpret the three patterns of ethnic behavior, we return briefly to Fig. 2, where it is seen that all speakers over 60-- Italian, Irish, and Jewish--use [ɒ] almost exclusively (>85%) in casual speech. Older speakers form a homogeneous group of dialect users; only for speakers under 60 is there significant variation in the use of [ɒ] and [o] in casual speech. What emerges, then, is a historical change in the use and evaluation of the or-variable. This change may be described as a change in pragmatic competence (Bailey 1973:29-30), i.e. in a speaker's knowledge of the situational appropriateness of using [ɒ] vs. [o] in Class II words. The change may be reconstructed as in Figure 5.

About 70 years ago, [ɒ] in Class II words was the correct form in Boston for all three ethnic groups. Class II words were phonetically distinct from Class I words. This word class distinction, and the general acceptance of [ɒ] as correct for Class II words, was valid for the whole population, as evidenced by the wide range of occupations and educational levels of older speakers (cf. Table 2).

The first change to occur was the emergence of the new variant [o] for Class II words. This variant had two labels: it was the unique Boston and standard English term for Class I words, and it was also the standard English form for Class II words. Thus the introduction of [o] as an alternate variant for Class II words was not a borrowing from Class I--since there is no motivation for such a change--but rather an inversion of standard English into Boston dialect phonology. The differential behavior of the three ethnic groups may then be interpreted as a measure of how the new variant [o] in Class II words was accepted by each group. In more formal terms, the linguistic behavior of the three groups reflects the shifting of pragmatic labels--stigmatized, correct, neutral--which each group assigned to the older [ɒ] and the newer [o] variant.

The course of linguistic change is often characterized by phonological variation corresponding to gross stylistic stratification

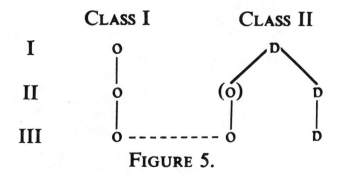

FIGURE 5.

(Labov 1972:172-4). This variation may be a precursor of change, since it testifies to the linguistic insecurity of that segment of the population which has two norms for a variable. We observe this stylistic stratification in the large PPD's of highly-educated Irish speakers (Fig. 4). We also find it, even more sharply, among several of the OLDER Jewish speakers indicated by the arrows in Fig. 4. Two of these speakers with educations beyond high school have large PPD's--43 points for Bim B., 67, and 52 points for Stel B., 65--whereas all younger Jewish speakers have low PPD's reflecting [o]. It is among these older Jewish speakers with high PPD's that we find the beginnings of the change in the *or*-variable, i.e. in the recognition of [o] as acceptable for Class II words. Thus Irish speakers with high PPD's are now at the stage of change where these older Jewish speakers were 40 years ago.

4. A THREE-STAGE MODEL. The patterns of variation and change in the *or*-variable may be explained in terms of a model which takes ethnic group membership as its principal component, and educational level as secondary. In Stage I, ACQUISITION, some members of a group obtain higher education in significant numbers; in so doing, they are exposed to standard English variants for certain of their dialect variables. These speakers assign a positive label to the standard variant, which is PASSIVE for them, and a negative label to the dialectal variant, which is their ACTIVE speech form. The assignment of opposing pragmatic labels results in high PPD's for these speakers.

In Stage II, TRANSMISSION, speakers with high PPD's transmit their variants, with pragmatic labels, to some younger speakers of the group. Younger speakers make a production reversal: they adopt as correct and active the variant, here [o], which was correct and passive for their elders. The second variant, [ɒ], which earlier had been active and stigmatized, now becomes passive and stigmatized.

In Stage III, SPREAD, all younger members of the group adopt the variants with their new labels. For speakers at this stage, [ɒ] becomes a mark of negative prestige of speakers or groups who have not begun to participate in the stages of change.

In the historical progression of Stages I-III, Jews as a group are at Stage III, Irish at Stage II, and Italians at an early Stage I. The older Jewish speakers in the study acquired their high PPD's when they were in their 20's, as a result of educational exposure (Stage I). They then transmitted variants and pragmatic labels to those younger speakers with whom they came into contact (Stage III), so that we find younger Jewish speakers of several educational levels and occupations using [o] and stigmatizing [ɒ]. If a group has reached this stage of change, then even older speakers such as Ben S. and Sam G., who have low PPD's reflecting dialect [ɒ], will consider [ɒ] highly stigmatized and claim that they never use it.

Italian speakers have apparently just begun to be affected by the phonetic and pragmatic changes in *or*. Among speakers

with a college education, two have high PPD's.   Debbie L., 24,
with a PPD of 30, considers her speech poor; but she maintains
emphatically that it is a reflection of her heavy East Boston
accent, rather than a 'Boston' accent.   (East Boston has for
many years been a largely Italian working-class community.)
Two other college-educated speakers, Marcello C., 52, and Marc
C., 22--father and son--have low PPD's reflecting dialectal [ ];
in this respect they do not show behavior different from that of
Italian speakers with fewer years of education and less prestigious
occupations.   When we contrast this pair with Irish and Jewish
parent-child pairs (Pat B., low PPD = [ɒ] vs. Mike B., high
PPD; Bim and Stel B., high PPD's vs. Ellen B., low PPD =
[o]), we see quite clearly that Italians are just entering Stage I:
they have low PPD's reflecting [ɒ], and recognize both [ɒ] and
[o] as correct.

The basic assumption of this study has been that ethnic
divisions can be of primary importance in linguistic variation and
change, and that they are paralleled by educational divisions.
It should follow that occupational grouping will also be parallel to
ethnic divisions.   This view finds strong support in the large-scale
sociological study of Boston by Thernstrom (172-3).   U.S. Census
data for 1950 indicate that second-generation sons (ages 25-44)
of Jewish fathers were much more likely to enter white-collar
professions and to be college-educated than sons of Irish or
Italian fathers.   For first-generation fathers of all three ethnic
groups who had little schooling (where median years of education
were 5.2 for Italian, 8.3 for Irish, and 8.1 for Jewish), 18% of
the Irish and Italian fathers had white-collar jobs, as compared
with 54% of Jewish fathers.   Thus 'despite their lack of education,
Jewish immigrants [and first-generation residents] moved rapidly
into white-collar callings' (Thernstrom, 173).   In the next (second)
generation, of men who were 25-44 in 1950, 21% of the Irish sons
and 11% of the Italian sons had one or more years of college, as
compared to 44% of the Jewish sons.   The occupational figures
run parallel to the educational figures: 19% of Irish and 17% of
Italian sons entered white-collar occupations, whereas 46% of Jewish
sons did.

The distribution of standard and dialectal variants of *or* thus
finds correlation in the demographic data of Boston.   The group
which received college educations first and which was the first
to enter white-collar professions in large numbers, namely the
Jewish immigrants, was also the first to adopt the standard variant.
The fact that Irish rather than Italian speakers are currently in
the second stage of the three-stage model finds parallels in the
educational and occupational figures of these groups.   Italians
lagged somewhat behind Irish residents in immigrant and first-
generation college experience (11% vs. 21%), and in second-generation white-collar occupations (17% vs. 19%).

5.   CULTURAL FORCE.   The three-stage model accounts for
a complex pattern of phonological variation over time, affecting
subparts of a population at different rates.   But there is another,

more subtle, factor in human behavior which leads me to believe
that neither Irish nor Italians will complete the three-stage cycle
predicted by the model, and that neither will end up with a
sharp age-break trajectory. This factor is CULTURAL FORCE,
the influence which an ethnic group may exert on the political,
social, and occupational behavior of its members (Thernstrom,
160-75).   Ethnic and religious groups tend to form subcultures
within larger cultures.   Part of the 'institutional completeness'
(167) of subcultures is their distinguishing and highly-valued
occupational, educational, and linguistic traits. Furthermore, the
occupational and linguistic values which are held in esteem by a
subculture may or may not correspond to the values of the larger
mainstream culture.

Given this background, we may postulate that the dialect
variant [ɒ] has become a valued trait of Irish and Italians in
Boston.   It is clearly their linguistic feature--a mark of identity
for them.   The explanation for this may lie in the fact that
Jewish speakers had the briefest association with [ɒ] as a norm
of correctness, since they were the first to adopt the standard
variant, associated with the values of the larger society, through
educational exposure.   Irish and Italian speakers had a longer
period of intimate association with [ɒ], which resulted in its
accumulating positive values for them.

Linguistic evidence for this hitch in the three-stage model
comes from subjective reactions to the *or* variants.   All speakers
were given a judgmental task involving minimal pairs, as shown
in Table 4.   One word of each pair was an *or*-word, the other a
short-*o* word with the vowel [ɒ] in the Boston dialect (cf. § 1).
A pair could thus be homophonous if the *or*-word belonged to
Class II (e.g. both *short* and *shot* as [šɒət]).   Other pairs
could never be homophonous because the *or*-word belonged to
Class I (e.g. *cord* [koəd] ≠ *cod* [kɒəd]).   The pairs were presented
in a randomized list, and speakers were asked to make three
judgments: (1) Which pairs can be pronounced the same? (2)
Would you pronounce them the same? (3) Who pronounces *short*
with [ɒ], who with [o]?

TABLE IV.

Class I Words		Class II Words	
[o]	[ɒ]	[o/ɒ]	[ɒ]
cord	cod	short	shot
fort	fought	stork	stock
source	sauce	corn	con
court	cot	dorm	Dom
port	pot	corner	Connor
corpse	cops	shorty	shoddy
sore	saw	order	odder
		orphan	often

First, all subjects except two younger Jewish speakers had perfect dialect intuitions about homophonous vs. non-homophonous pairs, whether or not they themselves pronounced the pairs alike in non-reflected speech. But the reactions of speakers with high PPD's were most revealing. Older Jewish speakers uniformly reported that [ɒ] was stigmatized, and that they would never merge *short* and *shot* etc. (although they all did so, almost exclusively in casual speech). Irish and Italian speakers, however, reacted either neutrally or positively to [ɒ], stated that most Class II pairs were probably homophonous for them, and found this situation acceptable. Most made the distinction, however, that in alternating words like *short* and *forty*, [ɒ] was the form one used in speaking, [o] in reading. These speakers recognize a stylistic difference between [ɒ] and [o]; and it is this difference, rather than a stigmatized/prestigious distinction, which they are transmitting.

The Boston data thus show, contrary to Labov's finding in New York (1972:130), that the highest use of a stigmatized variant does not always correlate with the greatest negative reaction to that variant. The subjective reaction of a dialect speaker to a dialect feature like [ɒ] depends upon the status of that feature within the speaker's social group. The stigma attached to [ɒ] by Irish and Italian speakers with high PPD's was much milder, where it existed at all, than that attached to it by Jewish speakers.

Jewish speakers who used [ɒ] tended to associate it with lack of education, poor speaking habits, or an Irish accent--but only under duress did they associate it with themselves (Stel B., after prodding: 'Yes, I guess we do say that in Boston.') Irish and Italian speakers made virtually no ethnic association with [ɒ], but rather associated it with speaking as opposed to reading ('putting the r's in'), with ease and naturalness, and with themselves.

The strongest negative reaction to [ɒ] from an Irish speaker came from John McC., 22, who said he tried to avoid [ɒ] because it marked him as being a 'townie' (he came from a suburb). Mike B., 28, also Irish, reported that he had conditioned himself, since college, to 'say r (i.e. [oə]) when I see it, but it's easy to fall back'.

The two Italian speakers with relatively high PPD's, Debbie L., 24, and Bob C., 30, reported that they always tried to speak correctly, but did not associate that activity with the [o] variant, and did not consider [ɒ] stigmatized. In *cord-cod* of the minimal-pair test (a pair which would never be homophonous), Bob C. felt that an Irish person would say *cord* as [knəd]--thus indicating that the ethnic association of [ɒ] with an 'Irish accent' may in fact be more deeply ingrained in the Boston population than any interview could reveal.

Bob C. reported that he 'cringes' at the heavy Boston accent he hears on TV or radio talk shows. This attitude is characteristic of a dialect speaker who is 'upwardly mobile in the larger society', and for whom the values of the 'institutionally complete' subculture

(Thernstrom, 167) have become questionable. Such a speaker will use the very dialect features which he stigmatizes in the speech of others.

In contrast to Irish and Italian speakers, younger Jewish speakers who claim to have corrected their childhood [ɒ]'s to [o] appear in fact to have done so.

The conditions for Stage III of the model of change require that the population with high PPD's stigmatize the dialect variant; they should transmit not just stylistic labels but, more crucially, stigmatized/correct labels. But in Boston only Jewish speakers fit this criterion. Thus it LOOKS as if Irish speakers at Stage II are undergoing the change predicted by the model, and it is probable that some will complete it. However, in the very process of change, [ɒ] has become a characteristic which is to some extent held in esteem by Irish (and probably Italian) speakers, or at least has a much milder taboo than among Jewish speakers.

It may be accidental which group gains access to higher education first and thus enters the model first; but the very fact that any model of change involves time lapse allows cultural force to develop a counter-effect to the blind working of linguistic processes.

6. A NOTE ON LANGUAGE ACQUISITION. When dealing with a community where dialect and standard forms occur, we are led quite naturally to questions of first-language acquisition. Under what circumstances do some speakers acquire dialect variants as their native system? Do they learn standard variants simultaneously, or do they learn them later, as low-level additions to their grammars? From what source do other speakers acquire standard variants as a first system, with a simultaneous passive knowledge of dialect forms? What in fact are the relative contributions of a child's family and his peer group to the acquisition of dialect and standard variants?

In Boston, the acquisition of variants and their active and passive deployment in speech is determined, at least in part, by the pragmatic labels which a speaker's ethnic group attaches to those variants. There appears to be a strong tendency for children to look to members of their ethnic/social group for transmission of linguistic values.

An ethnic group is a family par excellence. It comprises an extended circle of relatives and acquaintances of all ages who are often bound together by an ancestral language, country, food, and folklore. These elements may be reinforced by social-religious organizations--including youth groups, which provide the CULTURAL FORCE to transmit the group's particular esteemed educational, occupational, and linguistic values. The Boston Data thus lend support to a theory of language acquisition which ascribes the primary transmission of language to the family (Halle 1962), but in the larger sense of the 'ethnic family'.

The cohesiveness and partially exclusionary character of ethnic-religious groups in Boston is to some extent reinforced by 'neighborhoods' (Thernstrom, 163-5). It is part of both fact and local folklore that the North End is 'Italian', that South Boston is 'Irish', that Chelsea and Brookline are 'Jewish', and that Revere's turf is divided between Jews and Italians. Actually, these areas are not exclusively populated by one group each, and many areas of the city have an ethnically mixed population. But the fact remains that they have an ethnic identity and flavor in the eyes of the general population, and that that flavor is reinforced by the many public ethnic festivals (including Greek, Armenian, Chinese, West Indian, Portuguese etc.) encouraged and sponsored by the mayor's office in Boston and surrounding towns.

While the transmission of values through the larger ethnic 'family' clearly plays a role in many children's linguistic development, the influence of the peer group has also been shown to be a factor in children's linguistic behavior (Labov 1972:304-7). If a child's peer group is also his ethnic group, then we would expect that the values of that group would be doubly reinforced. The relative influence of familial (whether maternal or ethnic) input vs. peer-group input is not certain, but it is clear that each source provides models for a child's choice of linguistic variants. If, however, the ethnic model proposed here is accurate, then we would predict that it should hold for ethnically mixed as well as homogeneous neighborhoods. That is, in neighborhoods with a clearly delineated ethnic mixture, where the linguistic values held in esteem by a child's ethnic group conflict with the values of his playmates, the pressure to talk like one's peers should be neutralized by the linguistic values of the ethnic group.

The hypothesis that values of the ethnic-familial group are stronger than those of the peer group in linguistic behavior needs to be tested on a large scale. I can offer in evidence only isolated examples which bear on the hypothesis, and which will provide a first step in its investigation.

A joint interview was conducted with three 15-year-old high-school students, two Irish (Roberta and Barry, cf. Table 2) and one Chinese (Linda C., who was, of course, not included in the figures discussed earlier). All had grown up together, attended the same public high school, and were close friends. All were from working-class families, and planned to attend college. Both Barry and Roberta used [ɒ] heavily in casual speech (about 80%), but considerably less informal speech, with a fairly high PPD of 30. Their behavior conforms to the *or* pattern of Irish speakers who have pursued (or, in this case, intend to pursue) higher education. In contrast to her friends, Linda used no [ɒ] in any of the speech styles, although she as well as her friends had other features of Boston dialect phonology. Linda's parents were not native speakers of English and thus could not provide her with a model; yet in this variable, her peer group also did not provide a model. I will assume that it was her older siblings who provided the model of the standard variant, since they were actively encouraging her in intellectual endeavors including college preparation (they were college students), and in the formal study of Toissinese, her familial Chinese speech form. Both Roberta and Barry acknowledged that Linda spoke a little differently from them, in that she sometimes 'put her r's in'; but they placed no value judgment on this behavior.

A second example demonstrates ethnic behavior among older speakers. Marcello C., 51, and Eli G., 53, both grew up in Revere, a working-class community. As children of immigrants, they had, as home languages, Italian and Yiddish respectively (besides English). Educationally and professionally, Marcello outranks Eli (cf. Table 2). In terms of the *or*-variable, Eli considers the [ɒ] of his youth stigmatized, and does not use it much in casual speech. Marcello, who considers himself upwardly mobile and is extremely conscious of speaking well, is an [ɒ] user in all styles. Both speakers acknowledge their Boston accents and feel comfortable with them.

The parents of these two men could not have provided native first-language input; rather, I believe that the ethnic group, as the larger 'family', provided that input. Higher education in the form of college and graduate school did not produce a high PPD for Marcello C., although it is doing so in younger Italian speakers. He had less than one year of college, yet has a low PPD reflecting [o], and is aware of a stylistic and social difference between [ɒ] and [o]. These are isolated examples, but they provide initial material for the further investigation of the ethnic/familial influence on language acquisition and variation.

FOOTNOTES

[1]All interviews were recorded on a Uher 4000 Report, using a lavalier microphone.

[2]Two of the older speakers, Ben S. and Stel B., came to Boston before the age of seven, from Latvia and Rumania respectively, and had Yiddish as the home language. Both spoke native Boston English, as did Marcello C. and Vera F., for whom Italian was the home language. Sam G. and Eli G. had also had Yiddish as the home language.

ACKNOWLEDGMENTS

I wish to acknowledge with gratitude the critical suggestions of Catherine Chvany, Joshua Fishman, Paul Kay, Barbara Moslin, Gillian Sankoff, Stephan Thernstrom, and Lee Williams. An earlier version of this paper was presented at the NWAVE VI meeting held at Georgetown University, October 1977.

REFERENCES

Bailey, Charles-James N. 1973. *Variation and linguistic theory*. Washington, D.C.: Center for Applied Linguistics.

Fisher, John L. 1958. "Social influences in the choice of a linguistic variant." *Word* 14.47-56.

Goldberg, Isaac. 1929. "A Boston boyhood." *American Mercury*, vol. 17, no. 67. [Reprinted in *The many voices of Boston*, ed. by Howard M. Jones & Bessie Z. Jones, 345-55. Boston: Little, Brown, 1975.]

Haas, Mary. 1944. "Men's and women's speech in Koasati." *Lg*. 20.142-9.

Halle, Morris. 1962. "Phonology in generative grammar." *Word* 18.54-72.

Labov, William. 1963. "The social motivation of a sound change." *Word* 19.273-309.

Labov, William. 1966. *The social stratification of English in New York City*. Washington, D.C.: Center for Applied Linguistics.

Labov, William. 1972. *Sociolinguistic patterns*. Philadelphia: University of Pennsylvania Press.

Thernstrom, Stephan. 1973. *The other Bostonians: poverty and progress in the American metropolis, 1880-1970*. Cambridge, MA: Harvard University Press.

Trudgill, Peter J. 1974. *The social differentiation of English in Norwich*. Cambridge: University Press.

Wolfram, Walter A. 1969. *A sociolinguistic description of Detroit Negro speech*. Washington, DC: Center for Applied Linguistics.

THE RELATION BETWEEN BLACK

AND WHITE SPEECH

IN THE SOUTH

Ralph W. Fasold

THE ISSUES

In investigating a topic with emotional overtones, like race and speech, it is perhaps more necessary than usual to specify exactly what the issues are, what are to count as facts, and what methodology is to be used in addressing the problem. There are two major points of controversy about black-white speech relations in the South. One is the extent to which such differences exist, and the other is the history of the speech varieties involved.

To oversimplify a bit, the extent-of-differences issue has two opposite poles. At one pole is the belief that the speech of blacks and the speech of whites, even in the South, are very different entities, even distinct languages (Loflin 1971, Luelsdorf 1975). At the other pole is the position that the alleged language differences between blacks and whites are simply the result of comparing populations that differ on other criteria than race, in particular, lower-class Southern black in-migrants to Northern cities with middle-class Northern whites. If the speech of socio-economically comparable blacks and whites within the South is investigated, these alleged differences would all but disappear (McDavid and Davis 1972, McDavid and McDavid 1951).

The historical issue revolves around the creole-origin hypothesis. This hypothesis posits a Plantation Creole spoken in the antebellum South by slaves, but not to any significant degree by whites, from which modern black English has developed by decreolization (Dillard 1972, Stewart 1970). Others deny that such a creole played a role in the development of modern black English and maintain instead that differences between black and white language that cannot be explained on the basis of regional and social factors result from the differential preservation of British

From *American Speech* 56:163-189, 1981. Reprinted with permission.

dialect features brought to North America by colonists (Davis 1969).

Wolfram (1971) has pointed out that either position on one of these issues can be held concurrently with either position on the other. There are four possible combined positions. The first position (different +, creole +) is that modern black English is substantially different from any variety of white English because it developed from the Plantation Creole and no white dialects did. The second position (different -, creole +) would be that, although there was a Plantation Creole, decreolization has proceeded so far that no significant differences between Southern black and white speech survive when the social status of the speakers are comparable. The third position (different +, creole -) would be that, although there was no Plantation Creole, black and white language systems have so diverged over the years because of racial discrimination and segregation that the two varieties are now substantially different systems. The fourth position (different -, creole -) is that there was no Plantation Creole and there were no other factors to cause substantial speech differences, so that in fact there are none. Only the first and fourth positions are actually held: the first position by such scholars as Stewart and Dillard and the fourth by Raven McDavid and the many linguists who have been influenced by him.[1]

Another group of investigators, who fall outside the four positions outlined above, consists of educators and psychologists who think that there are socially disadvantaged speakers, the great majority of whom happen to be black, whose linguistic systems are so seriously underdeveloped as to cause serious cognitive and linguistic deficits (for example, Bereiter, Osborne, and Reidford 1966). I return to the language development issue in another connection, but I know of no linguists who take the extreme version of this position seriously, so I say no more about it here. [2]

PREVIEW OF MY POSITION

The data I have investigated and the methodology I endorse have led me to an intermediate stance on both issues. To the question of whether or not there exist significant differences between black and white language in the South, I would answer, "Yes, to some degree, for some features." When the relevant data are investigated sufficiently carefully, it appears that some aspects of some variables show significant differences in the speech of blacks from what is to be found in the speech of whites. These differences are of sufficient theoretical interest that they should not be ignored, but they by no means indicate widespread deep differences in grammar and phonology.

As far as history goes, the conclusion I have come to is that the creole hypothesis seems most likely to be correct, but it is certainly not so well established as Dillard (1972), for example, would have us believe. Decreolization, however, seems to have progressed so far as to have obliterated most of the original creole features. I would like to emphasize that my intermediate view is not motivated by a desire to find a position acceptable to both sides of this debate; indeed, it seems likely that the position will be a source of irritation to both. The moderate position is simply where the facts seem to lead.

METHODOLOGY

It is somewhat puzzling that reputable scholars should have arrived at such divergent conclusions on the two major issues of black-white speech relations. The historical question is indeterminate, perhaps necessarily so, given the absence of linguistically sophisticated documentation on what black and white language was like during slavery. The earlier linguistic systems have to be reconstructed on the basis of incomplete data, and so there is room for disagreement. But the extent-of-difference issue is another matter; apparently it could easily be resolved by listening to Southern blacks and whites speak and observing whether there are differences. At bottom, of course, that is the solution, and everyone involved in the controversy claims to have paid attention to language data of some kind. The reason there are such sharp disagreements on the difference issue has much to do, in my opinion, with methodology. Everyone has data, but the data have not been collected or analyzed in the same way. In particular, two types of methodology have been used that are unlikely to give accurate results.

One unreliable method is used by those, such as Luelsdorf (1975), who adhere to a strict code-switching view of language variation. In this method, whenever variation is found in the language of black speakers, the more exotic or nonstandard form is assumed to be the real output of the black speaker's grammar, while the standard form is assumed to be the result of interference from the standard language, in which the speaker also has competence to some degree. The methodological result is that forms not maximally different from those readily found in familiar varieties of white language are systematically ignored. It is not surprising that the assumption of strict code-switching would lead to the conclusion of maximum differences between black and white speech. The use of this method is quite mistaken and seriously misleading, as has been pointed out before (Fasold 1978; Labov 1972b, pp. 188–90).

The other unreliable method is the use of data based on Linguistic Atlas techniques. Atlas methodology is inappropriate, not because it is mistaken or misleading, but because the data were collected for a different purpose and under constraints imposed by the technology of an earlier time. As McDavid and Davis (1972, p. 307) themselves point out:

> . . . the Atlas has concentrated on short-answer questions, of vocabulary, pronunciation, and morphology; syntactic items are few, because it is difficult to frame questions that would give an unequivocal response. And, in the absence of mechanical aids, it was hard for even the best investigator in the 1930's to record extended phrases from free conversation.

Since the genuine differences between black and white language are in part statistical and are sensitive to aspects of the surrounding linguistic environment, it is rare for Atlas records, or newer data collected in the same style, to contain sufficient examples of the crucial types.[3]

What is required is substantial amounts of speech, tape-recorded from an adequate number of speakers all from the South and of as closely comparable social status as possible. Furthermore, these recordings must be examined in considerable detail, with due attention paid to the nature of the forms involved and the environments in which they occur. To anticipate the following discussion, it is not enough to ask whether copula deletion occurs in both black and white Southern speech; it occurs in both, but we need to know whether the copula form is *is* or *are*, whether it is followed by *gonna*, and the proportion of copulas deleted by speakers from the two groups. Clearly, both black and white speakers use invariant *be*, but we need to know whether it refers to prediction distributed in time and whether the appropriate auxiliary is *do*, *will*, or *would*. The same degree of care is required in the analysis of each linguistic feature that may represent a difference. Any analysis that is not painstaking enough to lead to the discovery of details of this type or is based on data that are not extensive enough to support this kind of analysis will simply not be adequate.

THE NOTION "FEATURE OF VERNACULAR BLACK ENGLISH"

The debate on black-white speech relationships unfortunately sometimes founders on a misunderstanding of the term "feature of vernacular black English." The source of this misunderstanding is not too difficult to find and correct. A feature of any language variety is simply any structure that can be observed in the speech of those who use it. Even those who believe that vernacular black English (VBE) is a separate language from English would be forced to admit that many of its features are the same as those found in English.

For example, speakers of VBE place adjectives before the nouns they modify, as in *red apple*, in the same way that white English speakers do. The syntax of adjectives is thus a feature of VBE in spite of the fact that it is shared with nearly every other variety of English. Other features of VBE are proscribed by educators, grammar-book writers, and other guardians of the purity of the language and are more or less rare in the speech of socially advantaged speakers, but are nonetheless readily found in the nonstandard English spoken by whites. Since they occur in VBE, they are accurately described as features of that variety of English. It is however, a third category of features of VBE that is of interest to the present discussion. It comprises those features that are actually unique features of VBE, not occurring in other nonstandard varieties. The features of VBE are therefore of three types: (1) unmarked features, in the sense that they do not differ from the corresponding structures in standard English, (2) nonstandard features shared with other nonstandard varieties, and (3) unique, also nonstandard, features.

This threefold distinction is often not made in the literature, especially in books and articles designed to be read by educators in Northern cities. There the focus is on problems of language-arts education. Writing for teachers who, because of migration and desegregation, find themselves responsible for teaching lower-class black children, authors discuss the features in the last two categories, which comprise the information teachers need. Usually the distinction between shared and unique nonstandard features is not made, since it is irrelevant to the audience. For the investigation of black-white speech relations, however, attention to this distinction is important since without it an author can be taken as claiming that all nonstandard features of VBE are unique features. It is essential to distinguish between those features of VBE that are not of interest for our purpose since they are to be found in white nonstandard English and those that are of interest because they differentiate between VBE and Southern white nonstandard English.

SHARED FEATURES OF VBE: PHONOLOGY

Numerous features are mentioned in discussions of VBE, but most are found also in other kinds of English.[4]   Some of them are scarcely to be considered nonstandard. One of these is the neutralization of [ɪ] and [ɛ] before nasal consonants, as exemplified by the well-known homophony of *pin* and *pen*. This feature is quite common in English, especially Southern English, and it is not reasonable to consider it nonstandard in the dialect areas where it occurs. The vocalization or deletion of postvocalic [r] (*car* pronounced as [kaə] or [ka:]) and the perhaps less common deletion of postvocalic [l] ([kou] for *coal*) are two others. Again, there is no point in considering these features as nonstandard. Another example is the Southern pronunciation of the articles, allowing *a* and [ðə] for *the* before both vowels and consonants (*a apple*, *the* [ðə] *apple*), which is also shared by VBE but is part of the regional standard. "G-dropping," as in *walkin'* for *walking*, is certainly to be found everywhere there are English speakers, though perhaps statistically correlated with lower-class speakers and informal styles and perhaps statistically more frequent in the South than in the North. In any case, it is by no means unique to VBE. The voiced alveolar stop pronunciation of *th* ([douz] for *those*) is, like "g-dropping," a widespread feature, though statistically correlated with class and style. The voiceless equivalent ([trou] for *throw*) may be more common in Northern nonstandard varieties than in either VBE or Southern white dialects.

The use of labiodental fricatives for their dental counterparts in non-initial position ([bouf] *both*, [ifə] *ether*, [briv] *breathe*, [məvə] *mother*) is somewhat more doubtful. The voiceless examples have been observed in white Southern speech (Dorrill 1977) and seem to be more frequent and more widely distributed in VBE than the voiced ones. I am not aware that [v] for [ð] in noninitial position has been reported for Southern white speakers, but I have informally observed it in the speech of a middle-class white Southerner. There may be a statistically important difference between the use of this pronunciation rule by black and by white Southerners. I would not, however, at present wish to claim that it is an interesting feature. The deletion of word-final stops, especially voiced ones (*ba'* for *bad*), has frequently been observed in VBE, but may well occur in other varieties of English, and I will consider it not of interest.

SHARED FEATURES OF VBE: GRAMMAR

VBE features shared by other varieties of English are not, of course, limited to phonology. The use of nonstandard verb forms for the past tense and past participle is one such case. Sentences like *I seen it*, *I knowed him*, and *They had came* have been documented for white nonstandard dialects too often to require citation. Absence of concord for finite forms of *be* in the present tense (*They is fine*) and even more frequently in the past tense (*They was in the house*) has also frequently been reported for dialects other than VBE. *Ain't* is another shared feature, although the use of *ain't* for standard English *didn't* (*He ain't go*), which occurs in at least some varieties of VBE, has not, so far as I know, been reported for white speakers. Other VBE features that are not of interest for black-white speech relationships include *it* for expletive *there* (*It's a rabbit in the garden*), completive *done* (*He done left*), double modals (*I might could do it*),[5] and auxiliary inversion in indirect questions (*I wonder does he like me*).

Another shared feature is the deletion of a relative pronoun functioning as subject of the subordinate clause. Standard English allows the deletion of a relative-pronoun object (*He's the guy I met*), but not of a subject (**That's the boy delivers our newspaper*). No such restriction exists in VBE. But the same phenomenon has been reported for speech communities as widely separated as Appalachia (Wolfram and Christian 1976) and Cessnock, N.S.W., Australia (Shnukal 1979). Quite obviously, this is not a distinctively VBE syntactic feature.[6]

Negative concord (the "double negative" shibboleth) is, of course, one of the most widely distributed syntactic features of nonstandard English, and so appears to be unlikely as an interesting difference. Yet the possibility has been explored in two connections. First, Labov (1972a) found that in the most favorable environment (in which the second negative is an indefinite pronoun following the verb in the same clause, as in *He don't know nothing*), negative concord is not variable but obligatory for "core" speakers of VBE when interacting with their peers. There is no environment for which it is obligatory in any of the white nonstandard New York dialects that he investigated. Thus obligatory negative concord in this environment may indicate black versus white ethnic membership. However, aside from the fact that the obligatory nature was found for only one restricted kind of negative concord, there are two reasons why I do not propose it as an example of an ethnic difference. In the first place, as Labov (1972a, p. 181) points out:

> Any speaker is potentially capable of omitting the
> rule and producing sentences with   . He hears
> the standard form and can interpret it, and in
> his careful speech he usually shifts away from
> 100 percent use of negative concord. Even in
> casual speech many adults have shifted away from
> BEV and lost consistency in negative concord.
> And most importantly, consistent use of negative
> concord is the characteristic of core speakers of
> BEV in their peer-group culture and isolated in-
> dividuals ("lames") do not show consistent negative
> concord.

In addition to the fact that not all speakers of VBE have obligatory negative concord in this environment, those who do have it do not use it in all styles. In the second place, it has yet to be demonstrated that there are no Southern nonstandard speakers who have obligatory negative concord in the appropriate environment and style.

The second aspect of negative concord that seemed for a while to be a unique feature of VBE was the possibility of applying the rule to verbs in two clauses of the same sentence, as in *When*

it rained, nobody don't know it didn't   (Labov 1972a, p. 150).
It has recently been shown that this kind of negative concord
also exists in white Southern nonstandard English. Feagin (1979,
p. 229) recorded examples like the following from white speakers
in Anniston, Alabama:

> No, I'm not gon stay home when I ain't mar-
> ried; me and my kids and my husband can go on
> campin' trips.

Negative concord seems to be a feature shared in all respects by
VBE with other nonstandard dialects.

Finally, the rule of negative preposing that allows sentences
like *Can't nobody whip me in a fight* is a VBE feature that is well
documented for nonstandard English used by white speakers, both
North and South (Feagin 1979, Labov 1972a).

UNIQUE FEATURES OF VBE: THREE EXAMPLES

There are other features of VBE that seem to be unique--that
are not found in the speech of white Southerners even of lower
social classes.   The data available and the amount of space that
can be devoted to their discussion are insufficient to allow a
detailed analysis of all of them, so I concentrate on a few, with
a brief treatment of the others.   One such briefly considered
example in pronunciation is the devoicing of final stops in stressed
syllables.   The black English treatment of this feature is apparently
not paralleled in white speech, but some careful distinctions must
be made.   First, it is clear that in all varieties of English,
surface voicelessness of final stops is common, with the voiced/
voiceless distinction being carried by contrastive lengthening of
the preceding vowel when the underlying stop is voiced.   Thus,
the distinction between *bet* and *bed* is often manifested by the
pronunciations [bɛt] for the former and [bɛ:t] for the latter.
In black English, however, there is a noticeable fortis glottal
coarticulation with the stop, so that *bed* is pronounced [bɛ:əʔt].
Furthermore, this feature is not limited to vernacular black English, but is common in standard black English as well.   Second,
the ethnic distinction is limited to stressed syllables, since pronunciations of *hundred* and *salad* with final [ʔt] are common in white
speech, both North and South.

Other features treated briefly here are two of the suffixes
that appear in written standard English as *-s* and *-es*.   One of
these is the marker of nonpast tense when the subject of the
verb is third person singular, as in *he walks* or *he kisses*.   It is
well known that this morpheme is very frequently absent in VBE
(Fasold 1972a, Labov 1972a), but so is it in white nonstandard
speech.   In a study of whites and blacks of comparable lower
social class, Wolfram (1971, p. 145) reported that among his
Lexington, Mississippi, informants, black speakers lacked the suffix

87 percent of the time in connected speech, while white speakers lacked it 15 percent of the time. The statistical difference is surely remarkable.

An even sharper stratification of Southern blacks and whites for this feature was found by Sommer and Trammel (1980). Using data from sixth-grade children in Atlanta, they found that verbal -*s* was absent at a frequentcy of 76.8 percent in the speech of lower-class black children, most of whom can be expected to be VBE speakers. Upper-middle-class black children deleted verbal -*s* only 6.5 percent of the time, and the figure for lower-class white children was 2.3 percent. Upper-middle-class white children did not delete -*s* at all.

The relative rarity of verbal-suffix deletion in Southern white nonstandard English is attested also by Wolfram and Christian's study of Appalachian English (1976, p. 79) and by Feagin's study of rural working-class speakers in Anniston, Alabama, among whom deletion was observed only 4 percent of the time. Feagin remarks (1979, pp. 189-90): "In no case, however, was its occurrence in the Anniston data anywhere near that of the figures for the black adolescent gang members of Harlem who averaged 64% (699/1089) - deletion. . . . This difference between Black English and Southern White Nonstandard is especially striking because of the many other similarities between the two in regard to verb morphology and syntax." The statistical discrepancy between black and white speakers for this feature appears to demand an explanation beyond an appeal to differential educational and social opportunities between poor blacks and whites in the South. The creole hypothesis seems to be a good candidate.

Another -*s* or -*es* suffix marks the plurality of nouns in English. The absence of this suffix has been reported for VBE (Labov et al. 1968, Wolfram 1969), although at frequencies much lower than those for the verbal suffix. Plural suffix deletion also occurs in white nonstandard speech, but there seems to be a difference. In Appalachian English, at least, plural suffix deletion is rare and sporadic except for measure terms, such as *pound*, *mile*, and *mouth* (Wolfram and Christian 1976). Although plural deletion has not been carefully tabulated for black Southerners, Wolfram's VBE speakers in Detroit (Wolfram 1969), many of whom migrated from the South or were only one generation removed from their Southern origins, frequently lacked the suffix for all types of plural nouns, although most often for measure nouns.

UNIQUE FEATURES OF VBE: FIVE MORE EXAMPLES

There are several other features for which I offer somewhat more detailed discussion. They are remote-aspect *been* (*He been went*), the possessive suffix (*John's hat*), the simplification of

certain final consonant clusters (*des'*), copula and auxiliary deletion (*He big*, *He going home*), and distributive *be* (*He always be
doing that*). For the first of these features, data on Southern
white speech of the type I consider crucial are not adequate,
but the data for VBE are striking enough to raise the distinct
possibility that a black-white language difference does exist. In
the case of the other four, data on Southern white nonstandard
language has been collected and a black-white difference is clearly
indicated.

REMOTE-ASPECT "BEEN"

The use of *been* as an aspect marker is likely to be different
in black and white language varieties. Although now used relatively rarely in VBE, utterances like *You won't get your dues that
you been paid* (uttered in an account of what happens when one
leaves a club one has belonged to) have been observed. The
function of this construction is to indicate something that began
a long time ago and is still relevant (Dillard 1972, Labov 1972a,
Rickford 1975, Wolfram and Fasold 1974).
Due to the construction's relative infrequency, examples are
hard to find in VBE and, so far as I know, have not been
actively searched for in white Southern speech, but Rickford has
shown that there are striking differences in the way white and
black speakers interpret *been* sentences. Rickford asked groups
of black and white speakers from diverse geographical areas (mostly
from the Northeast, but some from North Carolina) to complete a
questionnaire that included a series of questions on the interpretation of *been*. Those questions were the following (Rickford 1975,
p. 172):

1. Someone asked, "Is she married?" and someone else answered,
"She BIN married." Do you get the idea that she is married
now? ____ Yes ____ No
3. Bill was about to be introduced to this guy at a party, but
when he saw him, he said, "Hey, I BIN know his name!" Which
of these three things do you think he's most likely to say next?
    a. Give me a minute and I might remember it.
    b. He's John Jones. I saw his picture in the papers
       yesterday.
    c. He's John Jones. I've been hearing about him for years.
So what do you think Bill meant when he said, "I BIN know his
name"? Choose the one [of the following interpretations] that is
closest to what you think.
    d. Used to know.
    e. Already knew.
    f. Know, but can't quite remember.

TABLE I: Consistently Appropriate Responses

	Number	Yes to 1	Yes to 1 C to 16	Yes to 1 C to 16 C to 3	Yes to 1 C to 16 C to 3 H to 3
Blacks	25	21	21	19	15
Whites	25	4	4	1	1

  g.   Know right now.
  h.   Have known for a long time, and still do.
  i.   Other:
16.   Frank asked his friend if he had paid off the bill on his
new stereo, and got the answer, "I BIN paid for it."   Does he
mean:
  a.   I've already paid for it.
  b.   I was paying for a long time, but I'm finished now.
  c.   I paid for it long ago.
  d.   I've been paying for it for a long time, and
       haven't finished yet.
  e.   Other:

     The appropriate answers were *yes* to 1, *c* and *h* to 3, and *c* to
16.   The performance of the black and white respondents in
giving consistently appropriate versus consistently inapporpriate
responses is given in tables I and II (Rickford's tables II and
III).   Whereas 15 black respondents gave appropriate responses
to all of the questions, only 1 white speaker did.   None of the
black speakers gave inappropriate responses to all of the questions,
but 10 of the 25 whites did.   It is possible that a group of white
speakers all from the South might do better (in fact, Rickford
points out that the one white speaker who gave all appropriate
responses was from North Carolina).
     Williamson (1971) cites examples, both from works of fiction
set in the South and from speech she has informally heard and
noted, in which Southern white speakers use *been* constructions.
With one exception, the *been* form in those examples either is a
copula with a noun phrase or a locative as complement or is an
auxiliary with the main verb in *-ing*.   These sentences could
easily have been derived by contraction and deletion of *have*.   In

TABLE II: Consistently Inappropriate Responses

	Number	No to 1	No to 1 C to 16	No to 1 C to 16 C to 3	No to 1 C to 16 C to 3 H to 3
Blacks	25	2	1	0	0
Whites	25	17	14	12	10

fact, Williamson cites Atwood (1953) and McDavid and McDavid (1960) as proposing precisely this analysis. So analyzed, the construction is not particularly black English, nor particularly Southern, nor even particularly nonstandard.

The form that is a candidate as a unique feature of VBE is *been* in constructions with a verb that is either uninflected or a past form (*I been know your name, I been paid my dues*) and distinctively refers to remote time. Although this form is similar in meaning to the present perfect (*have*) *been*, Rickford's results show that it is nonetheless distinct. The very similarity, in fact, could go a long way toward accounting for the survival of VBE *been* as a creolism, if that is what it is. The exception among Williamson's examples is *I been had it*, precisely the putative VBE form, although spoken by a white bus driver. It is difficult to make a case on the basis of one example; the bus driver might have learned the form from black speakers, as Rickford's one consistent North Carolina white respondent probably did (he reported extensive contacts with black people).

Herndobler and Sledd (1976) cite data from Newfoundland that is more seriously damaging to the candidacy of *been* as a unique VBE feature. They cite six examples from Noseworthy (1972) which are exactly parallel to the VBE form, but which are hardly likely, given the geographical area in which they were collected, to have originated in VBE. Herndobler and Sledd find it unlikely that these forms should have developed independently or be traceable to a creole spoken by blacks, but Dillard (1975) argues that there was a Maritime Creole from which both the American Plantation Creole and the creole-like forms observed in such places as Newfoundland could have been derived. Nonetheless, as Herndobler and Sledd point out, "the history of [*been*] is still quite confused and obscure."

THE POSSESSIVE

The absence of the possessive suffix, standardly spelled *'s*, is well-known as a variable feature of VBE; possessive *'s* is absent less often than verbal *-s* but more often than plural *-s*. Miller (1977) examined the speech of two black and two white speakers in the Augusta, Georgia, area for this feature (among others) and found that it occurred only in the speech of the two black informants. However, he reports it is "quite common in white CSRA [Central Savannah River Area] speech." The only example he cites is not entirely convincing, though, since it is a place-name-- *Clark's Hill*, the name of an Augusta reservoir. A speaker who says *Clark Hill* could very well suppose that to be the name of the reservoir, rather than have any variability in the possessive construction.

Among the Atlanta sixth-graders investigated by Sommer and Trammell (1980), there was a striking difference in the use of the possessive suffix between the VBE-speaking lower-class black children and the others. The lower-class black children had zero suffixes in 52.2 percent of their possessive constructions. Only one upper-middle-class black child had any instance of zero possessive, and that child used the zero variant only once. None of the white children used any zero possessives.

A close investigation of 18 ten-to-twelve-year-olds and 16 adolescents in my study of VBE in Washington, D.C. (Fasold 1972a), indicated the absence of the possessive suffix and an incomplete mastery of the standard possessive rule. That investigation included an exercise to probe the possessive, in which the informant was shown a drawing of a person or animal with some object and was told, for example: "This man has a hat. It's not the woman hat. It's the _____." A possessive noun phrase was to be elicited. The test included a man with a hat, a girl with a bike, a dog with a bone, a mouse with some cheese, a person named Jack Johnson with a car, and a person named Derrick Black with a toy. The test revealed not only absence of the suffix, but also difficulty in forming the possessive for the word *mouse*, which ends with a sibilant, and for the proper names *Jack Johnson* and *Derrick Black*. Some speakers used the plural *mice* (*mice cheese*) or attached the suffix to the first name alone or to both names (*Jack's Johnson car*, *Jack's Johnson's car*). Trouble with possessive formation was experienced by 17 of the 18 younger children and by 12 of the 16 adolescents. Table III shows the results for the two groups.

The data show that the standard rule for possessive formation was far from established among most of the younger children. The rule was better mastered by the adolescents, but most of them still did not give the standard forms for at least one of the more difficult nouns. These results are consistent with the hypothesis that possessive formation is variable in VBE grammar. If it is variable, younger speakers will hear a smaller number of

TABLE III: Number of VBE Speakers in Washington, D.C., Who Used Certain Possessive Forms

		adolescents
all standard possessives	1	4
Jack Johnson car*	13	5
Man hat**	8	0
mouse cheese	12	4
mice cheese	2	4

*Also Jack's Johnson car, Jack's Johnson's car, Derrick Black toy, Derrick's Black toy, or Derrick's Black's toy.
**Also girl bike or dog bone.

suffixed forms from which they can derive the standard rule for possessive suffixation; however, as they grow older and become exposed to more and more standard English, the rule should become better fixed. The results are consistent with this hypothesis, but they do not prove it.

An alternate hypothesis could be offered along the lines of the deficit theory sometimes espoused by educators and psychologists. According to this theory, the VBE-speaking youngsters suffer from underdeveloped language due to a deprived environment. This idea is unattractive because it requires that language acquisition be delayed until pre-adolescence and beyond. Such a long delay in the acquisition of simple morphology runs counter to what is known about children's facility for the acquisition of even intricate aspects of syntax. The argument that the acquisition of possessive formation in VBE grammar is different from that in other varieties can be judged only by further data on children who do not speak VBE, especially, for our purposes, children who speak Southern white nonstandard English.

FINAL CONSONANT CLUSTERS

The simplification of final consonant clusters is similar in some respects to the omission of the possessive ending. When the final consonant is a stop that agrees in voicing with the preceding consonant, simplification is possible in all varieties of English, even those used by speakers of prestige varieties. Very few English speakers, for example, would consistently say [wɛst saɪd] for *west side*. The normal pronunciation would be [wɛs saɪd]. For most varieties of English, variation between simplified and intact clusters establishes beyond a doubt that the final consonant is deleted by a rather low-level rule of phonology. An elicitation exercise with some of the same Washington, D.C., speakers who supplied the possessive data revealed surprising evidence that some of them might not have internalized the standard underlying cluster at all.

The exercise was based on the fact that, for most speakers of English, clusters are not deletable if they appear in a form to which a suffix beginning with a vowel is added. Speakers who frequently delete the final [t] from *test*, for example, never delete in the word *testing*. To elicit vowel-suffixed forms, the interviewees were given a series of sentences in the simple present tense. They were then given examples of the appropriate response, which was to repeat the sentence and to give the equivalent sentence in the *be* + verb + *ing* form. For example, to *They write things* the appropriate response was *They write things, They are writing things*. None of the examples had verbs ending in a simplifiable consonant cluster, but all of the test items did. Five of the verbs (*bust*, *lift*, *paste*, *rest*, and *test*) ended in *st* or *ft*, two (*ask* and *risk*) in *sk*, and one (*clasp*) in *sp*. The setting of the exercise focused upon language; the children were interviewed by an adult middle-class interviewer, so that self-monitoring of speech would have been at a high level; and the linguistic environment of the clusters, before -*ing*, is one least favorable to deletion. Nevertheless, 11 of the 18 children simplified clusters in one or more of the test items. One child deleted the final consonant in all eight items and one deleted in six items. That is, unexpected responses like *They are ressing* and *They are rissing their lives* were elicited.

Even more startling was the fact that, when they pronounced a second consonant at the end of the relatively uncommon items *risk* and *clasp*, a majority of the children supplied [t]. That is, they said, *They are risting their lives* and *They are clasting their hands.* In fact, *risting* was the most common response to the *risk* item, supplied by 12 of the 18 children. Two more omitted the final consonant entirely, and only four said *risking*. For *clasping*, only one child pronounced *sp*, four gave *clasting*, five avoided the cluster entirely by substituting *clap* or *clapping*, and the rest either gave *classing* (with no final consonant) or gave no response. In the case of the common *ask*, none of the children supplied a final [t], although five avoided the critical cluster by supplying the dialect variant *aksing*.[7] These results are summarized in table IV.

The fact that a majority of the subjects had only one stem-final consonant in some responses, even under the most favorable conditions for the appearance of two, indicates that they may not have underlying final consonant clusters in these words. The fact that [t] appeared in the items *risking* and *clasping* points to another possible stage in the development of standard English consonant clusters. These responses could be taken to indicate that [t] is the only possible underlying final stop in clusters.

TABLE IV: Participial Forms of Verbs Used by 18 Black Children

bust*	bussing	bussing, busting	bussing, busting	bussing,	busting
ask	assing	aksing	asking	asking, aksing	asking
risk	rissing	rissing, risting	risting	risking	risking
clasp	classing	classing, clap	classing, clasting, clapping	classing, clasting, clapping	clasping
Number of children responding as above	1	4	9	3	1

*Similarly lift (with f for s), paste, rest, test.

Common items like *ask*, for those speakers who do not have *aks*, would be lexical exceptions. If this interpretation is correct, there could be a significant difference between VBE and other dialects in the phonology of final consonant clusters. Evidently, there is a basilectal form of VBE in which final clusters ending in stops do not exist in the underlying forms, or are limited to those with final [t], with a few lexical exceptions. This system would contrast with the usual one in English, both standard and nonstandard, in which the final clusters are clearly in the under-lying forms, but are deleted by a relatively late rule. Such a VBE variety would fit well in a model of the decreolization of black English, as observed below.

The 18 Washington speakers, furthermore, are not the only VBE speakers who seem to lack underlying final clusters. Wolfram (1971) reports that lower-class black children in Lexington, Missis-sippi, participating in a similar exercise, demonstrated the same tendency to pronounce only a single final consonant on verbal bases followed by a suffix beginning with a vowel, specifically the agentive suffix *-er*.[8] Wolfram was later able to replicate these results in a research project conducted in Meadville, Missis-sippi.[9] This time, however, similar data from lower-class white children of the same town were collected, with a marked difference in the results. There were 72 children aged 7 to 18 years (36 white, 36 black), who each provided 4 responses (a total of 144 for each group). The whites lacked [t] in 4.2 percent of their responses and had it in 94.4 percent (1.4 percent of the responses were irrelevant to the question). The blacks lacked [t] in 37.5 percent of their responses and had it in 56.9 percent (with 5.6 percent irrelevant responses). The few single-consonant responses from white children may be errors in performance. No white children omitted [t] in the verb *lifting*, but only in verbs ending [st]. Their simplification of [st] could result from assimilating [t] to the preceding homorganic [s]. In any case, the difference is striking enough to demand an explanation.

The verb *ask* casts some doubt on my interpretation of the use of *risting* and *clasting* by the Washington speakers. None of the Washington children used *asting*, but in the Meadville data, white speakers used it three times and black speakers twice. The uninflected form of *ask* can be *ast* for some Southern speakers, as in the sentence *I'll go ast 'er*, spoken by a white motel-deskclerk in Memphis, Tennessee. John Algeo (personal communication) has suggested that *ast* could be a generalization based on the frequent pronunciation of the preterit *asked* as *ast*. If this is the correct explanation for *ast*, there is no reason to suppose it could not also explain *risting* and *clasting*, which would then not have a place in the discussion of black-white speech differences with respect to final consonant clusters. More data are needed to see if *ask* is lexically unique in this respect or if other *s* plus consonant clusters pattern in the same way. The disparity between the speech of blacks and whites with respect to the <u>absence</u> of final consonants before vowel suffixes is not affected, however, by *ast*.

As with the data on the possessive, an explanation could be sought in an appeal to delayed language acquisition. But accounting for the observed difference in that way is, if anything, even less attractive than it was for the possessive, since there are data from white children of the same region and age and of comparable social status. Granted that poor black children might be more economically and educationally deprived than even the poorest white children, it seems extremely unlikely that the difference in deprivation is just enough to have an effect on the acquisition of final consonant clusters, but not enough to affect other phonological structures, say, initial consonant clusters. It is more reasonable to propose that the performance of the black children represents a relatively early stage in the decreolization of the language of their community.

COPULA AND AUXILIARY ABSENCE

The absence of present-tense forms of *to be* has been carefully studied in the South by Wolfram (1974) and Feagin (1979). No one would seriously claim that Southern white speakers do not sometimes omit these forms. In fact, absence of *are* is extremely common in Southern white speech. The absence of *is* is not unheard of, especially in certain linguistic environments. Labov (1969, 1972a) proposed that contraction accounts for the absence of *are* in dialects that have vocalization and deletion of [r]. Contraction, a pan-English rule, has the effect of deleting the unstressed vowel in certain auxiliary and copula forms. For speakers who have [a] for *are*, the form is reducible of [ə] when unstressed, after which contraction would remove it without a trace. To delete *is*, a further rule is required to delete [z]; and it is this deletion rule, the argument runs, that is unique to VBE. Wolfram (1974) has shown convincingly that Labov's analysis cannot stand and that a rule to delete the [r] of *are* is needed in white Southern speech, in addition to the more general rules for the vocalization and deletion of [r]. This special deletion rule that is often applied to [r] is, to say the least, severely inhibited in its application to the [z] from *is* in Southern white speech, although far less inhibited in VBE. This difference is too substantial to be ignored.

Even when *is* deletion is the focus, further linguistic details must be carefully examined. One such detail is the environment in which original *is* is preceded by a word ending in a sibilant (for example, *This is the place*). Contraction of *is* would leave [z] following a sibilant (*This's the place*), where it would be a prime target for assimilation, leaving no remnant of *is*. This process does not require a special consonant deletion rule, and so occurs commonly in the speech of white speakers as well as VBE. Another environment in which *is* is fairly readily deleted in white speech is before the form *gonna* (Wolfram 1974, pp. 514-16). This deletion seems to result from a lexical constraint independent of phonology. [10] Wolfram's study of the present-tense forms of *to be* in Mississippi white speech showed that deletion of *are* is extremely common. Of his 33 subjects, 9 deleted *are* 100 percent of the time; 14 more deleted in 60 to 80 percent of the time; and, for the entire sample, white speakers deleted it 64.2 percent of the time. He concludes that "*are*-deletion is well established among white varieties in the deep South" (p. 512). The picture for *is* deletion is quite different. Of 45 speakers who used *is* five times or more, only 15 deleted it at all. Only 2 of them deleted it more than 25 percent of the time, and the overall rate of deletion was only 6.5 percent. Wolfram's results show that there are Southern white speakers, a clear majority of his sample, who delete only *are*, never *is*. Those who delete *is* do so very infrequently. [11]

The results from Feagin's (1979) study of white Southern speech in Anniston, Alabama, closely parallel what Wolfram found in Mississippi. Her rural working-class subjects, the group most prone to do so, deleted *are* 56.3 percent of the time and *is* only 6.8 percent of the time.

Neither Wolfram nor Feagin reports data on copula deletion for Southern black speakers, but the Sommer and Trammell (1980) study in Atlanta shows that the lower-class black children deleted the copula 32 percent of the time, whereas the white and upper-middle-class black children deleted it less than 2 percent of the time. It is not clear whether Sommer and Trammell's tabulation of deleted copulas included both *is* and *are*. Deletion of *is* is much more frequent in VBE outside the South than it is in the speech of Mississippi and Alabama whites. For example, Wolfram's lower-working-class black speakers in Detroit deleted *is* overall 37.1 percent of the time (Wolfram 1969, p. 174). The study of Harlem VBE by Labov et al. (1968), p. 219) shows *is* deleted with 37.7 to 54 percent frequency, depending on the peer group. Although none of those black speakers lived in the South, one would not expect Southern blacks to have substantially less deletion of , especially if the distinctive characteristics of Northern VBE are explained as displaced Southern dialect features.

No doubt white Southern speakers delete present-tense forms of *to be*; they delete *are* very frequently and some delete *is* occasionally. But the fact remains that there are many Southern whites who delete only *are* and, of those who delete *is*, almost none delete it as often as blacks do. These qualitative and quantitative differences should not be ignored, but how are they to be accounted for? The answer, I suggest, is that absence of *to be* forms in VBE represents the remnants of the earlier creole, in which their absence was a syntactic phenomenon. For white speakers, deletion of *are* is diachronically related to the fact that their speech is "r-less" and *are* deletion is, for some, being generalized to *is*, with possible reinforcement from contact with VBE speakers.

DISTRIBUTIVE "BE"

The last feature of interest to be discussed is distributive *be*, as in utterances like *He always be around here*. Like the other features, it is well documented in VBE. And like the other features, it must be examined with care if the question of its unique status in VBE is to be properly answered. If we are not to go astray, we must pay attention to two aspects of this form: its semantic force and the auxiliary associated with it in constructions demanding an overt auxiliary. Invariant forms of *be* are common to all English speakers. Aside from imperatives, *be* after modal auxiliaries, infinitive constructions, and the rare subjunctive (*Bring forth your wife, if such she be!*), all of which require invariant (uninflected) *be* in standard English, there are instances in colloquial English in which an apparently indicative *be* arises from the reduction and loss of *will* and *would*. All of the examples cited by Williamson (1971) as having been actually observed by her are of this type: *She be fifteen in November* (*will* reduction) and *I be glad to help you* (either *will* or *would* reduction) are two of them. Her two literary examples could also be explained in the same way. Such cases are obviously not unique to VBE. We must also distinguish the mysterious construction I have called the "buried imperative" (Fasold 1972b), as in *If you be good, I'll give you a lollipop*, which is not unique to VBE. There is also the stock phrase *There you be*, which I have observed in the speech of both blacks and whites and which ill fits the distributive semantics of the VBE usage. There are other uses of *be* in dialects of British English, most of which are easily distinguishable from the VBE construction on semantic grounds. One exception is its use in Irish English, which is similar to the VBE *be* and quite possibly played a role in the development of the latter (Rickford 1974).

In actual use, VBE distributive *be* sometimes comes close in function to invariant *be* from *will* and *would* reduction (Fasold 1972a, pp. 155-59; Wolfram 1974, pp. 517-21). As with the remote-time *been* construction, which sometimes comes close to the standard colloquial *have been* construction with *have* deleted, a potential ambiguity may contribute to the maintenance of the non-standard form--here, distributive *be*. Sometimes an uninflected *be* is clearly not distributive *be*, but at other times the distinction is hard to make.

There are, however, environments in which *will* and *would* cannot be contracted and therefore cannot be deleted. In these environments, distributive *be* shows up unmistakably because the auxiliary *do* will appear with it, whereas uncontracted forms of *will* and *would* are obligatory if they are part of what the speaker intended to say. Wolfram (1974) used this fact to test familiarity with distributive *be* in his research in Meadville, Mississippi. One such environment is negative sentences. The negative of distributive *be* is *don't be*, whereas that of the modal phrase is *won't be* or *wouldn't be*. Wolfram asked his subject to supply negative counterparts to three affirmative stimuli involving invariant *be*. The three stimulus sentences were the following:

He be in in a few minutes.
Sometime Joseph be up there.
Sometime his ears be itching.

The first example is a reasonably clear instance of *will* reduction (*He'll be in in a few minutes*). The other two are also capable of being interpreted as instances of reduced *will* or *would*, but the frequency adverb *sometime* tends to cue VBE speakers that distributive *be* is intended, since the meaning of the adverb is very consistent with the meaning of that verb. Wolfram's results are reported in table V (1974, p. 522, table IX).

There is a striking agreement between blacks and whites on their interpretation of the first sentence and a clear difference in their treatment of the other two. Although a minority of the whites supplied the appropriate auxiliary for the negative distributive *be* sentences, most of them either interpreted the forms to mean *will be* or gave some other response, usually an inflected *be* form. A majority of the black informants, on the other hand, interpreted the last two sentences as containing distributive *be* and provided the expected *do not* form, even though doing so required the use of a stigmatized form in a fairly formal context. There are white Southerns who demonstrate competence in the grammar of distributive *be*, but a much larger proportion of black Southerns show that they are at home with it. It seems

TABLE V: Negative Paraphrases of Affirmative Invariant <u>Be</u> Sentences

	Negative Paraphrase by Whites		
	do not	will not	other
He be in in a few minutes	0	53	2
Sometime Joseph be up there	11	23	21
Sometime his ears be itching	3	21	31
	Negative Paraphrase by Blacks		
	do not	will not	other
He be in in a few minutes	0	50	3
Sometime Joseph be up there	34	6	13
Sometime his ears be itching	32	2	19

hard to avoid the conclusion that distributive *be* is a VBE form, and that some whites have learned about it from contact with blacks.

DECREOLIZATION

There is evidence, then, that some aspects of VBE distinguish its speakers from even the most sociologically comparable white speakers in the South.   What is known about some of those features is consistent with the hypothesis that they arose from a creole language and their current place in VBE grammar can be understood as the result of decreolization.   Detailed proposals tracing possible steps in the decreolization of two of them, copula and auxiliary absence (Fasold 1976) and distributive *be* (Rickford 1974), have been presented elsewhere.   I give one further example here--the possible decreolization of syllable structure and final consonant clusters.

It is a wide-spread feature of pidgin and creole phonology that syllable structure favors alternating consonants and vowels. In final position, clusters of two or more consonants are particularly unlikely.   If there was a Plantation Creole, there is little doubt that clusters of final consonants were disallowed by the morpheme-structure constraints.   Words like *test* and *desk* would have been *tes* and *des*, both in surface phonology and underlying form.

A major force in decreolization is continued language contact between the creole and the standard language from which it derived most of its vocabulary.   Thus speakers of a creole that did not allow final clusters would sometimes hear words which were close cognates of items in their lexicon but which did contain such clusters.   Some creole speakers would imitate the final-cluster words when they wished to sound sophisticated, but that imitation would not affect their basic phonological system, being rather true code-switching.   The words with final clusters would be borrowed whole from the standard system.

As such imitation became more frequent, some of the words with final consonant clusters might have become part of the creole lexicon, but as lexical exceptions.   That is, in general, words were allowed to end in only one consonant, but some were exceptions.   When enough such exceptions had accumulated, a primitive new morpheme-structure rule might have developed to allow final clusters, but only of a restricted type.   I mentioned above that some of the Washington, D.C., children showed evidence of allowing only final [t] in clusters; that restriction could be a survival of this stage in the decreolization process.   A speaker at this stage would have some words with final clusters ending in [t]; words in the standard language that ended in clusters with other final consonants would end in the creole wither with [t] or with only one consonant. [12] For example, *desk* might be *dest* and *flask*,

flas. Furthermore, any underlying final cluster would be simplifiable by a general final-stop deletion rule operating at high
frequency. This stage would be a major step in the decreolization
process. Speakers would be a major step in the decreolization
process. Speakers would hear their elders occasionally say words
ending in final clusters. As far as the older generation was
concerned, these words were borrowings that did not affect their
internal rule system; the younger generation, however, would
treat the words as regular lexical entries and interpret their
usual pronunciation without a final consonant cluster as a result
of a deletion rule. Speakers at this stage would produce patterns
like those of the five children in the first two columns of table
IV.

As time passed, the creole speaker would acquire a few lexical
exceptions with consonants other than [t] in final clusters.
Words like *desk* and *ask*, for example, might have underlying [k],
while less common words, perhaps *flask*, would be lexically *flas*
or *flast*. These new clusters would be simplified very frequently
by the general stop-deletion rule inherited from the previous
stage. These speakers' patterns would match those of the nine
children in the middle column of table IV (with *ask* as a lexical
exception) and the three in the fourth column (with *ask* and *risk*
as exceptions).

Later, essentially all the underlying clusters would match
those of standard English. The rule deleting final stops would
be blocked in bases followed by a vowel suffix, so that *testing*
and *tesser* would be used to the exclusion of *tessing* and *tesser*.
Final stops would often be deleted, but the only difference between
the language of this stage and varieties that had never been
creoles would be statistically higher frequency of deleted stops.
This situation is that of most VBE today, and the child in the
fifth column of table IV would be typical. Table VI outlines this
decreolization process. Although the process is somewhat speculative, it does no violence to what we know of pidgin and creole
patterns and of decreolization, and it accommodates the facts in
table IV.

CONCLUSION

The features considered in this study are all in segmental
phonology and in morphology and syntax. There are other areas
in which some black-white speech differences might be found.
One of these is intonation and pitch level. Hansell and Seabrook
(1978), using data from Californians, found some differences in
this area, as well as in rules for discourse. Lexicon is another
area not addressed here that might be very fruitful. Perhaps
most significant would be differences in the ethnography of communication. It is possible that black and white speakers, in the

TABLE VI: Putative Decreolization of Final Consonant Clusters

Stage 1 (Creole)

Phonotactics:	Final clusters disallowed
Final-stop deletion rule:	None
Origin of words with final clusters:	Borrowing

Stage 2

Phonotactics:	Only clusters ending in [t] allowed
Final-stop deletion rule:	Extremely frequent application, not blocked by vowel suffix
Origin of words with final clusters:	Normal lexical entries for clusters ending in [t], borrowing for others

Stage 3

Phonotactics:	Only clusters ending in [t] allowed
Final-stop deletion rule:	Very frequent application, not blocked by vowel suffix
Origin of words with final clusters:	Normal lexical entries for clusters ending in [t], other clusters entered as lexical exceptions

Stage 4 (Modern VBE)

Phonotactics:	Same as for standard English
Final-stop deletion rule:	Frequent application, blocked by vowel suffix
Origin of word with final clusters:	Normal lexical entries

South and elsewhere, follow different rules for interruptions, simultaneous talk, mitigation and aggravation of disagreements in conversation, the construction of narratives, and the use of verbal art forms.

The linguistic features discussed here indicate that the two ethnic groups differ in their grammar and phonology but that the differences are relatively few and rather subtle. One might ask, if this is the case, what does it matter? To the extent that the differences support the creole hypothesis, a comparison of modern VBE and white nonstandard English can be interesting for the study of decreolization. Present-day VBE may well be an example of what a late postcreole looks like; the study of it can therefore add to our knowledge of creole phenomena.

To turn to less purely scholarly concerns, it is worth asking about the implications of black-white speech relationships for language-arts education. Whether we believe it is best to maintain ethnic and regional varieties or to teach all children the use of standard English, it is important to know about the differences between such varieties and the standards with which they contrast. Even if nonstandard dialects are to be encouraged or at least tolerated in spoken language, it could be important to know whether some children are thus discriminated against in learning to read and write the standard language. In this connection, I believe that a disproportionate amount of attention has been paid to VBE; if linguistic differences work to the disadvantage of black children in school, then they presumably affect children who speak other nonstandard varieties as well, and they would deserve attention, too.

But if the differences between VBE and standard English are as few and subtle as I believe they are, a real question arises about their importance in education. Research on potential reading problems for VBE speakers is, at best, inconclusive (Somerville 1975). When we look elsewhere in the world, for instance, in Switzerland, where the differences between Swiss German and the standard language of education are of about the same order of magnitude as the differences between VBE and standard English but where literacy is nonetheless high, real doubts arise about how crucial such differences are. We have lived through ten or fifteen years of intensive attention to VBE in education with precious little to show for it in terms of educational advancement. The recent Ann Arbor, Michigan, court decision, in which the school system was found not to discriminate against black children, but nonetheless was ordered to provide teachers with special in-service training about the effect on reading of the language of black students, was, in my judgment, a mistake that should not be repeated.

I do not advocate giving up, or not addressing the fact that lower-class black children often do not read as well as more-advantaged students. It seems to me that it is time to look elsewhere than in purely linguistic differences for answers. Linguists and anthropologists still have a contribution to make toward the solution of this complex problem, but most likely in the study of interaction rules, patterns of conversational strategy, and learning styles. Perhaps we would discover where the culturally appropriate behavior of black and other minority children may prove offensive to their teachers, creating a climate of hostility in which learning to read or learning anything else is likely to be made more difficult. Linguistic factors do exist and do play a role, and it is no doubt good for VBE-speaking youngsters to have a teacher who is aware of the structure of their linguistic system and who knows how to deal with it in a positive way. I do question, however, whether this good is great enough to be worth the

effort that was put forth in Ann Arbor.   If one wanted to
reduce the death rate in traffic accidents, to use an analogy, a
major effort to develop stronger automobile bumpers would probably
be misplaced.   Stronger bumpers would help a little, but tactics
like lower speed limits, breakaway road signs, and air bags are
likely to be more productive.   Similarly, I expect research on
the ethnography of communication to lead to better results in
improving education for minorities than continued worry about
deleted copulas and the homophony between *pin* and *pen*.

FOOTNOTES

[1] Philip Luelsdorf and Marvin Loflin take the position that
black and white language systems are extremely different,
but appear not to be interested in the historical issue.

[2] Readers who are interested in a linguist's criticism of
this view are referred to Labov 1972a, pp. 201-40.

[3] Data collected for the Linguistic Atlas of the Gulf States
has been tape-recorded and more emphasis has been placed
on connected free speech than had been the case in the past.
These data may well be adequate for the type of analysis en-
dorsed here.

[4] In listing forms that are "shared," I am being somewhat
conservative.   Although these features are found in Southern
white speech, it is possible that detailed analysis of some of
them might show subtle differences in distribution along the
lines of racial ethnicity.   In the absence of such detailed studies, I assume that no such differences exist.

[5] A double modal construction I have observed in south-
central Pennsylvania but have not found reported for other
regions is *won't can* (*He won't can come tomorrow*).   Somewhat
surprisingly, speakers of this dialect find *will can* ungrammatical.   This construction does not exist in VBE.

[6] Sommer and Trammell (1980), however, found that lower-
class black Atlanta sixth-grade children used this feature
38.1 percent of the time, whereas upper-middle-class black
children and upper-middle and lower-class white children used
it at frequencies of less than 10 percent.

[7] The [ks] cluster is not simplified, because the final
consonant is not a stop.

[8] Although Wolfram does not say so, his data contain no
evidence that final clusters are limited to those ending with
the stop [t], since all the test items ended in [st] in standard
English.

[9] These data served as the basis of Wolfram's (1974) study
of copula and auxiliary deletion and distributive *be*.   Although
consonant clusters were not discussed in that study, a tabulation

was made from the data by Deborah Hendrix. Wolfram graciously made these data available to me.

[10] An analysis in which *gonna* is taken as a "quasi-modal" with no *is* in the underlying form is falsified by such sentences as *He gonna be there, I know he is*.

[11] Wolfram excluded from tabulation all utterances in which a sibilant preceded the *is* slot. He included utterances with *gonna* following that slot.

[12] The use of *ast* for *ask*, discussed above, might ultimately cast doubt on the existence of stages in which [t] is the only possible final consonant in underlying clusters.

REFERENCES

Atwood, E. Bagby. 1953. *A Survey of Verb Forms in the Eastern United States*. Ann Arbor: Univ. of Michigan Press.

Bereiter, Carl; Osborne, Jean; and Reidford, P. O. 1966. "An Academically Oriented Pre-School for Culturally Deprived Children." In *Pre-School Education Today*, ed. Fred. M. Hechinger, pp. 105-37. New York: Doubleday.

Davis, Lawrence M. 1969. "Dialect Research: Mythology and Reality." *Orbis* 18: 332-39.

Dillard, J. L. 1971. *Black English: Its History and Usage in the United States*. New York: Random House.

Dillard, J. L. 1975. *All-American English*. New York: Random House.

Dorrill, George T. 1977. "Phonological Features in Negro and White Speech in Two South Carolina Communities." Paper presented at the Conference on Language Variety in America, Univ. of Chicago, April 1977.

Fasold, Ralph. 1972a. *Tense Marking in Black English: A Linguistic and Social Analysis*. Arlington, Va.: Center for Applied Linguistics.

Fasold, Ralph. 1972b. "A Look at the Form *Be* in Standard English." *Languages and Linguistics Working Papers* 5: 95-101. Washington, D.C.: Georgetown Univ. Press.

Fasold, Ralph. 1976. "One Hundred Years from Syntax to Phonology." In *Diachronic Syntax*, ed. Sanford Steever, Carol Walker, and Salikoko Mufwene, pp. 79-87. Chicago: Chicago Linguistic Society.

Fasold, Ralph. 1978. Review of *A Segmental Phonology of Black English* and *Linguistic Perspectives on Black English*, by Philip A. Luelsdorf. *Language in Society* 7: 438-45.

Feagin, Crawford. 1979. *Variation and Change in Alabama English: A Sociolinguistic Study of the White Community*. Washington, D.C.: Georgetown Univ. Press.

Hansell, Mark, and Seabrook, Cheryl. 1978. "Some Conversational Conventions of Black English." In *Proceedings of the Fourth Annual Meeting of the Berkeley Linguistics Society* pp. 576-87. Berkeley, Calif.: Berkeley Linguistics Society.

Herndobler, Robin, and Sledd, Andrew. 1976. "Black English: Notes on the Auxiliary." *American Speech* 51: 185-200.

Labov, William. 1969. "Contraction, Deletion and Inherent Variability of the English Copula." *Language* 45: 715-62.

Labov, William. 1972a. *Language in the Inner City* . Philadelphia: Univ. of Pennsylvania Press.

Labov, William. 1972b. *Sociolinguistic Patterns.* Philadelphia: Univ. of Pennsylvania Press.

Labov, William; Cohen, Paul; Robbins, Clarence; and Lewis, John. 1968. "A Study of the Non-Standard English of Negro and Puerto Rican Speakers in New York City." United States Office of Education Final Report. Cooperative Research Project No. 3288.

Loflin, Marvin D. 1971. "On the Structure of the Verb in a Dialect of American Negro English." In *Readings in American Dialectology*, ed. Harold B. Allen and Gary N. Underwood, pp. 428-43. New York: Appleton-Century-Crofts.

Luelsdorf, Philip A. 1975. *A Segmental Phonology of Black English.* The Hague: Mouton.

McDavid, Raven I., Jr., and Davis, Lawrence M. 1972. "The Dialects of Negro Americans." In *Studies in Honor of George L. Trager*, ed. M. Estellie Smith, pp. 303-12. The Hague: Mouton.

McDavid, Raven I., Jr., and McDavid, Virginia Glenn. 1951. "The Relationship of the speech of American Negroes to the Speech of Whites." *American Speech* 26: 3-17.

McDavid, Raven I., Jr., and McDavid, Virginia Glenn. 1960. "Grammatical Differences in the North Central States." *American Speech* 35: 5-19.

Miller, Michael J. 1977. "A Brief Outline of Black-White Speech Relationships in the Central Savannah River Area." Paper presented at the Conference on Language Variety in America Univ. of Chicago, Chicago, Ill., April 1977.

Noseworthy, Ronald. 1972. "Verb Usage in Grand Bank." *RLS: Regional Language Studies* (Dept. of English, Memorial Univ., St. John's, Newfoundland) 4: 19-24.

Rickford, John. 1974. "The Insights of the Mesolect." In *Pidgins and Creoles: Current Trends and Prospects*, ed. David DeCamp and Ian F. Hancock, pp. 92-117. Washington, D.C.: Georgetown Univ. Press.

Rickford, John. 1975. "Carrying the New Wave into Syntax: The Case of Black English BIN." In *Analyzing Variation in Language*, ed. Ralph W. Fasold and Roger W. Shuy, pp. 162-83. Washington, D.C.: Georgetown Univ. Press.

Shnukal, Anna. 1979. "A Sociolinguistic Study of Australian English: Phonological and Syntactic Variation in Cessnock, N.S.W." Ph.D. dissertation, Georgetown Univ.

Somervill, Mary Ann. 1975. "Dialect and Reading: A Review of Alternative Solutions," *Review of Educational Research* 45: 247-62.

Sommer, Elizabeth, and Trammell, Robert. 1980. "On the Distinctness of Southern Black and White Speech." Paper presented at the 22d meeting of the Southeastern Conference on Linguistics, memphis State University, Memphis, Tenn., March 1980.

Stewart, William A. 1970. "Toward a History of American Negro Dialect." In *Language and Poverty* , ed. Frederick Williams, pp. 351-79. Chicago: Markham.

Williamson, Juanita V. 1971. "Selected Features of Speech: Black and White.: In *A Various Language: Perspectives on American Dialects*, ed. Juanita V. Williamson and Virginia M. Burke, pp. 496-507. New York: Holt, Rinehart, Winston.

Wolfram, Walter A. 1969. *A Sociolinguistic Study of Detroit Negro Speech*. Washington, D.C.: Center for Applied Linguistics.

Wolfram, Walter A. 1971. "Black-White Speech Differences Revisited." In *Black-White Speech Relationships* , ed. Walt Wolfram and Nona H. Clarke, pp. 139-61. Washington, D.C.: Center for Applied Linguistics.

Wolfram, Walter A. 1974. "The Relationship of White Southern Speech to Vernacular Black English." *Language* 50: 498-527.

Wolfram, Walt, and Christian, Donna. 1976. *Appalachian Speech*. Arlington, Va.: Center for Applied Linguistics.

Wolfram, Walt, and Fasold, Ralph W. 1974. *The Study of Social Dialects in American English*. Englewood Cliffs, N.J.: Prentice-Hall.

A REEXAMINATION OF THE BLACK ENGLISH COPULA

John Baugh

INTRODUCTION

All facets of Afro-American behavioral research have obvious social implications. Undoubtedly, the catalytic impact of the civil rights movement has influenced this social orientation. In the case of linguistics, however, some of the most significant theoretical advances of our time can be linked directly with Black English Vernacular (BEV) research. In spite of the fact that scholars have typically approached BEV in a delicate and diplomatic manner, controversies rage at both professional and lay levels with regard to the viability and legitimacy of BEV research. This is not surprising because BEV is a stigmatized dialect and as such represents a highly personal and consequently an emotional topic. Though there are strong social concerns, and in some instances social consequences, involved in BEV analyses, affiliated linguistic issues also continually crop up. As a result we are forced to review the limitations, appropriateness, and social applicability of contemporary introspective linguistic theories. The present discussion, although rooted in a socially important topic, will stress linguistic concerns. This is not to suggest that the social aspects of BEV are being dismissed as unimportant, merely that they are not of primary concern here.

The present analysis reexamines the nature of copula variation in BEV and is cast in the tradition of the earlier copula research by Labov (1969) and Wolfram (1974). This analysis differs from previous examinations, however, in that more constraints have been introduced and the Cedergren-Sankoff computer program for multivariant analysis has been employed.

The data are from the Cobras, an adolescent peer group that was interviewed by John Lewis ("KC") as part of Labov's earlier BEV research. Having conducted fieldwork of my own in a Los Angeles BEV community, I am aware of the stifling effect that the interview can have on the vernacular corpus. After reviewing Lewis's interview, however, I feel that the authenticity of the

data is clear.   At this point, let it suffice to say that Lewis
showed an acute ethnosensitivity in all of the interviews that he
gathered.   Although these data are synchronic, the present
analysis reveals some diachronic implications as well.   To my
knowledge, this investigation represents one of the first times
that multivariant analysis has been used with regard to BEV for
historical purposes.

Linguistic Variation and Linguistic Theory

When the variable rule was first introduced (Labov, 1969),
the full potential of variable analysis for linguistic purposes could
not be known.   That its potential has been gradually maturing is
seen in the works of Trudgill (1971), G. Sankoff (1974), Cedergren
and Sankoff (1974), Wolfram (1974), Lavendera (1975), and others.
In a sense one might view variable analysis as traditional in
linguistic research; after all, what could be more natural or traditional than entering the speech community, gathering a corpus,
reviewing the corpus for paradigms, and reporting the nature of
linguistic systematicity wherever it is found?   In spite of this
traditional orientation, however, influential linguists have stressed
the theoretical restrictions imposed by nonideal corpora.   As a
result, systematic variation--henceforth variation--has typically
been viewed as free variation.   In this instance it will be most
beneficial to review affiliated theoretical and methodological concerns as they relate to BEV.
The research on BEV differs from the more formal research
in linguistics because the latter analysis is usually inductive.
Depending on one's theoretical perspective, this can be seen as
a blessing or a curse.   Whereas the evolution of formal linguistic
research has resulted in a condition where many scholars turn to
themselves as informants, there are few, if any, trained linguists
whose intuitions about BEV are reliable for descriptive purposes.
Another difficult choice must therefore be made.   Should we
strive to train speakers of Nonstandard English to become linguists
so that they can then introspect about their language, or should
we strive to enhance our empirical methodologies?   Unquestionably,
the only feasible alternative available to BEV is to continue with
the empirical tradition.   In training nonstandard speakers to become
introspective linguists we would inevitably bombard their native
intuitions with preconceptions to the point where the validity of
these intuitions would be questionable.
What, then, does this have to do with linguistic theory?
Quite simply, when we look at advances in linguistics, we see
that the methodologies employed in introspective research are not
generally applicable even in the first approach to a language.
In turn, the scholar who is interested in BEV and in related
social concerns finds that contemporary methodologies and theories
are often not suited to the task.   This is not a new point by

any means; Hymes has repeatedly indicated that we must take ethnographic considerations into account when conducting linguistic investigations, simply because ethnographic factors *directly* affect the language (cf. Hymes, 1962).

Returning to the special needs confronting BEV, then, there is an obvious need to enhance inductive methodologies. One could argue that these empirical needs have been in existence for many years, but in the case of BEV there seems to be a sense of urgency. A desire to rectify methodological and theoretical inadequacies does not lead immediately to rapid reassessment and revision. Nevertheless, significant strides are being made on several linguistic fronts and the resulting innovations can now be applied or reapplied as necessary. At this point in linguistic evolution, that is, with the maturation of variable research, it is safe to say that the incorporation of variable phenomena is a requisite for thorough descriptive purposes. And the greatest value lies in identifying the most significant constraints on these phenomena. A related concern must focus on what is meant by the term "Black English." In this chapter, for the sake of brevity, this issue is not treated in depth; Black English is used to refer to the vernacular dialect, namely, the dialect that is native to most working-class black Americans and that reflects the usage of "some or all of the features which are distinctive [in the colloquial dialects of these black Americans]."[1]

If we refine the accuracy of variable rules in the linguistic realm, the structural relations between Standard English (SE) and BEV will become clearer. In turn, such findings will bear directly on educational issues such as bidialectalism and linguistic-dialectal interference. Furthermore, the common concerns associated with English research in general must be considered. Given that BEV is structurally similar to SE, it stands as an important point of structural contrast and as such provides an excellent basis for comparing aspects of language change, language acquisition, and concepts of competence, both "linguistic" and "communicative" (cf. Hymes, 1974).[2] At present, linguistics is able to address these highly emotional topics with a high degree of objectivity. When valid linguistic correspondences or differences can be revealed, we can hope to approach social and educational concerns with a higher level of accountability. I am suggesting that wherever systematic linguistic relationships can be identified, no matter how large or how small, those relationships should ultimately be addressed. To the extent that a given linguistic phenomenon cannot be examined or substantiated at the level of the informants within a speech community, one should question the legitimacy of the description.

The final point that I would like to make with regard to linguistic theory and variable linguistic phenomena is a perssonal one and closely related to BEV concerns generally. Many scholars who have little or no formal linguistic training have used the nonstandard speech of Afro-Americans as an indicator of communicative deprivation, cognitive limitation, and the like (cf. Bereiter and Engelmann, 1966). Although this is fallacious from a linguistic perspective, the nature of contemporary introspective linguistic methodology is coincidentally such that it implicitly supports the elitist perspective that assumes BEV to be an "inferior" dialect. I am not advocating as a moral obligation that we enhance empirical methods; rather, it would seem that BEV and many other stigmatized dialects throughout the world cannot be accurately described for social, educational, or other purposes until the descriptive limitations of introspective research are clearly exposed.

Field Methods

We have seen that there is a definite need to reestablish strong contacts in the speech community; it is equally important to recognize that the task of the fieldworker, especially the urban fieldworker, is difficult and often precarious, and requires an intimate ethnosensitivity to the speech community and to one's informants. This may seem to be an added burden, but in those instances where inductive evidence is the only legitimate source of data social obstacles are unavoidable.

Scanning the BEV literature written over the past decade, one is struck by the fact that much of the descriptive emphasis is focused on younger members of the community, with the data usually having been gathered by strangers (i.e. outsiders to the community) in unfamiliar surroundings. Efforts to justify these limited procedures have been based on the claim that children tend to be less formal than adults, and that, consequently, for descriptive purposes, the vernacular corpora of children represent the purest BEV forms. Such procedural limitations have been discussed before (cf. Wolfram, 1974; Mitchell-Kernan, 1971) and need not be further discussed here. However, the role of the BEV fieldworker needs to be reviewed more carefully.

The role of the fieldworker should be stressed if for no other reason than the accuracy of a final empirical analysis, but for BEV the significance of the fieldworker is critical. Ironically, there has been minimal concern--at least in the overwhelming majority of BEV research--with the importance of data gathering. It has been as if the desire to describe the language has taken precedence over the need to insure the accuracy of the corpus. Effective fieldwork can--and must--be carried out on Black English at all social levels. But the gathering of the vernacular of the city streets is fundamental for an accurate view of social, historical, and educational issues.

As has been mentioned, most of the data used in this study were gathered from the Cobras by John Lewis (KC), who is an excellent fieldworker for BEV. Lewis, a black man, has lived through many of the same experiences as the Cobras, and is therefore intimately familiar with native topics of interest; he was able to argue with informants without social difficulty. These

special skills were particularly useful because the Cobras lived
in a situation where the ability to handle oneself in verbal confron-
tations was highly prized. Thus, Lewis's own verbal skill clearly
increased his effectiveness as a fieldworker. Throughout these
data, two factors seem to enhance Lewis's interviews: his intimate
understanding of his informants' social perspectives, and his close
contacts with the Cobras in a variety of social situations--not
merely in the interview.

The study of BEV has been plagued by shortcuts in the
field and quiet dismissals of many adult informants for social
reasons alone. Undeniably, the task of gathering BEV data is
often difficult and this too is a social fact, but if we intend to
address BEV in a traditionally sound manner, then we must enhance
our field methods in general. Like KC, we must be able to take
the time to gain the trust of several representative informants.

THE BEV COPULA: A BRIEF REVIEW OF
PREVIOUS RESEARCH

Before moving on to the current analysis, let us review the
implications of previous copula research. Although a variety of
works on the copula have emerged in broader contexts, the present
remarks are intended primarily with BEV and West Indian Creole
(WIC) examinations in mind. In early statements of the creole
position, Bailey (1965) and Stewart (1969) proposed that BEV
had a zero copula. Although arguments for a zero copula, with
emphasis on zero, have since been seen as greatly overstated,
Bailey and Stewart established the importance of looking closely
at the African and WIC roots of contemporary BEV.[3] Examining
black-white linguistic relationships with emphasis on the creolist
position. Stewart reviewed the grammatical relationship between
SE and white nonstandard dialects in opposition to BEV and Gullah,
and found that the auxiliary had unique and similar markings in
both Black dialects. In addition, examining another distinctive
BEV feature (be), he questioned the possibility of European (Irish)
influence:

> But if that is the origin of the Negro-dialect use
> of be (i.e., borrowed by Negroes, let us say,
> from Irish immigrants to North America), then
> why is it now so wide-spread among Negroes but
> so absent from the still somewhat Irish-sounding
> speech of many direct descendants of the Irish
> immigrants [1969, p. 16]?

For the purpose of the present discussion, concern necessarily
concentrates on the historical influences that affect copula variation. But dialect borrowing need not be restricted to a single
contact group. The Irish presence as indentured laborers and
their subsequent role as slave overseers could easily explain the

necessary dialectal contact. Nevertheless, the creolist position appears to be quite strong as well. It is quite possible and even likely that contemporary BEV dialects contain linguistic influences from both the Irish and the West Indians (cf. Traugott, 1972). These historical issues, although relevant to the current discussion, will be presented in greater detail at a later point in the chapter.

Labov (1969) found variation in the copula to be the result of a series of grammatical and phonological rules that were parallel to those of colloquial deletion in SE. Deletion in BEV was possible only in environments where contraction was possible in SE. Furthermore, the variable constraints on the contraction and deletion rules were parallel except for the phonological effects which opposed the deletion of a vowel to the deletion of a consonant. Labov's initial analysis has been confirmed and reduplicated in several studies (e.g., Legum et al., 1971; Wolfram, 1969; Mitchell-Kernan, 1971).[4] Carrying the research further by building on the work of Labov, as well as aspects of his own research in Detroit, Wolfram (1974) examined the nature of copula variation in a comparison of white and black Southern speech.

But, although these studies have led to a synchronic understanding of copula variation, numerous historical questions still remain unanswered. Recognizing the complexity of the diachronic issues that surround this particular problem, Fasold (1976) proposes an alternative historical solution that takes both the creole and SE origins into account. Citing evidence from Botkin's narratives (1945) as a structural point for historical reference, as well as the contemporary works of Labov, Stewart, and his own previous discussion of the phenomena (1972); Fasold posits that the copula may have originally been omitted as a grammatical feature because of BEV's African and creole origins, but that this deletion was later transformed into a phonological rule. Furthermore, his argument suggests that the transition from initial grammatical constraints to more current phonological conditionings could have taken place with minimal changes in the surface forms. We will return to Fasold's position shortly, but for the moment, let us say that his argument seems quite plausible given the strength of the arguments that have been presented from both sides of the diachronic debate.

THE PRESENT ANALYSIS

The Cobra data are excellent from a synchronic standpoint owing to the handling of the data and the Cobra's collective command of BEV. But significant strides have also been made beyond the realm of field procedures: It is, appropriately, the advanced analytic techniques that have been developed by Cedergren and Sankoff, (1974) that now provide the necessary tools to look at these variable phenomena in more detail (cf. Griffin, Guy, and Sag, 1973.

The Sample

These data were gathered in the mid-1960s. Since that time, some of the Cobras have ended up in jail or been killed or wounded in urban disputes. Most of the members are now in their mid to late twenties and, as far as I know, are still living in and around Harlem. I should also point out that KC did not record all of the 26 taped conversations of which the analyzed corpus is composed. Some of the interviews were conducted by Clarence Robins,[5] and some of the group interviews were success- fully conducted by combinations of black and white investigators. For the most part, however, it was KC and the Cobras.

During the mid-1960s the primary concern of the Cobras was the defense of their "turf" against rivals, most notably the "Jets."[6] There came about a noteworthy philosophical change in the Cobras, however, with the members of the group striving to become more aware of their plight as Afro-Americans; consequently, they began to spout the rhetoric of black awareness and cultural taboos.[7] More generally, these transitions in attitude caused the Cobras to question their outlook on society and several of the interviews contain the theme of "the plight of black America(ns)." In all, the data contained 578 tokens (i.e., environments where we would anticipate the presence of a copula in other dialects). Table I shows the breakdown of the totals in relation to the following grammatical constraints.

ANALYTIC PROCEDURE

The first version of the Cedergren-Sankoff program for multi- variant analyses was run on the Cobra data in two series of

TABLE I: Sample Totals for the Cobras: Based on Following Grammatical Constraints

gon(na)	Verb + ing	Loc/Adj		NP		Misc.
108	122	134		162		53
		locative	adjective	NP Det.	# NP	
		48	86	126	36	

Total = 578

calculations: (a) calculations that measured the same constraints as were measured by Labov and Wolfram; (b) a series of calculations that introduced new and subdivided constraints. Since Labov's original analysis employed an additive model, and Wolfram's analysis concentrated on white informants, it was felt that the synchronic clarification of BEV copula variation would be enhanced at this time by employing the Cedergren-Sankoff program.[8]

Once having conducted an initial series of calculations on the familiar constraints, it was necessary to repeat the calculations incorporating the following adaptations:

1. Question/non-question: Each token was identified as either a question or non-question and was submitted under this new factor group.

2. Miscellaneous factor for following grammatical constraints: It was necessary to introduce a miscellaneous category for those instances where the arbitrary factors were insufficient. For the most part these were adverbs of manner.

3. The subdivision of __ NP: Previously, following NP had been calculated as a single factor. The secondary calculations dividing this factor into:

(a) __ NP
(b) __ Det. # NP (i.e., *a* and *the*)

4. The separation of __ Loc/Adj: Heretofore, the analysis of __ Loc/Adj. appeared as a single constraint owing to quantitative confines. The Cedergren-Sankoff program, however, allowed the present separation of these features.

COMPARABLE CALCULATIONS

At first blush, the need for a comparable series of calculations might seem dubious, and cumbersome, but it was felt that a parallel series of calculations would substantiate and/or clarify previous synchronic assessments and show whether the original relations were preserved in a multivariant analysis with extended (i.e., finely divided) constraints. Thus, the first series of calculations was purposely designed to mesh with the previous analyses of Wolfram and Labov, in that identical factors were analyzed. Parenthetically, Cedergren and Sankoff developed their computer methods--at least in part--by reexamining Labov's 1969 data, and they found that their fit of prediction with observation reliably identified those environments that favored both contraction and deletion.

Table II shows that, as in Labov, 1969, a preceding pronoun subject heavily favors contraction and somewhat less strongly favors deletion. The phonological effects do not show the reversal

TABLE II: Feature Weights for the Comparable Series of Calculations for All Measured Constraints

	Contraction	Deletion
-C___	0.000	0.000
-V___	.396	.239
___C-	.465	.525
___V-	0.000	0.000
NP___	0.000	0.000
Pro___	.919	.622
___gon(na)	1.000	.567
___Vb + ing	1.000	.375
___PA/Loc	.336	.868
___NP	.430	0.000

for contraction and deletion, but preceding vowels still tend to
favor both rules.   However, the differential effect on both rules
will emerge as the analysis proceeds.   The following phonological
consonant appears to have an increased effect, but this will
diminish in later analyses as well (see Table III).   The significant
revisions of the original examination concentrate on the following
grammatical constraints; these will therefore be of primary concern
here.

The percentages from Labov's original research for the Cobras,
of full, contracted, and deleted forms of *is* according to the
preceding and following grammatical environments are given in
Figure 1.

The current contours, based on feature weights from the
nonapplications probability model, appear in Figure 2   (Labov's
illustrated contours are separated with regard to preceding grammatical constraints, whereas the present multivariant analysis does
not need to make this kind of separation since all groups are
considered simultaneously.)   With the exception of the PA/Loc, [9]

TABLE III: Feature Weights for Phonological Constraints

		Contraction	Deletion
Labov	-C___	.410	.800
	-V___	.900	.410
Present			
analysis	-C___	0.000	.061
	-V___	.408	0.000
	___C-	.522	.322
	___V-	0.000	0.000

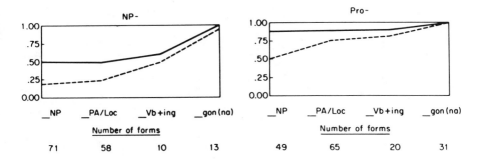

Figure 1.   Percentage of full, contracted, and deleted forms of is according to preceding and following environments for the Cobras: ——, *percentage contracted;* ----, *percentage deleted. (From Labov, 1972, p. 92.)*

the orderings from the multivariant anslysis are substantially the same with regard to the relative impact of following grammatical constraints on the contraction and deletion rules. Wolfram's analysis of white Southern speakers reflects similar patterns as well.

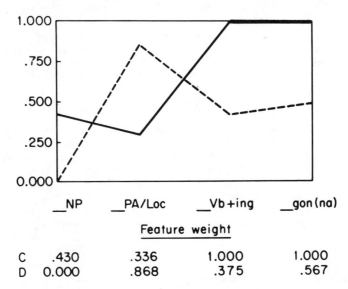

Figure 2.   Probability of full, contracted, and deleted forms of is based on feature weights according to following grammatical constraints for the Cobras: ——, φ *contracted;* ----, φ *deleted.*

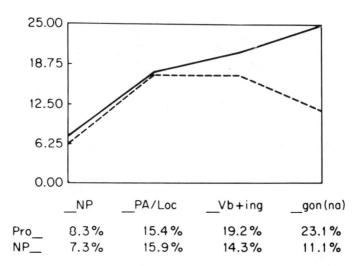

	__NP	__PA/Loc	__Vb+ing	__gon(na)
Pro__	8.3%	15.4%	19.2%	23.1%
NP__	7.3%	15.9%	14.3%	11.1%

Figure 3:   Percentage of is absence in Pro—and NP—by following environments for white southern speakers: ——, Pro----; ----, NP ——. (From Wolfram, 1974, p. 514.)

The patterning of *is*-deletion, although restricted in terms of the proportion of informants who realize the rule and the frequency with which it occurs for these informants, does appear to be a process found among some white Southern dialects.   From a qualitative viewpoint, it appears to be a process quite similar to the one observed for VBE [Wolfram, 1974, p. 514].

Before shifting the focus to the second series of calculations we might ask ourselves about the structural similarities and what they mean.   First of all, given the increased potential and analytic accountability of the Cedergren-Sankoff program, we see that, by and large, previous assessments were legitimate in their rule orderings.   But, additionally, the present confirmation now allows us to look at the nature of each constraint more closely.   Thus, leaving aside the factor revisions that we mentioned, the remaining constraints in the second series of calculations were the same (see Figure 4).

PHONOLOGICAL CONSTRAINTS

Beginning with preceding phonological constraints, we find the following (see Table III).

In the earlier analysis, the following phonological environment was significant only for adults; here it appears that both contraction and deletion are favored by a following consonant, which

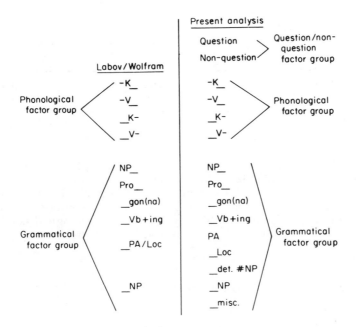

Figure 4:   Factor group revision.

indicates the likelihood that an underlying copula is present.
    It is important to recall that -C___ factors appear less frequent-
ly than do -V___ factors since all relevant pronouns end in vowels.
Nevertheless, the comparative findings clearly indicate con-
sistencies with regard to implications for the preceding phonological
conditionings;   namely,   -V___ favors   contraction   over   deletion,
whereas the reverse is true for -C___ .   The difference that is
illustrated here, however, would indicate that the phonological
constraints are not the strongest constraints with regard to either
rule.   At the same time, the weighting for -V___ (.408 contraction)
is the stronger phonological constraint and this accentuates the
comparability with previous assessments.
    The preceding phonological factors, in spite of the vocalic
appearance as a "slight" constraint are significant because they
confirm the preference of a CVC pattern (cf. Labov et al., 1968;
Labov, 1969).   The maintenance of a CVC pattern is further
supported when we consider that much of the evidence of pidgins
and creoles has suggested that CVC contours are generally present
in contact vernaculars (cf. Hall, 1966).   From the standpoint of
a more general picture of the phonological conditioning for BEV,
consider the case as stated by Labov, 1972 (see Table III):   "In
any case, the way in which contraction and deletion are opposed
with respect to the preceding vowel clearly demonstrates that
both contraction and deletion are phonological processes . . [p.

TABLE IV: Feature Weights for Question Constraints

	Question	Nonquestion
Contradiction	1.000	0.000
Deletion	1.000	0.000

106]." The present research, although still upholding this position, does not emphasize phonological conditioning in a *primary*
sense. The point will be examined further when the independence
of phonological and grammatical constraints is reviewed, but for
the moment it is significant to note that the phonological conditioning is maintained although it does not receive primary emphasis.

QUESTIONS AS A FACTOR GROUP

The situation with regard to questions is fairly complex, owing
to the phonological, morphological, and syntactic issues that relate
to the general class of questions proper and the issues that
relate specifically to those questions occurring in copula constructions. From the standpoint of phonology, final *ts* clusters have
been shown to have a unique effect on rule application; consequently, *it's*, *that's*, and *what's* are generally omitted in this type
of analysis (cf. Labov, 1969; Wolfram, 1974), as they have been
here. But given the importance of *what* in the broader context
of questions, its omission necessarily limits the extent to which
the impact of questions can accurately be assessed with regard
to contraction and deletion. Also, considering the exclusive focus
on *is* here, the scope of the question factor is further restricted
(see Table IV).

GRAMMATICAL CONSTRAINTS

The grammatical arguments surrounding copula variation are
by far the most interesting. In the past, it has primarily been
the grammatical constraints, and, more specifically, the explanations surrounding various grammatical conditionings, that have
lent viable support to both the creole and the English diachronic
perspectives. Although the historical alternatives are not of
primary importance at this point in the discussion, it is significant
to note that the grammatical issues cover a tremendously wide

TABLE V: Effect of Preceding NP or Pro on Contraction and Deletion as Shown by Feature Weights

	NP__	Pro__
Contraction	0.000	8.56
Deletion	0.000	.714

range of diachronic and synchronic territory. This is clearly the case because scholars have been able to construct feasible, yet different, explanations from similar synchronic evidence. With the complexity of grammatical features having been noted, the nature of their conditionings may now be described.

Preceding Grammatical Constraints

Table V shows that a preceding pronoun favors both rules, with contraction receiving primary emphasis. This is not surprising given the discussion surrounding pro__:
> it is plain that contraction is heavily favored when the subject is a pronoun. But the effect is much stronger than for other noun phrases ending in vowels. In the case of deletion, it can be seen that the rule operates much more often when a pronoun precedes . . . [Labov, 1972, pp. 106-107].

A further significant finding here that confirms previous analyses is the replication of the powerful constraint exerted by preceding NP. And, whereas Wolfram and Labov examined the nature of following grammatical conditionings based on separate analyses of the preceding factors, the present analysis has the advantage of being able to identify the overall conditioning. We can therefore see the relative impact of preceding grammatical elements without sacrificing other facets of the analysis.

Following Grammatical Constraints

Unchanged factors
The only factors to remain the same in the following grammatical factor group were (a) __gon(na) and (b) __ verb + *ing*. Both of these factors reflect the same conditioning and rule orderings that have been identified in the past: Following *gon(na)* strongly favors contraction and has a significant effect on deletion; verb + *ing* also favors contraction with a somewhat lesser effect on

TABLE VI: Effect of Following Gon(na) and Verb + ing on Contraction and Deletion Feature Weights

	__Gon(na)	__Verb + ing
Contraction	1.000	1.000
Deletion	.601	.402

deletion (see Table VI). Stated simply, in the final analysis the
relation of __ gon(na) and __ verb + ing to other constraints
remains unchanged when all analyses are considered.

The subdivision of following NP

With the complementary factors indicating similar rule orderings, we can now review the implications of the adjusted factors
beginning with the following NP. Previous analyses have examined
__ NP as a single constraint. The present analysis, however,
has subdivided __ NP into two factors.

Labov/Wolfram

Thus, the implications that have been posited with regard to
a following NP can now be reviewed more closely. Consider the
rule conditionings that have been suggested thus far (see Figures
1, 2, and 3). As these findings stand, their impact would
suggest __ NP as the least favored environment--within the realm
of the following grammatical factors--for the application of either
rule. With the division of the factor, however, another picture
emerges (Table VII). We can see, therefore, that it is necessary
to subdivide __ NP in the preceding manner because the true
nature of the conditioning is camouflaged until this is done.
The significance of this separation is further amplified because
__ Det. # NP now emerges as a primary factor in the application

TABLE VII: Effect of a Following NP or Det. # NP on Contraction and Deletion as Shown by Feature Weights

	__NP	__Det. # NP
Contraction	0.000	1.000
Deletion	0.000	.741

of both rules. The other side of the coin finds residual __ NP
as a low level constraint; in fact, __ NP is the least favored
following grammatical factor.

Further confirmation of the independence of phonological and grammatical conditioning

At this stage of the discussion, it is beneficial to look back
at some of the concerns that have been raised with regard to the
independence of phonological and grammatical constraints (cf.
Fraser, 1972). In spite of the importance of the various historical
options that have been aired, there still remains some confusion--
and some justifiable concern--as to the independence of analyzed
constraints. We find grammatical criteria and phonological criteria,
and numerous questions as to their mutual dependence or independence. The subdivision of our __ NP constraint, however,
clearly emphasizes the independence of previously discussed phonological factors, namely, the preference for CVC sequences. The
phonological conditioning is clear, but, more than that, the present
analysis suggests that grammatical and phonological factors are
independent. Turning our attention to grammatical concerns,
then, we are again faced with the prospect of an either/or hypothesis: grammar or phonology. The reweighting of the subdivided
__ NP constraint, however, would suggest that an either/or
approach is insufficient,[10] consider the phonological relations as
illustrated here:

$$\text{\_\_Det. \# NP} \quad
\begin{cases}
\text{-- } a \text{ NP} \quad \text{--- Obligatory vocalic status} \\
\text{-- } the \text{ NP} \text{ --- Obligatory consonantal status}
\end{cases}$$

Given the rule-favoring strength of the __ Det. # NP factors
(i.e., contraction [1.000], deletion [.741]), we clearly see the
overriding impact of the grammatical conditioning. This being
the case, the obvious question shifts to what might be perceived
as a conflict between the preference for CVC contours and the
grammatical conditioning. The point that is being emphasized
here is that *no such conflict exists*; rather, these findings suggest that both grammatical and phonological conditionings are
operating simultaneously. Undoubedly, this simultaneity is selectively conditioned and therefore should not be generalized. Thus,
the present analysis, while providing additional insights into the
synchronic nature of copula variation, has also confirmed that
phonological conditionings and grammatical conditionings are operating simultaneously. It will be necessary to return to this point
with regard to Fasold's historical discussion, but for the moment
it is significant to note the independence of grammar and pho-
nology--that is, the reconfirmation of their independence and,
more importantly, the fact that both condition rule application in
selective ways.

Separation of Locatives
and Adjectives

The final grammatical features that must be reviewed are the following locatives and adjectives. Heretofore, PA/Loc. has been measured as a single constraint. The limitation in the past was simply a quantitative barrier. "Because the total number of forms is considerably reduced for each group (even when single and group styles are combined), the following predicate adjectives and locatives are given together [Labov, 1972, p. 92]." Wolfram (1974) also measured locatives and adjectives as a single constraint, stating:

> Although there may be justification for categorizing
> this set on a different basis (e.g., considering
> adjectives as verbs, treating locatives as a
> separate category, etc.), it (i.e., the classification
> of factors) is considered here in the more tradi-
> tional classification for the sake of comparability
> with previous studies [p. 505].

Whereas previous samples may have been considered too small, they are not so rare that their isolated conditionings cannot be accurately assessed at this time.

In the case of locatives, the conditioning is similar to the combined conditionings that have been reported in the past (see Table VIII). The contraction rule is strong and is also favored over deletion. In addition, the ordering of these rules would strongly suggest an underlying copula, at least in this environment. With adjectives, an unexpected result appears. The rule orderings are emphatically reversed. Reflecting momentarily on the implications of the combined constraints, we see that the true nature of the conditioning was previously obscured. It is of course important to note that previous efforts combined these factors out of procedural necessity; however, with the difference now revealed, we must turn to the more complicated questions of how and why.

For the sake of discussion, let us assume for the moment that the unexpected did not occur: that locatives and adjectives reported similar weightings and, by extension, indicated rule orderings as suggested in previous analyses. The situation would

TABLE VIII: Impact of Following Locative and Adjective on Contraction and Deletion as Shown by Feature Weights

	Locative	Adjective
Contraction	1.000	.116
Deletion	.682	1.000

merely be one of synchronic clarification. Since the rules are emphatically reversed, however, the historical question of an underlying copula in BEV becomes more complicated and, by extension, requires further diachronic perusal. Now that adjectives have been shown to favor deletion in a rather convincing manner (deletion = 1.000; contraction = .116), the crossover pattern of the rule orderings suggests dialectal influence from at least two sources (see Table VIII). The implication for adjectives is that deletion must have predated "the emergence of contracted forms for this environment."

Based on the illustrated examples, we can see that previous assessments suggest consistent rule orderings with regard to all of the following grammatical constraints (Figures 1 and 3). Moreover, the historical implications that such an ordering supports would lead one to the conclusion that an underlying copula was a general feature of BEV at an earlier point in history. However, with adjectives favoring deletion over contraction, it is quite possible that a ZERO COPULA did exist in protoforms. This possibility is further reinforced by the relatively slight influence that adjectives have on the contraction rule. This does not imply that we should posit a zero copula in all environments any more than that we should assume an underlying copula was automatically present. Rather, the new locative and adjectival findings would again suggest that phonological and grammatical conditionings are operating independently yet simultaneously, with emphasis, of course, on environmental--and possibly historical--selectivity. The diachronic implications of these findings are unavoidable given the rule reversals that have been identified. It is important to maintain caution in this diachronic regard, and to recognize the limits that such speculation has previously brought to bear. Wolfram (1974) states the case concisely:

> This historical question of how VBE and Southern white speech arose, and how the relationship between black and white speech has developed since the settlement of the United States. In spite of the polemic with which the various historical options have been aired, evidence at this point still tends to be fragmented and anecdotal [p. 522].

SOME HISTORICAL IMPLICATIONS

In this instance, my proposed historical explanation is not based on speculation alone. Recalling the orientation of Fasold's recent discussion, namely, that both grammatical and phonological influences can account for fluctuations in the BEV copula, we can see that his position receives further confirmation based on the final analysis presented here. Let us now consider aspects of Fasold's discussion:

Proponents of the Creole history of Vernacular
Black English often disagree with linguists who
have studied the dialect synchronically over the
degree to which decreolization has progressed
. . .Accepting Labov's analysis of the modern dialect is not tantamount to a denial of the Creole
origin hypotehsis, but simply to recognize that
BVE has reached a late post-Creole stage.

Fasold goes on to outline a "hypothesized development of present
tense *be* deletion in Black English." For the purpose of the
discussion at hand, his concluding remarks are illuminating:

It is interesting to note, if I am correct in the
historical analysis of *be* forms, that while substantial changes in rules are going on in the background, the surface forms change little. From
Stage 3 on, once *da* is relexified as *is*, there continues to be variation between *is* and deletion up
to the present day.

As the situation stands now, with Fasold's position reinforced
by the present analysis, we would posit that European versus
African perspectives on the diachronic origins of BEV are far too
simplistic. What is needed is evidence that substantiates a position
that further considers both the African and European influence;
but for the moment let us consider the linguistic consequence of
West Indian contact.

Based on a comparison of two Creole varieties, Holm (1976)
examined the grammatical hierarchy of following grammatical constraints. Concentrating on Jamaican (Le Page and De Camp,
1960) and Turner's description of Gullah (1949), Holm found that
the syntactic environments where copula deletion were favored
differed from the orderings initially identified by Labov. Holm's
analysis is illuminating, and the constraint orderings that he has
identified are given in Table IX.

Holm's research is quite similar to the present analysis because
of his quantitative methodology. But more immediately relevant
to my purpose is Holm's demonstration of the importance of

TABLE IX: Grammatical Hierarchy Based on Percentage of Deletion for Jamaican and Gullah

Jamaican	Percentage	Gullah	Percentage
__Adj.	66	_gonna	88
__gonna	32	_Adj.	52
__NP	22	_V	52
__V	17	_Loc.	22
__Loc.	17	_NP	11

separating locatives and adjectives.   The orderings that Holm has identified tend to confirm the altered grammatical conditionings that have been identified in the present analysis.

In an effort to further resolve the issue, let us turn our attention to Bailey's (1966) description of Jamaican Creole English (JCE).   Bailey has identified the nature of locatives and adjectives in JCE as follows:
1.   Locatives: "the locating verb (V_L) de, 'be'. . . *must* be followed by a locative complement or modifier [emphasis my own]."

    (a)   *im de a yaad*
        'She is at home.'
    (b)   *jan no de ya nou*
        'John is not here now.'
    (c)   *wan trii de batamsaid me hous*
        'There is a tree below my house.'

2.   Adjectives: The adjectives in JCE operate similarly to those used by the Cobras, that is, the *be* form is absent.

    (a)   *di kaafi kuol*
        'The coffee is cold.'
    (b)   *di tiicha gud*
        'The teacher is good.'
    (c)   *di bos faas*
        'The bus is fast' [pp. 43, 64].

If we keep in mind the inverse relationship observed in Table IX and how the present assessment differs from the implicit historical perspective presented by Labov (see Figure 1), the diachronic aspect of this variation becomes clearer.   In the case of locatives, the $\underline{de}$ + loc. constructions that Bailey has outlined in JCE are structurally similar to the overriding number of full and contracted forms that have been used by the Cobras.   One would necessarily attribute this to an underlying copula, as seen in JCE.   Thus, this particular environment in BEV unquestionably reflects structural similarities to JCE (see the relationships presented in Figure 5).

The argument is further strengthened when applied to adjectives because, with the strength of the deletion rule now revealed, related historical concerns must come to the fore.   This being the case, the adjectival evidence from JCE, which is structurally similar to the corresponding evidence from the Cobras, lends additional support to the position that there was no copula before adjectives.   This also reinforces the creole origin hypothesis. When we consider the overall implications of the preceding investigations, the quantitative confirmation that emerges from the present analysis establishes the creole ancestry of contemporary BEV beyond any doubt.

At this point, however, it is wise to look at the historical implications a little more closely.   Although it is necessary to

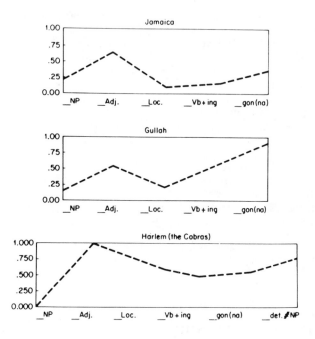

Figure 5: The impact of following grammatical constraints on deletion in Jamaica, Gullah, and Harlem (the Cobras).

recognize that creole origins have been posited before, it is equally important to recognize that many of these positions were presented prior to concise verification of the historical, empirical, or quantitative facts.   The present confirmation, then, stresses the need for this type of validation, especially given the social importance of these historical questions and the availability of new analytic techniques.

CONCLUSION

The historical perspective that is revealed here can be simply stated in spite of the rather elaborate steps that have brought us to this point.   It appears that the synchronic status of BEV copula variation has been influenced by West Indian creoles, as

well as by SE.   Based on the evidence presented, this seems to
be the only feasible alternative.   Moreover, when all of the structural and phonological facts are weighed, arguments for African
versus European origins must again be seen as overly simplistic.

There are unavoidable limitations to the diachronic scope of
research on stigmatized languages.   This is simply because many
of today's stigmatized dialects and languages were the languages
of the poor and uneducated classes of yesteryear.   The present
analysis and discussion attempts to take a step forward with the
recognition that new diachronic tools must continually be forged
for stigmatized languages.   We have justifiably been distracted
by the linguistic machinery that seems to operate so quickly,
cleanly, and efficiently in more prestigious languages.   The question is, are we to let the efficiency of prestigious linguistics
dictate the focus, direction, and overall development of these
new and special tools?

The fact that BEV should not be viewed in a monogenetic
fashion is not surprising considering the wide range of embryonic
explanations which have been debated at such length.   The difference that I wish to stress focuses on accountability.   Based on
the needs of linguistics, and for that matter those of all the
behavioral sciences, as well as the needs of those who are the
object of our scientific investigations, we must continue to strive
to maximize the level of accountability before we neglect available
data from real world contexts.

It is easy to see how linguists, influenced by a desire to
pursue theory, have in large part tried to avoid the descriptive
limitations imposed by inductive corpora.   However, we must focus
our efforts on through linguistic descriptions.   As long as scholars
are willing to dismiss empirical evidence under the banner of
"performance" our descriptions will never reflect the complete
structure of *langue*.   As long as systematic variation exists, and
as long as these phenomena are beyond the introspective grasp
of the analyst, we must be willing to reestablish the empirical
traditions that will expose such phenomena; otherwise, our descriptions cannot possibly represent *langue* in an actual sense.

In the case of BEV, however, the situation is even more
complex.   The social inequities and problems that were responsible
for the initial hubbub about Afro-American research, or lack of
it, are still with us today.   In fact these concerns are more vital
than ever because many Afro-Americans still differ from poverty
and, by extension, from its social and cultural side effects.
The unemployment figures from any urban city in the United
States will substantiate my point.   Those of us who are concerned
with the social consequences of linguistic research are confronted
with several decisions.   Even when confined to the realm of
obligatory empirical research, these decisions cannot be taken
lightly.   The need to enhance methodologies and theories is clearly
desirable whenever and wherever possible, especially considering
the subjective tradition within the field.

When one considers the extraneous factors that can influence the impetus and direction of future BEV research, it is important to recognize the unique position in which linguistics finds itself. In the case of BEV, we should make every effort to capitalize on strict linguistic principles to insure that our socially relevant concerns are not distorted by preconceived notions. We have a rare opportunity to make precise statements about an aspect of human behavior. Furthermore, we can hope that such information will benefit native members of the speech community.

ACKNOWLEDGEMENT

I am grateful for comments on earlier versions of this chapter from Gillian Sankoff, William Labov, and John Holm.

FOOTNOTES

[1]I have expanded Fasold's (1969) definition in an effort to incorporate an implicit interactional dimension into the definition. It is, after all, the interactional component that Bloomfield has identified as instrumental in defining the speech community (cf. Bloomfield, 1933, p. 42).

[2]This does not imply that we should stay at the level of analyzing purely linguistic constraints. Rather, I suggest that we take full advantage of an accurate linguistic statement prior to incorporating constraints that cannot be defined with the same accuracy as linguistic phenomena.

[3]Again, we must appreciate that their remarks came at a time when the social atmosphere was such that the "awareness level," if you will, of many blacks was such that African origins were not only palatable but preferred.

[4]A number of other works centering on the copula have treated it in broader linguistic and social contexts, for example, Day's work on Hawaiian Creole (1972) and Ferguson's multilingual comparative survey on the absence of the copula (1971).

[5]Clarence Robins worked closely with John Lewis in gathering BEV data. Robins was also one of the co-authors of Labov et. al., 1968.

[6]The Jets were also studied in Labov's original work and a detailed description of the peer group can be found in Labov et al., 1968.

[7]I am using "black rhetoric" here because the Cobras were obviously imitating popular rhetorical styles and as a result would often contradict themselves on a variety of ideological points.

[8]At the 1976 NWAVE conference at Georgetown University, Pascale Rousseau presented advances in the computer program that have not been included in this analysis; however, the revised program is available for general use at this time. She and David Sankoff are most responsible for the many technical improvements in variable rule research.

[9]Those who are familiar with previous analyses will immediately recognize that the new implications of the PA/Loc. reversal are not a trivial matter. The situation has changed, or rather, the assessment of the situation has changed, because of a complete analysis. Please recall that previous analyses for the Cobras did not account for all of the available data: ". . . the data presented here do not exhaust all the material which is available for the Jets and Cobras . . . [Labov, 1972, p. 91]." The present analysis does exhaust the Cobra data in a multivariant analysis, and the difference that has emerged results from the thorough analysis. It is important, therefore, that the difference illustrated in Figure 2 is not construed as a conflict with earlier research.

[10]Traugott (1972, p. 5) has discussed the limits of an either/or perspective with regard to the historical issues before. The new findings presented here tend to reinforce her position.

REFERENCES

Ashen, F. 1969. *Speech variation among Negroes in a small Southern community*. Unpublished doctoral dissertation, New York University.

Bailey, B. L. 1965. Toward a new perspective in Negro English dialectology. *American Speech*, , 171-77.

Bailey, B. L. 1966. *Jamaican creole syntax*. London: Cambridge University Press.

Bereiter, C., and Engelmann, S. 1966. *Teaching disadvantaged children in the pre-school*. Englewood Cliffs, N.J.: Prentice-Hall.

Bloomfield, L. 1933. *Language*. London: George & Unwin.

Botkin, B. A. 1945. *Lay my burden down: A folk history of slavery*. Chicago: University of Chicago Press.

Cedergren, H. J., and Sankoff, D. 1974. Variable rules: Performance as a statistical reflection of competence. *Language*, 50, 333-355.

Day, R. 1972. *Patterns of variation in the use of tense, aspect and diathesis in the Hawaiian Creole continuum*. Unpublished doctoral dissertation, University of Hawaii.

Fasold, R. W. 1969. Tense and the form *be* in Black English. *Language*, 45, 763-776.

Fasold, R. W. 1972. Decreolization and autonomous language change. *Florida FL Reporter*, 10: 9-12, 51.

Fasold, R. W. 1976. One hundred years from syntax to phonology. Chicago Linguistic Society, University of Chicago.
Ferguson, C. A. 1971. Absence of copula and the notion of
simplicity: A study of normal speech, baby talk, foreigner
talk and pidgins. In D. Hymes (Ed.), *Pidginization and
creolization of languages*. Cambridge: University Press.
Fraser, B. 1972. Optional rules in grammar. *Monograph Series
on Languages and Linguistics, Georgetown University, 25*, 1-16.
Griffin, P., Guy, G., and Sag, I. 1973. Variable analysis of
variable data. *University of Michigan Papers in Linguistics,
I*.
Hall, R. A., Jr. 1966. *Pidgin and creole languages*. Ithaca,
N.Y.: Cornell University Press.
Harris, Z. 1951. *Methods in structural linguistics*. Chicago:
University of Chicago Press.
Holm, J. 1976. Variability of the copula in Black English
and its creole kin. To appear, *American Speech*.
Hymes, D. 1962. The ethnography of speaking. In T. Gladwin
and W. C. Sturtevant (Eds.). *Anthropology and human be-
havior*. Washington, D.C.: Anthropological Society of
Washington.
Hymes, D. 1974. *Foundations in sociolinguistics*. Philadelphia:
University of Pennsylvania Press.
Labov, W. 1969. Contraction, deletion and inherent variability
of the English copula. *Language, 45*, 715-762.
Labov, W. 1972. *Language in the inner city*. Philadelphia:
University of Pennsylvania Press.
Labov, W., Cohen, P., Robins, C., Lewis, J. 1968. *A study
of the non-standard English of Negro and Puerto Rican
speakers in New York City*. USOE Final Report, Research
Project No. 3288.
Lavendera, B. 1975. *Linguistic structure and sociolinguistic
conditioning in the use of verbal endings in si-clauses
(Buenos Aires Spanish)*. Unpublished doctoral dissertation.
University of Pennsylvania.
Legum, S. E., Pfaff, C., Tinnie, G., and Nicholas, M. 1971.
The speech of young black children in Los Angeles. Technical
report 33. Inglewood, California: Southwest Regional
Laboratory.
LePage, R. and DeCamp, D. 1960. *Jamaican creole (creole
language studies I)*. London: Macmillan.
Mitchell-Kernan, C. 1971. *Language behavior in a black urban
community*. Language-Behavior Research Laboratory Mono-
graphs, 2. Berkeley: University of California.
Sankoff, G. 1974. A quantitative paradigm for the study of
communicative competence. In R. Baumann and J. Sherzer
(Eds.), *Explorations in the ethnography of speaking*.
London: Cambridge University Press.

Stewart, W. A. 1967. Sociolinguistic factors in the history of American Negro dialects. *Florida FL Reporter*, 5: 2, 11, 22, 24, 26.

Stewart, W. A. 1969. Historical and structural bases for the recognition of Negro dialect. *Monograph Series on Languages and Linguistics, Georgetown University*, 22, 515-524.

Traugott, E. C. 1972. Principles in the history of American English--a reply. *Florida FL Reporter*, 10: 5-6, 56.

Trudgill, P. J. 1971. The social differentiation of English in Norwich. Unpublished doctoral dissertation, University of Edinburgh.

Turner, L. 1949. *Africanisms in the Gullah dialect.* Chicago: University of Chicago Press.

Wolfram, W. 1969. *A sociolinguistic description of Detroit negro speech.* Washington, D.C.: Center for Applied Linguistics.

Wolfram, W. 1974. The relationship of white southern speech to vernacular Black English. *Language, 50*, 498-527.

MEXICAN-AMERICAN ENGLISH: SOCIAL CORRELATES OF REGIONAL PRONUNCIATION

Roger M. Thompson

When urbanized Mexican-Americans in Texas communicate in English, do they use Spanish-influenced, regional, or "nonregional" (standard or network) English?[1] In her dialect study of San Antonio, Janet Sawyer compared the speech of seven Mexican-Americans and seven native speakers of English. Her Mexican-American informants were second-generation, permanent residents of San Antonio, varying in age, education, occupation, and economic status. She found that, although even the most fluent bilingual had not adopted regional vocabulary, he was adopting San Antonio regional pronunciation. She concluded that San Antonio regional pronunciation is the prestige model for assimilating bilinguals. However, my work with Mexican-Americans in nearby Austin suggests that because of her sampling procedures, she may have overlooked some interesting social correlates of regional pronunciation in Mexican-American English.

Austin is a rapidly expanding city of 300,000 inhabitants, located 80 miles northeast of San Antonio. No comprehensive dialect study of the city has been completed, but an informal investigation I conducted confirmed that, as in San Antonio, the regional speech of the long-term residents blends features of Southern and Midland dialects of American English. There are of course many other English dialects heard throughout Austin. As the State's capital and the location of its largest university, the city has attracted residents not only from Texas but also from the rest of the nation. According to the 1970 census, 20 percent of the 65,000 who moved to Austin between 1965 and 1970 came from outside Texas and the South. Although a blend of Southern and Midland speech may predominate, there is currently a mixing of American English dialects.

In the midst of this dialect mixture are more than 40,000 Mexican-Americans who reside in Austin largely as a result of migration from rural areas in Texas rather than immigration from Mexico. They live in all sections of the city, but there are several neighborhoods where they form more than three-quarters

From *American Speech* 50:18-24, 1975. Reprinted with permission.

of the population. A sociolinguistic study of the language loyalty in the largest of these neighborhoods that I conducted in 1971 revealed that English is becoming the language of the home of the second and third urban generations.[2] Within this neighborhood, Spanish-influenced, regional and nonregional English can be heard seemingly in random variation.[3] However, Labov demonstrated in his study of English in New York City that, by using sociologically sound population-sampling procedures to select informants, it is possible to identify underlying rules or patterns in what appears to be random variation. Such sampling procedures were used in the following study to identify those social factors that correlate with the adoption of Spanish-influenced, regional, or nonregional English by these Mexican-Americans.

METHOD

In my original 1971 study of language loyalty, there were two surveys.[4] In the first, approximately 10 percent of the Spanish-surname households in the neighborhood were randomly selected and the occupants questioned concerning their language loyalty. In the second survey, I selected from the initial respondents 66 male heads of households who had been raised in Austin but whose parents had been raised elsewhere, in other words, the urban second generation, and interviewed them in their homes. For the present analysis, 40 who had been raised in the neighborhood were selected from the sampling of those raised in Austin. A 15 to 20 minute section of the second interview, which had been recorded on magnetic tape, was transcribed and analyzed for items of regional and Spanish-influenced pronunciation.

Because of the nature of the interview, I assume that formal rather than casual speech was elicited. I was an anglo conducting a brief formal interview.[5] Guided by an open-ended questionnaire, we discussed topics such as education, occupational advancement, and ethnic identification. The introduction of the microphone reinforced the formality of the situation. No attempt was made to elicit different levels or styles of pronunciation.

The Spanish-influenced pronunciation was identified by the occurrence of [s] where word-final [z] would be expected, for example, in nouns, *jazz* [jæs]; verbs, *analyze* [ænɑlɑys]; plural endings after vowels and voiced consonants, *cans* [kæns], *dishes* [disɑs]; or third-person singular verbs under the same conditions, *goes* [gos], *depends* [dipɛns]. Sawyer pointed out that such devoicing was the most persistent feature of a Mexican-American "accent" in her study.[6] Other pronunciation variables could have been used, for example the loss of /i/ ~ /I/ and /u/ ~ /U/, or /š/ becoming [s] or [č]. However, the devoicing variable was used because it seemed to predict the presence of other features of Mexican-American "accent." The word-final [z] variable influenced devoicing should use the standard rather than the regional pronunciation of /ay/ is to be expected because the nonregional pronunciation of /ay/ also occurs in Spanish, as in the word *paisano*.

SOCIAL CORRELATIONS

These assimilating Mexican-American men, who are second-generation inhabitants of Austin and are life-long residents of the same neighborhood, are adopting three different dialects of English: SE, RE, and SIE. It might be suggested that the pronunciation being adopted reflects differences in ethnic or language loyalty. However, there is no significant difference between the men in their preference for Mexican-American cultural items such as food and music. They do not differ in their attitudes towards the preservation of Spanish.[7] Speakers of SIE tend to use more Spanish in the home with their wives and children; however, the difference between speakers of SIE and the other groups is slight. English is the most frequently used language in the home. In all cases, most of the children speak only English at home, even when spoken to in Spanish. There is no correlation with age. The majority of the speakers of all three dialects are between 18 and 35 years of age, and the next largest group consists of those between 36 and 50. There is also no relationship to the amount of interaction the speakers have had with blacks either during childhood or at work.

Three social variables that do correlate with pronunciation are presented in table 1.[8] Almost all speakers of SIE usually speak Spanish at work, whereas most speakers of the other dialects use English. Typically, speakers of RE attended high school, whereas speakers of SE and SIE dropped out of school by the ninth grade. Speakers of SE and RE are equally affluent, whereas speakers of SIE are lower in socioeconomic status. Socioeconomic status in table 1 is not based on occupational classification alone. Ranking the men by general occupational classification results in no significant correlations. This is not surprising since socioeconomic status is generally derived by combining occupation, educational attainment, and income. No one of these criteria is sufficient in itself. Since the income of the Mexican-Americans in this study was not known, Bureau of the Census scores for ranking occupations were used. These scores are based on average levels of education and income for males in the United States in all occupations.[9] These scores may not be entirely valid for ethnic minorities, but they probably provide a better indication of the relative socioeconomic status of an occupation that would otherwise be obtainable.

also could be expected to occur more frequently in the conversations than the other features.

The speakers were ranked by dividing the total possible number of final [z] segments into the number that were devoiced. Since the devoicing of final [z] after /r/ sometimes occurs in the speech of many Anglos in Austin, zero percent devoicing would not be expected as the norm for non-Spanish-influenced speech. Over half of these Mexican-American speakers averaged between 10 and 15 percent devoicing with nearly all of it after /r/. Comparable figures for Anglo speech are not available. The other speakers ranged from 35 to 75 percent devoicing. Twenty-five percent devoicing was chosen to divide the speakers into those using Spanish-influenced English and those using standard English because it represents the break in these rankings.

The regional dialect of English that is typical of Austin was identified by the diphthong /ay/ as in the word *five*. In the Austin area, the /α/ is fronted to [a]. This fronting may or may not be accompanied by the dropping of the glide. When the glide is dropped, Northerners mistake the vowel for [æ]. However, *fine* and *fan* remain a minimal pair. This dipthong was chosen primarily because it occurred most frequently in the interviews. Speakers of Northern dialects would probably name fronting in /ay/ as the most characteristic feature of this regional dialect. Therefore, if these Mexican-Americans are consciously patterning their speech after a regional model, this feature would probably be one of the first to be adopted.

As in the case of devoicing, the speakers were ranked by dividing the total possible number of /ay/ segments into the number that were fronted. Only the fronting itself, rather than fronting accompanied by glide deletion, was considered. For the majority of speakers, fronting occurred less than 10 percent of the time. For the others, it occurred in up to 75 percent of the total possible occurrences. Twenty percent was chosen to divide the informants into speakers of regional and nonregional English.

RESULTS

The two pronunciation variables allow for the identification of four classes of speakers: speakers of standard English (SE), who do not devoice final [z] and do not front /α/ in the diphthong /ay/; speakers of regional English (RE), who do not devoice final [z] but front the /α/; speakers of Spanish-influenced English (SIE), who devoice final [z] yet have the standard English pronunciaiton of /ay/; and speakers of Spanish-influenced regional English (SIRE), who both devoice and front. In this neighborhood the speakers are divided almost equally among the first three categories: 11 SE, 12 RE, and 14 SIE. Only 3 speakers are classified as speakers of SIRE. That nearly all speakers with the Spanish-

TABLE I.   Pronunciation and Three Social Variables

		Pronunciation Type			
		SE	RE	SIE	SIRE
Language used	Spanish	3	5	12	0
at work	English	8	7	2	3
Highest grade	0-9	7	3	11	1
at school	10+	4	9	3	2
Socioeconomic	Lower	3	4	13	0
status	Upper	8	8	1	3

Arbitrarily, the score of 50 was chosen for dividing the statuses into upper and lower. The score of 50 ranks about halfway between the average score for machine operators and kindred workers and the score for craftsmen, foremen, and the like. In other words, 0-49 represents the lower working class and the lower half of the upper working class; 50-100 represents the upper working class and the middle class. That the upper working class and the middle class are equal in socioeconomic status in this neighborhood seems to be confirmed in the notes I made regarding the quality of housing.

One of the most interesting correlations concerns the English language attitudes of these speakers. Table 2 presents, according to socioeconomic status, the number who answered "yes" to the question, "Do you think that people without a Spanish accent can find better work?" When table 2 is compared with the bottom third of table 1, it is apparent that in the upper status, most who have regional pronunciation feel that pronunciation is important whereas nearly all who speak SE feel that it is not.

TABLE II.   Attitude towards Pronunciation

Question: "Do you think that people without a Spanish accent
            can find better work?"

Answer: "Yes."

		Pronunciation Type			
		SE	RE	SIE	SIRE
Socioeconomic	Lower	0	1	6	0
status	Upper	2	5	0	3

When asked why they answered "yes" or "no" to the question, those with regional pronunciation typically supported their "yes" answers with remarks like the following: "In school I noticed they made fun of Mexicans who had accents." "It is important in work where there is contact with the public." Those with SE pronunciation supported their "no" answers with comments that ability and training were the key rather than speech. When the occupations of RE speakers are compared with the occupations of SE speakers, it appears that the attitudes coincided somewhat with the type of occupation. Speakers of SE generally work with machines rather than people. On the other hand, half of those with regional speech deal with the public in areas such as sales, teaching, or social work.

Interestingly, nearly half of the SIE speakers also answered "yes." In the lower socioeconomic rankings they were almost the only ones to do so. However, the reasons for their affirmative responses differed fundamentally from those in the upper rankings. Without exception, their answers indicated that to them being "without a Spanish accent" meant being able to speak English rather than speaking with Anglo pronunciation. Typically they remarked that it was necessary to speak English so they could "talk to the boss," or "if you can't speak English, you can't get a good job."

SUMMARY

Assuming that the majority of the Anglos in Austin speak a distinctly Southern or Midland regional variety of English, it is interesting that only a third of these assimilating Mexican-American males do. The others are adopting SE or SIE. Generally, the speakers of RE attended high school, have higher socioeconomic status, have occupations that deal with the public, and feel that accent is important for socioeconomic advancement. Speakers of SE have equally high socioeconomic status but did not attend high school, do not deal with the public, and do not feel accent is important. Speakers of RE and SE generally use English at work. Speakers of SIE have had limited linguistic contact with the English-speaking world and seem to be unaware that there are different English dialects. They dropped out of school before high school, have lower socioeconomic status, and usually speak Spanish at work.

A word of caution should be given before applying these results to the up-coming generation. A key factor in the acquisition of RE seems to be attendance at high school. All forty of the men first learned English upon entering elementary school. They reported that these schools were predominantly Mexican-American. Therefore it would be expected that they had limited contact with speakers or RE. Those who attended high school reported that Mexican-Americans were in the minority. Therefore they had daily contact with fellow students who were speakers of RE. If high school is where they first developed the attitude that the acquisition of RE has social and economic rewards, this situation may have changed. A larger percentage of Mexican-Americans now attend high school, and in at least one high school they form a majority of the population. Today there may be less pressure to conform linguistically with speakers of RE in order to succeed. This potential change may be confirmed by further investigation.

This study should remind dialectologists of the importance of sampling procedures in urban dialectology. It was necessary to randomly select 200 households in the neighborhood in order to identify 40 adult speakers of the same sex and ethnic background who had been raised in the same neighborhood, had attended the same schools, and were members of the urban second generation. Too frequently in dialect studies, rather than beginning with a larger random sampling of the population and then carefully controlling the variables to select the informants, the dialectologist decides according to his own ad hoc criteria who the representative speakers should be. Relevant information may be uncovered, but its significance may not be realized. In Sawyer's study, for example, the fact that some Mexican-Americans were adopting regional pronunciation was identified. But because of her small sampling, she missed the significance of the educational level and the type of occupation of her informants, the two key factors in the acquisition of RE uncovered in this study in nearby Austin. Her informants who had adopted the most distinctly regional English were the two most highly educated ones, followed by the informant who had worked with the public as a saleswoman. The fact that some Mexican-Americans may be following a nonregional model was overlooked. By using sociologically sound sampling procedures, it was possible in the Austin study to establish that regional pronunciation is not the only prestige model. Instead, within the same neighborhood different dialects of English are being adopted according to identifiable sociolinguistic variables.

FOOTNOTES

[1]Janet B. Sawyer, "Aloofness from Spanish Influence in Texas English," *Word*, 15 (1959), 270-81.

[2]Roger M. Thompson, "Mexican American language loyalty and the validity of the 1970 census," *International Journal for the Sociology of Language*, 2 (1974), 7-18 (also in *Linguistics*, 128 [1974], 7-18).

[3]William Labov, *The Social Stratification of English in New York City* (Washington, D.C.: Center for Applied Linguistics, 1966).

[4]For complete details, see Roger M. Thompson, "Language Loyalty in Austin, Texas: A Study of a Bilingual Neighborhood," Diss., University of Texas at Austin, 1971.

[5]In the Southwest, the term *Anglo* is used to refer to English-speaking Americans who are not of Latin American ancestry.

[6]Sawyer, p. 278.

[7]A similar lack of correlation between English proficiency and Spanish language loyalty has been found in El Paso, Texas. See Jacob Ornstein, "Relational Bilingualism--A Socio-Educational Approach to Studying Multilingualism among Mexican Americans," presented to the Seventeenth International Congress of Anthropological and Ethnological Sciences, 23 August-8 September 1973, Chicago, Illinois.

[8]Because there are only three speakers of SIRE, statements concerning correlations of variables will be made only for the other three dialects. However, data on SIRE speakers will be presented in the tables.

[9]U.S. Bureau of the Census, *Methodology and Scores of Socioeconomic Status*, Working Paper no. 15 (Washington, D.C., 1963).

HISTORICAL DEVELOPMENT AND LANGUAGE CHANGE

The relationship between historical development and language change has become an important topic in linguistics in general and in dialect and language variation studies in particular. The three selections in this section describe three approaches to this topic. In the first one Guy Jean Forgue argues against the commonly held position of the 18th century, also expressed by J. L. Dillard in *All-American English* (New York: Random House, 1972) that American English spoken at the time of the American Revolutionary War had no dialects. He offers evidence that English in America was influenced by the language of the settlers, both the English and the non-English speakers. In providing a method by which students can use spelling anomalies of public documents and pronouncing dictionaries to reconstruct the American pronunciation of the second half of the 18th century, Forgue exemplifies some regional differences.

While it is sometimes felt that sound change is no longer active in modern urban societies and that American dialects are merging because of mass media, William Labov and his co-workers have found this not to be true. In 1968 Uriel Weinreich, Labov, and Marvin Herzog ("Empirical Foundations for a Theory of Language Change," in *Directions for Historical Linguistics*, ed. Winfred Lehmann and Yakov Malkiel. Austin: The University of Texas Press) divided the problem of understanding linguistic change into five parts: (1) locating universal constraints, (2) determining the mechanism of change, (3) measuring the effects of structural embedding, (4) estimating social evaluation, and (5) searching for causes of the actuation of sound changes. The work in Philadelphia reported by Labov, Malcah Yaeger, and Richard Steiner in *A Quantitative Study of Sound Change in Progress* (NSF Contract NSF - GS - 3287, 1972) located three universal constraints for vowel chain shifts: (1) tense or long nuclei rise, (2) short or lax vowels fall, and (3) back nuclei move to the front. In the study included in this book, Labov finds a reason for sound changes occurring at a particular time by searching for the social location of the innovators.

The third topic examined in this section is the nature of language change as evidenced in pidgin and creole languages. Washabaugh warns against Bickerton's position that innovations in pidgin and creole languages are the result of natural changes in that the innovative variants result from the language universal *faculté* and each variant is a result of the natural language

509

acquisition device.   Instead, Washabaugh argues that changes
occur and are maintained only when social conditions are ripe for
the seeds of change to sprout.   While natural change can occur
without influence from social factors, Washabaugh is convinced
that no innovation can be maintained without social pressures.

In addition to the works already mentioned, students interested
in American English at the time of the American Revolution should
consult

Marckwardt, Albert. *American English*, rev. by J. L.
Dillard. New York: Oxford University Press 1980.

Sen, Ann Louise.   "Reconstructing Early American
Dialects," *Journal of English Linguistics*, 12 (1978), 50-62.
Those interested in language variation and sound change should
consult

Kroch, Anthony.   "Towards a Theory of Social Dialect
Variation" in this anthology.

Labov, William.   "Resolving the Neogrammarian Controversy," *Language* 57, (1981) 267-308.
Those interested in pidgins and creoles and the nature of
language change should consult

Bickerton, Derek. *Roots of Language.*   Ann Arbor,
Michigan: Karoma Publisher, 1981.

The Genesis of Language, ed. Kenneth C. Hill.   Ann
Arbor, Michigan: Karoma Publisher, 1979.

Readings in Creole Studies, ed. Ian F. Hancock, in
collaboration with Edgar Polome, Morris Goodman, and
Bernd Heine. Ghent, Belgium, 1979.

AMERICAN ENGLISH AT THE TIME

OF THE REVOLUTION[1]

Guy Jean Forgue

Most of the attacks to which American English was subjected by Britons took place after the War of Independence and flared up anew when the war of 1812 was over. Those attacks were due to the wave of chauvinistic self-consciousness that swept the new nation after the Revolution as well as to British resentment at the loss of a colony. This is not to say, however, that American peculiarities had gone unnoticed during the 18th century. Oddly enough, early observers emphasized differences less than they wondered at the high level of uniformity and the general excellence of the English that prevailed among New World speakers. Nearly all Americans were described as talking alike at all social levels; dialects were slurred over and, when pointed out, seemed less deviant than those in the mother country. In spite of his antiamericanism, Jonathan Boucher could write in 1777:

> In North America there prevails not only, I believe, the purest pronunciation of the English tongue that is anywhere to be met with, but a perfect uniformity.

In the same year, another resident of three years' standing, Nicholas Cresswell, had this to add:

> Though the inhabitants of this country are composed of different nations and different languages, yet it is very remarkable that they in general speak better English than the English do.

Not were the colonists slow to brag that they held the palm of excellent English; some went as far as to compliment visiting Britons on the purity of their utterance whenever it happened to be "free of an English brogue" and contained a reasonable proportion of "aspirated" H's. In his *Dissertations on the English Language* (1789), Noah Webster proclaimed in a moralistic, prophetic tone:

> Nothing but the establishment of schools and some uniformity in the use of books can annihilate dif-

From *Revue des Langues Vivantes* 43:253-269, 1977. Reprinted with permission.

ferences in speaking and preserve the purity of
the American tongue. A sameness of pronunciation
is of considerable consequence in a political view;
for provincial accents are disagreeable to strangers
(...) and excite ridicule (and) disrespect. Our
political harmony is therefore concerned in a uniformity of language. As an independent nation,
our honor requires us to have a system of our
own, in language as well as in government. Great
Britain, whose children we are, and whose language we speak, should no longer be *our* standard;
for the taste of her writers is already corrupted,
and her language on the decline. But if it were
not so, she is at too great a distance to be our
model, and to instruct us in the principles of
our own tongue. Within a century and a half,
the continent will be peopled with hundreds of
millions of men, *all speaking the same language*.
Place this idea in comparison with the present
and possible future bounds of the language in
Europe (...), anticipate the period when the
people of one-fourth of the world will be able to
associate and converse together like children of
the same family. Compare this prospect, which
is not visionary, with the state of the English
language in Europe, almost confined to an Island,
and to a few millions of people; then let reason
and reputation decide, how far America should
be dependent on a transatlantic nation, for her
standard and improvements in language.

The English editor of Dr. David Ramsay ascribed American
linguistic purity to "the number of British subjects assembled in
America from various quarters, who, in consequence of their
intercourse and intermarriages, soon dropped the peculiarities of
their several provincial idioms, retaining only what was fundamental and common to them all--a process which the frequency or
rather the universality of school-learning in America must naturally
have assisted" (1791).

The fact is that American English had begun to diverge from
the mother tongue for over a century and a half through the
addition of foreign terms, the application of new senses to already
existing English words and phrases, and the retention of archaic
or provincial features against the new fashions that prevailed in
London at the court and on the stage. Boucher's and Cresswell's
opinion that there were no dialects in North America had no
basis in reality. As early as 1746, reservations had been made
about the lingo of New Englanders; Virginia negroes were found
by a traveler to speak "a mixed Guinea-English dialect". When
the Revolution came along, the linguistic Yankee as well as the
Southern colored types were well acknowledged, although Western
varieties would not be pointed out until after the War of 1812.

Not all Englishmen agreed as to the chastity of American. In 1756, Samuel Johnson had reviewed an American book and deplored that it contained "some mixture of the *American* dialect, a tract (trace) of corruption". To deter Gibbon from writing in French, David Hume argued in 1767 that "our solid and increasing establishments in America, where we need less dread of the inundations of Barbarians, promise a superior stability and duration to the English language", and some of the keenest commentators could already envision an enormous market for English books and dictionaries in the ever-expanding colonies; but others more pessimistically prophesied mutual unintelligibility: thus Boucher, the Marquis de Chastellux, whose 1786 *Voyages* contain remarks on the Americans' aversion for the English and their attempts at finding another common language (such as French or Hebrew), and of course Noah Webster, whose chauvinism could only gloat at the prospect of America ruling English at the expense of Britain.

When one examines the record, not much is actually known about the state of American English at the end of the 18th century. Let us try to piece together the fragmentary information which exists and sort it out, in the hope that something of a clearer picture will emerge.

Robert J. Menner wrote in 1915 that "the number of native-born Americans at the time of the Revolution whose pronunciation was exactly the same as that of Englishmen was exceedingly small". Such a statement is meaningless, unless one assumes that all Englishmen pronounced their language in the same way, which all records indicate is incorrect. it is more prudent to agree with Eilert Ekwall (*American and British Pronunciation*, Uppsala, 1946) that "educated American pronunciation on the whole remained at the stage which standard British pronunciation had reached about the time of the Revolution, while modern British pronunciation has left that stage far behind". For obvious reasons, the important changes that affected British pronunciation after the late years of the 18th century were not shared by the Americans. But the majority pronunciation in America today (sometimes called "General American"), derived from the Middle States, shows remarkable similarities to educated Northern English rather than to Eastern or London English, which are closer to the minority types of American heard in coastal New England and the South. It remains true, however, that at the time, American English must have been fairly close to whatever standard was beginning to prevail in the British Isles, including the North of England, where many settlers came from. Such influence must have existed, despite the geographical separation, because of the close links, administrative and cultural, that united the mother country and its plantations abroad, not to mention the overwhelming numerical superiority of the Britons, who outnumbered the Americans two to one, or almost three to one if we discount the Negro slaves.

The pronunciation of English in the colonies is fairly well known, although the absence of a clear system of phonetic transcription makes it only tentative. Obviously, American pronunciations derived from the British dialects spoken by the English-speaking settlers. What prevailed in the 1770's was this situation: in New England, around Boston and East of the Connecticut River, a mixture of southeastern English dialects--East Anglia and the counties adjoining London--for about two-thirds, the remaining third being divided among Southwestern England and other parts of the British Isles; the coastal South was apparently peopled by a slight majority of Londoners and southeasterners, with the rest a mixture of other Englishmen. The Boston area, the lower Hudson valley and the Southern Tidewater sections were clearly influenced by the fashionable English of the 18th century. Such varieties of American English are no longer dominant, though they exercised great influence in the early days of the Republic; but, even then, they were in direct competition with the English of the Middle States (New Jersey, Pennsylvania, Delaware), which exhibited totally different characteristics, such as the heavy retroflex postvocalic preconsonantal /r/ and the flattening of the /æ/ phoneme before a sibilant, as in *half*, *past*, *bath*, etc. This kind of English (a blend of Northern and Western English, with a heavy addition of Scotch-Irish and later German) was destined to become, if not the norm, at least the most frequently spoken variety in America. Those immigrants settled in the Piedmont of Virginia and the Carolinas as well as Western New England (upstate New York and the Western Reserve); from their ranks emerged the hordes that were to conquer the West and give it its peculiar speech. Spelling and middle-class pronunciations would later become increasingly common, as the new Americans relied essentially on the printed word (Noah Webster's "Blue-back Speller") and handbooks or dictionaries that put a premium on proper syllabication; teachers were more often than not small farmers, city clerks, workmen, indentured servants and, in some areas, ex-convicts; not a few schoolmasters were Scottish or Scotch-Irish and, as such, equally withstood provincial dialects and aristocratic affectations. Clarity and a precise utterance (with Webster as a cheerleader) became the ideal goal, and this goal was reinforced in the 19th century by the need to quickly assimilate and Americanize wave upon wave of foreign immigrants.

The mention of immigration should remind us that English had not always been the sole undisputed language of the colonies. This was true especially in the Middle Colonies. From his study of newspaper advertisements for runaway slaves and indentured servants, Allen Walker Read has shown that foreign languages were widely known, and even sometimes exclusively so, by a sizable fraction of the lower classes. In 1753, Benjamin Franklin had worried about the status of German in Pennsylvania, and written: "Few of their children in the country know English. They import many books from Germany [...] Advertisements, intended to be general, are now printed in Dutch [= German] and English. The signs in our streets have inscriptions in both languages, and in some places only German". We thus see the proletariat of the Middle Colonies occasionally conversant with

German, French, Spanish, Welsh and Irish.   In the Province of
New York, Dutchmen's servants had to learn Dutch before, or
instead of, English. Whenever they could speak nothing but the
latter idiom, the fact was mentioned as a distinctive trait. Read
concluded:

> The cosmopolitan spirit engendered by the
> prevalence of many languages was an element in
> the pattern of colonial American culture, and no
> doubt contributed to the breaking down of
> old loyalties culminating in the American Revolu-
> tion.

To this we may add the evidence afforded by Dr. Alexander
Hamilton's *Itinerarium* (1744).   Hamilton was a Scotsman from
Baltimore who rode over 1,600 miles along the Atlantic coast to
the North with his loyal Negro slave Dromo.   Dutch was still
often encountered along the Hudson, much to the annoyance of
the patriotic doctor; this conversation (the first ever recorded
in America between two colored people) is an example of this
situation:

> Dromo stopped at a house, where, when I
> came up, I found his discoursing a negroe
> [sic] girl, who spoke Dutch to him.
> 'Dis de way to York?' says Dromo.   'Yaw,
> dat is Yarikee', said the wench, pointing to
> the steeples'.   'What devil you say?' said Dromo
> again.   'Yaw, yaw' said the girl.   'You a damn
> black bitch', said Dromo, and so rid on.

In the same book we also find one of the earliest bits of "Black
English", as Dromo requests the skipper on a Rhode Island ferry-
boat to "*t*row away his stones" (which prevented the horses from
getting in), "*d*e hors*e be* better ballast".

Not only foreign accents, but a British one could be a dead
giveaway, or even a liability, in the new nation; Read's ads
abound in descriptions of runaways "with a thick Northern",
"broad", or "flat" English.   From this evidence it seems that by
the mid-18th century, speaking some English dialects (but not
East or Southeast of England) was a notable deviation from the
great body of the American vernacular.

There is a tale of an Englishman who sought asylum among
local folks beleaguered by Indians, and who was denied admittance
on the ground that he must have been French or Indian owing to
his peculiar accent; and another of a Boston merchant who had
lived in Britain too long and acquired its manners, so that he
had to rescue his business from bankruptcy by explaining and
defending his pronunciation in the local paper.

Bostonians and New Englanders in general were exposed to
mockery because of their accent, so well documented in Lowell's
Biglow Papers.   In 1764, Lord Adam Gordon noted that Boston
was "more like an English old town than any in America--the
language and manner of the people very much resemble the old
country, and all the neighboring lands and villages carry with

them the same idea." Practically each region was identified by its people's tone, as Boucher indicated in 1775: "One striking peculiarity in American elocution is a slow, drawling, unemphatical and unimpassioned manner". Boucher denied the existence of dialects, yet excepted:

> scanty remains of the croaking, guttural idioms of the Dutch, still observable near New York; the Scotch-Irish [...] in some of the back settlers of the Middle States; and the whining, canting drawl brought by some republican, Oliveran and Puritan emigrants from the West of England, and still kept up by their undegenerated descendants of New England.

From the spelling anomalies of public documents and such pronouncing dictionaries as Samuel Johnson Jr's and John Elliott's (1800) or Richard S. Coxe's (1813), it is possible to form an idea on how some Americans pronounced English in the second half of the 18th century.

Perhaps the most widely noted feature was the still lingering confusion between /a/ and /ə:/ as in *varmint, marcy, parson* (person), *clerk* and *sargeant* (in which case alone the /a/ sound still prevails); Webster was strongly opposed to such deviations from what he considered the norm set by the more polite people. /a/ and /e/ tended to be confused in words like *Amarica, rassle* (wrestle), *ketch* (catch)--an indecision that still exists today in some areas, particularly in the West, where *marry* has the same stressed vowel as *merry*. /i/ was often centralized under stress, resulting in a homophony of *pen* and *pin* (as today in the south), and such spellings as *sperit, git, sence, kittle*; Benjamin Franklin himself transcribed *get* and *friend* as *git* and *frind* in his little-known attempts at phonetic notation. Centralization (the neutralization of vowels by the loss of their full value) was also responsible for *shulling, bushup* (shilling, bishop), etc.

Most of the authors, especially Webster, strongly advocated /u/ for /ju/ or /iu/ after some consonants; the lexicographer actually regarded *kjub, mjute, blju, dju* (cube, mute, blue, due) as English "corruptions", on a par with *gjarden, kjind, pjower* (garden, kind, power) where the guttural is palatized after the fashion of London snobs and the New England "yeomanry". *Room, goold, obleege* (Rome, gold, oblige), still common at the time, were denounced by Webster on the grounds of analogy or propriety--whichever best served his deeply-ingrained prejudices. Likewise, the doughty New Englander rejected the Virginian /ju/ sound in *new* as well as the dropping of postvocalic /r/, which could lead to such confusions as *dust-durst, mash-marsh*, etc. Conversely, he favored the /hw/ sound in words beginning with *wh-* (*whale, which, why*, etc.), but his recommendations were, and still are not followed by at least half of the Americans.

For the "short O" vowel of *off, soft, God, drop, crop, because, naughty, strop*, the lexicographer rejected the Scotch-Irish pronunciation /a/, equally in vain, since it now prevails among a sizable minority of Americans. *Deef* for *deaf*, *heerd* for *heard*, *berd* for *beard*, *sarse* for *sauce* and *dater* for *daughter* were equally stigmatized by him, and whenever present today, are confined to rustic oldtimers and not admitted as standard.

The ending in *-ing* seems to have been reduced to *-in* almost uniformly, as it often is today in casual utterance: hence the spellings *linning*, *garding*, *kitching*, *chitlins* (linen, garden, kitchen, chitterlings) in some records made by hardly literate clerks. Curiously enough, Webster wrote nothing about the vowel *a* in words such as *ask*, *aunt*, *half*, *chance*, *example*, *can't*, *command*, etc., where it seems from other sources that at least some educated Americans had a "broad" /a/, as in the South of England today; on the other hand, a "short /æ/ was usually preferred in words beginning with kw + A(U); thus *quality*, *quantity*, *quarry*.

The /əɪ/ diphthong still varied freely with /aɪ/ in *bile-boil*, *pint-point*, *pison-poison*, as a scholastic piece of doggerel reminds us:
   "The sound of *oi* custom reconciles
   With that of *i* spoke long, as witness *toils*"
Equally uncertain was the status of the semivowels /j/ and /w/. Against the Wellerisms *weal* or *wery* (veal, very), common in Philadelphia and Boston, we find a slurring of the /w/ in *soon*, *awked*, (swoom, awkward), analogous to British pronunciations of *Norwich*, *Greenwich*, and a similar absence of /j/ in *Willam*, *critten*, *paster*, *indentered*, *unusal*, *regelar* (William, creature, pasture, indentured, unusual, regular), where *-ure* endings were then expected to have their full value (*-joor*), as now in American *literatyoor*.

Lieutenant was articulated in the English manner, but with *lootenant* gaining ground; *nephew* was still sounded with a *v*. Webster strongly recommended an *ee* sound in *either*, *neither*, *deceit*, *conceit*, but an /e/ in *leisure*, after the model of *pleasure*. He made a strong case for *advertisement* stressed on the penultimate, as well as *admirable*. If *skeptic* seemed pedantic to him, *schedule* was indifferently *skedule* or *sedule*. *S* and *sh*, by the way, tended to be confused as they still are in some pronunciations today, such as *licorish* (licorice). Dead set against Middle States forms, Webster railed at the literate who said *oncet* or *twicet* for *once*, *twice*; he somewhat arbitrarily condemned "unaspirated" *human*, *humble* and *hospital* at the same time as he accepted (*h*)*umor* or (*hj*)*erb*.

Obviously, despite the grammarian's stern admonitions, an area of uncertainty still shrouded many words in America: *idea* and *identity* could begin with an /i/ or an /ai/ sound; *chew* was almost universally *chaw*; *reason* rhymed with *raisin*. Word endings remained uncertain: the unstressed *schwa* could be rendered as /ə/ or /i/, as witness *Canady*, *sofy* (sofa), *monerca* (Monarchy) and, today, the doublets *Missouri-Missoura*, *Cincinnati-Cincinnata*. Final consonants tended to be dropped, so that *mile* and *mild* or *cold* and *coal* would sound alike. Excrescent consonants, conversely, were not uncommon: *gownd* (gown), *drownded, hunderd, coren* (corn), *aiern* (iron). However, most of these pronunciations are now dying out, and the obstinacy of the Connecticut school-master must be credited for the relative uniformity that now reigns in the United States. The rule of analogy and the pre-dominance of an educated vulgate have allowed a standard American pronunciation to emerge, with sufficient variety to vindicate the democratic spirit.

*
**

If American peculiarities in pronunciation (all of them actual British provincialisms) struck the observer's ear from early days, American words surprised visitors even more, since they required no phonetic ability to be detected. Innumerable authors have described the considerable additions made by the American colonies to the mother tongue before the end of the 17th century. One English traveler had critized the use of *bluff* for a steep river bank in 1735, and many other strictures had been made here and there about the exotic vocabulary of the Colonists. But the first serious commentator was a Scottish Presbyterian, a lineal descendant of John Knox, John Witherspoon, who was for twenty years (until his death in 1794) the President of what is now Princeton University. From his 1781 contributions to a Pennsyl-vania gazette we have a fair number of observations on the state of American in post-Revolutionary days as seen by an educated Scots with a flair for language.

After pointing out that English was spoken throughout the United States, even though there was no single standard because of the equality and independence of each State, Witherspoon observed that "the vulgar in America speak much better than the vulgar in Great-Britain [because] being much more unsettled and moving frequently from place to place, they are not so liable to local peculiarities, either in accent or phraseology". But among the educated, he discerned that he was the first to style "ameri-canisms", or speechways different from those of the corresponding class in Britain, although he was careful to distinguish between the speech of the vulgar and that of the cultivated. Among literate oddities, he mentioned:

"the U.S., or *either of* them" (for: any of)
"this is to *notify* the publick" (for: notify a thing to the public)
"fellow countrymen", a redundancy which was already the staple of political orations, about which Boucher would remark a few years later that their volubility showed "more fluency than correction".
"these things were ordered delivered" (*to be* delivered).
"I don't consider myself equal to" (instead of: as equal), a turn of speech allegedly favored by Thomas Paine.

Witherspoon also noted the shift in meaning which affected *clever*, meaning almost anything but "capable"; Hamilton writes that even after he had been "drilled into the use" of this adjective, he was stunned to hear of "a gentleman having moved to a *clever* house, of another succeeding to a *clever* sum of money, of a third embarking in a *clever* ship and making a *clever* voyage, with a *clever* cargo". *Mad*, as another word for *angry*, also surprised travelers. A number of the items denounced by Witherspoon as local or substandard have now found their way into cultivated speech, sometimes on either side of the Atlantic; thus: "I'm going to" (instead of: to do it), "once in a while", "to have occasion to" and to "tote". "Cant phrases", which we could call "colloquial" or "slang", included "to be taken in", "to bilk", "to be a hit", "to be the thing" (or "not the thing"). "Personal blunders" were "silent disdain" (foreboding Dan Moynihans's "benign neglect") and "total" in the sense of "absolute, unreserved", probably an ancestor of today's much-touted "total woman".

Witherspoon's articles spawned other remarks from fellow philologists; some mentioned "nice" for "handsome", "grand" for "excellent", "a power of" for "much, many" and "frontier" as a felicitous alternative for "back settlements", since it was not at the back, but in the forefront of civilization in its westward progress. Not all observations, however, were dispassionate. More often than not, novelties were roundly condemned, even by Americans; for instance, Franklin, who had lost touch with his native language during his many years in Europe, wrote Witherspoon in 1789 to stigmatize Americanisms such as "to improve" (utilize), "to notice", "to advocate", "to progress", "to be opposed to"--thus showing himself as much of a linguistic conservative as he was enlightened in politics and the sciences. Despite the multitudes of new words that appeared during the 18th century, strictures were almost always confined to a small number of shibboleths, which were ascribed to the Puritans of New England. An unnamed correspondent wrote:

> The advantages of a distinct language must strike every unprejudiced person. It will prove the best *palladium* of our independence and [...] lessen British influence, which continues to endanger our freedom, and justly excites the most serious apprehensions in the bosoms of our wiser patriots [...] Whilst we retain the language of Britain, we cannot forget that we were once a colony; and the painful recollection of our former vassalage is sufficient, if not to extinguish the flame of liberty, at least to obscure its brightness. To coin new words, or to use them in a new sense is, incontrovertibly, one of the unalienable rights of freemen; and whoever disputes this right, is the friend of civil tyranny, and an enemy to liberty and equality. (1801)

But the alleged laxity of American English and the proliferation
of new terms failed to enchant the purists, who looked upon
neology as a corruption instead of a gain. John Adams, much
less of an innovator in English than his contemporary Thomas
Jefferson, addressed the President of the U.S. Congress in 1780
to urge the creation of an "American Academy" in the hope
of "refining, improving and ascertaining the English Language".
In his *Six Months in America* (1832), Godfrey Thomas Vigne
poked fun at the American habit of all-purpose words:

> There are about half a dozen words in
> constant use to which the English ear is un-
> accustomed in the sense that they are meant
> to convey; such as to fix, to locate, to guess,
> to expect, to calkilate, etc. The verb 'to
> fix' has perhaps as many significations as
> any word in the Chinese language. If anything
> is to be done, made, mixed, mended, bespoken,
> hired, ordered, arranged, procured, finished,
> lent, or given, it would very probably be
> designated by the verb 'to fix'.

By the early years of the 19th century, and as a direct
outcome of national independence, the spelling and the lexicon
had changed from the British norms. Webster's *American Spelling
Book* of 1783 has become, and would long remain, America's lay
Bible; his 1806 dictionary had introduced novel forms, among
which a few were destined to remain: *honor*, *theater*, *mold*,
plow, *controller* (for: comptroller). Glossaries had become a
necessity as early as 1801, when a correspondent of the Philadelphia *Portfolio* mentioned such novelties as *spry* (active),
lengthy, *elegant* (fine), *sauce* (vegetables), *caucus*, *illy* (badly),
to belittle, *Miss* (for Mrs or Miss), *to gun*, *to tarry*, and many
others. In David Humphrey's *Yankee in England* (1815), we find
to boost, breadstuffs, *cent*, *chores*, *cuss*, *cute*, *dilly-dally*,
duds, *gal*, *gimcracks*, *glib*, *granny*, *gumtion*, *knack*, *mainly* (mostly), *muggy*, *outlandish*, *to peek*, *pluck* (courage), *to snap*, *a
sneaking notion*, *spook* (ghost), *spunk* (courage), *to stump* (challenge), *to swap*, *a mare's nest*, *to pluck up stakes*, *fine as a
fiddle*, *it's raining pitchforks*, and many more, explained in
the addendum, or quietly used. Boucher's amusing *Absence* (1775)
is replete with local Americanisms from Maryland, as well as Philip
Freneau's *Poems Written and Published During the American
Revolutionary War* (1809), where most of the Americanisms are
unexplained, and hence taken for granted.

*
**

We may now ask ourselves the question: what did the
Revolution *as such* directly contribute to American English?
First of all, certainly, a new attitude toward language, with a
proud assertion of Americanisms against "Briticisms" and a

harsh reaction against the old social order, in brief, national
pride and individual self-respect.   English titles naturally
died out after the withdrawal of the British troops.   John
Adams' letter to the Scottish Baronet Sir John Sinclair illustrates
this:

> If you, Sir John, will do us the honor
> to come and see us, you will be treated with a
> cordial civility, notwithstanding your title.

The new Americans became very sensitive about their social
status.   Equality demanded that everybody be, or pretend to
be, as good as the next fellow.   The Old World "peasant" was
replaced by *farmer*, although he was a landowner exempt from
rent or tithes.   The word thus became dignified, and justly so,
since, as J. F. Cooper later observed, nine-tenths of the American
legislators were indeed farmers.   As for *servant* and *master*, the
following dialogue will show the strong feelings held by some
citizens (1807):

> Is your master at home?
— I have no master.
— And who are you then?
— Why, I am Mr —'s *help*.   I'd have you to know, *man*,
> that I am no *sarvant*; none but *negers* are *sarvants*.

Help (1630) and *hired* (*man*) (1694) had carried no trace of
euphemism before the Revolution, not had *hand* (1724), which
designated slave labor; but they later dignified free domestics
or manual workers.

The amusing thing, however, is that the common folk exhibited a parallel propensity to apply to themselves grandiose
appellations.   Already before the war, Edward Kimber had
noted in 1746:

> Whenever you travel in Maryland (as
> also in Virginia and Georgia), your Ears are
> constantly astonished at the number of *Colonels*,
> *Majors* and *Captains*, that you hear mentioned:
> in short, the whole Colony seems at first to
> you a Retreat of Heroes.

Another observer, struck by the number of "colonels" in 1744,
wrote: "It's common saying here that a man has no title to that
dignity unless he has killed a rattlesnake".   During the Revolution,
(*the*) *Honorable* was applied to members of at least some of the
colonial legislatures and to those of the 1777 Continental Congress;
soon, it would be used for Governors, bishops and many lesser
dignitaries.   Said the *American Museum* for that year: "Nothing
shows the propensity of Americans to monarchy more than their
disposition to give titles to all our officers of government.   *Honorable* and *Esquire* have become as common in America as *captain* in
France, *count* in Germany, or *my lord* in Italy."   *Esquire* and
Gentleman did not survive the Revolution, but *Doctor*, among other
titles, became so current as to be almost synonymous today with
"unemployed".

The events and the new institutions that accompanied American independence naturally swelled the stock of existing Americanisms. It would be idle to list them at any length here, but we may want to have a look at some of the more striking terms that presumably emerged during the second half of the 18th century.

Blue Laws (1781, prohibiting entertainment on Sundays in the New Haven area); *buckshot* (1775), which caused great damage among the British and Hessian troops during the Revolutionary battles; *shotgun* (1776); *statehouse*, originally the capitol of a colony, then of a State; *Tory* (1769), an American partisan of the Crown, with Franklin's coinage *Toryess* (1777); *caucus* (1763), of unknown origin, used by John Adams to designate a political club; *antiamerican* (1773); *yankee doodle* (1767), thus evoked in a 1775 letter:

> When the 2nd [British] brigade marched out of Boston to reinforce the first, nothing was played by the fifes and drums but Yankee Doodle [...] Upon their return to Boston, one asked his brother officer how he liked the tune now.

To these we may add *congressional, to run for office, administration, Bill of Rights, abolition society* (1790), *plurality, the Mason and Dixon's Line, Blue-skin* (an ardent supporter of the Colonists' cause), *aid(e), antifederalist, appropriation, admission* (1777: the formal acceptance of a new state in the Union), *apportionment, Senate*; and again Jefferson's coinages: *anglomania, anglophobia, War-hawk, Anglo-American* (first used for the Canadians); Franklin's *to anglify* (1751); John Jay's *to Americanize* (1797): "I wish to see our people more Americanized, if I may use that expression; until we feel and act as an independent nation, we shall always suffer from foreign intrigue". *Brother Jonathan* (1776) derided the patriotic American, as had *Yankee* (1775, in its derogatory sense), and later *Uncle Sam* (1813), the American answer to John Bull. *Land office* (1681) came into general use after the Revolution, when public lands were distributed to veterans. A whole mode of life disappeared, such as the charming custom of *bundling*, or sharing the same bed in one's small clothes while "sparking it", or courting. Sterner days were ahead, with *gouging* (1774) "a brutal practice very common several years ago in the less civilized parts of some of the Southern States, in which it was the first object of the assailant to deprive his antagonist of his eyesight" (Freneau, 1809); nor did the Yankees lag behind, with *tarring and feathering* (1769), while the Virginians took the law into their own hands and invented *lynching* (1782), which was to endure until this century.

American inventiveness did not please everybody. Jefferson was reviled for *to belittle*, and Webster for *lengthy, to advocate, to demoralize*. Whenever such creations endured, the English were quick to claim them as their own, tracing them back to a distant native past. But it is true that the language of the new nation must have seemed rather uncouth. Some found the idiom flaccid and inaccurate (as for instance *bug* to signify any kind of insect). The Marquis de Chastellux opined that: "La partie de la langue créée aux Etats-Unis est extrêmement pauvre. Tout ce qui n'avait pas de nom anglais n'en a reçu ici qu'un simple désignatif (geai: oiseau bleu, etc)"--a gross exaggeration. But grandiloquence and bombast were soon noticed in a nation that prided itself on its size and democratic practices. John Adams had written in 1780:

> The constitutions of all the States in the Union are so democratical that eloquence will become the instrument for recommending men to their fellow-citizens, and the principal means of advancement through the various ranks and offices of society.

Hence some bragadoccio, which industrial and commercial expansion were to swell beyond all bounds in the 19th century and after. "The greatest in the world", "mammoth" are traced to postrevolutionary years; the abundance of Latin-based locutions and empty rhetoric was also unfavorably commented upon.

Since most revolutions are puritanical, it would be nice to conclude that 1776 began an era of chastity in America. It would be nice, but, as a recent President put it, it would be *wrong*: in 1775, John Adams was assigned by the Continental Congress the delicate task of drawing up rules for the regulation of the Navy, and he consequently recommended to punish profane or blasphemous sailors "by means of a wooden collar or a shameful badge". This was tantamount to battling the winds. The same fate awaited George Washington in 1776 as he lamented in an order to the Army "the growth of the wicked practise of profane cursing and swearing", probably oblivious of the well-established fact that he himself, in addition to being a notoriously bad speller and grammarian, was very free with *damns* and *hells* in his private discourses--a habit matched only by the American clergy's vulgarity and profanity. From the Revolution on, American English would diverge in two opposite, albeit reconcilable directions: the prudish "Victorianism" of the early 19th century, such as the bowdlerization of the Johnson and Elliott Dictionary in 1800, and euphemisms like "launched into eternity" for "hanged" (more American, "hung"), or again, "optical indecision" for "squinting"; and, on the other hand, the bold, untrammelled lingo of the frontiersmen, later replaced by the city slickers' slang that represent the bulk of American English as it is known today. For the American idiom, as for American politics and destiny, the Revolution was only a moment, if a decisive one.

FOOTNOTE

[1]Lecture given at The University of Liège on April 22, 1976, under the auspices of Centre d'enseignement et de recherche en études américaines.

THE SOCIAL ORIGINS OF SOUND CHANGE[1]

William Labov

INTRODUCTION

The past century of phonetic research has illuminated our understanding of the production of sounds, the properties of the acoustic signals, and to a certain extent, the perception of speech sounds. But the search for the originating causes of sound change itself remains one of the most recalcitrant problems of phonetic science. Bloomfield's position on this question is still the most judicious:

> No permanent factor . . . can account for specific changes which occur at one time and place and not at another. . . . Although many sound changes shorten linguistic forms, simplify the phonetic system, or in some other way lessen the labor of utterance, yet no student has succeeded in establishing a correlation between sound change and any antecedent phenomenon: the causes of sound change are unknown [1933, p. 386].

In spite of Bloomfield's warning, linguists have continued to put forward simplistic theories that would attempt to explain sound change by a single formal principle, such as the simplification of rules, the maximization of transparency, and so on. But at the Second International Congress of Nordic and General Linguistics, King rejected his own earlier reliance on simplification (1972), and recognized the point made 50 years earlier by Meillet (1921), Saussure (1922), and Bloomfield (1933): that the sporadic nature of sound change rules out the possibility of explanation through any permanent factor in the phonetic processing system. It seems clear that any explanation of the fluctuating course of sound change must involve the continual fluctuations that take place in the structure of the society in which language is used.

The approach to the explanation of linguistic change outlined by Weinreich, Labov, and Herzog (1968) divides the problem into

five distinct areas: locating universal constraints, determining
the mechanism of change, measuring the effects of structural
embedding, estimating social evaluation, and finally, searching
for causes of the actuation of sound changes.   The quantitative
study of sound change in progress by Labov, Yeager, and Steiner
(1972) located three universal constraints on vowel shifting,[2] and
developed the mechanism by which these chain shifts take place
in phonetic space, expanding the view of structural embedding
outlined by Martinet (1955).   Our current studies of sound change
in progress in Philadelphia (1973-1977) have developed further
the measurement and mathematical analysis of vowel shifts, with
the end in view of attacking the actuation problem itself.   We
have approached the problem of why sound changes take place at
a particular time by searching for the social location of the innovators: asking which speakers are in fact responsible for the
continued innovation of sound changes, and how their influence
spreads to affect the entire speech community.

It is often assumed that sound change is no longer active in
modern urban societies, and that local dialects are converging
under the effect of the mass media that disseminate the standard
language.[3]   One of the most striking results of the sociolinguistic
studies carried out since 1961 is to show that this is not true:
On the contrary, new sound changes are emerging and old ones
proceeding to completion at a rapid rate in all of the speech
communities that have been studied intensively.   Evidence for
sound changes in progress has been found in New York, Detroit,
Buffalo, Chicago (Labov, Yeager, and Steiner, 1972), Norwich
(Trudgill, 1972), Panama City (Cedergren, 1973), Buenos Aires
(Wolf and Jimenez, 1978), and Paris (Lennig, 1978).   This evidence
is provided by distributions across age levels (change in apparent
time), and by comparison with earlier reports (change in real
time), following the model of Gauchat, 1904 and Hermann, 1930).

Whenever these changes in progress have been correlated
with distribution across social classes, a pattern has appeared
that is completely at variance with earlier theories about the
causes of sound change.   If one looks to the principle of least
effort (Bloomfield, 1933, p. 386) as an explanation, then it follows
that sound change would arise in the lowest social classes.   The
principle of local density put forward by Bloomfield (1933, p.
476) points to discontinuities in networks of communication as a
determinant of the patterns of propagation of a change: Here it
would follow again that the lowest social class, which is most
isolated from the influence of the standard language, would be
most free to innovate in a direction distinct from the standard.
If however, the theorist focuses on the laws of imitation (Tarde,
1873) and the borrowing of prestige forms from centers of higher
prestige, then it would follow that new sound changes will be
the most advanced in the highest social classes.

In a first approach to the mechanism of linguistic change
(1965), I found no reason to favor either of these two notions
about the social locus of change, and indicated that sound change

could proceed from any location within the social spectrum. As Sturtevant (1948) had first suggested, the change would then follow a path determined by the social structure, adapted successively by those speakers that took the originating group as a standard of social value. However, Kroch (1978) pointed out several years later that no case had been found in which the highest social group was the originator of a systematic linguistic change, and argued that systematic (or "natural") sound changes would always be expected to originate in the working class. This insightful observation marked the beginning of a more determined search for the social location of linguistic change.

A wide variety of sociolinguistic studies carried out since 1965 showed no case contrary to Kroch's position. [4] It is true that older sound changes, like stable sociolinguistic variables, are often aligned with the socioeconomic hierarchy, so that the lowest social class uses the stigmatized variant most often, and the highest social class least often. But whenever age distributions and earlier reports indicate that there may be sound change in progress, the highest social class lags behind. Furthermore, it also appeared that the very lowest social group was less advanced, a finding not anticipated in Kroch's argument. In each case of sound change in progress located, the variables display a curvilinear pattern of social distribution, where the innovating groups are located centrally in that hierarchy: the upper working class or lower middle class.

Some of the data that support this observation was assembled in the general discussion of the role of socioeconomic class in linguistic change in Labov, 1972 (pp. 294-296). In New York City, the lower middle class was the most advanced in the raising of long open o in *lost*, *talk*, *law*, etc. (Labov, 1966, 1972). The same pattern was found in the backing of (ay) and the fronting of (aw) in that city. In Norwich, Trudgill found that the backing of short e before /l/ in *belt*, *help*, etc., showed a rapid development among younger speakers, and was most advanced in the upper working class (1974). In Panama City, Cedergren found that one of five sociolinguistic variables studied showed an age distribution that we now know is characteristic of sound change in progress. The lenition of (ch) in *muchacha*, *macho*, etc., showed a strong peak in the upper working class and lower middle class (Cedergren, 1973; Labov, 1972, pp. 293-294).

The number of cases that supported the curvilinear pattern was not very great. The quantitative data was drawn from three speech communities: New York City, Panama City, and Norwich; only six linguistic variables were involved, and for some of these [New York City (aw) and (ay)] the impressionistic data did not represent a systematic sampling. To confirm the existence of the curvilinear pattern, it seemed best to take a new community with a number of changes in progress, and develop techniques of sampling and measurement that would reduce the chances of error to a relatively low level. At the same time, the project could be designed to generate the kind of social information that would help to explain this surprising curvilinear pattern, if it were replicated. The earlier studies referred to were based on single interviews with individuals, and the reconstruction of the patterns of social communication that could lead to such a result was therefore quite limited.

Our project on linguistic change and variation[5] selected Philadelphia as a site for the further study of this problem, since it appeared that almost all of the Philadelphia vowels were in motion, and all of the basic patterns of chain shifting found in English and French could also be located in Philadelphia. The main data base for the Philadelphia investigation is a series of long-term neighborhood studies in working-class, middle-class, and upper-class areas, involving repeated interviews and participant-observation of the speech community. To this is added a geographically random survey of telephone users, with short, relatively formal interviews. Any convergence of findings from these two data bases, which have complementary strengths and sources of error, will provide strong confirmation of the results.[6]

THE MEASUREMENT OF SOUND CHANGE

The measurement of vowel nuclei [7] was carried out by a preliminary frequency analysis, using a real-time frequency analyzer, followed by linear predictive coding of the frequency domain to derive more exact estimates of the central tendencies of F1, F2, F3, and F0. Complete vowel analyses were carried out for the spontaneous speech of 113 subjects in the neighborhood studies and 60 subjects in the telephone survey, with 150-200 vowels measured for each subject. The mean values for each subject were then submitted to three normalization programs: uniform scaling methods using the geometric mean as developed by Nearey (1977) or vocal tract length estimate (Nordstrom and Lindblom, 1975), and a three-parameter method developed by Sankoff, Horrock, and McKay (1974).

Stepwise regression was carried out on the unnormalized and the three normalized series, deriving equations that predicted F1 and F2 mean positions from age, sex, social class, social mobility, ethnicity, neighborhood, communication patterns, and knowledge of other languages. We searched for the method of normalization that showed the maximum clustering to eliminate the effects of differences in vocal tract length, and the minimum tendency to eliminate variation that was known to be present in the data by independent means. Uniform scaling based on the geometric mean (Nearey, 1977) was selected by these criteria and will be used as the basis for the discussions to follow.[8]

Figure 1 shows the mean positions of the Philadelphia vowels for 93 speakers in the neighborhood series, using the Nearey normalization. It also shows vectors representing the significant

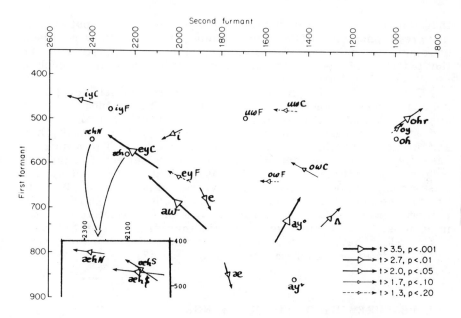

Figure 1: Neighborhood study of 93 speakers. Regression coefficients for influence of age on F1 and F2 of Philadelphia vowels, projected 25 years ahead and 25 years behind mean values. (-F) free; (-C) checked (æh) allophones: (æhN) before nasals, (æhS) before fricatives, (æh$) before stops.

age coefficients of the regression equations for F1 and F2. The age coefficient for each formant for each vowel is multiplied by the chronological age of the subject, for example,

$$F2(aw) = 2086 - 5.39 \times Age. . .$$

where the numbers may be read as F2 values in Herz. Thus the first and most significant coefficient shown above predicts that the difference in mean F2 positions for two speakers 50 and 25 years old will be 25 times 5.39 Hz: That is, the expected mean of F2 for the younger speaker is 135 Hz greater than for the older speaker. The vectors on Figure 1 represent the result of projecting the sound change 25 years ahead of the mean value and 25 years behind. The age coefficient shown above is highly significant, with a t value of 4.5 ($p < .001$); the significance of all age coefficients in Figure 1 is shown by the size of the triangles and the heaviness of the vector lines.

These age vectors fit in with evidence derived from earlier records and synchronic characteristics of the current data that

allow us to set up five strata of sound change in Philadelphia:
1. Recently completed changes: for example, the backing
of /ahr/ in *car*, *part*, etc.
2. Changes nearing completion: for example, the raising
and fronting of (aeh)[9] in *man*, *hand*, etc.
3. Middle-range changes: the fronting of (uw) and (ow) in
too, *moved*, *go*, and *code.*[10]
4. New and vigorous changes, not reported in earlier records:
the raising and fronting of (aw) in *house*, *down*, etc. from [au]
to [e']; the raising and backing of (ay) before voiceless consonants
in *fight*, *like*, etc. from [ai] to a back central nucleus; the
raising of (ey) in checked syllables in *made*, *lake*, etc., from
[eˇi] to [eˆɨ].[11]
5. Incipient changes: for example, the lowering of the
short vowels /i/, /e/, and /ae/.

Turning now to the random sample of telephone users, we
have the view of Philadelphia sound changes shown in Figure 2.
As we expected, there are fewer significant effects: Given the
brief and formal character of the interchange, and the noisy and
limited telephone channel, some of the minor patterns of age
distribution have been eliminated. But the effects that do appear
are quite consistent with the neighborhood study of Figure 1.
The oldest level of sound changes show no age correlations (e.g.,
/ahr/) or only a small age vector (/ohr/). Free and checked
/(ow/) are typical of the middle-range changes; they show a
moderate fronting effect. The new and vigorous changes identified
in the neighborhood studies are also the largest and most significant vectors here. There are some differences in the raising
and fronting of (ay°). The middle-range fronting and raising of
(aeh) before voiceless fricatives appears to be slightly stronger
in these data, and the raising and fronting of (aw) not quite as
strong. But with these small differences. Figure 2 shows the
convergence that we had hoped for. It follows that the sources
of error in the neighborhood studies and the telephone survey
are indeed complementary, and neither set of errors are powerful
enough to prevent the consistent view of age distributions from
emerging here.

The convergence of these two sets of data, combined with
the earlier reports on Philadelphia phonology, allows us to conclude
that we have obtained a fairly accurate portrait of sound change
in progress.

SOCIAL STRATIFICATION

Conclusions from earlier studies would lead us to associate
curvilinear social patterns with Stratum 4, the new and vigorous
changes represented by the long, heavy vectors in Figure 1.
Further terms in the regression equation show that this is the

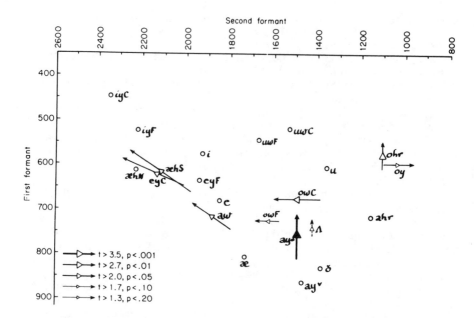

Figure 2: Telephone survey of 60 speakers. Regression co-efficients for influence of age of speaker on F1 and F2 of Philadelphia vowels projected 25 years ahead and behind the mean.

case. Extending the equation for F2 of (aw) to the three next most significant coefficients, we have: [12]

$$F2(aw) = 2086 - 5.39 \times Age + 126 \times Female \ [t = 3.5]$$
$$- 261 \times Social\ Class\ 9 \ [t = 3.1]$$
$$- 253 \times Social\ Class\ 13\text{-}15 \ [t = 2.5]. \ . \ .$$

The social-class scale is a 16-point index based on education, occupation, and residence value: In the most generally used terminology, Class 9 is the "upper working class." Regression coefficients for the full range of social classes are plotted in Figure 3A: Here both the F1 and F2 coefficients are combined to give the resultant vectors plotted along the front diagonal, parallel to the course of sound change. At the zero level is the lowest social class group (0-3 combined), which forms the reference level for the others. The most advanced sound change is shown by the significant peak in Class 9, and the least advanced status is shown by the significant low point of the upper middle class. The less significant values show a smooth curvilinear pattern around these points.

Figure 3B shows the class distribution for the fronting of checked (ey) in the neighborhood studies. This is a broader

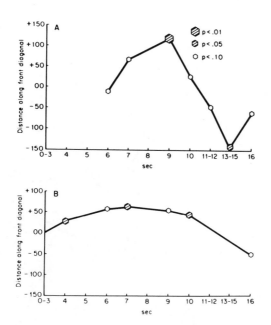

Figure 3: Projection along front diagonal of regression coefficients for F1 and F2 (A) of (aw) and (B) of (eyC) for all
socioeconomic classes compared to SEC 0-3; data from 93 speakers
in Philadelphia neighborhood study.

curvilinear pattern with a significant peak in the middle working
class (Class 7), and two other points significantly higher than
the lower class reference level in groups located symmetrically
above and below Class 7. Again, the less significant points form
a smooth, curvilinear pattern.

It is evident that the retrograde movement of checked /ey/
is not as vigorous as the raising and fronting of (aw), and the
class stratification is also not as sharp. The parallels between
the two patterns can be seen more clearly by abstracting from
this detailed class distribution, and dividing the social class
gradient into five groups: lower working class, 0-5; upper working
class, 6-9; lower middle class, 10-12; upper middle class, 13-15.
The upper class, discretely separated from the others, is given
an arbitrary rating of 16.

By dividing the working class and middle class into two groups
each, we will be able to make the closest comparison with the
various sociolinguistic studies that have documented change in
progress, particularly Trudgill, 1973; Cedergren, 1973; and Labov,
1966. Figure 4 shows the result of this reduction. Since the F1
vectors are in general less significant than the F2 effects for the
vowels considered here, F2 coefficients are plotted here without

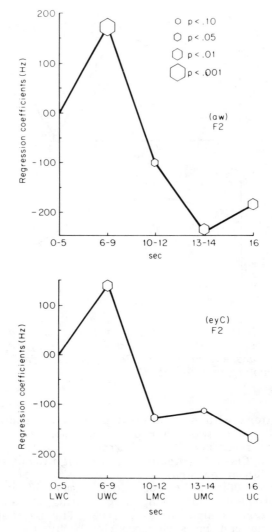

Figure 4: Regression coefficients for socioeconomic classes in Philadelphia neighborhoods: (aw) and (eyC). 0-5 is residual class.

F1 to maximize confidence in the results. The patterns of F2 of (aw) and (ey) are strikingly parallel to each other and to the curvilinear results of the earlier studies. They are typical of the general pattern for all the Philadelphia sound changes: None of them show an initiative from the lowest social group or from the highest; while the most vigorous changes, that have not yet met with social correction, are advancing most rapidly in the highest sections of the working class.

The third new and vigorous change, the raising and fronting of (ay°), shows no significant class distributions of this type. It is worth noting that this is also the only change where men are in the lead (Labov, 1978b). For most of the linguistic changes that have been traced so far, we find that women are about one generation ahead of men--at least in the early stages of the process. This is true in Philadelphia as well, except in the case of (ay°). There may be a connection between the normal curvilinear class pattern and the dominance of women in the advancement of sound change, but this direction of inquiry would carry us beyond the scope of the present report.

FURTHER DIRECTIONS OF EXPLANATION

Given the confirmation of earlier evidence that systematic sound changes generally arise in centrally located social groups, we can ask how this fact bears on the causes and motivations of sound change. Instead of speculating on the psychological motivations of the upper working-class innovators, it will be more fruitful to probe more deeply into their social roles and relations to others in the community. A further investigation of the problem is based on evidence from communication networks in the neighborhoods (Labov et. al., 1980). Although the full results of this inquiry are again beyond the scope of the present report, it may be helpful to indicate their general direction. It appears that the speakers who are most advanced in the sound changes are those with the highest status in their local community, as the socioeconomic class patterns indicate. But the communication networks provide additional information, discriminating among those with comparable status. The most advanced speakers are the persons with the largest numbers of local contacts within the neighborhood, yet who have at the same time the highest proportion of their acquaintances outside the neighborhood. Thus we have a portrait of individuals with the highest local prestige who are responsive to a somewhat broader form of prestige at the next larger level of social communication.[13] Through further studies of this process, we hope to discover how sound changes are generalized throughout the community and how local values are transmitted to create a relatively homogeneous urban dialect.[14]

The functions of language reflected in these sound changes cannot be limited to the communication of referential information. We are clearly dealing with the emblematic function of phonetic differentiation: the identification of a particular way of speaking with the norms of a local community

The identification of the innovators of these sound changes allows us to rule out some of the explanations that have been offered in the past for the phenomenon of sound change. Their advanced social position and the high esteem they hold in the local community rule out the traditional charge of careless ignorance of the norms of society. Their reputation as vigorous and effective users of the language, combined with the nature of the vowel shifts themselves, makes any discussion of the principle of least effort beside the point. The central position that they hold in local networks of communication gives new life to the principle of local density, though we cannot project any discontinuity between these speakers and the exponents of the upper middle-class standard that they are leaving behind in their development of local sound changes. Once we are willing to refine our notion of prestige to give full weight to the local prestige associated with the Philadelphia dialect, Tarde's laws of imitation gain in respectability. But we must be ready to recognize that such a local prestige, which appears primarily in behavior and rarely in overt reactions, is powerful enough to reverse the normal flow of influence, and allow the local patterns to move upward to the upper middle class and even to the upper class.[15]

None of these considerations provide an answer to the riddle of actuation. What is the force that has led to the continued renewal of sound change? Why have Philadelphians of the past few decades pushed the local vowel system even further along its traditional path, diverging even more from the dialects of other cities? The data generated by our neighborhood studies supports the earlier suggestion (Labov, 1965) that it is the entrance of new ethnic and racial groups into the community that provides the motivating forces behind this renewed diversification. In Philadelphia, as in New York, we are now witnessing a third wave of ethnic immigratiion. The Irish and German influx of the mid-nineteenth century was followed by a massive entrance of Italians, Jews, Ukrainians, and Poles at the end of the nineteenth century and the beginning of the twentieth; and in the middle of the twentieth century, the movement of large numbers of Southern rural black citizens into the Northern cities has created a city that is 33% black and inner city areas that are sharply divided between segregated black areas and traditional ethnic enclaves.

The renewed emphasis on local identification is accompanied by a strenuous reassertion of local rights and privileges by the ethnic groups who hold them, and a continued resistance to the pressure from black citizens of Philadelphia for their share of the jobs, housing, and political priorities in the city. The division of the city into two distinct communities by political, educational, and economic barriers is mirrored by the increasing divergence of the white and black dialects. Young black speakers do not participate at all in the evolution of the vowel system that is described here; instead, they clearly show their allegiance to a nationally based black English vernacular that is extraordinarily uniform in all the cities of the North.[16]   It is unlikely that the further evolution of the Philadelphia vowel system can be understood without reference to this striking parallel between the linguistic divergence of the black and white communities, and the political, economic, and educational barriers that divide the city so sharply in so many ways.

Through the further study of communication between racial and ethnic groups, and the communication patterns that connect local neighborhoods, we hope to delineate more closely the social pressures that are responsible for the dissemination and further advance of sound change, and thus isolate the driving force behind the continuing divergence of languages and dialects. There is no reason to believe, however, that this divergence will continue indefinitely. The current linguistic situation in Philadelphia is bound to be affected by changes in job opportunities and residential patterns that affect black-white relations. We have found evidence of mutual influence of black and white speech patterns where there is daily contact and the cultural values of the opposing groups are recognized and viewed as accessible. The current divergence in the Philadelphia speech community is the product of long-standing linguistic trends and the pressures of the immediate social situation; the future evolution of the local dialect will be determined by a similar interaction between general constraints on language structure and the changing social context. The validity of any explanation of linguistic change will depend upon our ability to grasp the most relevant data in both areas and integrate our observations in a theory of language change that has the same wide scope and compelling character as the events themselves.

FOOTNOTES

[1]The research reported here was supported by the National Science Foundation under contracts to the University of Pennsylvania SOC-750024-1 and BNC-76-15421. A more complete account of this research is available in W. Labov, A. Bower, D. Hindle, E. Dayton, A. Kroch, M. Lenning, and D. Schiffrin, *Social Determinants of Linguistic Change*, Technical Progress Report to the NSF (1980). The work reported here is the joint product of these authors and a number of others, most notably Arvilla Payne, Bruce Johnson, Shana Poplack, Gregory Guy, Sally Boyd, and Anthony Kroch. Kroch's study of the upper class of Philadelphia, supported by a post-doctoral fellowship from the National Institute of Mental Health [MH-05536], forms an integral part of the data that this report is based on. Kroch has made a number of substantial contributions to the analysis of the Philadelphia data and the general issues of sound change, which are gratefully

acknowledged here. A condensed version of this article was prepared for the Ninth International Congress of Linguists at Copenhagen, August 1978.

[2]The three major principles state that in chain shifts, (I) tense or long nuclei rise, (II) short or lax nuclei fall, and (III), back nuclei move to the front. These principles were foreseen by Sweet (1888), but applied to individual vowel movements rather than to chain shifts, where they have much greater predictive value.

[3]This general impression is in fact reinforced frequently by the statements of dialectologists who collect data from rural areas. A journalistic account of a dialect society meeting states that "differences in the way Americans talk seem to be wearing away . . . towards the standard national blandness of a radio announcer," and cites David Reed and Frederick Cassidy to this effect (*Philadelphia Inquirer*, 15 February 1978, p. 10-E). The findings of traditional dialectology appear to reflect the general decline of rural societies with loss of population, rather than general linguistic processes.

[4]The cities where sociolinguistic structure has been studied systematically now include Detroit (Shuy, Wolfram, and Riley, 1966; Wolfram, 1969), Salt Lake City (Cook, 1969); Glasgow (Macaulay, 1977), Belfast (J. Milroy and L. Milroy, 1977); Bahia Blanca, Argentina (Weinberg, 1974), Buenos Aires (Lavandera, 1975), Montreal (G. Sankoff and H. Cedergren, 1971), Paris (Lennig, 1978), and Teheran (Modaressi, 1978). In none of these cities do we find systematic innovation by the highest social group. In some cases, retrograde movements will show the upper middle class in the lead; this is particularly so in Lennig's study of Paris, where women speakers show a generalized rotation that reverses the direction of the traditional working class dialect. But here of course the upper middle class began in the rear, and so in retreat is very likely to be found in the lead.

[5]Supported by the National Science Foundation as noted in Note 1. Research conducted by this project in Philadelphia covers a wider range of issues concerning linguistic change in Philadelphia than are presented here. Payne (1974, 1977) reports the acquisition of phonetic and phonological rules by children with varying exposure to the Philadelphia dialect. Guy (1975) analyzes the constraints on consonant cluster simplification that differentiate Philadelphia from New York. Poplack examines the social influences on the English vowels used by Puerto Rican children (1976) and the functional constraints on deletion of final consonants in Spanish (1977). Experiments testing categorical perception of short a (Labov, 1977) show the perceptual consequences of the creation of new phonemic boundaries in mid-Atlantic dialects.

[6]The methods followed here are in accordance with the general principles presented in Labov, 1972, pp. 208-209, which confront the fundamentally irreducible "observer's paradox": Our aim is to observe how people speak when they are not being observed.

The general solution is to approach the object of investigation from radically different perspectives, so that the errors of one method of observation are not duplicated by the errors of another.
[7]The neighborhood data were recorded on a Nagra III or IVS tape recorder at 3 3/4"/sec. using Sennheiser dynamic MD214 or 404 condenser microphones. The spectral analyzer is the Spectral Dynamics 301C, synthesizing 165 filters every 16.7 msec over 3300 Hz for men, 180 filters every 18 msec for women; data is averaged over 50 msec. LPC analysis was carried out on a PDP 11/10, with programs based on Markel, 1971 and Makhoul, 1975.
[8]For further data on the normalization procedures and methods used to compare them, see Hindle, 1977; Lennig and Hindle, 1977; Lennig, 1978; and Labov et al. 1980.
[9]The parenthesis notation ( ) designates linguistic variables --phonetic units that show structured variation. Slashes / / and brackets [ ] indicate phonemic and phonetic units, respectively, where variability is not at issue.
[10]Philadelphia (ow) and (uw) are not fronted before liquids /l/ and /r/, and show no upglides before these liquids.
[11]In Figures 1 and 2, checked vowels are indicated by a following C, and free vowels by a following F. For the middle range vowels (uw) and (ow), as well the corresponding front vowels (iy) and (ey), the free vowels are lower and more centralized than the checked vowels. In the earlier stages of diphthongization under chain shifting principle II, the free vowels move more rapidly than the checked vowels. This is true in Philadelphia, but not in all of the cities where this type of chain shifting is found.
[12]The figures shown here are based on the regression analysis with the finest division of the social class continuum. All regression analyses used a stepwise procedure (Draper and Smith, 1966) which examines each variable as if it were the last to be entered into the equation, and results are independent of the order in which the variables are presented to the program.
[13]These patterns in the communication of linguistic influence appear to be parallel to the two-step flow of influence isolated by Katz and Lazarsfeld (1955) in their study of personal influence.
[14]Weinreich, Labov, and Herzog (1968) argued that the basis for an empirical theory of linguistic change must be recognition of the heterogeneity of the speech community. Full competence in the use of the language requires that a speaker be able to recognize and interpret the differences within and across speakers that occur in his speech community, though he or she may use only a part of that range of variation in production. Thus the obverse of heterogeneity in production is homogeneity in normative structures, and a speech community may be defined as a group of speakers who share a set of norms for the interpretation of speech. Labov (1966) showed that New York City was such a community. The same can be said for Philadelphia, where subjec-

tive reaction tests of native residents show internal agreement and sharp disagreement with the reactions of outsiders, and the direction of style shifting is uniform for all speakers who have been studied. But, as in New York City, these statements apply to the white community only; the black and Puerto Rican speakers form distinct communities which fail to recognize many of the norms of the white community, and show many understandings that are perceived only dimly if at all by white speakers living in the same area (see Note 16).

[15] The sample of 20 upper class speakers studied by Anthony Kroch showed a surprising conformity to the Philadelphia vowel system and clearly form a part of the speech community. Though the upper-class speakers use phonetic variants that are quite removed from the more advanced groups, it is clear that the overall rotations of the vowel system have affected upper-class speakers, and the distributional sets used by upper-class speakers in spontaneous speech follow the Philadelphia system exactly. The oldest upper-class speaker and the oldest Irish speaker from Kensington, both born in the 1880s, show the same complex distributions of short a into tense and lax classes. Communities may show heterogeneity in phonemic distributions, almost inevitably in the course of mergers, tensing or laxing processes; but where we do find a resultant uniform template, it provides strong evidence for participation in a single speech community.

[16] The older Philadelphia black community appears to have participated in the Philadelphia vowel and consonant system, and it is still possible to find individual black speakers who use the Philadelphia vernacular. But the overwhelming majority of the black community now show no use at all of the Philadelphia vowel and consonant variants, or of the special grammatical features of the Philadelphia dialect. In the predominantly black high schools, there is almost no trace of the white Philadelphia vernacular described here. Instead, blacks participate in a nonlocal, nationally oriented linguistic and cultural framework; the phonology and grammar used in North and West Philadelphia appears to be identical with that used in New York, Detroit, Chicago, New Orleans, or Los Angeles.

REFERENCES

Bloomfield, L. 1933. *Language.* New York: Henry Holt.
Cedergren, H. J. 1973. *The interplay of social and linguistic factors in Panama.* Unpublished doctoral dissertation, Cornell University.

Cook, S. 1969. *Language change and the emergence of an urban dialect in Utah*. Unpublished doctoral dissertation, University of Utah.

Draper, N. R. & H. Smith. 1966. *Applied Regression Analysis*. New York: Wiley.

Efroymson, M. A. 1966. Multiple regression analysis. In A. Ralston and H. S. Wilf (eds.), *Mathematical methods for digital computers*. New York: Wiley.

Gauchat, L. 1905. l'unite phonetique dans le patois d'une commune. In *Festschrift Heinreich Morf* . Halle: Max Niemeyer.

Guy, G. 1975. Variation in the group and the individual: The case of final stop deletion. [*Pennsylvania Working Papers* I, 4. Philadelphia: U.S. Regional Survey.]

Hermann, E. 1929. Lautveraenderungen in der individual-sprache einer Mundart. *Nachrichten der Geselllsch der Wissenschaften zu Goettingen*, Phil.-his. Kll., 11, 195-214.

Hindle, D. 1978. Approaches to vowel normalization in the study of natural speech. In D. Sankoff (ed.), *Linguistic variation: Models and methods*. New York: Academic Press.

Katz, E. Lazarsfeld, P. 1955. *Personal Influence* . Glencoe, Ill.: Free Press.

King, R. 1972. *Historical linguistics and generative grammar*. Englewood Cliffs, N.J.: Prentice-Hall.

King, R. 1975. Integrating linguistic change. In K. H. Dahlstedt (ed.), *The Nordic languages and modern linguistics*. Stockholm: Almqvist and Wiksell.

Kroch, A. 1978. Towards a theory of social dialect variation. *Language in Society*, 7:17-36.

Labov, W. 1966. *The social stratification of English in New York City*. Washington D.C.: Center for Applied Linguistics.

Labov. W. 1972. *Sociolinguistic patterns* . Philadelphia: University of Pennsylvania Press.

Labov, W. 1977. Categorical discrimination along a new phonemic boundary. Paper given before the annual meeting of the Linguistic Society of America, Chicago.

Labov, W. 1978a. The measurement of vowel shifts. Paper given before the annual meeting of the American Association of Phonetic Sciences, San Francisco.

Labov, W. 1978b. The role of women in linguistic change. Paper given before the annual meeting of the Linguistic Society of America, Boston.

Labov, W., Bower, A., Hindle, D., Dayton, E., Kroch, A., Lennig, M., and Schiffrin, D. 1980. *Social determinants of sound change*. Philadelphia: U.S. Regional Survey.

Labov, W., Yaeger, M., and Steiner, R. 1972. *A quantitative study of sound change in progress*. Philadelphia: U.S. Regional Survey.

Lavandera, B. 1975. Linguistic structure and sociolinguistic conditioning in the use of verbal endings in *si*-clauses Buenos Aires Spanish). Unpublished doctoral dissertation. University of Pennsylvania.

Lennig, M. 1978. Acoustic measurement of linguistic change: The modern Paris vowel system. Unpublished doctoral dissertation. University of Pennsylvania.

Lennig, M., and Hindle, D. 1977. Uniform sealing as a method of vowel normalization. Paper presented at the 94th meeting of the Acoustical Society of dissertation.

Macaulay, R. 1977. *Language, social class, and education.* Edinburgh: University Press.

Makhoul, J. 1975. Spectral linear prediction: properties and applications. *IEEE Transactions on Acoustics, Speech and Signal Processing.* ASSP-23, No. 3.

Markel, J., and Gray, A. H. Jr. 1976. *Linear prediction of speech.* Cambridge, Mass.: Bolt, Beranek and Newman.

Martinet, A. 1955. *Economie des changements phonétiques.* Berne: Francke.

Meilllet, A. 1921. *Linguistique historique et linguistique genreale.* Paris: La societe linguistique de Paris.

Milroy, L., and Milroy, J. 1977. Speech and context in an urban setting. *Belfast Working Papers*, 2, p. 1.

Modaressi, Y. 1978. A sociolinguistic analysis of modern Persian. Unpublished doctoral disseration. University of Kansas.

Nearey, T. 1977. Phonetic feature system for vowels. Unpublished doctoral dissertation. University of Connecticut.

Nordstroem, P. E., and Lindblom, B. 1975. A normalization procedure for vowel formant data. Paper 212 at the Eighth International Congress of Phonetic Sciences, Leeds.

Sankoff, D., Shorrock, R. W., and McKay, W. 1974. Normalization of formant space through the least squares affine transformation. Unpublished program and documentation.

Sankoff, G. and Cedergren, H. 1971. Some results of a sociolinguistic study of Montreal French. In R. Darnell (ed.), *Linguistic diversity in Canadian society* . Edmonton: Linguistic Research, 1971.

Saussure, F. de 1922. *Cours de linguistique générale* . 2nd ed. Paris.

Shuy, R., Wolfram, W., and Riley, W. 1966. A study of social dialects in Detroit. Final Report, Project 6-1347. Washington, D.C.: Office of Education.

Sweet, H. 1888. *A history of English sounds.* Oxford: Clarendon Press.

Tarde, G. 1973. *Les lois d'imitation.*

Trudgill, P. 1972. *The social differentiation of English in Norwich.* Cambridge: University of Cambridge Press.

Weinberg, M. 1974. Analisis sociolinguistico de un aspecto del Espanol Bonaerense: la -*s* en Bahia Blanca. *Cuadernos de Linguistica.*

Weinreich, U., Labov, W., and Herzog, M. 1968. Empirical foundations for a theory of language change. In W. Lehmann and Y. Malkiel (eds.), *Directions for Historical Linguistics*. Austin: University of Texas Press.

Wolf, C., and Jimenez, E. 1978. A sound change in progress: The devoicing of Buenos Aires /z/ into /s/. Unpublished paper.

Wolfram, W. 1969. *A sociolinguistic description of Detroit Negro speech*. Arlington, Va.: Center for Applied Linguistics.

ON THE SOCIALITY OF CREOLE LANGUAGES

William Washabaugh

INNATE BLUEPRINTS

For some years now Derek Bickerton has been issuing a clarion
call for a return to an autonomous linguistics, a linguistics independent of sociology. He has presented unambiguous statements
like: "The creole continuum is first and foremost a LINGUISTIC
and not a SOCIAL phenomenon" and "At the level of *parole*,
social forces do have an effect on language; at the level of
langue they hardly ever do" (Bickerton 1979:13f); "The kind of
blueprint that we have wired into our heads is not a blueprint
which defines language negatively in terms of formal universals,
but rather one that defines language positively . . . people
already have a first language". All these statements leave no
doubt as to Bickerton's position which is that, in both creolization
and decreolization, the brain is running the show. These linguistic
processes either flow directly from, or are guided by, universal
cerebral blueprints for language acquisition. These processes
are cerebral from the first and then social only after the fact
and in a trivial sense: "Once they HAVE happened, a kind of
post-hoc folk linguistics swings into action, and social values are
assigned to various forms and structures irrespective of what
kind of linguistic change brought these forms and structures to
birth." In Bickerton's program, the brain is the mother who
gives birth to language, whereas society is the father who just
stands by and waits for his chance to smile or frown on the
product of the mother's efforts.

The results of Bickerton's program have certainly advanced
our understanding of creole languages by giant steps. His program
is exciting, and that excitement is due in large part to its simplicity. However, I will show here that Bickerton's simple program
is, when scrutinized, simplistic, and that the excitement which it
engenders is, in part, euphoric. My argument is divided into
two parts; first, I will lay bare the intellectual roots of Bickerton's
program, and I will show that these roots are neither thick nor
deep; second, I will examine certain creole phenomena which I

From *The Genesis of Language: The First Michigan Colloquium 1979*, Karoma Publishers, 1979, pp 125-139.

believe raise doubts about the empirical adequacy of Bickerton's cerebral linguistics.

ON THE SOCIALITY OF LANGUAGE

Bickerton's terminology (e.g., *faculté de langage* , *langue*, *parole*) reflects a certain commitment to a Saussurean paradigm[1]-- not to say that he is in agreement with the linguistic program outlined in the *Cours de Linguistique Générale* (CLG), but only that he is committed to some major principles of linguistic analysis which date to that seminal work. It would be correct enough to say that he is one of a school of linguists who are out to refine and clarify the contributions of Saussure and to rectify the inadequacies of Saussurean linguistics.

But with painful regularity disciples, who struggle to clarify and rectify a master's model, purge from that model subtleties which, in the first formulation, may appear as ambiguities or contradictions. Bickerton's program, along with the bulk of contemporary linguistic orthodoxy, seems to have fallen into this trap. Specifically, the clarity and power of Bickerton's program suggest that, while smelting the ore, he has lost some of the iron of Saussure's linguistics.

I will first assay the raw Saussurean model and then follow that model through its post-Saussurean transformation in which it gained power and simplicity but lost subtlety. The objective of this presentation is to recover the valuable ideas which were relegated to the slag pile during the post-Saussurean transformation, and to recycle them toward a subtler linguistics.

Saussure, with his head twisted back toward the 19th century, was smitten by three major views on language. First, there was neogrammarian universalism to which he had made no small contribution himself. According to that view, language is a collection of units of speech which result from universal, involuntary mechanical laws. Second, he was impressed by the sociologism of W. D. Whitney whose work was set squarely against the view that language is a natural organism regulated totally by involuntary laws. For Whitney, language is an institution arrived at through social interaction and convention. Third, Saussure was certainly subject to the psychologism which was in the air at the end of the 19th century (Hughes 1961)--not the mechanistic psychologism which surfaces in H. Paul's *Principles*, but a phenomenological psychology such as that born of Rickert and Dilthey.

Saussure twisted and turned his program of linguistics to try to bring these three major views into line. By 1894, his program had a shape. He saw that the regularities uncovered by the neogrammarians were not so much regularities of physical events, but of psychological states, *états de conscience* (Saussure 1974:24, 40). Accordingly, he divided linguistics into two sci-

ences--one of which addressed empirical events, and the other of
which, statics, addressed psychological states.

Saussure argued that linguistic statics was a branch of the
more general study of human symboling. Yet he was not so
concerned with the psychology of symbol production as with the
relations between symbols, and relations between symbols in Saussure's view were products of social conventions (Whitney's
sociologism is apparent here). This, the foundation of his
program, is apparent in Saussure's notes of 1894.

But for the rest of his life, Saussure struggled with, and
cannot be said to have solved, the question of the relative contribution of the individual and the society to language states. His
concepts of *la langue* and *la parole* reflect the struggle. In his
first course in general linguistics (1906) Saussure maintained that
la langue was an individual fact and that *la parole* was the
social fact of language. All that enters *la langue* must arrive
from the social sphere of *la parole* where linguistic elements are
"consecrated through use." In his second course (1908) he turned
about and argued that *la langue*, being the product of the social
consecration, was a social fact. *La parole* was the individual's
realization of *la langue* as well as the game field in which individual
variants vied for admission to *la langue*. In this second course,
la faculté du langue was introduced, but never developed, and
was described as the psychological potential extant in every
individual to acquire *la langue*. It is a universal psychological
condition, not a linguistic fact; it is a condition necessary for
the social institution of language. In the CLG, the relations
between *la langue*, *la parole*, and *la faculté* are left unresolved,
though they are cosmetically resurfaced to give the appearance
of consistency. Still, the principle remains that "there is nothing
in *la langue* which has not entered through *la parole*."

It should be apparent that the CLG is an unfinished work
(Koerner 1973:327). It offered a crooked path which had to be
straightened by Saussure's followers. And one of the most confusing of its confusions was certainly the distinction between the
psychological and the social in *la parole* and *la langue*.

The post-Saussurean resolution of this confusion between the
psychological and the social marks the birth of European structuralism, a birth foreshadowed in, but only adumbrated by, the
embryonic CLG. And for our purposes, it should be noted that
the delivery of structuralism from the embryonic CLG would have
been impossible without a stiff injection of Husserlian
phenomenology which had the effect of spotlighting the psychological while soft-pedaling the social.

> The structural trend in general linguistics
> which took root with the International Con-
> gresses of the late twenties and early thirties is
> now being reproved for its supposed estrange-
> ment from philosophy, whereas in reality the
> international protagonists of this movement had

close and effective connections with phenomenology in its Husserlian and Hegelian versions
(Jakobson 1970:13).

The precise nature of the contribution of phenomenology to
European structuralism is not so mysterious. That contribution
is the notion of the "transcendental ego," the Husserlian subject,
the view that the structure of knowledge, including linguistic
knowledge, derives from the very faculties of the knower.
Husserl's project "assumes that language is one of the objects
supremely constituted by consciousness and that actual languages
are very special cases of a possible language which consciousness
holds the key to" (Merleau-Ponty 1964:84). The cerebralism,
universalism, and mechanism of European structuralisms derive,
in large part, from Husserl's notion of the consciousness of the
subject.

A similar program--one founded on the same notion of
"transcendental ego"--when tendered by Chomsky, exploded American linguistics which had not been primed by the philosophical
inquiry that had always accompanied European linguistics.

Chomsky developed a notion which follows very
closely the idea of the subject in Husserlian
phenomenology. His explicit reference to this
subject is symptomatic of the fact that Husserlian
philosophy has been at the basis of signification
theories in this century, and, consciously
or not, explicitly or not, at the basis of modern
linguistics (Coward and Ellis 1977:129).

We look upon generative linguistics as "Chomsky's Revolution,"
but it is in reality Chomsky's continuation of the structuralist
revolution.

Bickerton is heir to this principle of the centrality and
transcendentality of the ego, and to the view that language is an
object which is constituted prior to experience. His understanding
of *la langue* and *la faculté* parallels with unnerving consistency
the Husserlian project described above (Bickerton 1975:179). In
fact, he is a good deal more consistent in his commitment to this
principle than other linguists who work within the generative
linguistic program. Specifically, he is critical of "correlational
sociolinguists" who advocate the generative program but whose
methods run contrary to the phenomenological principles of that
program. He argues that "choice of style is governed, not by
any inter-subjective and objectively perceptible features in the
situational context, but by the autonomous and fluctuating feelings
of the speaker" (Bickerton 1975:184). "Thus, as with most linguistic phenomena of any interest, switching turns out to be an
internal rather than an external process--to have its locus, not
in society, but in the mind" (Bickerton 1977a:16).

The cerebralism which surfaces so regularly in Bickerton's
linguistics is not a quirk, a whim, or a fetish. His "brainstorming"
is not at all a carking after an unrealistic theoretical goal.
Rather his cerebralism is well-measured; it is built upon no small

linguistic and philosophical foundation. His program is nothing less than the continuation of the structuralist revolution and the transformation of contemporary linguistic theory into one which is consistent through and through with the fundamental phenomenological principle of the "transcendental ego."

Bickerton seems to be a Copernicus (Bickerton 1975) trying to convince the skeptics that the ego, like the sun, is not determined, but is central and determining. However, whereas the Copernican revolution won the day, the structuralist revolution falters even at its inception. Husserl backed off from his pure phenomenology (Roche 1973), and the European structuralists have now set for themselves the goal of de-constructing the ego.

> In this development, a Cartesian grammar would become redundant and linguistics would have to orient itself to a different view of the subject, one in which the subject is destroyed and re-made in the signifier--a theory which, as we have seen already, both Marxism and psychoanalysis would favor (Coward and Ellis 1977:130).

So instead of being a Copernican prophet who is discovering a revolutionary path toward a new understanding of the linguistic cosmos, Bickerton may be one of a crew of linguists which is now straightening and extending the path which the structuralist pioneers charted with the aid of their Husserlian compasses. Only that crew has not yet realized that the pioneers got lost in the woods.

CREOLE LANGUAGE CHANGE AND
THE SOCIALITY OF LANGUAGE

This is not the occasion on which to offer an alternative to the whole structuralist, cerebralist program. Instead I would like to get creole language studies "out of the woods" by returning to the subtle embryonic structuralism of Saussure and by rediscovering there principles for calming the current "brainstorms." Specifically, I will return to a program based on Saussure's seminal observation that *la langue* is a social fact.[2] I will apply this dictum--that language is a social fact--to creole phenomena which Bickerton would explain by appealing to the notion of innate blueprint. My purpose is to demonstrate that alternative explanations are available for these creole language phenomena which on first glance seem apt for this universalist explanation.

The phenomena to be presented here are not facts about creolization--the genesis of a creole language. Rather they are facts about changes that appear in creoles consequent to their genesis. Some such changes--namely, those which occur by borrowing--will be set to one side here. These changes by borrowing for which an explicit model or target exists will not be discussed. Instead we will consider internally motivated changes which are not modeled on an explicit target language.

In Bickerton's view (1979) such internally motivated changes are directed by an innate blueprint, the same innate blueprint which guides creolization. Just as creolization wherein "the child . . . has to make up the deficit [of an absent model]; so the child has recourse to things which are somehow already in its knowledge", so, too, in internally motivated changes the guidance system is cerebral, not social. The speaker is guided in his changes by things which are somehow already in his knowledge. It is as if internally motivated change were an ineluctable juggernaut which forces its way into *la langue* regardless of the extra-cerebral conditions of the speaker.

Bickerton does not refer to such change as a juggernaut, but such a word does not exaggerate his view. He argues, for example, that the vowel denasalization change which, as I reported (1978), accounts for the *mɛ̃-me* variation in the past tense marker of Providence Island Creole (PIC) is altogether cerebrally initiated and promoted. "The change came about through a regular phono-logical process, and the result HAD to be socially classified some-how" (Bickerton 1979:14). Bickerton's own emphatic use of HAD implies that the change which is to be classified has all the force of a linguistic juggernaut.

My objective here will be to demonstrate that the maintenance of this and of other internally motivated changes in PIC is a social rather than a cerebral affair, and that such changes might not be maintained if the selfsame PIC were displaced into different social settings--indeed, the *mɛ̃-me* variation is evidently not realized in many similar varieties of Caribbean English Creole (CEC). That objective will be achieved by showing that not only the *mɛ̃-me* variation but also at least four other innovations are curiously collocated in PIC. Whereas linguistic conditions in other varieties of CEC are enough like those of PIC to support all these same innovations, no other variety finds them so far advanced. My conclusion will be that these innovations perform a special social function for the people of Providence Island.

First, there is the *men fi* innovation. By this innovation PIC speakers subtly intensify the impact of a sentence by adding modal force. In (1) the placement of *men* before *fi* says that indeed the rock was intentially tied on to hit the baby. The *fi* in the *men fi* construction is a complementizer which is governed by a deleted modal verb marked for past tense. The past tense marker *men* is made to carry the modal force of that deleted verb. Bickerton (1979) disagrees with this description,[3] but he does not disagree with the fact that this construction is rather rare in varieties of CEC. That last fact, on which there is agreement, is a crucial fact and one which is not accounted for by an innate blueprint.

(1) *Im tai a rak men fi go lik dong bis biebi.*
     He tied a rock to go hit down this baby.

A second innovation pertains to the directional complementizer *go* which occurs with verbs of motion in Caribbean English Creole (CEC) (2).   My argument (Washabaugh forthcoming) is that this directional complementizer derives, through reanalysis, from the motion verb used in a serial verb construction.   Some varieties of CEC have extended the reanalysis process from *go* to *kom* and *gan* (3), and have bleached the resulting complementizer of all features of directionality (4).   This reanalysis process spreads to *kom* and *gan* in a pattern which bespeaks guidance by a cerebral gyroscope.   But again, the furthest reaches of the extension of the innovation are found in PIC, and that fact will not be attributable to the brain.

(2) *She wash aut di swet an pres it an keri go gi im* PIC).
     She washes out the sweat and presses it and carries it to give it to him.
(3) a. *Firs ting im go go pap af i haan bogota* (PIC).
         The first thing you know he will go break his arm in Bogota.
     b. *Dem kom ko saach mi hier* (PIC).
         They came to search my hair.
     c. *Dem ah gan ga tiif aut presh pinuts bota* (PIC).
         Then I went to steal P's peanut butter.
(4) *Ai mos kom aut go luk waif* (PIC).
     I must come out to look for a wife.

A third innovation has to do with the sentence-initial interrogative tag in CEC (5a).   Roberts (1977) argues that such a tag is a recent spontaneous development in JC.   I (Washabaugh 1977) showed this "spontaneous development account" to be false by presenting evidence for the existence of a lexically distinct but syntactically identical tag in PIC (5b).   I can conceive of two alternatives to the "spontaneous development account," namely, a "survival account" and a "natural change account."   The evidence for such a "survival account" is twofold.   First, sentence-initial interrogative tags are quite infrequent in languages of the world. Second, the West African languages, Fante and Mandinka, are two among the handful of languages in which sentence-initial interrogative tags appear.

(5) a. *Duont a tuu poliis faada ya av?*
         You have two fathers who are policemen, don't you?
     b. *Ent mi ponkin vain da gro?*
         My pumpkin vine is growing, right?

One might argue for a "natural change account" as an alternative to both the "spontaneous development account" and the "survival account."   Evidence supporting the "natural change account"

is two-fold.   First, Roberts observed that the higher frequency
of sentence-initial tag use appeared among children.   Children
are typically the purveyors of natural changes in languages.
Second, I have recently observed frequent and regular use of
sentence-initial tags in the speech of four-year-old American
children (6) despite the fact that such utterances are unacceptable
to most adult speakers of English.   Such sentences support the
"natural change account" since natural change is hypothesized to
correspond inversely to the directionality of child language acquisition.

(6) Right mosquitoes can't eat up clothes?

If the weight of further evidence should tip the scales toward
a "natural change account" of interrogative tags, then again we
would be confronted with a situation in which the creole speakers
are promoting an innovation which leads their language away from
both the historical basilect and the acrolect.   And again, PIC is
one of the few varieties of CEC in which this innovation has
been observed.
A final innovation is the development of an iterative aspect
marker in PIC.   Whereas Bickerton (1976, 1977b) has argued
that the iterative aspect is marked in all creole varieties, D.
Taylor (1977:179) has shown that JC and Haitian Creole are
exceptions.   Like JC, basilectal PIC conveys iterative aspect with
an unmarked verb.   Whereas this gap in the evidence for Bickerton's hypothetical universals is problematic in its own right, it is
not the focal point of the discussion here.   The lack of a marker
of the iterative in PIC is merely the stage on which the focal
innovation plays itself out.
The innovation itself involves the reanalysis of the adjective
stodi (*stodi-sodi-todi*) to serve as a marker of the iterative
aspect as in (7).   When so used, *stodi* combines with an unmarked
verb and is never found in combination with another aspect marker.
To add to the complexity of the description, I should note the
existence of sentences (8a) and (8b) in which the adverbs *kiip*
and *pyur* are used to mark iterativity.   But in most instances
these adverbs combine with the aspect marker *de* which regularly
marks the continuative aspect.

(7) a.   *Him stodi rait pan piepa an gi wi* (PIC).
         He is always writing on paper and giving it to us.
    b.   *Di kau stodi mek im iirz go so.*
         The cow is always making his ears go so.
    c.   *E. stodi bring mango fi dem.*
         E. always brings mango for them.
(8) a.   *Ah kiip de bai saks.*
         I am always buying socks.
    b.   *Im pyur de ron baut.*
         He is just running about.

A plausible explanation based on the facts presented above is that *stodi* is the first or earliest marker of iterativity in PIC. The variable appearance of *kiip* and *pyur* with *de* indicates that, through decreolization, the iterative aspect is occasionally signaled by the marker *de* rather than by *stodi*. Since the iterative *de* is not distinct from the continuative *de*, the adverbs *kiip* and *pyur* are combined with just the iterative *de*. As a later development, the iterative *de* may be deleted leaving only the appended adverbs *pyur* or *kiip* to mark iterativity.

The central feature of the innovation is that an iterative aspect marker *stodi* is developed in PIC at some point later than the creolization process. This development of the iterative aspect marker is a natural change, since it proceeds by a reanalysis of a formative which already exists in the language. And here again, the innovation occurs in PIC though not in other varieties of CEC, at least not in the same way. (Such an innovative use of *todi* is not mentioned by LePage and Cassidy [1967:446]; though see Baugh [1976] for a discussion of *steady* in BE.)

All these innovations are natural changes. In each, the innovative variants pop out of the language universal *faculté*, and each variant is built into the grammar gradually under the guidance of the cerebral gyroscope. But whereas these innovations may be natural, they are not inevitable. Their progress is not ineluctable. One single observation will make this clear. Bailey (1973:67) has argued that natural changes spread in waves; innovations move outward from a central point. The lects at the epicenter of a series of innovations will contain the most recent changes; lects most peripheral to the center of change will contain the fewest innovations. Such a principle would lead us to place PIC, replete as it is with innovations, at the epicenter of natural changes in CEC. But that seems most unlikely since, as we will note below, Providence Island is among the youngest and most isolated of CEC communities.

My argument is that despite their cerebral provenance, natural changes are maintained only if "consecrated by use." Like so many seeds which have fallen to the ground, these innovations will sprout of their own nature. But they will only take root when conditions are right. Each innovation has undoubtedly sprouted in other, maybe all, varieties of CEC. But the question remains, why have they not taken root everywhere? Or again, why have they taken root so tenaciously in PIC? The cerebral linguist is at a loss to answer these questions. But a sociologist will point out some facts about Providence Island which, although independent of the foregoing linguistic observations, coincide with them more neatly than chance would have it.

A first fact: The foundation of the Providence Island community was laid according to the basic West Indian blueprint. There were the well-moneyed and landed British who set the limits within which the black slaves could function (Mintz and Price 1976). But because of the geographical isolation of the island, the ties of the landowners to Britain, characteristically

strong in other British West Indian communities (Mintz 1971),
were weakened. Accordingly, the Providence Island British could
not rejuvenate their social and cultural commitments, not to mention
their political and economic relationships, to the motherland.
The British influence, the British model, the British goal for
social mobility were all drastically attenuated by the simple fact
of geographical isolation.

A second fact: The Providence Island community since its
founding has been held in the political pocket of Colombia. The
last 150 years of its history witness unbroken Colombian hegemony
in Providence Island, and that has to be significant given that
the community is only about 190 years old.

A third fact: The island has spent most of its last 150
years in cultural limbo. The Colombians governed it but did
not, until recently, follow up that governance with social interven-
tions in island affairs. The reason for that is clear enough.
Providence Island is just as geographically removed from Colombia
as it is from the other West Indian communities.

These three facts, when taken together, create the image of
a people who are British enough to know that they do not want
to be identified with Africans (Price 1970), and who are free
enough from Colombia not to be immediately hispanicized. But
they are isolated enough from everyone that all their social and
linguistic models and targets are fuzzy. The islanders' response
to this situation is ambivalent. On the one hand, they are
moving toward the weak and fuzzy model supplied by the British
and, more recently, by American language and culture. This
movement surfaces as decreolization. But, on the other hand,
they are moving toward a distinctive identity which is neither
American nor African. The collocation of unusual linguistic innovations in PIC symbolizes that distinctive identity. Their "innovated"
language shows the people of Providence Island "that they belong
to a place" (LePage 1977:110) which is neither an acrolectal "place"
nor a basilectal "place," neither a "place" with the Anglo, nor a
"place" with the African. Their "innovated" language shows the
people of Providence Island that they belong to a distinct "place"
and that they have a distinct identity.

Such a movement could be unusually strong in Providence
Island where there are not such clear economic and political benefits
to be derived from assimilating to the Anglo model as in other
West Indian communities. The sense of unity and equality of all
islanders (Wilson 1973:44ff.) is stronger in this community which
is not clearly divided by class lines (Davenport 1961). So, the
pressure to establish markers of their identity and their unity is
strong in Providence Island, and that pressure fertilizes the ground
in which innovations sprout. The maintenance of these natural
changes in Providence Island is a product, not of cerebral forces,
but of a suitable social situation for the nurturing of innovations.

With this analysis I am not impugning Bickerton's distinction
between natural change and decreolization. It is certainly helpful
to see how innovations originate. But I am arguing that he has

carried the distinction too far by arguing that "natural change" proceeds without influence from social factors. My argument is that no innovation is maintained in a language without some pressure from factors external to the brain.

FOOTNOTES

[1] I am aware of the controversy which has been engendered by Koerner's talk (1972) of a Saussurean-Chomskyan paradigm. But I doubt that my adoption of Koerner's notion for rhetorical and heuristic purposes affects the substance of my argument.

The historiographical analysis outlined here is more fully explicated in Washabaugh (1974; 1976).

[2] As I have indicated in Washabaugh (1976), Saussure's notion of the sociality of language is irremediably flawed. Specifically, the idea that the sociality of *la langue* consists in its distribution to each member of the language community is an overly mechanical concept of sociality. So when I suggest that we must return to Saussure's seminal observation that *la langue* is a social fact, I mean only that we must return to the spirit of that observation, not to its substance.

[3] Bickerton argues that sentence (1) contains an embedded sentence whose verb *go* is combined with the modal auxiliary *fi* and which is marked for anterior aspect by *men*. I, on the other hand, have argued that *fi* in (1) is an infinitive marker bearing the force of a deleted verb which is marked for past tense (or anterior aspect).

Bickerton argues against my analysis by citing evidence to show that nonfinite sentences do not exist in contemporary CEC basilects. Another way of stating this same claim is to say that CEC basilects lack a raising transformation which would move a subject out of an embedded clause leaving the verb subjectless or nonfinite. But I have strong doubts about this claim.

My doubts should not be misconstrued as the obverse of a belief that all *fi*'s, aside from *fi* prepositions, are infinitive markers. I do not subscribe to such a claim. In fact, I have argued at length (Washabaugh 1975) that in historical basilects of CEC, now irrecoverably eroded, *fi* was not an infinitive marker. I argued, using sentences like (9), that *fi* is a complementizer which marks a sentence from which the subject has not been raised. My argument is that (9) is a sentence in which the *fi* complementizer marks an embedded finite sentence.

(9) *Ah waan di rien kom fi ah don go huoam* (PIC).
I want the rain to come so that I won't have to go home.

Sentences like (9) are rare in most contemporary varieties of CEC, but they are frequent enough in older texts. The frequency of sentences like (9) in older texts warrants the claim that the *fi* infinitive marker, which is so prevalent in all varieties of CEC, derives from the *fi* which in the past marked embedded finite verbs. That latter *fi* in turn is derived from a preposition. In sentences like (9), *fi* is a complementizer, the use of which does not imply the application of a raising transformation. All other uses of the *fi* complementizer of which I am aware do imply an application of a raising transformation.

That having been said, let us consider Bickerton's argument that raising does not apply in other types of *fi* sentences in CEC basilects. First, he presents the sentence (10) (see his p. 8) to demonstrate that the pronoun of an embedded sentence could not have been raised. By observing that the presence of the pronoun *am* renders sentence (10) ungrammatical, Bickerton concludes that subject to object (S-O) raising cannot apply in GC. One might extent this same sort of argument to the French sentence *je crois qu'il est riche*, and one might conclude that because **je le crois etre riche* is ungrammatical, that French lacks S-O raising. But such an argument would overlook the acceptability of *je le crois riche* which indicates that raising apples in French under certain conditions which need not be specified in English (Eckman 1975). Bickerton's sentence (10b) seems to be ungrammatical for just the same sort of reason that is, (10b) is ungrammatical not because (SO) raising is unavailable in GC, but because the raising of *am* without deletion of the aspect marker *a* violates the universal "specified subject constraint."

(10) a. *Mi sii i a kom.*
      I saw him coming.
   b. **Mi sii am a kom.*
(11) *Mi sii im kom.*
   I saw him coming.

Second, Bickerton has tried to maintain his claim that raising cannot apply in CEC by parrying my argument that the applicability of S-S raising in CEC, as in (12), implies the applicability of S-O raising (Eckman 1975). Bickerton (1977c:355) replies to this argument that S-S may apply at the mesolectal level and still be inapplicable at the basilectal level. And so, by reason of the variability in the creole continuum, the implicational relationship between S-S and S-O raising does not hold. My rebuttal to Bickerton's reply is that whereas the implicational relationship may not hold for the creole continuum, it should hold for individuals within the continuum. So, for example, sentence (13) is produced by Miss Kate, an 80-year-old Bottomhouse woman, whose speech I would impressionistically classify as basilectal. But Miss Kate also produced sentence (12), and regularly produces such sentences, in which S-S raising has been applied. Now if Miss Kate has acquired an ability to apply S-S raising systematically, she should, by implication, also have an ability to apply S-O raising. I suggest that sentence (13) is just such an example of a sentence in which S-O raising has been applied.

(12) *I (gras) haad fi ded.*
    That grass doesn't die easily.
(13) *Ai ekspek me fi go tu mista R. haus yeside.*
    I expected to go to Mr. R.'s house yesterday.

But perhaps Bickerton would want to argue that even if Miss Kate could apply both S-O and S-S raising, sentence (13) is not a sentence in which either raising has been applied. Perhaps he would want to argue that whereas *fi* in some sentences is re-analyzed as a complementizer, the *fi* in sentences like (13) is still a verb. Such a situation of incomplete reanalysis of a formative is not unknown for creoles (Roberts 1975).

However, such a suggestion would be most unlikely unless Bickerton would be willing to argue that some *fi*'s, and their *to* reflexes, are never reanalyzed within the creole continuum. For it is a fact that sentences like (14) appear everywhere in the Providence Island continuum through to the acrolect. In such sentences the *men* and *fi* are replaced by *waz* and *tu* , but the sentences nevertheless exhibit the same structural arrangement of formatives as those of (13) and (8). Unless Bickerton is willing to argue that *tu* in the sentences (14a) and (14b) is a verb, then his argument will founder on those sentences. My description of the structure of (8) is that it contains an infinitive marker *fi*; I would carry over that same argument and apply it to (14), saying that *tu* in these sentences is an infinitive marker.

(14) a. *I told you was to invite Bill.*
    b. *You promise was to sell me some coconut.*

I will admit that the variability of structures in the creole continuum places formidable methodological obstacles in the way of cogent syntactic argumentation. So formidable are they that Bickerton's own arguments against the applicability of S-O raising in CEC occasionally trip over them. Bickerton argues that the pronoun in sentence (9) above is not raised out of the embedded sentence. (He argues this despite the fact that this is a sentence which I already grant that raising does not apply to.) But his argument against raising is based on the fact that the pronoun following *fi* exhibits a subjective rather than an objective form. This is the weakest of his arguments, for Bickerton should recognize that the form of a pronoun in PIC is highly variable and certainly subject to some hypercorrection. So at the basilect level there is no *ah/mi* pronominal distiction, as in sentence (15); at another level of the continuum the use of *ah* may be over-generalized as in the nearly acrolectal (16). Sentence (16), along with the collection of sentences like (9) which appears in Washabaugh (1975:118), should be sufficient to illustrate that the forms of pronouns in PIC are highly variable and will not provide any firm foundation for a syntactic argument.

(15) *Di bwai kos mi se mi krebm.*
     The boy cussed me saying that I am craven.
(16) *Yu gaiz nat fier.   Un wudn let ai vuoat.*
     You guys are not fair.   You wouldn't let me vote.

On a number of counts then, Bickerton's case against raising in CEC is weak.   First, his evidence for the inapplicability of raising in GC is too restricted.   Second, his argument that the variability of the creole continuum nullifies the implicational relationship between S-S and S-O raising founders on the observation that both types of raising are applied by a single individual who frequently uses the *men fi* construction.   Third, his argument that *fi* in CEC undergoes reanalysis from a verb to an infinitive marker, and that, as reanalysis proceeds, the *men fi* construction is lost, fails to account for the existence of the structurally similar *waz tu* construction throughout the creole continuum.

My analysis of the *men fi* construction avoids, on the one hand, all these difficulties, and yet it accords, on the other hand, with a variety of facts besides those which directly motivate it.   First, my analysis accounts as neatly as Bickerton's for the fact that the *men fi* construction never occurs without the application of EQUI deletion to the clause marked by *fi*.   Let me demonstrate the argument with sentence (17).   Bickerton's hypothetical sentence (17a) is ungrammatical because such a sentence would have to be derived from something like (yong mahn past-se)$_{S3}$(mi past-oblige)$_{S2}$(fi me past-tel yu)$_{S1}$.   But such an underlying string could never be generated because of a selection restriction on *oblige* which requires that its subject and the subject of the caluse which it dominates be identical (Perlmutter 1971:9f.).   Note, however, that a sentence like (17b) is grammatical because it is derived from (yong mahn past-se)$_{S3}$(mi past-oblige)$_{S2}$(fi me past-tel yu)$_{S1}$ which does not violate such a selectional restriction.   The postulation of an underlying abstract verb *oblige* was independently motivated in Washabaugh (1975).   The task of accounting for the ungrammaticality of (17a) follows straight-forwardly from that argument and observes that if the verb dominating *fi* is *oblige*, then the subject of the clause dominated by *oblige* will always be subject to EQUI deletion because of the "like subjects constraint" attached to *oblige*.

(17) a.   **Yong mahn se men fi mi tel yu se mis missi ded.*
     b.   *Yong mahn se mi men fi tel yu se mis missi ded.*
          The young man said that I should tell you that Miss Missi is dead.

Second, I claim that the *fi* infinitive marker in (8) exhibits a certain verbiness only because it shares the force of a deleted verb.   This claim accords with Huddleston's (1971:295) analysis of *to* in English (18) which also has a certain verbiness about it. Huddleston argues that the *to* in (18) is an infinitive marker, and that the *are* is a modal auxiliary. Would Bickerton contravene that argument and say that for English (18), as he has for PIC (14), the *to* is a verb?

(18) You're to leave immediately.

Finally, my claim that the *fi* complementizer in (8) derives historically from a preposition rather than from a verb squares with masses of evidence which have demonstrated affinities between complementizers and prepositions (Washabaugh 1975: 134).

REFERENCES

Bailey, Charles-James. 1973. "The state of 'steady': aspectual marking in Black English." Paper presented at the convention of the Linguistic Society of America, Philadelphia.

Bickerton, Derek. 1973. "The nature of a Creole continuum." *Language* 49:640-669.

Bickerton, Derek. 1973. "Creolization, linguistic universals, natural semantax, and the brain." *University of Hawaii Working Papers in Linguistics* 6:3.124-141.

Bickerton, Derek. 1975. *Dynamics of a Creole System*. London and New York: Cambridge University Press.

Bickerton, Derek. 1976. "Creole tense-aspect systems and universal grammar." Paper presented at the conference of the Society of Caribbean Linguistics, Georgetown, Guyana.

Bickerton, Derek. 1977. "Pidginization and Creolization: Language acquisition and language universals." In *Pidgin and Creole Linguistics*. Ed. by Albert Valdman, pp. 49-69. Bloomington, IN: Indiana University Press.

Bickerton, Derek. 1979. "Putting back the clock in variation studies." *Language* 53.353-361.

Coward, Rosalind, and John Ellis. 1977. *Language and Materialism: Developments in Semiology and the Theory of the Subject*. Boston: Routledge and Kegan Paul.

Davenport, W. 1961. Introduction. *Social and Economic Studies* 10(4).

Eckman, Fred. 1975. "On explaining some typological facts about raising." Paper presented at the convention of the Linguistic Society of America, San Francisco.

Hughes, H. Stuart. 1961. *Consciousness and Society: The Reorientation of European Thought 1890-1930*. New York: Knopf.

Koerner, F. F. K. 1972. "Towards a historiography of linguistics." *Anthropological Linguistics* 14.255-275.

Koerner, F. F. K. 1973. *Ferdinand de Saussure: Origin and Development of His Linguistic Thought in Western Studies of Language*. Braunschweig: Viewig.

LePage, Robert B. 1977. "De-creolization and Re-creolization." *York Papers in Linguistics* 7.103-128.

LePage, Robert B., and Frederic G. Cassidy. 1967. *Dictionary of Jamaican English*. New York: Cambridge University Press.

Merleau-Ponty, Maurice. 1964. *Signs*. Evanston: Northwestern University Press.

Mintz, Sidney W. 1971. "The socio-historical background of pidginization and creolization." In *Pidginization and Creolization of Languages*. Ed. by Dell Hymes, pp. 481-496. London: Cambridge University Press.

Mintz, Sidney W., and R. Price. 1976. *An Anthropological Approach to the Afro-American Past: A Caribbean Perspective*. Philadelphia: Ishi.

Perlmutter, David M. 1971. *Deep and Surface Structure Constraints in Syntax*. New York: Holt, Rinehart and Winston.

Price, Thomas. 1970. "Ethno-history and self-image in three New World Negro societies." In *Afro-American Anthropology*. Ed. by N. Whitten and J. Szwed. New York: The Free Press.

Roberts, Peter. "The adequacy of certain theories in accounting for important grammatical relationships in creole languages." Paper presented at the International Conference on Pidgins and Creoles, Honolulu, Hawaii.

Roberts, Peter. 1977. "*Duont*: A case for spontaneous development." *Journal of Creole Studies* 1.1.101-108.

Roche, Maurice. 1973. *Phenomenology. Language and the Social Sciences*. Boston: Routledge and Kegan Paul.

Saussure, Ferdinand de. 1974. Notes inedits sur Linguistique Generale. Fascicle 4 of *Cours de Linguistique Generale, Edition Critique par R. Engler*. Wiesbaden: Harrossowitz.

Taylor, Douglas. 1977. *Languages of the West Indies*. Baltimore: Johns Hopkins University Press.

Washabaugh, William. 1974. "Saussure, Durkheim and sociolinguistic theory." *Archivum Linguisticum* 5.25-34.

Washabaugh, William. 1975. "On the development of complementizers in creolization." *Working Papers on Language Universals* 17.109-140.

Washabaugh, William. 1976. "The history of linguistics and the theoretical status of inherent variability." *Proceedings of the Mid-America Linguistics Conference*, pp. 515-554. Lawrence, KS: University of Kansas Press.

Washabaugh, William. 1977. "A note on 'duont'." Mimeographed.

Washabaugh, William. 1978. "Complexities in creole continua." *Lingua* 46.245-261.

Wilson, Peter. 1973. *Crab Antics*. New Haven: Yale University Press.

DIALECTS AND EDUCATION

Prescribed space restrictions at first seemed to dictate dropping the proposed section on Dialects and Education. But some excision elsewhere made possible the retention of at least three desirable articles.

As Riley Smith and Donald Lance suggest in the first article, school recognition of language variation has until recently existed only in terms of absolute contrast between "Good English" and "Bad English." Bad English included the whole range of regional and social variation, along with various colloquialisms and, of course, slang. More than one textbook author allowed personal prejudice and regional bias to enter into a decision about words and forms to be condemned. A speech director of New York City listed the common pronunciation of post-vocalic and vowel /r/ as inexpressibly vulgar; and one textbook writer, surely a Midland speaker, must have begun a textbook trend by listing as undesirable the Northern *sick to the stomach* in contrast to his presumably acceptable Midland *sick at the stomach*.

In the 1930's the so-called Battle of Usage, heralded by Charles C. Fries's *Teaching of the English Language* in 1927 and speared by the NCTE monograph by Sterling Andrus Leonard, *Current English Usage*, in 1933, did stress that some "Bad English" items were in good use, but the social range of regional variation was ignored.

Indeed, it was Kurath's *Linguistic Atlas of New England* and the derivative publications by Kurath, McDavid, and Atwood that finally made possible a factual treatment of American dialects in schoolbooks. McDavid's chapter in W. Nelson Francis's *The Structure of American English* in 1958 helped to make knowledgeable the several thousand English teachers for whom the book had been a classroom text. The senior editor of this collection early sought to encourage English teachers to include discussion of regional variation with an article, "The linguistic atlases: our new resource" (*English Journal* 45 (1956):188-194) and to show teachers of English as a second language that such discussion was relevant to them in "Language variety and TESOL" (*TESOL Quarterly* 7 (1973):13-23. The American Dialect Society recently has been presenting programs at the NCTE annual conventions for the purpose of helping teachers to incorporate dialect units in their classes. Recent textbooks now do contain some dialect content, but most ignore it.

Quite the contrary situation obtains with respect to at least one social dialect, that now often called Black Vernacular English or BVE, discussed by several writers in the two preceding sections. The volcanic political situation in the early 1960's created explosive and exploding attention to BVE in the teaching of English and in teacher preparation. A court decision in Ann Arbor, Michigan, adjured teachers to study BVE features as a means of eliminating a negative attitude toward Black students. The Conference on College composition and Communication, a component of NCTE, supported a resolution, as Smith and Lance reported, demanding recognition of BVE and other dialects as valid for student use without prejudice or condemnation. But in 1982 the CCCC executive committee, seeking to avoid a divisive controversy at the 1983 annual convention, tabled a special committee report that called for implementing the resolution by wide-front action in teacher preparation, textbook writing, and community involvement.

Among the authors listed in the Smith and Lance bibliography the following are recommended for relevant further reading: Abrahams, Dillard, Fasold and Shuy, Smith, and Wolfram and Fasold.

A heretofore unconsidered aspect of the BVE issue in the schools is treated by the junior editor and Gene Piché. It is clear that there is a correlation between the acceptance of BVE as a valid dialect and the attitude of white students toward the speakers of Black English. That there is some indication of greater acceptance in recent years may be taken as encouraging.

Then an educational issue lacking conspicuous public attention but clearly of critical importance to thousands of Americans is presented in the article by William Leap. Although this anthology does not focus upon bilingual education as such, it is certainly relevant to bilingual education that a social dialect is being produced by the influence of native Indian speech upon English. Leap's article raises the pertinent question whether this social dialect is not entitled to the same consideration that is sought for BVE as a valid language variety.

STANDARD AND DISPARATE VARIETIES

OF ENGLISH IN THE UNITED STATES:

EDUCATIONAL AND SOCIOPOLITICAL

IMPLICATIONS

Riley B. Smith and Donald M. Lance

There are fewer varieties[1] of the national language in the United States, showing fewer differences among each other and diverging less from the standard, than is the case in any other industrialized nation.   There exist, in addition, both a national standard and several regional standards of American English whose norms may, but seldom do, conflict with each other.   Language varieties are not only to some extent socioregional, as in England - reflecting class membership as well as region of domicile (Halliday et al. 1964:18) - but also, when they do survive pressures toward language conformity, are increasingly socioethnic - reflecting both class membership and ethnic identity (Labov 1972:300).   And since America is perhaps unique in the intensity with which it perceives schooling as the principal agent of benevolent social change through class leveling (Marckwardt 1973:206), the persistence of some language varieties is widely interpreted as a social problem, reflecting an ethnic diversity which is undesirable because it marks a rejection of the dominant cultural values and is of itself a denial of an important American myth: cultural uniformization through mere exposure.

These American peculiarities can best be described by briefly tracing them to (1) the historical settlement of North America and to subsequent internal migration, (2) the dynamics of American social attitudes which are partly a function of demographic history and (3) developments in dialect research and official policy toward language variety - principally recent ones touching on education.

The first settlers in what is now the United States were overwhelmingly English-speaking (Bähr 1974:196) - significant exceptions being Dutch speakers in the Hudson Valley and in New York City, German speakers primarily in Pennsylvania, and Black

From *International Journal of the Sociology of Language* 21:127-140, 1979. Reprinted with permission.

speakers of various west African languages (and Pidgin English)
mainly in the coastal South (Dillard 1972). But unlike most
other languages in North America, English remained part of its
larger linguistic community - dominated, in this case, by the
speech of London and southeastern England - for well over a
century, or until after the revolution of 1776 (Williams 1975:105).
American English was thus a participant in the eighteenth century
rush toward standardization (Halle and Keyser 1971:124) which
grew out of the English Industrial Revolution, with its attendant
urbanization and upheaval of social class structure. But the
English of America already showed far greater homogeneity, both
geographically and socially, than did that of the mother country,
despite the fact that English-speaking settlers came from many
regions of the British Isles, from many social classes, and from
both urban and rural societies (McDavid 1973:7-8). That it so
quickly achieved much more than a spoken interintelligibility over
a wide area must be attributed largely to the massive population
mixtures in settlement patterns and to the unprecedented geographical and social mobility of the American people.[2]

The standardization process, i.e., the acceptance and codification of a norm based on the vernacular language of the culturally
dominant people (Haugen 1966:98), was comparatively uncomplex
in the case of American English, then, because it was in many
respects virtually complete by the time of independence. The
retention of some regional differences was assured by the great
distances between early population centers, as well as by the
strong feelings of distinction which had always existed among the
former colonies. The survival, moreover, of a few minor and
unthreatening language communities within the United States, some
of them kept alive only through continuing immigration and surviving in spite of strong assimilationist pressures, perhaps contributed to a general toleration of what diversity there was within
the English language. America's literary and linguistic legacy
from Britain could never, of course, be completely denied,[3] in
spite of the intensity of cultural separatist feelings throughout
the nineteenth century. The United States, alone among the
major industrialized nations, has a colonial and *Abstand* language
(Kloss 1967).[4] But because of the nation's early political break
with Europe and its two centuries of separate, often self-preoccu-
pied, development, it has almost completely escaped domination
by the standard language of the mother country - a dependency
which burdens Australian English to this day (Platt and Platt
1975:43 ff).

In its national context, standard American English is a norm
referring almost exclusively to those forms of inflectional morphology and syntax which are universally undenigrated. In these
respects it differs but in minor details from the norm accepted
elsewhere in the English-speaking world. Pronunciation, on the
other hand, though it has always had some social significance
nationally - the range of acceptable variation being ultimately limited - is a largely regional matter.[5] In the national context,

disparate pronunciations, provided they can be associated primarily with region, are generally tolerated and often even expected. Phonetic and phonological divergences from a supraregional pronunciation norm – though the existence of such a norm has never been strongly claimed except by foreigners – do not approach being the social markers in America that they are in Britain; no American *accent* has the prestige of RP (Halliday et al. 1964:18).

Of those features which count as markers of acceptability within the standard, lexis seems to rank high only in those societies where diglossia either obtains or is approached. Although it is normally weaker than either morpho-syntactic or phonological markers, vocabulary does have some stigmatizing potential in most of the other developed nations, especially the English-speaking ones. This contrasts markedly with the situation in the United States, where the word as such plays little role as a social marker. This fact is reflected in American dictionaries and lexicons, where, as Atwood notes (1963:180), 'there is little distinction between dialect and standard speech'. In the public mind, very few items of vocabulary are ever marked, in and of themselves, simply 'nonstandard' and hence dismissed as unacceptable for use (except under unusual circumstances). Words recognized as divergent are sometimes identified as regionalisms, but even these are seldom thought to exist apart from the acceptable word-stock of the language – no matter how rustic their connotation. If such words are in widespread use, they are normally tagged as vernacular colloquialisms at various levels of informal style, some of them highly innovative, some now primarily associated with specific ethnic groups.[6] There is the general feeling among Americans that the word-stock of their language – no matter how restricted individual words may be to particular levels of style, usage or 'register' – is a common storehouse to which every speaker has at least access, his word choice being dependent merely on the range of his stylistic repertory.[7]

Indirect evidence of this feeling is the outrage which greeted *Webster's Third New International Dictionary* (1961), an outrage now largely attributable to the editorial abandonment of many of the traditional lexicological 'status labels', markers felt to be indispensable clues to the area of a word's *stylistic*, not of its *general*, acceptability, or to its range of usage appropriateness (Wells 1973). That the naked word – apart from grammatical contextual or phonological factors – is rarely sufficient of itself to signal either acceptability or opprobrium with respect to the standard language can be demonstrated by looking at those few items which even *Webster's Third* felt obliged to tag with its few 'status labels'.[8] The overwhelming majority deviate from the standard either in their inflectional-morphological structure or in their syntactic relationships; a few merely reflect phonological deviations from the standard. But virtually all violate canons of the national standard other than the purely lexical, and it is to these violations that their unqualified exclusion from the standard language must

be attributed. Even slang, that almost peculiarly American lexical
category, derives its connotations from other than purely lexical
factors.

Standard American English is a rather imprecisely definable
notion, then, which encompasses those forms of the language
which are nationally accepted: the national *Schriftsprache* in a
wide range of styles and almost all regional forms of the spoken
language which do not violate the canons of this written language.
Those linguists who deny the existence of an American national
standard (McDavid 1966:38 ff) include pronunciation as one of
the main linguistic elements figuring in judgments concerning standardization in general, and, from a nationwide perspective, it is
clearly not the case that pronunciation should be so included.
The confusion made here is of the regional 'standard' of the *speech
community* - more sensitive to oral markers of social diagnosticity
(Bailey 1973b:65) - with the more general standard of the larger
language community - in this case the nation - in relation to which
the standard language is normally defined.   Since standardization
in America never went through those processes which normally
give rise to *accent* - that 'compromise between the standard language and the dialect' (Leopold 1959:362), which refers to the
phonetic features of one's native dialect when speaking the standard
language - *accent* in American has been elevated, not only by
scholars but to some extent in the public mind, to *dialect*.
These terms themselves are now hardly distinguished except on
the connotative level, since the 'water[ing] down' of a '*dialect* to
an *accent*' (Haugen 1966:100) had never been much of a dilution
to begin with.

The study of American English dialects has a respectable
history in that it was not initiated, and until recent times has
not been sustained, by clearly perceived political or educational
motives.   Although early studies of regional speech - a milestone
being the founding, in 1887, of the American Dialect Society - seem
to have been largely the result, after the British example, of
antiquarian interests,[9] research in regional dialects shortly came
under the influence of the essentially philological traditions of
European dialect geography.   Field and analytic techniques which
had been developed in Europe were transplanted, and some modifications were made to sensitize the linguistic corpus to the more
fluid North American social structure.   Their first fruit was
Linguistic Atlas of New England (Kurath et al. 1939-1943); plans
were also laid during the 1930s - the decade of the zenith of
scholarly interest and activity in this tradition - for further research.   Until the 1960s, however, the most interesting and influential dialect studies were those which grew directly from the
earliest field work in the eastern United States (Kurath 1949;
Atwood 1953; Kurath and McDavid 1961).   Although a large number
of projects have been and continue to be carried through (Cassidy
1973), research activities within this tradition progressively waned
for complex reasons - the most important ones being methodological
and philosophical.

For our purposes, the important findings of this research are as follows. On the basis of the clustering of lexical isoglosses, three major speech areas of the eastern United States were delimited, and eighteen minor ones (Kurath 1949:fig. 3).[10]   The existence of a variety of English traditionally termed 'General American' was hereby unfounded and denied (though see Van Riper 1973 for a history of the persistence, despite some 'ambiguity', of the term). In addition, a 'Midland' dialect was clearly set off from a 'Northern' one, eastern New England speech and the speech of New York City were grouped with other 'Northern' dialects in a major area, and the dialects of the Appalachian region were declared to be 'Midland' rather than 'Southern'. Although Kurath's basic regional divisions have influenced almost every publication on the topic of American English since, they have never been uncritically accepted, either in the public mind or by students of American English. In view especially of our current knowledge of the complexities of language variation, linguists generally agree that emphasis on the geographical aspects of dialects is, at best, misleading.

Apart from these complexities, there was also a mismatch between the methodology of European dialectology and the facts of the American linguistic situation which no technical modifications in the field work could correct. Not only was American folk language, by the time of the survey, 'highly undifferentiated' (Weinreich 1954:310, fn. 20), but the influence of the standard language on dialect informants, no matter how carefully chosen on the basis of their isolation, was unavoidable. The ultimate unfruitfulness of Kurathian dialectology, for either historical or sociolinguistic enlightenment, is traceable to its failure to disclose patterns of internal variation, largely in the urban centers of the North (Maurer 1969). For this, entirely new research methods needed to be developed.

If the Kurathian tradition of empirical research in language variation is termed 'philological', then the impetus behind the second burst of scholarly interest and research in language variation, which reached its peak in the late 1960s and early 1970s, might be termed 'sociological'. Though conscious of its debts to Kurath and the European tradition, this new wave of research, dominated by William Labov, developed a new approach toward the solution of the problems of urban language variation. Labov sought to discover and formalize principles of the social dynamics of both language change (1963) and the synchronic fluctuation of language varieties (1966), and he found those patterns by correlating individual speech variations - largely phonetic - with separatedly defined social and stylistic parameters.

The linguistic sophistication of the urban research of Labov and his colleagues triggered an interest in what are now called 'social dialects' (Wolfram and Fasold 1974:33) - virtually a codeword for the variety of English spoken by the majority of Black people throughout the United States.[11]   (For reviews of the historical connections between Black English studies and develop-

ments in sociolinguistics, see Smith 1976; Dittmar 1976:240-249.)
The concurrent widening of the research interests of Caribbean
creolists to include American Black English contributed to an
intensification of this research focus (Dillard 1972). But it was
the historical and social facts themselves, the massive out-migration
of Southerners, mainly Black, during and after World War II
which kept the attention of American linguists directed toward
'social dialects'.

The social problems which this migration led to were immense,
and, by the late 1950s and the early 1960s, some of its effects
were realized in the educational failure of Black children. Because
of the strong American traditions of schooling as – at its most
basic level – instruction in the standard language (Marckwardt
1973:204), this failure was perceived as correctable only through
a variety of special language programs. That so much financial
support was available, from both government agencies and private-
foundations, for research in 'social dialects' eventually advanced
our knowledge of Black English and ultimately furthered research
in sociolinguistics; it also attests to the educational and social
importance ascribed to this demographic problem.

We now know that population resettlements on a large enough
scale can restructure the social hierarchy of language varieties
within the speech community, the usual pattern being for negative
attitudes to be either strengthened or created anew toward the
language of the immigrant population (DeCamp 1959:596). This
is what happened in the case of Southern varieties of English
transplanted in the North and West. Of these varieties, Black
English, with its apparent morphological and syntactic differences
from standard English, was marked as clearly nonstandard and
its speakers as uneducated. Since education is the first step,
though a major one, toward the American goal of assimilation,
the persistence of social and educational problems surrounding
urban Blacks in the North (now coupled with understandable
movements for ethnic identity) corroborated for most Americans
the direct connection between nonstandard English and ineducabil-
ity. This one variety of English has become, not surprisingly,
essentially a socioethnic dialect of Black culture, with a marked
uniformity throughout the United States. It is now virtually a
'caste dialect' (Labov 1972:299) whose identity is further confirmed
when described as a system of speaking behavior (Abrahams 1973:
228).

The role of the school in English-language instruction to native
speakers, traditionally unquestioned in its insistence on the primacy
of standard English, came under attack, in the late 1960s, from
the entire American linguistics establishment (Center for Applied
Linguistics 1974:1 ff), which condemned traditional methods as
'eradicationist' (Fasold and Shuy 1970:ix). More sharply attacked
as even more repressive (Labov 1969) were the various 'compensa-
tory' language programs developed in response to the educational
failure of 'disadvantaged' lower-class – mainly Black – children.
A number of alternative proposals were made and experimented

with by linguists, their overt goals ranging from (1) developing 'bidialectalism' to (2) developing literacy through the use of specially devised 'dialect readers' to (3) motivating the student toward literacy and a general appreciation of the written language by creating a pride in his own vernacular (Smith 1976:27 ff).

These proposals all represent the positions of factions spread along a generally *liberal* political continuum: they have in common a belief that the associations of language variety and social-class membership (or ethnicity) are accidental rather than essential. Educational approaches to nonstandard varieties based on the contrary belief - either a traditional one or any of the versions of the language-deficit hypothesis advanced by Bernstein (Trudgill 1974:52 ff) - were damaging to the nonstandard speaker's self-esteem, in this view, and merely contributed, through the process of 'stereotyping' (Abrahams 1969:11), to the perpetuation of this association of language and class. The only educational policy which might be effective in breaking down the linguistic support of class divisions, then, would be one which sought to divest language varieties of their accidental associations of prestige or denigration. Only the most extreme liberal position treats ethnic or linguistic diversity as a positive political or social goal, the promotion of linguistic pride in speakers of nonstandard varieties being merely a necessary stage in any program having as its goal the 'leveling' of language attitudes. It is this attack exclusively on language attitudes, which are seen as pernicious but ultimately vulnerable, that characterizes the most radical of these liberal positions. But none of these factions ignores language attitudes as a social and educational problem.

The recent emphasis by empirical linguists on attitudinal studies (Ford 1974) - and the neglect of purely descriptive studies - bears further witness to the dominance of this liberal position among American linguists. Marxist critics of the American sociolinguistic scene (Dittmar 1975; 1976) are only partly correct in ascribing to them the view that the social system is 'stable and permanent' (1975:249), and that such linguistic phenomena as *prestige*, *stigmatization*, and *hypercorrection* are to be treated as natural 'facts isolated from the social system' (1975:264). And they are quite wrong in their assertion that American sociolinguists are socially 'unconcern[ed]' (1976:245).

One important resolution with respect to nonstandard dialects of English, that which was adopted in 1974 by the Conference on College Composition and Communication (*College Composition and Communication*, 1974) - an important branch of the prestigious National Council of Teachers of English - can be understood only in this somewhat political context.[12] It represents the leftmost position of American linguists and educationists with respect to nonstandard language. Otherwise, it is a remarkable document only because it is a pedagogical *mea culpa* and promulgates views at variance with those which one normally associates with English teachers and their organizations. Stewart (1974) may be correct in his prediction that the resolution will have a counter-productive effect. More likely it will simply come to naught, since the effects of teaching, either on the general level of language skills or on language attitudes, are usually overstated by teachers themselves.

Regardless of the policy which American education ultimately adopts toward nonstandard language, it will probably have less effect either than its advocates wish or than its opponents fear. It will almost certainly not arrive again at an unequivocal 'eradicationist' policy - either traditional or Marxist. The liberal tradition seems too firmly rooted in American education for such a radical change. But both the public school and higher education in American have long served as responsive and often willing agents for the correction of what are perceived as social ills not touching on their main business (e.g., busing, Affirmative Action), and a general reaction can already be seen to have set in. Especially vulnerable to the destructive impact of such a reaction is the public school, more directly controlled by and thus more responsive to conservative social elements than higher education.

'Social change comes before, not after, language change', says James Sledd (Murphy and Ornstein 1976:451), and Jencks is convincing in his demonstration that there are 'rather modest relationships [in America] between schooling on the one hand and status and income on the other' (Jencks et al. 1972:11). A language education policy, no matter how well conceived and implemented, will never 'overcome racial prejudice [n] or do away with economic and social injustice' (Spolsky 1971:5). Skeptical though we are that a language policy can have more than a negligible effect on language attitudes, we would like to believe that linguistics can make a contribution to both the general enlightenment and curing of some of society's ills. Conscience constrains us, in any event, to condemn policies which we judge to be either wrongheaded in conception or unjust in their effects.

Whether language varieties will continue to be leveled toward the standard in America, or whether some varieties will be stabilized in contrast with the standard - this may be a social question with respect to whose outcome neither linguists nor educators hold very strong hands. Traditional demographic tendencies favor continued leveling, whereas some social realignments in modern industrial societies seem to favor the revitalization of certain language varieties (Cooper and Fishman 1974:9). But from a social point of view this is essentially an unimportant question. The paucity of varieties of English in America, in contrast with the large number or varieties of the national language in other large industrialized nations, fails to mirror a concomitant social equality. With Halliday, we hold that 'wherever human behavior is perceived as variable, social value tends to attach to the variants; language is no exception' (1974:190). It is unlikely that language variation, even in America, will ever be so leveled as to defy perception.

FOOTNOTES

[1] We use the term *variety* instead of *dialect* only partly because of the pejorative connotations of the latter (see Haugen, 1966:100). The sociolinguistic phenomena themselves are different enough in America to need a different term.

[2] McDavid points out that the varieties of English in America were never so disparate as in England from the beginnings of the settlement because (1) village life, which alone normally provides for the survival of dialects in most nations, never took root in English-speaking America (1971:48-50), and (2) neither the rural peasantry nor the upper classes were represented in any numbers among the colonists (1973:7-8). Cassidy links the rapid leveling of varieties to the normal 'social realignments' which take place in 'developing colonies', the 'aberrant speech characteristics [being] rubbed away while the broad similarities are generalized' (1973:77).

[3] For an account of early American efforts toward standardization, especially the influence of Noah Webster, who supported vernacular underpinnings (as opposed to almost every other American of rank - Thomas Jefferson excepted - who looked to the authority of British speech and letters for their models), see Mencken (1963:3-30).

[4] With the possible exception of the Gullah dialect, all varieties of spoken English in America have been subsumed under the general rubric 'English'. The recent 'creolist' position that Black English should be recognized, for structural reasons, as a separate system (Dillard 1972) has been neither accepted nor indeed understood by society at large - most notably not by the Black community itself.

[5] This generalization must be read in its contrastive context. Labov has shown (1966) how even minor differences in pronunciation have, on a regional level, considerable social signifcance. And some regional pronunciations - e.g., the epenthetic vowels in *athlete*, *film*, *elm* (Liles 1972:293), and the excrescent [r] *wash* - may be seen as nationally nonstandard.

[6] English has a history of hospitality to lexical borrowing. American English has especially lacked hostility to alien vocabulary, with respect both to the immigrant languages in its midst and to its own regional and social varieties. Although most American slang, notes Maurer (Mencken 1963:705), 'emerges from the subcultures of the criminal', even this is seen as a vital element in the American vocabulary.

[7] The indifference, or puzzlement, with which American linguists have treated Bernstein's notion of two distinct 'codes' - where the acquisition of a learned vocabulty (as opposed to a strictly native one) plays such a strong role in marking the 'elaborated code' of the middle class - may be partly explained by the American characteristic of having a relatively open wordstock.

[8] As a brief sampling, the items *them* (adj.), *drownded, hisself, oncet* (/ wənzt /), *ain't* (< has/have not), *like to* (=came near), and *substantiate* (with the pronunciation /-nchə wat/) are all marked 'substandard'; *ary* (< ever a), *onliest, knowed, heighth*, *everwho*, and *done* (adv.) are marked 'dialect' but are unqualified as to region.

[9] Folkloristic interests have also played a role in scholarly research in regional American dialects, and some of it has been surprisingly excellent (e.g., Randolph and Wilson 1953).

[10] These major divisions and many of the minor ones were said to be largely confirmed by patterns of pronunciation among 'cultured' informants - 'speakers of the local forms of the standard dialect' (Cassidy 1973:84) - which were abstracted from the earlier lexical survey (Kurath and McDavid 1961:11-22).

[11] Empirical linguists of this 'urban' school have now belatedly turned their attention to the 'social dialects' of whites with such studies as Wolfram and Christian (1976).

[12] The resolution reads as follows: 'We affirm the students' right to their own patterns and varieties of language - the dialects of their nurture or whatever dialects in which they find their own identity and style. Language scholars long ago denied that the myth of a standard American dialect has any validity. The claim that one dialect is unacceptable amounts to an attempt of one social group to exert its dominance over another. Such a claim leads to false advice for speakers and writers, and immoral advice for humans. A nation proud of its diverse heritage and its cultural and racial variety will preserve its heritage of dialects. We affirm strongly that teachers must have the experiences and training that will enable them to respect diversity and uphold the right of students to their own language' (*College Composition and Communication*, 1974:2 ff).

REFERENCES

Abrahams, Roger D. (1969), "Black talk and Black education", *The Florida FL Reporter* 7 (1):10-12.

Abrahams, Roger D. (1973). "'Talking My Talk': Black English and social segregation in Black American communities", *African Language Review* 9 (for 1970-1971):227-254.

Atwood, E. Bagby. (1953). *A Survey of Verb Forms of the Eastern United States*. University of Michigan Press, Ann Arbor.

Atwood, E. Bagby. (1963). "The methods of American dialectology", *Zietschrift für Mundartforschung* 30:1-30. [Cited from rpt. in H. Hungerford, J. Robinson, and J. Sledd, eds. (1970), *English Linguistics*. Scott, Foresman, Glenview, Ill. Pp. 176-216.]

Bähr, Dieter. (1974). *Standard English und seine geograph- ischen Varianten*. Wilhelm Fink Verlag, Munich.

Bailey, Charles-James N. (1973). *Variation and Linguistic Theory*. Center for Applied Linguistics, Arlington, Va.

Cassidy, Frederic G. (1973). "Dialect studies, regional and social", in T. A. Sebeok (ed.), *Trends in Linguistics*, Vol. 10: *Linguistics in North America*, Part I. Mouton, The Hague. Pp. 75-100.

Center for Applied Linguistics. (1974). "LSA reaffirms Labov resolution", *The Linguistic Reporter* 16(3):1, 3, 11.

College Composition and Communication. (1974). "Students' right to their own language", 25 (Special Issue).

Cooper, Robert L., and Fishman, Joshua A. (1974). "The study of language attitudes", *International Journal of the Sociology of Language* 3:5-19.

DeCamp, David. (1959). "The pronunciation of English in San Francisco", *Orbis* 8:54-77. [Cited from rpt. in J. V. Williamson and V. M. Burke, eds. (1971), *A Various Language: Perspectives on American Dialects*. Holt, New York. Pp. 549-69.]

Dillard, J. L. (1972). *Black English: Its History and Usage in the United States*. Random House, New York.

Dittmar, Norbert. (1975). "Sociolinguistics - A neutral or a politically engaged discipline?", *Foundations of Language*. 13: 251-265.

Dittmar, Norbert. (1976). *Sociolinguistics: A Critical Survey of Theory and Application*. Edward Arnold, London.

Fasold, Ralph W., and Shuy, Roger W. (1970). *Teaching Standard English in the Inner City*. Center for Applied Linguistics, Washington, D.C.

Ford, James F. (1974). "Language attitude studies: A Review of selected research", *The Florida FL Reporter* 12(1 & 2): 53-54, 100.

Halle, Morris, and Keyser, Samuel Jay. (1971). *English Stress: Its Form, Its Growth, and Its Role in Verse*. Harper and Row, New York.

Halliday, M. A. K. (1974). "The context of linguistics", in F. P. Dineen, ed., *Linguistics: Teaching and Interdisciplinary Relations*. (Georgetown University Roundtable on Languages and Linguistics) Georgetown University Press, Washington, D. C. Pp. 179-197.

Halliday, M. A. K., McIntosh, Angus, and Strevens, Peter. (1964). *The Linguistic Sciences and Language Teaching*. Longmans, London. [Cited from partial rpt. in R. W. Bailey and J. L. Robinson, eds., (1973), *Varieties of Present-Day English*. Macmillan, New York. Pp. 9-37.]

Haugen, Einar. (1966). "Dialect, language, nation", *American Anthropology* 68:922-935. [Cited from rpt. in J. B. Pride and Janet Holmes, eds., (1972), *Sociolinguistics*. Penguin, Harmondsworth. Pp. 97-111.]

Jencks, Christopher et. al. (1972). *Inequality: A Reassess-
ment of the Effect of Family and Schooling in America.* Pen-
guin, Harmondsworth.
Kloss, Heinz. (1967). "'Abstand' languages and 'Ausbau' lan-
guages", *Anthropological Linguistics* 14 (vii):27-41.
Kurath, Hans. (1949). *A Word Geography of the Eastern United
States.* University of Michigan Press, Ann Arbor.
Kurath, Hans, dir. and ed. et al. (1939-1943). *Linguistic
Atlas of New England,* 3 vols. in 6 fascicles. Brown Univer-
sity, Providence, R.I.
Kurath, Hans and McDavid, Raven I., Jr. (1961). *The Pro-
nunciation of English in the Atlantic States.* University of
Michigan Press, Ann Arbor.
Labov, William. (1963). "The social motivation of a sound
change", *Word* 19:273-309.
Labov, William. (1966). *The Social Stratification of English
in New York City.* Center for Applied Linguistics, Washing-
ton, D.C.
Labov, William. (1969). "The logic of nonstandard English",
The Florida FL Reporter 7(1):60-74, 169.
Labov, William. (1972). *Sociolinguistic Patterns .* University
of Pennsylvania Press, Philadelphia.
Leopold, Werner F. (1959). "The decline of German dialects",
Word 15:130-153. [Cited from rpt. in J. Fishman, ed.
(1968), *Readings in the Sociology of Language.* Mouton,
The Hauge. Pp. 340-364.
Liles, Bruce L. (1972). *Linguistics and the English Language.*
Goodyear Publishing Company, Pacific Palisades, Calif.
Marckwardt, Albert H. (1973). "General educational aims of
native language teaching and learning", in T. A. Sebeok,
ed., *Trends in Linguistics ,* Vol. 10: *Linguistics in North
America,* Part 1. Mouton, The Hague. Pp. 206-227.
Maurer, David W. (1969). "The importance of social dialects",
Newsletter of the American Dialect Society 1(2):1-8.
McDavid, Raven I., Jr. (1966). "Sense and nonsense about
American dialects", *PMLA* 81:7-17. [Cited from rpt. in H. B.
Allen and G. N. Underwood, eds., (1971), *Readings in Amer-
ican Dialectology.* Appleton-Century-Crofts, New York.
Pp. 36-52.]
McDavid, Raven I., Jr. (1971). "The urbanization of American
English", *Jahrbuch für Amerikastudien* 16:47-59.
McDavid, Raven I., Jr. (1973). "The English language in the
United States", in T. A. Sebeok, ed., *Trends in Linguis-
tics,* Vol. 10: *Linguistics in North America ,* Part 1. Mou-
ton, The Hague. Pp. 5-39.
Mencken, H. L. (abridgement by Raven I. McDavid, Jr., with
the assistance of David W. Maurer). (1963). *The American
Language.* Alfred A. Knopf, New York.

Murphy, R. Paul, and Ornstein, Jacob. (1976). "A survey of research on language diversity: A partial who's who in sociolinguistics", in P. A. Reich, ed., *The Second LACUS Forum 1975*. Hornbeam Press, Columbia, S.C. Pp. 423-461.

Platt, John T. and Platt, Heidi K. (1975). *The Social Signifi-cance of Speech*. North Holland Publishing Company, Amsterdam.

Randolph, Vance, and Wilson, George P. (1953). *Down in the Holler: A Gallery of Ozark Folk Speech*. University of Oklahoma Press, Norman.

Smith, Riley B. (1976). "Research perspectives on American Black English: A brief historical sketch", *American Speech* 49:24-39.

Spolsky, Bernard. (1971). "The limits of language educa-tion", *The Linguistic Reporter* 13(3):1-5.

Stewart, William A. (1974). "The laissez-faire movement in English teaching: Advance to the rear?", *The Florida FL Reporter* 12(1 & 2):81-90, 98-99.

Trudgill, Peter. (1974). *Sociolinguistics*. Penguin, Harmonds-worth.

Van Riper, W. R. (1973). "General American: An ambiguity", in H. Scholler and J. Reidy, eds., *Lexicography and Dialect Geography: Festgabe for Hans Kurath*. Franz Steiner Verlag, Wiesbaden. Pp. 232-242. (*ZDL* - Beihefte Nr. 9.)

Webster's Third New International Dictionary (1961). Mass., G. & C. Merriam Company, Springfield.

Weinreich, Uriel. (1954). "Is a structural dialectology possi-ble?", *Word* 10:388-400. [Cited from rpt. in H. B. Allen and G. N. Underwood, eds., (1971), *Readings in American Dia-lectology*. Appleton-Century-Crofts, New York. Pp. 300-313.]

Wells, Ronald A. (1973). *Dictionaries and the Authoritarian Tradition*. Mouton, The Hague.

Williams, Joseph M. (1975). *Origins of the English Language: A Social and Linguistic History*. Free Press, New York.

Wolfram, Walt, and Fasold, Ralph W. (1974). *The Study of Social Dialects in American English*. Prentice-Hall, Engle-wood Cliffs, N.J.

Wolfram, Walt, and Christian, Donna. (1976). *Appalachian Speech*. Center for Applied Linguistics, Arlington, Va.

BLACK AND WHITE ADOLESCENT
AND PREADOLESCENT ATTITUDES
TOWARD BLACK ENGLISH

Michael D. Linn

Gene Piché

Perhaps Professor Higgins' reaction to the speech of Liza Doolittle in George Bernard Shaw's *Pygmalion* is the best-known change of a listener's attitude towards a speaker when he changes dialect. While *Pygmalion* is a fictional account of such changes in attitudes, a number of recent studies furnish evidence that listeners do evaluate a speaker's personality, ethnicity, education, intelligence, and ambition on the basis of relatively small samples of spoken language. More recently, social scientists have argued that spoken language is an identifying feature of members of a national or cultural group and that any listener's attitude toward that group should generalize to the language that the group uses. In effect, "evaluational reactions to a spoken language . . . should be similar to the reactions elicited in an interaction with those perceived as members of a group that uses it" (Anisfeld, Bogo, & Lambert, 1962, p. 223). Because the use of a particular language is a feature of all members of a national or cultural group, any reactions to the language per se should reflect the stereotyped characteristics of the group that speaks it.
This stereotyping appears to be a feature of group prejudices developing in children as early as seven or eight. Allport (1954) found that this ethnocentrism reached its peak at early puberty.
As children grow older, they normally lose this tendency for total rejection and overgeneralization. As Allport writes,
> Thus, after a period of total *rejection*, a stage
> of differentiation sets in. The prejudices grow
> less totalized. Escape clauses are written into
> the attitude in order to make it more rational
> and more acceptable to the individual. (p. 309)
Thus, children, when they are learning adult categories of rejections, are not able to make appropriate subcategories or exceptions.

PURPOSE

The purpose of the present study was to describe the attitudes of black and white, male and female, middle and lower class adolescents and preadolescents to tape-recorded samples of Standard English (SE) and Black English (BE). Specifically, it sought to determine if the major processes of social change have had an effect on black and white Americans. If such changes have altered the attitudes of blacks toward themselves and of whites toward blacks, the changes should be reflected in their attitudes toward BE. This study combines the matched guise technique pioneered by Lambert and the specific language cues of the Labov (1966) studies. In order to determine what stereotypic responses black and white, male and female, adolescents and preadolescents held toward BE, two speech streams were prepared: one in SE and the other in BE. The two were the same except that the one in BE contained the approximate percentages of BE features that Wolfram (1969) described in his Detroit study. Both speech samples were read by three middle class black males into a tape recorder. The speech samples of each reader were separated from his/her other sample by a speech sample of each of the other readers. The tapes were then played to high school and grade school students who then marked their responses on a semantic differential that was developed for this study.

PROCEDURES

A. The Speech Sample

To achieve as natural a simulated casual speech sample as possible, the speech sample of a male high school senior was recorded. Because Shuy, Wolfram, and Riley (1968) found that asking informants to describe recent movies and television programs was a good source of casual speech, the high school senior was asked to describe the movie, *The Sea Hawk*, which he had just seen in film class. After this speech sample was described, it served as the basis for the tape-recorded sample stimulus both in the construction of the semantic differential and in the main study. If was edited for such things as false starts, interviewer interference, and repetition, and was adjusted slightly for the order of the discussed events.

The BE version was developed by using the approximate percentage of actual versus potential occurrence of these selected grammatical features: nonoccurrence of the copula, the third person singular [Z], the plural [Z], and the possessive [Z], and the approximate number of occurrences of multiple negation. In addition, one occurrence of the invariant *be* was included in the

BE sample.   Because of the fairly short length of utterance
necessarily employed here, the percentages of occurrence did not
in all cases exactly match Wolfram's percentages.   However, this
was felt to be insignificant because the variation was slight and
was well within the range of individual speakers of BE.

The initial tape-recorded samples were shortened after their
use in the preliminary study where it was observed that most of
the students finished their descriptions before the end of the
tape-recorded sample.   In the preliminary study, the five black
male speakers each recorded the speech sample using both guises.
However, time and attention factors resulted in a decision to
employ three speakers each using both guides in the final study.
This number was tested to make certain that the speakers' alternate
guises would not be identified as being uttered by the same
speaker. In a trial run they were not.

B.   Construction of the Semantic Differential

The written material, a narrative account of a movie, from
which the stimulus tape was made, consisted of two passages.
One passage was written in SE and the other in BE.   Each
passage, approximately a minute and a half in length, was read
by five middle class, male bidialectal black speakers.   To prevent
the subjects from learning that the same speaker was using two
separate guises, the two guises of the same speaker were separated
from each other by one guise of the other four speakers.   The
students apparently did not associate the same speaker with each
of his/her two guises, but some students did think that two
different speakers using the same guise were the same speaker.
A tape was prepared containing samples of both SE and BE.
This tape was then played to a senior high school English class
and to a sixth grade English class.   The high school class had a
total of 27 students: 16 males, 11 females, 12 middle class, 15
lower class, 20 white and 7 black.   The sixth grade sample was
made up of 16 students: 8 males, 8 females, 10 lower class, 6
middle class, 8 white, and 8 black students.   While the groups
were not composed of an equal number of members, they did
represent a subset of the groups to be tested.
To be certain that the semantic differential represented the
attitudes of the subjects, it was constructed by using descriptors
given in free responses from the 27 high school and 16 sixth
grade students to the BE and SE stimulus materials.   To obtain
these free responses, the subjects were asked to write a description
of the speaker immediately after hearing each taped speech sample.
Each subject described every speaker in both guises in this
fashion.   The tape recorder was stopped between samples while
the subjects wrote their descriptions.   A form was provided for
this purpose.   The adjectives and descriptive phrases occurring
in the written responses were collected and tallied.   Only the 15
most frequently occurring items were used to construct the semantic

differential. It was arbitrarily decided that no item occurring fewer than 10 times would be included.

C. The Main Study

Because it was evident from the preliminary study that some students regarded outsiders with suspicion, particularly when biographical questions were asked, it was decided that more reliable results would be obtained if the stimulus materials were presented as a regular classroom activity; therefore, the classroom teachers presented the stimulus material in their own classes for the main study. Before the teachers presented the stimulus material, the experimenter went over the material with them so that there would be uniformity of presentation. All that was necessary for the teacher to do was to help the students fill out the personal data sheet and to read the directions to the subjects. The teachers answered questions about the personal data sheet. It was emphasized that the personal information was for statistical purposes only and that no names were to be put on the papers. After the personal data sheets were filled in, the following directions were read aloud:

> We all make judgments about a person when we hear his voice. For example, when a stranger calls you on the phone, don't you start to form a mental picture of him? You are now going to hear six voices describe a movie, *The Sea Hawk*. Pretend that the voice you hear is some one talking to you on the phone. On each of the following six pages is a list of characteristics that describe the speaker. After you have heard him, put an X in the space on the seven-point scale that you feel best describes him. Be sure to mark all fifteen items for each speaker.

The teacher then answered any questions.

Next, the teacher went over the directions in the front of the test booklet:

> After you hear the speaker, place X in the appropriate blank. For instance, if you thought the speaker was very mean, you should mark it
> Mean X : __ : __ : __ : __ : __ Nice
> If you thought he was very nice, you should mark it
> Mean X : __ : __ : __ : __ : __ Nice
> If you had no opinion or could not tell, you should mark it
> Mean X : __ : __ : __ : __ : __ Nice
> If you thought he was kind of nice, but not very nice, you should mark it
> Mean X : __ : __ : __ : __ : __ Nice

If you thought he was kind of mean, but not
very mean, you should mark it
Mean   X :   :   :   :   :   Nice
After the directions were explained, the teacher played the section
of the tape that contained the first speech sample of Speaker 1.
The teacher then stopped the tape machine and read the semantic
differential aloud while each student marked the evaluation of the
speaker. This process was repeated until all BE and SE speech
samples were evaluated. The time required to run the experiment
was 45 minutes so that the entire experiment was run in a single
class period.

D. Subjects

For the main study, the final tapes and the revised personal
data sheet were presented to 12 high school English classes and
to 12 grade school English classes in the Richmond, Virginia,
area. In order to prevent any undue racial bias that might
result from the race of the teacher, two black teachers and two
white teachers were selected from each level. Each of the eight
teachers presented the material to three of her own classes.
The total number of subjects tested was 501. There were 217
sixth grade students and 284 high school students. The data
from 13 sixth grade students and 10 high school students were
not usable because they were incomplete, unreadable, or unclassifi-
able. Because equal cell size was necessary for the Statistical
Analysis System (SAS) program of the IBM 360 computer used
for analysis of the items on the semantic differential, only 240
subjects were used in the final analysis. All 15 middle class
black female preadolescent subjects were maintained, with subjects
in the other cells selected from the subject pool by means of a
random numbers table so that each cell had 15 members. Social
class categories were based on the features described in *Social
class and mental illness* by Hollingshead and Redlich (1958).

RESULTS

The main effects of sex, social class, race, age, and guise
and the interactions thereof were analyzed by a separate analysis
of each rating scale. The ANOVA of these separate rating scales
revealed that black students regarded BE more favorably than
did white students and that black preadolescents regarded BE
more favorably than did black adolescents. Whenever there were
significant differences in the mean scores, BE was rated as being
braver, dumber, a better fighter, and black, as well as being
more prejudiced and using poorer English. Also, SE was generally

marked as being nicer, smarter, better educated, and using good English. Blacks tended to rate BE as having more friends, being better liked, and being good looking. Whites tended to rate SE in the same manner. Because there was no clear objective way to relate results obtained on each scale to the results obtained from the other scales, a factor analysis was run to determine if any significant patterning of variables occurred. To compensate for any sampling errors, Rao's cononical factoring was used. A varimax orthogonal rotation with 99 iterations reduced the data to three factors as shown in Table I. As can be seen from the factor loadings in Table 1, certain scales stood out with particularly high correlations with one factor and lower ones on the others. For example, Factor I reflects the common use of such scales as

```
Do you think the speaker is
Dumb......................................Smart
Well Educated.................... Poorly Educated
Ugly...............................Good Looking
Poor........................................Rich
Black.....................................White
Do you think he has
Good English .......................Poor English
```

Factor II, by comparison, reflects a correlation between the following scales:

TABLE I: Varimax Rotated Factor Matrix

Semantic Differential Scale	Factor I	Factor II	Factor III
1. Mean............Nice	0.20636	-0.62014*	0.05087
2. Tall............Short	0.01231	-0.01675	0.2896
3. Brave...........Cowardly	-0.12183	0.15414	0.60486*
4. Dumb............Smart	0.62455*	-0.38650	-0.11461
5. Well educated....Poorly educated	-0.78477*	0.27179	0.08519
6. Ugly............Good looking	0.40940*	-0.51941*	-0.21462
7. Good athlete.....Poor athlete	0.09209	0.21026	0.62386
8. Good fighter.....Poor fighter	0.00564	0.13925	0.77962*
9. Poor............Rich	0.46386*	-0.37689	-0.04509
10. Black...........White	0.40914*	0.00687	0.45752*
11. Prejudiced.......Unprejudiced	0.18363	-0.46078*	0.05945
12. Good English.....Poor English	0.57095*	0.25236	0.09247
13. Few friends......Many friends	0.03725	-0.57426*	-0.33826
14. Cares about			
other people.....Only himself	0.22694	0.60455*	0.11641
15. Like him........Dislike him	0.24572	0.72307*	0.18582
Percent Total Variance	61.9	23.8	14.3

*High loading scales

Do you think the speaker is
Mean .... Nice
Ugly................................Good looking
Prejudiced......................... Unprejudiced
Has few friends ....Has many friends
Do you think you would
Like him............................. Dislike him

For Factor III the principal scales were

Do you think he is
Brave .... Cowardly
A good athlete....................A poor athlete
A good fighter ....A poor fighter
Black.......................................White

Based upon the meanings which the scales suggest for each factor, these factors were labeled School Failure, Popularity, and Physical Prowess.

Using the Statistical Package for the Social Sciences (SPSS), a cross tabulation was run to discover if a few subjects with scores at the extreme ends of the markers would skew the results. To determine if these factors were statistically significant, the responses were standardized by subtracting each response from the average and then dividing by the standard deviation. Next, the three factor scores were computed and standardized by subtracting the average from each individual response and dividing by the standard deviation. The final factor scores were rounded off to 0.5. These results demonstrated that the results of the factor analysis were not skewed by a few subjects with scores at the extreme ends of the scale. The level of significance was tested with both Chi square and Kendal Tau B and C, and all interactions were significant at $p < .001$.

By reversing the high loading scales with negative correlations and combining them with the high loading scales with positive correlations in Factor I, School Failure, a high positive score indicates that the speaker is viewed as high in School Failure or as a combination of dumb, poorly educated, poor, black, and using poor English. A low or negative score indicates the opposite: the speaker is viewed as low in School Failure. For Factor II, Popularity, a high or positive score indicates a rating of popularity: the speaker is perceived as nice, good looking, unprejudiced, having many friends, caring about people, and being liked. A low or negative score indicates the opposite. For Factor III, Athletic Prowess, a high or positive score indicates that the speaker is perceived as having athletic ability or having a combination of being brave, a good athlete, a good fighter, and black. A low or negative score indicates the opposite. The speaker is perceived as lacking in physical prowess. Because the main effect of guise, the two-way interactions, and three-way interactions do not add information to that combined in the four-way and five-way interactions, they will not be discussed except to

say that guise and all two-way and three-way interactions scored
BE higher in Factor I, school Failure, and Factor III, Physical
Powess, and lower in Factor II, Popularity.

As Tables II through VI indicate, BE is generally rated higher
for Factor I, School Failure, and for Factor III, Physical Prowess.
Thus, the SE guise is perceived as being more successful in
school and as being more popular, and the BE guise as having
more physical prowess. Preadolescents, especially white middle
class males, tended to rate their own guise more favorably, just
as Allport suggests.

TABLE II: Summary of Differences of Percent Responses at Median (Sex x Race x Class x Guise)

Interaction	Guise	Factor I	Factor II	Factor III
Female lower class black	BE	63.3	51.1	85.6
	SE	43.4	73.3	66.6
	Diff.	19.9	-22.3	19.0
Female lower class white	BE	80.9	35.6	83.5
	SE	39.9	71.1	61.1
	Diff.	41.0	-35.5	21.4
Female middle class black	BE	82.2	32.1	80.1
	SE	50.0	67.7	51.0
	Diff.	32.2	-35.6	29.1
Female middle class white	BE	91.0	48.8	90.0
	SE	42.6	77.7	55.6
	Diff.	47.4	-28.9	34.4
Male lower class black	BE	80.1	43.3	92.3
	SE	55.5	67.7	71.1
	Diff.	24.6	-24.4	21.2
Male lower class white	BE	92.3	25.6	80.0
	SE	48.9	67.7	55.6
	Diff.	43.4	-42.1	24.4
Male middle class black	BE	73.3	41.1	87.6
	SE	48.9	76.7	66.7
	Diff.	24.4	-35.6	20.9
Male middle class white	BE	98.9	7.8	75.4
	SE	53.3	67.7	45.5
	Diff.	45.6	-59.9	29.8

A. Four-Way Interactions

In the Sex x Race x Class x Guise interaction, all groups rated BE higher for Factors I and III and lower for Factor II. All black groups, except middle class females for Factor II, had smaller differences than did their white counterparts for all three factors. The harshest ratings for BE by whites was for Factor I, School Failure. All of the white groups rated BE much higher, in comparison to SE, on School Failure than did any of the black groups. For all of the white groups, there was a 40% difference in the median score. Furthermore, male and female middle class whites and male lower class whites all had more than 90% of their responses on the positive side of the median. For Factor II, middle class white males were especially harsh on BE. Only 7.8% gave BE positive scores, indicating a very negative reaction. The least difference in scores was registered by female and male lower class blacks and by female middle class whites. For Factor III, Physical Prowess, all groups rated BE more favorably, and there was not a great deal of difference between the groups.

In the Sex x Class x Age x Guise interaction, female lower class preadolescents had the least stereotyping, as well as being the only group to rate SE more positively (although not appreciably) than BE for Factor III. Male and female middle class adolescents and male lower class adolescents showed the most stereotyping. For all three factors, adolescents had larger differences in scores than did their preadolescent counterparts.

In the Sex x Race x Age x Guise interaction, all groups rated BE higher for Factors II and II and lower for Factor III. However, there was only a slight difference between scores for BE and SE for Factors I and II for either male or female black preadolescents and no appreciable difference for male white pre-adolescents for Factor III, indicating support for Allport's thesis. However, overall, black preadolescents had lower differences, indicating less stereotyping than the other groups, and white male adolescents had the largest differences, indicating the most stereotyping. Interestingly, the white adolescent females deviated noticeably from the other white groups in that they did not rate BE as negatively as the rest of the white groups did on the Popularity Scale. Particularly interesting is the fact that there is no appreciable difference between the scores for BE and SE in Factor I for either male or female preadolescents, indicating that they might regard SE as the appropriate speech for school.

In the Class x Race x Age x Guise interaction, there was no appreciable difference between the scores for BE and SE for lower class black preadolescents for any of the three factors. However, they were the only group to rate SE higher than BE for Factor III. While lower class black preadolescents seem to have the least stereotypic attitudes, white middle class males seem to have the most stereotypic views; they had the largest differences for all three factors. Assuming that School Failure is a negative value and that popularity and physical prowess are positive values, middle class black adolescents seem to have a much more negative attitude toward BE than do middle class black preadolescents as shown by their having larger differences for Factors I and II and smaller differences for Factor III. The most negative attitude toward BE was exhibited by middle class white preadolescents who rated BE high for School Failure and very low for Popularity and who had little difference in the scores for Physical Prowess.

B. Five-Way Interaction

For the five-way interaction, Sex x Class x Race x Age x Guise, there was no appreciable difference in scores between SE and BE for female lower class black preadolescents for any of

TABLE III: Summary of Differences of Percent Responses at Median (Sex x Class x Age x Guise)

Interaction	Guise	Factor I	Factor II	Factor III
Female lower class	BE	61.1	57.8	71.0
preadolescent	SE	42.2	70.0	76.6
	Diff.	17.9	-12.2	-5.6
Female lower class	BE	83.3	52.1	89.9
adolescent	SE	40.0	88.9	72.2
	Diff.	43.3	-36.8	17.2
Female middle class	BE	84.4	43.3	86.6
preadolescent	SE	52.2	76.6	55.5
	Diff.	32.2	-33.3	31.1
Female middle class	BE	88.8	20.0	83.4
adolescent	SE	39.9	75.5	51.1
	Diff.	48.9	-55.5	32.3
Male lower class	BE	81.1	63.3	85.5
preadolescent	SE	47.8	64.4	74.4
	Diff.	24.4	-22.3	11.1
Male lower class	BE	91.1	19.9	86.6
adolescent	SE	47.8	64.4	52.1
	Diff.	43.3	-44.5	34.5
Male middle class	BE	78.8	36.6	79.1
preadolescent	SE	53.2	74.4	64.4
	Diff.	24.6	-37.8	17.4
Male middle class	BE	94.5	12.2	84.4
adolescent	SE	43.9	70.0	47.8
	Diff.	50.6	-57.8	36.6

the three factors, indicating that they probably have the least stereotyping of any group; middle class white adolescent males and females have the largest differences, indicating that they probably have the most stereotyping. However, if we look at the difference in attitudes represented by the three factors, white male middle class preadolescents have the most negative attitude toward BE. They rated it lowest in popularity (only 6.6% gave it a positive rating) and had the largest difference between BE and SE. In addition, 100% rated it positive for Factor I (School Failure). While there was only a 37.8% difference in scores between SE and BE at the median (0.0), at the next level (0.5) there was a 57.5% difference with 93% rating BE positively. In addition, they showed less difference between SE and BE for Factor III (Physical Prowess) than any other group; in fact,

TABLE IV: Summary of Differences of Percent Responses at Median (Sex x Race x Age x Guise)

Interaction	Guise	Factor I	Factor II	Factor III
Female black preadolescents	BE	65.5	52.2	84.4
	SE	57.7	63.4	62.2
	Diff.	8.8	-11.2	22.2
Female black adolescents	BE	80.0	31.0	81.0
	SE	36.6	76.6	55.5
	Diff.	34.4	-45.6	25.5
Female white preadolescents	BE	80.0	34.4	87.7
	SE	38.9	75.5	70.0
	Diff.	41.1	-41.1	17.7
Female white adolescents	BE	92.1	52.2	85.6
	SE	43.4	74.4	46.6
	Diff.	48.7	-22.2	39.0
Male black preadolescents	BE	65.5	64.4	91.2
	SE	55.5	74.4	73.3
	Diff.	10.0	-10.0	17.9
Male black adolescents	BE	87.9	20.1	88.8
	SE	49.0	69.9	64.6
	Diff.	38.9	-49.8	24.2
Male white preadolescents	BE	93.3	21.1	73.3
	SE	54.4	70.0	65.6
	Diff.	28.9	-49.8	7.7
Male white adolescents	BE	97.8	12.2	82.2
	SE	47.7	64.5	35.6
	Diff.	50.1	-52.3	46.6

there is no appreciable difference between the two scores, indicating very strong support for Allport's thesis.

Female black middle class adolescents and all of the white groups except female lower class preadolescents were particularly harsh for BE for Factor I.   Also for Factor I, adolescents, except for female middle class whites where there was no appreciable difference between age groups, had noticeably higher differences than their preadolescent counterparts.   In addition, all groups of blacks, except female middle class adolescents who had no appreciable difference in scores from their white counterparts, had significantly lower differences than the white groups.

For Factor II, Popularity, all groups rated BE less popular than SE, but the differences were not significant for female and male lower class black preadolescents.   The four middle class white groups had appreciably larger differences than the other

TABLE V: Summary of Differences of Percent Responses at Median (Class x Race x Age x Guise)

Interaction	Guise	Factor I	Factor II	Factor III
Lower class black	BE	63.3	64.4	71.2
preadolescents	SE	57.7	67.8	78.8
	Diff.	5.6	-3.4	-7.6
Lower class black	BE	80.0	30.0	90.1
adolescents	SE	41.0	73.3	58.9
	Diff.	39.0	-43.3	31.2
Lower class white	BE	78.8	42.3	83.4
preadolescents	SE	42.2	80.0	72.1
	Diff.	36.6	-37.7	11.3
Lower class white	BE	94.5	18.8	80.0
adolescents	SE	46.6	67.1	44.4
	Diff.	47.9	-48.3	35.6
Middle class black	BE	67.7	52.2	87.8
preadolescents	SE	54.4	69.9	56.7
	Diff.	13.3	-17.7	31.1
Middle class black	BE	87.8	21.1	80.0
adolescents	SE	44.4	73.4	61.1
	Diff.	43.4	-52.3	18.9
Middle class white	BE	94.4	13.3	77.0
preadolescents	SE	51.0	73.3	63.3
	Diff.	43.4	-60.0	13.7
Middle class white	BE	95.7	11.1	87.8
adolescents	SE	44.5	72.2	37.7
	Diff.	51.2	-61.1	50.1

TABLE VI: Summary of Differences of Percent Responses at Median (Sex x Class x Race x Age x Guise)

Interaction	Guise	Factor I	Factor II	Factor III
Female lower class black preadolescent	BE	51.1	66.7	86.7
	SE	48.8	71.1	80.1
	Diff.	2.3	-4.4	6.6
Female lower class black adolescent	BE	75.5	35.7	84.5
	SE	37.7	75.5	53.4
	Diff.	37.8	-39.8	31.1
Female lower class white preadolescent	BE	71.2	48.9	84.5
	SE	37.8	69.0	71.1
	Diff.	33.4	-20.1	13.4
Female lower class white adolescent	BE	91.0	22.2	82.2
	SE	42.3	75.5	48.8
	Diff.	48.7	-53.3	37.8
Female middle class black preadolescent	BE	80.1	37.8	82.2
	SE	64.4	53.3	44.4
	Diff.	15.7	-15.5	37.8
Female middle class black adolescent	BE	84.1	26.6	78.8
	SE	35.5	77.7	57.7
	Diff.	48.6	-51.1	20.1
Female middle class white preadolescent	BE	89.0	20.0	91.0
	SE	39.9	82.2	66.7
	Diff.	49.1	-62.2	24.3
Female middle class white adolescent	BE	93.4	13.3	88.9
	SE	44.5	73.4	44.5
	Diff.	48.9	-60.1	44.4
Male lower class black preadolescent	BE	75.6	62.3	88.9
	SE	66.6	64.4	77.7
	Diff.	11.0	-2.1	11.2
Male lower class black adolescent	BE	84.1	24.5	95.6
	SE	44.6	71.1	64.4
	Diff.	35.5	-46.6	31.2
Male lower class white preadolescent	BE	86.7	35.5	82.2
	SE	46.7	85.5	71.1
	Diff.	40.0	-50.0	11.1
Male lower class white adolescent	BE	97.7	15.5	77.8
	SE	51.1	57.8	39.9
	Diff.	46.6	-42.3	37.9
Male middle class black preadolescent	BE	55.5	66.6	93.6
	SE	44.4	84.5	68.9
	Diff.	11.1	-17.9	24.7

TABLE VI (continued)

Interaction	Guise	Factor I	Factor II	Factor III
Male middle class black	BE	91.0	15.6	82.2
adolescent	SE	53.2	68.8	64.5
	Diff.	37.8	-53.2	17.2
Male middle class white	BE	100.0	6.7	54.6
preadolescent	SE	62.0	71.2	60.1
	Diff.	37.8	-64.5	4.4
Male middle class white	BE	97.8	8.9	86.6
adolescent	SE	44.5	71.2	31.2
	Diff.	53.3	-62.3	54.4

groups. For blacks, preadolescents had noticeably lower differences between SE and BE; and for whites there were no appreciable differences except for the female lower class where the adolescents had appreciably larger differences.

For Factor III, Physical Prowess, neither male middle class white preadolescents nor female lower class black preadolescents had a significant difference between the two guises. All other groups rated BE as having significantly more physical prowess with the largest differences being exhibited by male and female middle class white adolescents. Both female and male middle class black preadolescents had larger differences than did their adolescent counterparts; while for all the other groups, adolescents had larger differences, again indicating some support for Allport's thesis.

CONCLUSION

While earlier studies (Harms, 1961; Hurst & Jones, 1966; Buck, 1968, Tucker & Lambert, 1969; Bronstein et. al., 1970) did indicate whites and blacks agreed upon the preference for SE as compared to BE, it is difficult to compare these studies with the present study because the dimensions along which these studies solicited information differed from the present one. However, if Anisfeld, Bogo, and Lambert (1962) are correct in their assumption that any reaction to the language of a national or cultural group should reflect the stereotyped characteristics of the group that speaks it, these earlier studies indicate a lack of ethnic pride on the part of blacks and a lack of respect on the part of whites.

The present study indicates that BE is no longer considered the "shuffling speech of slavery" by either white or black grade school or high school students. As Williams (1970) suggested, complicated aspects of social change over the past two decades have created a greater feeling of pride among blacks and some change in regard for blacks by whites. Both black and white students demonstrated a respect for BE. Both white and black students rated BE more favorably than SE on the Physical Prowess factor. These qualities are those eulogized in the popular song "Bad Leroy Brown, the Meanest Man in the Whole Damn Town." Because of the attitude toward physical prowess, one might expect that there would be a negative correction with school success. Good athletes and good fighters are often stereotyped as lacking in school success.

SE was marked more favorably by both whites and blacks on the education factor. Claudia Mitchell-Kernan (1972) reached the same conclusion in her ethnographic study of a black community in the San Francisco Bay area. She reported that "some of the variants labeled Black English by the linguist are referred to as *flat, country,* and *bad English* by native speakers. The antonyms for these terms are *proper* and *good English* (Mitchell-Kernan, 1972, p. 196). She found that *good English* was viewed by the black community as "educated and intelligent, whereas using *bad English* tends to give the impression that one is un-educated and to some degree unintelligent" (Mitchell-Kernan, 1972, p. 201); the same results were found in this study. SE was also rated more favorably on the Popularity factor than was BE. However, the differences were not significant for lower class black preadolesents.

This study also tends to support Allport's (1954) and Lambert, Frankel, and Tucker's (1960) contention that children reach the zenith of ethnic identity at the beginning of puberty. Male middle class white preadolescents in particular support this thesis in the way they rated BE particularly low on school success and popularity and SE proportionally higher on physical prowess than did the other groups. Unexpectedly, this study indicates that adolescents, particularly white male middle class ones, tend to stereotype more strongly than do any of the other groups. However, this does not conflict with Allport's thesis because they also rated BE the highest of any group on the Physical Prowess factor, an area which high school males consider prestigious. Females, particularly lower class black preadolescents, seem to have the fewest stereotypes. Middle class black female adolescents seem the harshest of all black groups on BE. This may result from the schools' insistence upon the preference for SE, coupled with society's having less tolerance for females using nonstandard English than for males.

Finally, this study demonstrates that students do judge speak-ers in significant ways on the basis of speech cues alone. The judgments tend to result in certain, albeit inaccurate, stereotypes. Research alone will not rid students of these stereotypes. How-ever, research can be used to determine what attitudes various groups hold toward each other so that steps can be taken to counteract attitudes that are clearly erroneous and irrelevant.

ACKNOWLEDGEMENT

The authors would like to thank Ray Sansig, formerly of the Mathematical Science Department of Virginia Commonwealth University, now of the United States Bureau of Standards, for his help in the statistical design of this paper.

REFERENCES

Allport, G. *The nature of prejudice* . Cambridge, Mass.: Addison-Wesley, 1954.

Anisfeld, E., Bogo, N., & Lambert, W. E. Evaluational reactions to accented English speech. *Journal of Abnormal and Social Psychology*, 1962, 65, 223-231.

Bronstein, J. et al. A sociolinguistic comment on the changing attitudes toward the use of Black English and an experimental study to measure some of those attitudes. Paper presented at the 56th annual convention of the Speech Communication Association, New Orleans, December 1970. Also in ERIC: ED 051 226.

Buck, J. F. The effects of Negro and White dialectal variations upon attitudes of college students. *Speech Monographs*, 1968, 35, 181-186.

Harms, L. S. Listener judgments of status cues in speech. *Quarterly Journal of Speech*, 1961, 47, 164-186.

Hollingshed, A. B. & Redlich, F. C. *Social class and mental illness: a community study* . New York: John Wiley & Sons, 1958.

Hurst, C. G., Jr. & Jones, W. L. Psychosocial concomitants of sub-standard speech. *Journal of Negro Education*, 1966, 35, 409-421.

Labov, W. *The social stratification of English in New York City* . Washington, D.C.: Center for Applied Linguistics, 1966.

Lambert, W. E., Frankel, H., & Tucker, G. R. Judging personality through speech: A French Canadian sample. *Journal of Communication*, 1960, 16, 305-321.

Mitchell-Kernan, C. On the status of Black English for native speakers: An Assessment of attitudes and values. In C. B. Cazden, V. P. John, & D. Hymes (Eds.), *Functions of language in the classroom* . New York: Teachers College Press, 1972, 195-210.

Shuy, R. W., Wolfram, W., & Riley, K. *Linguistic correlates of social stratification in Detroit speech* . Final Report 6-1347. Washington, D.C.: United States Office of Education, 1968.

Tucker, G. R., & Lambert, W. E.   White and Negro listeners'
    reactions to various American English dialects.   *Social
    Forces*, 1969, 47, 463-468.
Williams, F.   Language, attitude, and social change.   In F.
    Williams (Ed.), *Language and poverty*.   Chicago: Markham,
    1970, 380-399.
Wolfram, W. A.   *A sociolinguistic description of Detroit Negro
    Speech*.   Washington, D.C.:   Center for Applied Linguistics,
    1969.

AMERICAN INDIAN ENGLISH AND ITS

IMPLICATIONS FOR BILINGUAL EDUCATION

William L. Leap

This paper is concerned with some aspects of language pluralism found within the membership of contemporary American Indian tribes and communities. It also deals with some of the consequences of that pluralism, with which educational policy and bilingual theory are concerned.

1. At the present time, we estimate that some 206 different languages and language dialects are being spoken in Indian country. The results of a survey by Wallace Chafe, published in 1962, provide a sense of the range of fluency which may be subsumed under this figure: 49 of these languages have fewer than 10 speakers, all over 50 years of age; 6 of these languages have more than 10,000 speakers within all generational groupings in each community. Fluency in the remaining 151 languages may fall at any point between those two extremes. Fluency is not, as some suspect, an open-and-shut, yes-no matter. And, of course, social and cultural factors will also affect the placement for each group--as in the instance where a person knows how to carry out his/her religious responsibilities in the native language, but does not use the language for any purpose outside of that context.

Levels of English language fluency within the tribes and communities may be similarly wide ranging. It is not uncommon to find, within any given community, persons who speak virtually no English at all. Usually, if such statements can be made for such a highly heterogeneous population, the younger members of the tribe tend to be the more fluent in English and/or rely on English more frequently as the medium of conversation and discussion. The increase in locally available schooling opportunities, which replaces the older practice of off-reservation, boarding school instruction; the creation of federal work-incentive programs which encourages Indians to seek employment in the off-reservation, urban context; the availability of Sesame Street and other English-dominated media packages; and other such factors have all had a hand in shaping the distribution of English fluency

Leap, William L. 1979. American Indian English and its implication for bilingual education. In *Georgetown University Round Table on Languages and Linguistics 1979*. Edited by James E. Alatis. Georgetown University Press. Pp. 657-659. Used by permission of the publisher.

within each tribal and community context. Thus the differences in levels of English facility from one tribe to the next, can be traced in part to the differences in impact which one or more of these factors may have had on any particular locale.

Still, some generalities about the English of Indian people can be drawn. One of these, as described in the Havighurst report (see Fuchs and Havighurst 1972:206-212) and in subsequent studies, has to do with the priority which Indian people place on having their children acquire English language skills. A second, as reported in the U.S. Civil Rights Commission's *Southwest Indian Report* (1973) and elsewhere, refers to the continuing perception by many non-Indians of the inadequacy of the English language skills of Indians. The BIA, for example, continues to treat the strengthening of its students' English skills as one of its highest educational priorities, since, by their report,

> . . . [M]ost Indian children entering BIA schools
> continue to be tribal speakers first and speakers
> of English as a second language second [and] .
> . . are closer to tribal life-ways than students
> enrolled in the public schools (Benham 1977:31).

These data may seem to be contradictory--e.g. how can there be an increase in English fluency, high levels of interest in maintaining English fluency, and still be reported inadequacy of English fluency, all within the same population? The answer lies in part in the level of generalization which must be used to talk about the common problems of the memberships of over 400 politically autonomous and culturally separate Indian tribes. It lies also in the persisting stereotypes of unsocialized Indian behavior reinforced by the media, the textbooks, and other social institutions. Indians have been portrayed as 'poor unfortunates' for so long that it may be difficult for people to see anything other than poverty and misfortune even when they are confronted with facts to the contrary. Witness, for example, the assumption in the passage just cited, that BIA students tend to be closer to tribal lifestyles than Indian students in public schools--when, as of latest count, well over 70 percent of all Indian children are enrolled in public schools, regardless of where they reside. The procedures used for testing levels of language proficiency, which often base their conclusions on nothing more than the results of vocabulary identification tasks, certainly make their contribution. But the contradictions also refer us to some facts about the nature of the English spoken by persons in many Indian communities.

One hundred years ago, familiarity, to say nothing of fluency, with English was a novel thing in most Indian communities in the west. See, for example, DuBois' comment that: 'for the period 1846-1880, Spanish was the vehicle for communicative interaction with Anglo-Americans . . . particularly with the Mescalero' (1977: 191). By the beginnings of this century, the prime mandate of the Indian school had become defined around developing speaking, reading, and writing skills in English. Any carryover of native language arts instruction, as had been the case in Choctaw and Cherokee schools, for example, was eliminated by federal fiat. School classrooms and dormitories were set up in the off-reservation contexts, specifically to encourage the use of non-Indian codes. Persons from differing tribal backgrounds were often placed in the same classroom and dormitory, to prevent continued reliance on the student's ancestral language as the means for conversation. Schooling policies, in addition, forbade the use of Indian languages for any public purpose, and punished students who violated the restriction. This added significantly to the pressure to use English as the exclusive means of student communication.

What emerged from this context, as we currently understand it, was a set of English language 'codes' based, to certain extents, on the speaking knowledge which the students had already mastered--the skills in ancestral language expression. As reflected in student term papers and examination essays from Haskell Indian school in 1916 (see Malancon and Malancon 1977 for discussion), sentence constructions, details of spelling (and therefore, pronunciation as well), and vocabulary usage began to show direct Indian language influence, almost as if the students were forming English expressions with non-English grammars. The students obtained a kind of English fluency in this fashion, yet the fluency remained distinct from the sense of fluency defined and expected by Standard English speakers. Tribally distinctive English codes emerged--each formed off the grammar of the particular Indian language. They all utilized a common core of English vocabulary words, with various lexical items from the speaker's Indian language (i.e. Indian loan words) enriching the potential for expression of each code, something which was highly appropriate given the nature of the sentence formation process underlying each code.

The students who went through this process of 'creative construction' are among the grandparents and great-grandparents of today's tribal and community membership. Their children (persons in today's parental generation) learned both their Indian language and their parents' 'Indian English' at home. The schools continued to construct their language arts curriculum in terms of the language needs of Standard English speakers. This, in turn, bypassed the specific language arts needs which the students brought with them into the classroom. And it also did something else. For the curriculum to have impact on the level of the students' English fluency, instruction would have to make direct inroads into the Indian language grammar underlying that fluency. Growth (i.e. standardization) of English skills resulted in a weakening and ultimately a loss of Indian language skills in many instances. Maintenance of Indian language fluency required resistance and rejection of Standard English influence in the grammar, and this Standard English convention in their speech.

Consider now the contemporary consequences of this situation. Students in the present generation encounter the local variety of Indian English, influenced by the ancestral language tradition of the community, as the first language in the home. They may also be exposed to the ancestral language of their community, depending on the situation within the home and the tribe. Yet even if this does not occur, since the English being learned shows ancestral language influence, the children are able to become passively fluent in their Indian language (i.e. receptively, though not necessarily productively, competent) through the acquisition of their locally appropriate, Indian English code. This helps explain why so many nonspeakers in the contemporary Indian communities can understand what parents and grand-parents say to them in their native/ancestral tongue, even though they are not able to respond to the speaker in the same linguistic terms. The children's English may in fact allow them to be predisposed to learning (or relearning) Indian language fluency, something which will greatly assist them in later life, if, for example, they decide to become active members of tribal government and/or to participate more extensively in the tribe's ceremonial life.

The less positive sides of Indian English fluency may emerge within school-related contexts in a variety of ways. Fluency in the local Indian English code may, for example, lead a student to use sentences such as (1)-(5) in written compositions.
    (1) Two womens was out there fighting.
    (2) Since the church close down, we been goin to mass in
        Pajarito.
    (3) You do not record none of your wills or any of your
        transactions with BIA.
    (4) Any fiestas which we might have are given early in the
        summer.
    (5) The individual pick out their own cattle.
Each of these sentences reflects a construction type common to the spoken English at one community in the United States South-west, but quite inappropriate as far as written (or spoken stan-dard) English expression is concerned. Similarly, Indian English fluency may lead the student to interpret material on the printed page in terms quite different from those intended by the writer; familiar 'problems' in reading comprehension reported in the litera-ture on Indian schooling can often be traced to such causes. Other examples could be suggested; the point is clear. Without adequate control over the kinds of basic English skills expected and assumed by educational authorities, impediments to educational progress can be predicted. The record on leaving school, test-score placements, and other signs of the so-called 'under-achieve-ment' of the Indian student all bear out the validity of this prediction.

2. The impact of the Indian student's English language skills on his/her educational progress has long been recognized by schooling authorities and by language planners and researchers. As Fuchs and Havighurst noted in the summary volume of the National Study of Indian Education (1977:208ff.), two solutions--intensive programs of ESL instruction, and programs offering (transitional) bilingual education, have come to be relied upon to

bring about the necessary strengthening of English language skills which effective classroom performance appears to require. Until the 1970s, however, the nature of the English language 'problem' toward which these remedial strategies were to be directed was presented in the literature in terms of a subtractive (or outright deficiency) model--identifying what Standard English conventions were not present in Indian English speech; or in terms of a contrastive model--identifying what problem areas in English fluency might be present within the English of a given Indian community. To my knowledge, it was not until 1971 that serious attempts to describe and account for the linguistic and sociolinguistic details actually present in any variety of American Indian English were initiated.

My own study of the varieties of English spoken at Isleta pueblo, New Mexico, began during this period as an outgrowth of dissertation-related studies of Isletan Tiwa, the ancestral language of that community. The first suggestion that Isletan English might have a logic independent of that of Standard English came with the conclusion of an analysis of the surface-level phonology of the English of several adult speakers. While English vocabulary was being employed in their speech, the words and phrases were pronounced in terms of Tiwa, and not English, phonological constraints. (See Leap 1973 for discussion.)

This was not, then, a case of Isletan Tiwa interference with an otherwise intact English phonological pattern: if anything, Isletan phonology has preempted the English pattern, not just selected portions of it. Elaboration of this comment is provided in Leap (1977c) and in Stout's (1977) analysis of the Keresan English of Santa Ana, New Mexico.

The phonological analysis also highlighted a series of Isletan English sentence constructions which seems to be directly influenced by Tiwa grammatical constraint. Additional papers (Leap 1974b and 1974c) reviewed several of these constructions to show how Tiwa grammatical rule was taking precedence over English grammatical rule in Isletan English sentence formation. The creative synthesis of Tiwa and English syntax present in this English code continued to be the topic of subsequent analysis. Instances appeared such as in the contrastive use of single vs. double negation in the code, where Tiwa semantic rules were being directly replicated in Isletan English. Cases also appeared, as in the formation of sentences with cognate object constructions, where both a Tiwa and an English language explanation could be used to account for the particulars of the derivation. These implied that criteria for selecting between the explanations needed to be developed in the analysis, possibly replicating the decision-making which the Isletan English speaker has to carry out when initiating the act of derivation. (For discussion, see Leap 1977d.)

Constructions also appeared where the source could not be traced either to Isletan Tiwa grammar or to the grammatical component of Standard English: the use of uninflected *be* in Isletan English shows some decided parallels to the use of *be* in Black

English vernacular, for example. Analysis showed, in fact, that a close association between this aspect of the deep structure of these two nonstandard codes could be established, provided Fasold's definition of distributive *be* were brought into closer harmony with the absence of tense-specification reflected in his own data but not highlighted in his discussion of theme. (See Leap 1975 for the details.)

While some of the affinities between Isletan and other varieties of nonstandard English were beginning to be explored through such interdialectal comparisons, the limitations of using typological characteristics of one nonstandard code when describing or interpreting the features of a second also were becoming clear. In a recent paper (Leap 1977a), I show how the absence of tense-marking on Isletan English verbs may reflect any number of grammatical constraints. Thus to assume that tenseless verbs in Isletan English are derived through phonological simplification, as is the case in some Black English dialects, is as inappropriate as it is premature.

The uniqueness of the Isletan English code was beginning to be highlighted in the interdialectal comparisons. Speaker assessments of a set of Isletan English sentences, following the elicitation technique outlined in Fasold (1969), proved to be markedly distinct from those given by speakers of Anglo and Spanish American English varieties common to the communities immediately adjacent to the Isletan reservation. (See Leap 1977e, for further discussion.) Arguments that Indian English codes merely represent some variant of regionally appropriate American English are seriously weakened by these findings.

Intertribal comparisons of Indian English forms yielded similarly useful perspectives on the uniqueness of Isletan English. I had been advised on numerous occasions that Indian people in the southwest and elsewhere could place a person's tribal background merely by listening to the way he/she spoke English. (See, in particular, the anecdote reported in Leap 1974a.) Comparison of these specifics of word-final consonant cluster reduction in Isletan and Cheyenne English (Leap 1977b); Penfield's (1975, 1977) several papers on the continuing autonomy of four Indian English varieties --Navajo, Ute, Mojave, and Hope, within the same classroom; Stout's continuing analysis of syntactic details and their sociolinguistic correlates within the English of elementary students at Laguna pueblo, New Mexico (much of which is summarized in Stout 1978), and Miller's (1976) study of English language acquisition among children on the Pima reservation, have provided ample evidence to support the language-specific nature of each community's Indian English variety. A study of the English of school children from San Juan and Laguna pueblos, New Mexico, currently ongoing at the Center for Applied Linguistics under support from the National Institute of Education promises to add additional support to these claims, especially where the impact of Indian English fluency on school performance is concerned. Natalie Kuhlman's work on Papago and Pima English (Kuhlman and Longoni

1975, Kalectaca and Kuhlman 1977) achieves the same end, in spite of her continuing reliance on subtractive/deficiency models in her descriptions.

In the light of these studies, my argument (Leap 1973, passim) that there are as many different kinds of American Indian English as there are American Indian language traditions becomes readily understandable. Descriptive data, comparative insights, tribal opinion, and speaker assessments of grammaticality and sentence acceptability all combine to support the claim. The arguments of Mary Jane Cook (1973, passim) and others who continue to interpret the English of Indian people in the southwest strictly in terms of shared, area-wide phenomena must be dismissed in the light of this conclusion.

3. The argument that there are as many kinds of Indian English as there are Indian language traditions--that is, a minimum of 206 different Indian English varieties, carries with it some particular implications for the interests of this year's Georgetown University Round Table and I want to explore several of those implications in the following paragraphs.

Taken uncritically, the claim might seem to imply that speakers of Indian English are also speakers of their appropriate ancestral languages. Such is not always the case, as the argument and statistics in the first section of this paper have already suggested. I am personally aware of instances in Indian country where the control over ancestral language grammar contained in the knowledge of the local Indian English code is the only reflex of Indian language skill which the community membership (or a significant portion of that membership) now possesses. At some phase in the transmission of language skills within the community, Indian English must have begun to be acquired autonomously--i.e. successful acquisition was not dependent on the presence of an existing Indian language grammar or Indian language speaking skill. We might, for this reason, want to view Indian English as some kind of creole if, in the strict sense of the term, its predecessor was some sort of pidgin. Then, we would want--as Stout and Erting (1977) have done for uninflected *be* in Isletan English--to interpret the English language dynamics in the community in terms of a post-creole model. Doing this would detract from the more critical point: the grammar being transmitted autonomously is a whole grammar, whatever its origin--that is, it is systematic enough to be learnable, and complete enough to be learned in the same (or comparable) form by various segments of the community membership, through reliance on the same range of cognitive skills which all human beings employ in the natural language acquisition process. While the codes may have had their original basis in some process of relexification or other form of 'creative construction', such processes do not appear to be necessary for their successful maintenance or their successful transmission.

The complexity faced by language arts programs in American Indian schools can, I believe, best be interpreted in these very terms. Given the diversity in range and level of language fluency

which may occur within any Indian speech community, the local
classroom may contain, at minimum: (1) students who have learned
Indian English and have little, or no, control over their ancestral
language; (2) students who speak both their ancestral language
and some variety of English; and (3) students fluent in their
ancestral language but showing minimal fluency in English. Schooling authorities tend to view the language condition of their students
through a much more unified perspective--building the language
profile around greater or lesser degrees of evidenced English
fluency. The BIA continues to estimate the number of speakers
of Indian languages in its schools by extrapolating from the number
of students who speak English as a second language--see the
statistics reported in Fuchs and Havighurst 1972:207-208, or the
conclusions of the survey of bilingual education needs of Indian
children, carried out by the National Indian Training and Research
Center (1975). Here lies the basis for the oft-reported divergence
between institutional and parental expectations where the student-
general need for strengthening English language skills exists,
while the parents (and students) express concern about unad-
dressed, student-specific Indian language fluency.   And even
when native language instruction is included in the school curriculum, the justification advanced for doing so emphasizes a promised
growth in student English facility, rather than the strengthening
of student native language arts.

The school-based perspective on student language needs has
some serious consequences for interests in ancestral language
maintenance as well.   For, regardless of the level of ancestral
language fluency which the student brings into the first grade
classroom, the general pattern in Indian country shows a marked
reduction in (if not elimination of) that fluency by the time the
student completes the sixth grade. The causes for this reduction
extend far beyond the failure of school to include ancestral language instruction in the curriculum.   As argued in an earlier
section of this paper, by focusing attention only on English language questions, and by attempting to rework the students' existing control of English into a more standardized format, the school
is literally undermining student fluency in his/her ancestral lan-
guage--the grammar underlying his locally appropriate English
code and the grammar underlying his ancestral fluency being, in
essence, one and the same.

Under current practice, and I would include here the various
transitional bilingual programs funded under the Bilingual Education
Act (Title VII, ESEA), a successful program of English language
instruction in any Indian school virtually guarantees native language genocide. This will continue to be the case, until educational policy and classroom practice cease treating the Indian
English question as something totally autonomous from the remaining
portions of the Indian student's verbal repertoire.

4.   What kind of educational strategy is appropriate for students with fluency in some variety of American Indian English?

It is not appropriate merely to ignore the differences in structure and usage convention which distinguish the student's Indian English grammar from that of the standard code. To present the students with exercises highlighting the differences between the past tense forms of *lay* and *lie*, when the student may not ever use *laid* or *lay* (or, more generally, the [d] morpheme or verbal ablaut) to mark past tense expression for these verbs (if, in fact, he/she defines tense/aspect distinctions in temporal terms at all) is both an inefficient and irresponsible use of the student's schooling experience--to say nothing about the previously noted impact such instruction could have on the Indian language skills he/she already controls.

Still, speaking situations outside the home community and tribal context often require some evidence of Standard English expression as a precondition for effective mobility within their context. Educational programs which fail to provide Indian students with opportunities to gain stronger control over Standard English conventions are therefore equally inefficient and equally irresponsible.

The school's task is to find an educational strategy which will integrate Standard English into the student's verbal repertoire without detracting from the native language skills already evidenced within that repertoire, or allowing Standard English to supersede the English usage patterns already familiar to the student. The school also needs to help the student distinguish between sentence variants, so that he/she can select the sentence form most appropriate to any given speaking situation. And, because the student's existing English fluency is, to a large part, governed by the grammar of his/her ancestral language, it will also be necessary for the school to provide instruction in Indian as well as English language arts. The more secure the student is in the language skills she/he already controls, the more prepared she/he will be to integrate new speaking tasks into the scope of his verbal repertoire.

In effect, what is being called for here is a program of bilingual education, if by that term is meant an education strategy which starts with the students' existing language skills--in this case, those subsumed under the phrase 'Indian English', and then directs those skills toward the building of language fluencies deemed appropriate by the membership of the home community as well as by persons in the surrounding society. Such an educational strategy is highly appropriate for schooling programs in Indian country, regardless of specific locale; it is often said that Indian people have their feet in 'two worlds'. If so, it is only fitting that their children gain control over the verbal codes basic to mobility and movement within each sphere.

But a problem remains: the kinds of language needs described here are not viewed as appropriate for bilingual services under current HEW practices. The Lau Remedies, the provisions of the Bilingual Education Act (Title VII, ESEA), and other federal programs facilitating the development of bilingual/bicultural instruction

in the nation's schools define student eligibility for federally supported bilingual services in terms of the presence of 'limited
English-speaking ability'. LESA, when used in reference to an
individual, refers to someone who has difficulty speaking and
understanding instruction in the English language because his/her
dominant language—i.e. the language most relied upon for communication in the home—is other than English; and whose educational
progress can be shown to be impeded as a result of that difficulty.

As this discussion has shown, the Indian English-speaking
student may experience the same kinds of difficulties in speaking
and/or in understanding English language instruction in the classroom, and may find his/her educational progress impeded as a
result of those difficulties—even though the language relied upon
for communication in the home is Indian English, and not the
student's ancestral tongue. As a result, Indian participation in
the Title VII network has never been extensive—in FY 1976, for
example, of the $135 million disbursed for basic program support
under this Act, only $3.25 million, approximately 2.5 percent of
the available monies, were awarded to LEAs serving Indian students—even though Indian students could benefit equally well
from Title VII services currently made available to non-Indian
LEAs whose students show closer conformity to the description of
language need defined in the Title VII regulations.

There has been, in recent months, much discussion about
the need to rewrite the Title VII act so that it could become
more sensitive to the language needs of the nation's linguistic
minorities. In the present case, a simple change in the definition
of limited English-speaking ability will allow for greater Indian
eligibility for Title VII support without requiring extensive changes
in the original mandate and purpose of this legislation: Section
703(a)(1)(B) should be revised to allow LESA to refer to 'individuals who come from environments where a language other than
English has had measurable or demonstrable impact on their level
of English proficiency'. Following that passage with the remainder
of section 703(a)(1) as presently worded will allow Indian students
to become eligible for Title VII services provided the students
are speakers of their community's Indian English code.   Such
will clearly be the case for students in many Indian communities,
whether they are fluent in their ancestral language or not. The
change suggested here would facilitate the introduction of bilingual
instruction into the schooling programs serving these communities,
and remove the language barrier which so often impedes the
progress of the 'monolingual-English-speaking Indian' through the
American education system.   And I am pleased to report that
Resident Commissioner Baltasar Corrada has included it in the
proposed reauthorization of the Bilingual Education Act which he
introduced to the 95th Congress; and that Senators Dominici and
Hart have included the same definition in the text of the comparable
legislation introduced in the U.S. Senate.

AUTHOR'S POSTSCRIPT

This paper was written in the spring of 1978 and contains in its final paragraphs some comments about possible (as of that writing) changes in the wording of the Bilingual Education Act (Title VII, ESEA). It is worth noting that the definition of eligibility for Title VII services *was* modified by the Congress later that summer to allow:

> individuals who are American Indian and Alaskan Native students and who come from environments where a language other than English has had a significant impact on their level of English language proficiency . . .

to be eligible to receive bilingual instruction through Title VII support programs *whether these students are speakers of their ancestral languages or not*. A larger number of schools serving American Indian students had already begun to receive Title VII funding after 1976, due in large part to the outreach services provided to schools and to tribal governments through the network of Title VII Resource Centers. The introduction of new eligibility criteria intensified this trend. By 1979, more than twice the amount of the allocation for American Indian projects in 1976 was needed to support Title VII services in American Indian education. Since that time, funding for American Indian projects has remained between eight and ten-percent of the total appropriation for support of basic projects during each fiscal year.

(Jan. 1, 1985)

ACKNOWLEDGEMENTS

I want to thank Rosario Gingras, Lance Potter, Paul Murphy, and Angui Madera for their help in preparing this statement, and to dedicate the paper to Rudy Troike, former director of the Center for Applied Linguistics, under whose tutelage many of the insights being explored here were originally conceived.

REFERENCES

Benham, William J., Jr. 1977. *Education in the Bureau of Indian Affairs*. Research and Evaluation Report Series No. 52. Washington, D.C.: Bureau of Indian Affairs, Office of Indian Education Programs.

Chafe, Wallace. 1962. *Estimates Regarding the Present Speakers of North American Indian Languages*. IJAL 28.162-171.

Cook, Mary Jane. 1973. "Problems of Southwestern Speakers in Learning English." In: *Bilingualism in the Southwest*. Edited by Paul Turner. Tucson: University of Arizona Press. 175-198.

DuBois, Betty Lou. 1977. "Spanish, English and the Mescalero Apache." In: *Studies in Southwestern Indian English*. Edited by William L. Leap. San Antonio: Trinity University Press. 175-198.

Fasold, Ralph. 1969. *Tense and the Verb BE in Black English*. Lg. 45.763-776.

Fuchs, Estelle, and Robert J. Havighurst. 1972. *To Live on this Earth: American Indian Education*. New York City: Doubleday.

Kalectaca, Milo, and Natalie Kuhlman. 1977. *Sacaton School District Language Assessment Project*. San Diego: National Training Resource Center. Multilith.

Kuhlman, Natalie, and Robert Longoni. 1975. "Indian English and Its Implicationss for Education." In: *Southwest Languages and Linguistics in Educational Perspective*. Edited by Gina C. Harvey and M. F. Heiser. San Diego: Institute for Cultural Pluralism. 333-348.

Leap, William L. 1973. "Language Pluralism in a Southwestern Pueblo: Some Comments on Isletan English. In: *Bilingualism in the Southwest*. Edited by Paul Turner. Tucson: University of Arizona Press.

Leap, William L. 1974a. "Ethnics, Emics, and the 'New' Ideology: The Identity Potential of Indian English." In: *Social and Cultural Identity*. Edited by Thomas Fitzgerald. Athens: University of Georgia Press. 51-62.

Leap, William L. 1974b. "Grammatical Structure in Native American English: The Evidence from Isleta." In: *Southwest Areal Linguistics*. Edited by Garland Bills. San Diego: Institute for Cultural Pluralism. 175-188.

Leap, William L. 1974c. "On Grammaticality in Native American English: The Evidence from Isleta." *International Journal of the Sociology of Language* 2. 79-89.

Leap, William L. 1975. "'To Be' in Isletan English: A Study in Accountability." Presented at the International Conference on Pidgins and Creoles, Honolulu.

Leap, William L. 1976. "How Isletan, Isletan English?" Presented at the annual meeting of the Southwestern Anthropological Association, San Francisco.

Leap, William L. 1977a. "A Note on Subject-Verb Agreement in Isletan English." In: *Studies in Southwestern Indian English*. Edited by William Leap. San Antonio: Trinity University Press. 121-130.

Leap, William L. 1977b. "On Consonant Simplification in Isletan English and Elsewhere." In: *Studies in Southwestern Indian English*. Edited by William Leap. San Antonio: Trinity University Press. 45-54.

Leap, William L. 1977c. "The Study of American Indian English: An Introduction to the Issues." In: *Studies in Southwestern Indian English*. Edited by William Leap. San Antonio: Trinity University Press. 3-20.

Leap, William L. 1977d. "Two Examples of Isletan English Syntax." In: *Studies in Southwestern Indian English*. Edited by William Leap. San Antonio: Trinity University Press. 65-78.

Malancon, Richard, and Mary Jo Malancon. 1977. "Indian English at Haskell Institute, 1916." In: *Studies in Southwestern Indian English*. Edited by William Leap. San Antonio: Trinity University Press. 141-154.

Miller, Mary Rita. 1977. *Children of the Salt River: First and Second Language Acquisition Among Pima Children*. Bloomington: Indiana University Language Science Monographs, Vol. 16.

National Indian Training and Research Center. 1976. *Bilingual Education Needs of Indian Children, A Survey*. Research and Evaluation Report No. 36. Washington, D.C.: Bureau of Indian Affairs, Office of Indian Education.

Penfield, Susan. 1975. "A Grant Proposal: Suggestions for Dealing with Mojave English." In: *Southwest Languages and Linguistics in Educational Perspective*. Edited by Gina Harvey and M. F. Heiser. San Antonio: Trinity University Press. 335-364.

Penfield, Susan. 1977. "Some Examples of Southwestern Indian English Compared." In: *Studies in Southwestern Indian English*. Edited by William Leap. San Antonio: Trinity University Press. 23-44.

Stout, Steven O. 1977. "A Comment on Selective Control in English Expression at Santa Ana." In: *Studies in Southwestern Indian English*. Edited by William Leap. San Antonio: Trinity University Press. 55-64.

Stout, Steven O. 1978. "Aspects of the Indian English of Laguna Elementary School, New Mexico." Unpublished doctoral dissertation. The American University, Washington, D.C.

Stout, Steven O., and Carol Erting. 1977. "Uninflected BE in Isletan English: Implicational Scaling and the Relationship of Isletan English to Other Ethnically Identifiable Varieties of English." In: *Studies in Southwestern Indian English*. Edited by William Leap. San Antonio, Trinity University Press. 101-120.

U.S. Civil Rights Commission. 1973. *The Southwest Indian Report*. Washington, D.C.: Government Printing Office.

INDEX

Boldface numerals indicate an article by the author. An added n = footnote, b = bibliography, and def = definition.